The Rowman & Littlefield Handbook of Women's Studies in Religion

....

The Rowman & Littlefield Handbook Series

This contemporary series of academic handbooks provides an authoritative guide to relevant and emerging topics across the humanities and social sciences. To encourage greater dialogue across disciplines, this series engages high-quality, original, and multi-disciplinary research on topics, themes, and key debates in academia today.

- Each handbook draws together newly commissioned work to provide a comprehensive benchmark for a field or subdiscipline
- The individual handbooks include an international team of contributors, with valuable expertise, knowledge, and perspective in their fields
- Handbooks in this series correspond to the latest topics on courses around the world

Each Handbook is available for purchase in both print and digital formats. For more information, see www.rowman.com.

The Rowman & Littlefield Handbook of Christianity in the Middle East
   Edited by Mark A. Lamport and Mitri Raheb
The Rowman & Littlefield Handbook of Media Management and Business
   Edited by L. Meghan Mahoney and Tang Tang
The Rowman & Littlefield Handbook of Policing, Communication, and Society
   Edited by Howard Giles, Edward Maguire, and Shawn L. Hill
The Rowman & Littlefield Handbook of Women's Studies in Religion
   Edited by Helen T. Boursier

The Rowman & Littlefield Handbook of Women's Studies in Religion

....

Edited by
Rev. Dr. HELEN T. BOURSIER, PhD

ROWMAN & LITTLEFIELD
Lanham • Boulder • New York • London

Published by Rowman & Littlefield
An imprint of The Rowman & Littlefield Publishing Group, Inc.
4501 Forbes Boulevard, Suite 200, Lanham, Maryland 20706
www.rowman.com

86-90 Paul Street, London EC2A 4NE

British Library Cataloguing in Publication Information Available

Library of Congress Cataloging-in-Publication Data

The previous edition was catalogued by the Library of Congress as follows:

Names: Boursier, Helen T., 1960– editor.
Title: The Rowman & Littlefield handbook of women's studies in religion / edited by Helen T. Boursier.
Description: Lanham : Rowman & Littlefield, 2021. | Includes bibliographical references and index. | Summary: "The handbook offers interreligious and multicultural perspectives on women's studies in religion in conversation with specific contextualized gender-biased justice challenges. Contributing authors address 25 current and trending themes from their diverse socio-cultural-religious backgrounds. The handbook is practical, contemporary, and relevant as it moves theory to practical application" — Provided by publisher.
Subjects: LCSH: Women and religion.
Classification: LCC BL458 .R69 2021 (print) | LCC BL458 (ebook) | DDC 200.82—dc23
LC record available at https://lccn.loc.gov/2020054158
LC ebook record available at https://lccn.loc.gov/2020054159

ISBN 978-1-5381-5444-1 (cloth)
ISBN 978-1-5381-8091-4 (pbk.)
ISBN 978-1-5381-5445-8 (ebook)

Dedicated to all of our mentors, encouragers, and sheroes whose wisdom, courage, love, visionary leadership, selflessness, and dedication to gender justice have inspired us. Thank you. May our words honor you.

Contents

SECTION ONE · A FIRMLY FLUID FOUNDATION FOR WOMEN'S STUDIES IN RELIGION

SECTION TWO · ETHICAL CONNECTIONS

SECTION THREE · **RELIGIOUS DIVERSITY AND WOMEN'S STUDIES IN RELIGION**

SECTION FOUR · **CHALLENGING AND CHANGING SYSTEMIC GENDER INJUSTICE**

SECTION FIVE · **FUTURE MOVEMENT—THE BECOM*ING* OF WOMEN'S STUDIES IN RELIGION**

Acknowledgments

··

I offer my profound gratitude for the contributing authors' passion, commitment, and dedication to this project. Many of them completed writing their chapters during spring 2020 when the COVID-19 pandemic began. Despite all of the added stressors during this unpredictable season with remain-in-place orders, which included scrambling to reformat classroom teaching to online learning and traditional worship services to virtual experiences to provide spiritual connection amid COVID-19 uncertainties, these dedicated authors pressed on with the race that was before them. They completed their work for on-time submission and on-time arrival to the publisher. Their perseverance to their individual research and writing themes overflowed into their commitment to completing this volume. Each author appreciates and respects the significance, relevance, and necessity of this collective witness of, for, and with women's studies in religion. They remained diligent because, for each one of these contributing authors, the work to transform systemic injustice against females, because they are females, remains a pressing urgency. It undergirds their work and was the individual and collective incentive to complete the chapters for this handbook despite COVID-19. Each chapter exemplifies the author's selflessness and commitment to further the progress for women's studies in religion. I am particularly grateful to Yudit Kornberg Greenberg for graciously stepping up at the zenith hour to write an essay on women in the Jewish tradition, diligently and selflessly filling what otherwise would have been a gaping hole in this manuscript. Finally, I am grateful to Rolfe Janke, who invited me to submit a proposal for this handbook. I never would have done so without his exuberant confidence and encouragement.

Rev. Dr. Helen T. Boursier, PhD

Foreword

....

In the Name of God All-Merciful, Most Compassionate

This is a book of explorations and experiments in the power of women in religion to change the world. A half century ago, when I was a young woman, such a book was scarcely conceivable. Now, it is indispensable.

I grew up in a highly secular, mostly Jewish suburb of Philadelphia where religion was about holidays and women's aspirations were modestly encouraged but clearly circumscribed. There were certain things a sensible girl simply wouldn't try for. One of them was a leadership role in a religious community. Another was an independent life that put spiritual striving first. But the borders of the realm of the mind, thank God, were even then open to every imagination—and that is how I came to find the original friends of my soul among people I encountered only in books.

I did not at first come upon any women scholars who were writing in the fields I cared about. Before the internet, they were not so easy to find! Instead, the thread leading out of the maze of psychic isolation was put into my hands by the works of Carl Jung. He was the first defender of women and the suppressed feminine that I ever read. I remember so clearly the wonder I felt when, in my teens, I came across his view that the formal adoption by the Catholic Church of the ancient belief in the Assumption of Mary (a doctrinal adjustment that occurred only in 1950) was the most important spiritual event in Europe since the Reformation. Yes, it was true, it dawned on me: it *must* be true. The reappearance of female power in sacred spaces from which it had been banished was going to transform everything.

And, now, of course, we are in the midst of that transformation. It is already undoing the centuries-old supremacy of European influence while challenging local social practices that have served to entrench systems of domination everywhere. From the steep global increase in female literacy to the struggles for agency under way in so many contexts, the planetary balance of power is slowly shifting, against fierce resistance, from the hierarchal toward the egalitarian vision. That is what the rise of the suppressed feminine does.

As this great realignment inexorably makes its way into our common consciousness, religions of all sorts must realign as well, sifting the wheat of their deep sustaining wisdom from the chaff of outdated adaptations to societies that have faded or are fading away. Such reappraisals are inevitably painful since they bring into doubt foundations of meaning that, for many people, are of life-or-death importance. *Is the way I live—is my*

....

religion—real? Is it about anything? If not, to what end have I suffered? On what, exactly, have I staked my trust? Questions like these can be agonizing, and, when change is rising, such suppressed questions will rise as well, surrounded by anger, fear, and despair. If the spread of the new vision is to bring the broad benefits to humanity and the planet that many of us long for, its proponents must offer compassionate answers to questions like these. We must be able to affirm that yes, all is not lost. There *is* wheat in our traditions, and it can still be ground and baked to make good bread. There can still be such a thing as good religion, which is not the opiate but the sustenance of the people. However, that bread will not come out of the oven until everyone is seated around the table. Religion cannot be an excuse for domination anymore.

These days, people of religion have got more important things to do than trying to compete for control.

Everyone awake in our era knows that we are in a race against time. To overcome the obstacles of inertia and reaction that confront us requires the marshaling of tremendous political will, and that will can be supported only by something that dissolves our cynicism and arouses our deepest commitment. A profound rediscovery of meaning is required. Human beings must recognize themselves again as essentially rooted in something that transcends them, something to which they are responsible, something that embraces them all. It is the job of religions publicly to insist that a human life is not a trivial thing. If people of religion are to be effective now, they must insist on this sincerely and together. There is so much more to being human than resentment, self-glorification, and greed! There has always been more. But there has never been a more urgent moment in which to proclaim aloud that elementary fact.

Women are taking the lead in this proclamation. As the earth is becoming known to us again as a real being and the great gateway to the holy—as earth is acknowledged as *already present in heaven*—women are regaining their spiritual authority. The Qur'ān tells us in the Chapter of the Great Convulsion that, when the earth casts off her burdens and begins to speak, *"Then whoever has done an atom's weight of good will see it/And whoever has done an atom's weight of evil will see it"* (99:7–8).

Much that was invisible is now clearly visible. Terrible crimes are revealed for what they are; wonderful new beauties are shown to be coming to birth. Some of these revelations, small and large, may be found in the volume before you. In the work of women like these—both our scholars and their subjects—the earth speaks her truth, and she will be heard. May you find here powerful new friends for your own soul, and may they aid you in your own work for the happiness of all.

Chaplain Rabia Terri Harris
Founder, Muslim Peace Fellowship
Co-Founder, Community of Living Traditions

Introduction

Gender injustice is an academic topic for rigorous research and writing, but its systemic manifestations also are very personal and real. It feels a bit unexpected and somewhat ironic that I came to edit a collection of women's studies in religion. I did not seek to be a feminist theologian per se. Instead, feminism claimed me from the gender injustice and sexual violation I have experienced because I am female. Thirty-five years before the #MeToo movement became the forthright public platform to protest sexual violations, I was raped by a family member in my childhood home when I was twelve—an atrocity that my psyche blocked from conscious memory for forty years. Then, as a young adult, each time I walked the length of the pier as a US Navy journalist with an assignment to photograph and write about a ship returning from deployment, I silently endured the humiliating catcalling contests among the male enlisted personnel who were stationed aboard the frigates already docked at this navy base.

Fast-forward twenty-five years later to when I told my minister that I sensed God calling me to vocational ordained ministry. I was literally stunned speechless when he immediately responded that he did not believe that the ordination of women was "biblical." Instead of offering guidance, prayers, counsel, or encouragement, he rejected me outright by using gender as a "regulatory norm" against females.[1] During the subsequent formal discussions with this pastor over an eight-month period, he gave me a 150-page study guide about whether the ordination of women was biblical, a "study" conducted by a segment of a denomination that later broke off from its mainline affiliate because its members did not believe that the ordination of women was biblical. The pastor told me to read this "study" and then "convince" him. While all this was happening, time ticked away for me to submit the appropriate paperwork to enroll in seminary for the upcoming fall term. These delay tactics are called the "debate and betrayal" process, as evil maintains itself by lengthening the time before a decision is eventually made that supports the initial view of the oppressor. It is a common gender injustice ploy and a gross misuse of power.[2] As the last-call admission deadline approached for the next academic year, I abruptly withdrew from that gender-biased delay game and submitted my application to a denomination and seminary that welcomed females to vocational ordained ministry.

Feminism claimed me throughout my seminary-to-ordination process when I was criticized for being "too aggressive," "too strong," and "too focused," reproaches numerous allies noted that my male colleagues would not receive. As the senior and organizing pastor of a new church, when I attended the otherwise all-male local ministerial alliance in my community (what I publicly referred to as "the men's club"), the theme song that bubbled up in my spirit and encouraged me came from one of the closing scenes in the 1964 film *Mary Poppins* when suffragettes marched through the house carrying placards and singing, "Votes for women; step in time!"[3] Feminist ideals continued to claim me during my graduate studies in practical theology with an emphasis on liberation theology and justice for the marginalized. I learned that, while the problem of gender injustice is personal, it also manifests in the grander scale through religious and secular systemic structures of dominion and power. Liberation theology's focus on the preferential option for the poor and marginalized shaped my sense of call to become a volunteer chaplain in 2014 with mothers and children seeking asylum who were fleeing targeted violence in Central America to seek safety with family members in the United States.

I began my volunteer chaplaincy in ignorance and naivete, but as I facilitated art as spiritual care with thousands of mothers and children while they were detained in a for-profit immigrant family detention center located seventy miles from my home, feminism claimed me more deeply. I sought to understand the depth of their pain and suffering, including the systemic connections related to why they fled their homelands, so I did the necessary rigorous academic work to move myself from *un*knowing to deep knowledge that was informed analytically and experientially, such that I now stand on the certainty of what I know to be true about femicide and US culpability to feminicide at the US–Mexico border (see chapters 17 and 18). After Immigration and Customs Enforcement rescinded my security clearance and shut down the all-volunteer art ministry on December 15, 2016, I continued to volunteer with asylum seekers in various

FIGURE I.1. Pastora Helena and four asylum seekers at a migrant shelter in Nuevo Laredo, Mexico on Ash Wednesday 2020. Wax resist with soap on black paper with colored pencils
© *Helen T. Boursier*

contexts outside of detention, including multiple pastoral care visits to migrant shelters along the US–Mexico border (see cover artwork and figure I.1). The gender injustice I have documented experientially and analytically informs my research, writing, pastoral care ministry of presence at the border, and advocacy and witness in the public square.[4] With so much public rhetoric demonizing asylum seekers as "killers, criminals, rapists, and drug dealers,"[5] I counter this biased false narrative through mixed media representations from my arts-based research, seeking to create each image to be a portal through which these beautiful families can bear witness.[6]

Feminist concerns also claim me as a professor. Like many of the contributing authors, I teach women's studies in religion. Some of these students take a course because women's studies in religion interests them; others sign up for a class because it fits into their schedule and/or they need to check off the religious studies requirement. Many of these students have a very limited knowledge or understanding about the depth, breadth, or intensity of gender injustice. They often remark insistently that they are *not* feminists. Some enter a course believing that gender injustice no longer exists. Typical justifications include that women can vote, get a job anywhere they want, serve in the military, and choose their marital status. By the end of the first unit, students realize that gender injustice continues to thrive, often hiding under the guise of religion.

FEMINISM AND WOMEN'S STUDIES

This handbook on women's studies in religion expresses and applies "feminist theology" and "feminism" in the broadest possible and most inclusive perspective, as the essays address a diverse scope of concerns. If feminist theory is worthwhile as a concept and discipline of study, then its ideals must be relevant, applicable, and transformative for all females, regardless of their social, economic, religious, political, or geographic location. Judith Butler explains, "It would surely be a mistake to gauge the progress of feminism by its success as a colonial project. It seems more crucial than ever to disengage feminism from its First World presumption, and to use the resources of feminist theory, and activism, to rethink the meaning of the tie, the bond, the alliance, the relation, as they are imagined and lived in the horizon of a counterimperialist egalitarianism."[7] In other words, to borrow a phrase (and book title) from bell hooks, *Feminism Is for Everybody*.[8]

Solidarity includes being vocal about any gender injustice that is being perpetrated to force it from social silence into the public consciousness, which will help to restore social order while also helping to heal the individual victims of oppression and marginalization.[9] The point is not to make the world a more kind, gracious, and just place for females alone. Rather, in uplifting the full humanity of females, it simultaneously enables, fosters, and empowers the full blessedness of all creation, with the long-held feminist value that what is at stake "is not only for the liberation of women, but for all who are broken, physically and in spirit, by the oppressions of our world."[10] The common denominator of gender injustice is patriarchy and the birth-rated authority of males over females. The birth ranking is exacerbated by intersectionality factors, such as socioeconomic, racial, cultural, political, geographical, and religious. It is noteworthy to highlight that, as ridiculous, archaic, and/or outdated as it is, the intersectional inter-religious commonality for gender bias continues to be that females are born female (and males are born male).[11] Religious traditions might differ on how they justify gender inequity, but the root origin still stakes its claim in the birth-ranked rationalization that males are predestined to wield power over females simply because boys are born boys and boys matter more than girls (or so goes the patristic argument).

CONTRIBUTING AUTHORS

The contributing authors have their very real experiences with gender injustice, an interreligious intersectional reality that guides each one's research, writing, advocacy, and public witness. Each contributing author views women's studies through a partic-ular lens, but the common denominator resonates with bell hooks's explanation: "Fem-inism is a movement to end sexism, sexist exploitation, and oppression."[12] Females are born with biases against them simply because they were born female, which confines females of all religions, races, and classes in what has been called "a ghetto of sorts."[13] With religious studies as the lens through the viewfinder of gender in/justice, the con-tributing authors argue for a preferential option for women, as they offer education and enlightenment on past, present, and trending gender injustice.

CONTENT OVERVIEW

The topics for this handbook address past, present, and evolving gender inequities so that emerging generations have the knowledge and tools to challenge and change micro and macro gender injustice. The chapters cover diverse religions and themes, though of course not every religion or gender injustice could be covered in a single volume. Contributing authors were asked to connect classroom theory to lived reality to assist readers to move forth from ideas about women's studies in religion to becoming agents of change. The goal is for feminism to claim the minds, hearts, and spirits of readers to move from whatever place of *un*knowing to being able to say, "I once was blind, but now I see" (Jn 9:25). In that seeing, together we can move forth into practical action, embracing Olive Schreiner's dream in 1890 "[to] make a track to the water's edge," making a "bridge that shall be built with our bodies," that shall become a bridge over which pass "[t]he entire human race" so that all creation can be healed and whole.[14] Long before feminist was classified as a term or formalized as an academic discipline, brave foremothers, sheroes[15] of diverse religious traditions, raised their voices and risked their lives to object to the oppressive gender norms of their day. They became part of the "track to the water's edge." The unfinished work must continue.

The handbook unfolds in five sections. Section One, "A Firmly Fluid Foundation for Women's Studies in Religion," provides the groundwork of what brought this discipline along the gender justice journey thus far. It gives a review of key themes from the past to the present and explains why using inclusive language of God matters. It includes an introduction to methodology for doing women's studies in religion and offers a Latina feminist example for how to include arts-based research for art and activism at the borders. Section Two, "Ethical Connections," brings in themes that intersect with ethics, including ecofeminism, economic sustainability, feminist ethics, and health care. Section Three, "Religious Diversity and Women's Studies in Religion," engages various religious traditions with the unique challenges that are indicative of particular religions. Readers will note the overlap of gender injustice between and among religious traditions. Section Four, "Challenging and Changing Systemic Gender Injustice," makes the connection between theory and action to move learning from the classroom or textbook into real life. It draws attention to interreligious and multicultural gender oppression, including sexual violence and the #MeToo movement, femicide and state culpability to feminicide through border controls and exclusion from asylum, a Mohawk feminist response to violations to Indigenous lands and women, and a religiopolitical witness for love and justice.

Section Five, "Future Movement—The Becom*ing* of Women's Studies in Religion," includes new and emerging themes, such as how to engage feminism and religion in the digital world; envisioning women's mosque spaces online; reimagining a universal human rights framework that reduces the viability or need for distinct gender identities; how a nomadic spirituality for survivors of childhood violence creates a space from spiritual homelessness toward spiritual homemaking; and the ultimate role, challenge, and charge to continue the vision for and work of women's studies in religion to foster the fullest possible humanity for all people with hope now. The closing chapter, "Resources for Clarification, Education, and Action," includes glossaries of hashtags, people, events, phrases, and organizations related to women's studies in religion. A bibliography of works cited follows each chapter.

Individually and collectively, the contributing authors invite readers to consciousness-raising in the fullest sense of this early expression of women's studies in religion, a consciousness-raising that includes moving from unknowing to informed active engagement to challenge and change gender injustice in all of its manifestations through participation in personal and public actions of solidarity with and for persons who are marginalized because of their gender. It is a handbook for education that transforms spirits and minds, ultimately moving readers to participation in practical actions of resistance, as we work together to create a more just universe whereby the humanity of all persons is respected, honored, and fulfilled to the fullest possible expression of selfhood. With this theme in view, I invited the contributing authors to self-identify as they desired for their byline on the opening page of each chapter. Each byline serves as an expression of selfhood by naming and claiming how each author self identifies, but it also is an action of solidarity with all those who have worked diligently, often struggling against criticism, minoritized oppression, and disrespect, while they pressed on to complete an academic degree and/or ordination or religious recognition.[16] These hard-earned honorific titles also are our affirmation for *you* to press on with the race that is before you, and to run that race with endurance (1 Cor 9:24).

The integrated education, examples, and suggestions for response ultimately call all people to stop using theology and religion as excuses for domination of one human being over another, offering the clarion cry: *"Ya!* Enough!" May feminist theology make its claim on you so that we walk together to the water's edge and build that bridge for all of humanity to cross.

Rev. Dr. Helen T. Boursier, PhD
June 15, 2020
New Braunfels, Texas

NOTES

1. Judith Butler, *Undoing Gender* (New York and London: Routledge, 2004), 53.
2. James Newton Poling, *Deliver Us from Evil: Resisting Racial and Gender Oppression* (Minneapolis, MN: Fortress Press, 1996), 10, 33, 34, 54.
3. Robert B. Sherman and Richard M. Sherman, composers, "Sister Suffragette," in *Mary Poppins,* directed by Robert Stevenson (Burbank, CA: Walt Disney Studios, 1964), DVD.
4. See, e.g., Helen T. Boursier, *The Ethics of Hospitality: An Interfaith Response to U.S. Immigration Policies* (Lanham, MD: Lexington Books, February 2019); *Desperately Seeking Asylum: Testimonies of Trauma, Courage, and Love* (Lanham, MD: Rowman & Littlefield, November 2019); *Willful Ignorance: Overcoming the Limitations of Christian Love for Refugees Seeking Asylum* (Lanham, MD: Lexington Books, forthcoming); and *Refugee Art: Testimonies of Immigrant Families Seeking Asylum* (blog), https://refugeeartblog.com/.
5. Caroline Moreno, "Nine Outrageous Things Donald Trump Has Said about Latinos," *The Huffington Post,* November 9, 2016, https://www.huffpost.com/entry/9-outrageous-things-donald-trump-has-said-about-latinos_n_55e483a1e4b0c818f618904b?guccounter=1&guce_referrer=aHR0cHM6Ly93d3cuYmluZy5jb20vc2VhcmNoP3E9dHJ1bXArcXVvdGUraW1taWdyYYW50cytyYXBpc3RzJmZvcm09RURHHTlRUJnFzPVBVNDJmN2aWQ9OGNmOTk4N2FkYzRkNGQ2ZThiNTYzM2FiZjljY2YyMTgmcmVmaWc9MDgyMDEyM2NhYTYxNDc3MzllNGE3MTRhYTc5MDVmZmIjNTZmM2FiYjAmY2M9VVNmbGFnZ1lbi1VUylbbHY9QVFqOTNPQWhEVGdkqSHpUdjFwYVVFkbmpndTJnMjZ4ZXRpcVl2b3RRDYjVDTEFjTTlKVVVNFOHdFblHHSWFBaWV1YkRGGR1Jld1dXeEFFUNjJrQkZYU3B6bGFW2bHdCVUdNd3Jqc1hk5TXBOOE0yZTJJnBsdmFyPTAmUEM9UEM M9RENUUuw&guce_referrer_sig=AQAAAC-22lJ5aSFL_nyCaiaklgYtYchcPqOKgRT8fFck9aoDOXzzEqESaqbdW7NaSHK7cnT3sIFhpPIWvNKFUNQpiLTX1XETlYY133topSaLuRH6aqNLrNwQBu4-EmVWIPZ84wqj8OQgYM01L6HIIltxwyZ5Z_1MXD_EQmTgovr2WZd.
6. See Helen T. Boursier, *Art As Witness: A Practical Theology of Arts-Based Research* (Lanham, MD: Lexington Books, 2021).
7. Judith Butler, *Precarious Life: The Powers of Mourning and Violence* (London and New York: Verso, 2004, 2006), 41–42.
8. bell hooks, *Feminism Is for Everybody: Passionate Politics* (New York and London: Routledge Taylor & Francis Group, 2015).
9. Judith Herman, *Trauma and Recovery: The Aftermath of Violence from Domestic Abuse to Political Terror* (New York: Perseus Books, 1992, 1997, 2015), 1.
10. Serene Jones, *Feminist Theory and Christian Theology: Cartographies of Grace* (Minneapolis, MN: Fortress Press, 2000), 6–7.
11. See, e.g., Elisabeth Schüssler Fiorenza, *Congress of Wo/men: Religion, Gender, and Kyriarchal Power* (Cambridge, MA: Feminist Studies in Religion, 2016).
12. bell hooks, *Feminist Theory: From Margin to Center,* 3rd ed. (London and New York: Routledge, 2014), xii.
13. Marilyn Frye, *The Politics of Reality: Essays in Feminist Theory* (Berkeley, CA: Crossing Press, 1983), 9.
14. Olive Schreiner, *A Track to the Water's Edge: The Olive Schreiner Reader,* ed. Howard Thurman (New York: Harper & Row Publishers, Inc., 1973), 53–56; originally published in *Dreams* (Cape Colony, South Africa: Matjesfontein, 1890).

15. I thank Reverend Natalie Webb, co-founder and co-director of Nevertheless She Preached for introducing me to this term.

16. See, e.g., Dr. Bertice Berry, "Call her Doctor," Facebook (video blog), December 13, 2020, (3) Watch | Facebook; Kara Alaim, "Attack on Jill Biden's 'Dr.' Title Is No Surprise for Women Scholars—and Proof that She Needs to Use It," Opinion, CNN, December 14, 2020, Attack on Jill Biden's 'Dr.' title is no surprise for women scholars—and proof that she needs to use it (Opinion) CNN; and Leah D. Schade, 'That's Rev. Dr.' to You, Kiddo: A Rebuttal to WSJ's Joseph Epstein," Pathos, *EcoPreacher* (blog) December 13, 2020, That's "Rev. Dr." to you, kiddo. A rebuttal to WSJ's Joseph Epstein | Leah D. Schade (patheos.com).

BIBLIOGRAPHY

Alaim, Kara. "Attack on Jill Biden's 'Dr.' Title is No Surprise for Women Scholars—and Proof that She Needs to Use It." Opinion. CNN, December 14, 2020. Attack on Jill Biden's 'Dr.' title is no surprise for women scholars—and proof that she needs to use it (Opinion) CNN.

Berry, Dr. Bertice. "Call her Doctor." Facebook (video blog), December 13, 2020. https://www.facebook.com/watch/?v=392789672168847.

Boursier, Helen T. *Art As Witness: A Practical Theology of Arts-Based Research*. Lanham, MD: Lexington Books, 2021.

———. *Desperately Seeking Asylum: Testimonies of Trauma, Courage, and Love*. Lanham, MD: Rowman & Littlefield, 2019.

———. *The Ethics of Hospitality: An Interfaith Response to U.S. Immigration Policies*. Lanham, MD: Lexington Books, 2019.

———. *Refugee Art: Testimonies of Immigrant Families Seeking Asylum* (blog). https://refugeeartblog.com/.

———. *Willful Ignorance: Overcoming the Limitations of Christian Love for Refugees Seeking Asylum*. Lanham, MD: Lexington Books, forthcoming.

Butler, Judith. *Precarious Life: The Powers of Mourning and Violence*. London and New York: Verso, 2004, 2006.

———. *Undoing Gender*. New York and London: Routledge, 2004.

Frye, Marilyn. *The Politics of Reality: Essays in Feminist Theory*. Berkeley, CA: Crossing Press, 1983.

Herman, Judith. *Trauma and Recovery: The Aftermath of Violence from Domestic Abuse to Political Terror*. New York: Perseus Books, 1992, 1997, 2015.

hooks, bell. *Feminism Is for Everybody: Passionate Politics*. New York and London: Routledge, 2015.

———. *Feminist Theory: From Margin to Center*. 3rd ed. London and New York: Routledge, 2014.

Jones, Serene. *Feminist Theory and Christian Theology: Cartographies of Grace*. Minneapolis, MN: Fortress Press, 2000.

Moreno, Caroline. "Nine Outrageous Things Donald Trump Has Said About Latinos." *Huffington Post*, November 9, 2016. https://www.huffpost.com/entry/9-outrageous-things-donald-trump-has-said-about-latinos_n_55e483a1e4b0c818f618904b?guccounter=1&guce_referrer=aHR0cHM6Ly93d3cuYmluZy5jb20vc2VhcmNoP3E9dHJ1bXArarcXVvdGUraW1taWdyYW50cyZmb3Jtcm09RURHTlRlUUJ1bXFzPVNDNDJmN2aWQ9OGNmOTk4N2FkYzRkNGQ02ZThiNTYzM2FiZjljY2YyMTgmcmVmaWc9MDgyMDEyM2NhYTYxNDc3MzllNGE3MTRhYTc5M2FhYjAmY2M9VVMmc2V0bGFuZz1lbi1VUyZlbHY9QVFFqOTNPQWhEVGkqSHpUdjFwYVYFkbmpndTJnMjZ4ZXRpbV3b3RDYjVDTEFjTTlKVVVNFOHdFblRHSWFBaWV1YkRGGRJld1dXeEFFUNjJrQkYU3B6WFd2bHdCdCVUdNQ3JqcXk5TXBOOE0yZTJ2JnBsdmFyPTAmUEM9RENUUUw&guce_referrer_sig=AQAAAC-22lJ5aSFL_nyCaiaklgYtYchcPqOKgRT8fFck9aoDOXzzEqESaqbdW7NaSHK7cnT3sIFhpPIWvNKFUNQpiLTX1XETlYY133topSaLuRH6aqNLrNwQBu4-EmVWIPZ84wqj8OQgYM01L6HIIIltxwyZ5Z_1MXD_EQmTgovr2WZd.

Poling, James Newton. *Deliver Us from Evil: Resisting Racial and Gender Oppression*. Minneapolis, MN: Fortress Press, 1996.

Schade, Leah D. "'That's Rev. Dr.' to You, Kiddo: A Rebuttal to WSJ's Joseph Epstein." Pathos. *Eco-Preacher* (blog) December 13, 2020. That's "Rev. Dr." to you, kiddo. A rebuttal to WSJ's Joseph Epstein | Leah D. Schade (patheos.com)

Schreiner, Olive. *A Track to the Water's Edge: The Olive Schreiner Reader*. Edited by Howard Thurman. New York: Harper & Row Publishers, Inc., 1973.

Schüssler Fiorenza, Elisabeth. *Congress of Wo/men: Religion, Gender, and Kyriarchal Power*. Cambridge, MA: Feminist Studies in Religion, 2016.

Sherman, Robert B., and Richard M. Sherman, composers. "Sister Suffragette." In *Mary Poppins*. Directed by Robert Stevenson. Burbank, CA: Walt Disney Studios, 1964. DVD.

A FIRMLY FLUID FOUNDATION FOR WOMEN'S STUDIES IN RELIGION

....

CHAPTER 1

A Work in Progress

···

Feminist Scholarship Shaping God's Image—Then and Now

Rev. Dr. Jacqueline J. Lewis, Middle Collegiate Church, New York

ABSTRACT

The opening chapter covers the ebb and flow of feminist theology from its conception with reflections on overlapping trajectories, varying research interests, and methodologies the foremothers engaged to further women's studies in religion. A work in progress sets the context with groundbreaking scholarship from the beginning years that shape present research topics and methods to influence future transformations for women in the world. It offers insights on how to define and build meaningful solidarities among women across faiths, ethnicities, and racialized groups.

WOMEN'S WAYS, BEGINNING WITH HAGAR AND MARY

As I write this chapter, it's April. We're just past Easter and Passover and in the middle of Ramadan. I was asked to do *The Today Show* with my friend, Rabbi Sharon Brous, to talk about holy days in troubling times. I love Sharon's keen mind and compassionate heart, so when she's going to show up, I'm showing up too. We have deep conversations about how to fix religion, about finding the feminist meanings in the text, and about women's bodies and our experiences and how they shape the way we read Torah and the Bible. Hope and resilience run through our conversations.

···

Our congregation just wrapped up our fourteenth annual Revolutionary Love Conference; 600 people attended to learn with some of the best thought leaders of our time, most of them women. Sikh activist and filmmaker Valarie Kaur called us to see no stranger and to consider whether the troubling times in our nation are the darkness of the tomb or the darkness of the womb. V, formerly known as Eve Ensler, talked about the powerful four steps of an apology as a model for healing our nation. Buddhist sensei Reverend angel Kyodo williams and Sister Simone Campbell had a conversation about overcoming threats to democracy while Muslim activist and author Linda Sarsour urgently reminded us that this is no time for bystanders. Kendi King, an 18-year-old actor, playwrite, and activist, stunned us with wisdom about the way art changes culture. Dr. Ruby Sales and Reverend Traci Blackmon talked with me about healing a divided nation; Sunita Viswanath and Reverend Dr. Damaris Whitaker were on a panel talking about breaking down walls and making borders permeable. Reverend Jennifer Butler and Reverend Amanda Hambrick Ashcraft brought feminist Christian critique of our culture to the table. Sharon, all of these women, and more—across generation, faith, and ethnicity—are leading a revolution of love and justice. Together, we are articulating a vision for a healed and whole world. Their particular experiences of the divine— experiences of resilience, resistance, and redemption; of wilderness wandering and healing and wholeness; of joy, sorrow, and hope—interrogating them is changing theological discourse and building movements because of their faith and beyond their faith. We are weaving new chapters of theological conversations that are rooted in our traditions and that are creating new ones.

Women have particular ways of prophetic sight, insight, and hindsight. Ways of seeing, of envisioning a world, of imagining Shalom, or the Reign of God on earth, or radical Dharma—this sight is accompanied by daring, prophetic speaking and writing. They are raising questions like *What if we are really to dismantle the ways we think systems need to function? What if this darkness is not so much about death, but about life? Everyone has hurt, where is yours? Who are you not to own your power?* Women have perceptions unique to each, experiences unique to each, and a particular way of speaking in tongues about the thing, putting new ideas and thoughts alongside the old. They dare to put new wine in old wineskins.

When I think of new perceptions and daring speech, Mary comes to mind. Which one? The one from Magdala. There are so many Marys in the gospels: Mary, the mother of Jesus; Mary of Bethany, sister of Martha and Lazarus; Mary, the mother of James and Joseph; and Mary, the wife of Clopas. But I am thinking of the first preacher, the one who told the other disciples that she had seen the risen Lord, the one who was finally, after Pope Gregory fully sullied her reputation, weaving together threads of Mary stories in the process, recognized by the Catholic Church as the Apostle's Apostle in 2016.

In some ways, the confusion about Mary is understandable. There was no court reporter taking notes, no journalist trying to get the facts right about the gospels. They were stories told about Jesus during his life, shared in community at the end of his life, and put to papyrus some 30–60 years after he died. The gospels are both eyewitness testimony and holy memory. There are so many stories of the women: Who birthed Jesus, who cared for Jesus, who poured perfume on his feet and dried it with her hair, who spoke to him at the well, who was healed of seven demons, who asked for her daughter to be healed, who talked him down from his ethnocentrism, who sat at his feet while her sister cooked, who stayed at the cross and who came to care for his body after the sabbath was over, who hosted him and the disciples, and who made space for the earliest gatherings in their homes. Women. Some named Mary, some unnamed. That their stories might be blurred and obscured is not surprising given all the givens.

But Pope Gregory smeared Mary in front of a bunch of people who could not read and who were trying to survive a plague and who trusted his telling of events. By the time he linked together a story about Mary and *Jesus Christ Superstar* captured our imaginations, she was a prostitute, who turned her life around, who did not know how to love Jesus, who had many men before in many different ways, who followed him, did not leave him, and preached the gospel to the men. Of course, the men were the "real" disciples, which is why even though she preached the first sermon, the rest of us should not talk in church, let alone preach . . . and you see how we get here. Mary is sexualized and stylized; she is a prostitute turned good girl who follows Jesus, but not good enough. Her voice did not really matter; the Gospel of Mary did not make it into the canon, and feminist and womanist theologians have been working against the constructs of theology—God talk—that made God a man, made men closest to God, most like God; gave them power to tell the story about God, and create rituals, institutions, and systems to concretize the theology, the liturgy, the cult of manhood, with God as head man. Feminist scholarship has been working against memory to re-member the revelation of God to Mary in that garden. She saw the Lord; she saw the Living God. She perceived an amazing moment and said it out loud; she put flesh on the word.

Hagar had a conversation with God in the wilderness (Gn 16:7). Put out of doors by Sarah with her and Abram's boy Ishmael, she met God in the wildness and was told she would be the mother of a nation. What did her epiphany mean for the talking of God? Was Hagar's naming of God, as Delores Williams wrote, "an act of *defiance* and *resistance* as well as an *expression of awe*?"[1] What might this womanist observation have to say about feminist scholarship; has it too been an act of defiance and resistance as well as an expression of awe?

Women's ways of seeing and saying, of perceiving and articulating the work of the Holy in their lives, in the world, in their communities of faith, and in the public square have set the world on fire, and we're not finished yet. What feminist scholarship imagines about God pushes Her out of the confines of maleness; it liberates Her.

THE PROBLEM WITH GOD'S IMAGE

As a psychologist of religion, I have been deeply influenced by the work of Ana-María Rizzuto in her book *The Birth of the Living God*.[2] As object relations theorists, we both subscribe to the suggestion of Donald Winnicott that God is both created and found. Found in the sense that parents, religious leaders, and the culture "present" God to us to be found. Rizutto writes, "No child arrives at the 'house of God' without his pet God under his arm." Everyone, even atheists, have a God representation, or God image. It is formed out of experience, images in houses of worship or nature, music, and art and in stories told to us about God in scripture, sermons, midrash, and stories enacted in the lives of the people around us.

God is created in that God is a mystery, and, for as long as there have been human beings, we have created God in the spaces where God is unknown. We've marveled at sunrises and sunsets; we've stood on sandy shores and been licked by the sea. We've seen clouds settle around the necks of mountains; we've seen the mouths of mountains ripped apart in lava spewing heat in the air. We've wondered about rivers crawling slowly through the land and asked ourselves from whence cometh this beauty and from whence cometh our help. We engaged our holy imaginations to build a relationship with the ineffable that we experienced as Holy Other and as Light and Love inside ourselves. We created metaphors from our lives. God was potter to our clay, shepherd to our wandering sheep-ness; God was a rock in a weary land, a fortress, a deliverer in which we could hide our face.

And we created God in our own image. And by "we" I mean men. We carved into the wood the faces of the strongest among us. We decorated pots and masks with fierceness we hoped would protect us. We were afraid, so we conjured a God deserving of our fear. We were punitive, so we created a God who would withhold love from us when we failed. We coveted the land of our enemies, so we put words about smiting them and conquering them in the mouth of our God. We did not understand either the draught or the flood, and we attributed the power we could not control to God and tried to control him with our sacrifices, prayers, and burnt offerings. The fiercest most powerful God won the God contests; the stories that shaped the God image were told by the fiercest in the land. And what was also said was the "he" was universalist and not meant to exclude the "she," but it does. Once the masculine is deified, the feminine is problematized.

Those who came behind *found* the God *created* by the powerful. He was all knowing, all powerful, sometimes benevolent. He was pleased by sacrifices and offerings. He was far away up on the mountain but would sometimes come down. You could see his feet. He would lead the people in a pillar of cloud or fire. He would hang out in the tent of meeting. He would hear and answer prayers but demanded obedience and allegiance.

The names we have for God, the characteristics we ascribed to God, the experiences and revelations we attributed to God, our theological musings about God have had the power to shape politics and policies, to define governments, constitutions, and courts. And, of course, because it is God, what He decides, what He wills, who He has revealed himself to be is truth, and incontrovertible.

FEMINIST INTERVENTIONS IN IMAGING GOD

Women have been doing theology since the early church, and the task of feminist theologians has been as much about giving sight and sound to the voices of women of the past as it has been about imaging and articulating God for themselves and their communities in the present and for the future. *The Woman's Bible,* a critique of Christianity produced in the 1890s by American suffragist Elizabeth Cady Stanton (1815–1902), was an important founding moment in Christian feminism.[3] Today, feminist theological reflection includes academic scholarship in theology and philosophy as well as music, liturgy, literature, art, and drama.

In an article called "The Human Situation: A Feminine View," Valerie Saiving asked questions about the nature of Christian concepts such as sin (pride, ambition, and self-centeredness) as influenced by masculine theology, thereby not reflecting feminine sins (self-denigration, triviality, and lack of focus).[4] Her essay is widely recognized as a pioneering analysis of the gendering of sin in the Christian tradition, beginning a move in which feminist theology began to question much of what had gone before not only in terms of women's roles in congregational life but also in the gendering of theological concepts.

The encounter between feminism and theology was given added impetus by the Second Vatican Council (1962–1965), which encouraged Roman Catholics to enter into a positive engagement with the non-Catholic world. Feminist pioneers such as Rosemary Radford Ruether, Mary Daly, and Elizabeth Johnson were Catholics working in the initially optimistic climate that followed the Second Vatican Council (1962–1965). Daly's 1968 book, *The Church and the Second Sex*, offered a hard-hitting feminist critique of Christian misogyny but still expressed hope that the Church could be transformed.[5] Later editions include disclaimers in which Daly makes clear her subsequent rejection of Christianity as irredeemably patriarchal.[6]

On May 1, 1983, the *New York Times* published an article written by Phyllis Trible, then professor of Old Testament at Union Theological Seminary, and the author of *God and the Rhetoric of Sexuality* and the soon-to-be-published *Texts of Terror: Literary-Feminist Readings of Biblical Narratives*. In the article "The Creation of a Feminist Theology," she reviewed *Sexism and God-Talk: Toward a Feminist Theology* by Rosemary Radford Ruether and *In Memory of Her: A Feminist Theological Reconstruction of Christian Origins* by Elisabeth Schüssler Fiorenza. About Ruether's work, Trible writes:

> Affirming human experience as the basis of all theology, Mrs. Reuther claims that historically such experience has been identified with and defined by men. The uniqueness of feminist theology is its use of women's experience to expose the male-centered bias of classical theology and articulate a faith that incorporates full humanity. Whereas the traditional paradigm begets domination and subordination, feminism seeks a mutuality that allows for variety and particularity in women and men. The goal is not to diminish males but to affirm both sexes whole, along with all races and social groups.[7]

According to Trible, Schüssler Fiorenza posits two forms of early Christianity: the "Jesus movement" in Palestine and the "missionary movement" in Greco-Roman cities. For her, "the Jesus movement had a vision of inclusive wholeness, with special concern for the poor; the sick and crippled; and tax collectors, sinners, and prostitutes. This group manifested "the feminist impulse within Judaism."[8] Indeed, it was a discipleship of equals that understood God "in a woman's Gestalt as divine Sophia (wisdom)." In Trible's assessment, Schüssler Fiorenza argues from its roots:

> The Christian missionary movement, unlike the Jesus movement, addressed people of different national, cultural, social and religious backgrounds. Its integrative symbol was the new Creation available to all through the work

of Jesus. Women were active as rich patrons and prominent leaders. The existence of churches in private houses provided equal opportunities for them, because the house was women's proper sphere. Moreover, according to the theology of the group, which turned on the power of the Spirit, all Christians, female and male, were equal. The pre-Pauline baptismal formula that in Christ there is no male and female, as the idea occurs in St. Paul's Epistle to the Galatians, expressed that ethos.

It's always interesting to me as a feminist that I am not so keen on Paul; he does not always survive my hermeneutic of suspicion around his own gender issues. But, in truth, his teachings, while still doing some bidding of empire, leaned toward gender equality.

Yet St. Paul himself, fearing . . . orgiastic behavior in worship like that in contemporary pagan cults, he restricted the role of women (but not of men) to insure decency and order. Further, through such concepts as "father of the community" and "bride of Christ," he paved the way for the transferal of patriarchal structures to the Christian community. While St. Paul made independence possible for women by encouraging them not to marry, he nevertheless subordinated them in marriage to their husbands. Thus, his views on women were double-edged.

And this double-edged commentary makes my point exactly. Still, for a man of his time, Paul did move the needle.

This argument concludes that to protect itself within the patriarchal structures of Greco-Roman society, the post-Pauline community eliminated any ambivalence. Complete subordination of women within marriage and church became the norm. Hence in time Christianity denied the Gospel to women. For Mrs. Schüssler Fiorenza, however, despite this sexist repression, the "good news" referred to in the word "gospel" survives for women to recover and claim.[9]

WOMEN'S EXPERIENCES SHAPING IMAGES

In 1992, Ruether defined "the critical principle of feminist theology" as "the promotion of the full humanity of women."[10] As many have observed, this definition has inspired a process of theological reflection that begins with women's experience in recognition of the fact that theology has been almost exclusively informed by the experiences of men. Feminists' critique of traditional theology observes the extent to which scripture and theological knowledge is shaped by the cultural location and physicality of the theologian, including his or her gender/gender performance. Acknowledging women's experience and ways of being/knowing is a corrective to previous theological discourse. Further, since male and female are both made in the image of God (Gn 1:27), then to fully know God requires the theological participation of both sexes and nongender-conforming participation as well.

AND WE ARE NOT FINISHED

The medieval theologian Hildegard of Bingen struggled to capture her vision of the Spirit of God with a cascade of vivid images and a mélange of metaphors.[11] The divine spirit, Hildegard wrote, is the very life of the life of all creatures; the way in which everything is penetrated with connectedness and relatedness; a burning fire who sparks, ignites, inflames, kindles hearts; a guide in the fog; a balm for wounds; a shining serenity; an overflowing fountain that spreads to all sides. As rendered by Elizabeth Johnson in the following passage, Hildegard's vision encompassed many of the themes that appear in the writing of twentieth-century feminist writers:

> She is life, movement, color, radiance, restorative stillness in the din. Her power makes all withered sticks and souls green again with the juice of life. She purifies, absolves, strengthens, heals, gathers the perplexed, seeks the lost. She pours the juice of contrition into hardened hearts. She plays music in the soul, being herself the melody of praise and joy. She awakens mighty hope, blowing everywhere the winds of renewal in creation.[12]

This, for Hildegard in the twelfth century, is the mystery of the God in whom humans live and move and have their being.

Eight centuries later, Native American poet, literary critic, activist, professor, and novelist Paula Gunn Allen wrote in similarly provocative language of the spirit that pervades her Laguna Pueblo / Sioux peoples:

> There is a spirit that pervades everything, that is capable of powerful song and radiant movement, and that moves in and out of the mind. The colors of this spirit are multitudinous, a glowing, pulsing rainbow. Old Spider Woman is one name for this quintessential spirit, and Serpent Woman is another . . . and what they together have made is called Creation, Earth, creatures, plants and light.[13]

These words make me think of Latina feminists like Gloria Anzaldúa and Ada María Isasi-Díaz.[14] I can hear them on the border—*en la frontera*—conjuring wisdom from the earth, the wind, the sea, and fire.

In this passage from *The Color Purple*, Alice Walker's character, Shug Avery, recounts to Celie the epiphany that came over her when she learned to get the old white man off her eyeball:

> It? I ast.
>
> Yeah, It. God ain't a he or a she, but a It.
>
> But what do it look like? I ast.
>
> Don't look like nothing, she say. It ain't a picture show. It ain't something you can look at apart from anything else, including yourself. I believe God is everything, say Shug. Everything that is or ever will be. And when you can feel that, and be happy to feel that, you've found It.[15]

What freedom Alice Walker takes as a novelist to use her Holy imagination to liberate Celie and Shug. Shug, a juke-joint singer, preaches a new gospel to Celie who has lived a life of abuse and neglect. Those feminists who continue the work of creating God-talk liberate women of all ages and strata to claim God for themselves, to see and say from their experiences and add to theology for all times.

In Ntozake Shange's poem, "A Laying On of Hands" in *For Colored Girls Who Have Considered Suicide/When the Rainbow Is Enuf,* Shange articulates the yearning for profoundly eminent God as she writes about a sense of what she is missing but what she cannot quite describe or name. There is a sense of almost-ness of her experience of loving men and women that approximates what she wants, what she needs. In her speaking and writing, she plays in the space of her imagination. She names the longing and walks herself to an insight: She had what she was looking for all along, and she declares:

> i found god in myself
> & i loved her / i loved her fiercely[16]

In my own holy musings, I've written, "My God is a curvy Black woman with dreadlocks and dark, cocoa-brown skin. She can rock a whole world to sleep, singing in her contralto voice. Her sighs breathe life into humanity. Her heartbreaks cause eruptions of justice and love." This to the delight of many, like Father Richard Rohr, whose Center for Action and Contemplation published the larger piece, to the outrage of some.[17]

What does God look like to you? What is God like for you? As feminists seek to enlarge the image of God for a world yearning to know Her more fully, we know we might delight, stretch, and enrage the people we engage. Still we must continue the feminist project of Mary and Hagar, articulating what we see and experience as acts of defiance and resistance and as expressions of awe. We can do this together as sisters in the wilderness, across faith, across ethnicity, across time.

NOTES

1. See Delores S. Williams, *Sisters in the Wilderness: The Challenge of Womanist God-Talk* (Maryknoll, NY: Orbis, 1993).

2. See Ana-María Rizzuto, *The Birth of the Living God* (Chicago, IL: University of Chicago Press, 1981).

3. Elizabeth Cady Stanton, *The Woman's Bible,* 1895; reprint available through CreateSpace, 2017.

4. Valerie Saiving, "The Human Situation: A Feminine View," first published in 1960 and later included in *Womanspirit Rising: A Feminist Reader in Religion,* ed. Carol P. Christ and Judith Plaskow (New York: HarperOne, 1979, 1992).

5. Mary Daly, *The Church and the Second Sex* (Boston, MA: Beacon Press, 1986).

6. See Daly, *The Church and the Second Sex.*

7. Phyllis Trible, *Texts of Terror: Literary-Feminist Readings of Biblical Narratives* (London and Minneapolis: Fortress Press, 1984).

8. Phyllis Trible, "The Creation of a Feminist Theology," *New York Times,* May 1, 1983, sec. 7, page 28.

9. Trible, "Creation of Feminist Theology," 28.

10. Rosemary Radford Ruether, *Sexism and God-Talk: Toward a Feminist Theology* (Boston, MA: Beacon Press, 1992), 18.

11. See, for example, Hildegard of Bingen, *Scivias*, trans. Mother Columba Hart and Jane Bishop, The Classics of Western Spirituality (New York: Paulist Press, 1990).

12. Paraphrase in Elizabeth A. Johnson: *She Who Is: The Mystery of God in Feminist Theological Discourse* (New York: Herder & Herder, 1992), 127–28.

13. Paula Gunn Allen, *The Sacred Hoop: Recovering the Feminine in American Indian Traditions* (Boston, MA: Beacon Press, 1986), 22.

14. See, for example, Gloria Anzaldúa, *Borderlands / La Frontera: The New Mestiza*, 25th anniv., 4th ed. (San Francisco: Aunt Lute Books, 2012) and *Making Face, Making Soul / Haciendo Caras: Creative and Critical Perspectives by Feminists of Color* (San Francisco: Aunt Lute Books, 1990); and Ada María Isasi-Díaz, *Mujerista Theology: A Theology for the Twenty-First Century* (Maryknoll, NY: Orbis Books, 1996), *En la Lucha/In the Struggle: Elaborating a Mujerista Theology*, 10th anniv. ed. (Philadelphia, PA: Fortress Press, 2004), and *Decolonizing Epistemologies: Latina/o Theology and Philsophy* (New York: Fordham University Press, 2011).

15. Alice Walker, *The Color Purple* (New York: Pocket Books, 1982), 177–78.

16. Ntozake Shange, "A Laying On of Hands," in *For Colored Girls Who Have Considered Suicide/When the Rainbow Is Enuf* (New York: Scribner, 1976), 63.

17. Jacqueline J. Lewis, "She Is God. She Is Love," *The Mendicant* 9, no. 2 (2019): 2. Center for Action and Contemplation, https://cac.org/wp-content/uploads/2019/05/theMendicant_Vol9No2.pdf.

BIBLIOGRAPHY

Anzaldúa, Gloria. *Borderlands / La Frontera: The New Mestiza*. 25th anniv., 4th ed. San Francisco: Aunt Lute Books, 2012.

———. *Making Face, Making Soul / Haciendo Caras: Creative and Critical Perspectives by Feminists of Color*. San Francisco: Aunt Lute Books, 1990.

Daly, Mary. *The Church and the Second Sex*. Boston, MA: Beacon Press, 1986.

Gunn Allen, Paula. *The Sacred Hoop: Recovering the Feminine in American Indian Traditions*. Boston, MA: Beacon Press, 1986.

Hildegard of Bingen. *Scivias*. Translated by Mother Columba Hart and Jane Bishop. The Classics of Western Spirituality. New York: Paulist Press, 1990.

Johnson, Elizabeth A. *She Who Is: The Mystery of God in Feminist Theological Discourse*. New York: Herder & Herder, 1992.

Isasi-Díaz, Ada María. *Decolonizing Epistemologies: Latina/o Theology and Philsophy*. New York: Fordham University Press, 2011.

———. *En la Lucha/In the Struggle: Elaborating a Mujerista Theology*, 10th anniv. ed. Philadelphia, PA: Fortress Press, 2004.

———. *Mujerista Theology: A Theology for the Twenty-First Century*. Maryknoll, NY: Orbis Books, 1996.

Lewis, Jacqueline J. "She Is God. She Is Love." *The Mendicant* 9, no. 2 (2019): 2. Center for Action and Contemplation, https://cac.org/wp-content/uploads/2019/05/theMendicant_Vol9No2.pdf.

Rizzuto, Ana-María. *The Birth of the Living God: A Psychoanalytic Study*. Chicago: University of Chicago Press, 1979.

Ruether, Rosemary Radford. *Sexism and God-Talk: Toward a Feminist Theology*. Boston, MA: Beacon Press, 1992.

Saiving, Valerie. "The Human Situation: A Feminine View." In *Womanspirit Rising: A Feminist Reader in Religion*, edited by Carol P. Christ and Judith Plaskow. New York: HarperOne, 1979, 1992.

Schüssler Fiorenza, Elisabeth. *In Memory of Her: A Feminist Theological Reconstruction of Christian Origins*. London, 1983.

Shange, Ntozake. "A Laying on of Hands." In *For Colored Girls Who Have Considered Suicide/When the Rainbow Is Enuf*. New York: Scribner, 1976.

Trible, Phyllis. "The Creation of a Feminist Theology," *New York Times*, May 1, 1983.

Williams, Delores S. *Sisters in the Wilderness: The Challenge of Womanist God-Talk*. Maryknoll, NY: Orbis, 1993.

CHAPTER 2

The Inclusive Language of God

Why It Matters for Women's Studies in Religion

Yudit Kornberg Greenberg, PhD, Rollins College

ABSTRACT

The language of God, or "God-talk," is integral to theology and philosophy of religion. While "God" is the primary subject matter of theology, scholars have shifted from analytic approaches, such as proofs about the existence of God and attributes of God, to the grammar and metaphors employed to designate, convey, and ascertain the divine. In cross-cultural investigation of the languages for the divine, it becomes apparent that these are largely androcentric, hierarchical, and sexist. The objectives of this chapter are 1) to provide examples from scriptures, liturgy, and other discourses that serve as evidence for the predominance of androcentrism in representing the divine; 2) to illustrate recent scholarly critical responses to historic God languages that have contributed to social hierarchy and exclusion of women from access to religious knowledge, authority, and leadership; and 3) to assess feminist strategies for ameliorating gender imbalances in religious life and thought through deconstruction and "hermeneutics of suspicion"[1] and construction of an inclusive language for theology in light of ethical values that respect differences across gender, race, ethnicity, class, and sexuality.[2]

INTRODUCTION

In this chapter, I investigate conceptualizations of the divine, with a focus on the Abrahamic traditions with some comparative examinations of Asian religions. I explicate gendered and androcentric language through the lens of critical feminist and cultural scholarship and examine alternative notions and imagery located in historical texts, as well as in contemporary feminist theology, that provide more inclusive approaches to the divine. In addressing scriptural, philosophical, mystical, and liturgical texts, I explore a multiplicity of perspectives within each religious tradition and highlight not only dominant trends but also voices that offer lesser-known images of the divine feminine, indicating that cultures and religions are fluid, and provide a range of meanings.[3]

Feminist theologians strive to liberate religion from the dominance of patriarchally shaped traditions, correcting gender imbalance and providing a religious worldview where women are represented and act as equals in matters related to doctrines, beliefs, and practices. An influential theory by anthropologist Clifford Geertz describes how religious language and symbols legitimate social systems, and, accordingly, feminists have shown that representation of the divine impact and shape social constructions of body, gender, and sexuality. The main concern of most feminist theologians is that the divine is usually represented in masculine terms. Even religions that have multiple gods and goddesses generally have a male supreme god to which all other gods and goddesses are subservient. The supremacy of the male god and the traditions that this divine hierarchy promulgates can be seen reflected in societies and the daily lives of their adherents. At the same time, the presence of goddesses in religions, such as Hinduism, has not always correlated to gender and social balance for women. To the contrary, sometimes, the order in the divine realm as conceived by spiritual adepts and theologians has been used by them as a justification for maintaining the social structure in which gender inequality has persisted.

God languages are analogous and metaphorical and the consequence of our attempts to convey an experience of something that transcends language.[4] It is therefore erroneous to take religious language about God literally or to believe that images of God correspond to the divine reality. The challenges of God language are especially relevant for Western feminists who work within the context of monotheistic and scripture-based religions.[5] Despite God being understood as neither male nor female in Abrahamic traditions, masculine God language has dominated their theology and liturgy. The core of the feminist critique in these contexts is the conviction that the language we use reflects and in turn shapes the way we construct our religious experiences. In this critique, we learn about the nature of religious symbols and the way in which issues of gender and sexuality are inseparable from them. Even more importantly, the use of religious language affects interhuman, interreligious, and human–nature relationships.[6]

Western and Asian feminist theologians and philosophers continue to wrestle with gender imbalances in their traditions, especially in terms of religious leadership and questions of authority and power.[7] This is a significant issue when we study God language in the context of social justice. This chapter concludes by underscoring the value of dialogue among feminists in our mutual work toward spiritual and material egalitarianism in our traditions for spiritual practice and revisioning women's status in their respective traditions.

Since inclusive God language is linked to justice and authority in human society, it is incumbent upon scholars in the field of women's studies in religion to examine scriptures and other sacred texts that inform us of the prevalence of masculine God language in these texts. Investigating the variety of concepts and metaphors for the divine then helps to correct or confirm the record of traditional God language and compose inclusive language that reflects diverse and pluralistic visions for the divine and that can be integrated into liturgy and other writings, thus helping to renew women's connection to spirituality and their historic religious communities.

THE LANGUAGES OF GOD IN JUDAISM

In the Hebrew bible, among God's numerous names, YHWH (without vowels) and *Elohim* are dominant.[8] God is also called *El Elyon*, literally God Most High. Here, not only the nouns but also the verbs are gendered as male. The reference to God as "the God of Abraham, Isaac and Jacob" (Genesis 50:24; Exodus 3:15) first indicates the superiority of masculine names and attributes, on which basis feminist Jewish theologians build their case that by apotheosizing the divine primarily as male, masculinity emerges as normative and women as other. At the same time, we should not ignore texts that are suggestive of a more egalitarian view. In the act of creation of humanity in the very first chapter of Genesis, when God created the first human being, God said: "Let us make Adam in our image, after our likeness. God created Adam in His image, in the image of God He created him; male and female God created them (Genesis 1:26–27). In addition, there are occasional representations in texts where God is depicted as a mother giving birth, feeding and comforting her children: "As one whom his mother comforts, so will I comfort you; and you will be comforted in Jerusalem."[9]

The notion of God's presence, the Shekhinah, with its feminine name and character, is notable but is nonexistent in the Bible.[10] It is only in rabbinic literature that the Shekinah as a concept is identified, signifying the immanence or the indwelling divine presence who follows the Jews in their exile and suffers with them.[11] As Jewish life in exile persisted, the Shekhinah is transformed into a separate emanation as an aspect of the divine, thus constituting an exception to the dominant trope of the male Jewish God.

Whereas in the eyes of the rabbis of the Talmudic era, God's presence, or the Shekhinah, dwells among the exiled community of Israel; the kabbalists in the 12th century imagined aspects of the divine in more embodied terms and claimed that the Shekhinah, among its other meanings, is both integral to the divine and represents the community of Israel. A key element in the symbolic universe of the kabbalah then is the emergence of the divine female, a figure within the divine-symbolic realm. One factor theorized by some scholars in the elevation of the divine feminine from presence to divine hypostasis in the kabbalah was the influential role of the cult of Mariology in Catholic theology and worship.[12]

Among her numerous functions in the Zohar,[13] the Shekhinah provides the source of life for the lower worlds. In addition to being identified as Malchut (kingdom), she is also called the bride of God, princess, the Sabbath, the Torah, the moon, the earth, and the apple orchard.[14] The Shekhinah in the Zohar is also imagined as a nursing mother, filled with milk, which goes out continuously, breastfeeding Israel with spiritual blessings.[15] The imagery of God as a nursing mother is also accompanied with the suckling act, which indicates the interdependence of human and divine; just as God's blessings flow from above, so do human prayers from below rise above.[16]

JEWISH FEMINIST THOUGHT

Theological, halakhic, and cultural scholarship have informed and shaped new perspectives and methodologies in interpreting, constructing, and democratizing an inclusive Judaism. Given the predominance of androcentric God language in Jewish texts, Jewish feminists provide a theoretical framework for re-envisioning the three pillars of traditional Judaism—Torah, God, and Israel—in all areas of Jewish life and thought, including gender, sexuality, theology, liturgy, and ethics. Furthermore, they aim to apply the moral imperative for inclusivity and equality not only for women but to all aspects of life. Among the earliest scholars were Rachel Adler, Judith Plaskow, Ellen Umansky, Marcia Falk, and Susannah Heschel, who centered their work around the critique of traditional male God language.[17]

Judith Plaskow's scholarship is the first systematic feminist Jewish theology that focuses on recovering women's history and redefining women's relationship with the sacred. Contributing to Susannah Heschel's anthology *On Being a Jewish Feminist* (1983), Plaskow declared that *The Right Question Is Theological*.[18] Written in response to Cynthia Ozick's essay "Notes Toward Finding the Right Question," Plaskow contends that theology, rather than Halakhah (Jewish law), is primary, whereas Ozick's focus is on Halakhah. According to Plaskow, Halakhic rulings result from theological presumptions, one of which is women's otherness.[19]

In *Standing Again at Sinai* (1990), Plaskow establishes the ways that patriarchal values define the nation of Israel and justify exclusively masculine God language and patriarchal understandings of body and sexuality. Embracing the goddess, she states, "The Goddess is, of course, God/She, but in a clearer and more powerful way. Not simply a feminine reworking of the masculine deity but an ancient power in her own right, she gathers to her all the qualities and prerogatives of the goddesses of many names. She is Asherah, Ishtar, Isis, Afrekete, Oyo, Ezuli, Mary, and Shekhinah. She is lover, creator, warrior, grantor of fertility, lawgiver, maiden, mother, and crone."[20] At the same time, Plaskow also problematizes replacing masculine images with female ones for God. Instead, she observes that feminists have yet to apply "the presence of God into empowered, egalitarian community."[21]

Plaskow challenges women and men to embrace the notion of Jewish transformation and is adamant that women must see themselves "standing again at Sinai" as recipients and partners of the covenant. This entails critiquing deeply embedded notions of hierarchy and exclusivity as these exist in the Torah, liturgy, and Halakha. Furthermore, as partners of the covenant, feminist theologians must redefine the Jewish community's ethics of inclusivity, ameliorate what they characterize as imbalanced God language, and create new midrashim and liturgy that reflect women's experiences and sensibilities. Rachel Adler is another major Jewish theologian whose book *Engendering Judaism: An Inclusive Theology and Ethics* (1999) furthers feminist thinking by focusing on creating egalitarian rituals, which men and women recreate and renew together as equals.[22]

Liturgy is a fundamental platform for liberating religious traditions from the yoke of patriarchy. The earliest gender-inclusive language in the Jewish prayer book was introduced in 1975 by the Reform Movement. A paradigmatic change was replacing "Blessed are you God and God of our fathers/God of Abraham, God of Isaac, God of Jacob" with "Blessed are you God and God of our ancestors/God of Abraham, God of Isaac, God of Jacob, God of Sarah, God of Rebekah, God of Leah and God of Rachel," adding the names of the biblical matriarchs.

Poet and scholar Marcia Falk contributed to alternative God language in Hebrew in her *Book of Blessings: A New Prayer Book for the Weekdays, the Sabbath, and the New Moon Festival* (1996). In composing new language for Hebrew prayers, she decided against employing male (or female) images of and metaphors for God. In her judgment, personal images of God, whether masculine or feminine, are limiting. In her emphasis on divine immanence, she created images such as eyn hachayim, "wellspring of life"; nishmat kol chai, "breath of all living things"; and nitzotzot hanéfesh, "sparks of the inner, unseen self" to serve as renewed metaphors for divinity.[23] Since the publication of her groundbreaking book, several prayers from *The Book of Blessings* have been featured in new Conservative, Reform, and Reconstructionist prayer books.

Jewish feminist scholars have contributed to ameliorating androcentrism in Jewish life and thought as demonstrated by the questions, responses, and creation of new languages to express an inclusive religiosity whether in theological reflections, midrashim, or the compositions of new prayers and rituals. They explored and implemented two primary approaches for reconstructing Jewish liturgy: 1) adding feminine nouns, pronouns, and names of the divine to existing masculine ones; and 2) removing personal pronouns and other gendered forms, replacing them with neutral and abstract metaphors. Other paradigm shifts in Jewish liturgy include a gynocentric approach, highlighting the Shekhinah and the ways in which divinity appears primarily in female form, such as the earth-based, embodied Jewish prayer book authored by the Kohenet (priestess) Institute.[24]

CHRISTIAN FEMINIST THEOLOGY

Christian women's organized opposition to ecclesiastical leadership and practice dates from the 19th century, with social critics who began to challenge the status quo. Among them is Elizabeth Cady Stanton's publication of the *Woman's Bible* in 1895, in which she disputes the scriptural suggestion that sin and death were introduced into the world by a woman. In the second half of the 20th century, Christian theologians began their activism and scholarship denouncing gender hierarchy and exclusion in the Church. In her classic manifesto of feminist theological consciousness, *Beyond God the Father*, Mary Daly critiqued the patriarchy of the Roman Catholic Church. Objecting to the phallocentric language used in both the Hebrew Bible and the New Testament, she coined the famous phrase "Since God is male, the male is God." Her "pragmatic yardstick or verification process" for God language is articulated thus: "In my thinking, the specific criterion which implies a mandate to reject certain forms of God-talk is expressed in the question: Does this language hinder human becoming by reinforcing sex-role socialization?

Expressed positively. . . . Does it encourage human becoming toward psychological and social fulfillment, toward an androgynous mode of living, toward transcendence?"[25]

While Mary Daly went on to reject Roman Catholicism and mainstream Christianity, Catholic feminist theologian Rosemary Radford Ruether committed to reforming Christian theology by identifying the transformative principle of feminist theology. Ruether sees the replacement of the transcendent male deity with an immanent female as insufficient. She integrates into its rubrics women's experiences, thus "exposing classical theology, including its codified traditions, as based on male experience rather than on universal human experience."[26] She states that "When the word Father is taken literally to mean that God is male and not female, represented by males and not females, then this word becomes idolatrous."[27] She extends her concern beyond Christianity to embrace the truths of other religious traditions and suggests that the focus of Christian goals and rituals should turn from the sole worship of "God the Father" to concern for Gaia, which represents the ecology of the earth. In her 1992 book *Gaia and God*, she advocates that Christians should embrace both Gaia and God as "two voices," as their role is maintenance of the earth given to us by the creator. The challenge is embracing a co-deity whose conceptual roots are so distinct from the tradition's God.

Elisabeth Schüssler Fiorenza's approach to feminist biblical interpretation follows the same reasoning, holding that a feminist critical hermeneutic must "reject those elements within all biblical traditions and texts that perpetuate, in the name of God, violence, alienation, and patriarchal subordination, and eradicate women from historical-theological consciousness."[28]

Sallie McFague is another well-known Christian feminist, whose book *Models of God: Theology for an Ecological, Nuclear Age* critiques the dominance of male and monarchical imagery in Christian God language and suggests alternatives that deify feminist values. She defines theological discourse as metaphorical, enabling new woman-centered imagery. Her book *The Body of God: An Ecological Theology* presents the earth as a single holistic system that is permeated by God, and thus as God's body, thereby emphasizing the interconnection and sacredness of all forms of life.

It is interesting to note that many of the themes that undergird the writing of 20th-century feminists are already present in earlier Christian women's writings. An example is Hildegard of Bingen, a medieval female saint, who shared her vision of the Spirit of God as the mystery of the way in which everything is penetrated with connectedness and relatedness.[29]

NEW CHRISTIAN LITURGY

Advocacy for the incorporation of women's experience and embodiment into theological discourse has resulted in major changes in the symbols and practices that define and sustain Christian communities. In her discussion of gender and liturgy in Catholicism, scholar Teresa Berger notes major issues linked to the priestly office and thereby to maleness in the Church. Yet she recognizes that this is an opportune time for change because "women have moved from liturgical consumption and reproduction to liturgical production, grasping liturgy as a crucial site for the negotiation of faith and women's lives."[30] She critiques what is an "optional reading" in the Sunday lectionary for the Roman Catholic dioceses in the United States: the parable in which Jesus likens the coming of God's reign to a woman baking (Matthew 13:33). She questions its optionality and advocates for change by making it integral since it is one of the few biblical texts that shows Jesus drawing on women's everyday lives to imagine God's reign.

Feminist scholar Christine Hoff Kraemer offers an extensive discussion of sexist language, concluding that inclusive language is political in nature.[31] She argues that ridding Christianity of masculine referents, particularly those for God, is a political position, just as is the traditional prohibition of female referents for God, as both have exclusionary potential. Instead, she advocates for the use of multiple metaphors with the goal of inclusivity in gender, ethnic, age, and class differences. The following is an example of a newly created woman-centered Christian prayer:

(1) One: Come, Holy Spirit, breath divine
All: Open us for your presence
(1) One: Refresh and give life to what is exhausted and tired
All: Drive away fear out of our hearts
(1) One: Come, Holy Spirit, Wind Divine
All: Wake up our longing, create a new beginning among us
(2) One: God, our mother and father, creator of women in your own image, loving foundation and heart of all beings, we are gathered here before you. Let us pray for all women around the world so that they may be blessed with:
All:
The strength to persevere,
The courage to speak out,
The vision to seek a renewed ministry,
The faith to believe in you beyond
All systems and institutions,
so that your face on earth may be seen in all its beauty.[32]

Some feminists have incorporated neopagan elements within their approach to reforming Christian theology and liturgy, although conservative Christians are opposed to the integration of nature-based metaphors. In response, neopagans insist that what they adhere to are in fact pre-Christian European pagan practices that absorbed many folk rituals and festivals. They justify their practices by explaining that the term *Easter* derives from Eostre, a goddess of fertility and rebirth. Similarly, the Christmas tradition of decorating an evergreen tree can be traced back to pre-Christian Winter Solstice celebrations, where the tree represented the promised rebirth of the Sun God.

As the feminist Christian movement grew, minority groups, such as Womanist, Latina, Asian, and LGBTQ+ theologians, emerged, with a focus on empowering and liberating their constituents.[33] While novelist Alice Walker coined the term *womanist*, Delores S. Williams was the first to use the term *womanist theology* in her discussions of Black women's oppression based on class, race, and sex.[34] More recently, in her search for suitable metaphors for representing Black women's experiences, Williams has rejected the Exodus model of Black theology, with its focus on liberation, and turned to wilderness imagery as a more suitable image of Black women's reality. For her, survival and productive quality of life represent the core of womanist theology, rather than Black theology's focus on liberation.[35]

An early vocal proponent for change for Latina theology is Cuban American Ada María Isasi-Díaz, a major scholar and activist of Mujerista theology, who affirms the presence of God amid Latina communities and their daily lives. According to her, Mujerista theology helps Latinas discover ways of combatting oppression so that God's ongoing revelation is disclosed in society. Her theology is based on the lived experience of the poor and the encounter with God in the messiness of life.[36] Asian theologian Kwok Pui-lan describes the merits of drawing inspiration from the traditional religions of one's own region and ethnic group in order to revitalize and expand Christian worship.[37] What is common to Womanist, Mujerista/Latina, and Asian Christian feminists is their refusal to maintain the status quo of God language and their alienation from dominant tropes in Christian theology. Their ideologies and theologies are a reminder that Euro-centric-derived white Christianity does not represent them nor does it serve them in their search for spiritual belonging and in their socioeconomic reality and everyday lives. Thus, engagement with God language encompasses not only gender and sexuality; moreover, God language represents color, race, ethnicity, and class.

ISLAMIC FEMINIST THEOLOGY

Islamic feminists argue that many Islamic communities violate the true teachings of Islam and the Qur'ān is in fact compatible with the ideas of gender equality. Riffat Hassan and Fatima Mernissi are among the earliest Muslim feminists based in the West and influenced by the liberal thinker Fazlur Rahman and his holistic reading of the Qur'ān in order to seek the spirit behind its literalism. For example, Riffat Hassan interrogates the Qur'ānic male interpretation that blames Eve for the fall of humanity. Despite a theological rejection of any form of gendered anthropomorphism, the Qur'ān and earliest Muslim theology employ the Arabic name for God or Allah and render it into the pronoun *huwa* ("He").[38] While God language has not been a topic of discussion, scholars have focused on the Qur'ānic concept of equality of all human beings and promoted the application of this theology to Islamic law. Saba Mahmood, a Pakistani-born Western-educated scholar, advocates for women mastering the discourse of classical Islamic texts and argumentation in order to reinterpret traditional texts.[39]

Amina Wadud, an American Muslim, and Sa'diyya Shaikh, a South African Muslim, interpret verses from the Qur'ān that express the equality between men and women, and they explain the subordination of women in the religion on the basis of patriarchal interpretations by conservative clergy and legal scholars. In a 2009 interview about mixed prayers she led in New York, Dr. Wadud states that "Islam gave me a language, and actually Arabic was an important part of it—it gave me the language of *tawhid*, the language of God's intimate relationship with the creation, but also the power to bring harmony to things which are disparate."[40]

Another approach taken by Sa'diyya Shaikh deploys Sufi thought and practice for creatively rethinking the ontological assumptions about gender embedded in Islamic law and legal reasoning, inspired by 13th-century Islamic thinker Ibn Arabi. In his writings, Arabi conjures the earth as the creative, benevolent, maternal source of good, thereby linking it to the divine. As he states it, "[The earth] gives all of the benefits from her essence [*dhat*] and is the location [*maḥall*] of all good. Thus she is the most powerful [*a'azz*] of the bodies. . . . she is the patient [*ṣabur*], the receptive one [*qabila*], the immutable one, the firm one. . . . it is the mother from whom we come and to whom we return. And from her we will come forth once again. To her we are submitted and entrusted. She is the most subtle of foundations [*arkan*] in meaning. She accepts density, darkness, and hardness only in order to conceal the treasures that God has entrusted to it."[41] Ibn Arabi focuses on feminine, and especially maternal, imagery and employs feminine metaphors of childbirth, particularly the act of contraction, to describe the origin of creation.[42] Despite gendered hierarchies in Islamic scriptures, their mystical writings are steeped in feminine imagery of the divine, providing a greater intimacy in the nexus of the human and the divine.

THEALOGY, NEOPAGANISM AND CROSS-CULTURAL VISIONS OF THE DIVINE FEMALE

Countering and correcting the patriarchal theology of the Abrahamic religions is *thealogy*, the discourse of the feminine divine (thea) in contrast to the male God (theo), providing a framework for giving voice to representations of the divine in a female form. Scholar Naomi Goldenberg first used this term in her book *Changing of the Gods* (1979). Thealogy has become widely known as a provocative term denoting a shift away from the androcentric theological paradigm. Like Christian and Jewish feminist theology, thealogy developed from radical feminist criticism of religion as the glorification of masculinity, and from reflection on women's experience and the sacral power of femaleness.

Thealogical narratives feature female divine archetypes, including Ishtar, Isis, Sophia, and the Virgin Mary. While thealogy is not associated with any one religious or spiritual tradition, it shares valuing the power of femaleness with neopaganism. Neopaganism, earth-based spirituality, and goddess-centered traditions are decentralized, possessing no clergy, holy books, or geographic centers. These traditions can also be characterized as pantheistic or panentheistic,[43] promoting the idea that the divine is immanent in the world. Since the divine permeates all, this creative life force is typically identified with nature, and thus with Gaia, or Mother Earth. Mother Earth, also revered as a goddess, provides the gifts of the earth that sustain all living things. Thealogy then stresses nurturing, motherhood, nature, and wisdom. This thinking subverts patriarchal notions of the divine and is aimed at liberating women from oppressive thinking and thus empowering them.

THE MAHADEVI (THE GREAT GODDESS) IN HINDU TEXTS

In Hindu philosophy and theology, we encounter the active and creative feminine principle, and the two primary manifestations of God—Vishnu and Shiva—are always with their feminine counterparts, Lakshmi and Parvati. Both Lakshmi and Parvati are also identified with the great goddess—Mahadevi—and the Shakti, or divine power.

As early as the Ṛig Veda (1900–1700 BCE), we find evidence for the feminine divine in a hymn known as the *Devi Suktam* ("Praise to the Divine Feminine," RV 10.125), which envisions the feminine divine as a supreme and pervasive divinity. Written by a renowned woman sage known as Ambhrani, her verses invoke the all-encompassing presence of the Devi: "I am the Queen, the gatherer of treasures, established in/as Ultimate Reality, the Primary Object of Worship. The Luminous Divine Powers (*deva*) have dispersed me in many places, having many abodes, causing me to be All-Pervasive."[44] A well-defined theology of the divine feminine identified as Shakti is found in the Devi Mahatmyam from the 6th century CE, where she is also recognized as Durga and Kali (see figure 2.1). She is convergent with her creation at its emergence (DM 1.57). She is the power (*Shakti*) and process of matter (*Prakṛti*) unfolding itself, comprising the principles of creation, destruction, and sustenance while underscoring her maternal qualities of compassion, love, and care.[45]

In the Hindu tradition, there are multiple approaches to the divine, including the Vedic notion of the Brahman, the Absolute and impersonal who is genderless; goddesses, such as Shakti; and gods and goddesses who are worshipped singularly or together as pairs, such as Krishna-Radha. Nonetheless, there is still the question of women's empowerment in the public sphere of religion. Goddesses do not necessarily offer liberating female models. The goddess Lakshmi, Shiva's wife, for example, has been the paradigm of the subservient wife. At the same time, in Bhakti Vaishnavism, the goddess

FIGURE 2.1. Durga in the eleventh century CE Rani ki Vav Stepwell in Patan, Gujarat.
© *Vasudeva Narayan*

Radha, Krishna's consort, was elevated to the level of supreme divinity among her devotees in 16th-century Bengal. As specialists in Hindu theology note, women's access to
and embodiment of spiritual authority in Hindu traditions varied throughout history in
different sects and movements, as seen in lesser or greater women's representations as
saints, gurus, and yoginis. Furthermore, since Hinduism has an important and vibrant
private home tradition of worship, women exercise their autonomy and express their
identity with the goddess directly. Despite the prevalence of the feminine principle and
the Devi in sacred Hindu, Jain, and Sikh texts, feminists continue to engage in critically
analyzing these in order to bring to light persisting theological and cultural imbalances.
Nonetheless, it is evident that the Hindu tradition offers many more representations of
the divine feminine than the Abrahamic traditions and could perhaps serve as a guiding
model for feminist engagement in religious studies.

TRADITIONAL AND FEMINIST BUDDHIST VIEWS OF GOD

Buddhism denies the existence of an eternal, omnipotent God, or the godhead who is the
creator and controller of the world. Early Buddhists denied Hindu gods and goddesses
and repudiated that Siddhartha Gautama (the Buddha) was a god. Thus, God language
in Buddhism is a nonissue for Buddhist philosophers and theologians. Nonetheless, as
Buddhism integrated into indigenous traditions, deities, such as Avalokiteśvara (literally, the Lord who gazes down toward the world) and Tara, his consort, were developed
in different Buddhist cultures as either gods or goddesses who embody the compassion
of the Buddha. Furthermore, androcentric beliefs, such as the idea that women cannot
achieve enlightenment and other patriarchal social structures, have been dominant in
Buddhist societies.

Constructing a counterpatriarchal thealogical framework in contemporary Buddhism, and in parallel with Western thealogies that feature empowered female figures,
the bodhisattva Tara has recently been elevated and popularized as the embodiment of
female compassion. In popular Tibetan Buddhism, Tara has provided a female substi-
tute for Avalokiteśvara, embodying the "four divine abiding," lovingkindness, compassion, sympathetic joy, and impartiality/equanimity, which were previously attributed
to him and have gained in popularity in contemporary Buddhist societies.[46] In addition
to popularizing this female bodhisattva, Buddhist feminists have worked to advance
gender equality in the treatment of women in Buddhist societies and in accounting for
the role of women in the history of Buddhism. Feminist scholars such as Rita Gross and
Miranda Shaw acknowledge a misogynist strand in early Buddhist texts but argue that
the core teachings of Buddhism promote gender equity.[47]

CONCLUSION

God language is integral to theology and religious studies and has been a fundamental subject of inquiry for feminists cross-culturally. Feminist theologians have critically
examined masculine and hierarchical language of the divine in scriptures and liturgy

and argued that traditional God languages perpetuate sexism and male-dominated power structures in religious institutions and beyond. Jewish and Christian scholars have been the earliest and most prolific activists and leaders in altering the landscape of Western theology and religious studies. In their reforms, they postulate a three-prong approach to God language: adding feminine nouns, pronouns, and names of the divine to existing masculine ones; removing personal pronouns and other gendered forms, replacing them with neutral and abstract metaphors; and, finally, adopting a gynocentric approach in which divinity appears primarily in female form.

While some feminist theologians work within their constituent traditions with a primary focus on ameliorating women's social and religious status, others have broadened their concerns and activism to combatting heterosexism, homophobia, and other deeply embedded biases. Thealogical constructive thought has been characterized by creativity, imagination, and courage to give voice and agency to women in the spiritual and public sphere and to issues of race and class. Feminists have also defined and elevated the spiritual connection between humanity and nature. Their care for mutuality and reciprocity and interdependence of beings has inspired new metaphors, new rituals, and new social contexts for speaking about and to the divine. In my hope to open an interreligious space among feminists cross-culturally, I brought into this conversation texts and voices from the Abrahamic traditions, as well as of Hindu, Buddhist, and other thealogies that offer a plethora of concepts of the feminine principle and the divine mother and include in their theological imaginary the creative and empowering force of the goddess. I believe that scholars of women's studies, religion, gender, and sexuality can gain inspiration from each other's activism in word and deed, thus contributing to interreligious understanding and mutual appreciation of our traditions.

NOTES

1. A feminist hermeneutics of suspicion in religion critically engages in biased representation of women in scriptures and traditional theology as well as with the absence of women's voices and experiences of the divine.

2. Inclusive language reflects a sensitivity to differences of individuals and communities in gender, race, class, age, physical differences, nationality, theological beliefs, culture, and lifestyle.

3. It is important to acknowledge the significant role of the American Academy of Religion in providing a platform for feminist work in theology and religion. See, for example, the annual contributions of scholars to Feminist Theory and Religious Reflection Unit and Women and Religion Unit and to the journal of *Feminist Studies in Religion*.

4. These are Sally McFague's terms in *Metaphorical Theology: Models of God in Religious Language* (Minneapolis, MN: Fortress Press, 1982).

5. The god of revealed religions is not the same as the Aristotelian god, who is the Unmoved Mover, whose being is independent of humanity. Abraham Joshua Heschel reminds us that the God in the Hebrew Bible, despite his primary masculine and hierarchical status, *needs* humanity for his realization, manifestation, and fulfillment.

6. The subject of ecofeminism integrates justice for ecology and women. On the interrelatedness of human beings and nature, see, for example, the ecofeminist theology of Carol Christ, "Ecofeminism and Process Philosophy," *Feminist Theology*, 14, no. 3 (2006): 289–310.

7. See, e.g., Alf Hiltebeitel and Kathleen M. Erndl, eds., *Is the Goddess a Feminist?: The Politics of South Asian Goddesses* (New York: New York University Press, 2000).

8. Hebrew is a gendered language in which every noun and verb is either masculine or feminine.

9. The Book of Isaiah 66:7–13.

10. Yet we find the verb designating the residence (*shkn*) of God among the Jewish people and in the temple in Jerusalem.

11. The term was first used in the Aramaic form, *shekinta,* in the Targums, written Aramaic translation and interpretation of the Bible.

12. On this theory, see Arthur Green, "Shekhinah, the Virgin Mary, and the Song of Songs: Reflections on a Kabbalistic Symbol in Its Christian Context," *AJS Review* 26, no. 1 (April 2002): 1–52.

13. The Zohar (13th-century Spain) is considered the most important works of the Kabbalah. A dominant theme in the Zohar is the concepts and meanings of the sefirot, the divine channels that connect the upper and lower worlds.

14. In various midrashim to Shir Ha-shirim (Song of Songs) especially in the Zohar, the female protagonist as the Shekhinah is an active agent in the mutual interplay with the masculine aspect of the divine, offering an alternative to the covenantal relational model as represented in prophetic literature.

15. For a discussion on the Shekhinah in the Zohar, see Ellen Haskell, "Bathed in Milk: Metaphors of Suckling and Spiritual Transmission in Thirteenth-Century Kabbalah," in Shubha Pathak, ed., *Figuring Religions Comparing Ideas, Images, and Activities* (New York: SUNY Press, 2013), 127.

16. Yet the Shekhinah in the kabbalah not only embodies positive traits, such as nurturing; at the same time, she is also associated with death and darkness. The Shekhinah has also been compared by leading scholars to the Hindu Shakti not only as the feminine counterpart of the male God but also as the ever-flowing universal feminine energy and wisdom, which enables the nexus of the human and the divine. Gershom Scholem, *On the Mystical Shape of the Godhead* (Berlin: Schocken, 1991), 174. See also Braj Sinha, "The Feminization of the Divine: Shakti and Shekhinah in Tantra and Kabbalah," *Journal of Indo-Judaic Studies,* March (2019).

17. Other key figures in the early years of the Jewish feminist movement include Sally Priesand, Blu Greenberg, Rebecca Alpert, Paula Hyman, Tova Hartman, and Judith Hauptman.

18. This is one of the earliest collection of essays addressing issues of Jewish identity and feminism and encompassing an array of salient issues from prayer to theology.

19. It should also be mentioned that male-God language is not only a problem for women in Judaism, as Howard Eilberg Schwarz argues in his work, *God's Phallus: And Other Problems for Men and Monotheism* (Boston, MA: Beacon Press), 1994. Schwarz reads the male god as legitimating masculine domination while at the same time creating tension between men's homoerotic relationship with the divine and their expected heterosexual social roles.

20. Judith Plaskow, *Standing Again at Sinai: Judaism from a Feminist Perspective* (San Francisco: Harper & Row, 1990), 146.

21. Plaskow, *Standing Again at Sinai,* 155.

22. She is committed to Halakha but at the same time recognizes the pervasive injustice toward women in rabbinic texts. Adler's agenda in developing her inclusive theology and ethics is not only to critique but also to offer alternative models of legally binding contracts. A primary example is her ethical commitment contract—brit ahuvim (lovers' covenant), based on the principle of mutuality—replacing the traditional marriage contract (Ketubah) and its language of acquisition with this alternative contract. She views her constructive Jewish theology and ethical praxis as Tikkun Olam (mending a shattered world).

23. Falk suggests that her theology of immanence both affirms the sanctity of the world and shatters the idolatrous reign of the lord/God/king. She further defined her monotheism as "the embracing of diversity within the unity of the greater whole."

24. See Kohenet Hebrew Priestess Institute, http://www.kohenet.com/, accessed May 1, 2020.

25. Mary Daly, *Beyond God the Father: Toward a Philosophy of Women's Liberation* (Boston, MA: Beacon Press, 1973), 21.

26. Rosemary Radford Ruether, *Sexism and God-Talk: Toward a Feminist Theology* (Boston, MA: Beacon Press, 1983), 13.

27. Ruether, *Sexism and God-Talk,* 66.

28. Elisabeth Schüssler Fiorenza, *In Memory of Her: A Feminist Theological Reconstruction of Christian Origins* (Crossroad, 1994), 22–23; and *But She Said: Feminist Practices of Biblical Interpretation* (Boston, MA: Beacon Press, 1993). Fiorenza and other feminist theologians with concern for liberating traditional male-centered Christian theology recognize that the books that comprise the Bible were written and chosen exclusively by men.

29. This reference appears in Nancy Frankenberry, "Feminist Philosophy of Religion," *The Stanford Encyclopedia of Philosophy* (Summer 2018 Edition), Edward N. Zalta (ed.), https://plato .stanford.edu/archives/sum2018/entries/feminist-religion.

30. See, for example, Teresa Berger, "The Contemporary Church and the Real Presence of Women: Of Liturgy, Labor, and Gendered Lives," Yale University, https://ism.yale.edu/sites/ default/files/files/The%20Contemporary%20Church%20and%20the%20Real%20Presence%20 of%20Women.pdf; Martin Stringer, "Text, Context and Performance: Hermeneutics and the Study of Worship," *Scottish Journal of Theology* 53 (2000): 365–79; Richard E. McCarron, "Pursuing 'How Liturgy Means': Liturgical Texts as Hypertext, Oral Text and Intertext," *Proceedings of the North American Academy of Liturgy Annual Meeting* (2002): 101–11.

31. See, for example, Christine Hoff Kraemer, "Ground of Being: An Earth-Centered Liturgy for Christian Churches," http://www.christinehoffkraemer.com/8festivalsX.html; Peter Berger and Brigitte Berger, "Femspeak and the Battle of Language," in *The Politics of Prayer: Feminist Language and the Worship of God*, ed. Helen Hull Hitchcock (San Francisco: Ignatius Press, 1992); and Elizabeth A. Johnson, *She Who Is: The Mystery of God in Feminist Theological Discourse* (St. Louis, MO: Crossroad, 1992), in which the author argues that, by introducing competing images of God into liturgy, we encourage believers to understand that these are metaphors.

32. This prayer was adapted from the Women's Ordination Worldwide opening prayer July 2011, Irmgard Kampmann, Germany, https://www.womensordination.org/programs/world -day-of-prayer/optional-inclusive-liturgies/.

33. For an extensive overview of womanist theology, see Emilie Maureen Townes, "Womanist Theology," https://ir.vanderbilt.edu/bitstream/handle/1803/8226/Townes-WomanistTheology .pdf?sequence=1&isAllowed=y.

34. See Alice Walker, *In Search of Our Mothers' Gardens: Womanist Prose* (Boston: Mariner Books, 1983); and Delores Williams, "Womanist Theology: Black Women's Voices," 1987, https://www .religion-online.org/article/womanist-theology-black-womens-voices/.

35. See Delores S. Williams, *Sisters in the Wilderness: The Challenge of Womanist God-Talk* (Maryknoll, MD: Orbis Books, 1993).

36. See, for example, Ada María Isasi-Díaz, *En la Lucha/In the Struggle: Elaborating a Mujerista Theology*, 2nd ed. (Minneapolis, MN: Fortress Press, 2003). For an explanation of the transition from "Mujerista" to the more inclusive "Latina feminist theology," see, e.g., María Pilar Aquino, "Latina Feminist Theology Central Features," in *A Reader in Latina Feminist Theology: Religion and Justice*, ed. María Pilar Aquino, Daisy L. Machado, and Jeanette Rodríquez (Austin, TX: University of Texas Press, 2002), 133–60.

37. Kwok Pui-lan, *Introducing Asian Feminist Theology* (New York: Bloomsbury Publishers, 2000).

38. At the same time, the attribution of *father* to the divine, common to both Jewish and Christian theology, is absent from Islamic writings.

39. Saba Mahmood conducted seminal research on the pious women of Egyptian women's mosque movement who reclaimed public religious spaces as part of pursuing Islamic knowledge.

40. "Interview with the Muslim Reform Thinker Amina Wadud: 'The Koran Cannot Be Usurped,'" https://en.qantara.de/content/interview-with-the-muslim-reform-thinker-amina -wadud-the-koran-cannot-be-usurped.

41. Cited in Sa'diyya Shaikh, *Sufi Narratives of Intimacy: Ibn 'Arabī, Gender and Sexuality* (Chapel Hill: University of North Carolina Press, 2012).

42. Here, Sufi and Lurianic Kabbalistic imagery of cosmogenic myth and the process of creation bear interesting parallels.

43. The belief or doctrine that God is greater than the universe and includes and interpenetrates it.

44. Quoted in Rita D. Sherma, "God the Mother and Her Sacred Text: A Hindu Vision of Divine Immanence," in *Bloomsbury Research Handbook of Indian Philosophy and Gender*, ed. Veena Howard (New York: Bloomsbury, 2019).

45. It is interesting to note that the Shekhinah in Judaism has been compared to Shakti as the ever-flowing universal feminine energy and wisdom that enables the nexus of the human and the divine. See, for example, the work of Gershom Scholem, one of the most important scholars of Jewish mysticism, *On the Mystical Shape of the Godhead* (Berlin: Schocken, 1991), 174. See also Braj Sinha, "The Feminization of the Divine: Shakti and Shekhinah in Tantra and Kabbalah," *Journal of Indo-Judaic Studies*, March (2019).

46. The development of Tara as a Tibetan goddess has been linked by scholars to the Brahmanical concept of Devi. For a discussion on Buddhist thealogy, see, for example, "15th Sakyadhita International Panel: Bee Scherer on *Buddhist Tantric Thealogy?*" http://awakeningbuddhistwomen.blogspot.com/2016/11/15th-si-con-scherer.html.

47. See Miranda Shaw, *Passionate Enlightenment* (Princeton, NJ: Princeton University Press, 1995).

BIBLIOGRAPHY

Adler, Rachel. *Engendering Judaism: An Inclusive Theology and Ethics*. Philadelphia, PA: Jewish Publication Society, 1999.

Aquino, María Pilar. "Latina Feminist Theology Central Features." In *A Reader in Latina Feminist Theology: Religion and Justice*, edited by María Pilar Aquino, Daisy L. Machado, and Jeanette Rodríquez, 133–60. Austin, TX: University of Texas Press, 2002.

Bell, Catherine. *Ritual Theory, Ritual Practice*. New York: Oxford University Press, 1992.

Berger, Peter, and Brigitte Berger. "Femspeak and the Battle of Language." In *The Politics of Prayer: Feminist Language and the Worship of God*, edited by Helen Hull Hitchcock. San Francisco: Ignatius Press, 1992.

Christ, Carol. "Ecofeminism and Process Philosophy." *Feminist Theology* 14, no. 3 (2006): 289–310.

Daly, Mary. *Beyond God the Father: Toward a Philosophy of Women's Liberation*. Boston, MA: Beacon Press, 1973.

Eskenazi, Tamara Cohn, and Andrea Weiss (eds.). *The Torah: A Women's Commentary*. New York: URJ Press, 2008.

Frankenberry, Nancy. "Feminist Philosophy of Religion." In *The Stanford Encyclopedia of Philosophy* (Summer 2018 Edition), edited by Edward N. Zalta. https://plato.stanford.edu/archives/sum2018/entries/feminist-religion.

Green, Arthur. "Shekhinah, the Virgin Mary, and the Song of Songs: Reflections on a Kabbalistic Symbol in Its Christian Context." *AJS Review* 26, no. 1 (April 2002): 1–52.

Gross, Rita M. *Buddhism after Patriarchy: A Feminist History, Analysis, and Reconstruction of Buddhism*. New York: SUNY Press, 1993.

———. *Feminism and Religion: An Introduction*. Boston: Beacon Press, 1996.

———. *Feminist Theology as Theology of Religions in a Garland of Feminist Reflections Book: Forty Years of Religious Exploration*. Oakland: University of California Press, 2009. https://www.jstor.org/stable/10.1525/j.ctt1pp1vn.19.

Gross, Rita M., Carol P. Christ, Grace G. Burford, Amina Wadud, et al. "Feminist Theology: Religiously Diverse Neighborhood or Christian Ghetto?" *Journal of Feminist Studies in Religion* 16, no. 2 (Fall 2000): 73–131.

Haskell, Ellen. "Bathed in Milk: Metaphors of Suckling and Spiritual Transmission in Thirteenth-Century Kabbalah." In *Figuring Religions Comparing Ideas, Images, and Activities*, edited by Shubha Pathak, 117–45. New York: SUNY Press, 2013.

Hiltebeitel, Alf, and Kathleen M. Erndl, eds. *Is the Goddess a Feminist?: The Politics of South Asian Goddesses*. New York: New York University Press, 2000.

Isasi-Díaz, Ada María. *En la Lucha/In the Struggle: Elaborating a Mujerista Theology*. 2nd ed. Minneapolis: Fortress Press, 2003.

Jantzen, Grace M. *Becoming Divine: Towards a Feminist Philosophy of Religion*. Bloomington: Indiana University Press, 1999.

Johnson, Elizabeth A. *She Who Is: The Mystery of God in Feminist Theological Discourse*. St. Louis, MO: Crossroad, 1992.

Jones, Serene. *Feminist Theory and Christian Theology: Cartographies of Grace*. Minneapolis, MN: Fortress Press, 2000.

Kamitsuka, Margaret D. "Toward a Feminist Postmodern and Postcolonial Interpretation of Sin." *Journal of Religion* 84, no. 2 (April 2004): 179–211.

Klein, Anne C. *Meeting the Great Bliss Queen: Buddhists, Feminists, and the Art of the Self*. Boston: Beacon Press, 1995.

Kraemer, Christine Hoff. "Ground of Being: An Earth-Centered Liturgy for Christian Churches." http://www.christinehoffkraemer.com/8festivalsX.html.

Kwok, Pui-lan. *Introducing Asian Feminist Theology*. New York: Bloomsbury Publishers, 2000.

McCarron, Richard E. "Pursuing 'How Liturgy Means': Liturgical Texts as Hypertext, Oral Text and Intertext." *Proceedings of the North American Academy of Liturgy Annual Meeting* (2002): 101–11.

McFague, Sally. *Metaphorical Theology: Models of God in Religious Language*. Minneapolis, MN: Fortress Press, 1982.

Meyers, Carol. "Female Images of God." In *Women in Scripture*. Boston, MA: Houghton Mifflin, 2000.

Plaskow, Judith. *Standing Again at Sinai: Judaism from a Feminist Perspective*. San Francisco: Harper & Row, 1990.

Ruether, Rosemary Radford. *Goddesses and the Divine Feminine: A Western Religious History*. Oakland: University of California Press, 2005.

———. *Sexism and God-Talk: Toward a Feminist Theology*. Boston, MA: Beacon Press, 1983.

———. *Women and Redemption: A Theological History*. Minneapolis: Fortress Press, 1998.

Saiving, Valerie. "Androcentrism in Religious Studies." *Journal of Religion* 56 (1976): 177–97.

Scholem, Gershom. *On the Mystical Shape of the Godhead*. Berlin: Schocken, 1991.

Schüssler Fiorenza, Elisabeth. *But She Said: Feminist Practices of Biblical Interpretation*. Boston: Beacon Press, 1993.

———. *In Memory of Her: A Feminist Theological Reconstruction of Christian Origins*. New York: Crossroad Publishing, 1994.

Schwarz, Howard Eilberg. *God's Phallus: And Other Problems for Men and Monotheism*. Boston, MA: Beacon Press, 1994.

Sered, Susan. *Women as Ritual Experts: The Religious Lives of Elderly Jewish Women in Jerusalem*. New York: Oxford University Press, 1992.

———. *Women of the Sacred Groves: Divine Priestesses of Okinawa*. New York: Oxford University Press, 1999.

Shaikh, Sa'diyya. *Sufi Narratives of Intimacy: Ibn 'Arabi, Gender and Sexuality*. Chapel Hill: University of North Carolina Press, 2012.

Shaw, Miranda. *Passionate Enlightenment*. Princeton, NJ: Princeton University Press, 1995.

Sherma, Rita D. "God the Mother and Her Sacred Text: A Hindu Vision of Divine Immanence." In *Gender and Indian Philosophy*, edited by Veena Howard. New York: Bloomsbury, 2019.

Sinha, Braj. "The Feminization of the Divine: Shakti and Shekhinah in Tantra and Kabbalah." *Journal of Indo-Judaic Studies*, March 2019.

Stringer, Martin. "Text, Context and Performance: Hermeneutics and the Study of Worship." *Scottish Journal of Theology* 53 (2000): 365–79.

Wadud, Amina. *Qur'an and Woman: Rereading the Sacred Text from a Woman's Perspective*. New York: Oxford University Press, 1999.

Walker, Alice. *In Search of Our Mothers' Gardens: Womanist Prose*. Boston: Mariner Books, 1983.

Walker Bynum, Caroline, Stevan Harrell, and Paula Richman, eds. *Gender and Religion: On the Complexity of Symbols Boston*. Boston: Beacon Press, 1986.

Williams, Delores. *Sisters in the Wilderness: The Challenge of Womanist God-Talk*. Maryknoll, NY: Orbis Books, 1993.

CHAPTER 3

Doing Women's Studies in Religion

A Methodology Primer for Moving from the Classroom into Real Life

Prof. Natalie Kertes Weaver, PhD, Ursuline College

ABSTRACT

Women's studies in religion become transformative when they enter the mainstream through virtually every imaginable vocational calling. This chapter helps readers to transpose the ideals of theory from a theological or academic discussion so they become transformative in one's professional or vocational calling. It guides readers to identify, discern, and make tangible steps to interpolate feminist theory such that it becomes one's lived reality in the workplace. The theory and practice of taking feminist theology from the classroom to encounters in the world shows readers how to build feminist theology from within a particular lived context, embracing interdisciplinary studies and making this theology relevant and applicable for the reader's lived reality.

This chapter invites readers to consider how women's studies in religion can move from the classroom into the living realities of women's day-to-day lives. It begins with an introduction to methodologies for studying women in religion and then asks how theory is formed by experience and in turn helps to inform and shape women's experiences in a more intentional way. By sensitizing readers to practical questions and thought processes that guide women's studies in religion, students are better equipped to take theory out of the classroom and apply it in concrete ways in women's lives and practice, in both religious and common settings.

In order to contextualize this discussion better, an introduction to methodology in women's studies in religion is helpful. *Methodology* refers to the study of methods. It is important to consider methodology because such consideration makes us aware of how we are going about our work. In the absence of an awareness of methodology, we might assume that whatever approach we happen to take is standard or obvious or universal. However, when we make methodology a self-conscious part of our investigations, we become aware not only of what we are studying but also of the manner by which we are going about it.[1] We become self-aware of our choices as researchers, and this helps us to be conscientious of important nuances we might otherwise miss.

When we think methodologically, we are required foremost to identify that we are making a choice about the kinds of questions we are asking and the types of materials we are turning to as primary sources and texts of authority, and we become mindful of the scope and limit of the studies we undertake. Beyond this, we also become more cognizant of *ourselves* as researchers. This means that we are required to confront our preferences in research (such as whether we prefer reading or interviewing); we are challenged to confront biases and predispositions we have based on our past exposures to the materials we are studying or lack thereof; and we become mindful of the limitations of the scope of our work, especially because we understand that there are many other avenues of research we could pursue that would yield different insights from those we discover.

Given that there are many approaches one can take to study women in religion, at the outset I would like to discuss three approaches to help sensitize the reader to something of the range of perspectives, all of which are valuable *and* necessary. These include what I will call 1) notable women in religious history, 2) ordinary women in religious history, and 3) textual traditions about women in religion.

First, one can begin by looking at *notable women in religious history*. In this kind of approach, one discusses important female figures in sacred literature and history in order to illustrate the critical role that women have always played in religions. This is an important thing for scholars to do because women frequently play key parts in their traditions, yet their stories are often subsumed under larger, male-dominant narratives. An example of this would be the historical re-visioning of figures such as the Virgin Mary in Christianity or the wives of the Prophet Muhammad in Islam. Research and recovery of how these female figures shape and inform the early traditions of Jesus and the Prophet Muhammad enable us to see women at the center of these religions, as opposed to seeing them as marginal figures with little significance or influence. This is an important strategy of recovery. A caveat to this approach is that, even while we may quickly identify important female religious figures, it is also true that the status of ordinary women in history is rarely on the same level as that of these leading women.

Therefore, a second important methodological approach is to tease out the *ordinary* roles and contributions that women have made. This is the approach I refer to as ordinary women in religious history. This method takes a great deal of creative re-envisioning because women's stories and practices are often undertold or hidden beneath the prevailing stories, philosophical texts, and practices and rituals of men. For example, in Jewish practice, a minyan, or quorum of 10 Jewish adults, was required for certain public rituals and prayers. While today in some communities, women may be accepted as part of a prayer quorum, in traditional practice only men counted toward that number. One could look at this situation and conclude that women were omitted from formal, public prayer and therefore from some of the most central practices of the Jewish faith. Similarly, in Roman Catholic practice, women cannot be ordained priests. On this basis, one could conclude that women cannot minister in the leading sacramental acts that constitute the essential worship life of the Catholic Church. To leave off here, however, would be a failure to see the centrality of women's participation in other, equally indispensable, dimensions of religious life. For Jewish women, perhaps that might be the rabbinically mandated lighting of the candles each week, as the family comes together to mark the start of the Sabbath. This role has traditionally been assigned to women. For Catholic women, perhaps that would be the long preparation of children for their First Communion. Although there is no law requiring that it be women, it is women who overwhelmingly work with grade school children in this kind of sacramental preparation. As such, while it is possible to analyze critically the places where women are omitted, it is equally important to discover, document, and elevate the places where ordinary women play an integral role in the ongoing function of the faith community.[2]

In addition to researching and documenting extraordinary women leaders as well as ordinary women operating within their faith traditions, a third methodological approach is *textual traditions about women in religious history*. Sacred texts, such as the Bible, Qu'rān, and Tanakh, and auxiliary texts, such as writings of the rabbis, Islamic jurists, and Christian theologians, have throughout time had a great deal to say about human life, its origins, its destiny, and moral instructions for human behavior. Such teachings have enormous influence on the way people understand the major features of life in society. That influence usually extends beyond the boundaries of a faith community and spills over into the larger normative cultural assumptions we hold about gender roles, sexuality, marriage, divorce, distribution of labor, access to employment and education, financial matters, and political participation.

Since the women's movement of the middle twentieth century, scholars of women in religion have scoured the textual traditions, often finding alarming levels of misogyny in the way that women are described and treated in sacred texts and theological treatises. Justifications for the pervasive social restrictions, subjection, separation, abuse, and unequal treatment of women are regularly made based on theological arguments about the allegedly inferior intellectual, spiritual, moral, and physical nature of females. Particularly androcentric (or male-centered) bias in texts has targeted women's reproductive capacity as manifestly divergent from normative humanity, which is to say, from male humanity. As such, taboos around women's menstruation, gestation, birthing, post-birthing, lactation, and even menopause can be found in almost every studied religious tradition. Such taboos, often glossed over as demarcating categorical differences, rather than qualitative differences, nevertheless are responsible for the restriction and marginalization of women from gainful and personally liberated access to life in the polis. To these same taboos can be traced restrictions on women's access to sacred places, religious ritual participation, and formal study of religion. Even more, the diminishment of women's public and ritual participation has translated into the subordination of women in marriage and family life, often leaving women with little or no voice to state preferences, to defend self and offspring against sexual and physical abuse, or to author one's own life. In short, study of religious texts reveals that religious beliefs and arguments about women have immeasurably contributed to the whole legal, societal, marital, and political shape of women's lives.

Studying women in religion includes a huge range of possible approaches beyond these three here mentioned. A few examples include studying women's contributions to and representations in religious art, music, and dance. Another includes studying women's practices and rituals as a discreet subject within religious studies. Still another might be an intersectional, anthropological study of women in context, where women's religious experience is framed as both formed and informed by larger demographic indicators. Here, for example, the diversity of religious experiences of women of the same faith in the same location could be analyzed in terms of varying socioeconomic factors that largely impact faith formation and practice.

In any of these approaches, studying women in religion in a formal, academic way has the merits of explaining how things came to be the way they are for women; disclosing the developmental history of ideas about women; and enriching our own current understanding of contemporary women's experiences. However, arguably the greatest merit of studying women in religion is the potential it has to empower and support the lives of real women, their families, and their communities. In this sense, a critically important task of the study of women in religion is the need to move study outside of the theoretical context of the classroom into real women's lives. One way of doing this is through the methodological approach that I call *praxis-based learning*.

Praxis-based learning involves a methodology that incorporates direct experience within the development, application, and assessment of theories.[3] It differs from traditional classroom models that might start with books and articles about women's experiences, insofar as it situates the initial focus of study in actual people's lives. Here, for example, rather than reading about women, students might talk to women, ask questions about their experiences, collect interview data, and make detailed observations about women's lives and practices. One very detailed, immersive model of this kind of study is called *ethnography*, wherein the researcher actually immerses herself for a period of time within the life of the community she is studying in order to understand how the research subjects perceive themselves and their practices from an insider's point of view.

A similar approach is taken when students of a foreign language visit and live for a time in the country where the language is spoken in order to gain fluency and to learn how the language is spoken idiomatically. Another ethnographic model involves developing a qualitative research questionnaire, or a series of well-developed questions, which is given to a statistically valid number of subjects. Responses to questionnaires are carefully recorded and studied, with the goal of extrapolating from the collected data dominant themes and insights that characterize the group's experiences and attitudes. In the study of women in religion, in both of these research methods, the goal is to collect information *from* women firsthand as opposed to *about* women from supposedly "objective" or authoritative sources, such as the Bible or theological texts.

This model relies on the all-important shift toward giving women their own voices to describe what they do, why they do it, and what it means to them. What is more, the very process of engaging women in the discussion and analysis of their own experiences, rather than talking about women, is deeply constructive for the religious self-consciousness of women. Since women are often omitted from leadership and authorial roles in ritual practice and religious study, there is a powerful psychological value in providing a forum for women to speak with authority about their own lives.

Once information is gathered about women's experience, beliefs, practice, and so on, from women themselves, that material can be reflected upon, both by the one conducting the study and by the subjects of that study. This practice is sometimes described as *theological reflection*. The reflective practice is an important step in the study because it allows both researcher and research subject to examine, discuss, and nurture the insights that surface from the initial data, interviews, and ethnographic immersion. It is also the time when theories can fruitfully be developed.

An example here from an undergraduate student taking a course in religious studies to satisfy a core curricular requirement will help to illustrate the fruitfulness of theological reflection based on lived experience. Some years back, I worked with a female Orthodox Jewish student who asked to study a select set of texts from the Hebrew Scriptures. This student was cautious about her course of study because she was mindful of the concerns her husband, family, and rabbi had about variant ideologies influencing her religious faith. During our time together, the student read feminist authors, including some who critiqued Orthodox women's practices of ritual bathing and separation during menstruation. While discovering that the practices were not inaccurately described, my student felt that critiques that represented these practices as oppressive failed to appreciate why women maintained them and the deep value the practices held for women both personally and communally. She decided to do a research study, collecting data from women in her community, wherein she ultimately developed an orthodox-feminist treatment of women's religious practices as being pro-woman and female-elected. While her thesis was interesting and informative to me, I was more impressed ultimately by the manner in which the student gained a strong sense of voice and value about her own religious identity. She was neither persuaded by the charges that the practices were oppressive, nor was she reliant upon male religious authorities to speak on behalf of the value of the practices. She empowered herself and the other women she studied with to speak to their experience, to build community with one another in their dialogue, and to arrive at a contemporary, gynocentric (or women-centered) interpretation of Orthodox women's traditions.

In this example, one sees how theological reflection leads to theories based on studied experience. Such theories can become the basis for transformational action. So, for example, another investigator could build upon the research my student conducted by broadening the pool of subjects studied or developing a community resource in which women have opportunities to catalog, share, study, and interpret their experiences from one generation to the next. When theory becomes tested and returned back to the community's experience, the full circle of *praxis-based learning* begins to come into sight. Theory that informs action in an intentionally formative way is praxis, and when that praxis-action occurs, new experiences follow, which in turn become the material for further theological reflection, novel theories, and revised behaviors. Some describe this methodology of praxis-based learning as manifesting a "hermeneutical circle," in which experience leads to reflection, reflection leads to theorizing, theorizing leads to praxis,

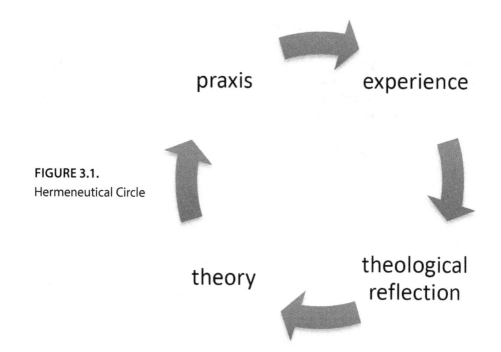

FIGURE 3.1.
Hermeneutical Circle

praxis   experience

theory   theological reflection

and praxis leads to new experience. The hermeneutical circle is regularly referenced and cited and imaged as in figure 3.1.

Based on these ideas, women's studies in religion might follow these steps to move from the classroom into real life. First, students should identify an area of interest about women's studies in religion. Preliminary research about the feasibility of a learning initiative or research project is always prudent. This includes determining whether one has access to speaking with women, whether the researcher will be welcomed to engage firsthand in the study, and how well prepared the student–researcher is to conduct the study. Early self-preparation includes identifying past personal experiences, the novelty of the subject, and potential biases and presumptions that might influence the study. This sort of self-intake is not to be feared but rather welcomed in the same way that one might welcome turning on the lights when entering a room in order to navigate the space without bumping into objects or knocking something over. Ideally, a brief prospectus of the study, including feasibility, subject access, and researcher-bias disclosure will enhance the project's ethical value, structural vision, and achievable outcomes.

Second, particularly important to this kind of study, students need to work in conjunction with their faculty mentors to determine the scope of a praxis-based learning project as well as responsible and safe parameters for carrying it out. Any study that involves living human subjects carries certain risk potential.[4] Risk factors can include such varied elements as the safety of a research location, response-preparedness to unintended triggering of trauma and posttraumatic stress in interview subjects, and the safety of research subjects when participating in discussions about their religious experiences as women. Research questions and immersion experiences should be carefully crafted with the guidance of mentors and institutional research boards in order to ensure that praxis-based learning experiences can be conducted safely for all involved. This note of caution, while in no way meant as a deterrent for praxis-based learning, is nevertheless seriously offered here because women's religious experience has historically been guarded, and often enforced with violence, by patriarchal power.[5] Where those traditional power structures are or appear to be challenged, there can be genuine risk.

Third, research should be joyfully undertaken. The use of the term *joyfully* is very intentional because *doing women's studies in religion* is a rare and wonderful opportunity to meet people, to come together as community, to form relationships, and to build knowledge. Any time people have the opportunity to listen to and learn from other people's lives, they are receiving a profound and unique gift of the transmission of human knowing. Studying women in religion means encountering the vulnerability of women sharing their purest convictions, sometimes their deepest sorrows, their frustrations with unfairness in life and society, their moral vision and hope, their families, and so much more. Particularly because formal praxis-based women's studies in religion constitute a still young discipline within institutions of higher education, any opportunity to build up knowledge about women's experiences from women's own voices is invaluable. This work is honorable and helps to complete the story of human beings and religious faith, which until recent decades has only been less than half told.[6]

Fourth, the research should be documented, recorded carefully, and content analyzed. Where possible, findings should be returned to the community to guarantee that the research accurately and adequately represents women's voices and experiences so that the research subjects recognize the study to be a fair and responsible representation of themselves. During such a time, theological reflections of both researcher and research subjects about their experiences together might be undertaken and shared in order to continue growing knowledge and insight about the work. Here, both researcher and research subjects will notice that the self is also developing, that preconceived notions are altering, and that the praxis-based learning through encounter is a transformational experience.

Last, the final research and experience can be shared publicly according to the conditions agreed upon at the outset of the project. This is where constructive knowledge building about women in religion is returned to the larger body of scholarship and also made available for further inquiry, innovation, and application. Insights garnered through praxis-based learning here have formative value in creating new ideas that can be implemented in practical ways for further study and analysis.

STEPS FOR *DOING* WOMEN'S STUDIES IN RELIGION

1. Identify an area of interest about women's studies in religion.
2. Do preliminary research about the feasibility of the project, conduct self-intake, and assess risk.
3. Conduct project joyfully.
4. Document, record, and reflect.
5. Share new knowledge, noting possibilities for continued work in your area.

Doing women's studies in religion is ultimately about learning from women themselves. The methodological shift to give voice to women interrupts long established patterns that until very recently reserved theological inquiry to be conducted by the empowered, religious elite who were typically men in nearly every, if not every, religious tradition. Turning to women to describe their own lives and seeing value in that work represents a tectonic shift in the nature of formal religious studies. The necessity and value of this kind of work cannot be overstated. What is more, doing women's studies in religion through praxis-based learning bravely innovates upon the traditional classroom model of hierarchical pairings between teacher and student or expert and learner. In the methodology considered in this article, those hierarchical pairings are replaced by the more democratic model of a community of learners who construct new knowledge together. The wisdom of people's lives is honored through dialogue and relationship building, and the learning process becomes one of facilitation and guidance between students and mentors that results in mutual discovery and growth. Doing women's studies in religion has the power to transform self- and other-awareness; to empower women for themselves and for the people they love; to build up communities of faith; to address problematic areas for women in religious practice; and, most importantly, to offer a long overdue correction to the story about women and God.

NOTES

1. See, e.g., Nicole Slee, Fran Porter, and Anne Phillips, eds., *Researching Female Faith: Qualitative Research Methods* (New York: Routledge, 2017).

2. See, e.g., Susan Ross, *Extravagant Affections: A Feminist Sacramental Theology* (Continuum, 2001). This work illustrates the point here through the examination of Roman Catholic sacraments in the larger light of preparation and reception with a community of women.

3. See, e.g., Leonardo Boff and Clodovis Boff, *Introducing Liberation Theology* (Maryknoll, NY: Orbis, 2013). This text of liberation theology provides an outstanding introduction to praxis-based learning and "doing" theology from the ground up.

4. See, e.g., Carl H. Coleman, Jerry Menikoff, Jesse Goldner, and Nancy Dubler, *The Ethics and Regulation of Research with Human Subjects*, 3rd ed. (Newark, NJ: LexisNexis, 2005).

5. See, e.g., Mary Daly, *Gyn/Ecology: The Metaethics of Radical Feminism*, rev ed. (Boston: Beacon Press, 1990). This classic work of feminist theology details cross-cultural patterns of violence against women in religion as a result of patriarchal power structures in church and academy.

6. See, e.g., Ada María Isasi-Díaz, *En la Lucha/In the Struggle: Elaborating a Mujerista Theology*, 10th anniv. ed. (Minneapolis: Fortress Press, 2004). This work illustrates powerfully the joyful process of doing theology from the perspectives of women themselves, as the author provides a forum for Latina/Mujerista women to speak about their moral attitudes about life and faith.

BIBLIOGRAPHY

Boff, Leonardo, and Clodovis Boff. *Introducing Liberation Theology*. Maryknoll, NY: Orbis, 2013.

Coleman, Carl H., Jerry Menikoff, et al. *The Ethics and Regulation of Research with Human Subjects*, 3rd ed. Newark, NJ: LexisNexis, 2005.

Daly, Mary. *Gyn/Ecology: The Metaethics of Radical Feminism*. rev. ed. Boson: Beacon Press, 1990.

Isasi-Díaz, Ada María. *En la Lucha/In the Struggle: Elaborating a Mujerista Theology*. 10th anniv. ed. Minneapolis: Fortress Press, 2004.

Ross, Susan. *Extravagant Affections: A Feminist Sacramental Theology*. London: Continuum, 2001.

Slee, Nicole, Fran Porter, and Anne Phillips, eds. *Researching Female Faith: Qualitative Research Methods*. New York: Routledge, 2017.

CHAPTER 4

Women's Creative Research Methodologies on the Periphery and at the Border

Latina Women's Restorative Interventions through Art and Activism

Rebecca M. Berru-Davis, St. Catherine University, St. Paul, Minnesota

ABSTRACT

This chapter critically engages ways a feminist perspective is reclaimed and interpreted through creative methodologies. Two examples of women's restorative interventions are a shantytown on the periphery of Lima, Peru, and one at the US–Mexico border. Within these liminal places, I illustrate how creative expression and activism inspired and organized by women as a collective enterprise is a means to respond to and process the challenges and trauma engendered by experiences of displacement, migration, mobility, and loss. These efforts enacted by women underscore the ways in which these methodologies are effective in bringing to light sociopolitical issues; raising awareness of the realities of women's lives in marginal or transitional spaces; and contributing to healing, recovery, and change.

As a Latina scholar, I recognize that research carried out in the academy involving a dialogical conversation between scholars and experts in the field is essential. I honor this methodology, but I am also committed to seeking out other places where significant insights and contributions are found. Thus, my research attempts or works to access the deep wells of wisdom that come from the margins where women are often located. I am drawn toward these edges that are both physical and metaphorical where those who live in obscurity often reside. In order to expand this essential conversation, I am inspired by the work of Latina theologians such as María Pilar Aquino (b. 1956), who asserts that what is needed is "a space for those who are socially marginalized and powerless to become active participants in articulating their interests, commitments and visions of justice."[1] Aquino further affirms that, no longer is it a matter of speaking about women, for women, or on behalf of women, but "Women are the makers of their own consciousness and experience. They want to work out their own theological perspectives, in order to inspire processes that promote fullness of life and encourage the march toward a new earth where men and women share equally and realize together their full humanity."[2] As a researcher, I seek ways to open up these spaces where wisdom resides.

In order to access these perspectives, creative methodologies are necessary. Clearly, the spiritual insights and theological acumen of women are not retrieved solely through discursive methods but are accessed in alternative ways and often found in women's expressive modalities of communication. In this chapter, I share examples that highlight the ways in which visual arts provide a lens for a firmly, fluid foundation for giving flesh to women stories and insights from these socially and physically peripheral spaces. I turn to the arts because they are a potent and underutilized source that informs and enlightens. Moreover, the arts have a powerful way of arresting our attention and directing fresh light on the intersectional complexities that exist for women.

ON THE PERIPHERY

In order to restore theological language to its capacity for touching vital centers of human existence, Latin American theologian Ivone Gebara (b. 1944) notes, "Feminist theological expression always starts from what has been lived, from what is experienced in the present." Gebara further asserts that it is essential to return "the poetic dimension of human life to theology, since the deepest meaning in the human being is expressed only through analogy; mystery is voiced only in poetry, and what is gratuitous is expressed only through symbols."[3]

The visual arts are a means to access this wisdom, and *Picturing Paradise* is one such project that I am engaged with that highlights the creative and artistic activity of Peruvian women artists from Pamplona Alta, a shantytown located on the outskirts of Lima, Peru. It is a project that utilizes an ethnographic methodology that begins with the quotidian experiences of women's lives. It attends to the interdisciplinary and intersectional nature of women's experiences, eliciting the distinct ways they perceive their agency and place in the world. As activist research, this project extends itself into other arenas, including exhibition and education, and is intentional in its means to support the women.

In 2006, while carrying out research for an art history thesis related to Latin American women's textile work, I met twenty-five Peruvian women artists from two art cooperatives located in Pamplona Alta, one the many *pueblos jovenes* (young towns) that encircle the city of Lima. The women were among the many residents, with histories of displacement from the interior because of terrorism, violence, or natural disasters. They had moved to the city in search of safety, better educational opportunities for their children, and economic prospects for themselves and their families. Daily, these women dedicated themselves to stitching together appliqued and embroidered fabric pictures, called *cuadros*, as a means to earn an income for themselves and their families (see figure 4.1).[4] These works of art sold in the markets, locally and abroad, depicted images of their past lives in the countryside and their current lives in the shantytowns. In my work with them, I recognized in these colorful works evidence of their skillful techniques, the resourceful use of materials, and a fluency with a visual language they had masterfully devised. What some may dismiss as tourist or popular art, I took seriously, noting the women artists were creating images of their personal and collective narratives of displacement and survival. For me, they were acts that reflected the deeper implications and expressions of the resilience and hope they held.[5] Attention to visual art created by women is attending to an alternative discourse to deliberate the women contexts, their lives, and their insights.[6]

To understand more about the significance of the art and the lives of these women, I turned to ethnography. It is a methodology that theologian Ada María Isasi-Díaz

FIGURE 4.1. *Cosecha* (Harvest); fabric art.
© *Rebecca M. Berru-Davis*

FIGURE 4.2. Closeup of hands sewing; fabric art.
© Rebecca M. Berru-Davis

(1943–2012) asserts is a means to understand the lived experiences of women. Using an ethnographic approach focused on the quotidian experiences of these women, fresh insights and pertinent questions arose related to the way theology and life are understood.[7] Since the project's inception, this method positions me, when in Peru, as one who accompanies the women throughout their daily tasks. It keeps me attentive to generative themes that emerge in conversation and in art.[8] I accompany the women on the ground, in their homes, and at their tables, alert to themes that emerge in conversation and in their activities (see figure 4.2). And in the process I become not merely observer but "witness," in a theological sense, to their struggles and joys, their wisdom and eloquence.[9] At the same time, I am always conscious of the thorny issues related to power, subjectivity, relationship, and voice. Although ethnography is disposed to the complexities, confusions, and unexpected turns of human relationships, creating at times what James Clifford calls "lucid uncertainty," I find it useful in that it begins with the experience of these women.[10] Through shared experiences and dialogical processes, it attempts to get at meaning and bring to light their sensibilities, understandings and perceptions. It assumes that knowledge is not limited solely to experts in the academy.

As I spent time with the women around their sewing tables, I noted their conversations, and, from this experience, an idea emerged to commission specific works of art related to the women's hopes and dreams. What transpired was a collection of revelatory works about what the women deemed most significant in their lives. A subsequent commissioned project inspired visual narratives of their inspiration and motivation for persisting and a third prompted images and themes that reflected their identity. These fabric pictures were assembled into an exhibit called *Picturing Paradise: Cuadros from the Peruvian Women of Pamplona Alta as Visions of Hope*. Included along with the art are photos of the women artists, their words, and images of the context in which they live and the world they envision (see figure 4.3). In ongoing consultation with the women, the exhibit continues to circulate throughout the United States in over twenty-five venues, and has been shown twice in Lima, Peru.[11]

This project also falls under the umbrella of activist research. The exhibit *Picturing Paradise* serves as a link between the northern and southern hemispheres because it reflects the realities of the women's lives and their creative work. It also engenders awareness of their ingenuity, resilience, and wisdom, and in the process a felt recognition of their challenges and sense of solidarity is created between the women artists

FIGURE 4.3. Botanica scene (flower garden); fabric art.
© *Rebecca M. Berru-Davis*

and others who "receive" their art.[12] In this way, the lives of women, normally invisible, are given voice, heard, and supported. In collaboration with a small women-run, nonprofit called Con/Vida, additional *cuadros* are made available for sale when the women's art is exhibited.[13] The proceeds assist over twenty-five women and their families in Pamplona Alta.

At one university where the exhibit was shown, the women's art was described as *destellos* (little sparks), suggesting their images evoke glimmer, twinkles, and sparkles of the divine.[14] Just as written text illuminates, so do images reveal God's presence in our world today. I find great affinity in these methods of seeking insights from ordinary people and heralding the conviction that all voices, particularly those overlooked, hidden, silenced, and marginalized, warrant attention in the theological discourse. In this case, a methodology that transverses and combines art, ethnography, and activism in new ways brings to light the lives and creativity of women living on the margins of society counting their art and their perspectives as important contributions. Peripheral places, such as shantytown, and liminal places, such as borders described below, prove salient spaces where women's creative methodologies are enacted.

AT THE BORDER

In her book, *Borderlands/La Frontera*, Chicana literary artist Gloria Anzaldúa (1942–2004) writes, "The U.S. Mexican Border *es una herida abierta* (is an open wound), where the Third World grates against the first and bleeds. And before a scab forms it hemorrhages again, the lifeblood of two worlds merging to form a third country—a border culture."[15] Written in 1987, her insights are even more cogent today as anti-immigration sentiment persists, and continues to be motivated by fear, all fomented by exclusionist policies, xenophobia, and racism.

The US–Mexico border is nearly two thousand miles long, stretching from the Pacific Ocean in California and Baja California to the Gulf of Mexico in Texas and Tamaulipas. Borders are spaces where individuals in transition, Anzaldúa asserts, live in a state of *"nepantla." Nepantla* is a descriptive Nahuatl word for an in-between, liminal state, that uncertain terrain one crosses when moving from one place to another.[16] For some, the border is a porous space; for others it is about firm lines of demarcation.

Navigating through this sociopolitically charged landscape is not an easy endeavor. Despite the proliferation of contentious upheavals, there are activists who continue to be diligent in responding to the desperate needs of migrants with humanitarian aid as well as advocating for substantive policy change through legal avenues. My focus here is on women's restorative interventions enacted on the border, and specifically those that include art. Noting that, as migration in the world becomes increasingly prevalent, my premise is that, for those dealing with the reality of mobility and displacement and the anxieties related to the insecurity of fluctuating border policies, opportunities for processing trauma and change is ever more pressing. Thus, creative methodologies that seek to address the undertold stories of life on the edges have something to contribute. In this case, it is the work of women artists who bring to light the palpable essence of deeply felt stories and experiences.

"Contemporary artists working within this border region have become powerful actors performing significant roles as agents and advocates of social justice," notes scholar Christina Aushana.[17] Art activists create works that critique the border politics of the region, sometimes engaging in provocative measures or political dissidence in order to make transparent social inequalities. As Anzaldúa writes, "Border artists *cambian el punto de referencia* (change the point of reference). By disrupting the neat separations between cultures, they create a culture mix, *una mestizada*, in their artworks. Each artist locates her/himself in this border *'lugar'* (place) and tears apart and rebuilds the 'place itself.'"[18]

To gain a perspective on how border artists continue to open up new ways to think about the border reality, I begin with an abbreviated trajectory of border art. This is then followed by two examples that illustrate how art, carried out cooperatively is a means to address the lives of individuals and communities in flux or ruptured by experiences of crossing borders.

Alongside the social upheavals of the 1960s and 1970s and in conjunction with the Chicano movement, border artists took up issues of affirming the presence, culture, and experiences of the Latino community, including the plight of immigrants. They also engaged in the practice of recovering and reclaiming narratives previously erased. For example, Aztlán, located in northwestern Mexico and the southwest United States, was understood as the historic and mythic homeland of the Mexica people who migrated to central Mexico to found Tenochtitlan. For Chicano artists in the 1960s, restoring the memory and claim to this ancient border homeland through visual language was central to justifying their presence.[19]

For Chicano artists at this time, printmaking was reinvigorated because it was a means of intentionally democratizing art by allowing for inexpensive and easy dissemination. Silkscreens by artists such as Rupert García (1973) were widely distributed among grassroots activists as posters and flyers. García's classic print ¡*Cesen Deportación!* (Stop Deportation!) used the salient symbol of the barbed wire, referencing both detention and incarceration.

A decade later in 1984, the San Diego–based Border Arts Workshop/*Taller de Arte Fronterizo* (BAW/TAF) was launched by a binational group of artists, activists, journalists, and scholars.[20] Most of the projects were carried out in Tijuana or at other points along the border. From the beginning, the group established itself by addressing the social tensions along the US–Mexico border by using conceptual art, performance, and techniques of parody to provoke the viewer into questioning the status quo. Their visual idioms drew on religious and indigenous sources and were informed by popular culture and *rasquache*, a bricolage, kitsch aesthetic claimed by Latino artists.[21] Among the founding members were Guillermo Gomez Peña and Coco Fusco, who juxtaposed Mexican and American popular culture and the coexistence of the realities on both sides of the border through art, literature, and performance. They intentionally carried out their provocations both inside and outside the museum. The BAW/TAF continued to confront the political tensions of the borderlands and challenged the pretenses of nationalist xenophobia and stereotypes for the next twenty years.

From the BAW/TAF emerged other artists who formed new coalitions. One such transnational women's group that functioned between 1988 and 1992 was called *Las Comadres*. It initially formed as a study group for discussing how art, theory, and politics could be used as tools for creating a dialogue concerning the US–Mexico border.[22] Emily Hicks, one of the founding members commented, "I wanted to be in a feminist group that was open to experimentation and focused on border/immigration issues. The diversity in *Las Comadres* was inspiring and as more women joined the group, I realized it would be possible to expand to showing our work. . . . I wanted *Las Comadres* to be an anti-racist, inclusive feminist art collective."[23] As self-declared feminists, with members coming from diverse cultural, ethnic, work, and disciplinary experiences, they cultivated a sense of trust and established an organic nonhierarichal way of functioning. Another member recounted, "*Las Comadres* brought a dimension of honoring women's perceptions and connections to the issues and to daily life, with a sensual and ritual aspect I had been longing for; an invitation and permission to explore and expand in political, metaphysical and social aspects."[24] Their aims came to fruition in a 1990 exhibition they curated at the Centro Cultural de la Raza called *La Vecindad*/The Neighborhood, a multimedia, multidisciplinary production. Their installation was staged to calculatedly critique *Los Vecinos*/The Neighbors, an exhibition at the San Diego Museum of Photographic Arts, which emphasized the poverty and criminality of immigrants.[25] *La Vecinidad* featured three principal spaces representing different frameworks, including a bright, multicolored kitchen contrasted with a completely black and white "conflict room," a border feminist library, and a video viewing room that included a performance piece, *Border Boda* (Wedding). "We explored what it meant to create border culture, a culture that instead of highlighting the alien and destitute celebrated the entire neighborhood."[26]

As illustrated here, early border artists democratized art through printmaking, confronted audiences through performance art, and critiqued the dominant rhetoric related to immigration through installation and the content of their exhibits. However, as artist and cultural critic Amalia Mesa-Bains notes in a 2015 interview, "We are in a new era now, where the larger political scene of anti-immigration and border politics is being played out within the backdrop of Latinos as America's largest ethnic majority. Even more now, the Mexican and US relationship must be understood, and Chicano artists and cultural workers are part of the web of relationship and cultural production that connects across the border."[27] Thus, those engaged as artists and social poets are critical actors in facilitating, accessing, and illuminating the palpable experiences of those living on the border. Artist-driven projects serve to sustain communities in flux and support those identities in transition.[28] Women's innovative and creative methodologies seek to attend to and apprehend the soul-felt pulse of communities and offer restorative interventions where art serves as a means to reflect, heal, and build community through a sense of solidarity. What follows are two specific examples.

ART MADE BETWEEN OPPOSITE SIDES (AMBOS)

Los Angeles–based, Tanya Aguiñiga (b. 1978) is a Latina artist who unites the worlds of art and activism. As a young girl growing up in Tijuana, she navigated a border daily for fourteen years in order to attend school in the United States. She then graduated with a BA in Applied Design from San Diego State University and completed her MFA at the Rhode Island School of Design. She says she utilizes a variety of media in order to "visualize a stigmatized society."[29]

Her initial work in the 1990s with the BAW/TAF shaped her community-based sensibilities in approaching her art initiatives. In 2018, she founded the socially driven project called AMBOS (Art Made Between Opposite Sides).[30] Aguiñiga describes her project as "an ongoing series of artist interventions and commuter collaborations that address binational transition and identity in the U.S./Mexico border regions, seeking to create a greater sense of interconnectedness while recording what it means to cross the border and what it means to live with or adjacent to it."[31]

AMBOS started as a monthlong activation at the San Ysidro border crossing in Tijuana. The project has grown to include other artists with strong ties to the border region and evolved into a multifaceted investigation and documentation of what life looks like along the entire length of the US–Mexico border. The overriding purpose of the AMBOS team is to capture an accurate representation of the sister cities and communities on both sides of the border and in the process transform the crossing into a more mindful space of transition, thus humanizing the act of border crossing. Aguiñiga explains, "It is part documentation of the border, part collaboration with artists, part community activism, part exploration of identities influenced by the liminal zone of the borderlands." She continues, "[AMBOS functions] as an emotional thermometer to gauge the emotive toll of ongoing policy changes and the transnational relationship between each community."[32] Aguiñiga and her assistants worked eastward from Tijuana/San Diego to Matamoros/Brownsville, Texas, inviting those crossing the border by foot or in cars to write their thoughts and emotions about the crossing on a postcard and tie a simple knot using two strands of fabric to record their presence and participation as a symbol of their relationship between the United States and Mexico. Aguiñiga claims that using a simple craft-based technique democratizes the making process because anyone can participate and it does not elevate one person's contribution over another. "I like the way craft connects a lot of us beyond identity and socio-economic class and gender," Aguiñiga explains. "I totally believe we have an intuitive body knowledge. . . . I believe in listening to our hands."[33] "Through these efforts, AMBOS recontextualizes and calls attention to the way craft and art can be used as a vehicle for community self-care and in the process meaningful artwork is created. AMBOS aim is to generate healthier cross-border relations by raising awareness of issues and opinion in the border region and amplifying them to an international audience."[34]

SPACE IN BETWEEN

Another project, now transformed into an exhibition called *Space in Between*, is a long-standing collaborative sewing and embroidery workshop project conceived by artist Margarita Cabrera (b. 1973).[35] The sculptures in the exhibition, made from disassembled Border Patrol uniforms, represent cactus plants native to the US–Mexico borderlands. The embroideries were created by Mexican immigrants inspired by their experiences of crossing the border. The exhibit's title *Space in Between* alludes to *nepantla*, "the space in the middle," the liminal place experienced by marginalized cultures and their strategies for survival as described by Anzaldua. *Nepantla*, as Cabrera elucidates, "is a mythological space and a metaphorical one. It is the physical geographical area between cultures; between relationships between people and even the space between breaths."[36]

Margarita Cabrera, herself an immigrant born in Mexico, began the workshops in 2010 in Texas as a way to foster dialogue between recently arrived immigrants and more established immigrants. She has staged additional workshops in New Mexico and North Carolina and, more recently, in Phoenix, Arizona, and Fresno, California. Cumulatively, around 100 sculptures have been produced.[37]

Wire armatures support the stuffed representations of life-sized desert plants made from sections of dark green US Border Patrol uniforms. The Border Patrol uniforms sourced from thrift stores are cut to duplicate the shapes of cacti and desert plants indigenous to the US Southwest. They are then arrayed in traditional Mexican terra-cotta pots. The pieces are sewn together by hand and machine, leaving uncut threads rough-hewn and dangling at seam ends and then embroidered and embellished using traditional sewing techniques. Pockets, buttons, identification patches, and labels remain intact. Cactus spines are simulated by tufts of yellow thread, and succulent flowers are fashioned with stuffed bright red fabric, all contrasting with the factory-made precision of the uniforms. Cabrera explains:

> Some see the Border Patrol uniform representing security and protection. Others see it as a symbol of resistance, violence or even death. The heart of this project is about taking these differing perspectives and coming together to transform it into something new—something that represents life, growth and the beautiful potential of people working together. With these works, we have created art pieces that serve as cultural and historical artifacts that value and document the experiences, struggles, and achievements of those who have found their way, often through migration and exceptional sacrifice, to new places where they now work to contribute meaningfully within their communities.[38]

Just as the work of *Picturing Paradise* takes place around tables, enabling dialogue among women, Cabrera's collaborative sewing project also promotes *charlas* (conversations) because women are encouraged to share their border-crossing stories as they work. Included in these exchanges are memories that deal with the deeply painful experience of separation from family and loss of loved ones as well as the jubilant ones of survival, persistence, and success. Ivonne Gebara notes that the collective ways of women working together at various crafts become cells for personal communal change. "[W]omen dare to talk about themselves, about social and political organization or disorganization. They have the freedom to reflect, agree or disagree and then their consciousness, lulled by the clatter of plates and pans, begins to awaken. It finds words and feels the urge to reorganize this world differently."[39] Like the women artists in Latin America who stitch their world on their own terms through fabric, "[t]his project," as Cabrera asserts, "is about telling the real stories of Latino communities and counteracting the stories that are told in the media that are pulling our communities apart. These are stories of hope, stories of dreams. We're breaking a barrier—a division—that may have been silencing some of these experiences and some of these conversations."[40]

Creative expression and activism inspired and organized by women as a collective enterprise is a means to respond to and process the trauma and challenges engendered by experiences of displacement, migration, mobility, and loss. The examples discussed here enacted by women underscore ways in which innovative methodologies are effective in bringing to light sociopolitical issues; raising awareness of the realities of women's lives in marginal or transitional spaces; and engendering efforts that contribute to healing, recovery, and change. As Anzaldúa asserts, "The border is the locus of resistance, of rupture, implosion and explosion, and of putting together the fragments and creating a new assemblage."[41] Disrupted lives on the periphery or at the border compel attention. These examples of crafting as record and stitching as memory work assist in making sense of what happens in women's lives inwardly and outwardly. Listening to women's sentiments expressed through their hands and hearing what is put into speech through visual art require the work of creative methodologies.

NOTES

1. María Pilar Aquino and Maria José Rosado-Nunes, eds., "Feminist Intercultural Theology: Toward a Shared Future of Justice," in *Feminist Intercultural Theology: Latina Explorations for a Just World* (Maryknoll, NY: Orbis Books, 2007), 25.

2. María Pilar Aquino, *Our Cry for Life: Feminist Theology from Latin America* (Maryknoll, NY: Orbis Books, 1993), 65.

3. Ivone Gebara, "Women Doing Theology in Latin America," in *Through Her Eyes: Women's Theology from Latin America*, ed. Elsa Tamez (Maryknoll, NY: Orbis Books, 1989), 45.

4. For sources that explore the significance of crafted works as valued works of art in the makeshift marketplace, see Ruth B. Phillips and Christopher B. Steiner, eds., *Unpacking Culture: Art and Commodity in Colonial and Postcolonial Worlds* (Berkeley: University of California Press, 1999); H. H. Nelson Graburn, ed., *Ethnic and Tourist Arts: Cultural Expressions from the Fourth World* (Berkeley and Los Angeles: University of California Press, 1976); Walter Morris, *Handmade Money: Latin American Artisans in the Marketplace* (Washington, DC: Organization of American States, 1996).

5. Women throughout the world turn to cloth as viable communication. See John Michael Kohler Arts Center, *Hmong Art: Tradition and Change exh. cat.* (Sheboygan, WI, 1986); Guy Brett, *Through Our Own Eyes: Popular Art and Modern History* (Philadelphia, PA: New Society Publishers, 1987). Or as in this "Memory Cloth" documents what a South African woman witnessed during apartheid. See Carol Becker, "Amazwi Abesifazone (Voices of Women)," *Art Journal* 63, no. 4 (2004): 117–34; Marjorie Agosín, *Tapestries of Hope, Threads of Life: The Arpillera Movement in Chile* (Lanham, MD: Rowman & Littlefield, 2008).

6. Art historian Janet Catherine Berlo explains that "[t]extiles are eloquent texts, encoding history, change, appropriation, oppression and endurance, as well as personal and cultural creative visions. For indigenous Latin Americans, especially women, cloth has been an alternative discourse." Janet Catherine Berlo, "Beyond Bricolage: Women and Aesthetic Strategies in Latin American Textiles," in *Textile Traditions of MesoAmerica and the Andes: An Anthology*, ed. Margot Blum Schevill, Janet Catherine Berlo, and Edward B. Dwyer (New York and London: Garland Publishing, 1991), 439.

7. Isasi-Díaz outlines *ethnomethodology*, a strategy that places value on *lo cotidiano* for understanding the everyday life of women and shaping a *mujerista* theology.

8. Ada María Isasi-Díaz, *En la Lucha/In the Struggle: Elaborating a Mujerista Theology* (Minneapolis: Fortress Press, 1993), 62–80.

9. I thank Dr. Joanne Doi for this insight. Doi develops this notion of "witness" in a theological sense as opposed to participant/observer in her dissertation *Bridge to Compassion: Theological Pilgrimage to Tule Lake and Manzanar* (Unpublished dissertation), Graduate Theological Union, Berkeley, CA, 2007, 23–27.

10. James Clifford, *Routes: Travel and Translation in the Late Twentieth Century* (Cambridge, MA: Harvard University Press, 1997), 13.

11. At this writing, the exhibit has been shown in the following places: University of St. Thomas Luann Dummer Center for Women, St. Paul, MN (May 2006); Basilica of Saint Mary Pope John XXIII Gallery, Minneapolis, MN (September 2–October 29, 2006); United Theological Seminary, St. Paul, MN (September–October 2007); Princeton Theological Seminary, Princeton, NJ (October 29–December 7, 2007); Bryn Mawr Presbyterian Church, Bryn Mawr, PA (January 2008); Dominican School of Philosophy and Theology Galleria, Graduate Theological Union, Berkeley, CA (January 26–March 20, 2009), The Muscarelle Museum of Art, College of William and Mary, Williamsburg, VA (April 8–May 17, 2009), the Miraflores Community Gallery, Lima, Peru (June 5–7, 2009); Chabot Community College Gallery, Hayward, CA (October 2009); the Northcutt Gallery, Montana State University-Billings, MT (February 2010); St. Gregory of Nyssa Episcopal Church, San Francisco, CA (July–August 2010); St. Mary's Notre Dame, South Bend, IN (September–October 2010); Notre Dame de Namur, Belmont, CA (September 20–October 22, 2011); UNIFÉ Universidad Femenina del Sagrado Corazón, Lima, Peru (May 23–30, 2012); Casa Loyola, Barcelona, Spain (June 2012); Libreria Claret, Barcelona, Spain (April 2013); Loyola Marymount University, Los Angeles, CA (Spring 2014); Carroll College, Helena, MT (Fall 2014); Haehn Art and Heritage Museum, College of St. Benedict (April–December 2015); Boston College (Fall 2016); Laramie Community College, Cheyenne, WY (Fall 2017); Northwest College, Powell, WY (Fall 2018); Schoolhouse Gallery, Colstrip, MT (Spring 2019); Holter Museum, Helena, MT (Fall 2019); Paris Gibson, Great Falls, MT (Winter 2020); MonDak Heritage Center, Sydney, MT (Spring 2020); and Hockaday Museum, Kalispell, MT (Fall 2020).

12. M. Shawn Copeland, *Enfleshing Freedom: Body, Race, and Being* (Minneapolis, MN: Fortress Press, 2010), 94.

13. *Con/Vida: Popular Arts of the Americas* is a nonprofit directed by Sister Barbara Cervenka, OP, and art historian Marion Jackson. For more information about Con/Vida and the exhibit *Picturing Paradise*, see www.convida.org.

14. I am grateful to Dr. Cecilia Gonzalez Andrieu, associate professor of theology, for this insight. *Picturing Paradise* was exhibited at Loyola Marymount University, March 10–June 27, 2014. See https://digitalcommons.lmu.edu/picturing-paradise/.

15. Gloria Anzaldúa, *Borderlands/La Frontera: The New Mestiza* (San Francisco: Aunt Lute Books, 1987), 3.

16. Gloria Anzaldúa, "Border Arte: Nepantla el lugar de la frontera," in *La Frontera/The Border Experience: Art About the Mexico/United States Border Experience*, ed. Patricio Chavez, Madeleine Grynsztejn, and Kathryn Kanjo (San Diego, CA: Centro Cultural de la Raza and the Museum of Contemporary Art, 1993), 110.

17. Christina Aushana, "Transborder Art Activism and the U.S.-Mexico Border: Analyzing 'Artscapes' as Forms of Resistance and Cultural Productions in the Frame of Globalization," *International Journal of Interdisciplinary Social Sciences* 6, no. 7 (2012): 130–41.

18. Anzaldúa, "Border Arte," 107.

19. For more on the visual history of Aztlán, see Virginia M. Fields and Victor Zamadio-Taylor, *The Road to Aztlán: Art from a Mythic Homeland* (Los Angeles: Los Angeles County Art Museum, 2001).

20. Founding members of the BAW/TAF were David Avalos, Sar-Jo Beran, Victor Ochoa, Isaac Artenstein, Guillermo Gomez Peña, Michael Schnorr, and Jude Ederhart. Many of these members were linked to San Diego's Centro Cultural de la Raza, a Chicano arts center founded in 1970, accessed December 30, 2020, http://www.galeriadelaraza.org/eng/exhibits2/archive/artists.php?op=view&id=60&media=info.

21. For more on *rasquache*, see Tomás Ybarra-Frausto, "Rasquachismo: A Chicano Sensibility," in Richard Griswold del Castillo et al., eds., *Chicano Art: Resistance and Affirmation, 1965–1985* (Los Angeles: Wright Gallery, UCLA, 1991).

22. Amalia Mesa-Bains, "Organizational Profiles," in *The U.S.-Mexico Border: Place, Imagination, and Possibility*, exh. cat., September 10, 2017–January 7, 2018 (Los Angeles, CA: Craft & Folk Art Museum and the Getty Foundation, 2017), 75.

23. Cathy Breslaw, "Las Comadres Collective Reassessed: Women, Artists, Scholars and Activists Talk About Four Life-Changing Years," *The Buzz*, April 17, 2017, https://vanguardculture.com/las-comadres-collective-reassessed-women-artists-scholars-activists-talk-four-life-changing-years/.

24. Las Comadres as described by founding members Graciela Ovejero Postigo and Cindy Zimmerman in Breslaw, "Las Comadres Reassessed."

25. These exhibits were staged at a time when anti-immigrant sentiment was at an increased and inflammatory high. *The U.S.-Mexico Border: Place, Imagination, and Possibility*, 75.

26. Aida Mancillas, Ruth Wallen, and Marguerite R. Waller, "Making Art, Making Citizens: Las Comadres and Postnational Aesthetics," in *With Other Eyes: Looking at Race and Gender in Visual Culture*, ed. Lisa Bloom (Minneapolis, MN: Minnesota University Press, 1999), 108.

27. Amalia Mesa-Bains, "Amalia Mesa-Bains Is an Artist and Cultural Critic Based in Northern California," interview by Lowery Stokes Sims, *The U.S.–Mexico Border: Place, Imagination, and Possibility*, 116.

28. Paul DiMaggio and Patricia Fernandez-Kelly, eds., *Art in the Lives of Immigrant Communities in the United States* (New Brunswick, NJ: Rutgers University Press, 2010), 14.

29. Alia Akkam, "The U.S.-Mexico Border, Art and Politics Collide at the Artist's New Show at the Museum of Arts and Design," *Architectural Digest*, May 30, 2018, https://www.architecturaldigest.com/story/tanya-aguiniga-us-mexico-border-museum-art-and-design.

30. The word, *ambos* in Spanish means *both*.

31. From the AMBOS project website: www.ambosproject.com. Its mission: "AMBOS seeks to express and document border emotion through art making on opposite sides by providing a platform to binational artists along the border," accessed November 14, 2018.

32. AMBOS, as described on its website: www.ambosproject.com.

33. Diana Budds, "To Better Understand the U.S.-Mexico Border, One Artist Is Tying Knots," *Curbed*, May 14, 2018.

34. AMBOS, as described on its website: www.ambosproject.com. This project has had various iterations, including *Border Quipu*, a collection of vibrantly colored knots that symbolize myriad individuals who have crossed the border. This project was featured in Tanya Aguiñiga's 2018 solo exhibition, *Craft and Care*, at the Museum of Arts and Design (MAD) in New York.

35. Margarita Cabrera was born in Monterrey, Mexico, and grew up in Mexico City; Salt Lake City, Utah; and El Paso, Texas. She earned her BFA from Maryland Institute College of Art and her MFA from Hunter College, CUNY. She is currently assistant professor of art at Arizona State University in Tempe. For more on Margarita Cabrera see https://www.margaritacabrera.com.

36. Julia Dupuis, "Margarita Cabrera: Breaking Down Borders with a Needle and Thread," March 7, 2018, https://www.hamilton.edu/news/story/margarita-cabrera-breaking-down-borders-with-a-needle-and-thread.

37. Maximiliano Durón, "Searching for the In-Between: Margaret Cabrera's Collaborative Thinks Beyond Borders," *Art News*, https://www.hamilton.edu/documents/Artnews_Searching%20for%20the%20In-Between.pdf.

38. Durón, "Searching for the In-Between."

39. Ivonne Gebara, "Option for the Poor as an Option for the Poor Women," in *Concilium 194 Women, Work, and Poverty*, ed. Elisabeth Schüssler-Fiorenza (Edinbugh: T&T Clark, 1987), 110–17.

40. Durón, "Searching for the In-Between."

41. Anzaldúa, "Border Arte," 107.

BIBLIOGRAPHY

Agosín, Marjorie, ed. *Stitching Resistance: Women, Creativity and Fiber Arts*. Kent, England: Solis Press, 2014.

Anzaldúa, Gloria. *Borderlands/La Frontera: The New Mestiza*. San Francisco: Aunt Lute Books, 1987.

Aquino, María Pilar, and María José Rosado-Nunes, ed. *Feminist Intercultural Theology: Latina Explorations for a Just World*. Maryknoll, NY: Orbis Books, 2007.

Azaransky, Sara. *Religion and Politics in America's Borderlands*. Lanham, MD: Lexington Books, 2013.

Berelowitz, Jo-Anne, "Border Art Since 1965." In *Postborder City: Cultural Spaces of Bajita California*, edited by Michael Dear and Gustavo Leclerc, 143–81. New York: Routledge, 2003.

Berlo, Janet Catherine, Edward B. Dwyer, and Margot Blum Schevill, eds. *Textile Traditions of Mesoamerica and the Andes: An Anthology*. New York and London: Garland Publishing, 1991.

Berru-Davis, Rebecca. "Picturing Paradise: Imagination, Beauty, and Women's Lives in a Peruvian Shantytown." In *She Who Imagines: Women, Beauty and Justice*, edited by Laurie Cassidy and Maureen O'Connell, 145–60. Collegeville, MN: Liturgical Press, 2012.

Collier, Elizabeth W., and Charles R. Strain with Catholic Relief Services. *Global Migration: What's Happening, Why, and a Just Response*. Winona, MN: Anselm Academic, 2017.

Di Maggio, Paul, and Patricia Fernández-Kelly, eds. *Art in the Lives of Immigrant Communities in the United States*. New Brunswick, NJ: Rutgers University Press, 2010.

Gebara, Ivonne. *Longing for Running Water: Ecofeminism and Liberation*. Minneapolis: Fortress Press, 1999.

Heyer, Kristin E. *Kinship across Borders: A Christian Ethic of Immigration*. Washington, DC: Georgetown University Press, 2012.

Illman, Ruth, and W. Alan Smith. "Fabric Arts in Peru as Identity." In *Theology and the Arts: Engaging Faith*, edited by Ruth Illman and W. Alan Smith, 81–96. New York and London: Routledge, 2013.

Isasi-Díaz, Ada María. *En la Lucha/In the Struggle: Elaborating a Hispanic Women's Liberation Theology*. Minneapolis, MN: Fortress Press, 1993.

Medina, Lara, "*Nepantla* Spirituality: My Path to the Source(s) of Healing." In *Fleshing the Spirit: Spirituality and Activism in Chicana, Latina, and Indigenous Women's Lives*, edited by Elisa Facio and Irene Lara, 167–85. Tucson, AZ: University of Arizona Press, 2014.

Segura, Denise A., and Patricia Zavella, eds. *Women and Migration in the U.S.-Mexico Borderlands: A Reader*. Durham, NC: Duke University Press, 2017.

SECTION TWO
ETHICAL CONNECTIONS

CHAPTER 5

Where Ecofeminism Meets Religions

Contributions and Challenges

Heather Eaton, PhD, Saint Paul University in Ottawa, Canada

ABSTRACT

Ecofeminism, short for ecological feminism, is the combining of ecological and feminist analyses and movements. Ecofeminism appeared in the 1970s predominantly in North America, although the expression was introduced by French feminist Françoise d'Eaubonne (*Le Féminisme ou la Mort*, 1974), where she called upon women to lead an ecological revolution. In 1975, theologian Rosemary Radford Ruether wrote, "Women must see that there can be no liberation for them and no solution to the ecological crisis within a society whose fundamental model of relationships continues to be one of domination" (Ruether, 1975, 204). Ecofeminism has expanded over the years, and it is currently experiencing a resurgence. Ecofeminism has become a composite, with different emphases on the ecology or feminist aspects. It represents numerous approaches and types of analyses and is multidisciplinary in method and global in scope. Moving from the assumption that both ecology and feminism are germane to contemporary religious reflections and analyses, this chapter discusses ecofeminism and its relevance to women's and feminist studies in religion and presents insights on future pathways.

WHERE ECOFEMINISM MEETS RELIGIONS: CONTRIBUTIONS AND CHALLENGES

Ecological feminism, or ecofeminism, represents multiple intersections between feminism and ecology and between women and nature. These involve ideas, ideologies, policies, and practices, and are historical, contemporary, contextual, culture dependent, and with distinct and divergent lived realities. Where and how ecology, feminism, women, and nature overlap with religions requires vast yet discerning discussions. The following is a reflection on places where ecofeminism meets religions, offering some general points for consideration.[1] The chapter is divided into three sections. The first is an overview of ecofeminism. The second addresses aspects where ecofeminism is germane to religion. The third and concluding section offers thoughts on the relevance of, and limits to, ecofeminist frameworks and suggestions for future pathways.

OVERVIEW OF ECOLOGICAL FEMINISM

Ecofeminism is about connections between ecological and feminist concerns: discerning multiple associations between the feminist and ecological movements and between the historical and contemporary oppression and domination of women and the natural world.[2] Ecofeminism is an insight, an exposition, and an ecopolitical strategy. It involves historical, ideological, and critical analyses; cultural critiques and visions; and, for many, political actions. Ecofeminism is an umbrella term that shelters distinct and multiple links between feminism and ecology and women and the natural world and is now a vast area of research and activities. Some considered it to be a third wave of feminism.

Much has been written about the emergence and development of ecofeminism and its many forms. The following is a synopsis of some of the key aspects, inclusive of those who focus on various ecology-feminist connections but prefer concepts such as feminist ecology, feminist social ecology, feminist green socialism, feminist environmentalism, feminist ecocriticism, women and environment, feminist green philosophy, and others. Noting that these distinctions are pertinent and that ecofeminism is not a preferred idiom for some, it is advantageous here to propose a broad, flexible, and comprehensive meaning to the term.

The axiom *ecofeminism* is deemed to have originated with French feminist Françoise d'Eaubonne in *Le Féminisme ou la Mort* (1974) when she called upon women to lead an ecological revolution to save the planet. Shortly after, Rosemary Radford Ruether wrote, "Women must see that there can be no liberation for them and no solution to the ecological crisis within a society whose fundamental model of relationships continues to be one of domination."[3] However, ideas about connections between women and nature are deep rooted. They were ideologically asserted within patriarchal dogmas, systems, and customs as they expanded and entrenched themselves, virtually globally, over a few thousand years.

Much early momentum for ecofeminism came from the research into the historical, symbolic, political, and economic relationships that exist between the denigration of the natural world and the oppression of women, mainly in Euro-Western cultures. Historical excavations revealed that, in general and in most religious and other cultural systems, women and the natural world have been interrelated, that is, that women were considered to be close to nature and nature was deemed to be feminine. At times, this association was lauded, but as Euro-Western societies became established, this women/nature nexus solidified, and both were considered inferior to men/culture. Publications such as Susan Griffin's *Woman and Nature*, Mary Daly's *Gyn/Ecology*, and Carolyn Merchant's *The Death of Nature: Women, Ecology and the Scientific Revolution* in the 1970s and early 1980s made the historical trajectories evident. Also, these works became the precursors to a range of ecofeminist academic work, especially in the fields of philosophy, theology, and religious studies. The association of women with nature and their mutual subordination—cross-cultural yet distinct and differentiated—became important historical foundations for ecofeminism. During the 1980s and 1990s conferences, publications, and interest grew around ecofeminism, with many voices contributing to the development and expansion. Vandana Shiva's work, including *Staying Alive: Women, Ecology and Development* (1988) and *Ecofeminism* (1993) with Marie Mies, became influential and indicated the multidisciplinary and multicultural usefulness of ecofeminist insights. Case studies revealed that the women/nature nexus and ecofeminist evaluations are not ideologically constructed, experienced, or lived out in identical ways in distinct cultures, as shown in *Ecofeminism and Globalization: Exploring Culture, Context and Religion* (Eaton and Lorentzen, 2003).

The exposure of hierarchical dualisms provided a vital catalyst for ecofeminist cultural analyses. Hierarchical dualisms—ways of perceiving the world in opposites or dualisms, such as heaven/earth, culture/nature, men/women, masculine/feminine, reason/emotion, spirit/matter, and mind/body—were exposed, challenged, and in general deconstructed by feminist scholars. Val Plumwood's book, *Feminism and the Mastery of Nature* (1993), became a decisive exposition and analysis of the parallel oppressions of women and nature. She, along with Karen Warren and others, exposed how the logic of dualisms is reproduced in a logic of domination, evidenced in social patterns and in economic, political, and spiritual relationships. Thus, the twin dominations of women and nature became justified and appear *natural*, reinforced by religion, philosophy, and cultural symbols. Ecofeminist research exposes that this matrix of domination and oppression has identifiable roots in anthropocentrism, androcentrism, misogyny, hierarchy, naturism, and the emergence of organized agriculture. It became clear that dominations are interlinked (race/ethnicity, class, gender, sexual orientation, colonialism, and ecological exploitation). The logic and practices of domination are mutually sustaining in ideological and material manners and are evident in cultural structures and customs.

Ecofeminist publications have continued to delineate new ways to understand the term, the associations, and the relevance. Theoreticians from philosophy, religions, sciences, social scientists, and humanities contribute. Many distinct voices are in the conversation, including conventional differentiations among feminisms (liberal, Marxist, cultural, materialist, socialist, womanist, mujerista, etc). Religious and/or spiritual activists and academics contributed from many standpoints (e.g., Wiccan, Goddess, Jewish, Christian, Hindu, Indigenous, and Islamic traditions).

A second basic claim within ecofeminism is empirical. In most parts of the world, environmental problems generally disproportionately affect women. Ecofeminist empirical claims scrutinize the sociopolitical and economic structures that restrict many women's lives to poverty, ecological deprivation, and economic powerlessness. From another angle, considerable empirical work in international and development studies and initiatives connect women/gender, environment/ecology, and development. Numerous women and development organizations make these connections, such as UN Women. Some see this work as part of a larger field of ecofeminism, while others separate the empirical from the theoretical efforts.

From the beginning, connections between women/nature and feminism/ecology were made by environmental, peace, and animal rights activists as well as by farmers, artists, teachers, and more. Eventually ecofeminism incorporated intersectionality as a cornerstone approach as well as approaches from critical race, queer, ethnicity, identity, disability, and numerous contextual-cultural and postmodern theories. In all the ways that ecological analyses and theories have developed, such as deep and social ecologies, environmental ethics, ecojustice, environmental racism, sustainability studies, environmental/ecophilosophies, ecocriticism, art, literature, and more, ecofeminism has advanced in tandem. All of this added much needed nuance, internal critiques, and assessments as well as reinforcing the validity and usefulness of ecofeminism as a lens, analysis, and insight. Ecofeminist thought and activism exist in India, Asia, Africa, and Latin America, and more.

As mentioned, ecofeminism is an umbrella term. Activists, academics, and theorists differ on foundational assumptions, on the nature of the relationship between women and the natural world, on ecological paradigms, on feminist approaches, on the roots of environmental crises, and on goals and the means of transformation. It is interesting to note that the meanings of ecofeminism developed with considerable fervor. There were publications, conferences, and activism, which opened debates about ecofeminist origins, development and theories, representation, activist or academic priorities, culture, context, the significance or not of religion and spirituality, essentialism, and more. Then, ecofeminism faded from view in the 1990s, although not entirely.

Since roughly 2010, further developments within ecofeminism have resurged, with numerous publications that assert the importance of the topic, analyses, and insights. Ecofeminism encompasses different forms of knowledge, embodied in the concrete, and has proven to be an enormously useful and flexible insight. Ecofeminism is a textured field of theoretical and experiential insights that connect ecology and feminism and assesses the power and practices related to the women/nature nexus that exists in most cultures and religions.

ECOFEMINISM AND RELIGION

Religions have been a dialogue partner with ecofeminism from the beginning. One reason is because the roots of any women/nature nexus are embedded in religious precepts. Some of the earliest ecofeminist texts in theology and religious studies examined the historical origins of patriarchy and the development of patriarchal religions and philosophies of the Euro-Western cultures. Many explored the expansion of classical religions and how their ideas, texts, religious structures, doctrines, and practices justified the domination of women and nature. The Christian traditions and their cultural legacies were studied in depth by ecofeminist researchers and exposed for influencing and reinforcing a women/nature nexus in Euro-Western cultural development.

Both oppressive and liberating elements were found in most traditions, and some, such as Indigenous, Goddess, and Wiccan, were seen to offer old and new insights relevant to ecofeminist ideals. As religions began responding to ecological issues, they had to address their historical and contemporary limits and insights. Although it is evident that religions are often fraught with bias, prejudices, narrow mindedness, and injustices, they can also be life affirming, liberating, and ethically sound. This ambiguous nature of religions must be discussed, without losing the power, potential, and profundity of religions as a social force. When it comes to feminist challenges to religions, the ambiguous nature is more obvious because, in general, religions have not been overly responsive to women's autonomy. Thus, the joint eco and feminist challenges are considerable and require comprehensive religious transformations. However, the problem of *religion* needs to be discussed.

There is often an assumption that when referring to *religion* there is an evident referent. Yet this is not the case. Departments of religious studies and theology and religious schools—thousands around the world—have no agreed upon definitions for or theories of religion(s). Although *everyone knows* religions exist and are powerful personal and social forces, there is no clear categorization. After decades of studying religions and proposing countless taxonomies—historical to contemporary, distinct/amalgams, comparative, world religions, or by structures (beliefs, rituals, texts, dogmas, and institutions), or by personal to social influence and impacts, or using philosophical, political, psychological, sociological, or spiritual frameworks—the quest for a substantial, meaningful and agreed-upon definition of religion has proven to be elusive. This plethora of theories used to describe, explain, analyze, deconstruct, or denounce religion(s) reverberate back to the problem of an absence of a definition.

What can be classified as traditional religions—Indian (Jainism, Hinduism, and Buddhism), East Asian (Confucianism, Daoism, and Shinto) Middle Eastern monotheism (Judaism, Christianity, and Islam)—is a poor taxonomy for several reasons. One, whatever *religions* are, they are always amalgamations of multiple historical, cultural, symbolic, and ideological systems. Two, religions have porous boundaries. They are historically and contextually fluid, mutable, and heterogeneous and have countless internal differentiations. For example, what exactly is Christianity? The countless historical and contemporary variations defy description in addition to the innumerable internal denominations: Baptist, Evangelical, Anglican, Catholic, United, Lutheran, Mennonite, Orthodox, Reformed, etc. Three, the traditions of shamanism, animism, Goddess worship, and countless Indigenous spiritualities and practices everywhere in the world are rarely included in the term *religion*. Four, what distinguishes *religions* from cultures, contexts, philosophies, and ideologies is murky to an extreme. Five, no two people adhere to or *live* a religion the same way: fervor, intensity, conviction, commitments, rituals, etc. Theories of lived religions, usually ethnographic, offer some stability in approaching the topic of religions, as they assess lived experiences, identity formation, and meaning making. But they do not deal with revelations, salvations, truth claims, texts, beliefs, rituals, and the gamut of realities that comprise *religion*.

This conundrum of religions is also present when ecofeminism enters the conversation. In addition, there are additional cautions. For example, publications on ecofeminism and religion(s) usually take the form of one author's views on a particular religion.

However, several questions ensue. How widespread are the views? If from the standpoint of an adherent, how much critical distance, or hermeneutics of suspicion, are in place? What is the knowledge base of the researcher? Is this a practitioner, a true believer or a skeptic, a religious leader or institutional representative, a scholar, or a combination? These are important aspects to consider in evaluating whatever is claimed at the intersection of ecofeminism and religion.

Ecofeminism ideas and analyses have seeped into many distinct religions or at least have been addressed by some voices within most traditions and in many parts of the world. From an initial publication, *Ecofeminism and the Sacred* (Adams, 1993), to the present, religion has been a dialogue partner, although at times at the periphery of the larger field of ecofeminism. There are publications and case studies from around the world and from many traditions and contexts exploring and, virtually always, affirming and advancing the relevance of ecofeminism. For example, in addition to North America and Europe, there are publications on ecofeminism in Sri Lanka, India, China, Korea, Taiwan, Chile, Brazil, and several African countries. Collectively, they address ecological issues, such as food, land, water, climate change, and animal studies. They address religious topics, such as God/Goddess traditions, rituals, homilies, ethics, spiritualities, and more. This points to the pervasiveness of women/nature constructs and the usefulness and elasticity of ecofeminism.

It must be noted that at times religious contributions to ecofeminism were disparaged. One reason is an assumption that essentialism is central to ecofeminism when it has always been a marginal view and is overall rejected. A second reason is people contributing with a cursory, inaccurate, or uninformed knowledge of ecofeminism. A third reason is when the political activism and social transformation dimension is disregarded. Last is the issue of spirituality and uncritical usages of this term. In fact, at times, all of ecofeminism was assumed to be tainted with essentialist uncritical spiritualities.

A further observation is to note that most of the academic efforts on ecofeminism and religion, including my own, have involved Christianity. This could be because ecofeminism developed predominantly in Christian-influenced cultures and overall in North America. In general, Christian traditions have been pressured to grapple with ecological and feminist challenges. Some have proven to be flexible and responsive to both. Others have been responsive to ecological issues but less so to feminism. Ecofeminism brings a combined challenge, which is problematical to conservative Christian elements, for example, in institutional Catholicism, Evangelical, and Orthodox groups.

Ecofeminist approaches within Christianity have included the retrieval of relevant texts and teachings, such as translating the works of Hildegaard von Bingen. Other efforts have addressed doctrines, offering constructive reinterpretations of creation as incomplete rather than fallen, for example. Several creative approaches include reinterpreting biblical themes and motifs, as evidenced in the prominent Earth Bible Series. Reconstructive efforts have necessitated a discontinuity with some widespread tenets, such as Christian supremacy, other-worldly orientations, and gender essentialism. Feminist and ecological ethics and gender, ecojustice, and climate justice are important and novel contributions, providing significant critiques of affluence, consumerism, poverty-sustaining economics, food insecurities, and all manner of intersecting injustices. All of this work, at the intersection of ecofeminism and Christianity, proliferated and is part of the overall ecological and feminist reformation of as well as new expressions of Christian traditions. The theoretical, theological, and practical influence of these intense efforts is difficult to assess but indicate the extent of transformation needed when ecofeminism confronts religions.

The work of retrieval, reinterpretation, and reconstruction, as well as incorporating new ideas and insights, is a broad description of how ecofeminism intersects with religions. Working with texts, teachings, practices, ethics, rituals, and symbols—a vast task—represents what has been and is occurring. Theoreticians and religious and theological scholars advance the ecological and feminist challenges in tradition-specific or multireligious realms, which often occur in universities, seminaries, conferences, and publications. Questions worth pondering concern the connections between such work and the leadership, authority, and institutional elements of a tradition. A further question is about the relationships between the theoretical and academic efforts and the communities who adhere to these religions in lived ways: materially, practically, contextually, and in culturally specific manners. Ecofeminism may seem far from their lived realities. Thus, it is crucial that the negative repercussions of the ideas surrounding a women/nature nexus be made apparent in the practical and material lived realities of communities as well as how ecological and gender issues are connected. Case studies are one way to make these evident; however, the question of the accessibility, relevance, and influence of such studies needs to be raised.

ECOFEMINIST HERMENEUTICS

Ecofeminism has been developing for forty years or so and, as seen in the above examples, is percolating into religious awareness. Because ecofeminism is many things—activism, analyses, and academia—and is both widespread and context bound, it may be useful to consider a few general hermeneutics that could bolster ecofeminist religious efforts:

1) *An in-depth awareness of the logic of domination, the interlocking patterns of oppressions, and the critical theories of liberation informing ecofeminist theory(ies).*

It is central to any ecofeminist approach to delve into the mutually reinforcing ideas of the women/nature nexus and how women's lives and the natural world are devalued and subjugated to myriad repressions. There is a logic and systematic and structural patterns to the limitations, and often overt abuse, surrounding women's lives. In order to dismantle oppressions, it is crucial to understand in depth how domination works in a given culture. It is insidious, not experienced by all, yet ubiquitous. A focus only on equality and other liberal feminist notions is incapable of dismantling domination, in spite of equality and equity being worthy goals. Ecofeminism is a liberatory and justice discourse that exposes and denounces domination and reveals the many dimensions of a women/nature nexus. The destruction of the natural world must also be seen as oppression and domination. The end goal of ecofeminism is liberation, broadly understood.

2) *A recognition of the multi- and interdisciplinary character, indeed of the breadth and depth of ecofeminist analyses and proposals.*

In order to bring ecofeminist analyses and insights to bear on religious traditions, it is wise to learn about the many approaches, disciplines, analyses, and issues under the ecofeminist umbrella. There is no one ecofeminist orthodoxy but rather a composite of the many ways ecology and feminism and women and nature are interconnected in both their oppressions and liberations. It is easy to be reductionist and work within one's customary and comfortable categories. However, from the beginning, ecofeminism is multiple and involves many insights and strategies for change. For example, while gender essentialism is overall refuted, patriarchal cultures may be intransigent to loosening any gender categories. Essentialism can be exploited as a strategy for change in some cultures.

3) *Critical appraisals of the destructive and liberating elements within the religious traditions, especially with respect to women and the natural world and what connects them.*

It is importance to be candid and conscientious about the negative legacies of religious heritages. There is a tendency, at times, to elucidate the religious texts and teachings that support women and ecological sustainability while side-stepping the more problematic elements. It is necessary to assess a tradition for both the strengths and insights as well as the weaknesses and shortcomings. All patriarchal religions have misogynist facets, which need to be exposed and denounced. Also, to be a liberatory project, connections between the ideological and lived realities need to be overt. If ecofeminist religious claims are detached from cultural realities, they may be offering prescription, albeit graceful, views with little or no political awareness, emancipatory potential, or social responsibility.

From an ecological stance, many traditions have profound teachings. Some have maintained practices of living within the rhythms and limits of the natural world. The ecological wisdom and ethics within religious traditions should be confirmed. Yet there are limitations in reworking religions that have accumulated misogynist notions and anti-ecological stances. The discontinuity required from core elements of some traditions from both the ecological and feminist evaluations is daunting. There is a tension between how far a tradition can be stretched and reinterpreted and the need for new religious sensitivities that can respond to the socioecological plight. To some extent, this tension mirrors the feminist ambivalence with patriarchal religions among those who modify existing systems, those who continue the analytic (deconstruction) work, and those who create new traditions.

4) *A rigorous understanding of the extent of the ecological crisis.*

Some ecofeminist analyses considering the ecological crisis do not seem to know many specifics. To speak of a generic ecological crisis is to ignore the contextual specificities as well as the range of issues involved. There are innumerable resources available and countless meticulous reports that give data on the ecological crises. Ecological literacy is needed. An appreciation for the exchange between science and religion and learning basic Earth sciences are useful and important to any ecoreligious discourse.

To intersect ecofeminism and religion and discuss only feminism or religion and omit how this will relate to or alleviate an aspect of the ecological crisis weakens the possibility of actual transformation. Often, the emphasis is more on feminism than ecology. However, the ecological crisis is restructuring the world/Earth and requires massive efforts to address, respond, and adapt. Thus, continuity needs to occur between religious symbols, such as water, earth, or air and the actual conditions of these elements. It makes little sense to write about the *waters of life* when water contamination is acute. The physical and spiritual must be considered together. Otherwise, the unintended consequences will be the transformation of religious ideas and nothing else.

5) *Openness to the insights of the myriad religious traditions, especially those that have developed a high degree of sensitivity to the natural world, and a willingness to be transformed by the dialogue*.

Religions are in transition, with increasing multireligious encounters. These implicitly or explicitly raise questions about religious or scriptural authorities, truth assertions, and the claims of universality. The realms of religious studies and theology, although both addressing ecology and at times gender, can be very different. Those who are unfamiliar with the historical and contemporary multiplicities of religions tend to reproduce presumed, unsubstantiated, and at times unexamined assumptions about their religion, the world, nature, revelation, and truth. When Christian ecotheologians, including ecofeminists, enter the field of religion and ecology, it is apparent that few have studied other religions, including the histories, diversities, and complexities. They may be inexperienced with the scholarly tools that probe religions through phenomenology, sociology, cultural studies, psychology, critical theories, imaginative or symbolic processes, and cognitive or somatic studies. In general, theology, although not alone, operates with deficient theories of religion. Religious contributions that are mired in their own imperialism and triumphalism are more detrimental than beneficial.

A lack of interest in or knowledge of the multiplicities of religions, the insights from animism, Indigenous spiritualities, or other traditions such as Jainism, that have an acute sensitivity to the natural world is not appropriate in contemporary global contexts. Genuine openness, dialogue, learning, and cooperation are crucial if religions are to be effectively engaged on ecological and gender issues.

6) *Commitment to politically relevant and engaged work, cognizant of the strained concrete and material realities of poverty, inequalities, and structural violence*.

Ecofeminists from affluent contexts can fall prey to myopia, with an excessive emphasis on theory and a lack of attending to the material injustices and their causes. This renders such ecofeminist religious efforts powerless in the face of the real issues they are addressing. Worse still, not only powerless, but indirectly participating in the destruction of the world while creating beautiful theories about alternative futures. While we need to attend to the internal perversions and rectifications of various religious interpretations and methods, the accelerating ecological crisis and the strenuous material relationships between women and the natural world increase. From the beginning, ecofeminism has a radical, activist, and transformative premise with political ramifications. Those producing ecofeminist theories, religious or otherwise, are ultimately about social change.

These few hermeneutics, and there are surely more, may help orient ecofeminist religious efforts to be comprehensive and relevant. The final section deals with reflections on future directions and general comments at the intersection of ecofeminism and religion.

GENERAL REMARKS AND FUTURE DIRECTIONS

Ecofeminist publications are proliferating, refining analyses on the genealogy and noting the large range of disciplines involved in ecofeminist thought and activism. Current views incorporate intersectionality and context culture–specific analyses as well as advancing and enriching ecofeminist theories. There are ecofeminist analyses on farming, food, climate change, animal studies, ecojustice, ecotourism, vegetarianism, governance, literature, education, and more. There are Queer, integral, holistic, critical, postcolonial, Indigenous, materialist modes of ecofeminism. Dissertations on ecofeminism abound, on countless subjects and from around the world. The list of publications is massive. However, religions are rarely a dialogue partner currently.

This chapter has described ecofeminism and intersections with religions. There are five additional inquiries to be mentioned, that suggest future pathways. Each offers challenges and opportunities to the intersection of ecofeminism and religions that could orient forthcoming work.

The first is that, in terms of the large field of women and religions, ecofeminism has not been a key topic. In fact, ecological issues, in general, have not made a significant impact on the research areas. Within *women and religions*, much has been explored, excavated, reviled, and reassessed. These efforts have established an academic and public presence for women within some religious traditions and spaces. Key themes have been *women and* religious texts, imagery, ritual, leadership, and a host of ethical concerns and injustices. It is evident that the field of women and religions has focused primarily on *women* as a contested category to be problematized, diversified, and celebrated. The same cannot be said of the category of *religion*. The aforementioned critical religion appraisals have barely touched the field of women and religions. In fact, it is startling how often and in innumerable publications *women* are scrutinized persistently, and *religion* is undefined consistently. Understandably, the entire gender enterprise is about exposing omnipresent androcentrism, with agreed-upon goals to discover, analyze, and integrate women into religions as participative subjects and to pressure religions to be an ethical social presence. Thus, unpacking *religion* was never a priority. Nonetheless, religion has not been sufficiently problematized and needs to be addressed. Furthermore, women's issues are not the only concerns ecofeminists need to address.

The second is that ecological issues are becoming acute, and ecological decline poses more challenges than any moment in human, and perhaps even Earth's, history. The biosphere is declining, and the planetary systems—hydrologic cycle, ocean vitality, climate systems, and biodiversity—are unraveling. The consequences are dire. In addressing ecological issues, anthropocentrism is the norm, yet life and planetary dynamics are fully integrated. Furthermore, humans emerged from, belong to, and exist and flourish within a vibrant biosphere. To persistently speak of humans and the *environment* as discontinuous is absurd in the face of interrelated biosphere dynamics.

For example, climate justice efforts tend toward anthropocentrism, where the planetary and the political rarely intersect. Climate justice is framed within discourses of structural violence and human rights, noting that climate change is and will affect those with the least political and economic power to mitigate the effects. Climate justice is attentive to governance and to oppressive patterns of ethnicity, gender, and poverty. It looks at the modalities of power, national security and political transparency, food, and land and water sovereignty and encourages community-led solutions. Climate justice is concerned with the impact of climate change on humans, tethered to human rights. It is often anthropocentric and rarely considers the effects of climate instability on other life communities within the biosphere.

This worldview shift from anthropocentrism to Earth centric is occurring but rarely in ecofeminism or in women and religion. Climate change is a good example of the need for this worldview shift. Humans live on a thin layer of culture within a vast expanse of nature. The natural world, ecological vitality, and biospheric integrity are the *determining* planetary dynamics and the life support system for any viable human communities. Ecological feminism has the potential to make significant ecological contributions but needs to ensure the ecological dimension is informed and potent as well as being cognizant of the limits of anthropocentrism.

The third inquiry is that shifts are also occurring in the realm of religions. Ecological issues are impacting religious understanding, within a range of responses addressed earlier. If one assumes that religions could be effective in curbing the ecological crisis, then, in addition to the internal work of retrieval and reconstructions and multireligious efforts, transformations on a larger scale are also considered. For example, Thomas Berry claimed that religions are a necessary, albeit insufficient, aspect of addressing the current planetary dilemma, and religions have the capacity to revive. From *Dream of the Earth* he wrote, "any effective response to these issues requires a religious context. . . . We cannot do without the traditional religions, but they cannot presently do what needs to be done. We need a new type of religious orientation."[4] Only this scale of transformation will be responsive to the magnitude of the ecological and social crises, which have to be fully understood and articulated. The transitions needed to respond to the current era—ecological, social, cultural, and religious—are massive. The Forum on Religion and Ecology represents a wide range of efforts to engage religions on ecology, including ecofeminism. It also includes views informed by Earth sciences, evolution, and cosmology, noting that becoming informed of these larger horizons propels a new type of religious orientation. Here, too the intersections of ecofeminism and religions could be increased and deepened and be more compelling.

The fourth challenge is to consider the proposals for planetary or global visions, for example, the efforts of biodemocracy, earth democracy, ecological civilizations, the Earth Charter, and biospheric egalitarianism. These initiatives are coming from different countries and contexts yet are recognizing that a planetary vision and common ground must be found. The challenges are acute, as postcolonial cultures continue to seek autonomy, self-determination and governance, and ecological and economic control. It is an ongoing struggle to resist past and present forms of cultural imperialism. Yet, not only are countries increasingly interdependent; many ecological problems cannot be remedied within nation-states. These global visions are attempts to develop a unifying image and strategy without erasing the multiplicities of cultural, power, identity, economic, or other differences. It is clear that such global platforms are developing, offering a way forward within the diversities and complexities of postmodern worlds and differentiated yet interconnected Earth communities. Those interested in ecofeminism and religions could take up this challenge. It would expand and fortify contributions.

The fifth challenge is a reflection on the meaning of a diverse global women's movement: women moving effectively into the social, political, and economic spheres. The insistence that women gain equity and autonomy has reverberated globally. It is uneven, with gains and losses, backlashes, and much more to do. Yet it is a revolution of massive proportions within human social structures, ideologies, and symbolic systems. It is arguably the largest shift of consciousness humanity has made since the Neolithic revolution and the emergence of symbolic consciousness. From this vantage point, feminism is not only an ethical claim or political movement. It is a revolution in cultural symbolic consciousness. It is a change of reference points of all forms of social organization, bringing forth a radically new perception of human capacity, differentiation, and complexity. Patriarchy has been the ruling social, ideological, and symbolic organization for thousands of years, virtually everywhere. Feminism is a direct challenge to patriarchy. But it is more than ethical and social transformations.

An understanding of humanity has to expand to incorporate women: our inherent value, variations, inclusion, and participation in the planetary project. What is also occurring is that the subjectivity, diversity, and elegance of the human, as a species, are being expanded and enhanced. In tandem with the image of humanity being stretched and redefined, we are discovering ourselves as members of an Earth community, in a dynamic and creative universe. The women's movement deconstructs the restricted symbol of *woman* and opens the possibilities of reinventing the social order. This opening of consciousness is also the opportunity for greater dimensions of reality to seep into our awareness, disorienting and reorienting the human community in the larger projects of the Earth and the universe. An inclusive social imaginary needs to be situated within a new ecological imaginary. As well, any ecological consciousness must embrace the women's movement.

It is also true that most of feminist work does not address ecological issues in depth. The women's movement needs to attend to what is emerging into human consciousness about Earth's processes and dynamics. It is a bleak future for women within a ruined planet. We can imagine more than equity and autonomy for women as planetary participants, and we cannot accept less.

CONCLUSION

This chapter discussed ecofeminism and its relevance to feminist and women's studies in religions. It provided an overview of ecofeminism, of intersections with religions, and several hermeneutics that could be useful as foundational for ongoing work. Several tensions were mentioned: as issues of essentialism, poor theories of religions, inherent limitations within patriarchal religions, and the question of who speaks for religion. The last section presented five inquiries that offer challenges and suggestions for future pathways. The lacuna within the field of women and religions, the severity of the ecological crisis, that religions are in transition, the emergence of ecological planetary consciousness, and the far-reaching and revolutionary impacts of global women's movements could be catalysts for new contributions at the intersection of ecofeminism and religions.

NOTES

1. Given the vast bibliography for ecofeminism, this chapter is written as a reflection, with few references.
2. See select ecofeminist books in bibliography.
3. Rosemary Radford Ruether, *New Woman, New Earth: Sexist Ideologies and Human Liberation* (New York: Seabury Press, 1975), 204.
4. Thomas Berry, *Dream of the Earth* (San Francisco: Sierra Club Books, 1988), 87.

SELECT BOOKS ON ECOFEMINISM

Adams, Carol, and Gruen, Lori. *Ecofeminism: Feminist Intersections with Other Animals and the Earth.* New York: Bloomsbury Academic, 2014.

Cudworth, E. *Developing Ecofeminist Theory: The Complexity of Difference.* Hampshire: Palgrave Macmillan, 2005.

Cuomo, C. *Feminism and Ecological Communities: An Ethic of Flourishing.* London: Routledge, 1998.

D'Eaubonne, Françoise. *Le Féminisme ou la Mort.* Paris: Pierre Horay, 1974.

Diamond, Irene, and Orenstein, Gloria, eds. *Reweaving the World: The Emergence of Ecofeminism.* San Francisco: Sierra Club Books, 1990.

Eaton, Heather. *Introducing Ecofeminist Theologies.* New York: T&T Clark International, 2005.

Eaton, Heather, and Lois Ann Lorentzen. *Ecofeminism and Globalization: Exploring Culture, Context, and Religion.* Lanham, MD: Rowman & Littlefield, 2003.

Gaard, Greta. *Critical Ecofeminism.* Lanham, MD: Lexington Books, 2017.

Gebara, Ivone. *Longing for Running Water: Ecofeminism and Liberation.* Minneapolis, MN: Fortress Press, 1999.

Griffin, Susan. *Woman and Nature: The Roaring Inside Her.* London: Women's Press, 1978.

Hunnicutt, Gwen. *Gender Violence in Ecofeminist Perspective: Intersections of Animal Oppression, Patriarchy and Domination of the Earth.* Abingdon, Oxon: Routledge, 2020.

Isla, Ana. *Climate Chaos: Ecofeminism and the Land Question.* Toronto: Inanna Publications & Education Inc., 2019.

Kheel, Marti. *Nature Ethics: An Ecofeminist Perspective.* Lanham, MD: Rowman & Littlefield, 2008.

MacGregor, S., ed. *Routledge Handbook of Gender and Environment.* Routledge International. Abingdon, Oxon: Routledge, 2017.

Merchant, Carolyn. *The Death of Nature: Women, Ecology and the Scientific Revolution.* San Francisco: HarperCollins, 1980.

Mickey, Sam, and Douglas A. Vakoch, eds. *Literature and Ecofeminism: Intersectional and International Voices.* London: Taylor and Francis, 2018.

Mies, Maria, and Vandana Shiva. *Ecofeminism.* London: Zed Press, 1993.

Murphy, Patrick. *Reconceiving Nature: Ecofeminism in Late Victorian Women's Poetry.* Columbia: University of Missouri Press, 2019.

Odih, Pamela. *Watersheds in Marxist Ecofeminism.* Newcastle upon Tyne: Cambridge Scholars Publishing, 2014.

Phillips, Mary, and Nick Rumens, eds. *Contemporary Perspectives on Ecofeminism*. London: Routledge, 2016.

Plumwood, Val. *Feminism and the Mastery of Nature*. London and New York: Routledge, 1993.

Ress, Mary Judith. *Ecofeminism in Latin America*. Maryknoll, NY: Orbis Books, 2006.

Ruether, Rosemary Radford. *Gaia and God: An EcoFeminist Theology of Earth Healing*. San Francisco: HarperCollins, 1992.

———. *Integrating Ecofeminism, Globalization and World Religions*. Lanham, MD: Rowman & Littlefield, 2005.

———. *New Woman, New Earth: Sexist Ideologies and Human Liberation*. New York: Seabury Press, 1975.

Stephens, Anne. *Ecofeminism and Systems Thinking*. London and New York: Routledge, 2015.

Stevens, Lara, Peta Tait, and Denise Varney. *Feminist Ecologies: Changing Environments in the Anthropocene*. Springer International Publishing, 2018.

Sturgeon, Noel. *Ecofeminist Natures: Race, Gender, Feminist Theory and Political Action*. New York: Routledge, 1997.

Vakoch, Douglas A., and Sam Mickey. *Ecofeminism in Dialogue*. Lanham, MD: Lexington Books, 2018.

Warren, Karen. *Ecofeminist Philosophy: A Western Perspective on What It Is and Why It Matters*. Lanham, MD: Rowman & Littlefield, 2000.

CHAPTER 6

Reconfiguring Economic Sustainability

A Feminist Ethic for Liberty and Justice for All

Dr. Sharon D. Welch, Meadville Lombard Theological School (Unitarian Universalist)

ABSTRACT

Feminist entrepreneurs, activists, and scholars are reconfiguring economics to create new forms of community economy that embody the values of gratitude, reciprocity, and responsibility and redefine economic success as seeking reciprocal plenitude, rather than exploitative and extractive growth. Feminist economists Juliet Schorr and J. K. Gibson-Graham and a botanist and member of the Pottawatomie Nation, Robin Wall Kimmerer, acknowledge the costs of extractive and exploitative capitalism but focus more on the ethical gifts and challenges of economies based on "belonging, not belongings." This move, from critique to construction, is also found in the work of women entrepreneurs who are managing businesses that embody social responsibility and environmental regeneration.

We live in paradoxical times. Growing numbers of people throughout the world are fully aware of the threat of ecocide, human-induced extinction of ourselves and other species, and the role of current forms of economic practices in creating this danger. Yet few people are aware of the growing numbers of concrete, regenerative solutions to this crisis. These solutions are not merely changes in values. They are embodied ways of living in just and balanced relations with each other and the natural world. There is the creation of community economies and new ways of doing business, producing food, building homes, and providing essential services that embody respect for other human beings and our interdependence with the natural world.

Our challenge is clear. Increasing numbers of people throughout the world are recognizing that we are now living in a human-induced climate emergency. Can we expand our sense of interdependence to the natural world, and can we do so in a timely enough and effective enough manner to stop ecocide? The journalist Elizabeth Kolbert claims that we may now be experiencing a "mass extinction caused by human beings." She writes that "the impact of human activity is so far-reaching that our era is now being called the Anthropocene."[1]

NEW FORMS OF COMMUNITY ECONOMIES

There are growing numbers of people seeing this ecological threat and responding to it with both humility and creativity.[2] It is here that we have much to learn from the work of the indigenous scholars and activists Carol Lee Sanchez and Robin Wall Kimmerer. In their work they state that who we are as human beings is as much *actually* destructive as *potentially* regenerative and ecologically and socially responsible. Sanchez is of Pueblo and Lebanese descent, raised in the Laguna Pueblo, and was an author, artist, and professor of American Indian Studies. In her writing and teaching, Sanchez shared with us the fundamental insight that the indigenous respect for the natural order is *not* simply natural and, in fact, is just the opposite. Reverence for the natural world is learned from hard-won lessons of what had gone wrong when there was a lack of respect for both the natural and the social order. Respect is maintained only through two ongoing social processes—telling the stories of environmental degradation and social inequity and checking the tendencies to repeat those patterns through specific rituals. In her teaching and writing, Sanchez did not share with us the rituals that were used by the people of the Laguna Pueblo but encouraged us to tell our own stories of disruption and to create our own rituals of respect and belonging, our own recognition of the necessity and power of the Beauty Way.[3]

We find the same wisdom offered by Robin Wall Kimmerer. Kimmerer is a botanist and a member of the Potawatomi Nation. In addition to seeing our gifts of belonging and reciprocity and learning to use them in responsible ways, Kimmerer challenges us to see and check our constitutive evil. She tells the story of the Windigo, a person driven by greediness with a heart as cold as ice and only focused on their own needs. Once focused only on one's own needs, the longing for more becomes both insatiable and ruthless, even leading one to experience pleasure in taking from others and causing them pain.[4]

Kimmerer provides a compelling account of the way in which the Windigo shape the lives of so many of us. She sees the Windigo at the core of rapacious globalization and exploitative and extractive capitalism. The wisdom here is pointed. We *can* see this greed and violence and contain it in others, and we *must* see it and contain it in ourselves: "Gratitude for all the earth has given us lends us courage to turn and face the Windigo that stalks us to refuse to participate in an economy that destroys the beloved earth to line the pockets of the greedy, to demand an economy that is aligned with life, not stacked against it. It's easy to write that, harder to do."[5]

Kimmerer states that, while we can find antidotes to the Windigo, we cannot destroy the ongoing threat of isolation and insatiable greed. The Windigo remains as a recurring temptation that can lead us away from a respectful grounding in the social and natural plenitude that could sustain us.[6] While Kimmerer extols both the beauty and the possibility of living in a covenant of reciprocity, she also is forthright in her acknowledgment that it may be too late for us to correct the damage caused by a culture of individualism and heedless exploitation of the human and natural world. While we may choose to accept the covenant of reciprocity, while we may choose to honor our responsibilities, Kimmerer is clear: we may not know how to restore damaged ecosystems or how to live with the natural world in a way that is equitable and regenerative.[7]

There are growing numbers of people who have as strong a critique of extractive and exploitative capitalism as Kimmerer. In her book, *Christianity and the New Spirit of Capitalism*, the feminist theologian Kathryn Tanner decries the new forms of finance capitalism and its degradation of the natural world and of human community. She states that finance capitalism is concerned only with shareholder value, "returning value to the owners of stock," not with the well-being of either employees or the larger community (19). She states that finance capitalism "foments . . . extreme income/wealth inequality, structural under- and unemployment, and regularly recurring boom/bust cycles in asset values."[8] In addition, it is highly individualized: "Economic success or failure becomes one's individual responsibility, revelatory of who one is as a person" (168). Has one worked hard enough, long enough, and smart enough to be financially rewarded (168)?[9]

As we reckon with the harm done by the past and current forms of economic life, many people are calling us away from the economic practices of the past and present to a definition of wealth and success, like that described by Kimmerer. We can find this transformative understanding of wealth in the work of the feminist economists Juliet B. Schor and J. K. Gibson-Graham. In her book, *Plenitude: The New Economics of True Wealth*, Juliet Schor describes our basic challenge as follows. Many of us are relatively skilled at identifying what is wrong with our socially and environmental destructive economic system, yet we are also limited by an inability to imagine plausible alternatives. As Schor states, "Climate destabilization, economic meltdown, and the escalation of food and energy prices are warning signs from a highly stressed planet. . . . But the mainstream conversation has been stalled by fatalism. We're better at identifying what can't be done than what we need to accomplish."[10]

In *Plenitude*, Schor describes an emerging, environmentally responsible economic order, one not built on sacrifice and scarcity but grounded in a deep appreciation of what creates genuine and regenerative bounty—the plenitude that is possible as we move from an economy of endless consumption and growth to responsible connections to other people and to the natural world.[11]

J. K. Gibson-Graham (Katherine Gibson, Australian National University in Canberra, and Julie Graham, University of Massachusetts, Amherst, who wrote as a single persona from 1992 until Graham's death in 2010) have described a new political imaginary. They analyze, nurture, and celebrate the reality, opportunities, and challenges of community economies. They state that people all over the world are finding ways of shaping their economic lives to recognize the power of interdependence, not a "common being" but a "being in common." J. K. Gibson-Graham describe the ways in which people embody interdependence in such economic practices as employee buyouts in the United States, worker takeovers in the wake of economic crisis in Argentina, the anti-sweatshop movement, shareholder movements "that promote ethical investments and police the enforcement of corporate environmental and social responsibility," the living wage movement, efforts to institute a universal basic income, and social entrepreneurship. These are all part of a community economy "that performs economy in new ways."[12]

J. K. Gibson-Graham built on the insights of queer theory and political and feminist theory and organizing, emphasizing that shared questions often lead to different answers. Just as there is no one way to be a feminist, there is no single way to perform economic relations justly. There are, however, salient questions, choices to be made in each situation. Here, the economy becomes the product of ethical decision making, different ways of answering the same questions:

what is necessary to personal and social survival:
how social surplus is appropriated and distributed
and how social surplus is to be distributed and consumed, and,
how a commons is produced and sustained.[13]

In answering these questions, J.K. Gibson-Graham make a claim as startling as that of there being no preferred model of economic justice: *it is as difficult for workers to live within community economies as it is for owners.* For all of us, the challenge of new forms of subjectivity, sociality, and interdependence are "best shaped by practical curiosity as opposed to moral certainty about alternatives to capitalism."[14]

B CORPORATIONS

Progressives are accustomed to seeing work for social justice and environmental sustainability being expressed in political advocacy and in direct service to victims of injustice. We often are not aware of the ways in which we are not alone in our work for justice but have allies in the business community. There are for example, growing numbers of Certified B Corporations that self-critically and creatively do business in a way that is environmentally regenerative and socially just. Unlike the world of finance capitalism criticized by Tanner, in which the sole concern is profit and shareholder value, B Corporations have a triple bottom line of people, planet, and profit. In order to subsume shareholder value to the well-being of the planet and justice for employees, B Corporations require a different form of legal incorporation. Regular corporations are required to put shareholder value first and may be sued by shareholders if they do not do that. B Corporations have a radically different structure and legal obligations.[15]

According to the B Corps website, "Certified B Corporations are a new kind of business that balances purpose and profit. They are legally required to consider the impact of their decisions on their workers, customers, suppliers, community, and the environment. This is a community of leaders, driving a global movement of people using business as a force for good."[16] The goals of B Corporations are clearly described in the B Corps Declaration of Interdependence:

As B Corporations and leaders of this emerging economy, we believe:
That we must be the change that we seek in the world.
That all business ought to be conducted as if people and place mattered.
That, through their products, practices, and profits, businesses should aspire to
  do no harm and benefit all.
To do so requires that we act with the understanding that we are each dependent
  upon another and thus responsible for each other and future generations.[17]

This is a movement that is sustained by those who create such businesses, work for them, invest in them, and buy from them. Their goal is compelling not merely to be an alternative form of economy but to fundamentally reshape the economic order: "Our ultimate vision is that one day there will be no B Economy—just a global economy that aligns its activities toward achieving our common purpose of a shared and durable prosperity for all."[18]

Some benefit corporations are Certified B Corporations. In addition to a commitment to environmental regenerative and social justice, they receive third-party certification to make sure that these goals are genuinely met. Among other measures, the test looks for a core commitment to a social purpose, whether in type of goods and services provided, or in groups that are employed, or both.

B Lab certified over 650 companies across the globe in 2019—the most certifications in one year—expanding the B Corp community to over 3,100 companies hailing from more than 70 countries and 150 industries. Together, these companies are working to harness the power of business to solve the biggest social and environmental challenges facing the world today.[19]

B Corporations must demonstrate equitable compensation of employees and are noted for paying from over 100 percent to 230 percent of the minimum wage to the lowest paid employees, having compensation ratios between lowest and highest paid employees that are equitable and far less that the average ratio in US companies. Here, we have a key recognition that the existing pay ratio is ethically bankrupt. In August 2015 the Securities and Exchange Commission enacted a rule that companies would have to disclose the ratio of their chief executive officer versus median workers' pay. While there is resistance to the rule, there is also voluntary compliance with it by some corporations and a determination to move to a more equitable pay ratio. In an article in the *New York Times*, Rachel Abrams reported on companies that have been making such reports already (Whole Foods, the NorthWestern Corporation, and Noble Energy). The companies that have voluntarily reported their ratios are far different from most. According to the Economic Policy Institute, in 2013 chief executives were paid nearly 300 times their employees, while the ratio 50 years ago was roughly 20 times. Whole Foods has moved back to that standard of 50 years ago, with a cap of 19 times pay for their chief executive as compared to the average worker.[20]

Here, we have business leaders voluntarily committing themselves and their companies to a higher and more rigorous definition of excellence and a radically different view of success. In order to better understand why someone would choose to run their business as a B Corporation, I interviewed Hannah Halwel.[21] Halwel is the marketing director of Ikaria Design Company, an office furniture making company that has been in operation for ten years, and she is now doing the work of applying for certification as a B Corporation.

Halwel said that, since its inception, Ikaria has followed many of the principles of B Corporations, valuing environmental sustainability and social responsibility and not seeking to maximize profits at any costs. The reason for the company itself is a manifestation of a commitment to social justice in daily life. Halwel stated that in the 21st century, sitting has become the new smoking. Many jobs are sedentary, and, as currently designed, most office chairs and desks are unhealthy. When people sit for up to eight hours a day, back pain is often the result, and this damage is not easily rectified

FIGURE 6.1. Hannah Halwel.
© Kim Wade

by exercise before or after work. Halwel also explained that, in looking at the causes of the opioid crisis in the United States, the problem is not only excessive drug use to treat chronic pain but requires us to look at the multiple factors that cause such pain. While sedentary work is not the only factor by any means, unhealthy and lengthy sitting is one cause of chronic pain that can be addressed and prevented.

In order to address this fundamental health need, the founder of Ikaria Design Company, Pack Matthews, worked with health care professionals to design a chair, the Soul Seat, that supports healthy functioning, even when working in an office job. In so doing, one of the core goals of being a B Corporation was met, the creation of a product designed for a social good. Halwel described the satisfaction of this work:

> It is really rewarding to be working for a business that cares about being a good business, and is working on B Corp certification. Every single decision includes thinking about how it's going to impact being fully sustainable, or helping more people, or doing more good, and not just making more profit. This is in sharp contrast to businesses where there is a façade of the customers being number one when your bottom line is number one.

Halwel also insisted that it is also clear that a healthy chair and a healthy desk can be created for the people who use them and created in a way that is healthy for the planet and respectful for those who make the products. She emphasized that the materials used to create the Soul Seat, their ergonomic office chair, are environmentally sustainable. The stool that holds the seat is made either of recycled stainless steel or bamboo, not wood. Halwel said that bamboo is as sturdy as conventional wood, as easy to work with, and is a readily renewable resource. The cloth that covers the seats is made in the United States by companies where the working conditions are socially just. Furthermore, she said that the people who make the chairs are also paid a fair wage, far more than simply a minimum wage or even a living wage. While not yet in place, one of the goals of Halwel and Ikaria Design Company is to implement profit sharing in the near future to ensure that the value produced is fairly distributed to all those who create the products.

In addition to a product that is good for human health and is produced in an environmentally responsible way, these products are built to last. Halwel was clear: "We design and create products that will last for decades and do not need to be replaced or upgraded. When there are problems with use, we help our customers make simple repairs, rather than discarding and replacing the Soul Seat."

Halwel described another dimension of the work of Ikaria that is essential to a B Corporation, the empowerment of women, women having a genuine voice in the vision and daily operation of the business. Halwel described this as essential to her decision to work for Ikaria. "Here I am doing work that in itself is good for others and good for the planet, and I am working in an environment where my voice, my insights, questions and criticisms are genuinely valued and sought out and acted upon." Halwel added that, while some might say this is only because the owner is her father, she disagrees. The respect that he shows her is the respect that he shows everyone who works for Ikaria.

In my conversation with Halwel, it was clear that Ikaria is different from exploitative and extractive capitalism in another way. Halwel was clear—they are not interested in cornering or controlling the market. They see themselves working in cooperation with, not in competition with, other companies that are creating similar products. They have no desire to be the only environmentally regenerative and socially responsible office furniture manufacturer but to be one in a community of businesses that are also following the same goals. They are also working to find partnerships that enable them to get ergonomic chairs into schools, from kindergarten through high school.

Another thing that Halwel finds meaningful about working for a B Corporation is the community that it entails, in three key forms. First, to be a B Corporation is to be part of a community of businesses, learning from each other how to do business in a way that is good for people and the planet. That cooperation takes two different, but closely related forms. It is not easy to be certified as a B Corporation. The standards are high, the standards are reasonable, and the process of certification itself is fair and rigorous. She emphasized that it is a process that holds you accountable to your best intentions and inspires you to do more. She said that one of the benefits of certification is finding how they were already meeting certain standards and, at the same time, discovering that there are other standards (such as profit sharing) that they do not yet meet but aspire to meet in the near future.

A second aspect of this work that Halwel finds compelling is being part of a community of social entrepreneurs who share the same goals. She said, "What has kept Dad going for the past ten years is the entrepreneurship community in Columbia. They meet regularly to support and challenge each other. This group is the opposite of shark tanks. These are other businesses, lawyers, bankers, who pitch ideas and get feedback from other people." She noted that "these people are not trying to outdo each other; they are all trying to help each other do better—there is a sense of this being a win-win situation. It is better for all if more businesses are also seeking to be socially and environmentally responsible."

A final reward that is crucial for Halwel is this: "I take great satisfaction in knowing that this is a growing movement. Like many others of my generation, I try to make sure that all of the products that I buy are made in a way that is environmentally regenerative and socially just. Why would I or anyone else do business with a company that does anything else?" She makes it clear that she is far from being alone in this commitment:

> Young people in general are more aware of climate change than their elders. It's more tangible to them. We have 11 years, maybe 15. That's soon to me. There are so many businesses that are popular now that do good, whether they are technically social enterprises or not. You see many more products that list ingredients and claim that they are not toxic and bad for the environment. It's so obvious to me and my friends. Of course, you're not going to use plastic bags when you go to the grocery store, you're going to bring your own. You're going to shop where people treat their workers well, why would you go somewhere that isn't? To me it seems so obvious, how can people be oblivious?

Halwel proudly declared, "This is increasingly easy to do, and I am grateful to be part of the movement that is making this possible for others in the products that we design and make."

Halwel's work reflects the professional application of what has been recognized by many analysts of current economic practices. In a March 2014 article in *Crain's Chicago Business* weekly, the advertising executive Andrew Swinard wrote that corporate social responsibility is the millennials' new religion.[22] Studies of millennials done in 2017 show that this commitment is deep; it is growing, and it is well aware and highly critical of corporate efforts that are mere window dressing or a cover for bad publicity.[23] While Halwel would not describe this as a religion for her, it is for her and for many others a guiding imperative in how they conduct their businesses and practice responsible and limited consumerism. As she described it:

> In contrast to those who see the environmental problem and feel total despair, in my generation, we see what is being done. The more small businesses that are doing well, that are transparent about the structure of their business and their manufacturing process, and having profit sharing, the more large corporations are going to have to follow suit or they will be left behind. It's silly to think that nothing can be done because clearly so much is being done!

The possibility of an environmentally responsible form of economy is increasingly viable because of another form of cooperative effort—scientists, business leaders, and government officials coming together to explore ways of living in balance with the natural order in healing the damage caused by existing economic practices to the environment. And, in these responses, many scientists, engineers, and policy makers are drawing directly on the indigenous wisdom of how to live in reciprocity with the natural world.

In 2017 Paul Hawken published *Drawdown*, a scientific and ethical response to our current ecological crisis: "Drawdown is a message grounded in science; it is also a testament to the growing stream of humanity who understands the enormity of the challenge we face, and is willing to devote their lives to a future of kindness, security, and regeneration."[24] Hawken explained that this is "the most comprehensive plan ever proposed to reverse global warming." It was compiled by a group of seventy teachers and scientists from twenty-two countries. He highlights the significance of the fact that 40 percent of the coalition are women. This group of experts did not create the solutions themselves but drew together the work of engaged citizens throughout the world who are creating innovative solutions in the areas of buildings and cities, energy, food, land use, materials, transport, empowering women and girls (educating girls, family planning, and women agriculture landowners). Eighty of these solutions are being implemented and can be scaled up; twenty are in the process of exploration. Most of the solutions are environmentally and socially sound, but there are some with significant trade-offs, and those trade-offs are clearly named.[25]

Hawken describes how this work is both a technological challenge and an ethical gift, the gift of seeing who we are now and who we may be as responsible partners in the life of the planet. His description of our challenge is stark and evocative: "We will either come together to address global warming or we will likely disappear as a civilization. To come together we must know our place, not in a hierarchical sense, but in a biological and cultural sense, and reclaim our role as agents of our continued existence."[26]

SOCIAL ENTERPRISE ALLIANCE

What does it take to create a community economy that acknowledges who we are as responsible and equitable partners in the life of the planet? This challenge is also being taken up in the growing world of social entrepreneurship. Social enterprises are businesses or nonprofits that strive to honor a larger common good in three ways:

- **Opportunity Employment:** organizations that employ people who have significant barriers to mainstream employment
- **Transformative Products or Services:** organizations that create social or environmental impact through innovative products and services
- **Donate Back:** organizations that contribute a portion of their profits to nonprofits that address basic unmet needs.[27]

Tamra Ryan is the CEO of a social enterprise, Women's Bean Project, and is the interim director of the Social Enterprise Alliance, an organization that provides support for such businesses, helping them learn from each other and find better ways to be financially sustainable and meet genuine social and environmental needs.[28] In her book about the Women's Bean Project, *The Third Law*, Ryan described the mission of this work.

> Founded in 1989, The Bean Project is an anomaly in the business world. It is a business that packages and sells bean soup mixes and other food products to stores across the country. But tucked inside these businesses is a human services organization designed to provide a safe and accepting work environment where impoverished women can learn the skill required for gainful employment.[29]

FIGURE 6.2. Tamra Ryan.
© *Ron Morin*

Women's Bean Project is a social enterprise that "is a transitional employment program serving women who have struggled to obtain and maintain employment. When we hire women, they enter the role of production assistant and work in our food manufacturing business, making and packaging all the products we sell." They offer "a combination of on-the-job training, life skills classes, career service assistance and case management."[30] For example, women take high school equivalency courses and classes in financial literacy and computer literacy. Women also participate in sobriety and recovery groups and women's empowerment workshops. This combination of services and business has impressive results. They hire an average of 62 women each year, and, as of 2019, "95 percent of the women . . . are employed one year after graduating from the program."[31]

Ryan began her work with Women's Bean Project as a volunteer.[32] She had a background in marketing and product development and was attracted to Women's Bean Project's business model: "the better the business did, the more the mission was advanced." Ryan has been CEO of the Women's Bean Project since 2003 and explained that the mission of the business remains compelling and that the ethical rewards are extraordinary. The Women's Bean Project directly addresses the effects of mass incarceration on women and the community. Ryan noted that, while the effects of mass incarceration on women were not as apparent in 1989 when Women's Bean Project was founded, as they are now, and addressing those effects is at the core of their mission.

> Between 1977 and 2004 the number of women incarcerated increased by 757%. When the Project was founded in 1989, this was happening, but we weren't seeing yet the impact of removing women from their children, and then mothers coming back to their families and trying to reestablish relationships. We now see women whose mothers had been incarcerated when they were children, and who grew up without a mother, and many who even grew up with both parents in prison at some point in their lifetime.

Women's Bean Project has long worked to give women paid job training to prepare them for ongoing employment. Under Ryan's leadership, they are increasing their efforts to empower women to support themselves and their families with a new project with the Colorado Department of Corrections.

> Beginning in 2020 we will hire women on work release from Denver Women's Correctional Facility. Within the last year of their sentence they will come to work with us every day. We expect the changes to be extraordinary given what is happening now. What does it look like when we release someone with support around them, instead of just being dropped at the bus stop with $50 and a trash bag containing their belongings, and an expectation to meet with their parole officer the next day?

Ryan highlighted the ethical challenges and rewards of this work. First, there is the challenge of empowering women themselves, and, second, the work never gets easier: "It's because we hire all the people that we know no one else will hire. We don't know if they will come to work every day, and we invest lots of money and energy in them, and once they become great employees, they leave for other full-time employment." Third, the rewards of that empowerment remain as great:

> It is transformative to see the results of this work. I often see a woman come in on the first day, and not look me in the eye, and come across as angry or defensive. Then, six months or so later, she has literally blossomed, and goes on from here and creates a great life for herself and her family. That gives me great satisfaction, to see that what we're doing has an impact beyond our little world.

Ryan described two other things that are essential in being a CEO of this kind of business. For her, as a white middle-class woman, it is an intentional recognition and political use of her class and race privilege to challenge those very forms of privilege and to directly rectify their costs.

> A couple of things that I've come to realize that I believe at my core. When you choose to make a community your home, you take on a responsibility to do what you can to make it better. You can do that in lots of ways, in your profession, or as a volunteer. We each have a responsibility, particularly when we're born with privilege. I can tell you that I've often sat across the table from women who, except for the accident of birth, we are not very different at all. I was born into a white middle class community in Colorado Springs, Colorado, and my mom tells me that when I was four years old, I asked when I could start kindergarten so I could go to college. That doesn't make me better, I was raised in an environment where I didn't question my ability to do that.
>
> When you realize that you are not that special, it presents you with the humility to say that you have a responsibility to use our privilege in a way that helps our communities.

As she has engaged in this work, Ryan has found it equally important to find the support of others who are managing businesses with similar commitments to social justice.

> When I first came to Women's Bean Project, I worked to find peers. I wanted to collaborate with them. We're going to be most powerful in changing the world if we work together and share knowledge.

In 2013 Ryan wrote that Women's Bean Project was an anomaly in the business world. As interim CEO of the Social Enterprise Alliance, she is working to change that by grounding and expanding an organization that is providing support for other social enterprises. The mission of the Social Enterprise Alliance is clear and comprehensive:

> Social Enterprise Alliance believes in using the power of business to change the world. So we support social enterprises that sell products and services aimed at effecting social change. By creating credibility through certification, providing technical assistance and bringing attention to our members from consumers, companies and governmental entities that will buy, we lift up the organizations we serve so they can change the world.[33]

According to Ryan, a core element of this work is addressing how to fundamentally reshape a consumer-driven culture.

> Our country is very consumer driven, yet the greater awareness of the generation coming into power is one of wanting to make purchases based on mission, or at least, not doing harm. Doing business as way of doing good is a greater percentage of people's consciousness than it was 15 years. People who are 25–40 know what it is and want to be part of it.

Ryan pointed out that at this moment in history there are two interrelated challenges. Many people are well aware of the dangers of our current forms of exploitative consumer-driven economics and yet are rightly critical about companies that say they are doing things differently yet continue to largely operate, literally, as business as usual. It is for this reason that the Social Enterprise Alliance is creating a certification process. They are considering taking as their standard adherence to the United Nations Sustainable Development Goals. In January 2012, the United Nations Conference on Sustainable Development "[produced a set of universal goals that meet the urgent environmental, political and economic challenges facing our world." The goals are comprehensive and intrinsically interrelated: "Dealing with the threat of climate change impacts how we manage our fragile natural resources, achieving gender equality or better health helps eradicate poverty, and fostering peace and inclusive societies will reduce inequalities and help economies prosper."[34]

Ryan stated that the role of the Social Enterprise Alliance in helping business fulfill these goals is by "providing technical assistance in an affordable way, hosting summits where people can come together, learn from each other, and make ongoing relationships where they continue to learn from each other. We believe in what our members are doing, so we want to help our members do more of it." They also play a key role in spreading the word about the transformative work that is being done, having an impact yourself and helping others do the same.

COOK COUNTY COMMISSION ON SOCIAL INNOVATION

In addition to the work that is being done by businesses and nonprofits to create community economies that are just and regenerative, there are also government and business partnerships that seek the same goal. One such partnership is the work of the Cook County Commission on Social Innovation. In 2016, former Cook County commissioner and now congressman, Jesus "Chuy" Garcia, created the Cook County Commission on Social Innovation, for job creation, workforce development, entrepreneurship, community revitalization, and industrial development, naming Marc Lane, an attorney who works to certify benefit corporations, as vice chairman. Together, they have assembled a cohort for the commission, now led by Cook County Commissioner Alma Anaya. Made up of thought leaders in the nonprofit sector, Cook County government heads of department, economic development experts, and community builders, the commission has a diverse body of participants. Lane described the work of the commission as follows:

This is the only government unit to help vet legislation and see how to help the county board make the most of their policy-making power. It puts into place a preference for procurement of social enterprises, for co-ops and crowdfunding, for local stores. For instance, we have a Good Food Initiative to put nutritious, local, sustainable foods in schools, jails, and hospitals. We are finding ways to encourage urban agriculture. All of this adds jobs and tax revenue while decreasing crime, homelessness, hunger, and a host of related ills.

We're marrying the social mission of a government program with the market-driven approach of business. It's all about engaging businesses to pursue market-driven strategies that have a financial and social return. When you hold out a helping hand, you help yourself, your tax base, your economy. You create safer neighborhoods. Everyone's lives get better when we do the right thing. The reality is, we're all "us." Poverty and ill health hurts us all down the road. Make your ripple effect a positive one.

Morgan Malone serves the commission as a commissioner and is the chairwoman of the Intellectual Capital Committee of the commission. She pointed out a key dimension of what it takes to create a different form of economy not only environmentally sound business practices but focusing on the transformative and generative human relationships that enable people to work together for a more expansive social good.[35]

The biggest political challenge is not one that people would even expect, jobs, housing, wages, environment. The biggest challenges are tackling intangible systems. We can tackle tangible systems, around issues like jobs and housing. We can legislate those, and we can create infrastructure, programs, and policies.

FIGURE 6.3. Morgan Malone.
© Lawrence Agyei

But those are peanuts compared to the game of the mind—the intangible factors, the beliefs, mindset, culture, emotions, the things that actually shift opinions about what is possible. That is the biggest political challenge and opportunity in our country and the world.

Malone has three objectives for her work with the Commission on Social Innovation that incorporate both the tangible and intangible dimensions of social change:

The first is reframing public engagement by identifying opportunities for government, businesses, and citizens to work together. This means creating resources for all parties to engage in participatory practices and creating space to amplify voices across Cook County in the discipline of transformative economic development. For this to happen, it is essential to find out who else is doing the work, and then "creating a culture of 'do,' versus a culture of 'can't,'" with people who are already doing so much. We can connect residents with county commissioners and county departments who can use more coalition partners to move critical initiatives forward.

A second objective is making sure that the commission is as representative and diverse as the city and county. It is, in fact, the radical openness to diversity by the leadership of the commission that has led Malone to this work.

I went to a public meeting of the commission and was impressed by the good people who were doing interesting things on community development and revitalization that I had never heard of. That day I went up to the chairman of the commission, Jesus Chuy Garcia, and said that while the work was impressive, that there could be more representation from young people, community voices, people of color and women of color. He said, "I think you're right. Do you want to do it?" Later, he interviewed me, and I was appointed with a diverse cohort that included two young midcareer Latina women entrenched in neighborhood level work, another young Black woman, and a midcareer young white man who does data privacy. I admire Congressman Garcia for using the power extended to him to create spaces of equity.

The third objective is nurturing public trust and engagement in a way that goes far beyond open meeting protocols. As Malone stated, "The Illinois Open Meetings Act is important, but people want to do more than comment in public hearings. How can we really participate in hard work together? How do we re-imagine and create genuine private/public partnerships?"

A key factor here is one of genuine engagement not just in responding to tangible proposals but doing the intangible work of creating projects together. Malone described this as a key lesson that she learned from her time with the Kettering Foundation:

You can present people with options, but as they're digesting the options it is important to amplify a spectrum of response. Responsiveness in decision making does not exist as a duality, yes or no, I support this or I don't. Responsiveness exists on a spectrum that includes certainty, uncertainty, neutrality, and room to say, "I am not informed enough to opine at this time." Without this spectrum, it is difficult for citizens to give an affirmative yes so uncertainty or lack of information becomes rejection. Affirmative support comes from creating options and actions together and, together deciding what is possible and what can be done. If you are able to shift people's mindset and expand their world view regarding about what is possible, we can do anything to shift the tangible systems with collective understanding.

If you have not built public goodwill and deep partnership surrounding what is possible and you propose a solution, many people will be skeptical or opposed to it because there was no prior change management. Too often we don't do a good job at being open and transparent and helping people think through what is possible. We don't support people on the journey of collective understanding and consciousness. But the work of using collective impact to shift intangible systems will make all of the difference in the risks that we can take to legislate tangible issues.

CONCLUSION

What are the multiple drivers of these forms of constructive social engagement? What leads people to take up the demanding, long-term work of institutional change? Here, we find an emerging, broad-based sense of what actually constitutes the abundant, flourishing life. Diverse publics may be motivated for closely related reasons: a concern with the integrity of good work (work that is socially equitable and ecologically regenerative) and the discovery of a larger good—the joy of being a part of a wider human community. It is here that we have a core element of socially responsible economic life, a fundamental redefinition of economic success and of what constitutes the abundant life. People throughout the world are moving away from endless material expansion to genuinely interdependent plenitude. The goal is no longer maximum short-term economic gains but socially just economic and environmental regeneration, and, in this work, many women, with courage, persistence, and creativity, are leading the way.

NOTES

1. Elizabeth Kolbert, *The Sixth Extinction: An Unnatural History* (New York: Henry Holt and Company 2014), 266. Kolbert states that this is a term invented by the chemist Paul Crutzen to describe our "human-dominated, geological epoch." She says that in 2002, Crutzen noted the following "geologic-scale changes" caused by human beings: "Human activity has transformed between a third and a half of the land surface of the planet. Most of the world's major rivers have been dammed or diverted. Fertilizer plants produce more nitrogen than is fixed naturally by all terrestrial ecosystems. Fisheries remove more than a third of the primary production of the oceans' coastal waters. Humans use more than half of the world's readily accessible fresh water runoff." Most significantly, Crutzen said, people have altered the composition of the atmosphere. Owing to a combination of fossil fuel combustion and deforestation, the concentration of carbon

dioxide in the air has risen by 40 percent over the last two centuries, while the concentration of methane, an even more potent greenhouse gas, has more than doubled (108).

2. For multiple descriptions of multiple forms of constructive social engagement and how they relate to the growth of authoritarianism and demonstrate the power of multifaceted strategic nonviolence, see Sharon D. Welch, *After the Protests Are Heard: Enacting Civic Engagement and Social Transformation* (New York: New York University Press, 2019).

3. Carol Lee Sanchez, "Animal, Vegetable, Mineral: The Sacred Connection," in *Ecofeminism and The Sacred*, ed. Carol J. Adams (New York: Continuum, 1993).

4. Robin Wall Kimmerer, *Braiding Sweetgrass: Indigenous Wisdom, Scientific Knowledge, and the Teachings of Plants* (Minneapolis, MN: Milkweed Editions, 2013) 7, 377.

5. Kimmerer, *Braiding Sweetgrass*, 377.

6. Kimmerer, *Braiding Sweetgrass*, 377.

7. Kimmerer, *Braiding Sweetgrass*, 304. For an explanation of the shift from "environmental sustainability" to "environmental regeneration," see, e.g., Leah Gibbons, "Regenerative: The New Sustainable?" *Sustainability*, July 7, 2020, https://doi.org/10.3390/su12135483.

8. Kathryn Tanner, *Christianity and the New Spirit of Capitalism* (New Haven: Yale University Press, 2019), 7. "Contemporary capitalism is finance dominated in several senses. First, simply, finance-generated profit . . . in the financial sector (for example, banking, insurance, real estate) is a growing percentage of national income when compared with the industrial or service sectors. . . . For example, car companies routinely make more money from loaning money to buy cars than from selling them" (110).

9. Tanner's alternative to finance capitalism is a Christian way of relating to God (204–19). I must admit that as a non-Christian, I do not fully understand this alternative and look forward to having conversations in which Tanner engages the type of economies of plenitude and reciprocity that are described below.

10. Juliet B. Schor, *Plenitude: The New Economics of True Wealth* (New York: Penguin Books, 2010), 1. See also Schor's book that provides case studies of people who are living economies of plentitude, *True Wealth: How and Why Millions of Americans Are Creating a Time-Rich, Ecologically Light, Small-Scale, High-Satisfaction Economy* (New York: Penguin Books, 2011).

11. Schor, *Plenitude*, 4–7.

12. J. K. Gibson-Graham, *A Post-Capitalist Politics* (Minneapolis: University of Minnesota Press, 2006), 80–81.

13. Gibson-Graham, *Post-Capitalist Politics*, 88.

14. Gibson-Graham, *Post-Capitalist Politics*, 159.

15. "A Year of Business as a Force for Good: 2019 in Review: Celebrating Major Shifts Toward a More Inclusive and Regenerative Economy," B Lab, December 19, 2019, https://bthechange .com/a-year-of-business-as-a-force-for-good-2019-in-review-8e744ed4d620.

16. "A Global Community of Leaders," https://bcorporation.net/.

17. "The B Corp Declaration of Interdependence," *About B Corps*, https://bcorporation.net/about-b-corps.

18. "The B Economy," https://bcorporation.net/b-economy.

19. "A Year of Business as a Force for Good: 2019 in Review," https://bthechange.com/a-year -of-business-as-a-force-for-good-2019-in-review-8e744ed4d620.

20. Rachel Abrams, "Companies See Benefits in Publicizing Pay Ratios," *New York Times*, August 5, 2015.

21. Hannah Halwel is my daughter and Ikaria was founded and is owned by Pack Matthews, her father and my former husband. All of the following quotations are from my interview with her conducted on December 8, 2019.

22. Andrew Swinard, "Corporate Social Responsibility Is the Millennials' New Religion," *Crain's Business Weekly*, March 25, 2014.

23. Deloitte Millennial Survey 2017, https://www2.deloitte.com/us/en/pages/about-de loitte/articles/millennial-survey.html.

24. Paul Hawken, *Drawdown: The Most Comprehensive Plan Ever Proposed to Reverse Global Warming* (New York: Penguin Books, 2017), frontispiece.

25. Hawken, *Drawdown*, x.

26. Hawken, *Drawdown*, 217.

27. Social Enterprise Alliance, "About," https://socialenterprise.us/about/.

28. Social Enterprise Alliance, "About."

29. Tamra Ryan, *The Third Law* (Denver, CO: Gilpin House Press, 2013), 6–7.

30. Women's Bean Project, "Program Overview," https://www.womensbeanproject.com/program-overview/.

31. Women's Bean Project, "The Impact," https://www.womensbeanproject.com/the-impact/.

32. I interviewed Tamra Ryan on December 20, 2019, and all of the following quotations and references are from that interview; shared by permission.

33. For a more detailed description of the work done by Social Enterprise Alliance, see https://socialenterprise.us/about/.

34. The seventeen goals are no poverty, zero hunger, good health and well-being, quality education, gender equality, clean water and sanitation, affordable and clean energy, decent work and economic growth, industry, innovation and infrastructure, reduced inequality, sustainable cities and communities, responsible consumption and production, climate action, life below water, life on land, peace and justice strong institutions, and partnership to achieve the goal.

35. All of the following quotations are from an interview with Morgan Malone that I conducted on December 19, 2019; shared by permission.

BIBLIOGRAPHY

Abrams, Rachel. "Companies See Benefits in Publicizing Pay Ratios." *New York Times*, August 5, 2015.

B Lab. "A Year of Business as a Force for Good: 2019 in Review Celebrating Major Shifts Toward a More Inclusive and Regenerative Economy." Accessed December 28, 2019. https://bthechange.com/a-year-of-business-as-a-force-for-good-2019-in-review-8e744ed4d620.

Gibbons, Leah. "Regenerative: The New Sustainable?" *Sustainability*, July 7, 2020. https://doi.org/10.3390/su12135483.

Gibson-Graham, J. K. *A Post-Capitalist Politics*. Minneapolis: University of Minnesota Press, 2006.

Kassoy, Andrew, Bart Houlahan, and Jay Coen Gilbert. "An Open Letter to Business Leaders." Accessed May 1, 2018. https://bthechange.com/your-business-should-be-a-force-for-good-an-open-letter-to-business-leaders-b6909beab17f.

Kimmerer, Robin Wall. *Braiding Sweetgrass: Indigenous Wisdom, Scientific Knowledge, and the Teachings of Plants*. Minneapolis, MN: Milkweed Editions, 2013.

Kolbert, Elizabeth. *The Sixth Extinction: An Unnatural History*. New York: Henry Holt and Company, 2014.

Ryan, Tamra. *The Third Law*. Denver, CO: Gilpin House Press, 2013.

Sanchez, Carol Lee. "Animal, Vegetable, Mineral: The Sacred Connection." In *Ecofeminism and The Sacred*, edited by Carol J. Adams. New York: Continuum, 1993.

Schor, Juliet B. *Plenitude: The New Economics of True Wealth*. New York: Penguin Press, 2010.

Schor, Juliet B. *True Wealth: How and Why Millions of Americans Are Creating a Time-Rich, Ecologically Light, Small-Scale, High-Satisfaction Economy*. Penguin Books, 2011.

Social Enterprise Alliance. Accessed December 28, 2019. https://socialenterprise.us/about/social-enterprise.

Tanner, Kathryn. *Christianity and the New Spirit of Capitalism*. New Haven, CT: Yale University Press, 2019.

UN Sustainable Development Goals. Accessed December 28, 2019. https://www.undp.org/content/undp/en/home/sustainable-development-goals/background/.

Welch, Sharon D. *After the Protests Are Heard: Enacting Civic Engagement and Social Transformation*. New York: New York University Press, 2019.

Women's Bean Project. Accessed January 5, 2020. https://www.womensbeanproject.com/program-overview/.

CHAPTER 7

Feminist Ethics and the Harms of Credibility Excess

Candace Jordan, Princeton University, PhD candidate

ABSTRACT

Just as testimony is distorted by unjust social relations, so too is moral imagination. One only need turn to the #MeToo movement and reports of sexual abuse and coercion within and outside Hollywood to understand the deep sympathy with male perpetrators and disbelief of and hostility toward testifying women. Sex-based harm is reinscribed in subsequent attempts for redress. While downgraded testimonies surely hurt testifying women, this chapter explores the harms traded among patriarchy's supposed beneficiaries. Confession and redemption first require apt descriptions of testimonies distorted by prejudice. Exploring the relationship among social power, recognition, and credibility, I conclude by considering the ways in which rich theorizing of the harms perpetrated among co-conspirators can motivate better calibrated responses across social positions.

THE KAVANAUGH EFFECT

Supreme Court Justice Brett Kavanaugh's September 2019 confirmation hearing was interrupted when his former classmate Dr. Christine Blasey Ford accused him of sexual assault while they were in high school in 1982. Situated amid the #MeToo movement, the accusation drew national attention. While the hashtag's founder Tarana Burke has worked for over a decade drawing attention to sexual abuse in the United States, the movement has seen renewed energy. High-profile cases have deployed the hashtag to illuminate rampant sexual impropriety in Hollywood and in US Olympic sports.

Many have gathered in support of testifying women. Harvey Weinstein was dismissed as co-chairman of his production company, expelled from the Academy of

Motion Picture Arts and Sciences and convicted of a first-degree criminal sexual act and third-degree rape. Dr. Lawrence Nassar was imprisoned after Judge Rosemarie Aquilina extended his hearing in order to allow each assault victim to speak her testimony via victim impact statements. The responses were markedly different to accusations against Brett Kavanaugh. On Twitter, South Carolina Senator Lindsey Graham condemned Dr. Ford's accusations and support garnered by liberal Democrats and activists, claiming that the "smear campaign" intended to destroy Kavanaugh would only end up destroying "Red State Democrats."[1]

PerryUndem, a nonpartisan public opinion research firm based in Washington, DC, describes the Kavanaugh effect differently from Senator Graham's prediction of public opinion. In a December 2018 survey of 1,319 registered voters, those who felt unfavorably toward Kavanaugh, in part stemming from the belief that he lied under oath about his behavior during his teenage years, were "motivated . . . to vote for the Democratic candidate for US House of Representatives—above and beyond typical factors, such as party affiliation."[2] The Kavanaugh effect affected Republicans, especially Republican men, differently. The report characterizes the sexism renewed among Republican men, at least in part as a result of the hearing.

> Two-thirds of Republican men (68 percent) now agree that "most women interpret innocent remarks or acts as being sexist" (an item used to measure hostile sexism). This is up 21 points from 2017 when 47 percent of Republican men agreed and up 24 points from 2016 when 44 percent agreed.
>
> Fewer than half of Republican men (45 percent) now considers sexism a problem in our society, down from 63 percent in 2017 and 58 percent in 2016.[3]

Republican men are also less likely to believe women in cases of sexual harassment and assault after Justice Kavanaugh's hearings. In November 2017, 80 percent of Republican men said they were more likely to believe women making allegations of sexual harassment or assault rather than men denying allegations (18 percent). Now, 59 percent of Republican men say they are more likely to believe women.[4]

DISTORTIONS IN THE ECONOMY OF CREDIBILITY

Recent grappling with sexual assault testimonies illuminate that in situations of oppression, epistemic relations are badly distorted. Social justice movements such as #MeToo and Black Lives Matter highlight the prevalence of gender- and race-based suffering and the unequal power distribution afforded women and persons of color.[5] Testimonies bearing witness to these inequalities are often met with suspicion. One need only turn to reports of sexual abuse and coercion to understand the deep sympathy with male perpetrators and disbelief of and hostility toward testifying women. Sex-based harms are reinscribed in subsequent attempts for redress. Sometimes, women's indictments raise doubts about their credibility as witnesses to their experiences and to the social facts that enable such injustices. Who is considered a credible and capable transmitter of knowledge so often depends upon one's social position.

Theorizing epistemic injustice has gained increasing scholarly appeal. Social and standpoint epistemologies consider knowledge inseparable from social identity. Scholars theorizing and activists championing these social phenomena are in part calling attention to the illusion that unequal social power is founded in essential facts about the persons to whom that power is distributed. For example, it is not that Dr. Christine Blasey Ford, *qua* woman, is not a credible testifier. Rather, as a woman, she suffers social stigmas (for example, that women are prone to hysteria, misinterpret male attention, invite male advances, or do not clearly communicate consent) that make her testimony less credible to prejudiced hearers. Attending to social power illuminates the cultural and structural forces that enable violence against women and later encourage women's silence and censure. Religious ethicists should welcome the work under way, as it attempts to address questions concerning contemporary religious studies. These debates include the social process of moral and character formation, the potential for character to become deformed, how we imagine life together, and how we ought to promote such a vision.

Writing in the tradition of feminist ethics, and in conversation with Christian ethics, the African American cultural tradition, and the tradition of social criticism, I enter conversations on gender hierarchy and sex-based violence with a commitment to theorizing phenomena involved in gender oppression and to use these descriptions to motivate ways forward in the fight for social justice. My methods include cultural and literary critique, philosophical analysis, and surveying contemporary case studies drawn from my current social milieu, which includes the gendered politics of the United States.

This chapter enumerates harms flowing from according credibility in excess of what is due. Though beneficiaries of credibility excess may not be disrespected in the same way as persons who are deprived due credibility, they suffer important harms. José Medina enumerates three vices that arise in those consistently accorded excess credibility—epistemic arrogance, laziness, and closemindedness.[6] Similarly, I highlight the personal and relational harms of excessive credibility. Not only does awarding excessive credibility due to positive biases associated with one's social group foreclose important opportunities for fraternal correction, but excess can also contribute to the maintenance of immaturity in the person to whom it is afforded. Further, granting excess credibility can draw the so-called beneficiary into complicity with pernicious webs of systemic injustice. If credibility excess can yield bad character in these and other ways and the moral, epistemic, and social consequences are severe, then it may not be apt to consider beneficiaries of excess credibility advantaged on the whole. This is the claim about which I aim to raise suspicion.

TESTIMONIAL INJUSTICE

Miranda Fricker is credited with bringing the phenomenon of epistemic injustice to the attention of analytic philosophers. It has been widely theorized under various other descriptions by Patricia Hill Collins, Charles Mills, Gaile Pohlhaus Jr., Kristie Dotson, Rachel McKinnon, and Kate Manne, among others. Species of epistemic injustice have been articulated by African American thinkers, such as W.E.B. Du Bois (in his articulations of "the veil," "second sight," and "double consciousness"), Audre Lorde (in her description of social power and systemic oppressions), and Womanist theologian Katie Cannon (in her description of the unique yet historically suppressed insights of Black women). Testimonial injustice, a species of epistemic injustice, arises when prejudices held by hearers causes a deflated judgment of a speaker's credibility.[7] Dr. Ford's censure can be considered an instance of credibility deficit (owing to biases associate with her gender) and, thus, testimonial injustice.

Identity-Prejudicial Credibility Deficit (IPCD)

Fricker advances the claim that identity-prejudicial credibility deficit is the paradigmatic form of testimonial injustice. While the aim is to award due credibility, hearers sometimes err. Hearers' prejudices can result in the speaker receiving more credibility than is due (credibility excess) or less credibility than is due (credibility deficit). Testimonial injustice occurs when, by virtue of one's perceived membership in a social group, one is accorded less credibility than one is due. Fricker asserts:

> Broadly speaking, prejudicial dysfunction in testimonial practice can be of two kinds. Either the prejudice results in the speaker's receiving more credibility than she otherwise would have—a *credibility excess*—or it results in her receiving less credibility than she otherwise would have—a *credibility deficit*. . . . The idea is . . . that prejudice will tend surreptitiously to inflate or deflate the credibility afforded the speaker, and sometimes this will be sufficient to cross the threshold of belief or acceptance so that the hearer's prejudice causes him to miss out on a piece of knowledge.[8]

Upon perceiving a speaker to be part of a social group or groups, the hearer of testimony miscalibrates another's credibility due to bias associated with membership in that group. Credibility is lowered, and sometimes this causes the hearer to miss out on the knowledge carried in the speaker's testimony.

Keenly aware of epistemic injustice's political stakes, Fricker captures the injustice of identity-prejudicial credibility deficit in her illustrative examples. Mayella Ewell, a white woman alleging assault in Harper Lee's *To Kill a Mockingbird*, is believed over the testimony of Tom Robinson, a Black man whose testimony and physical handicap serve as the ultimate exoneration against Mayella's charge.[9] The prejudices we hold impact whether or not we receive the bits of knowledge carried in testimony. That testimony and the knowledge to which it points can be excluded, marginalized, erased, and silenced alerts us to the fact that credibility is not meted out equally. This epistemic and social deformity is sometimes non-accidental. Prejudices retrieved and credibility withheld may be deliberate in order to preserve the authority of the status quo.[10] Silencing women's testimony and undermining their experiences is often an effort in part to reaffirm the authority of patriarchal discourse.

Identity-Prejudicial Credibility Excess (IPCE)

The opposite phenomenon of credibility deficit is credibility excess. It occurs when one perceives a speaker to be part of a particular social group or groups and subsequently upgrades the speaker's credibility based on those associated biases. The hearer or recipient of testimony miscalibrates another's credibility due to bias associated with one's perceived membership in a stereotyped group. In instances of identity-prejudicial credibility excess, credibility is raised beyond what is due.

Fricker argues that because identity-prejudicial credibility excess generally benefits those to whom it is accorded, it is not an instance of testimonial injustice. She writes:

> The idea is to explore testimonial injustice as a distinctly epistemic injustice, as a kind of injustice in which someone is *wronged specifically in her capacity as a knower.* Clearly credibility deficit can constitute such a wrong, but while credibility excess may (unusually) be disadvantageous in various ways, it does not undermine, insult, or otherwise withhold a proper respect for the speaker *qua* subject of knowledge; so in itself it does her no epistemic injustice, and *a fortiori* no testimonial injustice.[11]

According to Fricker, individuals accorded identity-prejudicial credibility excess are not disadvantaged as conveyors of knowledge, even if credibility excess proves disadvantageous on discrete occasions.[12] Their status as knowers is not degraded, so even when credibility excesses are accorded, the (unusual) harms they suffer are not of the relevant sort. Though they may suffer harms, they do not suffer as knowers, and so do not suffer epistemic injustice in general or testimonial injustice in particular.

Conversely, knowers who are deprived of credibility when it is due suffer an injustice *qua* subject of knowledge. Epistemic injustice tracks one being *wronged specifically in her capacity as a knower.* The crucial distinction Fricker draws between the injustice of IPCD and the benefits of IPCE is that, in the former case, knowers' testimonies are disbelieved not based on adequate measures of credibility and reliability but rather on prejudices associated with their perceived social identities. IPCE occurs by the same mechanism. However, the person offering testimony is neither undermined nor insulted and so is not disadvantaged in the relevant way. Thus, no epistemic injustice occurs, even if the credibility excess is ethically bad or harms in some other sense. I aim to raise suspicion about this claim.

Writing on distortions in self-trust caused by prejudicial dysfunction in testimonial practice, Karen Jones similarly finds that credibility deficit is harmful, while excess proves largely beneficial. She defines intellectual self-trust as "an attitude of optimism about one's cognitive competence in a domain. Self-trust manifests itself in feelings of confidence, in dispositions willingly to rely on the deliverances of one's methods and to assert what is believed on their basis, and in modulating self-reflection."[13] Not being taken seriously as one whose opinions and experiences deserve engagement deflates one's intellectual self-trust, while unearned credibility afforded due to one's privileged social position inflates one's intellectual self-trust.[14] Inflations of intellectual self-trust make the epistemically privileged more likely to perpetuate the unjust social relations that give rise to testimonial injustice.[15] Jones writes,

> Because credibility excess is generally beneficial to those who have it, it would be wrong to call it an epistemic injustice, distortion in the economy of credibility though it is (Fricker 2007, 19–21). Unearned credibility that is the mere result of membership in a privileged social group can have the cumulative effect of distorting the person's intellectual self-trust in a domain. Given that self-trust in a domain is characterized by a suite of dispositions that effectively privilege one's own epistemic perspective over that of others, an excess of self-trust is likely to give rise to testimonial injustice.[16]

Jones claims that identity-prejudicial credibility excess is likely to cause testimonial injustice. Because those who unduly benefit from credibility excesses habitually privilege their own epistemic capacities, they are prone to downgrade their interlocutors' capacities, thus giving rise to testimonial injustice of the relevant sort, namely, credibility deficit. Put simply, credibility excess is a cause, not an instance, of epistemic injustice.

Fricker and Jones offer three central claims. Each endorses that identity-prejudicial credibility deficit is the paradigmatic form of testimonial injustice. Each argues that identity-prejudicial credibility excess, what Jones and Medina call "spoiling," heaps social benefits on the person to whom it is conferred and is not testimonial injustice. Finally, Jones argues that identity-prejudicial credibility excess likely causes testimonial injustice. And yet how are we to make sense of the individual attributions or withholdings of credibility against the backdrop of hierarchies that rely on tacit and pervasive prejudices? Fricker herself gives us resources to begin to consider the ways in which credibility excess might bring persons low in ways that constitute epistemic harm. She writes:

> I do not think it would be right to characterize any of the individual moments of credibility excess that . . . a person receives as in itself an instance of testimonial injustice, since none of them wrongs him sufficiently in itself. It is only if enough of them come together in the semi-fanciful manner described that each moment of credibility excess takes on the aspect of something that contributes to the subject's being epistemically wronged over the long term.[17]

Surveying individual moments of credibility excess or deficit based on race or gender prejudices obscures that racism and sexism are systemic in nature. Rather than being "semi-fanciful," cumulative testimonial excess is precisely what is facilitated by retrieving entrenched prejudices that then influence an overawarding of credibility. Sexism, for example, is constituted through ritual practices that affirm the gender hierarchy to which it is faithful. It is not immediately clear that the totalizing prejudices retrieved are separable from the resulting individual attributions of credibility excess.

While the illustrations of testimonial injustice on Fricker's account are drawn from fictional texts, historical examples are readily at hand. Dr. Keri Day draws attention to the same phenomenon of credibility being meted out unevenly across social positions.[18] Day illustrates how we use identity markers, such as gender and race, to assign credibility and trustworthiness. She illuminates historical resonances between Justice Kavanaugh's Senate Judiciary Committee hearing and the lynching of Emmett Till. Till, a Black boy suspected of whistling at a white woman while visiting relatives in Mississippi in 1955, was neither formally accused of a criminal offense nor tried in court. Instead, the enraged lynch mob privileged whites' testimonies to the alleged assault because of their social privilege. The Kavanaugh effect and Day's analysis attest to social power's impact on believing or discrediting individual testimony.

Testimonial injustice is suffered uniquely by those whose social positions are vehicles of negative prejudice, such as women, people of color, and poor folk, to name a few. But what of the harms done to those who find membership in privileged social groups? If we care about the harms precipitated upon the marginalized, then right relationship of the privileged, to themselves and other privileged persons, matters a great deal. Below, I generate suspicion that credibility deficit, and not credibility excess, is the paradigmatic form of testimonial injustice.

THE HARMS OF CREDIBILITY EXCESS

American novelist and cultural critic James Baldwin's oeuvre is rife with a similar suspicion. His work often testifies to the ways in which excesses among white Americans stunts their ability to mature. Not only will reckoning with the myth of their superiority aid in the transformation of the lives of Black people, whites themselves can find personal maturity and liberation from the fiction of their superiority. He writes:

> the Negro's past, of rope, fire, torture, castration, infanticide, rape . . . —this past, this endless struggle to achieve and reveal and confirm a human identity, human authority, yet contains, for all its horror, something very beautiful. I do not mean to be sentimental about suffering— . . . but people who cannot suffer can never grow up, can never discover who they are. . . . He achieves his own authority, and that is unshakable. This is because, in order to save his life, he is forced to look beneath appearances, to take nothing for granted, to hear the meaning behind the words.[19]

Baldwin here addresses the importance of truth seeking ("looking beneath appearances," "hear[ing] the meaning behind the words") for maturity and authority. Black people have historically borne the burden of testimonial injustice (and countless other non-epistemic injustices), suffering others' withholding of credibility due to racial prejudice. Though Baldwin hesitates to romanticize Black suffering, it is instructive that maturation is contingent upon confrontation with ("[taking] nothing for granted") "appearances" and "meaning"—the very bits of information exchanged in testimony.

He writes further that "the American Negro has the great advantage of having never believed that collection of myths to which white Americans cling."[20] Finally, he offers:

> In great pain and terror one begins to assess the history which has placed one where one is and formed one's point of view. In great pain and terror because,

therefore, one enters into battle with that historical creation, Oneself, and attempts to recreate oneself according to a principle more humane and more liberating; one begins the attempt to achieve a level of personal maturity and freedom which robs history of its tyrannical power, and also changes history.[21]

Part of white supremacy's scandal is that the myth of superiority conceals whites from themselves.[22] So too with insidious mechanisms of gender violence against women, where men (and even women) are educated into participating in systems and practices that silence women. Persons are cut off from the self-knowledge and recognition, by self and others, upon which maturity depends. Though there surely is no straightforwardly analogous relationship between race and gender, similarities between the logic of gender violence and the logic of racial violence are many, including the efforts to maintain pernicious hierarchies. The harms of being downgraded are material, social, and epistemic. Yet, when credibility is overestimated to such a large extent, the domain of social knowledge suffers. For example, when women are systemically silenced, the pool of knowledge surrounding women's experiences becomes deprived. The #MeToo movement in part testifies to just this. Women and girls were abused, shamed, and compelled into silence. The movement uncovers and publicizes both the abuse and the enforced silencing. Now, we have access to testimonies that speak to the breadth of women's experiences.[23]

Baldwin presciently reminds us that authority is bound up in testimony a great deal. Attributions of excessive credibility are harmful in part because they undermine an important feature of what it means to claim authority over oneself and the knowledge that one possesses. We care a great deal that persons are not authoritative simply because of the social milieu in which they find themselves nor the social identities they claim or to which they are ascribed. Rather, the maturity of which Baldwin speaks requires persons formed in part by their social milieu to account for the privileges they enjoy. The process by which persons form, test, and revise truths matters. We care about the procedural processes of generating convictions, especially when those convictions bear heavily on matters of justice. When the political stakes involve sexual assault of women at disproportionate rates to that of men or incarceration of persons of color at disproportionate rates to that of whites, the process by which our beliefs are formed, tested, and evaluated matters.

Writing on recognition respect, Charles Taylor similarly argues that authenticity, a morally important contact with oneself, is generated dialogically, with those we love and others with whom we are in crucial contact. He affirms that "not only contemporary feminism but also race relations . . . are undergirded by the premise that the withholding of recognition can be a form of oppression."[24] There is no shortage of examples in the literature on the multiple and intersecting oppressions that these groups face. And yet Baldwin's and Taylor's insights help disrupt the intuition that credibility excess also does not undermine, insult, or otherwise withhold a proper respect for persons. If identities are formed on the social plane and recognition of them requires public others, then refusal of recognition can presumably happen in both upward and downward credibility distortions. Can severe and repeated upward distortions in credibility and recognition owing to privileged group membership, rather than the way individuals inhabit such groups, amount to misrecognition or non-recognition? Is there a sense in which recognition is importantly withheld from privileged persons? Part of the logic of white supremacy is a refusal to confront a person as an authentic conveyor of knowledge. Such misrecognition is a harm suffered by the person deprived due to credibility or receiving credibility in excess.

José Medina explores the nature of testimonial injustice with a particular eye to the social positions of the persons to whom excess credibility is afforded and those to whom credibility is denied. He analyzes the epistemic disadvantages of the privileged and the epistemic advantages of the privileged. Medina is helpful when considering the harms of IPCE in at least two ways. First, he helpfully connects credibility distortion with social injustice. Social injustices, such as racism and sexism, provide the occasion for epistemic deformities. Second, Medina enumerates the material and epistemic benefits reaped by those accorded more credibility in light of their access to information (that they have greater access to information, educational opportunities, and receive a greater share of the capacity to disseminate knowledge).[25] Conversely, those denied testimonial credibility are often cut off from just these resources, often based on biases associated with their social group. And yet Medina mines feminist and critical race theories to complicate the story. Oppressed persons, often those who receive less than their due share of epistemic authority, commanded in part through testimonial receipt, may cultivate epistemic virtues. These virtues, which I do not take up in detail here, are often inaccessible to those who receive credibility in excess. In light of Medina's enumeration of the vices of the epistemically spoiled (epistemic arrogance, laziness, and closed-mindedness), the question becomes, in what ways are recipients of excess credibility truly beneficiaries? Where countless harms can be enumerated, is it an apt description of credibility excess that it does not bring low the person to whom it is accorded?

HARMS OF TESTIMONIAL INJUSTICE

The capacity to impart knowledge to others is in part what is violated in identity-prejudicial credibility. If this giving of knowledge is meaningfully tied to the dialogic nature of authenticity, as Taylor suggests, then cases of credibility excess obscure whether credence is given to the individual as capable conveyor of knowledge or whether the individual is obscured by their social role or roles. When persons are collapsed into social positions, their testimonies are at least in part regarded in virtue of their social group membership. It becomes unclear whether their testimony is being regarded or if what is being (re)affirmed is the set of assumptions that accompany the testifiers' social role. Returning to the trial in *To Kill a Mockingbird*, while it is clear that Tom Robinson suffers testimonial injustice (his credibility is downgraded because he is a Black man and thus unable to be seen as a competent and sincere testifier), it ought to be contested whether or not Mayella Ewell is not also importantly harmed in the excess of credibility her testimony is afforded. Her collapse into her social role as white and female in part draws her into complicity with the racial dynamics of the day. Her testimony is not received on its merit but rather in an effort to reaffirm the racial and gender dynamics of her social milieu. It is unconvincing in this instance that the excess credibility she is accorded results from her peers considering her a sincere and credible transmitter of knowledge.[26]

Fricker counts among the harms of testimonial injustice that folks lose out on knowledge. This harm is incurred by both testifiers and hearers. Mayella Ewell (and other's in the Maycomb County courtroom) for example, lose out on the bits of knowledge that Tom Robinson's testimony and trial aim to impart. The community forecloses opportunities for fraternal correction, which might result if they were not so deeply epistemically arrogant (as José Medina might describe them). In relationships of gender discrimination, testifiers often taken at their word, when mitigating factors might demand otherwise, can become cut off from correction and the insights that may flow from that correction (both in the immediate interaction and in future exchanges of testimony). Similarly problematic is the way in which others are importantly implicated in depriving those to whom excess credibility is afforded. These so-called beneficiaries are deprived of the opportunity to interrogate the credence of their testimony. While recipients of excess credibility may benefit materially, socially, and otherwise, serious concerns remain about their competence as credible and sincere knowers, rather than persons who are regularly given the benefit of the doubt. Having one's status as a credible and sincere knower and communicator is taken for granted, which calls into question whether or not that capacity is adequately put to the test at all.

Howard Thurman also offers helpful resources with which to consider the harms of awarding credibility excess to men accused of gender violence. In *Jesus and the Disinherited*, Thurman argues that the logic and practices of white supremacy under Jim Crow, the way whites are habituated and disciplined into a particular kind of "white subject," cripples their moral and rational capacities and hinders their freedom as human beings.[27] State-mandated segregation makes whites unable to relate rightly to Black people. Consider the similar logic of patriarchy and misogyny. Knowers can he hindered in their capacity for proper discernment. But, as Baldwin and Thurman suggest, they are less capable of rightly relating to self due to the excesses they "enjoy." Medina, Fricker, and others offer compelling reasons why it is bad to be epistemically spoiled. Not only can it lead to the cultivation of vice, but it can restrict one's capacity to rightly accord credibility to themselves and others. If that is true, then it is also importantly harmful to the epistemically spoiled that others are implicated in the maintenance and cultivation of epistemic vice in him. According credibility in excess can importantly let others down. One way this happens is through drawing them into complicity with unjust systems of embedded systemic prejudices.

Though Fricker theorizes the epistemic injustice of token interpersonal cases of testimonial injustice, rather than the cumulative effects of cases, it is not clear that token cases are so easily separable from the cumulative attributions of withholdings of credibility. Fricker cares a great deal about both the cumulative and token effects of the harms of distorted credibility. That there was an entire courtroom that was unable to hear Tom Robinson's testimony in part enabled Fricker to describe the credibility deficit at play as systemic rather than token testimonial injustice. That is, credibility deficit is based in systemic injustice when the deficit tends toward persistence of prejudiced attitudes.[28] Even when presented with exonerating testimony, hearers' prejudice toward Tom Robinson persisted, a credibility deficit remained, and his hearers did not receive his testimony. It is unclear why Fricker regards these cumulative effects of credibility excess and deficit over time as "semi-fanciful," especially when she grounds the systematicity of credibility distortions in the persistence of the prejudices that animate them. Built into her account of credibility excess and deficit is the fact that identity prejudices are importantly persistent (over time), even when our beliefs do not necessarily track the biases present in the social imagination. It is suggestively conflicting that credibility excess is not epistemic injustice in token cases, yet part of what credibility excess entails is recourse to cumulative and systemic prejudice. Token and cumulative cases of credibility excess and deficit are not easily disentangled.

I suspect the impetus to consider credibility deficit as the paradigmatic epistemic injustice is in part due to Fricker's and Jones's desire to theorize from the position of the traditionally disinherited. This theorizing takes seriously that power does not affect persons equally. Historically marginalized groups continue to suffer social, economic, and psychological harms due to their testimonies being downgraded. Fricker in part aims to contrast these deficits with the benefits accrued by persons deemed more credible. It seems right to mark Mayella Ewell, Justice Brett Kavanaugh, and Emmett Till's lynch mob as benefiting from increased believability. Material benefits indeed flow from the epistemic privilege they are granted.

And yet I have here sought to raise doubts about the claim that credibility excess does not harm the testifier as one capable of sincere testimony. Exploring how credibility distortions are at work in downgraded testimonies of women reporting sexual assault and the upgraded testimonies of the men who stand accused has helped to show how credibility excess cuts persons off from important fraternal correction, recognizes their testimony in light of membership in a social group, and thus potentially inhibits confrontation with a more authentic and rigorous basis for credibility. Finally, I suggest that the identity-prejudicial component of credibility excess in part blurs the attempt to separate token from cumulative cases of credibility excess and deficit. When credibility is habitually accorded in excess, right relationship with self and others is compromised. Men, for example, draw others into complicity with violent logics of patriarchy, sexism, and misogyny, which harms not only the women whom they silence. It also brings low those who dominate socially, politically, and otherwise. While these accumulated benefits result from credibility excess, more work is needed to identify and remedy the harms of credibility excess and discover the nature of its injustice, if any. The work of so many women in religion, philosophy, and outside of the academy has been to center women's experience in the fight for social justice. That requires in part privileged persons to relate better to self and other privileged persons to see themselves clearly. The refusal to attribute credibility accurately continues to obscure persons from self and other. Injustice, perhaps epistemic in nature, looms.

NOTES

1. Irin Carmon, "How the Kavanaugh Hearings Changed American Men and Women," April 16, 2019, https://www.thecut.com/2019/04/new-study-reveals-how-kavanaugh-hearings-changed-americans.html.

2. PerryUndem, "The Immediate, Short-Term, and Long-Term Effects of the Kavanaugh Hearings on the Electorate," April 2019, https://view.publitas.com/perryundem-research-communication/kavanaugh-ford-survey-report_f.

3. PerryUndem, "Effects of the Kavanaugh Hearings," 10.

4. PerryUndem, "Effects of the Kavanaugh Hearings," 10.

5. These identities do not begin to capture the distinct yet intersecting forms of oppression heaped upon transgender, genderqueer, and non-binary persons. While I do not treat these communities sufficiently here, there is ample scholarly and activist work under way to theorize and ameliorate the particular harms faced by these communities.

6. José Medina, *The Epistemology of Resistance: Gender and Racial Oppression, Epistemic Injustice, and Resistant Imaginations* (New York: Oxford University Press, 2013).

7. Miranda Fricker, *Epistemic Injustice: Power and the Ethics of Knowing* (New York: Oxford University Press, 2007), 17.

8. Fricker, *Epistemic Injustice*, 17. Further, "Epistemological nuance aside, the hearer's obligation is obvious: she must match the level of credibility she attributes to her interlocutor to the evidence that he is offering the truth" (19).

9. Though a physical disability provides near conclusive evidence that Tom Robinson could not have executed the assault, the jury cannot (or refuses to) conceive that a Black man is the bearer of credible and sincere testimony. That the truth of Tom Robinson's testimony requires disbelief of his accuser, a white woman and her father, further cripples the likelihood that he will be regarded on the merit of his testimony rather than according to prejudices associated with his social position.

10. Just as misogyny aims to preserve patriarchy (see Kate Manne, *Down Girl: The Logic of Misogyny* [New York: Oxford University Press, 2018]), techniques of anti-Black racism in part aim to preserve white supremacy.

11. Fricker, *Epistemic Injustice*, 20.

12. Fricker, *Epistemic Injustice*, 18. Credibility excess can prove harmful in cases where an ethical burden results or where one is insufficiently prepared due to missing out on important bits of knowledge. She insists that, in such circumstances, credibility excess can be disadvantageous, though on the whole it is usually an advantage. Credibility excess is, at best, a case of distributive unfairness.

13. Karen Jones, "The Politics of Intellectual Self-Trust," *Social Epistemology* 26, no. 2 (2012): 237–51, 245.

14. Jones, "The Politics of Intellectual Self-Trust," 237.

15. Jones, "The Politics of Intellectual Self-Trust," 238.

16. Jones, "The Politics of Intellectual Self-Trust," 246.

17. Fricker, *Epistemic Injustice*, 21.

18. Keri Day, "White Boys Will Be Boys: Kavanaugh, #MeToo and Race," September 28, 2018, https://religionnews.com/2018/09/28/white-boys-will-be-boys-kavanaugh-metoo-and-race/.

19. James Baldwin, *The Fire Next Time* (New York: Modern Library, 1995), 98.

20. James Baldwin, "Letter from a Region in My Mind," *The New Yorker*, November 17, 1962, https://www.newyorker.com/magazine/1962/11/17/letter-from-a-region-in-my-mind.

21. James Baldwin, "The White Man's Guilt," in *Collected Essays* (New York: Library of America, 1998), 723.

22. In my exploration of credibility excess and deficit, I parallel the logic of white supremacy with credibility excess and the logic of anti-Black racism with credibility deficit. I find that they are at least in part apt systemic expressions of excess and deficit, borne out in interpersonal exchanges of meting out credibility in virtue of social group membership. Though I do not focus on defending this relationship here, I suggest that it is rather straightforward that white supremacy, expressed interpersonally as racial bias and structurally as systemic injustice, sometimes involves granting to whites more than is their due in virtue of their membership in the relevant social group. Similarly, anti-Black prejudice, enacted interpersonally or structurally, is the withholding of proper respect based on one's membership in the relevant social group. Taking the fictional example Fricker offers in *To Kill a Mockingbird*, unevenly distributed social power can lead to both whites meting out excessive credibility to whites in virtue of their being white, and Black persons not getting the credibility they are due in virtue of their being Black. This unequal relationship of social power is at play in distorting credibility upward (in the case of white supremacy) and downward (in the case of anti-Black racism). I take this connection between credibility excess

and white supremacy and credibility excess and anti-Black racism to be fairly uncontroversial, but further work developing these ideas of course is warranted. For a survey of the documented disadvantages suffered by non-whites living in America, including but not limited to disadvantages in health, education, housing, and employment, see Elizabeth Anderson's *The Imperative of Integration* (Princeton, NJ: Princeton University Press, 2010), especially chapters 2–4.

23. For more on the publicity of knowledge, see Rebecca Kukla and Mark Lance's *Yo! and Lo!: The Pragmatic Topography of the Space of Reasons* (Cambridge, MA: Harvard University Press, 2009).

24. Charles Taylor, "The Politics of Recognition," in *Multiculturalism and the Politics of Recognition*, ed. A. Gutmann (Princeton, NJ: Princeton University Press, 1992), 36.

25. Medina, *The Epistemology of Resistance*, 29.

26. For work on the phenomenon of white ignorance, see Charles W. Mills, "White Ignorance," in *Race and Epistemologies of Ignorance*, ed. Shannon Sullivan and Nancy Tuana (New York: State University of New York Press, 2007). For work on affected ignorance, see Michele Moody-Adams, "Culture, Responsibility, and Affected Ignorance." *Ethics* 104, no. 2 (1994): 291–309.

27. Howard Thurman, *Jesus and the Disinherited* (Boston: Beacon Press, 1996). I thank Dr. Keri Day for drawing my attention to this example.

28. Fricker, *Epistemic Injustice*, 29.

BIBLIOGRAPHY

Baldwin, James. *The Fire Next Time*. New York: Modern Library, 1995.
———. "Letter from a Region in My Mind." *The New Yorker*, November 17, 1962. https://www.newyorker.com/magazine/1962/11/17/letter-from-a-region-in-my-mind.
———. "The White Man's Guilt." In *Collected Essays*, 722–27. New York: Library of America, 1998.
Carmon, Irin. "How the Kavanaugh Hearings Changed American Men and Women." April 16, 2019. https://www.thecut.com/2019/04/new-study-reveals-how-kavanaugh-hearings-changed-americans.html.
Day, Keri. "White Boys Will be Boys: Kavanaugh, #MeToo and Race." September 28, 2018. https://religionnews.com/2018/09/28/white-boys-will-be-boys-kavanaugh-metoo-and-race/.
Fricker, Miranda. *Epistemic Injustice: Power and the Ethics of Knowing*. New York: Oxford University Press, 2007.
Jones, Karen. "The Politics of Intellectual Self-Trust." *Social Epistemology* 26, no. 2 (2012): 237–51.
Manne, Kate. *Down Girl: The Logic of Misogyny*. New York: Oxford University Press, 2018.
Medina, José. *The Epistemology of Resistance: Gender and Racial Oppression, Epistemic Injustice, and Resistant Imaginations*. New York: Oxford University Press, 2013.
Mills, Charles W. "White Ignorance." In *Race and Epistemologies of Ignorance*, edited by Shannon Sullivan and Nancy Tuana. New York: State University of New York Press, 2007.
Moody-Adams, Michele. "Culture, Responsibility, and Affected Ignorance." *Ethics* 104, no. 2 (1994): 291–309.
PerryUndem. "The Immediate, Short-Term, and Long-Term Effects of the Kavanaugh Hearings on the Electorate." April 15, 2019. https://view.publitas.com/perryundem-research-communication/kavanaugh-ford-survey-reportf.
Taylor, Charles. "The Politics of Recognition." In *Multiculturalism and the Politics of Recognition*, edited by A. Gutmann. Princeton, NJ: Princeton University Press, 1992.
Thurman, Howard. *Jesus and the Disinherited*. Boston, MA: Beacon Press, 1996.

CHAPTER 8

Do Not Pass Me By

A Womanist Reprise and Response to Health Care's Cultural Dismissal and Erasure of Black Women's Pain

Rev. Anjeanette M. Allen, Chicago Theological Seminary, PhD Student

ABSTRACT

An ordained minister, chaplain, and former public policy professional offers a womanist perspective on the historical and current dehumanization and medical mistreatment of Black women as they are disproportionately undiagnosed and untreated for pain and other medical maladies due to misbelief about their pain. As a response, the author proposes the construction of a womanist practical theology of health and health care referred to as "WomanistHealthCare" to advocate for the creation of safe spaces, rituals, and practices embodied by love, beneficence, and justice for Black women, specifically in health care settings. A WomanistHealthCare approach is a critical pedagogy that yields understanding on the nuances between space, place, and power by situating Black women's bodies and the spaces they inhabit for care as sites for radical resistance and redemptive healing. WomanistHealthCare makes operable the Hippocratic Oath for Black women and the Black community at large, and upholds the principle of non-maleficence, which asserts an obligation to not inflict harm or evil on others, which, in medical ethics, is associated with the maxim *Primum non nocere*, "Above all do no harm."

INVOCATION

Iopen with a reflection and song to invoke the power of the Holy Spirit to ground the solemnness of the subject of Black pain, specifically of Black women. *Pass Me Not, O Gentle Savior*, is a song often sung to comfort our pain and ease our anguish. It was written by the United Methodist psalmist Fanny J. Crosby in 1868, set to compositional music by William Doane, and first appeared in Doane's *Songs of Devotion* for Christian Associations in 1870.[1]

Pass me not, O gentle Savior,
hear my humble cry;
while on others thou art calling,
do not pass me by.

We find ourselves in a time when so many souls are suffering, with a profound cry in this dry land for a saving grace and healing balm. As societal institutions pass so many marginalized people by, including Black and brown people, women, the poor, etc., we call upon the Lord our God with a plea to see us in our wounding as we also seek survival through our own collective resilience.

INTRODUCTION

As an ordained Black female minister, chaplain, and former public policy professional, I am particularly sensitive to the social location of Black women and recognize how gender, race, class, and sexuality work in mutually constitutive ways to impact our embodied experiences within the church and in the world. Given the centrality of religious experience in Black women's lives[2] and data that demonstrates how Black women are disproportionately undiagnosed and untreated for pain acuities (as well as other medical maladies), I contend that there is a prophetic and moral imperative for the ecumenical community, counselors, chaplains, public health officials, and theologians to address Black women's holistic wellness. Theological, social, political, and medical frames and practices that denigrate and defile the lives of Black women (and girls) and promote, even if unwittingly, cultural violence against Black women's bodies need to be confronted.

In this chapter, I explore the dehumanization and medical mistreatment of Black women historically and discuss how the development of a womanist practical theology of health and health care, which I refer to as "WomanistHealthCare," may help rectify spiritual malpractice and health care maleficence concerning Black women's holistic wellness in its advocacy for the creation of safe spaces, rituals, and practices, including health care settings that embody love, beneficence, and justice for Black women and other marginalized people.

WomanistHealthCare is an expansion of the term "WomanistCare"[3] co-created by pastoral theologian Marsha Foster Boyd to include a focus on medical ethics, which social ethicist Emilie M. Townes refers to as a "Womanist Ethic of Care."[4] I will discuss these terms later in my chapter, which pivots on well-documented racial disparities in health care concerning how Black Americans, as compared to white Americans, are systematically underdiagnosed and undertreated for pain due to racial bias and false beliefs about pain tolerance of Black Americans.

A HISTORICAL REVIEW: BLACK WOMEN'S DEHUMANIZATION AND DEFILEMENT

Black women in America have suffered historically under the weight of slavery and subsequent cultural hegemony. American colonizers enslaved and subjugated indigenous Africans and their progeny and viewed them as uncivilized savage infidels who were evil. Enslaved Black women were perceived as "cursed," with their bodies rendered as reproductive commodities and "medical superbodies" subject to extreme sexual violence and torture.[5]

Practical theologian and psychoanalyst Phillis Isabella Sheppard orients our understanding of Black women's bodies in historical and psychological ways. Sheppard highlights how the legacy of slavery not only inscribed itself on Black women's bodies historically but "is also written on their psyches and in a multitude of relationships."[6] I refer to this as psychic wounding. This notion of psychic wounding is a form of cultural violence.

Such cultural violence may also be experienced through "white gaze" perhaps best exemplified by the post-colonial, critical race theoretical perspectives espoused by Frantz Fanon in his assertion of the indefensibility of the fact of Blackness, which dehumanizes Blacks (and by extension other people of color) in the ontological sense; W.E.B. DuBois in speaking of the "double consciousness" for Black people's duality of identity; and in George Yancy's discourse of "white gaze." White gaze attends to the interrogative surveillance of Black people by white persons resulting in a distorted racialized perception.[7] This type of psychological violence causes the Black body to enter into a disjointed relationship with itself, as "gaze" relegates the Black body to be dangerous, unruly, unlawful, criminal, and hypersexual.[8] This oppression is continuous, as "whiteness" becomes the default "transcendental norm" and an empowered beneficiary to an invisible knapsack of societal privileges inaccessible to non-white persons.[9]

Black bodies became symbolically saturated and socially constructed as humanly inferior and even evil, particularly Black women's bodies, through hegemonic intersections between theology and philosophy, which provided ideological justification for the Transatlantic slave trade.[10] With the expansion of European imperialism, through colonization, a Christian demarcation was applied to African people based on the belief that Africans were devoid of religion, law, and morality and hence outside of the human race. Early Christian writings linked spiritual darkness with concepts of sin and evil,[11] as illustrated when European colonizers, in the 1500s, misinterpreted the biblical story of Noah and his son Ham in Genesis 9:20–27 as the "Curse of Ham." Colonists harnessed this story to equate Ham (biblically deemed by some as cursed) with Africans and thus Blackness with slavery.[12]

With colonialism, African slave women, in particular, could be taken by force to supplant needed labor force in a burgeoning "new world" economy. As postcolonial feminist Kwok Pui-lan explains, "[t]he control of colonized women's sexuality as reproductive labor was key to the colonial enterprise."[13] The control, social construction, and dehumanization of the African slave woman in the American colonial context was predicated on the dismantling of her sense of placement, family structures, and spiritual belief systems through rape, enslavement, and forced acculturation. An even more heinous sub-context to the subjugation of the African slave woman (and her progeny) was that her very nature and being (as a Black woman) was evil.

From these accounts, we find "narratives of pain," which have been inscribed on Black women's bodies as "historical text" as well as inscribed in their psyches and inter-relationships. This is a historical text that reads of a sub-human infidel, a mule of a worker, the object of sexual gratification, and a breeder of future slaves. In social ethicist Emilie Townes's *Womanist Ethics and the Cultural Production of Evil*, she locates and interrogates the body, particularly Black women's bodies, as sites of memory. Townes seeks to understand gender, race, and memory by exploring negative images and stereotypes of Black women in American culture, which have been "shaped into 'truth' in memory and in history."[14] Black women carry historical wounds on their very bodies that are marked by the legacy of slavery, powerlessness, and resistance, which remains a modern-day reality for Black women in America, especially in the medical system.

MEDICAL RACISM AND MALEFICENCE: FROM SLAVERY TO PRESENT

The racist mistreatment of Black persons in America was not only relegated to the slave trade colonialist enterprise but was and continues to be prominent in the American medical system. A pernicious aspect of medical racism concerns the mistreatment of Black Americans as unwilling and unwitting experimental subjects of doctors and researchers, which undergirds the current distrust many Black people have of the medical establishment to include research and treatment. As medical ethicist and journalist Harriet Washington highlights in her seminal text *Medical Apartheid* how this lack of trust of medicine referred to as "iatrophobia" (fear of the healer) dates back "as early as 1997, [where] a few especially perceptive biomedical researchers placed black iatrophobia in the context of a longer history of research abuse and neglect."[15]

Washington speaks further about the syphilis study conducted by the US Public Health Service between 1932 and 1972 in Tuskegee, Alabama, in which 400 Black men were infected with syphilis so that government doctors could study the trajectory of this painful disease. However, many of the participants were unaware that they could pass the disease to spouses and children.[16] Washington notes that, despite the syphilis study in Alabama being the "longest and the most infamous," it was "hardly the worst—experimental abuse of African Americans."[17] Women, particularly racial and ethnic women, have also been used as experimental subjects without consent, like the men in Tuskegee, but many of the cases for Black women involved excruciating gynecological mutilation and sterilization under the scope of research and training.[18]

Between 1845 and 1849, physician James Marion Sims, who is widely revered as a "women's benefactor" and progenitor "father" of American gynecology,[19] "conducted years of nightmarishly painful and degrading experiments, without anesthesia or consent, on a group of slave women" he purchased in an attempt to correct vaginal fistulas.[20] After several failed attempts on other slave women, Sims "succeeded in repairing a fistula on a slave named Anarcha in 1849 in the thirtieth operation she had undergone in four years."[21] Sims invited physicians, to set their "white gaze" upon these enslaved Black women's naked bodies and genitalia, which was unheard of for white women deemed "virtuous" within the Victorian-laden Cult of True Womanhood.[22]

These women were further dehumanized by being forced to endure painful and risky experimental surgeries without the assistance of anesthesia "ether" for pain that was indeed used for Sims's white women patients. Similar to other physicians of his era, James Marion Sims chose not to use anesthesia because of the racist misbelief that Black people did not feel pain or anxiety as noted in the 1851 text *The Natural History of the Human Species*, which stated that "the American dark races bear with indifference tortures insupportable to a white man."[23]

Many Black women in America continued to be maligned by medical professionals and subject to sterilization promoted by the racist eugenics movement's the Negro Project. The eugenics movement in America was popularized by Margaret Sanger, founder of Planned Parenthood, who "exploited Black stereotypes in order to reduce the fertility of African Americans."[24] Sterilizations were often involuntary, with many Black women being sterilized, unbeknownst to them, while unconscious. This was such common practice in Southern states that it was referred to as the "Mississippi appendectomy," which civil rights leader Fannie Lou Hamer was subjected to.[25] Also, involuntary hysterectomies were commonly practiced in places like New York City and Boston on "poor black and Puerto Rican women with minimal indications to train residents."[26]

In *Breaking the Fine Rain of Death*, Emilie Townes focuses on the health care issues affecting African Americans and pays close attention to various racial, gendered, social, political, and spiritual variables that define the social location of African Americans. Townes describes the racist history of health care provisions in African American communities and the wide range of maladies and diseases that disproportionately affect African Americans and the sociopolitical and economic forces that impact health. Townes also sounds the alarm for Black women in managed care systems, who may be denied care, as "they are more likely to have conditions that are diagnosed as untreatable, given limited treatment options."[27]

Due to social media platforms, contemporary stories chronicling the disbelief of Black women's pain by medical staff are widely accessible. One such story involves Barbara Dawson, who collapsed while being escorted in handcuffs from a hospital emergency room in Florida on Monday, December 21, 2015, where she sought treatment for breathing difficulties.[28] Hospital camera footage shows that Dawson repeatedly said, as she pleaded with the police officer and medical staff, "I am not feeling good," "I can't even hardly breathe," and "Please don't let me die!" After medical staff discharged Dawson, stating that nothing else could be done, she was arrested for disorderly conduct and trespassing when she refused multiple requests to leave. About 20 minutes after Ms. Dawson was dragged out and on the ground in the parking lot, she was pronounced dead.

Also, on a web-based media site Tonic, six women shared their stories about not being believed by doctors concerning their pain and other ailments.[29] Bonita Rush shared her story:

> In 2012, I was having really bad headaches. They came out of the blue. I went to the ER three times in a seven-day period and every time they sent me home. They did a CT scan, which came back negative. But the headaches persisted. I ended up having a seizure, went back to the ER, and was adamant something was wrong. I said, "If you guys are not going to do an MRI, give me a neuro consult so I can get in fairly quickly because something isn't right." I got the neuro consult. The doctor said the CT scan was clear. I pushed for the MRI, and he said, "Let's see if we can get you in today." I ended up having blood clots in about 70 percent of the right side of my brain.[30]

Thankfully, due to social media platforms in recent years, overall awareness of health care racial bias, particularly in treating pain, has been well documented and is increasing overall awareness.

In a 2016 medical journal report, titled "Racial Bias in Pain Assessment and Treatment Recommendations, and False Beliefs About Biological Differences between Blacks and Whites," it was found that:

> . . . [a] substantial number of white laypeople and medical students and residents hold false beliefs about biological differences between blacks and whites and demonstrates that these beliefs predict racial bias in pain perception and treatment recommendation accuracy. [This report] also provides the first evidence that racial bias in pain perception is associated with racial bias in pain treatment recommendations. Taken together, this work provides evidence that false beliefs about biological differences between blacks and whites continue to shape the way we perceive and treat black people—they are associated with racial disparities in pain assessment and treatment recommendations.[31]

Disparities in pain treatment are attributed to implicit or unconscious bias. Beyond medical implications, the undertreatment of Black women's pain and false beliefs about high pain threshold of Black people is further unsettling, as it is fueled by the stereotypical trope of "the strong Black woman," which normalizes the concealment of Black women's pain and suffering as a sign of strength or as religious faithfulness, which I will discuss later.

A sobering reality is that, although health and health care disparities impact various social demographic groups, racial and ethnic minority groups experience such disparities at greater rates. As noted in the Institute of Medicine report, titled *Unequal Treatment: Confronting Racial and Ethnic Disparities in Health Care*, "Racial and ethnic disparities in health care . . . are consistent across a range of medical conditions and health care services, are associated with worse health outcomes, and occur independently of insurance status, income and education, among other factors that influence access to health care."[32] Black women experience amplified discrimination in health care due to implicit racial and gender bias. In *Invisible Visits: Black Middle-Class Women in the American Healthcare System*, Tina Sacks highlights from her research how Black women's "experiences indicate that structural discrimination negatively affects Black women's health across the board," regardless of their socioeconomic status.[33]

Other current realities exist regarding the disproportionate numbers of Black and brown pregnancy-related deaths, which cuts across class lines. Some may recall Serena Williams's story where she almost died after giving birth to her daughter, as doctors and nurses did not listen to her at first concerning her health care history of pulmonary embolisms and would not give her a CT scan with contrast. Recently, the American College of Obstetricians and Gynecologists reported that racial bias on the part of health care practitioners serves as a contributing factor in health outcomes and health care, including the disproportionate numbers of pregnancy-related deaths of minority women.[34] Other recent news suggests that racial bias in a medical algorithm sold by a leading health services company called Optum favors white patients over sicker Black patients.[35]

It is clear that Black people in America have experienced suffering and subjugated pain from historical racist maleficence in the American medical system and that Black people continue to be subjected to current racism in the American medical system. Dr. Martin Luther King Jr. even recognized before his death the pernicious nature of health care injustice. At the end of his march from Selma to Alabama, he said to an audience, filled with physicians attending to the injuries that marchers sustained from racist segregationists, that "of all the forms of inequality, injustice in health is the most shocking and the most inhumane."[36]

Though Black women have survived because of resilience, acts of resistance, and a faith in a God they could not see, Black women's narratives of pain linger from the residual effects of slavery and subsequent cultural hegemony. Black women and girls are routinely mistreated and subjected to spiritual malpractice and medical maleficence. This is why it is important that narratives transform into social action and a work of creative praxis. This work would be undertaken by those with the moral fortitude and sense of moral imagination to advocate for fair practices and policies in the American medical system for those most marginalized, which includes Black women. In my own theological imagination and as part of my theological task to help Black women and girls reclaim their holistic selves, I am channeling all of my rage, angst, and love to advocate for the development of a womanist practical theology of health and health care, which I refer to as WomanistHealthCare.

WOMANISTHEALTHCARE: A WAY FORWARD

As a reprisal and response to health care's dismissal and cultural erasure of Black women's pain, I am constructing a womanist practical theology of health and health care, which I refer to as "WomanistHealthCare." WomanistHealthCare is an expansion of "WomanistCare," co-created by pastoral theologian Marsha Foster Boyd and other Womanist caregivers convened by Linda Hollies,[37] and it also builds on Emilie Townes's focus on a "Womanist Ethic of Care." According to Foster Boyd:

WomanistCare is the intentional process of care giving and care receiving by African American women. It is the African American Woman finding her place and her voice in this world. It is the bold expression of that woman caring circle. . . . [I]n this process, the focus is on holistic care of the body, mind and spirit in order that healing and transformation occur for African American women and their circles of influence.[38]

A WomanistHealthCare builds on WomanistCare by considering how health care spaces, more specifically, need to become more intentional about privileging the voice, concerns, and pains of Black women. A WomanistHealthCare also incorporates Emilie Townes's Womanist Ethic of Care as a theological approach to health and health care[39] by first recognizing health as a social cultural production[40] and, second, by utilizing lament[41] as a necessary point of departure for a justice-oriented approach based on empathy and love.[42]

As an engaged pedagogy, WomanistHealthCare seeks to shape our understanding of the relations of space, place, and power by situating Black women's bodies and ALL spaces Black women inhabit for care as sites for radical resistance, revelation, redemption, and healing. WomanistHealthCare helps us reframe theological anthropology, public theology, and also our notions of soteriology. As Shawn Copeland notes, "the body incarnates and points beyond to what is 'the most immediate and proximate object of our experience' and mediates our engagement with others, with the world, with the Other."[43] WomanistHealthCare is also a critical ethnography in that it honors and centers a Black woman's story as the "dynamic present,"[44] from which to shape dialogue and inspire liberational thinking for what it means to be a thriving human being. It is vital that more narrative collective work be done by theologians, medical researchers, ethicists, and activists to unmask, track, and mobilize on health care injustices concerning Black women's expression of pain. Such historiography is foundational to Womanist ethics generally and, as Audre Lorde expressed, "Your silence will not protect you."[45]

A WomanistHealthCare approach also implicitly challenges the stereotype of "the strong Black woman," which normalizes the concealment of Black women's pain and suffering as a sign of strength and further complicates the needed treatment and belief of Black women's pain as stated previously. For Black Christian women, the concealment of their pain and suffering is often regarded as religious faithfulness and a standard-bearer for her Christian identity and personhood as noted by pastoral theologian Chanequa Walker Barnes in *Too Heavy a Yoke: Black Women and the Burden of Strength*.[46] This type of "self-sacrifice," which renders a person bereft of healing and wholeness, is spiritually deficient and morally reprehensible, yet such a perspective flourishes in the Black community and Black church, though not exclusively. How does this impact Black women's physical, emotional, and mental well-being? How does it affect her hope for healing and redemption—individually, collectively, and systematically?

One of the ways to address this fallacy is to re-imagine and re-construct the ways in which we consider what it means to be a human being, to be made whole, and to feel cared about. What conjures up in my mind is a place, a communal space, where Black women can feel safe and nurtured. For this to happen, spiritual and medical caregivers of Black women and girls have to meet them in their social location. From a Womanist theological perspective, women's personal stories must be self-honored first (radical subjectivity) and then validated in the context of their communities (traditional communalism).[47]

WomanistHealthCare seeks to uphold the principle of non-maleficence, which asserts an obligation to not inflict harm or evil on others, which, in medical ethics, has been closely associated with the maxim *Primum non nocere,* or "Above all do no harm." It seeks to make operable the Hippocratic Oath, which clearly expresses an obligation of non-maleficence and an obligation of beneficence (meaning to prevent and remove evil or harm and to do and promote that which is good).[48] WomanistHealthCare advocates to operationalize the Hippocratic Oath through community education and awareness and grassroots mobilizing both in and beyond religious spaces to include medical schools, nursing schools, chaplaincy training, and partnership advocacy efforts with progressive organizations, such as the Black Women's Health Imperative.

A WomanistHealthCare approach is also keenly aware of the spatial politics concerning the care and nurturing of Black women's bodies. Cultivating spaces where Black women are able to share their stories and be heard, affirmed, and loved is vitally important to their healing, redemption, and flourishing. Similar to how church spaces should operate as a place of deep hospitality and refuge, places designated for healing in health care should embody such characteristics as well. If "the classroom remains the most radical space of possibility in the academy,"[49] according to hooks in *Teaching to Transgress,* I contend that health care spaces can and should become active sites for radical resistance, revelation, redemption, and healing so that Black women's and girls' holistic wellness (body, mind, soul, and will) may be attended to.

A WomanistHealthCare builds on the concept of "shared community," which is important in womanist sensibilities and in keeping with the African proverb "I am because we are." Furthermore, I contend that the need for reconstructed health care spaces and practices, public and private, is a broader task of Womanist practical theology such that it, as Phillis Isabella Sheppard suggests, "creates spaces for the loving and appreciative gazes that celebrate, challenge, and work for the ongoing transformation of Black women and the contexts in which they live."[50] This is both a Womanist task and the broader task of Black practical theology.

A WomanistHealthCare, in many ways, seeks to confront, as Kelly Brown Douglas explains in her text *Stand Your Ground: Black Bodies and the Justice of God,* the "protected space for America's Anglo Saxon exceptionalism."[51] Such space is closely guarded and insulated by whiteness itself, which is why whiteness is treated as "cherished property of America's exceptionalism."[52] Through correlation, from an Anglo Saxon exceptionalism perspective, hospitals and health care centers often operate as "protected spaces" for "cherished" white persons—a default hegemonic norm. However, as Douglas notes, Christ stood with the oppressed in death, but "death does not have the last word."[53] Jesus stood with the oppressed in his life, death, and resurrection. Black women's lives, and ALL Black lives matter to God and as a valuable part of humanity. This is why WomanistHealthCare serves a theo-ethical corrective that advocates for health care equity in terms of accessibility and practice.

As a Womanist, I am concerned about the macro-structural and the micro-structural issues that affect Black women's and girls' lives and the varied spaces they occupy (physically, socially, historically, psychologically, etc.). In my theological task to help Black women and other disenfranchised persons reclaim their whole selves (mind, body, spirit, and will) and embody their self-liberation, I will continue to consider the utility and development of a womanist practical theological framework in WomanistHealthCare.

CONCLUDING REMARKS AND BENEDICTION

As I close this chapter, I offer a reflection on the part of my title, Do Not Pass Me By, which I selected from the hymn *Pass Me Not, Oh Gentle Savior* written by Fanny Crosby.[54] I put this in the title to ground the solemnness of Black women's pain. When we sing and declare *Pass Me Not, O Gentle Savior*, we sing to comfort our pain and anguish, and we do this also as a "SHOUT"—a Black church conjuring SHOUT of meaning-making, to render "a way to exorcise or externalize black pain" so that "our pain is more accessible and available for understanding," according to Debra Walker King.[55]

The life and work of Jesus, the Savior in the hymn, serves as a witness that he cared for those forgotten by others, including biblical women like Tamar, the bleeding woman, the Samaritan woman, lepers, crippled, etc., who were bridled by pain and deemed as outcasts in their day. They were seen by God, such as Hagar was, seen by a Jesus who believed their pain, attended to their needs, and thereby embodied the Hippocratic Oath to help and not harm. Jesus does not pass Black women's pain by and neither should health care.

> Pass me not, O gentle Savior,
> hear our humble cry;
> while on others thou art calling,

DOCTOR, NURSE, ALGORITHM, or ANYONE. DO NOT PASS US BY!

NOTES

1. Fanny J. Crosby, "History of Hymns: 'Pass Me Not, O Gentle Savior,'" Discipleship Ministries, https://www.umcdiscipleship.org/resources/history-of-hymns-pass-me-not-o-gentle-savior.

2. According to the Pew Research Center, "[m]ore than eight-in-ten black women (84%) say religion is very important to them, and roughly six-in-ten (59%) say they attend religious services at least once a week. No group of men or women from any other racial or ethnic background exhibits comparably high levels of religious observance." "A Religious Portrait of African-Americans," Pew Research Center, January 30, 2009, https://www.pewforum.org/2009/01/30/a-religious-portrait-of-african-americans/.

3. Marsha Foster Boyd, "WomanistCare," in *Embracing the Spirit: Womanist Perspectives on Hope Salvation, and Transformation*, ed. Emilie Townes (Maryknoll, NY: Orbis, 1997), 198.

4. Emilie M. Townes, *Breaking the Fine Rain of Death: African American Health Issues and a Womanist Ethic of Care* (Eugene, OR: Wipf and Stock, 1998), 185–86.

5. Deidre Cooper Owens, *Medical Bondage: Race, Gender, and the Origin of American Gynecology* (Athens, GA: University of Georgia Press, 2018), 7. The term "medical superbodies" was coined by historian Deidre Cooper Owens in her text *Medical Bondage* to highlight the complicated social context in which Black women were dehumanized and their bodies objectified while simultaneously deemed profitable in medical experimentation for the benefit of white women's reproductive health.

6. Phillis I. Sheppard, *Self, Culture and Others in Womanist Practical Theology* (New York: Palgrave Macmillan, 2011), 153.

7. George Yancy, *Black Bodies, White Gazes: The Continuing Significance of Race* (Lanham, MD: Rowman & Littlefield, 2008), 3.

8. Yancy, *Black Bodies, White Gazes*, 3.

9. Yancy, *Black Bodies, White Gazes*, 46.

10. James H. Cone, *God of the Oppressed* (New York: Orbis Books, 1975/1997), 81.

11. Joe Feagin, *Racist America: Roots, Current Realities and Future Reparations* (New York: Routledge, 2000), 71.

12. Feagin, *Racist America*, 73–74.

13. Kwok Pui-lan, "Mending of Creation," in *Post-Colonial Imagination and Feminist Theology* (London: SCM Press, 2005), 212.

14. Emilie M. Townes, *Womanist Ethics and the Cultural Production of Evil* (New York: Palgrave Macmillan, 2006), 3.

15. Harriet A. Washington, *Medical Apartheid: The Dark History of Medical Experimentation on Black Americans from Colonial Times to Present* (New York: Anchor Books, 2006), 181.

16. Emilie M. Townes, *Breaking the Fine Rain of Death: African American Health Issues and a Womanist Ethic of Care* (Eugene, OR: Wipf and Stock, 1998), 88.

17. Washington, *Medical Apartheid*, 181.

18. Townes, *Breaking the Fine Rain of Death*, 115.

19. Townes, *Breaking the Fine Rain of Death*, 51.

20. Washington, *Medical Apartheid*, 61.

21. Townes, *Breaking the Fine Rain of Death*, 51.

22. Washington, *Medical Apartheid*, 64.

23. Ranjani Chakraborty, "The US Medical System Is Still Haunted by Slavery: Medicine's Dark History Helps Explain Why Black Mothers Are Dying at Alarming Rates," VOX, December 7, 2017, https://www.vox.com/health-care/2017/12/7/16746790/health-care-black-history-inequality.

24. Washington, *Medical Apartheid*, 195–96.

25. Washington, *Medical Apartheid*, 204.

26. Washington, *Medical Apartheid*, 204.

27. Townes, *Breaking the Fine Rain of Death*, 117.

28. Christine Hauser, "Recordings Add Detail in Death of Woman Forced from Florida Hospital," *New York Times*, January 7, 2016.

29. Joanne Spataro, "Doctors Don't Always Believe You When You're a Black Woman: Six Black Women Tell Us How They Had to Advocate for Themselves in the Doctor's Office," February 2, 2018, https://tonic.vice.com/en_us/article/qvedxd/doctors-dont-always-believe-you-when-youre-a-black-woman.

30. Spataro, "Doctors Don't Always Believe You When You're a Black Woman."

31. Kelly M. Hoffman, Sophie Trawalter, Jordan R. Axt, and M. Norman Oliver, "Racial Bias in Pain Assessment and Treatment Recommendations, and False Beliefs about Biological Differences Between Blacks and Whites," in *Proceedings of the National Academy of Sciences of the United States of America* (PNAS), vol. 113, no. 16, April 19, 2016, 4296.

32. Briand D. Smedley, Adrienne Y. Stith, and Aland R. Nelson, eds., *Unequal Treatment: Confronting Racial and Ethnic Disparities in Health Care*, Institute of Medicine, Board of Health Sciences Policy, Committee on Understanding and Eliminating Racial and Ethnic Disparities in Health Care (Washington, DC: National Academies Press, 2003), 79.

33. Tina Sacks, *Invisible Visits: Black Middle-Class Women in the American Healthcare System* (New York: Oxford University Press, 2019), 55.

34. American College of Obstetricians and Gynecologists, "Racial and Ethnic Disparities in Obstetrics and Gynecology," Committee on Health Care for Underserved Women, Committee Opinion Number 649, December 2015 (Reaffirmed 2018), 2–3. This was also addressed in a *New York Times* article by Roni Caryn Rabin, "Huge Racial Disparities Found in Deaths Linked to Pregnancy," May 7, 2019.

35. Carolyn Johnson, "Racial Bias in a Medical Algorithm Favors White Patients over Sicker Black Patients," *New York Times*, October 23, 2019.

36. Washington, *Medical Apartheid*, 2–3.

37. Linda H. Hollies, *WomanistCare: How to Tend to the Souls of Women*, vol. 1 (Joliet, IL: Woman to Woman Ministries, 1991). Linda H. Hollies was an editor for the first book on WomanistCare in 1991, which served as an outgrowth of gathered Black women clergy, professors, chaplains, etc. Hollies notes, "We write for our sisters who care. Each writer is a caring sister who has academically prepared to assist the people of God to move toward wholeness and full potential development. However, because each writer is of the female gender, our care and ministry flows out of our womanist understanding and experiences of God" (v).

38. Foster Boyd, "WomanistCare," in *Embracing the Spirit: Womanist Perspectives on Hope Salvation, and Transformation*, ed. Emilie Townes (Maryknoll, NY: Orbis, 1997), 198.

39. Townes, *Breaking the Fine Rain of Death*, 185–86.

40. Townes, *Breaking the Fine Rain of Death*, 2, 49, 50, 111, 112, 119, 154.

41. Townes, *Breaking the Fine Rain of Death*, 25.

42. Townes, *Breaking the Fine Rain of Death*, 174.

43. M. Shawn Copeland, *Enfleshing Freedom: Body, Race, and Being* (Minneapolis, MN: Fortress Press, 2010), 17.

44. Paulo Freire, *Pedagogy of the Oppressed* (New York: Seabury Press, 1970), 44–45, 84. Freire notes that problem-posing education roots itself in the dynamic present and becomes revolutionary and even prophetically hopeful.

45. Audre Lorde, *Sister Outsider: Essays and Speeches by Audre Lorde* (Berkeley: Crossing Press, 2007), 41.

46. Chanequa Walker-Barnes, *Too Heavy a Yoke: Black Women and the Burden of Strength* (Eugene, OR: Cascade Books, 2014), 137–38.

47. Stacey Floyd Thomas defines the work of Womanism in *Deeper Shades of Purple: Womanist Approaches to Religion and Society* (New York: New York University Press, 2006) within four tenets: 1) radical subjectivity, 2) traditional communalism, 3) redemptive self-love, and 4) critical engagement.

48. Tom L. Beauchamp and James Childress, *Principles of Biomedical Ethics*, 5th ed. (New York: Oxford University Press, 2001), 113–115.

49. bell hooks, *Teaching to Transgress: Education as the Practice of Freedom* (New York: Routledge, 1994), 12.

50. Sheppard, *Self, Culture, and Others in Womanist Practical Theology*, 188.

51. Kelly Brown Douglas, *Stand Your Ground: Black Bodies and the Justice of God* (Maryknoll, NY: Orbis Books, 2015), 39.

52. Douglas, *Stand Your Ground*, 40.

53. Douglas, *Stand Your Ground*, 188.

54. Crosby, "History of Hymns."

55. Debra Walker King, *African Americans and the Culture of Pain* (Charlottesville, VA: University of Virginia Press, 2008), 127.

BIBLIOGRAPHY

American College of Obstetricians and Gynecologists. "Racial and Ethnic Disparities in Obstetrics and Gynecology." Committee on Health Care for Underserved Women, Committee Opinion Number 649, December 2015 (Reaffirmed 2018).

Beauchamp, Tom L., and James Childress. *Principles of Biomedical Ethics*. 5th ed. New York: Oxford University Press, 2001.

Chakraborty, Ranjani. "The U.S. Medical System Is Still Haunted by Slavery: Medicine's Dark History Helps Explain Why Black Mothers Are Dying at Alarming Rates." VOX. December 7, 2017. https://www.vox.com/health-care/2017/12/7/16746790/health-care-black-history-in equality.

Cone, James H. *God of the Oppressed*. Maryknoll, NY: Orbis Books, 1975/1997.

Cooper Owens, Deidre. *Medical Bondage: Race, Gender, and the Origin of American Gynecology*. Athens, GA: University of Georgia Press, 2018.

Copeland, Shawn M. *Enfleshing Freedom: Body, Race, and Being*. Minneapolis, MN: Fortress Press, 2010.

Douglas, Kelly Brown. *Stand Your Ground: Black Bodies and the Justice of God*. Maryknoll, NY: Orbis Books, 2015.

Du Bois, W.E.B. *The Souls of Black Folk*. New York: New American Library, 1982, 1903 reprint.

Fanon, Frantz. *Black Skin, White Masks*. New York: Grove Press, 2008.

Feagin, Joe. *Racist America: Roots, Current Realities and Future Reparations*. New York: Routledge, 2000.

Floyd-Thomas, Stacey. *Deeper Shades of Purple: Womanist Approaches to Religion and Society*. New York: New York University Press, 2006.

Foster Boyd, Marsha. "WomanistCare." In *Embracing the Spirit: Womanist Perspectives on Hope Salvation, and Transformation*, edited by Emilie Townes, 197–202. Maryknoll, NY: Orbis, 1997.

Freire, Paulo. *Pedagogy of the Oppressed*. New York: Seabury Press, 1970.

Hauser, Christine. "Recordings Add Detail in Death of Woman Forced from Florida Hospital." *New York Times*, January 7, 2016. https://www.nytimes.com/2016/01/08/us/recordings-add-detail-in-death-of-woman-forced-from-florida-hospital.html.

Hoffman, Kelly M., Sophie Trawalter, Jordan R. Axt, and M. Norman Oliver. "Racial Bias in Pain Assessment and Treatment Recommendations, and False Beliefs about Biological Differences between Blacks and Whites." *Proceedings of the National Academy of Sciences of the United States of America (PNAS)* 113, no. 16 (April 19, 2016): 4296–4301.

Hollies, Linda H. *WomanistCare: How to Tend to the Souls of Women*. Vol. 1. Joliet, IL: Woman to Woman Ministries, 1991.

hooks, bell. *Teaching to Transgress: Education as the Practice of Freedom*. New York: Routledge, 1994.

Johnson, Carolyn Y. "Racial Bias in a Medical Algorithm Favors White Patients over Sicker Black Patients." *Washington Post*, October 24, 2019. https://www.washingtonpost.com/health/2019/10/24/racial-bias-medical-algorithm-favors-white-patients-over-sicker-black-patients/.

Lorde, Audre. *Sister Outsider: Essays and Speeches by Audre Lorde*. Berkeley: Crossing Press, 2007.

Meghani, Salimah H., Rosemary C. Polomano, Raymond C. Tait, April H. Vallerand, Karen O. Anderson, and Rollin M. Gallagher. "Advancing a National Agenda to Eliminate Disparities in Pain Care: Directions for Health Policy, Education, Practice and Research." *Pain Medicine*, 13 (2012): 5–28.

Pew Research Center. "A Religious Portrait of African Americans." January 30, 2009. https://www.pewforum.org/2009/01/30/a-religious-portrait-of-african-americans/.

Rabin, Roni Caryn. "Huge Racial Disparities Found in Deaths Linked to Pregnancy." *New York Times*, May 7, 2019. Accessed November 4, 2019. https://www.nytimes.com/2019/05/07/health/pregnancy-deaths-.html.

Sacks, Tina. *Invisible Visits: Black Middle-Class Women in the American Healthcare System*. New York: Oxford University Press, 2019.

Shange, Ntozake. *For Colored Girls Who Have Considered Suicide/When the Rainbow Is Enuf: A Choreopoem*. New York: Scribner Poetry, 1977.

Sheppard, Phillis I. "Building Communities of Embodied Beauty." In *Black Practical Theology*, edited by Dale P. Andrews and Robert London Smith Jr. Waco, TX: Baylor University Press, 2015.

Sheppard, Phillis I. *Self, Culture and Others in Womanist Practical Theology*. New York: Palgrave Macmillan, 2011.

Smedley, Briand D., Adrienne Y. Stith, and Aland R. Nelson, eds. *Unequal Treatment: Confronting Racial and Ethnic Disparities in Health Care*. Institute of Medicine, Board of Health Sciences Policy, Committee on Understanding and Eliminating Racial and Ethnic Disparities in Health Care. Washington, DC: National Academies Press, 2003.

Spataro, Joanne. "Doctors Don't Always Believe You When You're a Black Woman: Six Black Women Tell Us How They Had to Advocate for Themselves in the Doctor's Office." *Tonic*. February

2, 2018. https://tonic.vice.com/en_us/article/qvedxd/doctors-dont-always-believe-you-when-youre-a-black-woman.

Takaki, Ronald. *Iron Cages: Race and Culture in Nineteenth Century America*. New York: Routledge, 1979/2000.

Townes, Emilie M. *Breaking the Fine Rain of Death: African American Health Issues and a Womanist Ethic of Care*. Eugene, OR: Wipf and Stock, 1998.

———. *Womanist Ethics and the Cultural Production of Evil*. New York: Palgrave Macmillan, 2006.

Walker-Barnes, Chanequa. *Too Heavy a Yoke: Black Women and the Burden of Strength*. Eugene, OR: Cascade Books, 2014.

Walker King, Debra. *African Americans and the Culture of Pain*. Charlottesville, VA: University of Virginia Press, 2008.

Washington, Harriet A. *Medical Apartheid: The Dark History of Medical Experimentation on Black Americans from Colonial Times to Present*. New York: Anchor Books, 2006.

Williams, Delores S. "A Womanist Perspective on Sin." In *A Troubling in My Soul: Womanist Perspectives on Evil and Suffering*, edited by Emilie Townes. Maryknoll, NY: Orbis, 1993.

Yancy, George. *Black Bodies, White Gazes: The Continuing Significance of Race*. Lanham, MD: Rowman & Littlefield, 2008.

RELIGIOUS DIVERSITY AND WOMEN'S STUDIES IN RELIGION

CHAPTER 9

Constructing Wicca as "Women's Religion"

A By-Product of Feminist Religious Scholarship

Dr. Michelle Mueller, Santa Clara University

ABSTRACT

Feminist religious scholars are partially responsible for Wicca's reputation as a "women's religion." Broadly speaking, Wicca is a religion whose practitioners affirm and worship a Goddess and a God, the latter often referred to as the former's consort. Feminism informs Wicca, and women outnumber men. However, partnership between women and men has been an influential theme since the earliest appearances of Wicca in southern England. In the 1970s, American female leaders adapted traditional Wiccan practices, forming new women's-only groups. Scholars' overemphasis on the radical feminist branches, without adequate contextualization, has contributed to Wicca's public image as a "women's religion." This chapter deals with the social responsibility of scholars as well as the constitution of a women's religion. Is it defined by exclusive female membership, or by a female majority, or by the centering of women's experience? In what ways is the classification of Wicca as a women's religion accurate, and in which ways is it flawed? The chapter highlights connections between the feminist study of religion and lived religion.

A new religious movement, dating to 1950s England, Wicca has included women as full religious leaders from its start, a characteristic that distinguishes it from most world religions. While many Protestant denominations, as well as Reform Judaism, ordain women to the highest rank of religious authority, the struggle for women's equality in their religious leadership is a recent memory. Wicca and the broader movement of contemporary Paganism stand out as uniquely feminist against other, more known religions.

Women outnumber men in Wiccan and Pagan groups. Since Wicca and contemporary Paganism have been informed by feminism, it is not surprising that the ratio of female members to male members would surpass the average sex ratio. However, the common, popular image of Wicca has become somewhat fixed around certain separatist women's groups that actually represent the extreme edges of Wicca and Paganism, rather than the movement's majority. These "extreme edges" are women's separatist Dianic Wiccan groups that emerged in the 1970s, predominantly under the leadership of Zsuzsanna "Z" Budapest, founder and high priestess of Susan B. Anthony Coven #1.

In scholarship, as well as in popular media, Wicca has been approached as a women's religion, as a women's practice, and as a feminine theological project.[1] But the classification of Wicca as a women's religion should be examined. A female majority cannot be enough to warrant the label of women's religion; all major Christian groups are constituted of more than 50 percent women, after all.[2] The focus of this chapter is on unpacking the meaning and applicability of the phrase *women's religion* in reference to North American Wicca. What is meant or suggested by the phrase *women's religion*? Are women's religions exclusive to women, or are women's religions ones that prioritize the needs and interests of women? Or are women's religions simply female-majority religious traditions? And, if the latter, what degree of majority is needed, and why might one use *women's religions* over *female-majority* or *female-dominated* religions? Finally, which of the above possibilities accurately describe(s) North American Wicca, and what are the politics of naming that are relevant to this case? In this chapter, I argue that the classification of Wicca as a women's religion has been a project taken up by feminist religious scholars and that it is time to step back and evaluate the stakes for feminist religious scholars in rendering, or branding, Wicca as a women's religion, the impact it has on a minor religious population, and the outcomes for feminist religious practice in North America and beyond.

Because this chapter requires that I criticize the actions of several of my favorite scholars, it feels important that I clarify that I have great (though not limitless) admiration for the individuals whose influence I track herein: Rosemary Radford Ruether, Z Budapest, Starhawk, and Carol P. Christ. This is also true for the feminist Witchcraft traditions I discuss, Dianic Wicca and Reclaiming Witchcraft. I have been an avid reader of these authors' work since I first began studying women and Paganism academically. This chapter is a project of accuracy and an invitation for scholarly self-reflection on our responsibilities and power. This chapter emphasizes scholars' roles in contributing to Wicca's brand or public image as a women's religion and the outcomes of this rendering for religious practice, including the outcomes for Wiccan religious practice and the outcomes of other religious groups now borrowing from an image of Wicca that has been packaged by feminist scholars. I focus on outcomes in North America, but the phenomenon of scholarly influence on the feminine image of Wicca is not limited to North America. In my analysis, I attribute the root of the imbalance of information to the feminist religious scholars experiencing what Krister Stendahl termed "holy envy." The women's-only religious groups were compelling to feminist religious scholars, who in turn perceived the women's-only groups as normative in Wicca. It is scholars' contributions to misrenderings of the breadth of the Wiccan religion that I am concerned with. My points are in agreement with new religions scholar Teemu Taira's observations that scholars have power in shaping the public's understandings and definitions of the category of religion.[3]

My critique takes place on somewhat dangerous territory, for claims of subjectivity and objectivity (or others' lack thereof) are highly problematic and have been addressed as such in feminist scholarship.[4] Nevertheless, my positioning has allowed me an insider view on the impact of scholars' selective emphasis on women-only Wicca or feminist Wicca for the greater Wiccan/Pagan movement and the ability to reflect on this and other limitations on religious practice that result from it.

Finally, this chapter would be amiss if I did not at some point recognize the role of popular culture in representing and shaping the public image of contemporary Witchcraft or Wicca as a women's religion. The 1990s and 2000s brought several television shows and movies about not only supernatural witches but supernatural witches who are self-proclaimed *Wiccan* witches, all but one of whom have been women. These have been *The Craft, Buffy the Vampire Slayer, Charmed, American Horror Story Coven*, and *The New Chilling Adventures of Sabrina*. The one exception to supernatural Wiccans on television being female is Lafayette Reynolds, a Black queer male Witch, from the HBO drama *True Blood*.

The influence of popular culture is strong, in this case, the representation of not just witchcraft but *Wicca* as a feminine practice. As a scholar of new religious movements, I have little influence over the media industry. Perhaps I might be consulted by Netflix as an expert at some point in my career, but, even then, my contributions would be used to further commercial gain rather than toward an educational objective. With this chapter, I focus on the influence of scholars in shaping the public image of Wicca because I optimistically believe that I can more effectively intervene in this project. In addition to this justification, the impact of mass media on the growth of Wicca, specifically among teenage girls and young women, has been much discussed in the scholarship, whereas, to date, I have not seen this specific scholarly bias addressed in the literature.[5]

"FEMINIST WICCA" AND "WICCA AS FEMINIST": MORE THAN A DISCURSIVE DIFFERENCE

Before going any further, I must address an important distinction made regarding various Wiccan traditions. From the beginning, Wicca has prioritized women's equality and spiritual authority. This is clear in Gerald Gardner's writings, in the memories of the living elders from early Gardnerian Wicca, and in Doreen Valiente's contributions to Gardnerian Wicca. Considering this, Wicca is inherently feminist. However, within 1970s North America, individual female leaders developed new Wiccan traditions that furthered the feminist leanings of the traditional religion by relying more overtly on traditions of radical feminism. Pagan studies scholar Chas Clifton is oft quoted: "It would be fair to say that England gave Wicca to the United States, but the United States then exported feminist Witchcraft back to the rest of the world."[6]

The phrases *feminist Wicca* and *feminist Witchcraft* have been used to identify these "radically feminist" religious traditions. The label *feminist Wicca* has been used for Zsuzsanna "Z" Budapest's women's-only Dianic Wicca (according to sociologists Berger, Leach, and Shaffer, "a small percentage" of the American Pagan population), as well as for the Reclaiming Witchcraft tradition, founded by Starhawk with others, which is a male-including tradition highly informed by ecofeminist values.[7] Feminist Wicca has therefore been used to identify *radically feminist* Wiccan traditions, in contrast with other forms of Wicca, despite that the other forms of Wicca, prioritizing gender equality in leadership and inclusion of female images of the divine, are feminist as well.

There were many feminist women who, even at the height of Dianic Wicca, chose male-including traditions or branches of Wicca that do not fall under the feminist Wicca subset. Examples of female contemporary Pagan leaders outside of so-called feminist Wicca include Margot Adler, Cora Anderson, Rosemary Buckland, Janet Farrar, Selena Fox, Alison Harlow, Judy Harrow, Jerrie Hildebrand, Diana Paxson, Maxine Sanders, Doreen Valiente, and Morning Glory Zell. Each of these women identified as feminist and suggested that feminism informed their religious worldviews, while they were practitioners of Wiccan/Pagan traditions beyond those labeled feminist Wicca. These female leaders are rarely mentioned in texts by feminist theological scholars, in contrast with leaders in feminist Wicca or feminist spirituality, particularly Z Budapest, Ruth Barrett, Carol P. Christ, and Starhawk.

I participate in the convention of referring to the explicitly radical feminist traditions as feminist Wicca (or feminist Witchcraft) because the distinction is important; feminist Wicca is a unique phenomenon, distinct from other Wiccan traditions. The terminology is imperfect because it suggests that other Wiccan traditions are non-feminist, which is not accurate. In the absence of a preferable term, I uphold the convention.

WHAT IS WOMEN'S RELIGION, ANYWAY?

In order to evaluate the identification of North American Wicca as a women's religion, I must in some way assess the meaning of the label. Is *women's religion* a religious tradition exclusively practiced by or available to women? Is *women's religion* a religion focused on the experiences of women (with or without men and/or non-binaries)? What constitutes *women's religion*? What variations of *women's religions* are possible?

In *Priestess, Mother, Sacred Sister*, anthropologist Susan Starr Sered examines the ontologies, rituals, and cultures of twelve religions she identified as being dominated by women. Among these was the example of North American Feminist Spirituality, which includes feminist Wiccans as well as spiritual feminists from other religions. Sered affirms that the phrase *women's religion* is ambiguous and could justifiably label different phenomena, and so she clarified her own usage. Sered discloses that she would "use the term 'women's religions' interchangeably with 'female-dominated religions.'"[8] Sered reports that, across her case studies, "women are the majority of participants and leaders, there is no higher level male authority that ultimately directs these religions, and that these religions focus on women as ritual actors."[9] Her examples share in common female majorities "both in terms of leadership and membership" and an absolute absence of "discrimination against women on any level of leadership or participation."[10] These details are important because Sered provides one possible rubric for assessing a women's religion. "Additionally," Sered writes, "in all these examples an awareness exists on the part of leaders and/or members that this is a women's religion."[11] This final point has direct bearing for the assessment of Wicca. If Wiccans themselves do not conceive of their practice as a women's religion, it would not fit within Sered's model for women's religions.

Foreseeing inquiries such as mine, Sered adds, "The implications of these distinctions [between male-excluding and male-including religions] are significant, and it may well be that future studies will narrow down the field of inquiry. In thinking about the religions described in this book, it is helpful to treat the diverse examples as points on a continuum, rather than as a strictly homogeneous group."[12] As I am interrogating the applicability of the term, I wrestle to a greater degree with its definition than Sered did. It is precisely my point that the term in usage has led to the public's misinformation and misperception. Therefore, the gray area Sered settled with is precisely where my analysis takes place. While I have not settled on definitive boundaries for the constitution of women's religion, I agree with Sered's general areas for such classification. The paradigm of *women's religion* might refer to a female majority or to a centering of women's experiences and/or women's needs, or some other characteristic.

One possibility for determination of women's religions might be a quantitative approach. If status as a women's religion has to do with a majority of female membership, the boundary needs to be determined. A definition of "more than half" cannot be sufficient, as that makes most religious groups women's religions. In evaluating the accuracy of the women's religion label, we might turn to discourse around the classification of "Black denominations" and "Black religions." The National Congregations Study uses the following double-pronged scheme: a group might be "Black Protestant" if it is "affiliated with a traditionally Black denomination/movement *or* if it is affiliated with a [White denomination] *and* has a membership that is 80% or more African American/Black."[13] Were we to translate this classification scheme for the present inquiry, it would read something like this: A group might be a women's religion if it is affiliated with a traditional women's denomination/movement *or* if it is affiliated with a men's or mixed-gender denomination *and* has a membership that is 80 percent or more female.

Applying this rubric to Wicca, and furthermore to Paganism, we find that, because men have always been involved (not affiliated with a traditional women's denomination/movement), neither traditional Wicca nor Paganism meet the first criterion. In fact, in British Traditional Wicca, men are necessary as the priests who complement the priestesses in ritual performances. As for the second criterion, sociologists Berger, Leach, and Shaffer use "Wiccans," "Pagans," and "Goddess Worshipers" as three main sects in US contemporary Paganism for their scholarly writeup after their "Pagan Census," which received 2,089 completed surveys.[14] The category of Goddess Worshipers includes Dianics as well as other Witches and Pagans who practice a Goddess-oriented tradition, in contrast with duotheism or polytheism. Not surprisingly, Berger, Leach, and Shaffer found a female majority in each of the sects. However, not even in the "Goddess Spirituality" category did the percentage of women exceed 80 percent. Women comprised nearly 70 percent of the Wiccans and nearly 70 percent of the Pagans in the study. Those coded as Goddess Worshipers in their study had a higher female-to-male ratio but actually by only a rather slight difference. If this research sample is representative of today's Pagan population, only Dianic separatism presents as a women's religion, in number and in quality.

In a recent study, Berger discovered that the population ratio, at least within solitary Pagans (those who practice independently rather than within groups), has skewed more toward the female (now at 71.6 percent) than did her sample from fifteen years prior.[15] Berger reports that she had "anticipated that the gender disparity would decrease in all forms of contemporary Paganism as more children were born to and remained in the religion."[16] The recent rise in female membership, however, speaks to my greater point that the representation of Wicca as female in popular media and scholarship has an effect. Berger having mentioned second-generation Pagans, it is entirely relevant to speculate that boys raised as Wiccans/Pagans are less likely than girls raised as Wiccans/Pagans to remain in the religion *because* of the media association of Wicca/Witchcraft with femininity.

Should the centering around women's experiences be the determinant for classification as a "women's religion," even the explicitly feminist tradition of Reclaiming Witchcraft seeks to counter forms of oppression well beyond women's oppression. About its founder, Berger, Leach, and Shaffer write, "Starhawk not only incorporates a strong feminist perspective, which places greater emphasis on the goddess than the god force, but also advocates direct political action for environmental, gay and lesbian, and women's issues."[17] The spiritual tradition seeks to liberate women from patriarchal patterns as well as liberating men and non-binaries from confining expectations and countering bigotry and discrimination faced by all oppressed groups. To reduce the tradition to a "women's religion" only is to mask the group's inclusion of all genders and the intersectionality taught by the group itself. The classification of Wicca as a women's religion belies the facts of Wicca. It dismisses men's experience in the religious movement and does not account for aspects of Wicca that are not gender specific or that are gender neutral.

WICCA IN ROSEMARY RADFORD RUETHER'S *GODDESSES AND THE DIVINE FEMININE* (2005)

In a chapter titled "The Return of the Goddess," Ruether covered primarily feminist Wicca. Even in the section "The Developing Neopagan Movement" (which follows the headings "The Beginnings of Feminist Wicca," "The Leadership of Z. Budapest and Starhawk," and "The Thealogy of Carol Christ"), Ruether omits the names of men who were founding leaders in the organizations she discusses: Covenant of the Goddess, Circle Sanctuary (and the Lady Liberty League), and EarthSpirit. In the chapter, Ruether never indicates that men are involved in the contemporary religious movement and selectively picked only female names. Save for her reference to Gerald Gardner (commonly recognized as the founder of modern Witchcraft) as a historic figure, she names only female leaders—Selena Fox and Starhawk—even while discussing Pagan organizations founded or co-founded by men.

While covering Wicca, Ruether reviews the spiritual progression of Carol P. Christ. However, Christ is an unusual figure in the history of female Wiccan leaders. Developing the biography as if an introduction to Wicca, Ruether instead details Christ's journey *out* of Wicca. Ruether writes, "As [Carol P.] Christ was drawn into the Goddess movement, she began to participate in rituals with Starhawk and also to create her own rituals and group. She experienced the Wiccan movement as 'coming home' to a worldview that had always been her deepest intuition."[18] Under the "tutelage of the Wiccan movement in the United States," Christ began her journey as a priestess of the Goddess. Over time, Christ developed a women's spirituality pilgrimage program and now leads tours to and women's rituals on Crete. According to Ruether, "Her [Christ's] more recent work brings together both her new stage of psychological development and her experiences of living in Greece and experiencing the Greek goddesses in their ancient home, allowing her to modify and nuance the understanding of the Goddess that she had drawn from the tutelage of the Wiccan movement in the United States."[19] Ruether then discusses Christ's "[rejection of the Wiccan idea of magic] as part of a very American and patriarchal quest for control, based on the belief that individuals can bend reality to their will."[20] Ruether does not provide the context for the reader to understand that Christ selectively drew Goddess worship from the Wiccan tradition, which has traditionally included female and male images of the divine as well as female and male practitioners and leaders. Ruether's depiction of Wicca relies on an important spiritual feminist leader who neither identifies nor is typically recognized as a Wiccan. Christ's leadership is relevant to Wicca but is not a strong example of Wicca or even of feminist Wicca. Ruether skipped out on the opportunity to detail the lives of active female Wiccan leaders as well as male practitioners.

Ruether then delineates the histories of "feminist Wicca" only, which would lead any reader who is not an expert on Wicca or Paganism to assume these branches to be fully representative. A close reader might pick up on the subtlety of Ruether's rhetoric in the statement "Starhawk does not accept the Dianic form of separatist witchcraft practiced by Z. Budapest, seeking instead to include both women and men in her covens."[21] Factually speaking, Starhawk has not only *sought* to include women and men; Starhawk *includes* women and men. Describing Starhawk as "seeking" to accomplish this goal, Ruether fails to represent the mixed-gender membership of Reclaiming Witchcraft. Ruether again does not depict men as members of Wiccan covens. Assuming the index is complete, this, and the quick gloss of Gerald Gardner, seem to be the two references to male Wiccans in the nearly four-hundred-page volume titled *Goddesses and the Divine Feminine: A Western Religious History*.

About the establishment of the Covenant of the Goddess, Ruether writes, "some forty witches from fifteen California covens came together in Oakland to explore their differences and commonalities."[22] While this is factually correct, Ruether does not include any ratio of female to male. Having only discussed female Goddess worshipers thus far, Ruether's coverage, by omission, served to paint a portrait of women only in the Covenant of the Goddess, whereas men, such as Gwydion Pendderwen and Aidan Kelly, were among the signers of the original 1975 Covenant of the Goddess Bylaws.[23] Adding to this, the common reader is likely to assume that the "witch" label applies only to female practitioners, which, in Wicca, it does not. As a representation of Wiccans' and

Pagans' involvement with the Parliament of the World's Religions, from 1993 to 2004, she quotes from Selena Fox's paper only, omitting contributions from male Pagans. She reported on "EarthSpirit in Massachusetts" without any mention of its male founder Andras Corban Arthen.[24] Arthen was a presenter for the 1993, 2004, and 2009 Parliaments.[25] Janet and Stewart Farrar, married clergy couple who authored several books influential to American Paganism, including *The Witches Goddess*, *The Witches God*, *The Witches Bible*, and *Eight Sabbats for Witches*, are never mentioned.

"WICCA/PAGANISM" IN *ENCYCLOPEDIA OF WOMEN AND RELIGION IN NORTH AMERICA* (2006)[26]

Rosemary Skinner Keller and Rosemary Radford Ruether together edited a three-volume *Encyclopedia of Women and Religion in North America*. On the subject of Wicca/Paganism, Keller and Ruether include a chapter from priestess Selena Fox, a highly recognized leader within Paganism. Fox founded Circle Sanctuary in Madison, Wisconsin, in 1974. Throughout her public ministry career, Fox has been the lead priestess with close-ranking priests. She lived with Jim Alan at the founding of Circle Sanctuary in the mid-1970s. By 1994, Dennis Carpenter (her current spouse) had become co-executive director of Circle.[27]

In spite of their inclusion of Fox's chapter, which itself evenly acknowledged female leaders and male leaders in Paganism (respectively to their individual contributions and influences), the editors, in their introduction to the three-volume encyclopedia, omit mention of male figures. Instead, they depict an image of Wicca as a women's (separatist) religion.[28] In addition to their textual references, Keller and Ruether's shaping is even evidenced in their centering of Z Budapest, the founder of women's separatist Wicca, on the cover of Volume 1 as the one photographic image of a Wiccan or of Wicca. Each volume of the encyclopedia features photographs of women in North American religious history. Another photograph of Z Budapest is included in Selena Fox's chapter within the volume, the only photograph of a Wiccan/Pagan leader in the three-volume set.[29] My concern is not that men are not depicted, but rather that only a separatist female leader is depicted, whereas women sharing leadership with men is more normative in American Wiccan/Pagan history.

In her chapter, Fox accurately represents Wicca as female-dominated but not exclusive to women and included references to male practitioners and male leaders:

> Many groups consist of women and men and others are women-only or men-only. Most groups have at least one female leader, usually a priestess who has been trained in group leadership. Traditionally in Gardnerian groups, a priestess must be present in order for a ritual to happen. Many Wiccan and Pagan groups have both a priestess and a priest, sometimes a partnered couple. Some mixed groups and all men's groups are led by men. All women's groups typically have two or more women leading.[30]

Fox specifically describes Wicca and other forms of Paganism as "equal opportunity religion[s]." It is possible that Fox's clear statement on this may have been a cautionary act of mitigating the bias she anticipated in Ruether and Keller's volume, perhaps

ENCYCLOPEDIA OF
Women and Religion
IN NORTH AMERICA

Edited by

Rosemary Skinner Keller and
Rosemary Radford Ruether

Marie Cantlon, Associate Editor

FIGURE 9.1. Book cover *Encyclopedia of Women and Religion in North America*, vol. 1.
© *Indiana University Press*

one she was familiar with in other existing coverage. Fox, a feminist Pagan leader, acknowledges that women find something in Wicca and Paganism that they lack in other religions—"[a pathway to ministry] without the discriminating against women clergy"[31]—but she does not represent Wicca or Paganism as a religion that offers something meaningful or of merit to women only.

In this fashion, Fox's approach is much like Margot Adler's was in the well-known (1979) *Drawing Down the Moon*. At the time of Adler's writing, feminist Witches, more traditional Wiccans, and other Pagans were developing traditions alongside each other. Contrasts between the groups were fermenting but were far more fluid and flexible than they have become with age. Still, even then, Adler was able to articulate that some newer American traditions were more intentionally, or perhaps strategically, feminist—some exclusive to women and others inclusive to all genders—yet even British Traditional Witchcraft (Gardnerian and Alexandrian covens) offered the promise of equal opportunity in leadership and the inclusion of a female deity or female deities in the worldview.

Despite the fact of their inclusion of a body chapter that depicted the breadth of Wicca and Paganism, the editors, in their introduction to the encyclopedia, portray female separatist Wicca in the center of the movement and those who "believe that men and women can come together to worship the Great Mother and her son-consort" on the sidelines. Keller and Ruether first address Wicca and other Pagan religions: "Some American feminist women, however, have felt the need to break with patriarchal religions entirely and to seek a women's religion untainted by patriarchy. Many of these women have turned to some forms of neo-pagan or Wiccan religions."[32] The theology (also called thealogy) they then describe, for which they cite Carol P. Christ (herself an alternative voice in Wicca/Paganism), is also very clearly influenced by Starhawk's. The editors write, "[Wiccans/Pagans] typically see the Goddess as an immanent divine power permeating the earth or cosmos and make a strong connection between the redemption of humanity from patriarchy and the healing of the earth from ecological devastation. Some of these groups have become social activist who join with others in struggles against militarism and ecological abuse."[33] While Starhawk's ideas and eloquent writing have influenced many forms of Paganism and are therefore embedded to some degree in many contemporary Pagan traditions, Keller and Reuther's quote reads like a direct description of Reclaiming Witchcraft like no other Pagan tradition.

Throughout their discussion of Wicca and Paganism, Keller and Ruether did not discuss images of the divine masculine, beyond the "son-consort" aforementioned, which are central alongside images of the divine feminine in other forms of Wicca.[34] In sum, the volume's editors belie the more informed chapter within the encyclopedia by continuing to represent Wicca and Paganism selectively as "women's religions." Inevitably, the introduction will be more widely read than any one body chapter, meaning that Keller and Ruether's portrayal weighs heavily next to Fox's accurate representation.

REPRESENTATIONS OF WICCA/PAGANISM IN OTHER WORKS

The practice of overemphasis on radical feminist and separatist Wiccans and the omission of references to male-including Wiccan leaders is quite common in scholarship written by those trained in theology or women's studies. As a test of the bias within feminist religious scholarship, I compared the index count of references to several Pagan and Goddess Spirituality leaders across works associated with feminist studies in religion and those by scholars firmly in Pagan studies. The purpose of this experiment was to test my hypothesis that scholars oriented in feminist studies of religion have represented Wicca and Paganism as more radically feminist than have scholars oriented in Pagan studies.

My selection of Pagan and Goddess Spirituality leaders includes leaders in feminist Witchcraft/Goddess religion (Z Budapest, Carol P. Christ, Mary Daly, and Starhawk) as well as other Pagan leaders (all but one female) from traditional/eclectic Wicca and Neo-Paganism (Margot Adler, Rosemary Buckland, Janet Farrar, Selena Fox, Doreen Valiente, Morning Glory Zell, and Oberon Zell). Margot Adler, a professional NPR radio journalist and Gardnerian Wiccan high priestess, joined her professional skills with her personal interests, authoring *Drawing Down the Moon*, a comprehensive study of American Paganism during the 1970s. Rosemary Buckland, along with her husband and high priest Raymond, was among the first to teach Craft, British Traditional Wicca specifically, in North America. As discussed, Z Budapest is the founder of Dianic women's separatist Wicca, and Carol P. Christ is a feminist theologian and leader in women's Goddess spirituality. Mary Daly was a radical feminist theologian, ex-Catholic, and leader in Witchcraft-as-women's-liberation. Janet Farrar, an Alexandrian Wiccan high priestess, co-wrote, with husband Stewart, several British Traditional Wicca books. Selena Fox is a priestess and founder of Circle Sanctuary. Doreen Valiente collaborated with Gerald Gardner as a high priestess of early Gardnerian Wicca and wrote *Witchcraft for Tomorrow* and other books. Morning Glory Zell was a priestess within Church of All Worlds, a bisexual advocate for polyamory, and life partner to Oberon Zell (who himself is founder and "First Primate" of Church of All Worlds).[35]

As for the works, I selected academic books published between 1986 and 2006 whose content was either entirely or partially devoted to American Paganism. I compared the index counts across works by feminist religious scholars (Keller and Ruether's *Encyclopedia of Women and Religion in North America* and Ruether's *Goddesses and the Divine Feminine*) with those of Pagan studies works (Margot Adler's *Drawing Down the Moon*; Berger, Leach, and Shaffer's *Voices from the Pagan Census*; Chas Clifton's *Her Hidden Children*; Ronald Hutton's *Triumph of the Moon*; Sabina Magliocco's *Witching Culture*; and Sarah M. Pike's *New Age and Neopagan Religions*).[36]

I tabulated the data and then calculated the average reference count for each leader among the two scholarly groups. The two charts show patterns that differentiate feminist studies in religion scholars from contemporary Pagan studies scholars. Z Budapest is discussed frequently by scholars in both fields. Starhawk is discussed frequently by scholars in both fields, but significantly more frequently by scholars in feminist studies of religion. Margot Adler, Rosemary Buckland, Janet Farrar, Doreen Valiente, Morning Glory Zell, and Oberon Zell are discussed regularly by Pagan studies scholars and hardly ever, if at all, by Keller and Ruether. Doreen Valiente and Margot Adler stand out as particularly important in the views of Pagan studies scholars and as not very relevant in the views of feminist scholars of religion. Selena Fox is discussed fairly evenly by scholars in the two camps.

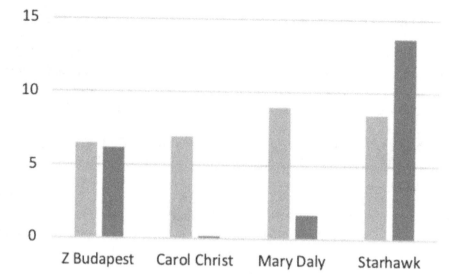

FIGURE 9.2. References to Leaders in Feminist Witchcraft/Goddess Religion

The privileging of Dianic Wiccans over other Wiccans/Pagans in scholars' representation of the Pagan movement can also be observed in the LGBTQ-Religious Archives Network (LGBTQ-RAN) projects. Directed by Mark Bowman, LGBTQ-RAN seeks to "preserv[e] history and encourag[e] scholarly study of lesbian, gay, bisexual, transgender and queer (LGBTQ) religious movements around the world."[37] The online archives consist of profiles and oral histories of LGBTQ leaders in religious history. Authors are welcome to submit profiles about themselves or other leaders in LGBTQ religious movements.

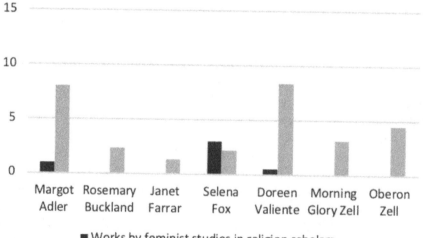

FIGURE 9.3. References to Leaders in Traditional/Eclectic Wicca and Paganism

The Pagans who have, to date, received profiles, whether submitted by themselves or others, are Z Budapest; Ruth Barrett, lesbian-feminist Dianic Wiccan priestess; Arthur Evans, a co-founder of the Minoan Tradition and leader in gay men's Witchcraft; T. Thorn Coyle, genderqueer Pagan author and ritual leader; Deryn Guest, a lesbian and eclectic Wiccan; Patricia Kevena Fili, a transgender trailblazer who began the journey of becoming a Pagan priestess upon being blocked from ordination within the Unitarian Universalist Association; Charles Redden Butler Neto, activist religious scholar, diversely trained Witch/Wiccan/Pagan, and a founding member of the Gay Men's Chorus of Washington, DC; and Jade and Falcon River, a lesbian couple who founded the Reformed Congregation of the Goddess, the "first legally recognized religious organization serving women's spirituality."[38] We might also count Mary Daly, the radical feminist theologian and feminist Witch, who was associated with radical feminism rather than with traditional Wicca. Dianics and other female separatist Pagans make up at least half of the Pagans represented in the profiles.

Pagans with LGBTQ-RAN oral histories are Ruth Barrett, Falcon River, and Jade River. When one filters the oral histories by "faith" using either "Wiccan" or "Women's Spirituality," the results are identical, which perpetuates the myth that these religious identifies are interchangeable. Absent are lesbian and bisexual priestesses who practiced Wiccan/Pagan traditions that included men, such as Morning Glory Zell and Alison Harlow.[39] Naturally, any such list (including mine) will be incomplete, and I do not fault LGBTQ-RAN or other organizations for specific cuts. However, the exclusion of non-separatist Witches from the records, consistent with the pattern inherent in feminist scholarly literature, is troubling, for it contributes to misinformation. Scholars have been particularly interested in Wiccan women's separatism and have allowed their interest to control the representation of Wicca as women's religion on important resources such as these.

THE ROLE OF "HOLY ENVY" IN THE CONSTRUCTION OF WICCA AS A WOMEN'S RELIGION

A concept from Krister Stendahl, the Harvard Divinity School dean emeritus turned (Swedish Lutheran) bishop, is central in my evaluation. It is Stendahl's concept of "holy envy." In 1985, prompted by others' prejudicial resistance to the establishment of a Mormon temple in Stockholm, Stendahl famously offered three principles for interreligious engagement. One of these was "Make room for holy envy." I argue that feminist religious scholar Rosemary Radford Ruether and others were moved by holy envy in their authorial decisions, which contributed to the image of Wicca as a women's religion. Whereas other researchers have emphasized the good virtue of Stendahl's "holy envy," I caution that too much unchecked holy envy can lead to misreading others' religious practices. My concern for holy envy in excess can be likened to Stephen Prothero's cautions around the dangers of perennialism in *God Is Not One* (2010). In the conclusion of the book, Prothero writes,

> For those who find [a religious or spiritual] path, it is tempting to lapse into the sort of naïve Godthink that lumps all other religious paths into either

opposites or mirror images of your own. The New Atheists see all religions (except their own "anti-religious religion") as the same idiocy, the same poison. The perennial philosophers see all religions as the same truth, the same compassion. What both camps fail to see is religious diversity. Rather than ten thousand gates, they see only one.[40]

Throughout her career, Ruether was committed to the path of the Christian feminist theologian. As an ecofeminist, Ruether was drawn to the work of Starhawk. In her work, *Gaia & God*, Ruether drew inspiration from earth-based religious traditions in an effort to "green" Christianity. A practicing Roman Catholic, Ruether was unwilling to part with Christianity, but she was willing to engage with feminist Wicca and to incorporate ecofeminist virtues from it into her own Christian practice.[41] After discussing Neo-Pagan feminism in *Goddesses and the Divine Feminine*, Ruether called Christians to "defend the religious liberties of Wiccans and pagans [sic], [for] Wicca is a positive movement that affirms the life values that Christians should also affirm, even if Christians might not agree with Wiccans on some aspects of their theologies or on some historical details."[42] Ruether continued by advising Christians to "also reject use of the language of [unjust Christian persecutions, which targeted poor and powerless women, men, and children,] against a contemporary religious movement that seeks to be life-affirming and to promote peaceful, harmonious relations among all peoples and the earth."[43] Ruether then suggested dialogue between Christians and Wiccans, stating, "many common values are shared by Wiccans and ecofeminists merging from Christianity and other mainstream historic religions. Is ecumenical dialogue possible between Christian ecofeminists and Wiccans? Is a new frontier of religious vision, largely shared across these religious communities today, emerging in response to the challenges of ecological crisis and militarism in modern societies and the questioning of traditional patriarchal religions?"[44]

When Ruether represented Wicca in these books, she did so while practicing inter-religious theology rather than a social-scientific analysis. She represented Wicca from her position as a Christian theologian interested in adopting teachings and practices that enhanced her own spiritual tradition. She packaged Wicca as "feminist Wicca" in order to enrich Christian feminism. Her practice was selective. She emphasized radicalism and separatism and overlooked male–female partnership, balance, and shared leadership as inherent and defining characteristics of Wicca. When she did acknowledge other forms of Wicca, she called these "male-dominated," implicitly referring to the critiques from Dianic and other radical feminist scholarly voices.[45] Empathizing with feminist Witches, Ruether writes that "It fell to Z. Budapest to synthesize the ceremonial practices of witchcraft, or Wicca, with the feminist liberation movement of the 1970s."[46] Ruether does not engage with other scholars' more moderate interpretations of Gardnerian Wicca, such as Jone Salomonsen's, which includes that:

> ... the Gardnerian Witches seemed to represent religious ideas befitting a new age: they worshipped a goddess as well as a god, ritualized on nights when the moon was full in small, autonomous and perfectly gender-balanced covens, and stripped off their clothes to dance in natural nakedness and ecstasy around the elements of nature: fire and earth. And even more peculiar, when compared

to the hegemonic position of the male priesthood in western congregations at the time: Witches not only obeyed a priest, but also a priestess. In fact, she was considered superior to him, as the "Great Goddess" was said to be to the "God," alternately her consort and son.[47]

In discussions of female superiority in Gardnerian Wicca, it is important to note that the idealization of the female is frequently male driven and does not necessarily equate to women's empowerment. Salomonsen addresses the problematics of what she refers to as the "conservative, androcentric lineage of European secret societies," a shaping heritage that other scholars have discussed as well. Still, Salomonsen was wise to note women's leadership as a significant characteristic of Gardnerian Wicca that still differentiates Wicca from most religions. Sociologists Berger, Leach, and Shaffer address the balance:

> Traditional Wicca as presented by Gardner had within it both the seeds of questioning traditional gender roles and the incorporation of an essentialist and romanticized notion of womanhood and manhood. It was in the United States that this religion became more clearly and openly feminist. Many of the people attracted to this religion were women seeking a female face to the Divine as part of their feminism. Some of these women became Dianics; others joined more traditional covens that were inclusive of men and women.[48]

I have chosen holy envy as an important hermeneutic here because Ruether clearly took personal interest in the woman-centered aspects of feminist Wicca. Ruether's personal interest in adopting the woman centeredness of feminist Wicca guided her shortsighted rendering of the greater Wiccan tradition (and of contemporary Paganism).

In addition to holy envy, *association* was a factor. Correspondence and conference announcements from American Pagan history evidence that Z Budapest, Selena Fox, Margot Adler, Starhawk, Rosemary Ruether, Ruth Barrett, and Carol Christ, among others, often attended or presented at the same events. Participation in religious feminist circles made feminist religious scholars more familiar with radical feminist Wicca than with more traditional forms of Wicca. Through association or exposure, they were familiar with feminist Witches and not with British Traditional Witches.

OUTCOMES OF THE WICCA-AS-WOMEN'S-RELIGION MYTH

My concern with feminist scholars' imposition of the women's religion construct is simple. The more we, as feminist scholars, contribute to the fiction that only women can be interested in a theological tradition that acknowledges deity in female form and ordains women, the more we ourselves limit possibilities for social progress. Furthermore, the perpetuation of the Wicca as women's religion myth comes with the risk of being a self-fulfilling prophesy, which blocks the growth of feminist religious practice among the general population. If members of the public perceive Wicca as an exclusive women's religion, both men and more moderate women who are not interested in separatism will assume that this group is not for them.

Feminist theology across denominations holds that feminist religion can change the world. Limitations on the potential growth of feminist religion, on account of misinformation, is counterintuitive for feminist religious scholarship, regardless of individual scholars' denominations. Unintended outcomes of the disproportionate emphasis on women's separatist Wicca can be even more grave: inadvertently contributing to male-dominated leadership *within* Paganism. Gwendolyn Reece discovered that contemporary Paganism, including Wicca, shares the same gender imbalance in religious leadership with other religious populations, meaning that the ratio of women to men in leadership is low, considering the ratio of women to men in membership. Reece recognizes that the imbalance might be attributed to certain branches of traditional Wicca requiring or preferring a male and female clergy team.[49] The existing discrepancy might be mitigated with more men in membership, thus bringing the ratio of male *leadership* to male *membership* more comparable to that for female leadership to female membership.

If it is agreed that Wicca, across its branches, is feminist—because of its inclusion of women in full leadership and inclusion of feminine imagery in its conceptualization of divinity—classifying Wicca as a women's religion simply on these grounds suggests that feminism is only for women and only serves women, presumptions with which I fundamentally disagree, as do many feminist Pagans. Conflating being informed by feminist praxis with serving women (exclusively or even predominantly), in my opinion, ends the conversation before it begins. If Wicca is instead recognized as a religion comprised of female and male practitioners *and* whose core values align with ecofeminism—as it is by the majority of its practitioners—Wicca could instead be highlighted, by journalists and the media, as an example of non-patriarchal religion that is appreciated and enjoyed by women and men alike. Knowledge about this example could influence other religious denominations in their own social progress. Feminist scholars' overemphasis on separatist branches, which are a minority in Paganism, has limited the feminist potential of such a religious tradition existing and thriving in the United States.

Religious scholars' "holy envy" can contribute to misinformation about religious populations. While many of us in education might agree that scholarship, in its best form, contributes to positive social change, certainly we must all agree that scholarship should communicate accurate information and contribute to well-rounded, robust knowledge. Yes, make room for holy envy. But do not allow holy envy to dominate how you interpret, evaluate, and represent religious traditions—your own or others—in scholarship.

NOTES

1. See, for example, Rosemary Skinner Keller and Rosemary Radford Ruether, "Introduction: Integrating the Worlds of Women's Religious Experience in North America," in *Encyclopedia of Women and Religion in North America*, ed. Rosemary Skinner Keller, Rosemary Radford Ruether, and Marie Cantlon, vol. 1 (Bloomington: Indiana University Press, 2006), xlvi; Judith H. Balfe, "Comment on Clarke Garrett's 'Women and Witches,'" *Signs* 4, no. 1 (1978): 202.

2. Michael O. Emerson, William A. Mirola, and Susanne C. Monahan, *Religion Matters: What Sociology Teaches Us about Religion in Our World* (New York: Routledge, 2016), 137.

3. Teemu Taira, "Religion as a Discursive Technique: The Politics of Classifying Wicca," *Journal of Contemporary Religion* 25, no. 3 (2010): 379–94.

4. I am also acutely aware of the ways in which I am guilty of very related activities to those for which I here criticize other scholars. Specifically, much of my research has been in the area of Mormon polygamy, a very small practice for contemporary, global Mormonism that is also over-represented by scholars purely because of *scholars'* interest. I therefore wrestle, on a very regular basis, with the very same problem that I challenge in this chapter.

5. Helen A. Berger and Douglas Ezzy, "Mass Media and Religious Identity: A Case Study of Young Witches," *Journal for the Scientific Study of Religion* 48, no. 3 (2009): 501–14; Julia Davies, "Wiccan Teens Online," in *Girl Culture: An Encyclopedia*, ed. Claudia A. Mitchell and Jacqueline Reid-Walsh (Westport, CT: Greenwood Press, 2007), 612; Lynn Schofield Clark, *From Angels to Aliens: Teenagers, the Media, and the Supernatural* (New York: Oxford University Press, 2003).

6. Chas S. Clifton, *Her Hidden Children: The Rise of Wicca and Paganism in America* (Lanham, MD: Rowman & Littlefield Press, 2006), 122; Kristy S. Coleman, *Re-Riting Woman: Dianic Wicca and the Feminine Divine* (Lanham, MD: Rowman & Littlefield Press, 2010), 15.

7. Helen A. Berger, Evan A. Leach, and Leigh S. Shaffer, *Voices from the Pagan Census: A National Survey of Witches and Neo-Pagans in the United States* (Columbia: University of South Carolina Press, 2003), 14.

8. Susan Starr Sered, *Priestess, Mother, Sacred Sister: Religions Dominated by Women* (New York: Oxford University Press, 1994), 12.

9. Sered, *Priestess, Mother, Sacred Sister*, 12.

10. Sered, *Priestess, Mother, Sacred Sister*, 3.

11. Sered, *Priestess, Mother, Sacred Sister*, 3.

12. Sered, *Priestess, Mother, Sacred Sister*, 12.

13. Gary J. Adler Jr. and Andrea L. Ruiz, "The Immigrant Effect: Short-Term Mission Travel as Transnational Civic Remittance," *Sociology of Religion: A Quarterly Review* 79, no. 3 (2018): 333.

14. Berger et al., *Voices from the Pagan Census*, 2.

15. Helen A. Berger, *Solitary Pagans: Contemporary Witches, Wiccans and Others Who Practice Alone* (Columbia: University of South Carolina Press, 2019), 21.

16. Berger, *Solitary Pagans*, 22.

17. Berger et al., *Voices from the Pagan Census*, 14–15.

18. Rosemary Radford Ruether, *Goddesses and the Divine Feminine: A Western Religious History* (Berkeley: University of California Press, 2005), 286–87.

19. Ruether, *Goddessses and the Divine Feminine*, 288.

20. Ruether, *Goddesses and the Divine Feminine*, 288.

21. Ruether, *Goddesses and the Divine Feminine*, 282.

22. Ruether, *Goddesses and the Divine Feminine*, 292.

23. "Covenant of the Goddess Annotated History of Policies 1975–2017," 50, www.members.cog.org, accessed March 26, 2020.

24. EarthSpirit, "Board of Directors," accessed January 15, 2020, http://www.earthspirit.com/about-was/board-of-directors.

25. "About Andras Corban Arthen," accessed January 15, 2020, https://www.parliamentofreligions.org/users/rev-andras-corban-arthen.

26. See Rosemary Skinner Keller, Rosemary Radford Ruether, and Marie Cantlon, eds. *Encyclopedia of Women and Religion in North America*, vol. 1. (Bloomington: Indiana University Press, 2006).

27. Circle Sanctuary, "History of Circle Sanctuary," accessed February 16, 2020, https://www.circlesanctuary.org/index.php/organization/history-of-circle-sanctuary.

28. Selena Fox, "Women in the Wiccan Religion and Contemporary Paganism," in *Encyclopedia of Women and Religion in North America*, ed. Rosemary Skinner Keller, Rosemary Radford Ruether, and Marie Cantlon, vol. 2 (Bloomington: Indiana University Press, 2006), 809–18.

29. Fox, "Women in the Wiccan Religion and Contemporary Paganism," 815.

30. Fox, "Women in the Wiccan Religion and Contemporary Paganism," 810.

31. Fox, "Women in the Wiccan Religion and Contemporary Paganism," 811.

32. Keller and Ruether, "Introduction," xlvi.

33. Keller and Ruether, "Introduction," xlvi.

34. Popular representations of the god in Wicca include Pan, Cernunnos, the Green Man, and Thoth. Other forms of Paganism are often ethnic reconstructionist traditions, such as Druidry or Heathenry; in these, the god-forms derive from the historic ethnic polytheistic tradition.

35. June Melby Benowitz, "Zell, Morning Glory (1948–)," in *Encyclopedia of American Women and Religion* (Santa Barbara: ABC-CLIO, 1998), 397; Oberon Zell, email to author, May 2, 2014.

36. Ronald Hutton, *The Triumph of the Moon: A History of Modern Pagan Witchcraft*, new edition (Oxford: Oxford University Press, 2001); Sabina Magliocco, *Witching Culture: Folklore and Neo-Paganism in America* (Philadelphia: University of Pennsylvania Press, 2004); Sarah M. Pike, *New Age and Neopagan Religions in America* (New York: Columbia University Press, 2004).

37. LGBTQ Religious Archives Network, "About LGBTQ-RAN," accessed March 1, 2020, https://lgbtqreligiousarchives.org/about.

38. Karen Moon, "The Reformed Congregation of the Goddess International and the Fork in the Road . . . ," May 24, 2017, https://foxrivermamas.com/2017/05/24/the-reformed-congregation-of-the-goddess-international-and-the-fork-in-the-road/.

39. Alison Harlow was a vocal feminist as well as a traditional Gardnerian Wiccan, a bisexual, and a founding member of Covenant of the Goddess. George Knowles, "Alison Harlow," Pagan Pioneers: Founders, Elders, Leaders and Others, accessed March 1, 2020, https://www.controverscial.com/Alison%20Harlow.htm; Margot Adler, *Drawing Down the Moon: Witches, Druids, Goddess-Worshippers and Other Pagans in America*, completely revised and updated (New York: Penguin Books, 1986), 226.

40. Stephen Prothero, *God Is Not One: The Eight Rival Religions That Run the World—and Why Their Differences Matter* (New York: HarperCollins, 2010), 334.

41. June Melby Benowitz, "Ruether, Rosemary Radford (1936–)," in *Encyclopedia of American Women and Religion* (Santa Barbara: ABC-CLIO, 1998), 296; Rosemary Radford Ruether, *Gaia & God: An Ecofeminist Theology of Earth Healing* (San Francisco: HarperCollins, 1994); Ruether, *Goddesses and the Divine Feminine*.

42. Ruether, *Goddesses and the Divine Feminine*, 296.

43. Ruether, *Goddesses and the Divine Feminine*, 297.

44. Ruether, *Goddesses and the Divine Feminine*, 297.

45. Ruether, *Goddesses and the Divine Feminine*, 277.

46. Ruether, *Goddesses and the Divine Feminine*, 277.

47. Jone Salomonsen, *Enchanted Feminism: Ritual, Gender and Divinity among the Reclaiming Witches of San Francisco* (New York: Routledge, 2002), 6.

48. Berger, Leach, and Shaffer, *Voices from the Pagan Census*, 14.

49. Gwendolyn Reece, "Pagan Leaders and Clergy: A Quantitative Exploration," *The Pomegranate* 19, no. 1 (2017): 32–33.

BIBLIOGRAPHY

Adler, Gary J. Jr., and Andrea L. Ruiz. "The Immigrant Effect: Short-Term Mission Travel as Transnational Civic Remittance." *Sociology of Religion: A Quarterly Review* 79, no. 3 (2018): 323–55.

Adler, Margot. *Drawing Down the Moon: Witches, Druids, Goddess-Worshippers and Other Pagans in America*. Completely revised and updated. New York: Penguin Books, 1986.

Balfe, Judith H. "Comment on Clarke Garrett's 'Women and Witches.'" *Signs* 4, no. 1 (1978): 201–2.

Benowitz, June Melby. "Ruether, Rosemary Radford (1936–)." In *Encyclopedia of American Women and Religion*, 295–97. Santa Barbara, CA: ABC-CLIO, 1998.

———. "Zell, Morning Glory (1948–)." In *Encyclopedia of American Women and Religion*, 397–98. Santa Barbara: ABC-CLIO, 1998.

Berger, Helen A. *Solitary Pagans: Contemporary Witches, Wiccans and Others Who Practice Alone*. Columbia: University of South Carolina Press, 2019.

Berger, Helen A., and Douglas Ezzy. "Mass Media and Religious Identity: A Case Study of Young Witches." *Journal for the Scientific Study of Religion* 48, no. 3 (2009): 501–14.

Berger, Helen A., Evan A. Leach, and Leigh S. Shaffer. *Voices from the Pagan Census: A National Survey of Witches and Neo-Pagans in the United States*. Columbia: University of South Carolina Press, 2003.

Clark, Lynn Schofield. *From Angels to Aliens: Teenagers, the Media, and the Supernatural*. New York: Oxford University Press, 2003.

Clifton, Chas S. *Her Hidden Children: The Rise of Wicca and Paganism in America*. Lanham, MD: Rowman & Littlefield Press, 2006.

Coleman, Kristy S. *Re-Riting Woman: Dianic Wicca and the Feminine Divine*. Lanham, MD: Rowman & Littlefield Press, 2010.

Davies, Julia. "Wiccan Teens Online." In *Girl Culture: An Encyclopedia*, edited by Claudia A. Mitchell and Jacqueline Reid-Walsh, 2:611–14. Westport, CT: Greenwood Press, 2007.

Emerson, Michael O., William A. Mirola, and Susanne C. Monahan. *Religion Matters: What Sociology Teaches Us about Religion in Our World*. New York: Routledge, 2016.

Fox, Selena. "Women in the Wiccan Religion and Contemporary Paganism." In *Encyclopedia of Women and Religion in North America*, edited by Rosemary Skinner Keller, Rosemary Radford Ruether, and Marie Cantlon, Vol. 2: 809–18. Bloomington: Indiana University Press, 2006.

Hutton, Ronald. *The Triumph of the Moon: A History of Modern Pagan Witchcraft*. New edition. Oxford: Oxford University Press, 2001.

Keller, Rosemary Skinner, and Rosemary Radford Ruether. "Introduction: Integrating the Worlds of Women's Religious Experience in North America." In *Encyclopedia of Women and Religion in North America*, edited by Rosemary Skinner Keller, Rosemary Radford Ruether, and Marie Cantlon, Vol. 1. Bloomington: Indiana University Press, 2006.

Magliocco, Sabina. *Witching Culture: Folklore and Neo-Paganism in America*. Philadelphia: University of Pennsylvania Press, 2004.

Pike, Sarah M. *New Age and Neopagan Religions in America*. New York: Columbia University Press, 2004.

Prothero, Stephen. *God Is Not One: The Eight Rival Religions That Run the World—and Why Their Differences Matter*. New York: HarperCollins, 2010.

Reece, Gwendolyn. "Pagan Leaders and Clergy: A Quantitative Exploration." *The Pomegranate* 19, no. 1 (2017): 25–46.

Ruether, Rosemary Radford. *Gaia & God: An Ecofeminist Theology of Earth Healing*. San Francisco: HarperCollins, 1994.

———. *Goddesses and the Divine Feminine: A Western Religious History*. Berkeley: University of California Press, 2005.

Salomonsen, Jone. *Enchanted Feminism: Ritual, Gender and Divinity Among the Reclaiming Witches of San Francisco*. New York: Routledge, 2002.

Sered, Susan Starr. *Priestess, Mother, Sacred Sister: Religions Dominated by Women*. New York: Oxford University Press, 1994.

Taira, Teemu. "Religion as a Discursive Technique: The Politics of Classifying Wicca." *Journal of Contemporary Religion* 25, no. 3 (2010): 379–94.

CHAPTER 10

For All Sentient Beings

....

The Question of Gender in Tibetan and Himalayan Buddhist Communities

Amy Holmes-Tagchungdarpa, Occidental College

ABSTRACT

Buddhist traditions are varied and diverse in their practice in communities throughout Asia, as is the position of women within them. While some communities emphasize the inferiority of the female body as a vehicle for reaching the end goal of enlightenment, others emphasize the inherent emptiness of the self and, therefore, the irrelevance of gender. This chapter will draw on work by Buddhist philosophers, historians, activists, and practitioners from Tibet and the Himalayas to explore how local Buddhist female-identified practitioners conceptualize gender in relation to Buddhist practice within and beyond monasteries. Engaging with the work and practice of varied communities reveals that, just as there is no one Buddhism, there is no one Buddhist feminism. In fact, many women in Tibetan and Himalayan Buddhist communities reject the label of feminist, positioning their goals on behalf of all sentient beings as being despite, or beyond, gendered expectations. This chapter will take into account multiple voices and perspectives in its exploration of the question of gender in Buddhism.

INTRODUCTION

Every Sunday, the Singyang Mani Lhakhang (Bhutia: *Zin g.yang ma ni lha khang*),[1] near the tourist town of Pelling in the eastern Himalayan Indian state of Sikkim, resounds with the sound of drums, bells, and chanting.

The rhythm is distinctive: it is the practice of Chöd (Tibetan: *gcod*), a famous contemplative tradition that is traced back to Machik Labdron (*Ma gcig lab sgron*, 1055–1149), an eleventh-century Tibetan woman. In this tradition, the practitioner visualizes herself offering parts of her body to hungry demons as an ultimate practice of detachment and compassion. It is now popular throughout areas of Asia where Vajrayāna Buddhism was practiced, including in Mongolia; Nepal; Bhutan; Tibetan cultural areas in China; and the Indian Himalayan states of Arunachal Pradesh, Sikkim, Himachal Pradesh, and Ladakh.[2] It is practiced in retreat centers and monasteries by monastic and Tantric practitioners in curriculums intended to transform the practitioner into a Buddha and realize emptiness. Despite its very Tantric visualizations, which involve imagining the carving up and offering of the body, the group at Singyang Mani Lhakhang are enthusiastic participants, practicing their chant and drum rhythm when they return home throughout the week and guiding each other in memorizing the texts.

Recent scholarship has noted a broader trend, one that is resonant with the Sunday practice sessions in Singyang: that in the last couple of decades, this practice has been enthusiastically taken up by women outside of monasteries.[3] The Singyang Mani Lhakhang practice group is made up of over twenty laywomen and less than a dozen men. However, the teacher of the practice is a male lama (*bla ma*), connected to the local Buddhist monastery, Pemayangtse (*Pad ma yang rtse*). This gendered student–teacher hierarchy may seem typical in Sikkim, where large non-celibate monasteries dominate the Buddhist religious landscape, and typical of Buddhism in the Himalayas, where women cannot be fully ordained. However, it is not typical: the Mani Lhakhang that hosts these weekly gatherings is home to a number of practice groups that are dominated by women, who teach and guide each other, give patronage to religious events, and read Buddhist texts and do ritual practice without the presence of male teachers.

The presence of such highly organized laywomen's practice groups is not specific to Sikkim and adds an additional dimension to how we understand gendered authority in Buddhist traditions. Women hold an ambivalent status in classical Buddhist texts as distractions and temptresses of male monastics.[4] The Buddha famously turned down requests for women to be ordained as part of his sangha,[5] his monastic community, three times before he agreed. Therefore, Buddhism is at times portrayed as sexist on an institutional level, even if the ultimate teachings state that enlightenment is beyond gender. These ultimate teachings have often been lauded by feminists and taken up as exemplary of how religions can promote gender equality and feminist goals.[6]

However, the contemporary institutional status of women in monastic Buddhism is considerably more complex. There is a strong transnational movement for women to be able to be fully ordained in countries where the lineages of full ordination have died out and critique that anything less is anti-feminist.[7] In response, scholars have noted that this movement often does not represent the desires of all Buddhist female monastics and has been considered imperialist, as many monastics focus on the well-being of "all sentient beings," *including, but not limited to*, women.[8] In surveying the field of scholarship recently, Amy Paris Langenberg observed an "elaborate textile of feminist discourse alongside an equally rich fabric of contemporary female monasticisms" in her exploration of two female monastic communities in Malaysia and Nepal. In her study, she found many female monastics reject the label of feminism but continue to "lead agentive, creative, and sometimes rebellious female lives," thereby resisting and also contributing "a new motif or fiber to the feminist weave."[9]

In this chapter, I will add to this elaborate textile noted by Langenberg by providing an overview of the diverse forms of practice that practitioners who identity as women from Vajrayāna communities in the Himalayas and on the Tibetan plateau participate in. In doing so, I intend to highlight women's agency in contemporary Buddhist communities and complicate assertions about androcentrism in Buddhism.

WOMEN IN BUDDHIST TRADITIONS

Why is this highlighting of women's agency necessary? Because, historically, Buddhism has been perceived as an androcentric religion that has contributed to the development of patriarchal authority in the sangha, the monastic community, and other forms of Buddhist institutions. This perception is based on the analysis of the central texts of Buddhism: the Pāli canon of Theravāda Buddhism and the Sanskrit Sūtras of Mahāyāna Buddhism and the translations of these sets of text into multiple classical and vernacular Asian languages that have taken place over the past 2,500 years. It is also based on important events from the Buddha's life, which are often taken as a centerpoint for understanding his dharma, or teachings. When he initially began his monastic community in ancient India, he turned down requests for women to join the sangha until he received three requests, and, when he did deign to admit women, he did so adding additional rules to the vinaya, the monastic commitments that the sangha aimed to uphold.[10]

Other literature in ancient Buddhist texts of the Theravāda tradition openly disparage women, seeing them as temptresses that distract male ascetics on the path. Even after this, in the Mahāyāna tradition, some Sūtras state that a woman cannot become a Buddha in a female body. To become a Buddha, "she has two options: (a) she can either be reborn with a physically male body and then born again into the body of a Buddha; (b) if she is far enough advanced along the bodhisattva path, she can self-elect to spontaneously change her sex in a show of her own magical prowess and then straightaway advance to Buddhahood."[11] Later texts in the Theravāda and Mahāyāna traditions continued to represent women as bags of pus and bile.[12] When the Vajrayāna tradition developed, some scholars argued that it represented a change in representation, as women were seen as yoginis, inherently enlightened and through sexual practices capable of initiating men into enlightenment.[13]

However, the above characterizations are complicated by attention to their respective historical contexts and the spread of Buddhism throughout Asia and around the world, where it has adapted to many new cultural and temporal concerns. Just as these texts can be read as androcentric or, in the case of Vajrayāna, gynocentric, they can also be read as the opposite. Other texts from the early Theravāda tradition, such as the collection of songs by early female monastics, known as the *Therīgāthā*, is full of examples of women extolling how the Buddhist sangha and dharma had liberated them from their restrictive social roles.[14] Similarly, the Mahāyāna concept of emptiness states that all concepts are ultimately beyond concept, *including* gender, which renders it an irrelevant consideration.[15]

Further complicating these claims is that fact that, since Europeans and Americans began studying Buddhism, they have also (in true Orientalist fashion) seen in Buddhism what they desired in their own societies. Liz Wilson has discussed how European and American writing on Buddhism and gender has reflected the waves of feminist scholarship and activism found in Europe and America. In the early twentieth century, the historical Buddha was represented as a social reformer, which coincided neatly with campaigns for women's suffrage.[16] Second-wave feminists of the 1960s and 1970s brought their concerns about "the range of social practices that bear on women's ability to exercise agency and self-fulfillment" to their Buddhist centers.[17] Rita Gross was an influential feminist scholar from this generation. Her classic book, *Buddhism after Patriarchy*, provided a critical discussion of Buddhist history and concepts from a feminist perspective that was intended to contribute to a "reconstruction" of Buddhism in a "post-patriarchal future."[18]

More recent scholarship, in line with third-wave feminism and new developments in gender studies (such as queer theory and masculinity studies), has critiqued the emphasis in these waves of scholarship on Euro-American, and particularly white non-heritage[19] Buddhist, concerns. As Wilson points out, these earlier waves of scholarship marginalized the voices of Asian women practitioners and the significance of devotional practice and flattened gender identities into simplistic binaries.[20] A number of scholars have incorporated insights from postcolonial feminist and gender theory into their studies of Buddhist communities. For example, there has been extensive scholarship dedicated to adding complexity to readings of historical Buddhist communities. There have also been critical scholarly discussions over the appropriateness of using feminism as a blanket concept for addressing issues of gender inequality in contemporary communities, especially since many Buddhist women do not consider themselves feminists but instead discuss their motivation in pursuing Buddhist soteriological aims through practice as concern for all sentient beings.[21]

AUTHORITY AND AMBIVALENCE: THE ORDINATION QUESTION

An area of scholarship where the different waves of feminist scholarship may be seen vividly is the debate about full ordination for women in Theravāda and Tibetan and Himalayan Buddhist societies. Full ordination lineages are considered to have historically died out in these cultures, and since the nineteenth century there have been movements to revive them.[22] The transnational impetus around their revival has become a centerpoint of the Sakyadhita, a Buddhist women's organization, which was founded in Bodh Gaya in 1987 by a number of heritage and non-heritage Buddhist women from different Buddhist traditions.[23]

Sakyadhita and other transnational initiatives aimed at reinstating full ordination for Tibetan and Himalayan nuns have been the center of controversy. Amy Paris Langenberg has discussed how feminism in such initiatives is far from univocal due to the complexity and diversity of perspectives and experiences present.[24] In her in-depth research into female ordination debates, Michelle Hannah has argued that these debates "are grounded in attempts to negotiate the complex intersections of Buddhism, global-ization, modernity, culture, religio-cultural identity politics, and gender (imaginaires). And so, the controversy about *gelongma* ordination resists simple explanation."[25]

While the debate over ordination remains an important and relevant discussion, the idea that ordination represents the only opportunity for women to exercise agency and gain equality in Buddhist societies ignores the contributions of the many women who have done so, and continue to, in contemporary communities. In this chapter, I intend to broaden the optics of discussions around gendered opportunities and include alternative perspectives by looking at Tibetan and Himalayan case studies where women have sought out the ultimate goals of Buddhism through various insti-tutional and noninstitutional pathways.

FREEDOM WITHIN MONASTIC INSTITUTIONS

Traditional practices and the institutions that transmit them continue to hold mean-ing and significance for women. However, they are by no means unchanging. There is flexibility within traditions and institutions. In March 2017, the Seventeen Gyalwang Karmapa (*Rgyal dbang kar ma pa o rgyan 'phrin las rdo rje*, b. 1985), spiritual leader of the Karma Kagyu tradition of Tibetan and Himalayan Buddhism, presided over the full ordination of nineteen nuns from his lineage.[26] In 2012, nuns from Tibetan and Hima-layan traditions began to be awarded with Geshema (*dge bshes ma*) degrees, equivalent to PhDs in Buddhist philosophy.[27]

Throughout the world, there are myriads of institutions where women carry out rit-uals, prayers, retreats, and other forms of service and new opportunities and positions for women continue to develop. In many of these institutions, female monastics are not provided with the same economic support as male monastics.[28] However, they still con-tinue in their practice and find it provides them with opportunities and fulfillment. Two well-known institutions in contemporary Tibetan cultural areas of China are Larung Gar (*Bla rung sgar*) and Yachen Gar (*Ya chen sgar*). Both of these institutions are located in remote parts of Kham (now Sichuan Province) and are home to large female monas-tic communities. Both Larung and Yachen have female teachers, known as khenmos (*mkhan mo*). Historian and ethnographer Padma'tsho has stated that in 2009 at Yachen there were thirty khenmos responsible for instructing female monastics in different forms of practice, including preliminary practices and rituals, but that "they have not yet received permission to give other Dharma teachings or explain the sutras on their own."[29] In 2019, Yasmin Cho, who has also conducted in-depth ethnographic research at Yachen, stated that there are over 10,000 female monastics who have migrated there since the 1980s.[30] Both Cho and Padma'tsho have noted the hard physical labor female monastics undertake as part of their practice at Yachen, including building their own living quarters.[31] Although, due to political interference, the size of the community changes over time, it is known for the dedication of its practitioners, who persevere in difficult physical circumstances.

In Nepal and India, the head of the Drukpa Kagyu tradition, Gyalwang Jikme Pema Wangchen (*Rgyal dbang 'jigs med pad ma dbang chen*, b. 1963), has instituted martial arts training in nunneries in his tradition. Several hundred nuns from Drukpa Kagyu institutions have been following Shaolin-style martial arts training for over a decade.[32] The Gyalwang Drukpa states that his motivation is to "take care of women and of nuns. . . . In our culture, no matter what they do, they are always second to men. I am fighting this attitude."[33] His support of female monastics has led him to include vocational training in plumbing and mechanics at his nunneries, but he is careful not to say he is dedicated to female empowerment since "that actually means I have the power to empower them. . . . I'm just removing obstacles, so they can come up with their own power."[34] Jigme Wangchuk, one of the female monastics training in martial arts, explained that Gyalwang Drukpa "thinks that we can be as successful as men. If we do our utmost, everything is possible."[35] She and her colleagues emphasize the feeling of strength and focus that come from their training. Even more directly, in another article, another female monastic, Jigme Palmo, stated, "We're not saying we hate men. But they've been above us for too long, and it's time we're all treated as equal."[36]

FREEDOM BEYOND MONASTIC INSTITUTIONS

Female practitioners also find meaning in alternative institutions beyond monasteries. A recent special issue of the journal *Revue d'Etudes Tibétaines* focused on diverse forms of female religious practitioners throughout Buddhist areas in Bhutan, Tibet, Nepal, India, and Mongolia. The editors Mona Schrempf and Nicole Schneider note in their editorial that, despite diversity, there are some shared themes among the women in these studies, including that they all bring about social change through their own agency and innovative means, that they eschew social expectations through different types of legitimation (including education, religious lineage, and supernatural recognition), and that there is fluidity between different types of roles.[37]

Another series of spaces for women's practice that share these characteristics that have not received much scholarly attention are Mani Lhakhangs in Sikkim in the eastern Himalayas.[38] Between 2006 and 2020, I have visited, supported, and participated in practice in these unique institutions in northeast India, specifically in the states of Sikkim and in Darjeeling and Kalimpong in northern West Bengal. These institutions derive their name—Mani—from the popular Vajrayāna Buddhist mantra "Om Mani Padme Hung" (*Om ma Ni padme hung*), and Lhakhang refers to a temple. These institutions are associated with the Mani mantra, as they were initially established as sites for a specific time of practice known as nyungne (*smyung gnas*). Nyungne is a fasting and prayer practice associated with the Bodhisattva of Compassion Avalokitesvara (*Spyan ras zigs*). Like Chöd, Nyungne was a practice developed by a historical female practitioner, Gelongma Palmo (*Dge slong ma dpal mo*, dates unknown).[39] Dedicated to the cultivation of compassion, Nyungne involves prayer, visualization, silence, intermittent fasting on every second day, and prostrations as part of a series of intensive contemplative techniques. Prayers include the mantra of Avalokitesvara and are accumulated on mala, or rosaries with 108 beads. Practitioners will also turn small handheld and larger prayer wheels, containing rolled-up repeated sets of mani mantra. Turning these wheels, along with intensive prayer, is intended to generate as many mantras as possible, which are dedicated to the well-being of all sentient beings. Nyungne practitioners are taught these practices by lamas, who give them vows and then transmit explanations of the prayers and practices word by word.[40]

Attending the Nyungne was a significant time commitment. For this reason, mostly older folk attended and, in particular, women.[41] These women became popularly known as *Mani Amlas* (Mani Mother) or *Nyungne Amlas* (Nyungne Amla). When I talked to women about why there was such an obvious age and gender trend at Nyungne retreats, they often responded that older women past menopause had grown children and therefore the time and energy to commit to Nyungne without distraction. Several women noted existential concerns that came with aging and anxiety over mortality. Participating in Nyungne was part of a preparation for clearing karmic obstacles and thereby having a peaceful death without regret.[42] Nyungne was also a long-term commitment; after taking vows, Nyungne practitioners are expected to adhere to specific dietary restrictions. These include avoiding freshly slaughtered meat and not consuming garlic, onion, meat, and eggs on important rituals days of the month.

While there is a long history of Nyungne practice in the region, in the 1990s, Mani Lhakhang began to be built or renovated in localities throughout the eastern Himalayas under the patronage of Tibetan lamas. In Sikkim, there were historically a number of Mani Lhakhangs. Hissey Wongchuk Bhutia has published on the history of one of these older Mani Lhakhang in Chumpong, west Sikkim, and its contemporary rituals. He describes how:

> Three times a month, the eldest women of the village of Nako, Chumpong and Arithang gather in the temple with its head-lama. On the eight and thirtieth day of each month, they make feast offerings (tshogs) and butter lamp offerings (mchod me) with goods brought from their own homes. They also bring rice, milk, butter, cheese, vegetables, biscuits, etc. for the single meal they take during these days.[43]

Bhutia discusses how the Mani Lhakhang also carries out annual rites, such as Drugpa Tsezhi (*Drug pa tshes bzhi*), the sacred text circumambulation ('*bum skor*), and the propitiation of the local land guardians (*gnas gsol*).[44]

The early 2000s led to a boom in the establishment of many new Mani Lhakhangs sponsored by local committees made up of Nyungne Amlas and their families, who coordinate fundraising, inviting teachers and preparing appropriate places for Nyungne to take place. According to the Ecclesiastical Department website, as of 2020 there are 163 recognized Mani Lhakhangs in the state.[45] These new Mani Lhakhangs have been established for a number of reasons. First, lamas and patrons have established them in smaller villages as a meritorious activity. Holding Nyungne in many villages makes it easier for local people from different socioeconomic classes to participate. In earlier times, when Nyungne were organized by Tibetan lamas and would take place in Siliguri and other towns in North Bengal, only wealthy families could afford to sponsor their mothers and grandmothers. Second, the appearance of multiple Mani Lhakhangs is a reflection of growing prosperity in Sikkim. The growing middle class in the state has the disposable income to sponsor these institutions and doing so brings social, as well as spiritual, capital. Singyang Mani Lhakhang is one of these newer Mani Lhakhang and was established in the 2010s.

Importantly, while male lamas do participate as leaders of Nyungne retreats, there are many other forms of informal teaching and guidance that take place at Mani Lhakhang between women. Women help each other with every step of their increasing familiarity with Nyungne preparation. I have seen groups of women correcting each other's posture, discussing how to hold and count their prayer beads, advising one another on the way they spin their mani while counting prayer beads, and talking in general about the benefits of reciting mani. This informal mentorship is more extensive than the teachings they receive from the lamas who lead the Nyungne retreats. And even during the retreats, community and collegiality is essential to survival. Tenzin Wangmo, a teacher in her early fifties, commented to me that the hardest part of Nyungne is "the fasting. It is so hard, sometimes your stomach is so painful, and we all get gas!" At that time, she says that encouragement (and surreptitious antacids!) from others is crucial to persevere and complete the retreat period.[46]

Why are women the predominant attendees and organizers of these events? The reasons for this are complex. One is institutional. In this part of Sikkim, men have many other Buddhist practice opportunities, as the local monasteries are administered and presided over by non-celibate male Tantric practitioners. Another is the gendered associations of Nyungne practice. As with devotion to Guanyin in China,[47] practices associated with compassion are gendered, and women are assumed to have higher amounts of innate compassion due to the constructed assumption of their "natural" motherly instincts. Women themselves do not explain it this way, though. They consider Nyungne as a soteriological opportunity and a space for female companionship and support. *Feminism* is not a term used by Nyungne Amlas in Sikkim. However, their leadership of Mani Lhakhang organizations and ritual expertise lead Mani Lhakhang to function as spaces of women's agency and opportunity. The rituals and texts of the practices of Avalokitesvara are not gender specific but act as opportunities for women to pursue spiritual freedom without social limitations.

CONCLUSION

This chapter has explored women's agency from varied perspectives within Buddhist communities on the Tibetan plateau and in the Himalayas. Engaging with the work and practice of varied communities reveals that, just as there is no one Buddhism, there is no one Buddhist feminism. In fact, many women in Tibetan and Himalayan Buddhist communities reject the label of *feminist*, positioning their goals on behalf of all sentient beings as being despite, or beyond, gendered expectations. Ultimately, within monasteries and beyond, in Mani Lhakhang and other lay practice communities, Buddhist practice continues to provide agency and fulfillment to women, despite its androcentric and patriarchal historical contexts, and allows women to not only imagine but actualize enlightenment.

NOTES

1. In this chapter, Tibetan, Bhutia, and other Himalayan language words will be transliterated according to local pronunciations and full transliteration according to the Wylie system for Tibetan spelling included after the first appearance of a term. This is a reflection of the fact that the areas under discussion share the classical language of Tibetan and use classical Tibetan script.

2. For more on Machik Labdron, see Michelle Sorensen, "Machik Labdron," *Treasury of Lives*, https://treasuryoflives.org/biographies/view/Machik-Labdron/TBRC_P3312. Accessed April 20, 2020. For more on the regional and international popularity on this practice, see Amelia Hall, "Revelations of a Modern Mystic: The Life and Legacy of Kun Bzang Bde Chen Gling Pa, 1928–2006," PhD diss., Oxford University, 2012.

3. On this phenomenon in Bhutan, see Francoise Pommaret, "Empowering Religious Women Practitioners in Contemporary Bhutan," *Revue d'Etudes Tibétaines* 34 (December 2015), 124–29.

4. Alan Sponberg, "Attitudes toward Women and the Feminine in Early Buddhism," *Buddhism, Sexuality and Gender*, ed. Jose Cabezon (Albany: State University of New York Press, 1992), 3–36; and Joze Cabezon, *Sexuality in Classical South Asian Buddhism* (Somerville, MA: Wisdom Publications, 2017).

5. In this chapter, widely known Pāli and Sanskrit Buddhist terms will appear in their most well-known spelling, without diacritics.

6. Rita Gross, *Buddhism beyond Gender* (Boulder: Shambhala, 2018).

7. These debates are covered in Liz Wilson, "Buddhism and Gender," *Buddhism in the Modern World*, ed. David McMahan (London and New York: Routledge, 2012), 257–72; and Thea Mohr and Jampa Tsedroen, eds., *Dignity and Discipline* (Somerville, MA: Wisdom, 2010).

8. Michelle Hannah, "Transmigratory Buddhism and Travelling Feminisms: Globalisation and Cross-Cultural Difference," *TAJA: The Australian Journal of Anthropology* 21, no. 3 (2010): 332–49, and "Colliding Gender Imaginaries: Transnational Debates about Full Ordination for Tibetan Buddhist Nuns," *Asian Journal of Women's Studies* 18, no. 4 (2012): 7–44; Emma Tomalin, "Buddhist Feminist Transnational Networks, Female Ordination and Women's Empowerment," *Global Development Studies* 37, no. 2 (2009): 81–100.

9. Amy Paris Langenberg, "An Imperfect Alliance: Feminism and Contemporary Female Buddhist Monasticisms," *Religion* 9, no. 6 (2018): 3. https://www.mdpi.com/2077-1444/9/6/190.

10. Chiung Hwang Chen, "Feminist Debate in Taiwan's Buddhism: The Issue of the Eight Garudhammas," *Journal of Feminist Scholarship* 1, no. 1 (Fall 2011): 16–32.

11. Stephanie Balkwill, "Why Does a Woman Need to Become a Man in Order to Become a Buddha: Past Investigations, New Leads," *Religion Compass* 12, no. 8 (2018).

12. Liz Wilson, *Charming Cadavers* (Chicago: University of Chicago Press, 1995).

13. Miranda Shaw, *Passionate Enlightenment* (Princeton, NJ: Princeton University Press, 1994).

14. Charles Hallisey, trans. *Therīgāthā: Poems of the First Buddhist Women* (Cambridge, MA: Harvard University Press, 2015).

15. Ogoshi Aiko, "Women and Sexism in Japanese Buddhism," *Japan Christian Review* 59 (1993): 19–25.

16. Wilson, "Buddhism and Gender," 258–59.

17. Wilson, "Buddhism and Gender," 260.

18. Rita Gross, *Buddhism after Patriarchy* (Albany: State University of New York Press, 1992), 4.

19. Jessica Falcone puts forth a convincing argument for a spectrum of Buddhist practice from "heritage" to "nonheritage" Buddhist practitioners. Heritage Buddhists are defined as having been "actively enculturated" into Buddhism by "at least one side of the family who raised them—a family whose connection to the traditions extends back at least a few generations." Jessica Marie Falcone, *Battling the Buddha of Love* (Ithaca, NY: Cornell University Press, 2018), 30.

20. Wilson, "Buddhism and Gender," 261–62.

21. Amy Paris Langenberg provides a great overview in her article, "An Imperfect Alliance: Feminism and Contemporary Female Buddhist Monasticisms," *Religions* 9, no. 6 (2018): 190, https://doi.org/10.3390/rel9060190.

22. For a discussion of the beginning of these movements in Sri Lanka, see Tessa Bartholomeusz, *Women under the Bo Tree: Buddhist Nuns in Sri Lanka* (Cambridge: Cambridge University Press, 1994).

23. Mavis L. Fenn and Kay Koppedrayer, "Sakyadhita: A Transnational Gathering Place for Buddhist Women," *Journal of Global Buddhism* 9 (2008): 47.

24. Langenberg, "An Imperfect Alliance," 3.

25. Hannah, "Colliding Gender Imaginaries," 11.

26. "History in the Making: The First Step toward Full Ordination for Tibetan Buddhist Nuns," *The Karmapa*, https://kagyuoffice.org/history-in-the-making-the-first-step-toward-full-ordination-for-tibetan-buddhist-nuns/. Accessed April 20, 2020.

27. Tibetan Nuns Project, "Geshema Degree," https://tnp.org/geshema-degree/. Accessed April 20, 2020.

28. Kim Gutschow, *Being a Buddhist Nun* (Cambridge, MA: Harvard University Press, 2004).

29. Padma'tsho, "Courage as Eminence: Tibetan Nuns at Yarchen Monastery in Kham," in *Eminent Buddhist Women*, ed. Karma Lekshe Tsomo (Albany: State University of New York Press, 2014), 188.

30. Yasmin Cho, "Yachen as Process: Encampments, Nuns, and Spatial Politics," *Frontier Tibet*, ed. Stéphane Gros (Amsterdam: Amsterdam University Press, 2019), 494.

31. Padma'tsho, "Courage as Eminence," and Cho, "Yachen as Process."

32. Dominique Butet, "The Druk Amitabha Kung Fu Nuns: Combining Martial Arts and Meditation," *Buddhist Door*, November, 14, 2014, https://www.buddhistdoor.net/features/the-druk-amitabha-kung-fu-nuns-combining-martial-arts-and-meditation.

33. Butet, "The Druk Amitabha Kung Fu Nuns."

34. Alisha Hardidasani Gupta, "Meet the Kung Fu Nuns of Nepal," *New York Times*, November 8, 2019, https://www.nytimes.com/2019/11/08/us/meet-the-kung-fu-nuns-of-nepal.html.

35. Butet, "The Druk Amitabha Kung Fu Nuns."

36. Nandita Singh, "The Kung Fu Nuns Think It's Time to Kick Gender Inequality in India to the Kerb," *The Print*, October 20, 2019, https://theprint.in/india/kung-fu-nuns-think-gender-inequality-india-to-kerb/307655/.

37. Mona Schrempf and Nicole Schneider, "Editorial: Female Specialists between Autonomy and Ambivalence," *Revue d'Etudes Tibétaines* 34 (December 2015), i–viii.

38. Three studies that are available regarding Mani Lhakhangs in the eastern Himalayas are Tanya Zivkovic, "Embodying the Past: Gelongma Palmo and Tibetan Nyungne Rituals," *Journal of Ritual Studies* 27, no. 2 (2013): 45–63; Amy Holmes-Tagchungdarpa, "The Legacy of a Female Sikkimese Buddhist Teacher: The Lineage of Pelling An Wangdzin and Gendered Religious Experience in Modern Sikkim," in *Eminent Buddhist Women*, ed. Karma Lekshe Tsomo (Albany: State University of New York Press), 159–68; and Hissey Wongchuk Bhutia, "The Precious Ocean of Amazing Faith: The History and Practices of Chumpong *Mani Lhakhang* (Temple)," *Bulletin of Tibetology* 47, no. 1–2 (2011): 69–76.

39. For more on this practice, see Ivette M. Vargas-O'Brian, "The Life of Dge slong ma dPal mo: The Experience of a Leper, Founder of a Fasting Ritual, a Transmitter of Buddhist Teachings on Suffering and Renunciation in Tibetan Religious History," *Journal of International Association of Buddhist Studies* 24, no. 2 (2001): 157–86.

40. In their studies of Nyungne rituals, Zivkovic and Vargas-O'Brian have also noted these patterns of activity. Zivkovic, "Embodying the Past," and Vargas-O'Brian, "The Life of Dge slong ma dPal mo."

41. This was also noted by Zivkovic and Vargas-O'Brian in their studies of Nyungne in Darjeeling and Nepal, respectively. Zivkovic, "Embodying the Past," and Vargas-O'Brian, "The Life of Dge slong ma dPal mo."

42. Interviews with participants of Nyungne at Gyalshing, Sindrang, Singyang, and Chombong Mani Lhakhangs between 2006 to 2020.

43. Bhutia, "The Precious Ocean of Amazing Faith," 73.

44. Bhutia, "The Precious Ocean of Amazing Faith."

45. The Ecclesiastical Department, Government of Sikkim, http://www.sikkimeccl.gov.in/. Accessed April 20, 2020.

46. Interview with Nyungne participant at Gyalshing Mani Lhakhang, 2019.

47. Yuhang Li, *Becoming Guanyin: Artistic Devotion of Buddhist Women in Late Imperial China* (New York: Columbia University Press, 2020).

BIBLIOGRAPHY

Aiko, Ogoshi. "Women and Sexism in Japanese Buddhism." *Japan Christian Review* 59 (1993): 19–25.

Balkwill, Stephanie. "Why Does a Woman Need to Become a Man in Order to Become a Buddha: Past Investigations, New Leads." *Religion Compass* 12, no. 8 (2018).

Bartholomeusz, Tessa. *Women under the Bo Tree: Buddhist Nuns in Sri Lanka.* Cambridge: Cambridge University Press, 1994.

Bhutia, Hissey Wongchuk. "The Precious Ocean of Amazing Faith: The History and Practices of Chumpong *Mani Lhakhang* (Temple)." *Bulletin of Tibetology* 47, no. 1–2 (2011): 69–76.

Butet, Dominique. "The Druk Amitabha Kung Fu Nuns: Combining Martial Arts and Meditation." *Buddhist Door.* November 14, 2014. https://www.buddhistdoor.net/features/the-druk-amitabha-kung-fu-nuns-combining-martial-arts-and-meditation.

Cabezón, José Ignacio. *Sexuality in Classical South Asian Buddhism.* Somerville, MA: Wisdom Publications, 2017.

Chen, Chiung Hwang. "Feminist Debate in Taiwan's Buddhism: The Issue of the Eight Garudhammas." *Journal of Feminist Scholarship* 1, no. 1 (Fall 2011): 16–32.

Cho, Yasmin. "Yachen as Process: Encampments, Nuns, and Spatial Politics." In *Frontier Tibet*, edited by Stéphane Gros, 489–516. Amsterdam: Amsterdam University Press, 2019.

Ecclesiastical Department, Government of Sikkim. http://www.sikkimeccl.gov.in/. Accessed April 20, 2020.

Faure, Bernard. *The Power of Denial: Buddhism, Purity and Gender.* Princeton, NJ: Princeton University Press, 2003.

Fenn, Mavis L., and Kay Koppedrayer. "Sakyadhita: A Transnational Gathering Place for Buddhist Women." *Journal of Global Buddhism* (2008): 45–79.

Gross, Rita. *Buddhism after Patriarchy.* Albany: State University of New York Press, 1992.

———. *Buddhism beyond Gender.* Boulder, CO: Shambhala, 2018.

Gupta, Alisha Hardidasani. "Meet the Kung Fu Nuns of Nepal." *New York Times*, November 8, 2019. https://www.nytimes.com/2019/11/08/us/meet-the-kung-fu-nuns-of-nepal.html.

Falcone, Jessica Marie. *Battling the Buddha of Love.* Ithaca, NY: Cornell University Press, 2018.

Gutschow, Kim. *Being a Buddhist Nun: The Struggle for Enlightenment in the Himalayas.* Cambridge, MA: Harvard University Press, 2004.

Hall, Amelia. "Revelations of a Modern Mystic: The Life and Legacy of Kun Bzang Bde Chen Gling Pa, 1928–2006." PhD diss., Oxford University, 2012.

Hallisey, Charles, trans. *Therīgāthā: Poems of the First Buddhist Women.* Cambridge, MA: Harvard University Press, 2015.

Hannah, Michelle. "Colliding Gender Imaginaries: Transnational Debates about Full Ordination for Tibetan Buddhist Nuns." *Asian Journal of Women's Studies* 18, no. 4 (2012): 7–44.

———. "Transmigratory Buddhism and Travelling Feminisms: Globalisation and Cross-Cultural Difference." *TAJA: The Australian Journal of Anthropology* 21, no. 3 (2010): 332–49.

Holmes-Tagchungdarpa, Amy. "The Legacy of a Female Sikkimese Buddhist Teacher: The Lineage of Pelling An Wangdzin and Gendered Religious Experience in Modern Sikkim." In *Eminent Buddhist Women*, edited by Karma Lekshe Tsomo, 159–68. Albany: State University of New York Press, 2014.

The Karmapa. "History in the Making: The First Step toward Full Ordination for Tibetan Buddhist Nuns." https://kagyuoffice.org/history-in-the-making-the-first-step-toward-full-ordination-for-tibetan-buddhist-nuns/. Accessed April 20, 2020.

Langenberg, Amy Paris. "An Imperfect Alliance: Feminism and Contemporary Female Buddhist Monasticisms." *Religion* 9, no. 6 (2018): 1–24.

Li, Yuhang. *Becoming Guanyin: Artistic Devotion of Buddhist Women in Late Imperial China*. New York: Columbia University Press, 2020.

Mohr, Thea, and Jampa Tsedroen, eds. *Dignity and Discipline*. Somerville, MA: Wisdom, 2010.

Padma'tsho. "Courage as Eminence: Tibetan Nuns at Yarchen Monastery in Kham." In *Eminent Buddhist Women*, edited by Karma Lekshe Tsomo, 185–94. Albany: State University of New York Press, 2014.

Pommaret, Francoise. "Empowering Religious Women Practitioners in Contemporary Bhutan." *Revue d'Etudes Tibétaines* 34 (December 2015): 124–29.

Schrempf, Mona, and Nicole Schneider. "Editorial: Female Specialists between Autonomy and Ambivalence." *Revue d'Etudes Tibetaines* 34 (December 2015): i–viii.

Shaw, Miranda. *Passionate Enlightenment*. Princeton, NJ: Princeton University Press, 1994.

Singh, Nandita. "The Kung Fu Nuns Think It's Time to Kick Gender Inequality in India to the Kerb," *The Print*. October 20, 2019. https://theprint.in/india/kung-fu-nuns-think-gender-in equality-india-to-kerb/307655/.

Sorensen, Michelle. "Machik Labdron," *Treasury of Lives*. https://treasuryoflives.org/biogra phies/view/Machik-Labdron/TBRC_P3312. Accessed April 20, 2020.

Sponberg, Alan. "Attitudes toward Women and the Feminine in early Buddhism." *Buddhism, Sexuality and Gender*, edited by Jose Cabezon, 3–36. Albany: State University of New York Press, 1992.

Tibetan Nuns Project, "Geshema Degree." https://tnp.org/geshema-degree/. Accessed April 20, 2020.

Tomalin, Emma. "Buddhist Feminist Transnational Networks, Female Ordination and Women's Empowerment." *Global Development Studies* 37, no. 2 (2009): 81–100.

Vargas-O'Brian, Ivette M. "The Life of Dge slong ma dPal mo: The Experience of a Leper, Founder of a Fasting Ritual, a Transmitter of Buddhist Teachings on Suffering and Renunciation in Tibetan Religious History." *Journal of International Association of Buddhist Studies* 24, no. 2 (2001): 157–86.

Wilson, Liz. "Buddhism and Gender." *Buddhism in the Modern World*, edited by David McMahan, 257–72. London and New York: Routledge, 2012.

———. *Charming Cadavers*. Chicago: University of Chicago Press, 1995.

Zivkovic, Tanya. "Embodying the Past: Gelongma Palmo and Tibetan Nyungne Rituals." *Journal of Ritual Studies* 27, no. 2 (2013): 45–63.

CHAPTER 11

Introducing Asian Transpacific North American Feminist Theology

Rev. Dr. Keun-Joo Christine Pae, Denison University

ABSTRACT

Conceptualizing the transpacific as a way to explain the US-Asian relations, I introduce Asian transpacific North American feminist theology. With attention to the grassroots organization Pacific Asian North Asian American Women in Ministry and Theology's work, this chapter elaborates on the idea of "interstitial integrity" as the buttress against the multi-layered oppression that has historically targeted Asian Pacific American women. Interstitial integrity articulates APA women's construction of a self in any culture, wisdom based on betwixt and in-between engaged relationships, anti-military and deimperial activism, and liberative image of God. The chapter also examines how APA women use their historical and diasporic memories in their feminist theology and ethics.

Keywords: interstitial integrity, transpacific, Asian Pacific American women, diaspora, historical memories, deimperialization, demilitarization, transnational feminist theology

At age five in 1905, Mary Paik Lee, with her family, crossed the Pacific Ocean first from Korea to Hawai'i and then to California. Lee's grandparents were among the first converts to Christianity in northern Korea. She would always proudly tell people that Dr. Samuel Moffett, one of the first American Protestant missionaries to Korea, baptized her entire family. The story about her grandmother, who opened the first school for girls in Pyeongyang, the current capital city of North Korea, only adds more pride to her family history.

Mary Paik Lee's memoir, *Quiet Odyssey*, begins with her narration of the political turmoil in Korea at the turn of the 20th century. Imperial Japan prepared to annex the

Korean Peninsula after its victories in the Sino-Japanese War (1894–1895) and the Russo-Japanese War (1904–1905), the historical events that she did not physically experience.[1] In Lee's memories, Korea and the United States were interconnected through Christianity and the transpacific migration of people and goods. The memoir highlights the transnational identity shared among Asian immigrants and their American-born children, the role of Christianity in Asian immigration and the Asian American community building, and endured racism marked with alienation and violence. Although Lee is one of a handful of Asian American women who recorded their lives on American soil in the early 20th century, she is neither the beginning nor the end of Asian women's transpacific migration. Neither is her odyssey quiet. Her odyssey, along with many courageous odysseys of Asian Pacific American (APA, hereafter) women, has been inscribed in the waves of the Pacific Ocean, the broadest and deepest body of water on Earth.

The Pacific Ocean connects Asia to the United States while seemingly separating the two continents. Geopolitically speaking, the Pacific Ocean silently remembers and embodies the history of Asian immigration to the United States, America's wars in Asia Pacific, tourism at the cost of exoticized Asian women, global trades, cheap female labor at sweatshops along the Pacific Coast, migrant laborers, endangered oceanic lives, and so forth. The Pacific Ocean is like Mother God, who continually creates life, holds tears and dreams of Her creation, and embraces silenced victims of history. How would feminist theology look if Asian and Asian American women's transpacific lives were considered seriously in theological reflection and imagination? For the last thirty-five years, this question has been central to the grassroots organization Pacific Asian North American Asian Women in Theology and Ministry (PANAAWTM).

With attention to feminist theo-ethical discourses proliferated by PANAAWTM, this chapter maps out Asian transpacific North American feminist theology. Promoting sisterhood among APA women in the Christian church and theological education, PANAAWTM has produced feminist religious knowledge. This knowledge is based on the feminist interrogation of the global power structure, questioning how the global power structure intersects with gender, race, class, sexuality, and religion and how neoliberal capitalism, industrialized militarism, and neocolonialism systematically exploit Asian women's gendered, racialized, and sexualized labor. The critical analysis of the global power structure has been a pivotal source for a feminist theology of liberation for and by APA women in solidarity with other marginalized groups of people for global peace and justice.

The primary goal of this chapter is to introduce Asian transpacific North American feminist theology. For this purpose, I first conceptualize the transpacific as the contact zone among multiple cultures and peoples. This concept justifies transnational approaches to feminist theology in the 21st century. Second, the history of Asian America through the lens of gender is discussed, as Asian women's historical experiences with the transpacific region are the invincible sources for doing feminist theology from an Asian and Asian American perspective. The last part of this essay elaborates on the liberative image of God through the idea of "interstitial integrity" articulated by PANAAWTM scholars. Interstitial integrity stresses wisdom rooted in betwixt and in-between engaged relationships and the feminist theological praxis of the demilitarization and deimperialization of the world, the transpacific, in particular.

ASIAN PACIFIC NORTH AMERICAN FEMINIST THEOLOGY AND TRANSPACIFIC STUDIES

In her essay, "Fishing the Asia Pacific," Kwok Pui-lan, feminist theologian and founding member of PANAAWTM, accentuates the importance of collaboration between Asian and Asian American feminist theologians. Different from the common belief shared in the American public, Asia and America are not two separate entities but ones that are "constantly influencing each other within the broader regional formation of the Asia Pacific."[2] The Pacific as a concept is inseparable from European, American, and Asian imaginations or fantasies of economic expansion, domination, a clash between civilizations, exoticized indigenous cultures and women, and military operations. For Asians, the Pacific is unthinkable without remembering European and American imperialism. China and Japan only add Asianized imperialism to the region while South Korea and Singapore have risen as regional powers, if not sub-empires.[3] In the meantime, the Pacific invokes imperialist nostalgia among Europeans and Americans—wars, conquest, and endless wealth. The term "transpacific" is the most recent effort at naming this often forced contact zone.[4]

How women have been historically positioned in the complex web of power relations in the transpacific is the salient point for Asian transpacific American feminist theology. In general, the tasks of Asian transpacific American feminist theology are threefold: (1) to complicate Asian Pacific American (APA) women's experiences of global power structures, (2) to search for solidarity among the marginalized (i.e., women, people of color, the poor, etc.) for global peace and justice, and (3) to imagine a liberative God.

Like other feminist theologies of liberation, Asian transpacific American feminist theology takes APA women's experiences of oppression seriously. These experiences, however, should not be treated as locally isolated events from larger global power structures built upon the complex intersection of race, gender, sexuality, class, and religion. Neither should be they seen as the ahistorical result of patriarchy, sexism, racism, or poverty. APA feminist theologians analyze oppression with a focus on its historical specificity while connecting it to the global power structure marked with colonialism, neoliberal capitalism, and transnational militarism. The analytical tools of race, gender, class, and sexuality enable APA feminist theologians to dissect the rules of imperial power. For example, discussing an American soldier's rape of the Filipina by the name of Nicole, Kwok Pui-lan warns her audience not to treat this rape case as a mere example of sexual violence against women in a patriarchal world. Instead, the case reveals a long history of US domination over the transpacific, the presence of the American military in the region, masculinist military power, corruption of national government, and the exoticization of Asian women's bodies as rapable colonized bodies.[5] As feminist theologians in the United States see how the US military power operates domestically and globally, they can consciously practice solidarity with Asian women like Nicole, whose lives are jeopardized by US bases in their countries.

The transpacific is the contact zone where dominant and subordinate groups and people with multiple identities interact with one another. However, interactions and contacts among diverse groups are often forced and, thus, create situations "full of tensions, fractures, and resistance."[6] In the contact zone, the analysis of power is crucial for the liberative mode of feminist theology. In the meantime, dialogue among diverse identities and negotiations with multiple identities and power groups are necessary. What Kwok calls "dialogical imagination" captures the fluidity and contingent character of Asian culture in the transpacific, including culturally and religiously hybridized Christianity practiced, theologized, and imagined among APA Christians.[7]

As seen in Mary Paik Lee's story, the transpacific is the space of diaspora. Asians have arrived on American soil through the Pacific passage. Diasporic memories transnationally and intergenerationally connect Asian Americans to Asia as well as to various places around the globe where Asians immigrated. Just as Mary Paik Lee narrates Korea's subjugation to Imperial Japan, which she did not physically experience, in *Haunting the Korean Diaspora*, American-born Korean sociologist Grace Cho interweaves the Korean War (1950–1953) with her family's stories. She depicts the war as the origin of her mother's relocation at Oakville through marriage with Cho's father, who was stationed in South Korea in the early 1970s.[8] Cho's diasporic vision flashes back to the survivors of the Japanese military "comfort women" system during World War II.[9] Despite the generational difference between Lee and Cho, their diasporic memories show how these memories traverse time and space, interweaving different people's varied memories together with their own, remembering what they (their ancestors) left behind and what remains in their psyche.

Like Cho, by engaging the Asian diaspora, APA feminist theologians and biblical scholars unpack unnarratable stories, such as racialized and gendered trauma, and suppressed memories scattered over the transpacific. Their reading of the Christian Bible often exhumes the silenced voices of the colonized and diasporic subjects, including female migrant workers. For example, Hebrew Bible scholar Gale Yee's reading of the Book of Ruth compares Ruth the Moabite to Asian immigrant women, who offer gendered and sexualized labor for the survival of their families and communities while being culturally forced to live up to a model minority stereotype.[10]

Diaspora studies interwoven with postcolonial studies challenge the construction of the center and the periphery by putting a diasporic (or displaced) subject in the center of knowledge production about war, colonialism, race, gender, liberation, and justice. "A diasporic consciousness," found among APAs who have been forcefully displaced from their homelands and live with the intergenerational memories of displacement and uprootedness, creates a mysterious space, where transcultural and transnational dialogue occurs and the followers of Jesus (*ochlos*) represent the corpus of the displaced and the uprooted.[11] In this space, culturally and historically specific stories of diaspora sound familiar, unfamiliar, transcendental, and often ambiguous. Christian New Testament scholar Jin Young Choi's postcolonial reading of the Gospel of Mark exemplifies how a diasporic consciousness enables her to interweave multiple stories of broken people and their embodied knowledge—the disciples of Jesus, the *ochlos*, which is compared to the Korean *minjung*, or commoners, and the transnationally displaced and replaced bodies of Asian descendants. Choi's biblical hermeneutics (*phronēsis*) disrupts the center and the periphery in the production of knowledge, as she prioritizes the embodied knowledge of Asian and Asian American women whose bodily memories of colonialism, neoliberal capitalism, and war haunt not only the Asian diaspora and American history but also biblical texts.[12]

A diasporic consciousness eventually leads us to the liberative images of God, born and reborn in Asian transpacific North American feminist theology. These images are ingrained in APA women's historically concrete experiences.

A HISTORY OF ASIAN AMERICA: OPPRESSION, RESISTANCE, AND ACTIVISM

Asian transpacific North American feminist theology is historically specific and contextual. While the mainstream Christian theology forgets and erases the presence of the colonized bodies of APA women in history, APA feminist communities of religion, such as PANAAWTM, make a collective effort to remember the experiences of these women intergenerationally and holistically. The intentional remembrance of the concrete is a form of feminist activism that allows PANAAWTM to remember the past, present, and future holistically and not to be disillusioned by false hope.[13] Hence, they theologically reflect on how racialized, gendered, and sexualized oppression of Asians in the United States has taken different forms in historically specific moments—from the 1882 Chinese Exclusion Act through the Japanese internment camp during World War II to attacks on Asians during the COVID-19 pandemic. Although APAs' collective memories and historical experiences of oppression are relevant sources for their critical feminist theology, their persistent social activism for peace and justice is what makes APA feminist theology distinctively a combination of feminist and liberation theology, connecting it to other theologies of liberation.

Throughout US history, APAs have endured the various forms of systematic oppression, built upon Euro-Americans' prejudices against Asians. To the American public, Asians were from the same region of Asia Pacific, the culturally, racially, and religiously unified region, having open borders. This Pacific is imbued with the "yellow peril"—unknown fear, danger, and threat to the United States from Asia. Whether the perceived threat appears as the forms of communism, economic domination, war, prostitution, or the huge influx of cheap labor force, the yellow peril surfaces whenever the United States has tensions with Asian countries or needs to take the public attention away from domestic problems. At the same time, "American Orientalism" colors Asian Americans with a perpetual foreigner stereotype, whose loyalty to the United States is suspect and who can never be fully assimilated with American culture, as "Orientalism" has been constructed as barbaric, exotic, alien, and racially different from and inferior to the West.[14] America's version of Orientalism has contributed to formatting the American national identity by excluding Asians from citizenship and portraying them as religiously dangerous, physically unsanitary, and disease stricken. Regardless of how long Asian Americans have lived in the United States, they have been considered foreigners and victimized by xenophobia. The rise of anti-Asian sentiments and attacks on Asian Americans, especially women, in the United States during the COVID-19 pandemic is the latest chapter of yellow peril and perpetual foreigner stereotypes. These negative stereotypes deeply ingrained in American culture and history have continuously challenged APA feminist theologians to investigate not only US domestic racism, sexism, and classism but also America's long history of imperial desire over the Asia Pacific.

Today, more than 19.5 million Asian Americans in the United States make up almost 6 percent of the US population.[15] According to Asian American historian Erika Lee, Asian American history, which had begun long before the United States was conceived as a country, includes global immigration history, race history, gender discrimination, and history of US citizenship and naturalization.[16] Lee further underscores the history of Asian Americans as a transnational history of America.[17] Asian Americans' immigration to the United States is connected to US foreign policy and relationships with diverse countries in East Asia, Southeast Asia, Central Asia, South Asia, Middle East, and the Pacific Islands. Asians' struggle for racial and gender equality in America is also integrated with their homeland politics. Being transnational and embodying multi-racial, ethnic, religious, and national identities are not merely being Asian but also being American.

APAs include long-term permanent residents "as far back as six generations."[18] Some people, such as Hawaiians, never migrated to the United States but became American after the US annexation of their islands. "Asian Americans" first meant those of East and Southeast Asian ancestry predominantly, but "Pacific" was added, as the term increasingly included South Asians and Pacific Islanders.[19] During the 1960s, the racially conscious pan-Asian identity arose among APAs who shared similar experiences of racial discrimination in the United States and political goals for justice and equality. Today, the APA identity should be understood both as a racialized and a political identity.

The APA women's history is tied with that of men, who started coming to the United States around 1763.[20] However, the transpacific migration of some 40,000 to 100,000 Asians from China, Japan, the Philippines, and South and Southeast Asia to Latin America happened during the 250-year history of the galleon trade (1565–1815).[21] The galleon trade connected Asia to New Spain through the movement of goods and peoples. By the end of the 19th century, Asian indentured laborers had gone to the Caribbean, Mexico, Costa Rica, and other places around the Americas.[22] The roots of Asian immigration to the United States extends back to Europe's search for Asia and the arrival of Asian sailors, slaves, and servants in New Spain. The mass movement of Asian laborers to the United States beginning in the 19th century connects to the arrival of Asian coolies in Latin America. Both mass migrations were intertwined with the increasing European and American presence in Asia and "the West's search for labor following the end of African slavery in the Americas."[23] For this historical reason, transpacific studies are often compared to transatlantic studies tied with the notorious Atlantic slave trade. However, the Atlantic passage of the slave trade does not hold the same stories with the Pacific passage of indentured Asian laborers. Their living conditions in the agricultural sector were comparable. However, different from enslaved Africans, the "coolies" were recruited in their hometowns, worked only for the contracted period, and had the freedom to move to different parts of the United States when the contract was over.

In the 19th century, a large number of Asian men crossed the Pacific Ocean to the United States as forced laborers (mostly in Hawaii and California), merchants, and gold prospectors. While Asian women were generally banned from entering the United States in the same period, in the early 20th century, Chinese and Japanese women were lured to prostitution in the country. From 1907 to 1924, 45,000 Japanese and 1,000 Korean picture brides arrived in Hawaii and California and married native men who were working on plantations and farms.[24] From 1890 to 1952, Asians could not be naturalized in the United States, although many of them spent their entire lives in the country. The series of Asian exclusion acts during this period made Asians become the first undocumented immigrants.[25] The Trump administration's militarized control over the Southwestern border with Mexico is an updated experience of what Asians (mostly Chinese and Japanese men) suffered when they crossed mountain deserts to enter the United States in the early 20th century. Their journeys through deserts also often ended with death.

Until 1968, when the Immigration and Nationality Act of 1965 was fully enacted, Asian American women were few in proportion to men. As the Asian American population grew in the United States, ethnic Asian churches functioned as the community center not only to preserve their respective cultures, languages, and Christian practices but also to promote their political interests. Especially in the early 20th century, Korean and Chinese American churchwomen were internationalists who worked on independence in their motherlands subjugated by European and Japanese powers.[26] At the same time, these churchwomen were actively involved in promoting women's rights in America. Three Asian women's organizations in San Francisco in the early 20th century are noteworthy: the Korean Ladies' Organization, founded in 1908; the Chinese Women's Jeleab (self-reliance) Association in 1911; and the Chinese YWCA (Young Women's Christian Association) in 1916. All these organizations maintained transnational identities of Asian American women amid harsh immigrant life in the United States.[27] Despite legally sanctioned discrimination against Asian Americans, their vibrant church communities sprang up across the United States.

World War II dramatically changed the United States—Asian relations, which affected the lives of Asian Americans, especially Japanese Americans. In response to the Japanese empire's attacks on Pearl Harbor in 1941, the US government set up concentration camps across the country where all Japanese Americans were incarcerated. At the same time, Japanese American men were forced to fight for the United States against Japan. In Japanese internment camps, women were the sustainers of life. The mass incarceration of Japanese Americans during World War II still traumatizes not only Japanese Americans but also any persons of Asian descent. Survivors from the Japanese American internment camp that was located in Crystal City, Texas, staged a protest rally March 30, 2019, outside of the nearby for-profit immigrant family detention center in Dilley, Texas, with the slogan "Never Again Is Now" (see figure 11.1).[28] Survivors shared stories about their long-time trauma, and they offered prayers for freedom for detained immigrant families as they hung paper swans on the fence outside the South Texas (Immigrant) Family Residential Center, which has the capacity to lock up 2,400 mothers and children (see figure 11.2).[29]

Another notable group of Asian female immigrants consists of military brides. America's wars in Asia Pacific brought many Asian war brides (mostly Japanese, Korean, Thai, and Vietnamese women) who were married to non-Asian servicemen. Due to their association with non-Asian men, their leadership for ethnic Asian churches has often been neglected. However, these women were the backbone of

FIGURE 11.1. Survivors of the Japanese American internment camp at Crystal City, Texas stage a protest rally outside of the for-profit South Texas (Immigrant) Family Residential Center March 30, 2019.
© *Helen T. Boursier*

FIGURE 11.2. During the peaceful protest that was held near the immigrant family detention center located in Dilley, Texas, Japanese American internment camp survivors hung 25,000 paper cranes, a Japanese symbol for healing, peace, and hope, as their symbolic prayers for the mothers and children detained inside Dilley.
© *Helen T. Boursier*

Asian American communities. In essence, they built their communities and churches when only a small number of Asians could legally immigrate to the United States until the 1965 New Immigration Law.

Since the Immigration and Nationality Act of 1965, the APA population has rapidly grown across the United States. The post-1965 immigrants from Asia are divided into highly educated professionals who have corresponded to a "model minority" stereotype and those who have constituted a critical low-paid workforce in the United States. The former is usually represented by APA churches as if APAs shared similar moral, religious, and cultural values inspired by Protestantism with the middle-class white Americans. The latter group, predominantly constituted of both US-born Asian and Asian immigrant women, is relatively hidden from the public.

For the last two centuries, the United States has constantly been opening markets, making wars, and building empire in the transpacific from the continents of Asia, Australia, the Americas, and the islands in the Pacific, including Guam, American Samoa, the Commonwealth of Northern Marianas, Hawai'i, the Marshall Islands, Okinawa, and Pitcairn.[30] America's empire building in the transpacific has affected APA women's lives. Asian war brides during World War II and the Korean War (1950–1953) embodied America's wars in the transpacific in an intimate way. Through the Korean War, the United States congealed its Cold War hegemony in East Asia, demonstrating its power to interpret and enter a Third World country's armed conflict.[31] America's war in Vietnam eventually forced the US government to open its door to Asians in 1965. Currently, 90 percent of Asian Americans are post-1965 immigrants and their children. In the meantime, the indescribable feelings of sorrow, loss, and grief associated with America's wars and empire building in Asia Pacific have haunted Asian Americans. APA feminist theologians courageously engage these visceral feelings in their theological work.

In the 1960s, APA communities were engulfed in civil rights activism, farm worker movements, and labor union movements. These movements articulate "Asian Americans" as a political identity. Yuri Kochiyama, Philip Vera Cruz, and Grace Lee Boggs, the three iconic Asian American activists in the 1960s, rejected the label "Orientals" and the model minority stereotype. They proclaimed themselves "Asian Americans, a pan-ethnic identity that emphasized commonalities across all Asian immigrant and ethnic groups."[32] Many APA church women supported these social justice movements and advocate for racial justice, LGBTQI rights, gender equality, economic justice, and immigrant rights. Since the 1960s, social activism has made and remade a new Asian America.

ASIAN TRANSPACIFIC NORTH AMERICAN FEMINIST THEOLOGY: INTERSTITIAL INTEGRITY

Metaphorically speaking, the vast Pacific Ocean is a hybridized space where diverse cultures and images of God find their own spaces without claiming rigid boundaries. They live harmoniously with one another, allowing currents and waves to intercross one another without fearing the emergence of hybridized spaces. Rita Nakashima Brock's articulation of "interstitial integrity" represents my construction of Asian transpacific North American feminist theology. This theology actively remembers, re-remembers, and retrieves the historical memories of APA women marred with European imperialism, war, patriarchy, racism, sexism, and neoliberal capitalism. This theology, more significantly, honors APA women's courage and activism for justice, equity, and peace, domestically and transnationally. According to Brock, "interstitial integrity more accurately describes how human beings construct a self in any culture"—this characterizes the story of the race (Native Americans, whites, blacks, APAs, Latino/as, and so forth) and immigration on North American soil.[33] All of our identities on American soil have been differently and yet intersectionally constructed by colonization, transplanted and, hence, hybridized in North America. Brock traces interstitial integrity in APA women's work for justice, which has lasted since the late 19th century. Instead of splitting us into Asians or Americans, we, APA women, have worked on both frontiers at once for justice for ourselves, our compatriots, and people in other countries.[34] As Brock further stresses, interstitial integrity helps us be attuned to the fullness and to participate in "its ever-changing rhythms and patterns rather than to be starved by unrealized hopes or a thin nostalgic past."[35]

Interstitial integrity fosters wisdom leadership with emphasis on human relationships, embodied by APA women. Su Yon Pak and Jung Ha Kim underscore that APA women remember, witness, and cultivate wisdom in between and among various human relationships—we are constituted by these relationships in friendships, in intergenerational relationships, and among members and leaders of the community.[36] What makes a person wise comes from "betwixt and between engaged relationships."[37] In interstitial integrity, we breed wisdom, holding together what is seen and unseen and refusing to let go of either seemingly different worlds.[38] This wisdom gives freedom to APA Christian women who often become firsts in the church and theological education—the first APA woman pastor, the first APA woman tenured faculty, the first APA woman academic dean, and so forth. When no one has left recipes for us, we create new dishes, bringing our foremothers' ingredients and recipes to the present and borrowing our friends' cooking skills and spices. Together, we are held in interstitial integrity. Wisdom born out of and nurtured in interstitial integrity empowers us to navigate life's uncertainties without fear while fostering the community built upon genuine friendships.

Finally, interstitial integrity, as feminist praxis, purports to deimperialize and demilitarize the world, the transpacific in particular, and Christian theology. Since the transpacific is a highly militarized and imperialized space by multiple empires and sub-empires, any feminist theology born out of this space necessitates the liberative process of demilitarization and deimperialization. Both of these actions require us to engage with Christian theology in relation to critical studies of US imperialistic militarism in Asia Pacific. Some 42 percent of Asian North Americans are associated with Christianity, which has offered religiously charged ideologies of Manifest Destiny and American Exceptionalism.[39] These ideologies have equated Christian triumphalism (e.g., Christ's victory over evil) with America's victory over American Indians, non-Christians, communists, and Muslims, justifying the imperialistic military expansion of the United States in Asia and beyond. Through critical Christian theology rooted in the Jesus movement as the people's movement against the ruling of the Roman Empire, we can learn to engage with Christianity differently—not as the center of hierarchical power but as the deimperialistic and demilitaristic movements of people beyond borders who have radically envisioned God's love and justice for all living beings.

CONCLUSION

This chapter emphasizes the importance of transnational perspectives in APA feminist scholarship on religion, especially Christianity, delineating how APA women's historical and diasporic memories have produced their embodied knowledge of God. The transpacific both as a concept and as a transnational space is cardinal for my construction of Asian transpacific North American feminist theology. The transpacific as a conceptual ground for feminist theology highlights Asia and America as an intersectional and hybridized space, rather than two separate continents or bodies of knowledge. Hence, Asian transpacific North American feminist theology promotes global solidarity and shared global responsibility for peace and justice, more specifically, demilitarizing and deimperializing the world, the transpacific, in particular. Feminist theologies for and by APA women are grounded in the Jesus movement as people's movement and does not conform to Christian triumphalism.

Interstitial integrity is both the feminist concept and praxis born out of APA women's historical and diasporic memories and experiences with the transpacific. Interstitial integrity articulates the construction of a self in any culture, emerging in between and betwixt engaged relationships. Courageously facing uncertainties, ambiguities, and dangers in their transpacific diaspora and life on American soil, APA Christian women have nurtured interstitial integrity. Interstitial integrity is the theological concept that best describes APA women's embodied wisdom and knowledge of God.

I conclude this chapter during the COVID-19 pandemic. The pandemic teaches vulnerability and the common destiny shared in the global community. In the United States, however, people of color, Blacks, Latinx, and Asians are disproportionately affected by COVID-19 due to the failure of the public health care system, anti-Asian attacks, and the poor management of the crisis by national leadership. In this time of risk, APA women's hard-earned knowledge of God as interstitial integrity will heal the global community from the traumatic suffering of the pandemic, eradicate xenophobic yellow peril, and grant the world wisdom to navigate life's uncertainties and ambiguities.

NOTES

1. Mary Paik Lee, *Quiet Odyssey: A Pioneer Korean Woman in America*, with an introduction by Sucheng Chan (Seattle, WA: University of Washington Press, 1990).

2. Kwok Pui-lan, "Fishing the Asia Pacific: Transnationalism and Feminist Theology," in *Off the Menu: Asian and Asian North America Women's Religion and Theology*, ed. Rita Nakashima Brock, Jung Ha Kim, Kwok Pui-lan, and Seung Ai Yang (Louisville, KY: Westminster John Knox Press, 2007), 9.

3. Viet Thanh Nguyen and Janet Hoskins, "Introduction: Transpacific Studies: Critical Perspectives on an Emerging Field," in *Transpacific Studies: Framing an Emerging Field*, ed. Viet Thanh Nguyen and Janet Hoskin (Honolulu, HI: University of Hawai'i Press, 2014), 2–4.

4. Thanh Nguyen and Hoskin, "Introduction," 2.

5. Kwok, "Fishing the Asia Pacific," 5.

6. Kwok Pui-lan, *Postcolonial Imagination and Feminist Theology* (Louisville, KY: Westminster John Knox Press, 2005), 43.

7. Kwok, *Postcolonial Imagination and Feminist Theology*, 43.

8. Grace Cho, *Haunting the Korean Diaspora: Shame, Secrecy, and the Forgotten War* (Minneapolis, MN: University of Minnesota Press, 2008).

9. Cho, *Haunting the Korean Diaspora*, 164.

10. Gale Yee, "'She Stood in Tears amid the Alien Corn': Ruth, the Perpetual Foreigner and Model Minority," in *Off the Menu: Asian and Asian North American Women's Religion and Theology*, ed. Rita Nakashima Brock et al. (Louisville, KY: Westminster John Knox Press, 2007), 45–65.

11. *Ochlos* is a Greek word for the crowd, which the author of the Gospel of Mark often uses to describe the commoners who followed Jesus.

12. Jin Young Choi, *Postcolonial Discipleship of Embodiment: An Asian and Asian American Reading of the Gospel of Mark* (New York: Palgrave Macmillan, 2015).

13. Keun-joo Christine Pae, "Three Tales of Wisdom: Leadership of PANAAWTM," in *Leading Wisdom: Asian and Asian North American Women Leaders* (Louisville, KY: Westminster John Knox Press, 2017), 128.

14. Kwok, "Fishing the Asia-Pacific," 4.

15. Erika Lee, *The Making of Asian America: A History* (New York: Simon & Schuster, 2015), 1.

16. Lee, *The Making of Asian America*, 2–9.

17. Lee, *The Making of Asian America*, 10.

18. Rita Nakashima Brock and Nami Kim, "Asian Pacific Protestant Women," in *Encyclopedia of Women and Religion in North America*, ed., Rosemary Skinner Keller and Rosemary Ruether (Bloomington, IN: Indiana University, 2006), 498.

19. Brock and Kim, "Asian Pacific Protestant Women," 498.

20. Brock and Kim, "Asian Pacific Protestant Women," 498.

21. Lee, *The Making of Asian America*, 20.

22. Lee, *The Making of Asian America*, 34.

23. Lee, *The Making of Asian America*, 35.

24. Brock and Kim, "Asian Pacific Protestant Women," 499.

25. Lee, *The Making of Asian America*, 192.

26. Brock and Kim, "Asian Pacific Protestant Women," 499–500.

27. Brock and Kim, "Asian Pacific Protestant Women," 500.

28. See, e.g., Mike Moffitt, "WWII Internment Camp Survivors to Protest Trump with 10,000 Paper Swans," *San Francisco Gate*, March 28, 2019, https://www.sfgate.com/bayarea/article/WWII-internment-survivor-to-return-to-13720509.php; Martha Nakagawa, "Japanese Americans Gather in Texas to Protest Family Detention at Border," *Nichi Bei Weekly*, April 11, 2019, https://www.nichibei.org/2019/04/japanese-americans-gather-in-texas-to-protest-family-detention-at-border/; and Robyn Ross, "The Legacy of Crystal City's Internment Camps," *Texas Observer*, January 14, 2018, https://www.texasobserver.org/otherness-among-us/.

29. An organizer said, "We asked for ten thousand cranes because it means 'more than you can ask for.' We got twenty-five thousand cranes." The organizer added, "Each crane represents one of our ancestors who was incarcerated," cited in Helen T. Boursier, *Art As Witness: A Practical Theology of Arts-Based Research* (Lanham, MD: Lexington Books, 2021). For information on the for-profit immigrant family detention center, see Helen T. Boursier, *The Ethics of Hospitality: An Interfaith Response to U.S. Immigration Policies* (Lanham, MD: Lexington Books, 2019), 162–63.

30. Jinah Kim, *Postcolonial Grief: The Afterlives of the Pacific Wars in the Americas* (Durham, NC: Duke University Press, 2019), 2.

31. Jodi Kim, *Ends of Empire: Asian American Critique and the Cold War* (Minneapolis: University of Minnesota Press, 2010), 150.

32. Lee, *The Making of Asian America*, 304.

33. Rita Nakashima Brock, "Cooking without Recipes: Interstitial Integrity," in *Off the Menu: Asian and Asian North American Women's Religion and Theology*, ed. Rita Nakashima Brock et al. (Louisville, KY: Westminster John Knox Press, 2007), 136.

34. Brock, "Cooking without Recipes," 139.

35. Brock, "Cooking without Recipes," 139.

36. Su Yon Pak and Jung Ha Kim, "Introduction," in *Leading Wisdom: Asian and Asian North American Women Leaders*, ed. Su Yon Pak and Jung Ha Kim (Louisville, KY: Westminster John Knox Press, 2017), 7.

37. Pak and Kim, "Introduction," 7.

38. Pak and Kim, "Introduction," 8.

39. Nami Kim and W. Anne Joh, "Introduction," in *Critical Theology against U.S. Militarism in Asia: Decolonization of Deimperialization*, ed. Nami Kim and W. Anne Joh (New York: Palgrave Macmillan, 2016), xiv.

BIBLIOGRAPHY

Boursier, Helen T. *Art As Witness: A Practical Theology of Arts-Based Research*. Lanham, MD: Lexington Books, 2021.

———. *The Ethics of Hospitality: An Interfaith Response to U.S. Immigration Policies*. Lanham, MD: Lexington Books, 2019.

Brock, Rita Nakashima. "Cooking without Recipes: Interstitial Integrity." In *Off the Menu: Asian and Asian North American Women's Religion and Theology*, edited by Rita Nakashima Brock, Jung Ha Kim, Kwok Pui-lan, and Seung Ai Yang, 125–43. Louisville, KY: Westminster John Knox Press, 2007.

Brock, Rita Nakashima, and Nami Kim. "Asian Pacific Protestant Women." In *Encyclopedia of Women and Religion in North America*, edited by Rosemary Skinner Keller and Rosemary Ruether, 498–505. Bloomington, IN: Indiana University, 2006.

Cho, Grace. *Haunting the Korean Diaspora: Shame, Secrecy, and the Forgotten War*. Minneapolis, MN: University of Minnesota Press, 2008.

Choi, Jin Young. *Postcolonial Discipleship of Embodiment: An Asian and Asian American Reading of the Gospel of Mark*. New York: Palgrave Macmillan, 2015.

Kim, Jinah. *Postcolonial Grief: The Afterlives of the Pacific Wars in the Americas*. Durham, NC: Duke University Press, 2019.

Kim, Jodi. *Ends of Empire: Asian American Critique and the Cold War*. Minneapolis: University of Minnesota Press, 2010.

Kim, Nami, and W. Anne Joh, eds. *Critical Theology against U.S. Militarism in Asia: Decolonization of Deimperialization*. New York: Palgrave Macmillan, 2016.

Kwok, Pui-lan. "Fishing the Asia Pacific: Transnationalism and Feminist Theology." In *Off the Menu: Asian and Asian North America Women's Religion and Theology*, edited by Rita Nakashima Brock, Jung Ha Kim, Kwok Pui-lan, and Seung Ai Yang, 3–22. Louisville, KY: Westminster John Knox Press, 2007.

———. *Postcolonial Imagination and Feminist Theology*. Westminster John Knox Press, 2005.

Lee, Erika. *The Making of Asian America: A History*. New York: Simon & Schuster, 2015.

Lee, Mary Paik. *Quiet Odyssey: A Pioneer Korean Woman in America*, with an introduction by Sucheng Chan. Seattle, WA: University of Washington Press, 1990.

Moffitt, Mike. "WWII Internment Camp Survivors to Protest Trump with 10,000 Paper Swans." *San Francisco Gate*, March 28, 2019. https://www.sfgate.com/bayarea/article/WWII-internment-survivor-to-return-to-13720509.php.

Nakagawa, Martha. "Japanese Americans Gather in Texas to Protest Family Detention at Border." *Nichi Bei Weekly*, April 11, 2019. https://www.nichibei.org/2019/04/japanese-americans-gather-in-texas-to-protest-family-detention-at-border/.

Nguyen, Viet Thanh, and Janet Hoskins, eds. *Transpacific Studies: Framing an Emerging Field*. Honolulu, HI: University of Hawai'i Press, 2014.

Pae, Keun-joo Christine. "Three Tales of Wisdom: Leadership of PANAAWTM." In *Leading Wisdom: Asian and Asian North American Women Leaders*, edited by Su Yon Pak and Jung Ha Kim, 125–137. Louisville, KY: Westminster John Knox Press, 2017.

Pak, Su Yon, and Jung Ha Kim, eds. *Leading Wisdom: Asian and Asian North American Women Leaders*. Louisville, KY: Westminster John Knox Press, 2017.

Ross, Robyn. "The Legacy of Crystal City's Internment Camps." *Texas Observer*, January 14, 2018. https://www.texasobserver.org/otherness-among-us/.

Yee, Gale. "'She Stood in Tears amid the Alien Corn': Ruth, the Perpetual Foreigner and Model Minority." In *Off the Menu: Asian and Asian North American Women's Religion and Theology*, edited by Rita Nakashima Brock, Jung Ha Kim, Kwok Pui-lan, and Seung Ai Yang, 45–65. Louisville, KY: Westminster John Knox Press, 2007.

CHAPTER 12

"I Am the One Who Will Change the Direction of the World"

A Female Guru's Response to Sexual Inequality and Violence in Hinduism

Antoinette E. DeNapoli, Texas Christian University

ABSTRACT

This chapter examines the leadership of a revolutionary, female guru named Trikal Bhavanta Saraswati, who is addressed by her followers as "Mataji," or "Holy Mother," and who has founded the first women's monastic society (*akhāḍā*) as a grassroots response to gender-motivated exploitation, inequality, and abuse in North Indian Hindu society. Based on five years of ethnographic research, this chapter makes three intersecting arguments. First, it suggests that the religious gender-motivated abuse against female ascetics (*sādhus*) and women devotees, more generally, to which Mataji's leadership heightens attention, is linked to received understandings of the female *sādhu* as inferior to the male *sādhu*. Second, the chapter contends that responsibly addressing and ameliorating gender inequality involves reforming Hindu society of the misogyny endemic to the running of religious institutions, in which gender hierarchies tacitly affirm women's secondary status and reinforce male and dominant caste hegemonies. Finally, it argues that Mataji's leadership as the female Shankaracharya advances the idea of the female *sādhu* as normative to the male *sādhu* in order to advocate gender equality in Hindu society.

Many religions today are at a moral crossroads. From the Roman Catholic Church to Tibetan Buddhism,[1] personal experience accounts of teachers, priests, and gurus committing pedophilia, rape, and various forms of harm have upended religious lives and worlds. Within contemporary cultures, there is a rise and pervasiveness of allegations of sexual misconduct, abuse, discrimination, and harassment by religious leaders and clergy. While this is not novel in the history of religions, across global landscapes, religions are embroiled in a "sex abuse crisis." "These are extraordinary times," writes the historian Wietse De Boer, in the context of the institution of the Catholic Church.[2] De Boer's observation can be cast more widely to other religions. Why, then, are issues around sex, gender, and violence a "crisis" now in religion?

Societies are no longer tolerating what they did long ago.[3] Modern-day communication has revolutionized human access to problems of sex and violence so that more people are aware of these problems and they are harder to hide. Religious sex scandals continue to supply the fodder for front-page headlines. Although the stigma related to reporting abuse has not gone away, the increasing global awareness of the problem may indicate shifting social attitudes. From another angle, as modernist discourses about human and civil rights and feminist and post-colonial identities evolve, so do people's understandings of systemic sexism, racism, and xenophobia. The current *avatār* of the information age we inhabit has enabled women as a class and historically marginalized identities to recognize and claim their fundamental right to be treated with equality, respect, and dignity because of their individual humanity. In an era of greater moral scrutiny, people are not only looking *at* religion for its role in the "sex abuse crisis," but they are also looking *to* religion as a constructive resource for responding to it.

This chapter illuminates the life, teachings, and activism of the revolutionary female guru named Trikal Bhavanta Saraswati, who is addressed as "Mataji" ("Holy Mother"), and the ways in which she is actively responding to this crisis within Hindu society. Mataji's grassroots quest to eradicate religious sexual inequality, discrimination, and violence is altering cultural mindsets about the value and rights of the female sex in northern India. As the third of four children born into a farming family in 1965, Mataji leads a relatively small, yet demographically diverse, community and lives in the popular pilgrimage town of Prayagraj (formerly Allahabad).

Taking my cue from Mataji's teachings, as well as from the literature on interpersonal violence, my use of the terminology "the sex abuse crisis" broadly references the interlinked problems of sexual inequality, discrimination, exploitation, and violence against women.[4] Based on ethnographic research I conducted with Mataji from 2014 to 2019 in Uttar Pradesh, a northern state in which Hindu nationalist ideologies are on the rise,[5] I will show that her leadership as the female Shankaracharya sheds light on the intersections of religion, sex, and violence in India. My analysis is drawn from Mataji's personal narratives, which I documented with a voice recorder; her religious discourses, which I also recorded or were videotaped and shared on social media by Mataji's devotees at her request; and the religious parliaments in which she participated and during which I conducted field research. Importantly, the office of the Shankaracharya characterizes the highest echelon of the traditional Hindu power structure. Until Mataji, it had been subject to the sole control of high-caste Brahmin men. Not only has Mataji declared herself to be the first female Shankaracharya without institutional sanction, but she has done so within a context of increasing religious chauvinism and male hegemony.[6]

Thus, through advocacy of gender equality and autonomy for female ascetics (*sādhus*), Mataji's leadership attacks entrenched misogynistic stereotypes concerning *sādhus* as morally "loose" and "dangerous" women by heightening associations between independent female power and the power of the divine feminine known as *śakti*. As a class of religious women who have relinquished the norms of marriage, family, and householding in order to worship divinity, female *sādhus* are especially vulnerable to problems related to the sex abuse crisis as it occurs within Hindu institutions (e.g., temples, ashrams, and monasteries). My data also suggests that their fundamental rights are being flouted in these and other contexts.[7]

Against this backdrop, I argue that Mataji's leadership radically addresses religious forms of the sex abuse crisis and, by implication, improves women's lowered status by advocating the equality and normativity of the female *sādhu* to that of the male *sādhu* in Hindu society. Additionally, her teachings advance an alternative narrative of virtuous femininity to that featured in the dominant Brahmanical discourse through emphasis on self-assertion, self-determination, and self-governance as capacities intrinsic to the "female as normative."[8] Mataji's female-centric theology, therefore, enlarges Indic visions of the "good woman."

If the escalating protests against the Indian Parliament's recent amendment to the Citizenship Act of 1955 are any indication, India is at a watershed moment.[9] Its Hindu nationalist government under Modi is, as the cultural anthropologist Tulasi Srinivas explains in an article published in *The Revealer*, "enacting and redacting constitutional laws in an attempt to delimit Indian citizenship." Not surprisingly, women's constitutionally protected fundamental rights have fallen under increased scrutiny and criticism amid such a tense and rapidly shifting political climate.[10] It behooves scholars to examine how the leadership of female gurus like Mataji combats misogyny, while furthering gender equality within Hindu society. By bringing Hindu women's voices and experiences to bear on emerging accounts of religion and the sex abuse crisis, scholars gain a nuanced understanding of its cultural complexities and the transformative potential of religion to redress a virulent issue in socially responsible ways.[11]

"AM I A BEAUTY OR A SANNYĀSĪ?": MATAJI'S PERSONAL STORY OF SEX AND VIOLENCE IN HINDUISM

Mataji's encounter with the sex abuse crisis in Hinduism began in the late 1990s, when she was a married householder with two children. During this period, she was employed in the social work sector. In the evenings after completing her household duties, Mataji attended religious programs held near the Triveni Sangam, a place extolled in popular and religious literature for its sacred power, as the holy Ganga, Jamuna, and Saraswati rivers are said to converge there. During one of these programs, Mataji met a guru named Baba M. His intense joy and love for God impressed her. Mataji felt safe around him and trusted him. She revealed to Baba M. her deepest secrets, sharing intimate details of her crumbling marriage due to the serial infidelity of her spouse. Every time Mataji came to Baba M.'s temple, alone or with others, he came running to her. Often, as Mataji says, he had tears in his eyes, exclaiming, "Hey Lord! My daughter has come!" Baba M. showered Mataji with the love and affection that a father might show to his child. He gifted her expensive silk sarees, blouses, woolen blankets, and wads of cash. He told Mataji to take the money and buy clothes and food for her family members.

But the more time that Mataji spent in Baba M.'s company, the more she realized that he was developing an unhealthy attachment to her. A guru's ascribed enlightened status is derived from the shared understanding that he or she has severed his or her ties to the world. From the viewpoint of renunciation, being detached from the worldly dualities of pleasure and pain, as well as from social practices that stoke the fires of sexual desire, prepares the guru to realize the ultimate and, hence, break free of the cycle of rebirth. Baba M., however, as Mataji says, "crossed his limits" and violated the guru–disciple relationship. He would call her at night, begging Mataji to meet him. He said that he couldn't bear another day without seeing her "beautiful face." Before giving talks, Baba M. would call Mataji into his private room and tell her "I love you." She knew from the look in his eyes that his so-called love was sexual in nature, ignited by desire for her. She had seen "that look" before in the eyes of men—uncles, cousins, brothers-in-law, and co-workers—who had touched her inappropriately. Mataji felt a deep and wounding sense of shame and humiliation as a result of Baba M.'s behavior. More debilitating was the constant fear and confusion that interfered with her judgment and thus kept her from confronting him. After leaving for London, Baba M. called Mataji and told her to come and live with him in the United Kingdom. She simply stopped answering his calls and has not heard from him since.

In the year 2000, Mataji left her husband and family, after the children were in college, and became a *sādhu*. While she lived in different ashrams until 2007, the year in which she settled at the temple where she currently lives, Mataji encountered the same situation of gurus' wanting to turn their spiritual relationship into one between "a husband and a wife." Not only would she have to satisfy the guru sexually, but she would have to clean, cook, and wash his clothes, too. One guru told her, "You are so beautiful. Beauty like yours should not go to waste." In response, Mataji asked the guru: "Am I a beauty or a *sannyāsī*?" Many of the gurus with whom Mataji studied were incapable of seeing her as a serious spiritual seeker of salvific knowledge. She says, "These gurus were called *yogīs*, but they were just *bhogīs* [lustful]."

As Mataji moved from one ashram to another, she met female *sādhus* who, like her, were facing similar personal circumstances, but who, unlike her, did not have the economic, material, or social resources to leave their situations. As renouncers, *sādhus* do not earn money. Rather, they generally rely on their devotees to sustain themselves physically and financially. In return, *sādhus* nourish their devotees spiritually through their religious knowledge, teachings, and blessings. Although there are female *sādhus* who run their own ashrams and temples and live on their temple's donations, the majority of the *sādhus* whom Mataji met depended solely on their male gurus for food, clothing, and shelter. For Mataji, however, years of sustained employment had enabled her to build a healthy savings. Most of that money she put toward her children's secondary and college education; the rest of it, though, she saved for herself. With that savings, Mataji was able to rent a small room in a dwelling close to the Triveni Sangam.

"A WOMAN WITHOUT A HUSBAND IS LIKE A LOOSE THREAD": SOCIETAL PERCEPTIONS OF FEMALE *SĀDHUS*

Her contact with female *sādhus* in and beyond Prayagraj enlarged Mataji's awareness of the physical, emotional, social, and economic hardships that women who leave behind home and family for spiritual reasons endure. In mainstream Indic society, women as a class are expected to marry and have families.[12] According to the dominant Brahmanical worldview, a woman's place is in the home. In childhood, a woman depends on her father for protection; in marriage, she depends on her husband; and in her old age, she depends on her son.[13] Orthodox Brahmanical discourse constructs virtuous femininity as a state of perpetual dependence on male kin for protection and economic sustenance. It eclipses the possibility for women to develop identities and aspirations independent of their prescribed roles and responsibilities. In this male-centric framework, a woman enjoys the highest status as a wife and mother of sons.[14]

From the conventional standpoint of Brahmanical Sanskritic Hinduism, the concept of the female *sādhu* is an anomaly.[15] Her renunciation of domesticity, which is understood to define and circumscribe the normative parameters for female identity and personhood, symbolically constitutes the negation of the "chaste woman." Consequently, female renunciation may be perceived as a transgression of the natural order (*dharma*). Without a home and a family to protect and preserve her virtue, a *sādhu's* moral character becomes suspect. The *Manusmṛti*, an orthodox Brahmanical treatise dealing with the subject of *dharma* (righteous behavior) and composed around the 2nd century BCE, warns female householders about the dangers of "being separated from their husbands" and of "wandering about" by themselves, by labeling these and other behaviors "corrupt."[16] Such textual proscriptions have acquired new *avatārs* in contemporary contexts. As a Rajasthani *sādhu* said to me, "A woman without a husband is like a loose thread. People want to get rid of it as quickly as possible, rather than let it be."

Societal perceptions of female *sādhus* as having a questionable moral character because of their unconventional lives reinforces their secondary status in Hindu society. Moreover, their economic dependency on others amplifies their vulnerability to sexual inequality and violence. Many of the *sādhus* whom Mataji met in Prayagraj and elsewhere had experienced some form of inequality, discrimination, and violence in their lives. Most of them disclosed their struggles with physical and emotional harassment by passersby and people whom they knew. According to Mataji, several of the women were raped by their gurus or by the disciples of their gurus; in instances where the *sādhu* became pregnant, her guru either paid for her to have an abortion or, in the majority of the cases, removed her from the ashram, kicking her out on the street. As Mataji said, "People don't respect female *sādhus*. They think, 'she has no male protector, so she has no virtue or dignity [*maryādā*].' They abuse her in so many ways. It's sexual terrorism."

"*TAN, MAN,* AND *DHAN*": CULTURAL COMPONENTS OF RELIGIOUS GENDER INEQUALITY AND VIOLENCE

Religious ideologies sanctioned by authoritative Hindu texts and underpinning guru devotion accentuate the primacy of the devotee's humility, surrender, obedience, loyalty, and reverence for the guru who is considered an enlightened soul and, hence, God incarnate. In localized North Indian contexts, this ideology is called "tan, man, and dhan." This means that the devotee offers his "body, mind, and wealth" as a show of loving devotion to the guru-qua-God. Implied here is the notion that the devotee's "body," the instrument through which she serves the guru; "mind," with respect to her thoughts and intentions, which should be focused on pleasing the guru; and "wealth" in the form of time, energy, and money represent offerings to the guru.

Mataji speaks at length about the dangers inherent in the "tan, man, and dhan" ideology of guru devotion. She sees it as a rationale for ill-intentioned gurus and others to breach the ethics of the guru–disciple relationship. What makes women more susceptible to inequality, abuse, and violence than men concerns the idea that the female epitomizes the ideal devotee because the virtues illustrative of guru devotion are considered intrinsic to the female sex. To that extent, Hindu religious imagination abounds with examples of renowned modern gurus, such as Sri Ramakrishna Paramahamsa, and gurus from the sixteenth century, such as Sri Chaitanya, the founder of Bengali Vaishnavism, approaching the ultimate by adopting female personas.[17]

Significantly, women's culturally ascribed capacity for guru devotion intersects with orthodox Brahmanical constructions of virtuous womanhood. Exemplifying the ideal woman is the self-sacrificing and self-effacing wife who worships her husband (*pati*) as her Lord (*deva*) by being sexually chaste, obedient, loyal, and respectful of his and his family's wishes. Brahmanical discourse accords the husband a superior position of power and authority over the wife. He symbolizes both a god and a guru for her. Loving devotion to him enacts a means for the wife to generate the spiritual merit that leads to a better rebirth. Like the guru, then, the husband represents a woman's gateway to the ultimate. And, like the ideal devotee, the ideal wife is expected to please her husband-qua-guru by offering him her *tan, man,* and *dhan*.

Given that the complementary ideologies of guru devotion and virtuous womanhood are deeply embedded in the cultural fabric of Indic society, their intersection can yield divergent interpersonal dynamics for guru–disciple relations. As the scholar–activist Shamita Das Dasgupta elucidates, "Cultural characteristics of a community affect people in significant and contradictory ways. . . . In a given situation, each cultural feature can be either a source of strength or a source of violence."[18] Mataji uses her platform as the female Shankaracharya to call attention to these ideologies as interlinked components contributing to the sex abuse crisis in Hinduism. She says,

> It is said that we should respect our elders. As the husband is elder to the wife, she has to obey him. She has to follow his orders. It is said that "the husband is God." We also have a saying in our Hindu religion that "Brahman is the guru of the whole world, and Brahman's guru is the *sannyāsī* [renouncer]. When a *sannyāsī* is the guru of Brahman, why wouldn't a woman worship him like a wife

worships her husband? [Mataji recites the verse:] Jagat Guru Brahman, Brahman Guru Sannyasi. They worship the guru to get God. They consider the *sannyāsī* God. He is God. Who wouldn't want to touch God? Who wouldn't want to eat with Him? Who wouldn't want to sleep with Him? These *sannyāsīs* are real gods for their devotees. . . . If the *sannyāsī* is the guru of the entire world, then what is the problem in worshipping him? This is the mentality of our culture.

Her teaching cues three points. First, guru devotion as a practice entails hierarchical structures of social relations, wherein the devotee desires intimate, physical contact with the guru-qua-God.[19] The scholar of religion Amanda Lucia terms these "structures of guru-disciple physicality," particularly as they pertain to normative practices that socialize "communal reverence" for the guru and devotees' need for proximity to the guru's physical body, "haptic logics."[20] More specifically, this desire for physicality, as Mataji explains, manifests by wanting to touch, feed, and "sleep with" the guru. Second, the twinned notions of husband as God and guru as (higher than) God lend themselves to legitimating misogynistic cultural attitudes and behaviors that increase women's risk for violence. That risk is pronounced for female *sādhus*, largely because of their lowered status compared with that of married women and male *sādhus*.

Furthermore, guru devotion operates on the premise of the devotee seeing and being seen by God incarnate as the guru. This is known as *darśana* in Hinduism. Built into that concept is the value of reciprocity, which reinforces the idea of *darśana* as a transformative, interpersonal encounter. As a conduit of/for the sacred, the guru transmits divine power simply by seeing the devotee, who, by absorbing that power, is said to become divine as a result. But just as importantly, divine power may be transmitted through the guru's speech (as when the guru says a *mantra* or gives a teaching), the guru's gaze, and the guru's touch. Such forms of sacred interaction illustrate the various means by which gurus initiate their disciples in Hinduism.[21] For gurus to show their devotees love and affection is considered a blessing.[22] In the best of circumstances, the guru's love, which is compared to ambrosia in Hindu texts and popular discourse, may uplift the devotee and quell her suffering. Mataji says the guru's attention:

> makes the woman feel special. She thinks that out of one-hundred people, he has selected me. There must be something special in me. . . . The guru praises her. Then he starts to give her dried fruits. Did you understand? He gives [her] the best things. Because of this special treatment, the woman does not know whether it is all a dream or reality. . . . It doesn't matter how good of a husband she has. Nothing compares to the guru's love.

In the worst of circumstances, the guru's showering the devotee with "dried fruits" (i.e., special treatment) may become a context for grooming (or "wooing," as Mataji describes it) her (or him), and thus for violating the boundaries of the guru–disciple relationship. Mataji explains:

> Can you imagine getting so much love? This is the guru's strategy. He will give money, love, care. Who wouldn't want that? You tell me! . . . Because of

such gurus, our Hindu religion is facing a huge loss. Those whom we worship as God are devils. They should be removed from their posts. To wipe out this evil, I have made myself a Shankaracharya. There is no one for the women. To reduce the disparities in our religion, I have given women their own society. I am the one who will change the direction of the world.

RESPONDING TO THE SEX ABUSE CRISIS IN HINDUISM: MATAJI'S FORMATION OF A FEMALE SOCIETY

In response her own and other *sādhu's* experiences related to the sex abuse crisis in Hinduism, Mataji says that she felt compelled by the gods and the people to whom she confided her ordeals to make herself the first female Shankaracharya of India. According to Mataji, she had a vision in which the deities Shiva and Shakti called her to lead in that position. She interpreted that call of the gods as her ritual initiation for the Shankaracharya leadership. Mataji announced her title in 2008, during the Magh Mela festival held in Prayagraj. Along parallel lines, she realized that female *sādhus* and women, more generally, need a *sādhu* society of their own, where they can live and practice their religion away from the male gaze and threats of male violence. So, in 2014, after a decade of building a constituency and raising funds from her speaking events, Mataji formed the first women's monastic society (*akhāṛā*) in India. She has named it Sarveshwar Mahadev Vaikunth Dham Mukti Dwar Akhara Pari, or Akhara Pari, in short, which may be translated as "The Army of the Free Birds." As a religious society, Akhara Pari, though woman oriented, is not woman exclusive. It accepts men and householders into its fold and has grown into a community of two hundred people. Located at Mataji's temple, it operates as a shelter for abused and homeless women and children and as a monastic center of learning, where women can study Vedic and other literature, perform rituals, and learn self-defense skills.

In 2019, three women, between the ages of thirty-five years and sixty-eight years, were living semi-permanently at Akhara Pari. Mataji has assigned each woman a role in its running and maintenance. For example, Lucky,[23] a middle-aged woman who was living alone on the streets before one of Mataji's devotees brought her to Akhara Pari, cooks for the residents; Khushi, an elderly widow who ran away from the home she shared with her son and his wife after they had physically abused and financially exploited her, cuts firewood for the ashram and cleans the temple space. Finally, Mani, who left her abusive husband, an alcoholic, came to the *akhāṛā* with her two children in tow and today performs rituals to the temple gods. It is unclear if these women will become *sādhus*; however, all of them have taken ritual vows of celibacy for as long as they stay at the *akhāṛā*. Because of their vow of celibacy, the women are called *brahmacārinīs* (celibate female students). Mataji requires celibacy of her residents. In her understanding, it exemplifies a powerful yogic discipline for teaching women the importance of self-respect and self-love, without which she says personal transformation is impossible.

By practicing celibacy, women can "see themselves" as spiritual aspirants (*yoginīs*), instead of being seen by others as sexual objects. Countering the Brahmanical discourse that lauds women primarily as procreators of the patriarchal family, Mataji says that women's duty (*strīdharma*) is to recognize their divinity. Celibacy allows women to know themselves as forms of the divine *śakti*, that is, the dynamic and creative female power of the universe, who are worthy of love, dignity, and respect. Similarly, it helps women to realize that the self-determining and self-governing impulses associated with *śakti* illustrate capacities intrinsic to the female as normative. Thus, celibacy affirms the normativity of female autonomy, while protecting the autonomy of *sādhus* living in a society that suspects independent female power.

CONCLUSION: "WHAT WOULD DURGA DO?"— A GURU'S REVISIONING OF THE "GOOD" WOMAN

Mataji's formation of Akhara Pari has emerged at a critical juncture in pan-Indian religious communities' responses to the sex abuse crisis. As shocking news of the brutal rape and murder of the twenty-three-year-old physiotherapy intern Jyoti Singh Pandey in Delhi in 2012 exacerbated mainstream fears about women's safety in India,[24] stories of lascivious gurus alleging their rape and abuse of women in 2013 inundated daily news coverage by the Indian and international media. It seems that Akhara Pari could not have come at a more compelling moment. Not only its creation but precisely its existence sends the potent message of the primacy, normativity, and equality of the female *sādhu* to that of the male *sādhu* in Hindu society. As the female Shankaracharya, Mataji reinforces the idea that female humanity is as normative as male humanity.[25] Through her leadership, she imparts to Indian women the vital knowledge that their lives and experiences matter. Her discourses, activism, and rituals variously underscore that *sādhus'* parity of opportunity to the Shankaracharya position in Brahmanical Hinduism, as well as their equal right to run an independent *akhāṛā*, demonstrates their birthright as female embodiments of *śakti*. Mataji forwards the notion that women deserve to live on their own terms and that autonomy precedes *and* exceeds their constitutional right to equality because it *is* the nature of the divine *śakti* incarnated as women. As Mataji says, "freedom is our most precious possession."

As cultural awareness of the interrelation of religion and sexual violence increases in India and elsewhere, Mataji strives to enhance her approach to addressing and eradicating systemic misogyny within Hinduism. Since the year 2015, she has been organizing and facilitating women's religious parliaments in northern India. During these events, Mataji, along with other invited female gurus, discuss and debate the parameters of ideal womanhood based on these leaders' readings of Hindu texts. In many of these parliaments, Mataji gives women across the life span permission to defend themselves from the people who hurt, mistreat, and abuse them. In one such event that was held in Delhi in July 2019, Mataji said to a mostly female audience that "No one ever tells a woman or a girl but she comes to know how a man sees and watches her. . . . When you see a man looking at you with a bad eye, you have the right and responsibility to protect yourself." In other parliaments, Mataji implores women to "speak out" against sexual inequality and violence. Drawing on the image of the great warrior goddess Durga, Mataji makes explicit that the *śakti* who defeats evil symbolizes the fierce power of the divine feminine inherent in the female as normative. She says that the warrior wisdom Durga has, women also have. In Mataji's words, "This knowledge is present in every mother, daughter, and sister. You can protect yourselves. You must take action against anyone who tries to hurt you." Mataji likes to pose the question, "What would Mother Durga do?" This phrase is quickly becoming women's *mantra* for revisioning femininity in Hindu society.

How powerful it must be for women, and especially young women, to hear words such as these pouring from the mouth of the first female Shankaracharya of India. Rather than tell women to depend on men for protection, which perpetuates received Brahmanical worldviews of the purported dependence, weakness, inferiority, and passivity of the female sex, she tells women, *sādhus* and householders alike, to see themselves as the rightful protectors of their own bodies. By doing so, Mataji shifts gender discourse on ideal femininity to foreground an alternative narrative of "women power" (*strī kī śakti*) in Hinduism. From the perspective of her teachings, the idea of female nature encompasses qualities commonly ascribed to the male sex, such as fierceness, autonomy, equality, self-discipline, and self-governance. Her theology accentuates that the concept of female dependence on men and, by implication, their second-class status to men, crystallizes the dominant Brahmanical interpretation of religious patriarchy, and not who women are. Mataji says, "Women are so powerful. They can do anything. They are power." The transformative vision of the female *sādhu* as normative concretized by her leadership offers women an interpretation of femininity with tremendous potential for changing *sādhus*' lives in tangible ways. Akhara Pari materializes one example of the changes that Mataji's leadership is motivating in contemporary Hinduism. Mataji reasons that the institutional shifts in female leadership happening within and beyond the Hindu traditions of India signify a broader (and concurrent) shift in cultural mindsets about gender norms. I am inclined to agree with her.

In sum, Mataji's leadership as the female Shankaracharya stitches into the fabric of an evolving Indic consciousness that "good women" can protect their own bodies, that they are entitled to develop and nurture independent identities and aspirations apart from those of the people with whom they share their lives, and that they must question oppressive viewpoints that threaten to imprison them in the cage of patriarchal ideologies and institutions.[26] Her life, teachings, and work dispel the illusion that female safety is a necessary function of male protection. Mataji calls this assumption "sweet poison." This means a conception about gender conventions that appears to benefit women but that ultimately disadvantages them. From where she stands, the idea that women need men's protection—that women require men to protect them from other men!—encourages the misogynistic view of female independence as non-normative, while legitimating male control over women's choices, bodies, and lives. It is an assumption that paralyzes people, particularly women, and traps them in the destructive web of fear and hatred. Mataji refuses to drink the poison.

By disrupting the problematic premise that India is unsafe for women, Mataji compels men and women across the spectra of class and caste to join "as equals" and together create a world where female flourishing is imminent. I dare to say that Akhara Pari points a way toward this horizon. For this reason, Mataji's revisioning of the boundaries of womanhood advocates that women must learn to safeguard their bodies and their rights. Mataji compares the cosmic field on which Durga battles the demons with the social "field of religion" (*dharmakṣetra*), where female *sādhus* and others are battling to protect and increase their right to equality of opportunity in religion. Her correlation of Durga's fight for cosmic order with the *sādhus*' fight for equality in Hindu society suggests Mataji's perception that the future and welfare of the women, men, and children of India, citizens and others currently being refused that right, hang in the balance.

So what would Durga do? Mataji's message is loud and clear: Durga would fight for the equality, autonomy, and justice of all. As Mataji says: "Until women's rights are respected and enforced in the *dharmakṣetra*, India cannot become a teacher to the rest of the world."

NOTES

1. Due to increased reporting, these religions have become the most visible players in the recent sex abuse scandal ripping news headlines, but they are not the only ones affected by it. For articles addressing this issue in the Roman Catholic Church see Kathryn Lofton, "Revisited: Sex Abuse and the Study of Religion," *The Immanent Frame*, August 24, 2018, https://tif.ssrc.org/2018/08/24/sex-abuse-and-the-study-of-religion/; and Julie Beck and Ashley Fetters, "Faced with an Ongoing Sexual-Abuse Crisis, What Are Catholic Parents to Do?," *The Atlantic*, March 17, 2019, https://www.theatlantic.com/family/archive/2019/03/catholic-church-abuse-crisis-how-parents-are-grappling/584866/. For articles addressing the issue in mainly convert Tibetan Buddhism communities, see Andy Newman, "The 'King' of Shambhala Buddhism Is Undone by Abuse Report," *New York Times*, July 11, 2018, https://www.nytimes.com/2018/07/11/nyregion/shambhala-sexual-misconduct.html; and Nick Brown, "Sexual Assaults and Violent Rages . . . Inside the Dark World of Buddhist Teacher Sogyal Rinpoche," *The Telegraph*, September 21, 2017, https://www.telegraph.co.uk/men/thinking-man/sexual-assaults-violent-rages-inside-dark-world-buddhist-teacher/.

2. Wietse De Boer, "The Catholic Church and Sexual Abuse, Then and Now," *Origins: Current Events in Historical Perspective* 12, no. 6 (March 2019).

3. I am grateful to June McDaniel for our conversations, which helped me to conceptualize the points discussed in this paragraph.

4. See, e.g., Tamsin Bradley, *Women and Violence in India: Gender, Oppression, and the Politics of Neoliberalism* (New York: I.B. Tauris and Company); Jillian E. H. Damron and Andy J. Johnson, "Violence against Women in Religious Communities: An Introduction," *Religion and Men's Violence Against Women*," ed. Andy J. Johnson, 3–14 (New York: Springer, 2017); Shamita Das Dasgupta, "(Un)Holy Connections: Woman Abuse in Hinduism," *Religion and Men's Violence Against Women*, ed. Andy J. Johnson, 371–382 (New York: Springer, 2015).

5. Emma Tomalin, *Religions and Development* (New York: Routledge, 2013), 7.

6. See Antoinette E. DeNapoli, "A Female Shankaracharya?: The Alternative Authority of a Feminist Hindu Guru in India," *Religion and Gender* 9, no. 1 (July 2019): 27–49.

7. Antoinette E. DeNapoli, "'What the Government Won't Give Us, God and the Courts Will!': Gender, Hinduism, and Female Empowerment in the Public Sphere—A Guru's Fight for Gender Equality in North India," paper presented at the Annual Meeting of the American Academy of Religion, Religion and Politics Unit, November 25, 2019, San Diego, CA.

8. Winnie Tomm, "Goddess Consciousness and Social Realities: The 'Permeable Self,'" vol. 1 of *The Annual Review of Women in World Religions*, ed. Arvind Sharma and Katherine K. Young (Albany: SUNY Press), 78, 90–91, 97–98.

9. The Citizen (Amendment) Act is a new and politically motivated law that denies Muslim immigrants in India citizenship, while further marginalizing Muslim and other religious minorities, like Tamil Sri Lankans, in the country. It came into effect on January 10, 2020.

10. Noorjehan Safia Niaz and Soman Zakia, *Reclaiming Sacred Spaces: Muslim Women's Struggle for Entry into Haji Ali Dargah* (Chennai, India: Notion Press, 2017).

11. While journalistic accounts of the religious sex abuse are plentiful, there is a paucity of scholarship on the subject in terms of its mechanics and religions' responses to it. Scholars are addressing this lacuna, and promising efforts are already under way to make the study of sexual violence central to religious studies discourse. Recently, the Henry Luce Foundation through its theology program awarded a team of religion scholars a $550,000 grant to study sexual abuse in religion. Named "The Religion and Sexual Abuse Project," the project's team consists of six main co-researchers who will "examine why and how this issue persists across a range of religions" (Tess Eyrich, "Grant Funds Study of Sexual Abuse in Religious Communities," *UC Riverside News*, August 6, 2019, https://news.ucr.edu/articles/2019/08/06/grant-funds-study-sexual-abuse-re ligious-communities). Each scholar will explore the issue from multiple religious and social-historical perspectives. They include Kent Brintnall, Holly Gayley, Ann Gleig, Andrea Jain, Amy P. Langenberg, and Amanda Lucia, who is leading the project from UC Riverside.

12. See June McDaniel, *The Madness of the Saints: Ecstatic Religion in Bengal* (Chicago: University of Chicago Press, 1989); Lisa Hallstrom, *Mother of Bliss: Anandamayi Ma (1896–1982)* (New York: Oxford University Press, 1999). See also Dasgupta, "(Un)Holy Connections," 377–78.

13. *The Laws of Manu*, trans. Wendy Doniger with Brian K. Smith (New York: Penguin, 1991), 5: 147–51 and 9: 2–3, 115, and 197.

14. Patrick Olivelle, *The Āśrama System: The History and Hermeneutics of a Religious Institution* (Oxford: Oxford University Press, 1993), 186.

15. Meena Khandelwal, *Women in Ochre Robes: Gendering Hindu Renunciation* (Albany: SUNY Press, 2004), 5.

16. Doniger and Smith, *The Laws of Manu*, 9: 14, 198. See also Olivelle, *The Āśrama System*, 189, for a discussion of the fines that Brahmanical *dharma* texts impose on men who have sex with female ascetics.

17. McDaniel, *The Madness of the Saints*; Rita DasGupta Sherma, "'Sa Ham: I Am She': Woman as Goddess," in *Is the Goddess a Feminist?: The Politics of South Asian Goddesses*, ed. Alf Hiltebeitel and Kathleen M. Erndl, 24–51 (New York: NYU Press, 2000).

18. Dasgupta, "(Un)Holy Connections," 375.

19. Amanda Lucia, "Guru Sex: Charisma, Proxemic Desire, and the Haptic Logics of the Guru-Disciple Relationship," *Journal of the American Academy of Religion* 84, no. 4 (2018): 953–88, https://doi.org/10.1093/jaarel/lfy025.

20. Lucia, "Guru Sex," 962.

21. June McDaniel, *Offering Flowers, Feeding Skulls: Popular Goddess Worship in Bengal* (Oxford: Oxford University Press, 2004), 94–95.

22. See also Lucia, "Guru Sex," 963, 970.

23. The names of the women mentioned in this paragraph have been changed.

24. See C. Mackenzie Brown and Nupur D. Agrawal, "The Rape That Woke Up India: Hindu Imagination and the Rape of Jyoti Singh Pandey," *Journal of Religion and Violence* 2, no. 2 (2014): 234–82.

25. Tomm, "Goddess Consciousness and Social Realities"; Rita Gross, "Is the Goddess a Feminist?," in *Is the Goddess a Feminist: The Politics of South Asian Goddesses*, ed. Alf Hiltebeitel and Kathleen M. Erndl, 104–12 (New York: NYU Press, 2000).

26. DeNapoli, "A Female Shankaracharya?," 49.

WORKS CITED

Beck, Julie, and Ashley Fetters. "Faced with an Ongoing Sexual Abuse Crisis: What Are Catholic Parents to Do?" *The Atlantic*. March 17, 2019. https://www.theatlantic.com/family/archive/2019/03/catholic-church-abuse-crisis-how-parents-are-grappling/584866/.

Bradley, Tamsin. *Women and Violence in India: Gender, Oppression, and the Politics of Neoliberalism*. New York and London: I.B. Tauris and Company, 2017.

Brown, C. Mackenzie, and Nupur D. Agrawal. "The Rape That Woke Up India: Hindu Imagination and the Rape of Jyoti Singh Pandey." *Journal of Religion and Violence* 2, no. 2 (2014): 234–82.

Brown, Nick. "Sexual Assault and Violent Rages . . . Inside the Dark World of Buddhist Teacher Sogyal Rinpoche." *The Telegraph*, September 21, 2017. https://www.telegraph.co.uk/men/thinking-man/sexual-assaults-violent-rages-inside-dark-world-buddhist-teacher/.

Damron, Jillian E. H., and Andy J. Johnson. "Violence against Women in Religious Communities: An Introduction." In *Men's Violence against Women*. Edited by Andy J. Johnson, 3–14. New York: Springer, 2015.

Dasgupta, Shamita D. "(Un)Holy Connections: Understanding Woman Abuse in Hinduism. In *Religion and Men's Violence against Women*. Edited by Andy J. Johnson, 371–82. New York: Springer, 2015.

De Boer, Wietse. "The Catholic Church and Sexual Abuse, Then and Now." *Origins: Current Events in Historical Perspective* 12, no. 6 (2019). http://origins.osu.edu/article/catholic-church-sexual-abuse-pope-confession-priests-nuns.

DeNapoli, Antoinette E. "A Female Shankaracharya?: The Alternative Authority of a Feminist Hindu Guru in India." *Religion and Gender* 9, no. 1 (2019): 27–49.

———. "'What the Government Won't Give Us, God and the Courts Will!': Gender, Hinduism, and Female Empowerment in the Public Sphere—A Guru's Fight for Gender Equality in North India." Paper presented at the Annual Meeting of the American Academy of Religion, Religion and Politics Unit, November 25, 2019, San Diego, CA.

Doniger, Wendy, and Brian K. Smith, trans. *The Laws of Manu*. New York: Penguin, 1991.

Eyrich, Tess. "Grant Funds Study of Sexual Abuse in Religious Communities." *UC Riverside News.* August 6, 2019. https://news.ucr.edu/articles/2019/08/06/grant-funds-study-sexual-abuse-religious-communities.

Gross, Rita. "Is the Goddess a Feminist?" In *Is the Goddess a Feminist: The Politics of South Asian Goddesses*. Edited by Alf Hiltebeitel and Kathleen M. Erndl, 104–12. New York: NYU Press, 2000.

Hallstrom, Lisa L. *Mother of Bliss: Anandamayi Ma (1896–1982)*. Oxford: Oxford University Press, 1999.

Johnson, Andy J., ed. *Religion and Men's Violence against Women*. New York: Springer, 2015.

Khandelwal, Meena. *Women in Ochre Robes: Gendering Hindu Renunciation*. Albany: SUNY Press, 2004.

Lofton, Kathryn. "Revisited: Sex Abuse and the Study of Religion." *The Immanent Frame: Secularism, Religion, and the Public Sphere*. August 24, 2018. https://tif.ssrc.org/2018/08/24/sex-abuse-and-the-study-of-religion/.

Lucia, Amanda. "Guru Sex: Charisma, Proxemic Desire, and the Haptic Logics of the Guru-Disciple Relationship. *Journal of the American Academy of Religion* 84, no. 4 (2018): 953–88.

McDaniel, June. *The Madness of the Saints: Ecstatic Religion in Bengal*. Chicago: University of Chicago Press, 1989.

———. *Offering Flowers, Feeding Skulls: Popular Goddess Worship in West Bengal*. Oxford University Press, 2004.

Newman, Andy. "The 'King' of Shambala Buddhism Is Undone by Sexual Abuse Report." *New York Times*, July 11, 2018.

Olivelle, Patrick. *The Āśrama System: The History and Hermeneutics of a Religious Institution*. Oxford: Oxford University Press, 1993.

Safia Niaz, Noorjehan, and Zakia Soman. *Reclaiming Sacred Spaces: Muslim Women's Struggle for Entry into Haji Ali Dargah*. Chennai, India: Notion Press, 2017.

Sherma, Rita DasGupta. "'Sa Ham: I Am She': Woman as Goddess." In *Is the Goddess a Feminist: The Politics of South Asian Goddesses*. Edited by Alf Hiltebeitel and Kathleen M. Erndl, 24–51. New York: NYU Press, 2000.

Srinivas, Tulasi. "Bathing the Gods in Bottled Water: An Account of Climate Change and Faith." *The Revealer*. February 4, 2020. https://therevealer.org/bathing-the-gods-in-bottled-water-an-account-of-climate-change-and-faith/.

Tomalin, Emma. *Religions and Development*. New York: Routledge, 2013.

Tomm, Winnie. "Goddess Consciousness and Social Realities: The 'Permeable Self.'" Vol. 1 of *The Annual Review of Women in World Religions*. Edited by Arvind Sharma and Katherine K. Young, 71–104. Albany: SUNY Press, 1991.

CHAPTER 13

Women in the Jewish Tradition

A Brief Overview of Jewish Feminism in the Last 50 Years

Yudit Kornberg Greenberg, PhD, Rollins College

ABSTRACT

Since the 1970s, Jewish women have gained access to and have been engaged in what were once off-limit religious practices. An integral part of the changing status of women in Judaism has been accomplished through projects aimed at providing women with a voice and access to worship, scholarship, and spiritual leadership roles. Feminist ideology and theology have raised fundamental questions regarding the androcentric nature of classical Jewish texts, including the prayer book. Jewish women scholars have transformed Jewish learning and the dissemination of knowledge through their study of history, archeology, Talmud, philosophy, biblical studies, creation of new midrashim, and the introduction of inclusive god language in liturgy and new rituals.

The recent phenomenon of women rabbis in the male-dominated Jewish tradition indicates that the sexual liberation movement of the 1960s had a major impact on the progress made toward spiritual leadership and egalitarianism in the Jewish community. Noteworthy in this context is that many of the leaders of the feminist movement in the United States in the 1960s were Jewish women, including Gloria Steinem, Bella Abzug, Betty Friedan, and Andrea Dworkin, all of whom helped shape the feminist movement.

The large number of Jewish women in the movement has been variously attributed to Jewish women's tendency to embrace progressive causes and their love of debate and relative comfort with being seen as "other" in a predominantly Christian society.[1]

Looking back, there is little doubt that their activism and ideologies served as a catalyst for the emergence of the Jewish feminist movement. The movement's origins can furthermore be traced to the increase in synagogue attendance by women and, with it, heightened awareness of and challenges to the inequities pertaining to women in the public sphere of religion.

Since the 1970s, Jewish women have gained access to and been engaged in what were once off-limit religious practices. In liberal Judaism, the desire and activism for full synagogue participation eventually translated into the ordination of women in the Reform rabbinate in 1972. The first Reconstructionist female rabbi was ordained in 1974. For the Conservative movement, the initial breakthrough was the decision in 1973 to count women in the Minyan (prayer quorum); the first female Conservative rabbi was ordained in 1985. It is estimated that, since 1972, more than 350 women have become rabbis in the Reform, Reconstructionist, and Conservative branches of American Judaism.[2] Rabbinic school classes at Hebrew Union College tend to have a 50/50 ratio of women and men, which matches other graduate programs in the country.[3] In the Jewish Reform, Conservative, Reconstructionist, and Renewal communities, the inclusion of women in all realms of synagogue and religious organizations, including their roles as rabbis and cantors, is now an established practice.[4] However, gender hierarchy remains, especially in women holding pulpits and serving as senior rabbis. As Professor and Rabbi Dvora E. Weisberg puts it,

> I see the progress Jewish women have made, both in the academy and in the religious arena, mirrored in my own experience. Thirty years ago, I began my graduate studies at a seminary that did not ordain women. All my professors were men, and I was advised to avoid anything having to do with gender or women when considering doctoral research. Today, the seminary in which I studied ordains women, and has many women on its Judaica faculty. I myself teach in a seminary where at least half of the tenured faculty are women, and where I serve as the director of the rabbinical school. My own research focuses to a great extent on gender, and a perusal of conference programs indicates that field is a rich and varied one.[5]

The road to ordination has been far more challenging to women in the Orthodox community, with only a handful having been privately ordained by Orthodox rabbis. The year 2013 marked a major milestone when three Orthodox women broke the Modern Orthodox glass ceiling and were formally and publicly ordained and recognized in their communities. They were given the title of Maharat (an acronym for the Hebrew words meaning leader in legal, spiritual, and Torah matters).[6]

An integral part of the changing status of women in Judaism has been accomplished through projects aimed at providing women with a voice and access to worship, scholarship, and spiritual leadership roles (see figure 13.1). Feminist ideology and theology have raised fundamental questions regarding the androcentric nature of classical Jewish texts, including the prayer book. Scholars have transformed Jewish liturgy through the introduction of an inclusive language of prayer and the creation of new rituals that center on women's experiences.[7] Among certain Modern Orthodox communities, we have

FIGURE 13.1. Rabbi Margaret Holub 2017.
© *Mickey Chalfin*

seen the emergence and growth of women's prayer groups.[8] Equally important have been innovations in the areas of education and scholarship. In addition to their roles as presidents of congregations and other communal organizations, women now hold spiritual and scholarly leadership roles, serving as rabbis and spiritual and Halakhic advisers, running Jewish day schools, directing and teaching Jewish studies programs at the university level and in rabbinical seminaries, and extensively publishing scholarly works in the growing field of Jewish studies.

FEMINIST THOUGHT AND THE DEPATRIARCHALIZATION OF LIBERAL JUDAISM

Since the emergence of the feminist movement, a critical transformation for women in Judaism has been scholarship, especially the academic study of Judaism in areas such as biblical studies, theology, philosophy, rabbinics, history, and literature. Jewish feminist thinkers began with questions of gender inequality but have since extended the parameters of their work to all areas of Jewish life and thought that pertain to gender, sexuality, and ethics. Feminist Jews in the 1980s debated the question, "What is the most fundamental and urgent area for Jewish feminist analysis, Halakha or Theology?" In retrospect, both theological and halakhic scholarship have informed and shaped new perspectives and methodologies in interpreting, constructing, and democratizing an inclusive Judaism.[9] Ozick's argument for the significance of halakhic justice, as well as Plaskow's premise that halakhic injustice toward women is rooted in a theology where women are absent or "other," validate the Jewish feminist project.

Feminist theology provides a theoretical framework for re-envisioning the three pillars of traditional Judaism—Torah, God, and Israel—and aims to apply the moral imperative for inclusivity and equality not only to women but to all aspects of life. Rabbi Margaret Holub reflects on the shifts that are occurring in theorizing about women and Jewish thought: "The whole understanding of gender is complex and becoming more fluid in this generation, so that the idea itself of 'women' is more interesting than it used to be. What is a woman's point of view? What are the power dynamics? Where are authority and privilege located?" She continues to remark: "Last year I was at a conference about hevra kadisha—it was in Berkeley, granted, but nevertheless I found myself at one moment chatting with three transgender rabbis. And the topic that brought us together wasn't even gender. As it happens, one of them was working on developing a hevra kadisha specifically oriented to working with transgender Jews when they die. That seems pretty interesting and, in its own way, deeply unsettling of categories that many of us have taken for granted."[10]

Plaskow's scholarship is the first systematic feminist Jewish theology that focuses on recovering women's history and redefining women's relationship with the sacred. One of Plaskow's ideas for transforming tradition is to replace the traditional idea of "chosenness" with the notion of Jewish distinctiveness. As she sees it, the notion of chosenness has perpetuated an environment that is antagonistic to pluralism and that has led to social inequality in the Jewish community.[11] One of the most important questions that Plaskow raises is whether feminism is actually transforming Judaism or only attaining equal rights while social and religious structures remain unchanged. She challenges women and men to embrace the notion of Jewish transformation and is adamant that women must see themselves "standing again at Sinai" as recipients and partners of the covenant. This entails critiquing deeply embedded notions of hierarchy and exclusivity as these exist in the Torah, in liturgy, and in Halakha. Furthermore, as partners of the covenant, feminist theologians must redefine the Jewish community's ethics of inclusivity, ameliorate what they characterize as imbalanced god language, and create new midrashim and liturgy that reflect women's experiences and sensibilities.

Rachel Adler is another seminal feminist Jewish scholar who juxtaposes Halakha, ethics, and theology in her work *Engendering Judaism: An Inclusive Theology and Ethics*.[12] She is committed to Halakha but at the same time recognizes the pervasive injustice toward women in rabbinic texts. Adler's agenda in developing her inclusive theology and ethics is not only to critique but also to offer alternative models of legally binding contracts. A primary example is her ethical commitment contract—brit ahuvim (lovers' covenant)—based on the principle of mutuality, replacing the traditional marriage contract (Ketubah) and its language of acquisition with this alternative contract. She views her constructive Jewish theology and ethical praxis as Tikkun Olam (mending a shattered world). Other pivotal feminist scholars include Ellen Umansky, Marcia Falk, and Rebecca Alpert. Umansky's theology centers around the critique of traditional male god language and on the creation of new and innovative rituals for women.[13] Marcia Falk offers creative innovations to the Jewish liturgy with her scholarly and poetic work on prayers and blessings.[14]

Sexuality played a pivotal role in women's struggles for religious equality. The sexual liberation in the 20th century helped to reveal problematic millennia held views of women and femaleness that identify them as Body in contrast with men and masculinity as linked with Mind, Spirit, and even God himself. The first distorted view of women was shaped by biblical hermeneutics that constructed the image of Eve as a weak-minded temptress who desired the forbidden fruit and whose punishment was painful childbirth and the desiring of her husband.[15] Modern and contemporary feminist views of sexuality aim to dispel religious concepts of impurity that stigmatize women's biological processes of menstruation, pregnancy, and childbirth. These two notions of women have been crucial in undermining women's social, political, and religious status and, with it, their exclusion from spiritual leadership roles.

A trend that hasn't nearly crested yet is the queering of Judaism. Feminist thought and activism have opened Jewish communal life to gay and lesbian Jews where they are slowly gaining acceptance and leadership roles. Lesbian Jewish feminists have made substantial contributions as rabbis, lay leaders, activists, and scholars.[16] Rebecca Alpert is one of the earliest thinkers and activists whose contributions to feminist Jewish theology are dedicated to the lesbian Jewish experience. Even though Jewish texts have been traditionally read as denouncing lesbians and gays, she chooses to remain in the realm of Jewish textuality by offering new readings and interpretive possibilities that incorporate lesbian and gay perspectives. Furthermore, she asserts that creating new stories stemming from lesbian and gay experiences is crucial to the transformation of Judaism as a whole.[17]

Alpert and other lesbian and gay thinkers are challenging notions of family, community, and religiosity by their presence within and outside the organized Jewish community. They question the criteria for membership in Jewish congregations and communal organizations; they engage in constructing new rituals, such as commitment ceremonies, and events to celebrate coming out in a Jewish context. They are also demanding that the Jewish community address homophobia and the impact of the AIDS epidemic on Jews.[18] The flagship organization of this movement is the World Congress of Gay, Lesbian, Bisexual, and Transgender Jews: Keshet Ga'avah (WCGLBTJ), which consists of member organizations in numerous countries. The Hebrew subtitle Keshet Ga'avah—Rainbow of Pride—emphasizes the importance of Hebrews and Israel to the World Congress. The Congress holds conferences and workshops representing the interests of lesbian, gay, bisexual, and transgender Jews around the world. An outgrowth of WCGLBTJ that demonstrates its growing impact on mainstream Judaism is the Institute for Judaism and Sexual Orientation (IJSO) of the Reform movement in its emphasis on social justice, holiness, and community.[19]

The Reform and Reconstructionist movements developed policies that sanctioned the ordination of lesbian and gay rabbis since the early 1980s and endorsed same-sex religious ceremonies and marriages since 2000. The Reconstructionist Movement was the first denomination to accept transgender students to the Reconstructionist Rabbinical College and ordain transgender rabbis. Most recently, Abby Stein, an ex-Hasidic Rabbi turned transgender activist, author, and teacher, has been influential in promoting awareness of LGBTQ+ issues on social media and in her memoir, *Becoming Eve: My Journey from Ultra-Orthodox Rabbi to Transgender Woman*. Rituals and prayers specific to the life events of transgender persons have been developed lately, such as "Transgender Remembrance Day, 100% in God's Image," Occupy K Street Judaism, McPherson Square, November 18, 2011,[20] and the beautifully crafted Sabbath prayer:

Opening Prayer: Twilight People

As the sun sinks and the colors of the day turn, we offer a blessing for the twilight, for twilight is neither day nor night, but in-between.

We are all twilight people. We can never be fully labeled or defined.

We are many identities and loves, many genders and none.

We are in between roles, at the intersection of histories, or between place and place. We are crisscrossed paths of memory and destination, streaks of light swirled together. We are neither day nor night. We are both, neither, and all.

May the sacred in-between of this evening suspend our certainties, soften our judgments, and widen our vision.

May this in-between light illuminate our way to the God who transcends all categories and definitions. May the in-between people who have come to pray be lifted up into this twilight.

We cannot always define; we can always say a blessing. Blessed are You, God of all, who brings on the twilight.[21]

As scholars and activists continue to work toward an inclusive and egalitarian Judaism, it behooves us to recognize and proclaim the well-known Jewish enjoinder: "May we go from strength to strength!"

NOTES

1. See Eryn Loeb, "Idle Worship," *Tablet Magazine*, August 15, 2011, https://www.tabletmag.com/sections/arts-letters/articles/idle-worship.

2. Pamela S. Nadell, "Rabbis in the United States," *Jewish Women: A Comprehensive Historical Encyclopedia*, February 27, 2009, https://jwa.org/encyclopedia/article/rabbis-in-united-states.

3. See Michael Meyer, *Response to Modernity: A History of the Reform Movement in Judaism* (Detroit, MI: Wayne State University Press, 1995).

4. However, there are challenges for both lay and clergy women in Conservative Judaism, including inconsistent requirements for ordained rabbis. On this issue, see Anne Lapidus Lerner, "Pacing Change," in *New Jewish Feminism: Probing the Past, Forcing the Future*, ed. Elyse Goldstein (Nashville, TN: Jewish Lights, 2008), 175–85.

5. Director of the School of Rabbinic Studies, Hebrew Union College, Jewish Institute of Religion, Los Angeles. Quoted in a private communication in 2012; shared by permission.

6. Eva Bilick, "Breaking the Modern Orthodox Glass Ceiling," February 20, 2013, *Jewish Women's Archive*, https://jwa.org/blog/breaking-modern-orthodox-glass-ceiling.

7. See especially the creative scholarship of Marcia Falk, *The Book of Blessings: New Jewish Prayers for Daily Life, the Sabbath, and the New Moon Festival* (New York: Harper Collins, 1996); see also the work of Rachel Adler, *Engendering Judaism: An Inclusive Theology and Ethics* (Philadelphia, PA: Jewish Publication Society, 1998). Imported from liberal Judaism in North America, interest in gender issues in prayer in Israel has increased in the past three decades.

8. Blu Greenberg, *On Women and Judaism: A View from Tradition* (Philadelphia, PA: Jewish Publication Society, 1981); and Susan Grossman and Rivka Haut, *Daughters of the King: Women and the Synagogue (A Survey of History, Halakhah, and Contemporary Realities)* (Philadelphia, PA: Jewish Publication Society, 1993).

9. See Susannah Heschel, ed. *On Being a Jewish Feminist: A Reader* (New York: Schocken, 1983).

10. Statement made by Rabbi Margaret Holub in 2012 in response to my request to reflect on the recent changes affecting women in Judaism; shared by permission.

11. Judith Plaskow, *Standing Again at Sinai* (San Francisco: Harper & Row, 1990); "Jewish Theology in Feminist Perspective," *Feminist Perspectives on Jewish Studies*, ed. Lynn Davidman and Shelly Tenenbaum, 62–84 (New Haven, CT, and London: Yale University Press, 1994); and "The Right Question Is Theological," in *On Being a Jewish Feminist: A Reader*, ed. Susannah Heschel, 223–33 (New York: Schocken, 1983).

12. See Rachel Adler, *Engendering Judaism: An Inclusive Theology and Ethics* (Jewish Publication Society, 1998). Her earlier essays include important and thought-provoking critiques, such as "The Jew Who Was Not There."

13. Ellen Umansky, "Creating a Jewish Feminist Theology: Possibilities and Problems," *Weaving the Visions: New Patterns in Feminist Spirituality*, ed. Judith Plaskow and Carol P. Christ, 187–98 (San Francisco: HarperOne, 1989); Ellen Umansky, "(Re)Imaging the Divine," *Response* 41–42 (Fall-Winter 1982): 110–19; and Ellen Umansky and Dianne Ashton, eds., *Four Centuries of Jewish Women's Spirituality: A Sourcebook* (Waltham, MA: Brandeis University Press, 2008).

14. Marcia Falk, *The Book of Blessings: New Jewish Prayers for Daily Life, the Sabbath and the New Moon Festival* (San Francisco: CCAR Press, 1996); Marcia Falk, "Notes on Composing New Blessings: Toward a Feminist-Jewish Reconstruction of Prayer," *Journal of Feminist Studies in Religion* 3 (Spring 1987): 39–53; and Marcia Falk, "Response to Feminist Reflections on Separation and Unity in Jewish Theology," *Journal of Feminist Studies in Religion* 2 (Spring 1986): 121–25.

15. In Genesis, Rabbah, and other rabbinic texts, the rabbis see Eve as having an overdeveloped sexual drive. For an extensive examination of Eve in rabbinic literature, see Wojciech Kosiór, "A Tale of Two Sisters: The Image of Eve in Early Rabbinic Literature and Its Influence on the Portrayal of Lilith in the Alphabet of Ben Sira," *Nashim: A Journal of Jewish Women's Studies & Gender Issues* 32 (2018): 112–30.

16. See, for example, Plaskow, *Standing Again at Sinai*; and Rebecca Alpert, *Like Bread on the Seder Plate: Jewish Lesbians and the Transformation of Tradition* (New York: Columbia University Press, 1997).

17. Alpert's writings include *Like Bread on the Seder Plate*; *Lesbian Rabbis: The First Generation*, edited with Sue Elwell and Shirley Idelson (Rutgers University Press, 2001); and *Whose Torah?: A Concise Guide to Progressive Judaism* (New York: The New Press, 2008).

18. This was a significant issue during the height of the epidemic in the 1980s.

19. Institute for Judaism and Sexual Orientation, "Mission and Vision," http://ijso.huc.edu/about/.

20. Liturgy prepared by Virginia Spatz, songeveryday.wordpress.com, for Occupy Shabbat DC.

21. Rabbi Reuben Zellman, "Transgender Shabbat Liturgy," *TransTorah.org*, May 3, 2020, https://www.keshetonline.org/resources/transgender-shabbat-liturgy/.

BIBLIOGRAPHY

Adler, Rachel. *Engendering Judaism: An Inclusive Theology and Ethics*. Philadelphia, PA: Jewish Publication Society, 1998.

Alpert, Rebecca. *Like Bread on the Seder Plate: Jewish Lesbians and the Transformation of Tradition*. New York: Columbia University Press, 1997.

———. *Whose Torah?: A Concise Guide to Progressive Judaism*. New York: The New Press, 2008.

Alpert, Rebecca, ed., with Sue Elwell and Shirley Idelson. *Lesbian Rabbis: The First Generation*. New Brunswick, NJ: Rutgers University Press, 2001.

Bilick, Eva. "Breaking the Modern Orthodox Glass Ceiling." *Jewish Women's Archive*. February 20, 2013. https://jwa.org/blog/breaking-modern-orthodox-glass-ceiling.

Falk, Marcia. *The Book of Blessings: New Jewish Prayers for Daily Life, the Sabbath, and the New Moon Festival*. New York: HarperCollins, 1996.

———. "Notes on Composing New Blessings: Toward a Feminist-Jewish Reconstruction of Prayer." *Journal of Feminist Studies in Religion* 3 (Spring 1987): 39–53.

———. "Response to Feminist Reflections on Separation and Unity in Jewish Theology," *Journal of Feminist Studies in Religion* 2 (Spring 1986): 121–25.

Greenberg, Blu. *On Women and Judaism: A View from Tradition*. Philadelphia, PA: Jewish Publication Society, 1981.

Goldstein, Elyse, ed. *New Jewish Feminism: Probing the Past, Forcing the Future*. Nashville, TN: Jewish Lights, 2008.

Grossman, Susan, and Rivka Haut. *Daughters of the King: Women and the Synagogue (A Survey of History, Halakhah, and Contemporary Realities)*. Philadelphia, PA: Jewish Publication Society, 1993.

Heschel, Susannah, ed. *On Being a Jewish Feminist: A Reader*. New York: Schocken, 1983.

Kosiór, Wojciech. "A Tale of Two Sisters: The Image of Eve in Early Rabbinic Literature and Its Influence on the Portrayal of Lilith in the Alphabet of Ben Sira." *Nashim: A Journal of Jewish Women's Studies & Gender Issues* 32 (2018): 112–30.

Ladin, Joy. *The Soul of the Stranger: Reading God and Torah from a Transgender Perspective*. Waltham, MA: Brandeis University Press, 2018.

Loeb, Eryn. "Idle Worship," *Tablet Magazine*. August 15, 2011. https://www.tabletmag.com/sections/arts-letters/articles/idle-worship.

Meyer, Michael. *Response to Modernity: A History of the Reform Movement in Judaism*. Detroit, MI: Wayne State University Press, 1995.

Nadell, Pamela S. "Rabbis in the United States." *Jewish Women: A Comprehensive Historical Encyclopedia*. February 27, 2009. https://jwa.org/encyclopedia/article/rabbis-in-united-states.

———. *Women Who Would Be Rabbis*. Boston: Beacon Press, 1998.

Peskowitz, Miriam, and Laura Levitt, eds. *Judaism Since Gender*. New York: Routledge, 1996.

Plaskow, Judith, "Jewish Theology in Feminist Perspective." In *Feminist Perspectives on Jewish Studies*, edited by Lynn Davidman and Shelly Tenenbaum, 62–84. New Haven and London: Yale University Press, 1994.

———. *Standing Again at Sinai*. San Francisco: Harper & Row, 1990.

Raveh, Inbar. *Feminist Rereadings of Rabbinic Literature*. Chicago: University of Chicago Press, 2015.

Stein, Abby. *Becoming Eve: My Journey from Ultra-Orthodox Rabbi to Transgender Woman*. Emeryville, CA: Seal Press, 2019.

Umansky, Ellen. "(Re)Imaging the Divine." *Response* 41–42 (Fall-Winter 1982): 110–19.

Umansky, Ellen, and Dianne Ashton, eds. *Four Centuries of Jewish Women's Spirituality: A Sourcebook*. Waltham, MA: Brandeis University Press, 2008.

Zellman, Rabbi Reuben. "Transgender Shabbat Liturgy." *TransTorah.org*. May 3, 2020. https://www.keshetonline.org/resources/transgender-shabbat-liturgy/.

CHAPTER 14

Muslimah Theology and Praxis

Huzur Mukhiani Dr. Zayn Kassam, Pomona College

ABSTRACT

Theological reflections on the part of Muslim women regarding their roles in Islam have been undertaken most famously by Azizah al-Hibri, Riffat Hassan, Amina Wadud, Asma Barlas, and Aysha Hidayatullah, among others. However, what has emerged as an interesting development is how Muslim women's religiosity is being played out as they deal with the messy world of theologically inflected and socially inscribed inequities. Organizations that explore theology-in-action are most notably Musawah, located in Indonesia, and reflect the turn to what Sa'diyya Shaikh has termed a "*tafsīr* of praxis."

As the novel coronavirus pandemic spreads throughout the globe, a newspaper headline and image capture my attention: "Myrtle Beach Mosque Hosts Drive-Through Supply Drive to Help During Coronavirus Quarantine," accompanied by an image of two hijab-wearing and thus identifiably Muslim women, one with a loaf of cellophane-encased bread in her hand while the other inclines her head, ostensibly focused on preparing to fill or filling a plastic bag with food. The image captures Muslim women as indispensable to the efforts of the Grand Strand Islamic Society in Horry County, Myrtle Beach, South Carolina, to live out the Islamic principle articulated by the Imam of the mosque, "that we should help each other as much as we can."[1] It also signals the participation and contributions of such migrant and racialized communities to American life, of which they are a part in this nation comprised so greatly of immigrants, historically and into the present.

Yet, for some, this story reinforces much of what they think is wrong with Islam and by extension Muslims: the women work away silently while a male Imam articulates what Islam is; the women are covered, a sure sign that their shariah or religious law controls women and sexualizes them so that they have to hide their beauty; and such charitable acts during a time of crisis bring to mind a crisis two decades ago when members of that same faith flew passenger planes into the Twin Towers in New York City in a suicide mission that unleashed American wars in Afghanistan and Iraq as well as a global War on Terror. Muslim women are also indispensable to such (mis)conceptualizations, for Islam as a faith is read as trampling on the rights of women and extending such violence to free societies across the globe; thus, to save the world from Islam is also to save its women. Such a misreading begs the question of how studies of Muslim women are framed.

HOW DO WE FRAME THE SUBJECT OF WOMEN IN ISLAM?

The first problem is the assumption that Muslim women share the same experiences and act in a certain manner because of their religion. Muslim women are by no means unified by their religion such that any Muslim woman anywhere in the world will experience the same strictures or privileges as her Muslim sisters elsewhere. Rather, the issue is more complex in that a Muslim woman's experience of being a woman and being a Muslim will differ depending on the specificities of her cultural, social, and economic location. The majority of the world's Muslim women live in South and Southeast Asia, followed by Muslim women in Africa, followed by the Middle East. Contrary to most expectations, more Muslims live outside the Middle East and most Muslims are not Arab. Depending on where in the world a Muslim woman lives, she is also affected by larger forces, such as economic globalization, increasing western cultural hegemony, a deteriorating global environment, war, migration pressures, and other such forces.

Second, it is often assumed that all third world women suffer privations due to the system of patriarchy in their culture or religion, which explains why women are oppressed "over there." Chandra Talpade Mohanty in a landmark essay first published in 1984 calls this:

> the "third world difference"—that stable, ahistorical something that apparently oppresses most if not all women in these countries. And it is in the production of this "third world difference" that Western feminisms appropriate and colonize the constitutive complexities which characterize the lives of women in these countries.[2]

Since the vast majority of Muslim women live in areas of the world that are not wealthy or, if they are, do not conform to western standards of social development, it takes a short step to suggest that Islam and Muslims perpetuate gender inequality and that Muslim women are viewed as victims of their religion, culture, and societies. The stereotype of the "The Muslim Woman" rests, on the one hand, on western "representations of [Muslim women] as backward, oppressed and politically immature women in need of liberation and rescue through imperialist interventions" and, on the other hand, internal Muslim "religious extremism and puritan discourses that authorize equally limiting narratives of Islamic womanhood and compromise [her] (their) human rights and liberty."[3]

Awareness of such prejudices and presuppositions in relation to Muslim women is essential to avoid making generalizations about all Muslim women and to avoid reducing the specificity of the historical, social, political, economic, and cultural contexts in which Muslim women live to the assumption that their situation is dictated solely by their religious adherence to Islam. This does not mean Muslim women through the centuries have not had to face struggles for gender equality and equitable treatment in their social institutions, including those created under religious guidance. It is here that thoughtful scholarship has sought to examine and understand the role that Islam and Muslim social institutions played in inscribing inequities for Muslim women.

THE TEXT, THE LAW, AND WOMEN: A BRIEF HISTORICAL CONSIDERATION

The first question we may ask is, Does the Qur'ān, Islam's holy book, make women secondary to men? Several verses affirm that the Qur'ān offers both sexes moral and spiritual equality and dignity. For instance, the Qur'ān makes no differentiation between the soul of a woman and the soul of man (Q. 4:1), holds female life to be intrinsically valuable (Q. 81:9), and views the creation of the woman as one of a pair because God creates all things in pairs (Q. 35:11 "Allah created you from dust, then from a little fluid, then He made you pairs"). No mention is made of the woman having been created from a male or to serve the male. Moreover, both men and women are judged on their piety and righteousness (*taqwa*) and are held equally accountable to God for their own moral decisions and actions (Q. 33:35).

However, there are verses pertaining to the social and legal spheres that Muslims have traditionally interpreted as giving men rights over women. For instance, Q. 4:34 states that men are a degree above women. Women are to inherit half the percentages allotted to men (Q. 4:11), and two women's testimony is worth that of one male (Q. 2:282). Q. 4:34 has also been read as authorizing husbands to beat their disobedient wives and Q. 4:3, as allowing men to marry up to four women. Yet, as Leila Ahmed notes in her magisterial work, "The unmistakable presence of ethical egalitarianism . . . explains why Muslim women frequently insist, often inexplicably to non-Muslims, that Islam is not sexist. They hear and read in its sacred text, justly and legitimately, a different message from that heard by the makers and enforcers of orthodox, androcentric Islam."[4]

The central or key issue here surrounds how the Qur'ān is to be interpreted. Are these verses binding for all Muslims over all time, or are they to be viewed as speaking to their historical context, as leading thinkers, such as the one-time Shaykh of al-Azhar, Muhammad Abduh (d. 1905 CE), have argued? In the Qur'ān itself only about 200 some verses out of 7,000 speak of legal matters. The medieval codes of Islamic law, or what has been called shari'ah, by and large formulated by the eleventh century, relied on (1) the Qur'ān as well as the commentaries on the Qur'ān, (2) the Tradition or Hadith literature, which narrates what the 8th- and 9th-century Muslim community remembers as the Prophet having said or done, (3) local custom (*adat*), (4) the independent reasoning of legal scholars (*ijtihād*), (5) the consensus (*'ijma*) of the learned community; and for some schools, (6) analogy (*qiyas*), and in Shi'i legal schools, the employment of logic (*mantiq*) to test the soundness of juridical reasoning.

Two important factors affect how Islamic law deals with women. First, the Qur'ān does not endow women with specific characteristics relating to their sex, what we call essentialism, the idea that women are inherently weak, inferior, emotional, etc. However, the rapid expansion of Muslims into Byzantine and Persian territories exposed Muslims to societies that were patriarchal long before the Qur'ān was revealed in the seventh century. Both patriarchal interpretations of the Qur'ān and patriarchal social institutions entered the Islamic intellectual and social arenas with the expansion of the Muslim empire, at the same time the Muslim legal schools were being formulated. A case in point, as has been so ably explored by Barbara Freyer Stowasser, is that, in the Qur'ān, the first female, named extra-Qur'ānically as Hawwa (the Eve figure) is not created from the rib of Adam, nor is she responsible for succumbing to Satan's lure, as is Eve in the Biblical tradition. However, male scholars who collected traditions of the prophet and wrote Qur'ānic commentaries imported such biblical notions from Jewish and Christian sources into the Islamic understanding of Hawwa, or Eve. As a result, the story that Eve was created from the rib of the male, Adam, was imported into Islam and, with it, attitudes toward women, which played a key role in how verses pertaining to women were interpreted by Muslims. Thus, even though the Qur'ān says no such thing, women were made not only subordinate to men, but, from Biblical sources, they also gave women characteristics such as being weak, in need of protection, ruled by their emotions, subject to the pain of childbirth, seductive, and responsible for the fall of men from their heavenly state. Jewish and Christian feminist women have had to reclaim their equality with men before God in pointing to another Genesis account, 1:26–27.

Muslim legal schools emulated the Byzantine and Persian societies in which they found themselves, where both veiling and seclusion were markers of high status for Jewish, Christian, and Zoroastrian women and served to distinguish "good" women from "fallen" women—indeed, women of economically lower class or women who wanted to signal that they were available for men—were either forbidden to veil or did not veil. Thus, medieval Muslim jurists drew upon verses in the Qur'ān to make the practices of veiling and/or seclusion applicable to all Muslim women in conformance with the traditions of the non-Muslim communities in the conquered domains. The verses they drew upon were verses such as the Qur'ān's command to Muslim women "to draw their scarves (*khumur*)[5] around their bosoms" (Q. 24:31) and "to draw their cloaks (*jilbab*) around themselves (when outdoors) so that they may be recognized and not be harassed" (Q. 33:59). The Qur'ān further asks that the wives of the Prophet be approached "from behind a curtain" (*hijāb*) (Q. 33:53), meaning a physical curtain that would divide space in a room, for example. Such verses were utilized by medieval Muslim jurists to turn a physical barrier—a *hijāb*—into a portable barrier, the veil, adopting conventions observed by the non-Muslim women in the conquered domains. Ironically, the spirit of protection underlying the cloak verse has today come to be viewed as a sign of oppression of Muslim women by their menfolk and their religion, in contrast to the original intent of the verses to uphold standards of modesty and afford protection to women in public spaces and that were, at that time, in keeping with the customs of upper-class Jewish, Christian, and Zoroastrian women. Thus, although veiling in the sense of covering one's head and, in some instances, the face, is not explicitly mandated by the Qur'ān, it marks a historical development in medieval Muslim legal and customary practice to signal prestige and conformance with local practices in the domains of the Islamic empire.

Let me turn to Islamic law to try to address two questions. First of all, although in commonplace usage, *shari'a* is used as a catch-all term to mean Islamic law, Islamic jurisprudence should properly be called *fiqh*. *Shari'a* denotes the divine and moral principles behind the system of Islamic law and is not monolithic. There are differences of interpretation and application across the various Sunni and Shi'a legal schools, so much so that there is in fact no singular *shari'a* law for women. Islamic law has continually been revised and added to over the course of centuries in keeping with the needs of society.

During the time of the Islamic empires, which lasted until the Ottoman Empire, which ended in 1919, the caliphs took over significant portions of the law under their control, including commercial law, constitutional law, and the laws governing foreign relations. Ironically, in the last centuries of three Muslim empires, the Persian, the Mughal, and Ottoman, the state legal system incorporated features of the French, the British, and the Roman codes of law and, in so doing, also imported their prejudices against women. Concomitantly, during colonial British rule over majority Muslim societies, such as Egypt and India, the British imposed a uniform secular administrative code but left clearly oppressive family laws in the hands of religious authorities by declaring that these were of divine origin and therefore should not be touched,[6] suggesting that in both cases attitudes toward male privilege were shared by colonial and Muslim administrations alike. Some would argue that the British were in fact retaining the patriarchal advantage because it was not in their interest to promote the rights of women. At the same time that they criticized Egyptian Muslims on how they treated Muslim women, they closed down schools for them, thereby ensuring that women would not have social advantages through education. Such "fixing" of legal codes meant that *shari'a* law, which until the modern period was not fixed and was continually able to adjust itself in paying attention to changing social needs, was now turned into a fixed, divinely ordained body of laws pertaining to women.

Muslim legal regimes "adopted (French or British) definitions of family and the family's role in the modern nation-state. The European model emphasized 'family stability' and limited divorce rights, largely on the basis of Christian doctrine, in order to solidify citizen relations for the ultimate purpose of state control and planning in the political and economic realms."[7] Such an emphasis on family stability and divorce rights contradicted Islamic marriage, which was at that point simply a contract among other contracts (and thus not "sacred") and not so rigidly defined.[8] Such British intervention has led to the internalization of the British-induced idea that family law is divinely originated. Therefore, changing family law became synonymous with trying to change Islam.

While earlier in the twentieth century, Muslim women had begun to take off the head covering, or *hijāb*, increasingly toward its end, Muslim women were taking on the veil. In part, the veiling or re-veiling of women is attributable to post-colonial developments. Every Muslim country has been under colonial rule with the exception of three: Saudi Arabia, which was under the British Mandate; Iran, which nonetheless saw much intervention in its affairs by the British, the French, and the Russians; and Turkey, which is what was left when the Ottoman Empire was disbanded by the Allied powers after the First World War. Lord Cromer, the British governor of Egypt, who opposed female suffragettes in England, nonetheless felt he had to be a feminist in Egypt. He identified Muslim societies as backward and in need of civilization and Christianization on the grounds that a sign of their backwardness was the manner in which such societies treated their women, by veiling and secluding them. Leila Ahmed, a Harvard historian of gender in Islam, has astutely observed how the resistance narrative of Muslims both reversed and ironically accepted the terms set in the first place by the colonizers.

In response to such attacks on their culture and religion, anti-colonial movements in Muslim societies reversed the colonial narrative, such that the adoption of the veil, whether enforced or voluntary, "came to symbolize in the resistance narrative, not the inferiority of the culture and the need to cast aside its customs in favor of those of the West, but, on the contrary, the dignity and validity of all native customs, and in particular those customs coming under fiercest colonial attack—the customs relating to women—and the need to tenaciously affirm them as a means of resistance to Western domination."[9] Doing so, however, re-entrenched Muslim patriarchal elites, and thus Muslim women find that their bodies are the battleground on which struggles for power and authenticity are being waged. Thus, the *hijāb* is suspended within a triangulated formation, with many Muslim women viewing it as a religious observance that also informs their self-identity as postcolonial Muslims; liberal western observers who continue to view it through orientalist lenses as signifying all that is wrong with Islam in terms of gender equity; and Muslim authorities who continue to operate from androcentric paradigms. When the *hijāb* carries over into the *niqāb*, a garment that extends the head covering to the face, leaving only the eyes visible to view, these tropes become magnified to the extent that some western governments have legislated against the wearing of face veils in public, notably Quebec, France, Germany, Austria, Belgium, Denmark, Bulgaria, Russia, and parts of Italy, Switzerland, and Spain.[10] COVID-19 has led one author to write an exposé on the hypocrisy of *hijāb* and *niqāb* bans in asking, "If we all start wearing masks does it mean we have succumbed to a form of oppression?"[11]

Contrary to Kipling's tired old trope that "East is East and West is West / never the twain shall meet"—a line strategically quoted in willful ignorance of the lines following—"But there is neither East nor West, Border, nor Breed, nor Birth, / When two strong men stand face to face, tho' they come from the ends of the earth!"[12]—a historical examination reveals that in fact East and West are more intertwined than one could have imagined. Thus, the Qur'ān's verses on women were interpreted in a patriarchal fashion largely due to the Byzantine Christian and Persian Zoroastrian contexts in which Muslims found themselves. Additionally, *shari'a* laws relating to women are not standard, varying as they do from Muslim-majority country to country, while the colonial fixing of legal codes had an adverse effect on laws pertaining to women, and the colonial representation of the backwardness of Islam has reinforced Muslim calls on women to veil in order to mark their difference from their former colonial masters, on the one hand, and to resist westernization, on the other.

It is against such a complex background that Muslim gender activists find themselves increasingly called to argue for reform on matters pertaining to personal status codes and family law by reinterpreting Islamic foundational and authoritative texts, rather than appealing to secular notions of nationhood or regimes such as the Universal Declaration of Human Rights. An appeal to secularism is seen simply as caving in to western values at a time when the memories of western colonization and the privations caused by western neoliberal economic globalization are being keenly felt, as evinced in the Arab movements (dubbed "the Arab spring"), which had as much to do with economics as they did with resistance against authoritarian political regimes.

Isobel Coleman in her study of women in Muslim societies (Saudi Arabia, Iraq, Iran, Afghanistan, and Pakistan) notes that progressive Muslim men and women, whom she terms "quiet revolutionaries," "are using Islamic feminism to change the terms of religious debate, to fight for women's rights within Islam instead of against it."[13] Two arenas in which Muslim activists are working for gender justice concern re-reading the Qur'ān to ascertain with a fresh eye and contemporary sensibilities what it says about women, and the second concerns how Muslim women are mobilizing to advance protections under their national legal systems.

QUR'ĀNIC FEMINIST HERMENEUTICS

While much work yet remains to be done, the twentieth century has seen a remarkable advance in the production of literature and analysis examining the scriptural underpinnings for gender justice in Islam, especially by North American Muslim academics. The Muslim feminist scholars Azizah al-Hibri and Riffat Hassan[14] argue, as their Jewish and Christian feminist counterparts did with respect to the Bible, that the Qur'ān is a scriptural text that offers women dignity and rights that Muslim societies have not always given to them and, further, that women are ontologically equal to men in the Qur'ānic perspective. Riffat Hassan lays the groundwork for the status of women in Islam in noting that the woman was neither created from the male, for the male, or as secondary to him. Her work opens up the possibility of considering the autonomous ethical imperative and agency that belongs to a woman, regardless of her biology, before Allah, despite the attempts of later Islamic discourses to curtail it largely as a response to prevailing cultural norms in the Byzantine and Sassanian territories conquered by the early Muslims.[15] The work of al-Hibri and Riffat Hassan has been continued by several scholars.[16] Amina Wadud and Asma Barlas sound some of the keynotes in feminist Qur'ānic hermeneutics.

Both Amina Wadud and Asma Barlas argue against reading Qur'ānic verses selectively and out of context, making the case instead that the Qur'ān has to be read holistically, within the context in which the relevant verses were revealed, and take into account the culture of seventh century Arabia as well as the presuppositions of the times in which the Qur'ān was interpreted. Not to do so, they argue, would compromise the Qur'ān's ability to be an eternally valid text of guidance for Muslims, regardless of time and place.

Wadud suggests that any Qur'ānic hermeneutic must distinguish between what she calls the "spirit" of the Qur'ān,[17] by which she means the [ethical] principles of the Qur'ān, and the socially regulatory verses of the Qur'ān that spoke to the seventh century Arabian contexts in which they were revealed. Thus, the goal of her work is to read the Qur'ān from "within the female experience and without the stereotypes which have been the framework for many of the male interpretations."[18]

For instance, she examines the wife-beating verse that has been interpreted to mean that all women must obey their husbands and, if they do not, they should be beaten.[19] By reading the Qur'ān in light of its principles concerning ethics and morals and social justice she opens up the possibility of "adapting the text to a multitude of culturally diverse situations in a constantly changing world of social communities."[20] Accordingly, she argues that this particular text must be read as being restricted to the particular seventh-century Arabian context. Furthermore, turning to the example of the Prophet himself, she finds that he "never struck a woman." Given the centrality of the paradigmatic example of the Prophet for devout Muslims, she argues that Muslim men cannot justify beating their wives based on Muḥammad's example. Islamic codes of law interpreted this verse as a restriction of such a beating, thereby confirming "a textual understanding against the use of it [that is, the verse] for unabashed spousal abuse or domestic violence."[21]

Asma Barlas examines the Qur'ān for examples of traditional patriarchy, especially in the form of patriarchal marriage, in which the distinction between the father and the husband is blurred. The father/husband is designated as God's surrogate on earth, establishing the woman/wife as his property/child and as someone over whom he has authority. She argues instead that "the Qur'ān not only does not link the rights of fathers and husbands in this way, but it also does not appoint either one a ruler or guardian over his wife (and children), or even as the head of the household. Nor does it designate the wife and children as the man's property or require them to be submissive to him."[22]

So, for instance, the Qur'ān counsels children to be kind to their parents in their old age (17:23–24) and re-emphasizes that even parents have no right to make children obey them in worshipping someone other than God (31:14–15). The verse suggests a human being, whether male or female, is free to disobey parents in matters of faith, thereby bringing home Barlas's point that the Qur'ān does not view "as legitimate the sanctity of the father's rule or traditional views of fathers as heads of the household."[23] That is, the Qur'ān does not regard the father as God's representative on earth, and, further, his authority is not regarded as an extension of God's authority. A close reading of the Qur'ān, therefore, suggests that traditional Muslim patriarchal understandings linking father-right and paternal privilege as symbolic of God on earth is a misreading of the Qur'ān. Verses such as these undermine medieval masculine interpretations of the Qur'ān that gave greater authority in all matters to men in keeping with their Christian and Jewish counterparts, who did the same in their religious traditions.

However, in *Feminist Edges of the Qur'ān*, Aysha Hidayatullah posits that the verses gesturing to mutuality between the sexes and those supporting hierarchy cannot be reconciled;[24] rather, it is quite possible that the Qur'ān upholds both mutuality and hierarchy. It is *our* expectation that the Qur'ān conform to our views on gender equity that makes such verses appear contradictory or needing an apologetic feminist reading. Rather, she posits that "it is time to imagine new ways to achieve Islamically grounded justice"[25] and identifies questions drawn from insights garnered from comparative feminist work to rethink how to seek "the liberatory potential of texts while also confronting their androcentric elements."[26] A similar contention is leveled by Sherine Hafez, who critiques Saba Mahmood's influential study of pious women in Egypt, articulated in *Politics of Piety: The Islamic Revival and the Feminist Subject*,[27] in which the latter argues for a non-liberal alternative to Islamist women's agency. Hafez contends that, given "the complex and mutually imbricated discursive history of Islam and secularism in the

Egyptian context,"[28] when "Muslim women 'cultivate' piety by wearing a veil, they are simultaneously inculcated by discourses of colonialism, nationalism, liberal modernity, and local and global politics, in which both liberal and nonliberal imbrications configure their choices and practices and even their articulations of piety and ethical forms."[29] Thus, both Hidayatullah and Hafez gesture toward the power of context and the contemporary in forming and reforming subjectivities that struggle with drawing upon tradition while reformulating it with a contemporary sensibility.

Within the larger context of scriptural gender hermeneutics, Muslim feminist scholars make the case that gender justice for Muslim women does not entail having to leave the faith. Rather, multiple possibilities exist within the rich Islamic scriptural and discursive tradition and within Islamic praxis to assure Muslim women a dignified place in Muslim and non-Muslim societies, despite the institutional and historical impediments they face. And, indeed, there are gender activists in different Muslim societies doing just that.

WOMEN'S ACTIVISM

In addition to the dissemination of the works of scholars, such as those considered above, the twentieth century also witnessed the growth of women's magazines as sites of rethinking authoritative texts and resistance to hitherto accepted patriarchal norms. It also saw the formation of women's organizations employing both discursive and practical strategies to address issues of gender equity and justice. Perhaps one of the most notable women's magazines deserving mention is *Zanan*, founded in Iran in 1992 under the Khatami regime by Shahla Sherkat and closed down under the Ahmadinejad regime in 2008. The magazine created a forum for translation into Persian of key feminist works, discussions of such topics as the nature of women's rights, the scope of freedom of the press, new interpretations of Islamic texts, and legal issues. Giving voice to a diversity of viewpoints, the women's press in Iran:

> . . . and especially *Zanan*, provide[s] a forum for the articulation of diverse views, including those that are officially unpopular. As such, the women's press and those Islamic feminists associated with it are playing an important role in broadening the discursive universe of the Islamic Republic and in expanding legal literacy and gender consciousness among their readership. Also noteworthy is that the Islamic feminists who run *Zanan* and *Farzaneh* publish the writings of secular feminists.
>
> The rereading of the Islamic texts is a central project of Islamic feminists . . . [who] engage in new interpretations of Islamic texts in order to challenge laws and policies that are based on orthodox, literalist, or misogynist interpretations.[30]

In North America, *Azizah*, a magazine that describes itself as being for "the contemporary Muslim woman," was founded in 2000 by Tayyibah Taylor, a Trinidadian who converted to Islam in 1971 and was born to a Christian family, and an Indonesian Muslim woman, Marlina Soerakoesoemah. Targeted at the American Muslim woman, *Azizah* features articles ranging from Islamic law, art, raising children, and recipes to fashion and sports as well as incorporating reader suggestions on articles they might like to see, such as on childbirth. It has paid special attention to Muslim feminist scholars, who, according to Taylor, "show how 'the beautiful *Qur'ānic* ideals [do not support] the oppressive treatment of women in many Muslim societies, [thereby] inventing a feminism that is neither conventionally Eurocentric nor secular in its nature.' In other words, they are shaping an *Islamic* feminist discourse."[31]

In addition to the women's press, Muslim women have also formed several organizations that are transnational in scope in order to address local, national, and international issues of gender equity. Perhaps the most significant of these is Sisters in Islam (SIS), formed in 1988 in Malaysia. Its mission is to promote "the principles of gender equality, justice, freedom and dignity in Islam and empower women to be advocates for change."[32] In addition to hosting a wide variety of programs, seminars, workshops, and activities designed to disseminate information on gender rights within an Islamic framework, it also undertakes research.

The combination of research and activism is critical to the work undertaken by the organization. As a multi-year project, SIS has conducted a survey on the impact of polygamy on the family institution. In 2019, it published *Perceptions and Realities: The Public and Personal Rights of Muslim Women in Malaysia,* based on interviews conducted with 675 women ranging from homemakers to professionals across Malaysia. SIS has also collaborated with other Muslim women's organizations around the world to create Musawah: Campaign for Justice in Muslim Family Laws, which was launched at a global meeting in Kuala Lumpur in 2009 (see www.musawah.org). Musawah predicates its struggle for justice on the axiom that "There cannot be equality in society without equality in the family" and hence makes activism for equality in the family its primary mission.

Although organizations such as Sisters in Islam and Musawah have begun to have an impact locally, nationally, and internationally in the twenty-first century, it is in the latter decades of the twentieth century that we find the fermentation and thinking that would seed the directions they now take and identify the key areas of their focus. Sisters in Islam's genesis lay in a group of professional women who came together to discuss the discrimination women were facing under the Islamic Family Law Act of 1984, as a subcommittee formed by the Association of Women Lawyers in Malaysia. Recognizing that religion was often the justification given for men's superiority and rights in cases dealing with child custody, polygamy, and domestic violence, the group sought out the guidance of Amina Wadud, then a professor at the International Islamic University in Kuala Lumpur, in order to study for themselves key Islamic texts pertaining to gender.

Their studies with Wadud and other renowned US-based scholars, such as Abdullahi an-Na'im and Fathi Osman, brought home the realization that "injustice toward Muslim women is incompatible with the spirit of compassion and justice in the Qur'ān."[33] In addition to acquiring strategies through which to address such injustice, SIS was able to see that while "the Qur'ān is divine, *fiqh* [Islamic jurisprudence] is not,"[34] thereby enabling them to identify the need to "fracture" Islamic discursive and legal hegemony by utilizing feminist methods of engaging Islam in the public sphere. Thus, they began to organize public symposia and to network with Muslim women's organizations nationally and internationally, writing to the media on contested matters, such as polygamy. Undertaking research projects, such as the ones mentioned, jointly with universities and providing legal advice to lawyers dealing with cases entailing *shari'ah* law has garnered SIS criticism for being too liberal or for not having the credentials to reinterpret Islamic law, challenges that SIS has successfully overturned. As Basarudin observes, "SIS's faith-centered intellectual activism is located within the transnational struggles of Muslim women because it illuminates the local and global as bounded and shared geographical spaces that subscribe to historical specificities yet simultaneously connect women's diverse experiences of negotiating Islam."[35]

The above examples reflect to some extent what Sa'diyya Shaikh has termed a "*tafsīr* of praxis"[36] in relation to her work on spousal abuse in South African Muslim communities to foreground "how a group of Muslim women think and speak in relation to the text and engage God, ethics, and religion through the realities of their suffering and oppression."[37] Julianne Hammer extends such experientially informed readings/ interpretations (*tafsīr*) of the Qur'ān to argue "that the activism of American Muslim women (and men) in relation to women's religious authority and leadership in American Muslim communities, including the woman-led prayer, can be understood as an embodiment of a *tafsīr* of gender justice and equality."[38] This chapter has sought to show that there are profound connections between the discursive and the practical in struggling for and realizing gender justice globally and locally for Muslim women in ways perhaps not dissimilar from the intellectual and activist efforts of women in other religious traditions. In this regard, it could be unequivocally said that the efforts of feminist or woman-centered scholars and activists in every faith tradition during the twentieth century have laid the groundwork for ongoing engagement with the reality of women's lives for the twenty-first century.

NOTES

1. Donovan Harris, "Myrtle Beach Mosque Hosts Drive-Through Supply Drive to Help During Coronavirus Quarantine," *ABC 15 News*, April 4, 2020, https://wpde.com/news/coronavirus/myrtle-beach-mosque-hosts-drive-through-supply-drive-to-help-during-coronavirus-quarantine.

2. Chandra Talpade Mohanty, "Under Western Eyes: Feminist Scholarship and Colonial Discourses," in *Third World Women and the Politics of Feminism*, ed. Chandra Talpade Mohanty, Ann Russo, and Lourdes Torres (Bloomington: Indiana University Press, 1991), 53–55. This essay was first published in 1984, updated for this volume, and subsequently revisited in "'Under Western Eyes' Revisited: Feminist Solidarity through Anticapitalist Struggles," in *Feminism without Borders: Decolonizing Theory, Practicing Solidarity*, ed. Chandra Talpade Mohanty (Durham, NC: Duke University Press, 2003).

3. Jasmine Zine, "Between Orientalism and Fundamentalism: The Politics of Muslim Women's Feminist Engagement," *Muslim World Journal of Human Rights*, 3, no. 1 (2006), Article 5, 1.

4. "Leila Ahmed and Women's Voices in Islam" (blog), March 1, 2013, http://blog.yalebooks.com/2013/03/01/leila-ahmed-and-womens-voices-in-islam/.

5. It is unclear whether the *khimār* (scarf), here mentioned in connection with its use for covering the bosom, also covered the head. The Qur'ān does not explicitly call for head coverings, which could suggest that either the practice was so commonplace as to need no explicit mention or that the historical adoption of the practice of veiling when Muslims emulated Byzantine and Persian practices of covering the head afforded a lens through which to read the Qur'ān retroactively as legitimating head coverings.

6. Srimati Basu, "Cutting to Size: Property and Gendered Identity in the Indian Higher Courts," in *Signposts: Gender Issues in Post-Independence India*, ed. Rajeswari Sunder Rajan (New Delhi: Kali for Women, 1999), 254–57.

7. Barbara Freyer Stowasser and Zeinab Abul-Magd, "*Tahlil* Marriage in Shari'a, Legal Codes, and the Contemporary *Fatwa* Literature," in *Islamic Law and the Challenges of Modernity*, ed. Yvonne Yazbeck Haddad and Barbara Freyer Stowasser (Lanham, MD: Rowman & Littlefield, 2004), 168.

8. Stowasser and Abul-Magd, "*Tahlil* Marriage," 168.

9. Leila Ahmed, *Women and Gender in Islam* (New Haven: Yale University Press, 1992), 164.

10. "The Islamic Veil across Europe," BBC News, May 31, 2018, https://www.bbc.com/news/world-europe-13038095.

11. Katherine Bullock, "We Are All Niqabis Now: Coronavirus Masks Reveal Hypocrisy of Face Covering Bans," *The Conversation*, accessed April 28, 2020, https://theconversation.com/we-are-all-niqabis-now-coronavirus-masks-reveal-hypocrisy-of-face-covering-bans-136030.

12. Rudyard Kipling, "The Ballad of East and West," in *A Victorian Anthology, 1837–1895*, ed. Edmund Clarence Stedman (Cambridge, MA: Riverside Press, 1895).

13. See Isobel Coleman, *Paradise beneath Her Feet* (New York: Random House, 2010).

14. Azizah al-Hibri published her landmark essay, "A Study of Islamic Herstory: Or How Did We Get into This Mess," in *Women's Studies International Forum* 5, no. 2 (1982): 207–19, while Riffat Hassan's reflections on gender issues entered the American scene in 1987 with her essay titled, "Equal before Allah? Woman-Man Equality in the Islamic Tradition," in *Harvard Divinity Bulletin* 17, no. 2 (1987): 2–4.

15. See Ahmed, *Women and Gender in Islam*; and Barbara Freyer Stowasser, *Women in the Qur'an, Traditions, and Interpretation* (New York: Oxford University Press, 1996).

16. Amina Wadud, Asma Barlas, Nimet Barazangi, Khalid Abou El-Fadl, Amira El Azhary Sonbol, Kecia Ali, and others.

17. A term invoked by an Indian sub-continental Muslim thinker, Syed Ameer Ali (d. 1928), at the turn of the twentieth century in his landmark book, *The Spirit of Islam* (Piscataway, NJ: Gorgias Press, 2001).

18. Amina Wadud, *Qur'an and Woman: Rereading the Sacred Text from a Woman's Perspective* (Oxford: Oxford University Press, 1999), 3.

19. Wadud, *Qur'an and Woman*, 99.

20. Wadud, *Qur'an and Woman*, 100.

21. Amina Wadud, *Inside the Gender Jihad: Women's Reform in Islam* (Oxford: Oneworld, 2006), 202–203.

22. Asma Barlas, *"Believing Women" in Islam: Unreading Patriarchal Interpretations of the Qur'ān* (Austin, TX: University of Texas Press, 2002), 167–68.

23. Barlas, *"Believing Women,"* 176.

24. Aysha A. Hidayatullah, *Feminist Edges of the Qur'an* (New York: Oxford University Press, 2014), 151.

25. Hidayatullah, *Feminist Edges*, 193.

26. Aysha A. Hidayatullah, "Feminist Interpretation of the Qur'an in a Comparative Feminist Setting," *Journal of the Feminist Study of Religion* 30, no. 2 (2014): 115–30.

27. Saba Mahmood, *Politics of Piety: The Islamic Revival and the Feminist Subject* (Princeton, NJ: Princeton University Press, 2005, 2011).

28. Sherine Hafez, *An Islam of Her Own: Reconsidering Religion and Secularism in Women's Islamic Movements* (New York: New York University Press, 2011), 11.

29. Hafez, *An Islam of Her Own*, 11.

30. Valentine M. Moghadam, "Islamic Feminism and Its Discontents: Towards a Resolution of the Debate," in *Gender, Politics, and Islam*, ed. Therese Saliba, Carolyn Allen, and Judith A. Howard (Chicago: University of Chicago Press, 2002), 15–52, 35.

31. Jamillah Karim, "Voices of Faith, Faces of Beauty: Connecting American Muslim Women through Azizah," in *Muslim Networks from Hajj to Hip Hop*, ed. miriam cooke and Bruce B. Lawrence (Chapel Hill: University of North Carolina Press, 2005), 169–88, 184.

32. Sisters in Islam, "Mission and Vision," https://sistersinislam.org/mission-and-vision/.

33. Azza Basarudin, "In Search of Faithful Citizens in Postcolonial Malaysia," in *Women and Islam*, ed. Zayn R. Kassam (Santa Barbara, CA: Praeger, 2010), 93–127, 103.

34. Basarudin, "In Search of Faithful Citizens," 103.

35. Basarudin, "In Search of Faithful Citizens," 116.

36. Sa'diyya Shaikh, "A Tafsīr of Praxis: Gender, Marital Violence, and Resistance in a South African Muslim Community," in *Violence against Women in Contemporary World Religions: Roots and Cures*, ed. Daniel C. Maguire and Sa'diyya Shaikh (Cleveland, OH: Pilgrim Place, 2007), 66–89.

37. Shaikh, "A Tafsīr of Praxis," 70.

38. Julianne Hammer, "Activism as Embodied *Tafsīr*: Negotiating Women's Authority, Leadership, and Space in North America," in *Women, Leadership, and Mosques: Changes in Contemporary Islamic Authority*, ed. Hilary Kalmbach and Masooda Bano (Leiden: Brill, 2011), 457–80, 460.

BIBLIOGRAPHY

Ahmed, Leila. *Women and Gender in Islam*. New Haven, CT: Yale University Press, 1992.

Al-Hibri, Azizah. "A Study of Islamic Herstory: Or How Did We Get into This Mess." *Women's Studies International Forum* 5, no. 2 (1982): 207–19.

Barlas, Asma. *"Believing Women" in Islam: Unreading Patriarchal Interpretations of the Qur'ān*. Austin, TX: University of Texas Press, 2002.

Basarudin, Azza. "In Search of Faithful Citizens in Postcolonial Malaysia." In *Women and Islam*, edited by Zayn R. Kassam, 93–127. Santa Barbara, CA: Praeger, 2010.

Basu, Srimati. "Cutting to Size: Property and Gendered Identity in the Indian Higher Courts." In *Signposts: Gender Issues in Post-Independence India*, edited by Rajeswari Sunder Rajan, 248–91. New Delhi: Kali for Women, 1999.

Bullock, Katherine. "We Are All Niqabis Now: Coronavirus Masks Reveal Hypocrisy of Face Covering Bans." *The Conversation*. Accessed April 28, 2020. https://theconversation.com/we-are-all-niqabis-now-coronavirus-masks-reveal-hypocrisy-of-face-covering-bans-136030.

Coleman, Isobel. *Paradise beneath Her Feet*. New York: Random House, 2010.

Hafez, Sherine. *An Islam of Her Own: Reconsidering Religion and Secularism in Women's Islamic Movements*. New York: New York University Press, 2011.

Hammer, Julianne. "Activism as Embodied *Tafsīr*: Negotiating Women's Authority, Leadership, and Space in North America." In *Women, Leadership, and Mosques: Changes in Contemporary Islamic Authority*, edited by Hilary Kalmbach and Masooda Bano, 457–80. Leiden: Brill, 2011.

Harris, Donovan. "Myrtle Beach Mosque Hosts Drive-Through Supply Drive to Help During Coronavirus Quarantine." *ABC 15 News*, April 4, 2020. https://wpde.com/news/coronavirus/myrtle-beach-mosque-hosts-drive-through-supply-drive-to-help-during-coronavirus-quarantine.

Hassan, Riffat. "Equal before Allah? Woman-Man Equality in the Islamic Tradition." *Harvard Divinity Bulletin* 17, no. 2 (1987): 2–4.

Hidayatullah, Aysha A. *Feminist Edges of the Qur'an*. New York: Oxford University Press, 2014.

———. "Feminist Interpretation of the Qur'an in a Comparative Feminist Setting." *Journal of the Feminist Study of Religion* 30, no. 2 (2014): 115–30.

Karim, Jamillah. "Voices of Faith, Faces of Beauty: Connecting American Muslim Women through Azizah." In *Muslim Networks from Hajj to Hip Hop*, edited by miriam cooke and Bruce B. Lawrence, 169–88. Chapel Hill: University of North Carolina Press, 2005.

Kipling, Rudyard. "The Ballad of East and West." In *A Victorian Anthology, 1837–1895*, edited by Edmund Clarence Stedman. Cambridge, MA: Riverside Press, 1895.

Mahmood, Saba. *Politics of Piety: The Islamic Revival and the Feminist Subject*. Princeton, NJ: Princeton University Press, 2005, 2011.

Moghadam, Valentine M. "Islamic Feminism and Its Discontents: Towards a Resolution of the Debate." In *Gender, Politics, and Islam*, edited by Therese Saliba, Carolyn Allen, and Judith A. Howard, 15–52. Chicago: University of Chicago Press, 2002.

Mohanty, Chandra Talpade. "Under Western Eyes: Feminist Scholarship and Colonial Discourses." In *Third World Women and the Politics of Feminism*, edited by Chandra Talpade Mohanty, Ann Russo, and Lourdes Torres. Bloomington: Indiana University Press, 1991.

Shaikh, Sa'diyya. "A Tafsīr of Praxis: Gender, Marital Violence, and Resistance in a South African Muslim Community." In *Violence against Women in Contemporary World Religions: Roots and Cures*, edited by Daniel C. Maguire and Sa'diyya Shaikh, 66–89. Cleveland, OH: Pilgrim Place, 2007.

Stowasser, Barbara Freyer. *Women in the Qur'an, Traditions, and Interpretation*. New York: Oxford University Press, 1996.

Stowasser, Barbara Freyer, and Zeinab Abul-Magd, "*Tahlil* Marriage in Shari'a, Legal Codes, and the Contemporary *Fatwa* Literature." In *Islamic Law and the Challenges of Modernity*, edited by Yvonne Yazbeck Haddad and Barbara Freyer Stowasser, 161–82. Lanham, MD: Rowman & Littlefield, 2004.

Wadud, Amina. *Inside the Gender Jihad: Women's Reform in Islam*. Oxford: Oneworld, 2006.

———. *Qur'an and Woman: Rereading the Sacred Text from a Woman's Perspective*. Oxford: Oxford University Press, 1999.

Yale University Press. "Leila Ahmed and Women's Voices in Islam" (blog). http://blog.yalebooks.com/2013/03/01/leila-ahmed-and-womens-voices-in-islam/.

Zine, Jasmine. "Between Orientalism and Fundamentalism: The Politics of Muslim Women's Feminist Engagement." *Muslim World Journal of Human Rights* 3, no. 1 (2006): 1–24.

CHAPTER 15

Homiletical Changes and Preaching Leadership of Women in the Christian Church

Rev. Dr. HyeRan Kim-Cragg, Emmanuel College,
University of Toronto

ABSTRACT

There has been a drastic shift in homiletical leadership and preaching scholarship since the 1960s as far as women's roles in Christianity are concerned. It has been an exciting time to witness barriers coming down that prevented women from being ordained in mainline Protestant churches. The 1960s was also an era that brought the second-wave feminist movement. Thus, the first part of this article will locate women's preaching leadership in the larger contexts of the four consecutive waves of the feminist movement in North American history. Then, we will examine four aspects of preaching that matter to women: experience, body, language, and biblical interpretation. How women preachers and feminist homileticians have contributed to enhancing the scholarship of homiletics will be explored next. Finally, a different way of preaching informed and developed by women preachers will be described. This alternative way of preaching is suggested as a feminist preaching practice that aims to overcome gender oppression and injustice.

INTRODUCTION

Since the 1960s, there has been a profound shift in homiletical leadership with regard to women's roles. This was a significant era when barriers preventing women from being ordained in mainline Protestant churches were significantly minimized.[1] Also, during this period, which Douglas Hall calls a period of creative chaos,[2] women's voices from the pulpit began to be heard in larger numbers. It is not a coincidence that this era overlaps with the second-wave feminist movement.[3] Thus, the first part of this chapter will review the women's movement beyond the church, however briefly, in order to locate women's preaching leadership in the larger contexts of the women's movement in North American history. Then, as a main part of the chapter, I will name four essential elements in preaching, which I regard as women preachers' contributions to the field of homiletics: experience, embodiment, language, biblical interpretation. I will demonstrate how these elements have shaped feminist preaching and also enhanced the entire scholarship in the area of preaching.

FOUR WAVES OF THE WOMEN'S MOVEMENT IN HISTORY: A NORTH AMERICAN VERSION

Canadian journalist Sally Armstrong calls the women's movement the longest revolution in human history. She traces the story of the struggle for women's emancipation all the way back to the Stone Age and argues that this struggle on the part of women has changed the landscape of humanity since that time.[4] Though the movement has lasted for millennia, Armstrong contends that an important shift occurred following the recent waves of the feminist movement that swept through the world over the last two hundred years. The suffrage movement (1848–1920), when women struggled to vote, is regarded as the first feminist wave. This movement enabled people to recognize women as persons, not a form of property owned by men. The second wave occurred with the development of the birth control pill (1963–1991) when women were able to achieve some control over their own bodies for reproduction. This movement enabled people to recognize that women are more than baby-making machines and that society should not confine them to that role at home in the domestic realms. The third wave came after 1991 when Anita Hill, a lawyer and academic testified against the US Supreme Court nominee Clarence Thomas, whom she accused of sexual harassment (1992–2010).[5] The movement, which this testimony sparked, enabled society to see how women's full dignity is still being ridiculed and violated in schools and workplaces. The struggle against sexual harassment continues to unravel into the 21st century. Most recently in September 2018, the psychologist professor Christine Blasey Ford alleged that then–US Supreme Court nominee Brett Kavanaugh sexually assaulted her in Bethesda, Maryland, when they were teenagers in the summer of 1982.[6] This case was right after Harvey Weinstein's long history of sexual harassment and assault was disclosed in 2017, and his charge was still unfolding in 2020.[7] We now live in the fourth wave of the movement, which took off with the advent of social media in 2012 and the era of Twitter, Facebook, and hashtags like #MeToo and #TimesUp.[8]

The women's movement has never been exclusive nor reserved for women only. It considers the oppression of women in relation to other oppressions, racism, classism, heterosexism, militarism, and colonialism, for example.[9] The importance of viewing feminism in this regard gained its momentum in this era of the fourth wave since the term *intersectionality* was first introduced in 1989 by legal scholar and human rights lawyer Kimberlé Crenshaw.[10] The wide use of this term is evidenced by its inclusion in the Merriam-Webster dictionary in 2017.[11] Women's studies in religion in general, and women's preaching in particular, need to be sensitized to the intersectionality of these different forms of oppression as a matter of principle and not as an optional way. There is a growing need for a keen attention to the intersectional nature of social categorizations, such as race, class, colonialism, gender, sexual orientation, and ability in women's studies of religion. Postcolonial feminist studies have contributed to calling for this attention.[12]

THREE CHANGES IN WOMEN LEADERSHIP IN PREACHING

Homiletician Eunjoo Mary Kim ascribes three changes to the Christian pulpit in North America over the last fifty years.[13] The first change is that the number of women seminarians are increasing. In 1993, for example, 61 percent of the graduates of the Master of Divinity from the Yale Divinity School were women. This new gender situation demands a different pedagogy for preaching and a different approach to preaching scholarship that takes women's experiences and perspectives seriously. The second change is the increase of numbers of sermons written by women clergy and active ministry not only in churches, but also in hospitals, military chapels, and spiritual care facilities. Their sermons offer a unique and profound reservoir of wisdom and insight as well as challenge and struggle. The third change is the growing number of women homileticians who made headway for feminist preaching scholarship influenced by feminist theory, feminist theology, and women's gender studies.[14] Their scholarly contributions are hard not to notice in homiletics. They pushed the scholarly boundaries, opened up more inclusive spaces, and critically examined male dominance and gender bias prevalent in homiletical scholarship and teaching. Some of their work will be presented in this chapter.

While a dramatic increase in female clergy and female church leadership during this time should be noted in a celebratory manner, it is unwise to believe that women preachers have only existed in the last century. Women preaching tradition goes back more than four hundred years. Anne Marbury Hutchinson (1591–1643), one of the first European women known to preach in New England in the United States, appears in the public record in 1644. Hutchinson was not a meek preacher but a headstrong leader who was behind the so-called the Antinomian Controversy. It became a controversy because she preached in ways that challenged the corrupt male clerical authority of that time.[15] She was one of the first woman preachers but not the last. There was a constant and steady stream of women preachers on the American frontier during the women's temperance movement, the women's voting rights movement, the child labor laws movement, and the civil rights movement in the United States. Since they, as itinerant preachers, preached not necessarily and only in the churches but in convents or less formal places,[16] their sermons were also less formal and more relational and intimate than those of their male counterparts, who tended to occupy the formal pulpit.[17]

Despite these persistent and outstanding models of female homiletical leadership over centuries, women preachers have not gained full equality to men in church even today. Far from it. There continues to be pushback against demands for increased equality in preaching leadership. For example, the first Southern Baptist woman clergy, Addie Davis, was ordained in 1964. But the Southern Baptist Convention again stopped ordaining women in 2000.[18] According to the Faith Communities Today 2010 national survey, only 12 percent of 11,000 congregations in the United States have a female as their senior or sole ordained preacher. In fact, the number of women in evangelical pulpits dropped to 9 percent.[19] History is instructive. It makes us vigilant. It teaches us where we came from, while, at the same time, signals that we may fall back to the wrongs of the past.

In short, tapping into the wisdom from history has demonstrated that major changes and breakthroughs of the women's movement have been achieved but are not guaranteed. Women preaching was a sign that women were obtaining gender equality and enhancing women's leadership in the Christian church as a part of the larger women's movement. But the struggle is not over. The women's movement must go on. With this historical review and lesson in mind, let us turn to examine four significant aspects that matter to women's preaching leadership in the Christian church today.

REDISCOVERY OF PREACHING AS TESTIMONY: EXPERIENCE MATTERS

In her examination of the preaching tradition as testimony, homiletician Anna Carter Florence notices the lack of female role models in the history of preaching. When one researches only the standard history of preaching, meaning mainstream-dominant history, women's voices as preachers are virtually silent, almost nowhere to be found. However, Florence notes that women preachers were *everywhere*[20] when one looks at the historical record of women preachers, especially their autobiographies. In 1620 and the settlement of New England Puritans, women were preachers.[21] This means both men and women preached. Yet women's preaching was not recorded in the normative preaching history books. The reason for the absence of women in the history of preaching is due to the historically dominant approach to homiletics that prefers a male-dominant preaching style. One aspect of this prejudice is the dismissal of women's approach to preaching as *testimony*. Preaching in the eighteenth and nineteenth centuries in North America was understood, and still is to some extent, to be predominantly scripture based and expository in style, absent of the subjective experiences of preachers and congregations.[22] This means preachers focus exclusively on the biblical text apparently on its own terms and apart from their own personal agendas.[23] In this strict view of expository preaching, testimony is not considered as preaching when it is preoccupied with sharing the preacher's personal experience in a confessional manner. That preaching-as-testimony tradition runs against the dominant homiletical tradition, which emphasized the impersonal and objective imposition of scriptural knowledge on the congregation. The challenge for preaching today is that this narrow, albeit dominant, view of preaching as the simple exposition of a biblical text followed by a practical application is still prevalent, though there has been a recent movement in homiletics where scholars claim that authenticity as self-disclosure is a key component in preaching.[24]

The self-disclosure of the preacher involves vulnerability and even weakness. It is the opposite of the dominant male preacher's image as the authority figure who is removed from the congregation and placed high on a pedestal. To some extent, claiming a personal and humble tact as a preacher challenges authority, which is traditionally and historically identified in the male preacher. Florence further probes the very assumption of preaching: "Does testimony challenge our assumptions about preaching in ways that are too disruptive, too dangerous, to explore?"[25]

To establish a homiletical tradition of preaching as testimony is to affirm a long history of preaching by marginalized Christians, including women, while shifting preaching authority and its power in the church. It is about validating the experiences of women and others whose experiences are overlooked and excluded as sources of homiletical knowledge for doing preaching, while contesting the notion of preaching as imparting objective biblical knowledge.

Again, the ancient biblical wisdom is deep when we look at the Gospel stories in the Bible about women proclaiming the Good News of the risen Christ. It was women who first witnessed the resurrection of Jesus and testified to what they saw. All four Gospels, despite their differences due to the multifaceted oral traditions of the early Christian communities, have one thing in common: it was the women who witnessed that the tomb was empty and that Jesus was risen from the dead. We can argue that this was the first and the oldest event of Christian preaching. For the homiletician Thomas Long, "bearing witness to the gospel" is the most primary and central meaning of preaching.[26] Preaching in the Gospel tradition was to testify what had been seen, even if it was frightening and terrifying, incredible and amazing.[27] That is why Florence calls *testimony* an old word in a new key. Not only is testimony the primary way many women preachers performed, but it is also the most courageous form of preaching, especially when we consider the testimony of martyrs. Etymologically, this makes sense because the word *witness* is derived from the Latin *testis*, which was turned into the Greek *marturia*, as the word combined with *testis* and *smer*, to remember, to be able to tell the truth, to bear witness.[28] In this linguistic understanding, preaching as witness is truth telling, is being able to remember what one saw and tell it, even if it may sometimes be a risk to one's life. In this regard, preaching is also a bold act; it is a dangerous, if not deadly, business. Kim agrees that preaching as testimony is not an easy task but a spirit-led vocation because it does not merely rely on philosophical speculation or scientific knowledge but depends on the grace of God "through her experience of encountering the living God, and with this conviction, she cannot help but preach."[29] Again, this profound biblical meaning of preaching as testimony and bearing faithful witness by women ancestors in faith affirms the importance of women's experience as a source of homiletical content and method. In short, experience in general, and women's experience in particular, matters in preaching.

ATTENTION TO THE PHYSICALITY OF PREACHING: BODY MATTERS

Despite the surge in the number of women in theological education and who have been ordained to ministries of Word and Sacrament in the last fifty years in North America, the pulpit is still a male place. The church has lurched between resistance and acceptance of women as preachers. According to the Hartford Institute of Religion Research, a survey (2010) estimates that only round 10 percent of American Protestant congregations have a female as their senior or sole ordained leader.[30] Women preachers "still are not widely recognized in mainstream Protestantism—and certainly not in Catholicism—as the equals of male preachers, and the greatest evidence of the fact is the limited opportunity for women to preach," Farmer and Hunter observe.[31]

It is true that not all preachers must be ordained. There have always been lay preachers. However, the ordination of women is crucial for preaching authority. Created in the image of God, equal to men, women have been called by God. God has called women and men as well as all gender identities equally to ordained ministry based on the baptismal declaration. That is the essence of the doctrine of the priesthood of all believers, a key Protestant theological conviction. And the role of the priest includes preaching.[32]

The church not only needs to increase the numbers of women preachers; it also must question what factors still unfairly prevent women from preaching. One of the factors is the perception of women's physical bodies, the so-called *look*. Women do not *look* like preachers because they do not fit the norm of the male preacher people have come to expect in the pulpit. It is not only in eyes of the beholder that this barrier exists. Pulpits have been physically built that way. They have been constructed for a tall, muscular male body. The churches were not made to fit the leadership of a petite 5-foot-tall woman. Even if the 1960s were the decade when the ordination of women took place in many mainline denominations and women preachers were out and about in congregations, the lingering mortar and bricks of the historic church buildings continued to stand as a barrier to them. This tenacious physical building is hard to change. The lack of imagination also remains tenacious.[33]

It is theologically imperative to pay attention to the physicality of preaching because Christian preaching is incarnational. The Gospel of John poetically captures this: "In the beginning was the Word, and the Word was with God, and the Word was God. . . . And the Word became flesh and lived among us" (1:1,14). Preachers are called to proclaim the Good News of Jesus Christ incarnated as the Word that is present in "the-flesh-and-blood, oral-aural, face-to-face synesthetic speech event of divine self-disclosure."[34] Preaching understood as the *divine* self-disclosure occurs through the *human* body of the preacher. The mystic Theresa of Avila in the Reformation era (1515–1582) captures this ironic and stunning reality. "Christ has no body now but yours. No hands, no feet on earth but yours. Yours are the eyes through which he looks compassion on this world. Yours are the feet with which he walks to do good. Yours are the hands through which he blesses all the world. Yours are the hands, yours are the feet, yours are the eyes, you are his body. Christ has no body now on earth but yours."[35] Avila's prayer is not merely pointed at preaching but extended to overall Christian service for God and to the world. Yet the emphasis on the role of the human body is instructive in that it prompts preachers to self-reflect on their bodies, from head to toe, and consider that their bodies, too, are conducive to preaching.

Nancy L. Gross, in assisting women preachers to become effective speakers in church, has the following to say: "In order to use the voice, women must feel that it is theirs to use; they must own it." Here, "the voice is a full-body instrument."[36] What this means is that the whole body matters in preaching. Like the piano keys cannot make amazing sounds without the solid foundation of the legs, preachers cannot make a powerful vocal sound without a firm physical base. Because pulpits often privilege tall people, women preachers of small stature often have to wear high heels, which not only cause physical pain if they stand too long but also emotional discomfort because of self-consciousness about their physical stature. When one appreciates the importance of standing posture for good preaching, an additional factor for many women preachers to consider what to wear, however trivial it may sound, should not be underestimated.

Mary Hilkert highlights that *bodily experiences*, such as menstruation, physical abuse, and rape, should be embodied in the act of preaching because such experiences are included in biblical texts. For preachers, both male and female, to bear faithful witness therefore, they must make a relevant reference to this in their sermon. To proclaim the good news by praising God incarnate means to honor women's bodily experiences that include but are not limited to pregnancy, birthing, miscarriage, and breastfeeding as much as to menopause and aging.[37] These are messy and mundane human affairs that are holy and sacred, life giving, life nourishing, and lifesaving as well as the loss of life and dying.

From a trivial matter of what to wear to serious bodily matters as bleeding, giving birth, and losing a body part, one may note that nothing is a small thing when it comes to the body. What is stressed here is that the preaching act aims at the integration of the "body-mind-personality-soul." It is to "bring forth your whole selves to the people of God."[38] That is what the Apostle Paul means when he says, "present your bodies as a living sacrifice [meaning offering in Hebrew], holy and acceptable to God, which is your spiritual worship" (Romans 12:1). The holistic understanding of the preaching act as offering may be extended to the meaning of hospitality. Homiletician John McClure identifies the role of the preacher as host by rediscovering an early homiletical tradition where the preaching event took place in conjunction with communal fellowship around the dinner table. But he also argues that the preacher should play the part of guest, too. The preacher as an itinerant evangelist has been hosted. In this way the preacher is inevitably both host and guest.[39] While different from McClure, Gross uses the same analogy of host and guest in teaching preaching to her students: "I encourage my students to extend themselves, to extend their voices to the congregation in the same way they would extend hospitality in their homes. . . . When we love ourselves, we are in congruence with ourselves, with our bodies, enabling us the freedom to speak. This freedom is manifested in posture, breath, vocal tone, and vocal gesture. When we lack self-love, we will find it difficult to . . . speak in congruence with the gospel."[40] This hospitality of homiletical practice is possible only when preachers love their neighbors as themselves.[41] It is where self-care and self-love of one's body matter in women's preaching leadership proclaiming God's love and the love of neighbors.

ATTENTION TO THE VOICE OF PREACHING: LANGUAGE MATTERS

The debate on the inclusive language in worship and preaching is another fruit born out of the second-wave women's movement with the rise of feminist theory and feminist theology in the 1970s and 1980s.[42] The first feminist preaching book as a bud in a garden of academia came to bloom in the 1980s, as more buds dealing with gender-inclusive language blossomed in the 1980s and 1990s.[43] Kim, however, argues that the inclusive language is not a twentieth-century invention but an issue that has been raised in the past. She traces the language issue back to the medieval era where women preachers challenged the patriarchal church and society through their creative use of theological language, including images of God that challenged the dominance of masculine metaphors. This, for instance, is found in the subversive rhetoric of Hildegard of Bingen in her preaching on the Trinity. Instead of thinking of God as father, Kim focuses on charity (love and mercy) as characters of God when she writes, "through this fountain of life came the embrace of God's maternal love, which has nourished us unto life and is our help in perils."[44] Kim, lifting up Bingen, and other women mystic preachers, including Julian of Norwich and Sor Juana Inés de la Cruz, contends that they remind us that language is to be taken seriously because language can create a new reality.

Geena Davis, the Hollywood actress, who advocates for women's visibility in the film industry, noticed that "68–78 percent of the incoming students in forensic science at universities are female. And about 78 percent of the young actors playing forensic scientists on TV are women."[45] Seeing is believing and seeing is becoming. If women can see themselves in TV, ads, and movies, they can become that. Theologian Elizabeth A. Johnson makes a similar point: "if God is [seen as] she as well as he, . . . a new possibility can be envisioned of a way of living together that honors difference but allows women and men to share life in equal measure."[46]

This possibility of creating new sermonic Christian language beyond gender bias is the work of metaphorical imagination and cannot be constrained by strictly literal interpretations. The bottom line is that God cannot be adequately described in human language. But language is reflective of reality. Our experience is partial, and so our language must evolve to give voice to what is in the process of becoming. With that in mind, it is critical that language be inclusive and that all preachers commit to using language that opens new possibilities for the understanding of the divine.

SIGNIFICANCE OF FEMINIST EXEGESIS: BIBLICAL INTERPRETATION MATTERS

It is essential to engage Scripture in preaching. To preach without engaging Scripture is like thinking one can start a car without the battery.[47] Scripture is the spark of the sermon. Yet many women preachers find that the battery is not properly connected to the engine. The vast majority of commentaries are authored by Western straight, white, middle upper-class, able-bodied men and inevitably reflect their limited experiences. Thus, those perspectives of non-Western non-White women and people from different classes, sexual orientation, and abilities may be painfully and unjustly excluded.[48] The dominance of the male perspective in biblical commentaries is worse than the male dominance of the pulpit. One may argue that, while only 10 percent of the pulpit is occupied by women preachers in Protestant churches, approximately only one in one hundred commentaries has been written by women and from a woman's perspective. In this regard, it is worth noting that the growing body of scholarship by women and people of color has been producing new approaches to interpreting the biblical texts.[49] One such example is the *Wisdom Commentary*, which is a work in progress under the leadership of Barbara Reid. As general editor, she writes, "The *Wisdom Commentary* is the first series to offer detailed feminist interpretation of every book of the Bible."[50] It is a daunting, painstaking, slow process, but, at the same time, it is an urgent and much needed task that is unprecedented. There has been nothing like this project before in terms of the scale and the scope, the people involved, and the levels of scholarly engagement. There is no other biblical commentary of similar size (it consists of fifty-eight volumes) written by women and men reflecting feminist female voices, however heterogeneous they may be. The first volumes were published in 2015, yet less than half of the volumes were complete in 2020. It may take more than ten years to complete the project. Previously, a smaller one-volume feminist commentary was published. Many of it deals only with the books and passages of the Bible that mention women.[51] While such efforts were necessary and instructive, they could not capture the vision of the feminist movement as one that serves and embraces more than women. Reid writes, "While issues of gender are primary in this project, the volumes also address intersecting issues of power, authority, ethnicity, race, class, and religious beliefs and practice."[52] As raised earlier, the attention to intersectionality is one of the most recent and valuable contributions of the fourth-wave women's movement to the church, academia, and activism. Thus, commentaries that fully embrace intersectionality are in still demand.

SEARCHING FOR DIFFERENT WAYS OF PREACHING

It should be clearly stated that there is no fixed and unchangeable difference between male and female preachers. A liberationist approach to women's experience questions and denounces false stereotypes and gender binaries as a product of the patriarchal system. For example, Naomi Goldenberg criticizes the Jungian feminine and masculine dichotomic distinction.[53] Instead of essentializing gender differences between female and male, what is essentially required for women preaching is how preachers are self-critically aware of their own social location, privilege, and positions of power as factors that control and limit or liberate and expand their hearing and preaching of the gospel.[54] That is what it means to take intersectionality seriously in preaching.

In a conversation with eight male and two female professors of preaching, homiletician Christine Smith has charted new territory for feminist homiletics and concluded that there is no decisive difference between male and female preachers. They are not inherently different, on the one hand. It does not mean, on the other hand, however, that there are no important differences between women and men. For example, Smith argues, there is a distinctiveness in terms of how women preachers consider intimacy and relatedness.[55] There is a gender-specific way of viewing authority and truth as well. In terms of articulating a unique quality of women preaching, Janice Riggle Huie finds that, when women preachers search for different images other than God the Father in their proclamation of the gospel, they are inspired to expand the sermonic metaphors in ways that are creative, imaginative, and evocative. Searching for new theological metaphors, preaching becomes participatory rather than authoritarian.[56] The language of God shapes the sermonic style. Preaching becomes a celebration of the community. Preaching is owned by the congregation rather than as a property of a solo preacher.

In short, ultimately, preaching, as far as women's leadership is concerned, is sharing the Gospel, Good News proclaimed as shared power, thanks to the grace and the goodness of God, who loves the world!

NOTES

1. For example, the Presbyterian Church in the United States started in 1956, while the Presbyterian Church in Canada followed in 1966. The Anglican Church of Canada ordained the first woman in 1973, followed by the Episcopal Church in the United States, which began ordaining women in 1976. The Evangelical Lutheran Church in the United States began in 1970, followed by its counterpart in Canada, which began ordaining women in 1976. Several other mainline denominations ordained women decades earlier. For example, Jarena Lee, born in 1783, is recognized as the first female preacher in the African Methodist American Church, the Wesleyan Methodist Church ordained the first woman in 1861, and the United Church of Canada, whose roots are in Methodism, ordained the first woman in 1936.

2. Douglas John Hall, "Christianity and Canadian Contexts: Then and Now," in *Intersecting Voices*, ed., Don Schweitzer and Derek Simon (Ottawa: Novalis, 2004), 19.

3. Joshua Clark Davis, *From Head Shops to Whole Foods: The Rise and Fall of Activist Entrepreneurs* (New York: Columbia University Press, 2020), 129–75.

4. Sally Armstrong, *Power Shift: The Longest Revolution* (Toronto: Anansi, 2019), 18.

5. Armstrong, *Power Shift*, 2.

6. In both cases, these public testimonies did not stem the tide from these two men being elected as Supreme Court justices, but created a watershed moment to make the public aware of how widespread sexual harassment is.

7. Daniel Victor, "How the Harvey Weinstein Story Has Unfolded," *New York Times*, published October 18, 2017, https://www.nytimes.com/2017/10/18/business/harvey-weinstein.html.

8. Armstrong, *Power Shift*, 2.

9. Christine Smith, *Weaving the Sermon: Preaching in a Feminist Perspective* (Louisville: Westminster John Knox, 1989), 69.

10. Kimberlé Crenshaw, "Demarginalizing the Intersection of Race and Sex: A Black Feminist Critique of Antidiscrimination Doctrine, Feminist Theory and Antiracist Politics," *The University of Legal Forum* 1, Article 8 (1989), http://chicagounbound.uchicago.edu/uclf/vol1989/iss1/8.

11. "Word We're Watching: Intersectionality," April 2017, https://www.merriam-webster.com/words-at-play/intersectionality-meaning.

12. Kwok Pui-lan, *Postcolonial Imagination and Feminist Theology* (Louisville: Westminster John Knox, 2005); Laura Donaldson, *Decolonizing Feminism: Race, Gender, and Empire-Building* (Chapel Hill: University of North Carolina, 1992); and HyeRan Kim-Cragg, *Interdependence: A Postcolonial Feminist Theology* (Eugene, OR: Pickwick, 2018).

13. Eunjoo Mary Kim, *Women Preaching: Theology and Practice through the Ages* (Cleveland, OH: Pilgrim, 2004), 2–5.

14. In chronical order, Smith, *Weaving the Sermon* (1989); Carol M. Norén, *Woman in the Pulpit* (Nashville: Abingdon, 1992); Lucy Rose, *Sharing the Word: Preaching in the Roundtable* (Louisville: Westminster John Knox, 1997); Mary Lin Hudson and Mary Donovan Turner, *Saved from Silence: Finding Women's Voices in Preaching* (St. Louis: Chalice, 1999); Jane V. Craske, *A Woman's Perspective on Preaching* (Nashville, TN: United Methodist Publishing, 2001); Jana Childers, ed., *Birthing the Sermon: Women Preachers on the Creative Process* (St. Louis, MO: Chalice Press, 2001); Roxanne Mountford, *The Gendered Pulpit: Preaching in American Protestant Space* (Carbondale: Southern Illinois University Press, 2003); Mary Catherin Hilkert, *Naming Grace: Preaching and the Sacramental Imagination* (New York: Continuum, 2003); Kim, *Women Preaching* (2004); Anna Carter Florence, *Preaching as Testimony* (Louisville, KY: Westminster/John Knox, 2007); and Nancy Lammers Gross, *Women's Voices and the Practice of Preaching* (Grand Rapids, MI: Eerdmans, 2017).

15. Florence, *Preaching as Testimony*, 5–17.

16. Catherine A. Brekus, *Female Preaching in America: Strangers and Pilgrims 1740–1845* (Chapel Hill: University of North Carolina, 1998).

17. John McClure, "gender" in *Preaching Words: 144 Key Terms in Homiletics* (Louisville, KY: Westminster John Knox, 2007), 42.

18. For an interesting and insightful online learning exercise, use your favorite search engine to conduct a quick historical survey of a particular denomination and its history of ordaining women.

19. Harford Institute for Religion Research, "A Quick Question: What Percentage of Pastors Are Female?," accessed January 25, 2020, http://hirr.hartsem.edu/research/quick_question3.html.

20. Florence, *Preaching as Testimony*, xix. Emphasis is in original.

21. DeWitte T. Holland, *The Preaching Tradition: A Brief History* (Nashville, TN: Abingdon, 1980), 51.

22. Florence, *Preaching as Testimony*, xix.

23. Harold T. Byrson, *Expository Preaching: The Art of Preaching a Book of the Bible* (Nashville, TN: Broadman & Holman, 1995).

24. Hudson and Turner, *Saved from Silence*; Richard L. Thulin, *The "I" of the Sermon: Autobiography in the Pulpit* (Eugene: Wipf and Stock, 2004).

25. Florence, *Preaching as Testimony*, xxii.

26. Tom Long, *The Witness of Preaching* (Louisville, KY: Westminster John Knox, 2005).

27. Kim, *Women Preaching*, 28–37.

28. Florence, *Preaching as Testimony*, xxi.

29. Kim, *Women Preaching*, 43.

30. Hartford Institute for Religion Research, "A Quick Question."

31. David Albert Farmer and Edwina Hunter, ed., *And Blessed Is She* (New York: Harper & Row, 1990), 3.

32. Hilkert, *Naming Grace*, 170.

33. Lillian Daniel, "Foreword," in Nancy Lammers Gross, *Women's Voices and the Practice of Preaching* (Grand Rapids, MI: Eerdmans, 2017), ix.

34. Charles L. Bartow, "Performance Study in Service to the Spoken Word in Worship," in *Performance in Preaching: Bringing the Sermon to Life*, ed. Jana Childers and Clayton J. Schmit (Grand Rapids, MI: Baker Academics, 2008), 215, 222.

35. Goodreads, "Teresa of Avila, Quotable Quote," accessed December 4, 2019, https://www.goodreads.com/quotes/66880-christ-has-no-body-now-but-yours-no-hands-no.

36. Gross, *Women's Voices and the Practice of Preaching*, 45.

37. Hilkert, *Naming Grace*, 174.

38. Gross, *Women's Voices and the Practice of Preaching*, 85.

39. John McClure, *The Roundtable Pulpit: Where Leadership and Preaching Meet* (Nashville, TN: Abingdon, 1995), 25, 27.

40. Gross, *Women's Voices and the Practice of Preaching*, 86–87.

41. HyeRan Kim-Cragg, "Home, Hospitality, and Preaching: A Need for the Homiletical Engagement of Migration," in *Religion and Migration: Negotiating Hospitality, Agency and Vulnerabiltiy*, ed. Andrea Biler, Isolde Karle, HyeRan Kim-Cragg, and Ilona Nord (Leipzig: EVA, 2019), 233–45.

42. One of the first writings is Mary Daly, *Beyond God the Father: Toward a Philosophy of Women's Liberation* (Boston, MA: Beacon Press, 1973); Letty Russell, *The Future of Partnership* (Philadelphia, PA: Westminster, 1979); Rosemary Radford Ruether, *Sexism and God-Talk: Toward a Feminist Theology* (Boston, MA: Beacon Press, 1983); and Elisabeth Schüssler Fiorenza, *In Memory of Her: A Feminist Reconstruction of Early Christian Origin* (New York: Crossroad, 1983).

43. Sallie McFague, *Metaphorical Theology: Models of God in Religious Language* (Minneapolis: Fortress, 1982); Gail Ramshaw, *Worship: Searching for Language* (Portland, OR: Pastoral Press, 1988); and Gail Ramshaw, *God beyond Gender: Feminist Christian God-Language* (Minneapolis, MN: Fortress, 1995).

44. Hildegard of Bingen, cited in Kim, *Women Preaching*, 60.

45. Armstrong, *Power Shift*, 235.

46. Elizabeth Johnson, "Naming God She: The Theological Implication," 2 *Boardman Lectureship in Christian Ethics* 5 (2000), http://repository.upenn.edu/boardman/5.

47. HyeRan Kim-Cragg, *Postcolonial Preaching: Creating a Ripple Effect* (Lanham, MD: Lexington Books, 2021), 105.

48. Gross, *Women's Voices and the Practice of Preaching*, 59.

49. Cain Hope Felder, ed., *Troubling Biblical Waters: Race, Class, Family* (Maryknoll, NY: Orbis, 1989); R. S. Sugirtharajah, *Voices from the Margin: Interpreting the Bible in the Third World*, 25th anniv. ed. (Maryknoll, NY: Orbis, 2016); Deryn Guest, Robert Goss, and Mona West, eds., *The Queer Bible Commentary* (London: SCM, 2015).

50. Barbara E. Reid, OP, "Editor's Introduction to Wisdom Commentary: She Is a Breath of the Power of God (Wis 7:25)," in *Hebrews*, Mary Ann Beavis and HyeRan Kim-Cragg, eds. (Collegeville, MN: Liturgical Press, 2015), xvii.

51. Carol Newsom, Sharon Ringe, and Jacqueline Lapsley, eds., *Women's Bible Commentary*, 3rd ed. (Louisville, KY: Westminster John Knox, 2012).

52. Reid, "Editor's Introduction to Wisdom Commentary," xvii.

53. Naomi Goldenberg, "A Feminist Critique of Jung," *Signs* (1976): 443–49.

54. Hilkert, *Naming Grace*, 172.

55. Smith, *Weaving the Sermon*, 27.

56. Janice Riggle Huie, "Preaching through Metaphor," in *Women Ministers: How Women Are Redefining Traditional Roles*, rev. ed., ed. Judith L. Weidman (San Francisco: Harper & Row, 1985), 51–52.

BIBLIOGRAPHY

Armstrong, Sally. *Power Shift: The Longest Revolution*. Toronto: Anansi, 2019.

Bartow, Charles L. "Performance Study in Service to the Spoken Word in Worship." In *Performance in Preaching: Bringing the Sermon to Life*, ed. Jana Childers and Clayton J. Schmit, 211–23. Grand Rapids, MI: Baker Academics, 2008.

Brekus, Catherine A. *Female Preaching in America: Strangers and Pilgrims 1740–1845*. Chapel Hill: University of North Carolina, 1998.

Bryson, Harold T. *Expository Preaching: The Art of Preaching a Book of the Bible*. Nashville, TN: Broadman & Holman, 1995.

Childers, Jana, ed. *Birthing the Sermon: Women Preachers on the Creative Process*. St. Louis, MO: Chalice Press, 2001.

Craske, Jane V. *A Woman's Perspective on Preaching*. Nashville, TN: United Methodist Publishing, 2001.

Crenshaw, Kimberlé. "Demarginalizing the Intersection of Race and Sex: A Black Feminist Critique of Antidiscrimination Doctrine, Feminist Theory and Antiracist Politics." *The University of Legal Forum* 1, Article 8 (1989).

Daly, Mary. *Beyond God the Father: Toward a Philosophy of Women's Liberation*. Boston, MA: Beacon Press, 1973.

Daniel, Lillian. "Foreword." In Nancy Lammers Gross, *Women's Voices and the Practice of Preaching*, viii–xii. Grand Rapids, MI: Eerdmans, 2017.

Davis, Joshua Clark. *From Head Shops to Whole Foods: The Rise and Fall of Activist Entrepreneurs*. New York: Columbia University Press, 2017.

Deryn Guest, Robert Goss, and Mona West, eds. *The Queer Bible Commentary*. London: SCM, 2015.

Donaldson, Laura. *Decolonizing Feminism: Race, Gender, and Empire-Building*. Chapel Hill: University of North Carolina, 1992.

Farmer, David Albert, and Edwina Hunter, eds. *And Blessed Is She*. New York: Harper & Row, 1990.

Felder, Cain Hope, ed. *Troubling Biblical Waters: Race, Class, Family*. Maryknoll, NY: Orbis, 1989.

Florence, Anna Carter. *Preaching as Testimony*. Louisville, KY: Westminster John Knox, 2007.

Goldenberg, Naomi. "A Feminist Critique of Jung." *Signs* (1976): 443–49.

Gross, Nancy Lammers. *Women's Voices and the Practice of Preaching.* Grand Rapids, MI: Eerdmans, 2017.

Hall, Douglas John. "Christianity and Canadian Contexts: Then and Now." In *Intersecting Voices,* edited by Don Schweitzer and Derek Simon, 18–32. Ottawa: Novalis, 2004.

Hilkert, Mary Catherine. *Naming Grace: Preaching and the Sacramental Imagination.* New York: Continuum, 2003.

Holland, DeWitte T. *The Preaching Tradition: A Brief History.* Nashville, TN: Abingdon, 1980.

Hudson, Mary Lin, and Mary Donovan Turner. *Saved from Silence: Finding Women's Voices in Preaching.* St. Louis, MO: Chalice, 1999.

Huie, Janice Riggle. "Preaching through Metaphor." In *Women Ministers: How Women Are Redefining Traditional Roles,* rev. ed., edited by Judith L. Weidman, 49–66. San Francisco: Harper & Row, 1985.

Johnson, Elizabeth. "Naming God She: The Theological Implication." *Boardman Lectureship in Christian Ethics* (2000): 1–24.

Kim, Eunjoo Mary. *Women Preaching: Theology and Practice through the Ages.* Cleveland, OH: Pilgrim, 2004.

Kim-Cragg, HyeRan. *Postcolonial Preaching: Creating a Ripple Effect.* Lanham, MD: Lexington Books, 2021.

———. "Home, Hospitality, and Preaching: A Need for the Homiletical Engagement of Migration." In *Religion and Migration: Negotiating Hospitality, Agency and Vulnerability,* edited by Andrea Biler, Isolde Karle, HyeRan Kim-Cragg, and Ilona Nord, 233–45. EVA, 2019.

———. *Interdependence: A Postcolonial Feminist Theology.* Eugene, OR: Pickwick, 2018.

Kwok, Pui-lan. *Postcolonial Imagination and Feminist Theology.* Louisville, KY: Westminster John Knox, 2005.

Long, Tom. *The Witness of Preaching.* Louisville, KY: Westminster John Knox, 2005.

McClure, John. *Preaching Words: 144 Key Terms in Homiletics.* Louisville, KY: Westminster John Knox, 2007.

———. *The Roundtable Pulpit: Where Leadership and Preaching Meet.* Nashville, TN: Abingdon, 1995.

McFague, Sallie. *Metaphorical Theology: Models of God in Religious Language.* Minneapolis, MN: Fortress, 1982.

Mountford, Roxanne. *The Gendered Pulpit: Preaching in American Protestant Space.* Carbondale: Southern Illinois University Press, 2003.

Newsom, Carol, Sharon Ringe, and Jacqueline Lapsley, eds. *Women's Bible Commentary.* 3rd ed. Louisville, KY: Westminster John Knox, 2012.

Norén, Carol M. *Woman in the Pulpit.* Nashville, TN: Abingdon, 1992.

Ramshaw, Gail. *God Beyond Gender: Feminist Christian God-Language.* Minneapolis, MN: Fortress, 1995.

———. *Worship: Searching for Language.* Portland, OR: Pastoral Press, 1988.

Reid, Barbara E. "Editor's Introduction to Wisdom Commentary: She Is a Breath of the Power of God (Wis 7:25)." In *Hebrews: Wisdom Commentary 54,* edited by Mary Ann Beavis and HyeRan Kim-Cragg, xvii–xxxv. Collegeville, MN: Liturgical Press, 2015.

Rose, Lucy. *Sharing the Word: Preaching in the Roundtable.* Louisville, KY: Westminster John Knox, 1997.

Ruether, Rosemary Radford. *Sexism and God-Talk: Toward a Feminist Theology.* Boston, MA: Beacon Press, 1983.

Russell, Letty. *The Future of Partnership.* Philadelphia, PA: Westminster, 1979.

Schüssler Fiorenza, Elisabeth. *In Memory of Her: A Feminist Reconstruction of Early Christian Origin.* New York: Crossroad, 1983.

Smith, Christine. *Weaving the Sermon: Preaching in a Feminist Perspective.* Louisville, KY: Westminster John Knox, 1989.

Sugirtharajah, R. S. *Voices from the Margin: Interpreting the Bible in the Third World.* 25th anniv. ed. Maryknoll, NY: Orbis, 2016.

Thulin, Richard L. *The "I" of the Sermon: Autobiography in the Pulpit.* Eugene, OR: Wipf and Stock, 2004.

CHALLENGING AND CHANGING SYSTEMIC GENDER INJUSTICE

CHAPTER 16

What's Religion Got to Do with Sexual Violence and the #MeToo Movement?

Rev. Dr. Marie M. Fortune, FaithTrust Institute

ABSTRACT

Women's studies in religion must address sexual violence as an all too common experience for many women (and some men) in the 21st-century United States and as an experience profoundly shaped by religious beliefs and practices. Where does #MeToo as a survivor movement come from? How has it intersected with religious practices and institutions? Where does the #ChurchToo movement emerge, and what is the history of addressing sexual abuse perpetrated by clergy and faith leaders? An understanding of the early 21st-century #MeToo movement requires some historical context in regard to both the legal and social response to sexual assault in society and to faith communities' response to sexual abuse and assault. All of this is shaped by sexism, racism, and patriarchal contexts shared by religious and secular communities alike.

Sexual violence and abuse are common experiences across faith traditions, including abuse perpetrated by faith leaders. Each tradition has its issues with theology, ethics, sacred texts, and doctrine. The challenges to various religious institutions are similar but also specific to each tradition. For example, the mechanisms of institutional oversight and authority over leadership in terms of professional ethics and boundaries vary among different traditions. Since faith is the individual and collective manifestation of religious doctrine and practice, in its many forms, it is significant in shaping a cultural understanding of sexual violence and of individual experiences of victimization or predatory practices.

In exploring questions about how #MeToo intersects with religious practices and institutions and the origin of #ChurchToo, no faith tradition is exempt from sexual violence and abuse, including abuse perpetrated by faith leaders. The religious context is important because, in US society, faith matters for the majority of people, whether victims, survivors, sex offenders, or bystanders. Each tradition has its issues with theology, ethics, sacred texts, and doctrine. The challenges to various religious institutions are similar but also specific to each tradition; for example, the institutional oversight and authority over leadership in terms of professional ethics and boundaries is shaped not only by polity but also by culture.

Violence against women, domestic violence, sexual abuse and harassment, rape, and intimate partner violence are all terms that address some aspect of gender-based violence experienced primarily but not exclusively by women in every setting of women's lives, public and private, secular and religious, across race, class, sexualities, age, ability, nationality, and status. From early religious texts, historical documents, personal diaries, and other sources, we know that gender-based violence has been a common experience for women (and some men) for eons and is the common thread that links women's lives: our fears and/or memories of sexual and physical violence. The link to religion and religious organizations has also been long standing.

In the 19th-century United States, Frances Willard helped to organize the Woman's Christian Temperance Union. It was a faith-based national organization that became the largest social movement in the United States whose purpose was to encourage abstinence from alcohol. But the real motivation for this social movement was to address domestic violence: women were suffering from domestic violence and reasoned that their husbands were coming home drunk and abusing them. If they could stop the alcohol, they believed the violence would end. Their strategy to view their individual experiences as part of a larger social problem was on target. Sadly, their analysis that ending alcohol consumption would end the domestic violence was misguided. But the lesson from history is that women organized a faith-based effort to address domestic violence.[1]

WHAT IS #METOO?

Tarana Burke was the first woman to use the phrase "me too." In 2006, she responded to a 13-year-old rape survivor, saying "me too." She then began to use the phrase on social media to advocate for "empowerment through empathy" particularly among women of color. She is now regarded as the founder of the #MeToo movement.[2]

In terms of the national impact of #MeToo, the next development came in late 2017 when women in the film industry began to disclose their accusations of assault and harassment by producer Harvey Weinstein. Actor Alyssa Milano posted on her blog, "If you've been sexually harassed or assaulted write 'me too' as a reply to this tweet," and reposted the following phrase suggested by a friend: "If all the women who have ever been sexually harassed or assaulted wrote 'Me too' as a status, then we would give people a sense of the magnitude of the problem."

As an actor and celebrity with a social media platform, Milano used her media access to expand a movement. The power of social media became apparent but also the importance of a strategy: "to give people a sense of the magnitude of the problem." Social science research had confirmed the magnitude of the problem of sexual assault and harassment of women and girls for years previously. But the research and the organizing of advocacy and support for women victims and survivors had not really pierced the public consciousness. Celebrity and social media advanced this effort significantly.

Milano was immediately made aware of Burke's original use of "me too," and she added the hashtag to what then has become #MeToo. Many more actors began to disclose abuse by Weinstein and other powerful men in the film industry. In doing so, they created space for other women to disclose and for some to take action to hold their perpetrators accountable. Subsequently a plethora of hashtags emerged, further expanding the awareness and networking among survivors of sexual assault and harassment from numerous sectors.[3]

The response from some women actors, producers, and directors (white women and women of color) with enough clout in the film industry to be able to not only speak out but to organize within the industry challenged the historic lack of accountability for male actors, producers, and directors who have persisted in their harassment of women and men. This response led to a new dimension of #MeToo: #TimesUp.

#TimesUp was formed in 2018 by 300 prominent women in Hollywood, among them producer Shonda Rhimes, director Ava DuVernay, and actor Reese Witherspoon. It was an effort to take #MeToo forward in analyzing and challenging the institutional basis of sexual harassment in the workplace. This step was critical in framing the issue of sexual harassment in the workplace as a systemic issue that flourishes in the context of gender inequity and not only an individual, personal experience.

In announcing the formation of #TimesUp, the women published a letter in the *New York Times*. "Now, unlike ever before, our access to the media and to important decision makers has the potential of leading to real accountability and consequences," the letter said. "We want all survivors of sexual harassment, everywhere, to be heard, to be believed and to know that accountability is possible."[4] #TimesUp has focused on the workplace writ large for women: from Hollywood to the fields, universities to the military. The TimesUpNow website clearly states a strategy that addresses sexual harassment and abuse as an institutional issue and a response based on social change organizing.[5]

HISTORICAL CONTEXT ADDRESSING VIOLENCE AGAINST WOMEN

The 21st-century efforts to address sexual harassment and abuse rest upon the foundation of work begun in the 1970s. As part of the second wave of feminist organizing in the United States, the painful facts of sexual and domestic violence were named in public discourse. One of the earliest important articles was "Rape: The All-American Crime" by Susan Griffin published in *Ramparts Magazine,* September 1971. Griffin asserted that rape was not an isolated, singular event perpetrated by a deviant individual but rather a crime against women as a class perpetuated and supported by sexism in society.[6]

Andra Medea and Kathleen Thompson published *Against Rape* in 1974 as a "survival manual." Medea and Thompson summarized an early social analysis and suggested practical precautions and support for victims/survivors. This book also began to document the early efforts to organize women to provide services and support for victims/survivors.[7]

In 1975, Susan Brownmiller published *Against Our Will: Men, Women and Rape*, in which she argued that rape is "a conscious process of intimidation by which all men keep all women in a state of fear." Brownmiller's book was not without controversy, but it did succeed in bringing the discussion of sexual violence to the fore.[8] The 1970s and 1980s saw the development of rape crisis centers, social science research, and legal advocacy to change antiquated laws that stood in the way of justice for victims and accountability for perpetrators.

But it was 1994 before there was a federal response to this widespread social problem of violence against women. The Violence Against Women Act of 1994 (VAWA) is a United States federal law[9] that provided $1.6 billion toward investigation and prosecution of violent crimes against women, imposed automatic and mandatory restitution on those convicted, and allowed civil redress in cases prosecutors chose to leave un-prosecuted. The Act also established the Office on Violence Against Women within the Department of Justice. This was a huge step forward because it provided funding for local and state programs addressing both sexual and domestic violence.[10] It has been repeatedly renewed (not without controversy), but, as of this writing (2020), its renewal languishes in the US Senate.

THE RELIGIOUS CONTEXT IN ADDRESSING GENDER-BASED VIOLENCE

Two primary issues must be considered when focusing on the intersection of religion and gender-based violence (GBV): the ways that religious teaching and practice have encouraged GBV and the ways that individual faith experiences and practices have shaped the experiences of victims, survivors, and perpetrators. For example, for Christian women suffering abuse (including rape) in their marriage, the biblical passage Ephesians 5:21–33 has frequently been invoked to excuse domestic violence and to justify a husband's "right" to dominate and control his partner. "Wives be subject to your husbands, as to the Lord" (v. 22). The frequent interpretation of this verse means that wives are to accept whatever behavior they experience at the hands of their husbands. A careful exegesis of this passage begins with considering verse 21: "Be subject to one another out of reverence for Christ." This verse can also be translated: "Accommodate to one another out of reverence for Christ." This verse is the foundation for the rest of the passage and contradicts attempts to use this passage to justify men's domination of women.[11]

In Hebrew scripture, the rape of a woman is addressed in the law as a property crime against the man to whom she "belonged," whether husband or father (Deuteronomy 22:23–28). Regardless of the circumstance, the victim is punished either with death or being forced to marry her rapist. Only if the rape occurred in the countryside is the woman not punished: it is assumed that she cried for help but no one heard her. This framing of rape does not provide support for victims nor accountability for offenders.[12]

The primary reason that faith and religious teaching matter when it comes to GBV is that the sexism that is built into texts and doctrines make it very easy to misuse teachings to blame victims and avoid holding offenders accountable. For example, a husband was charged with marital rape after he broke down a locked door and forced his wife sexually. His defense at trial was that he was Roman Catholic and the Church had taught him that, once he married, he had sexual access to his wife any time he chose. In reporting this incident, the reporter went to the local archdiocese and asked whether this was the teaching of the church. The reply was "of course not. We teach that husbands should respect their wives." But the spokesperson did not go on and state that the Church condemns marital rape and domestic violence and that the husband was wrong to assault his wife. This was a missed opportunity for the Church to use its authority to stand clearly with the victim and call the husband to account.[13]

Too often religious teaching and doctrine are misused and become *roadblocks* to responding to sexual violence victims. The challenge for faith traditions is to look within to find the teachings and practices that can be *resources and support healing*. It is the responsibility of scholarship and education to identify and remove roadblocks and to highlight and offer resources to victims/survivors for their healing and to offenders for their repentance. The literature that emerged in the 1980s and 1990s laid a foundation for further scholarship and education.[14]

SEXUAL ABUSE BY CLERGY AND LEADERS IN RELIGIOUS SETTINGS: A BRIEF HISTORY

Sexual abuse and exploitation carried out by religious leaders in all traditions is not a new phenomenon. But it lay hidden in silence until the latter 20th century when survivors began to speak out. Yet it was hidden in plain sight. In the 19th-century United States, Henry Ward Beecher (1813–1887) was a prominent, charismatic, and highly regarded preacher who held forth every week at Plymouth Church in Brooklyn, New York. He also frequently violated the sexual boundaries of his pastoral relationships with women, many of whom were the wives of his male friends and supporters. Paxton Hibbins's biography of Beecher, published in 1927, offers an unvarnished portrait of a clergyman who was unapologetically abusive. This portrait could describe many such faith leaders today.[15]

Contemporary information about abusive faith leaders began to emerge in the early 1980s in the United States. Survivors began speaking out. Many were searching for ways to find redress from their faith communities. Religious institutions, denominations, and organizations were not prepared to hear these disclosures from their members. Their all-too-common response was, and often continues to be, one of institutional protection: how to rally their resources to hide the "scandal" and "protect" the church from its people rather than protect its people from the corruption of its leadership.

At FaithTrust Institute, we received our first call from a survivor of abuse by a pastor in 1983. She briefly shared her circumstance and then asked whom in the United Methodist Church she should contact to file a complaint. This contact with her shattered my naivete and basic trust in faith leaders. More calls from survivors followed each week. We realized the need to try to equip faith communities to respond and to face up to this crisis in their midst. We began with training to formulate policies and procedures so that, when a victim came forward, she or he would have a mechanism to disclose her or his experience and expect a response designed not only to support the victim but also to ensure that this faith leader would not be able to harm others in the future. This effort sought to provide appropriate intervention and sanction for current perpetrators.

We soon added training directly to clergy and faith leaders on healthy boundaries based on our assumption that literally some of them did not know any better. They had had no training in seminary on healthy pastoral boundaries and were tragically ignorant of their responsibilities. This was our initial effort at prevention for individual congregations. FaithTrust worked directly with denominations, faith-based organizations, and seminaries to provide training in intervention and prevention. All of these efforts were based on framing the issue as more than "just an affair" or "a mid-life crisis" but rather as a violation of role, betrayal of trust, misuse of authority, and taking advantage of the vulnerable. The other significant assumption was clarity that this clergy misconduct violated the pastoral relationship and caused harm to individuals, families, and congregations.[16]

The work in the United States on sexual abuse by clergy focused primarily on Protestant denominations during the 1980s and 1990s. Running parallel to these efforts in the late 1990s were the beginnings of disclosures of child sexual abuse by priests in the Roman Catholic Church. These disclosures finally came to a head in 2002 when the US Conference of Catholic Bishops issued the *Charter for the Protection of Children and Young People*, which is a comprehensive set of procedures originally established by the USCCB in June 2002 for addressing allegations of sexual abuse of minors by Catholic clergy.[17] The charter, including guidelines for reconciliation, healing, accountability, and prevention of future acts of abuse, was revised in 2005, 2011, and 2018. Subsequently, disclosures of coverups and corruption among bishops in the United States and elsewhere laid bare the challenges for the institutional church more concerned with its image than with the well-being of its children.

Numerous lawsuits followed. In 2015, the movie *Spotlight* depicted the Boston Globe investigation, which began in 2001 and uncovered extensive sexual abuse of children by Catholic priests along with a major coverup by the Boston Archdiocese.[18] The film portrays the institutional corruption that has been disclosed again and again as the Catholic Church has sought to protect itself and its priests rather than protect its children.

In 1989, the Survivors Network of those Abused by Priests was founded to provide support for Catholic survivors who were beginning to disclose abuse they had experienced as children. The organization grew quickly and is now a major network for survivors abused by any faith leader as well as an activist network very effective in confronting the Catholic Church with demands for changes in policy and practice, including accountability for bishops who did not act to stop abusive priests.[19] In 2003, Bishop Accountability was formed. Using social media, this organization tracks accused priests, lawsuits, and disciplinary actions against church leaders.[20]

The 1990s also saw disclosures by Jewish survivors, which challenged the Jewish movements in the United States, including Reform Judaism, Conservative Judaism, and Modern Orthodox Judaism.[21] In the 2000s, Buddhist[22] and Muslim[23] survivors found their voices and came forward. FaithTrust Institute has worked with all of these groups to support establishment of policies and procedures based on texts and teachings of the particular group. This has been especially challenging for Buddhists and Muslims because their institutional structures are more focused on the local level with limited organizational hierarchy upon which to rely for direction.

#METOO PLUS #CHURCHTOO

When the #MeToo movement surfaced, the ground was fertile and ready for more public disclosures by survivors within religious settings. This has become the #ChurchToo movement primarily at the initiative of evangelical Christians. Emily Joy tweeted her disclosure of being abused by an evangelical youth pastor. The hashtag took off, resulting in allegations against numerous high-profile evangelical clergy.[24] Rachael Dehollander is an outspoken evangelical survivor who is challenging Christian colleges to train administrators to respond appropriately to victims and survivors and to take leadership in changing the cultural norms that support sexual violence.[25]

In 2008, Dr. Diana Garland from Baylor University directed the first national, random survey to try to measure the extent of sexual abuse by clergy. She documented the reality that so many survivors already knew:

> Of the entire sample, 8% report having known about CSM occurring in a congregation they have attended. Therefore, in the average American congregation of 400 congregants, there are, on average, 32 persons who have experienced CSM in their community of faith.[26]

We need more research to augment survivor testimonies, anecdotes, and lawsuits in order to examine the dynamics of power and privilege at work in each faith tradition that encourages and sustains sexual abuse by faith leaders.

WHERE ARE WE NOW?

The #MeToo and #ChurchToo movements represent a significant turning point. Silence no longer protects powerful people in leadership who exploit and abuse vulnerable people. The proliferation of survivor literature and social analysis and commentary is encouraging.[27] New young scholars are emerging like Hilary Scarsella and Stephanie Krehbiel.[28] The networking across faith traditions addressing abuse by leadership is very encouraging. These interfaith experiences have much to teach us. FaithTrust Institute provides an extensive bibliography begun in 2008 and maintained by Jim Evinger.[29] The scholarship is emerging based on survivor experiences and critique of organizational practices or lack thereof.

Most mainline Protestant denominations and Jewish movements now have intervention policies and prevention training in place. The Southern Baptist Convention is slowly taking steps to hold pastors and congregations accountable for pastoral abuse reports.[30] Roman Catholics are being pressed to clean up historic abuse situations as well as to address prevention. Buddhist and Muslim organizations are moving in that direction. The question remains whether religious institutions will press forward to address and reverse the ways that their structures, teachings, and doctrines continue to be roadblocks for both intervention and prevention of sexual violence and to proactively offer themselves as vehicles for justice and healing where brokenness and suffering of sexual violence have touched so many lives.

NOTES

1. History.com editors, "Women's Christian Temperance Union," History.com, updated August 21, 2019, Woman's Christian Temperance Union - HISTORY.

2. Me Too, "Get to Know Us: History and Inception," Me Too Movement | Get To Know Us (metoomvmt.org), accessed February 23, 2021.

3. See, Me Too, me too. Movement (metoomvmt.org).

4. Alix Langone, "#MeToo and Time's Up Founders Explain the Difference between the 2 Movements—And How They're Alike," *Time*, updated March 22, 2018, https://time.com/5189945/whats-the-difference-between-the-metoo-and-times-up-movements/.

5. "Safe, Fair, and Dignified Work for Women of All Kinds," *Times Up Now*, https://timesupnow.org/about/.

6. Susan Griffin, "Rape: The All-American Crime," *Ramparts Magazine*, September 1971, https://www.unz.com/print/Ramparts-1971sep-00026/.

7. Andra Medea and Kathleen Thompson, *Against Rape* (McGraw-Hill Ryerson Ltd., 1977).

8. Susan Brownmiller, *Against Our Will* (New York: Simon & Schuster, 1975).

9. Violence Against Women Act, Title IV, sec. 40001-40703 of the Violent Crime Control and Law Enforcement Act, H.R. 3355.

10. Lisa N. Sacco, "Violence against Women Act: Overview, Legislation, and Federal Funding," Congressional Research Service 7-5700, R42499, May 26, 2015, https://www.utsystem.edu/sites/default/files/offices/police/files/annual-promotional-exams/vawa.pdf.

11. Marie M. Fortune, *Keeping the Faith* (New York: HarperCollins, 1987), 14.

12. Marie M. Fortune, *Sexual Violence: The Sin Revisited* (Cleveland, OH: Pilgrim Press, 2005), 52.

13. Fortune, *Sexual Violence*, 85.

14. Marie Fortune's *Sexual Violence: The Unmentionable Sin* (1983) was the first book to address religion and sexual violence. The second edition, *Sexual Violence: The Sin Revisited*, followed in 2005. Fortune's *Keeping the Faith: Guidance for Christian Women Facing Abuse* (1987) was the first attempt to speak to abused women struggling with their Christian faith. Another significant contribution during this period was Pamela Cooper-White's *Cry of Tamar: Violence against Women and the Church's Response*. The first edition was published in 1995, and the second edition, in 2012. Traci West published *Wounds of the Spirit* (1999) to address the violence perpetrated against African American women and the role of the black church in response. Joy Bussert's *Battered Women: From a Theology of Suffering to an Ethic of Empowerment* (1986) was the first book to address religion and domestic violence.

15. Paxton Hibbins, *Henry Ward Beecher* (New York: George H. Doran Co., 1927).

16. Marie M. Fortune, *Is Nothing Sacred? When Sex Invades the Pastoral Relationship* (San Francisco: Harper & Row, 1989). This was the first book to frame the issue of pastoral boundary violations as pastoral misconduct and abuse.

17. United States Conference of Catholic Bishops, "Charter for the Protection of Children and Young People," http://www.usccb.org/issues-and-action/child-and-youth-protection/charter.cfm.

18. See, e.g., Jim Davis, "Church Allowed Abuse by Priest for Years," *The Boston Globe*, January 6, 2002. https://www.bostonglobe.com/news/special-reports/2002/01/06/church-allowed-abuse-priest-for-years/cSHfGkTIrAT25qKGvBuDNM/story.html.

19. Survivors Network of those Abused by Priests, https://www.snapnetwork.org; https://en.wikipedia.org/wiki/Survivors_Network_of_those_Abused_by_Priests.

20. Bishop Accountability, http://app.bishop-accountability.org.

21. Guila Benchimol and Marie Huber, "A Silence That Speaks: The Missing Discourse on Safety, Respect, and Equity," *Jewish Philanthropy*, January 28, 2020, https://ejewishphilanthropy.com/a-silence-that-speaks-the-missing-discourse-on-safety-respect-and-equity/.

22. Trudy Goodman, "Us Too," *Lion's Roar*, October 2, 2019, https://www.lionsroar.com/us-too/.

23. Aysha Khan, "'A Long Time Coming': The Muslims Are Bringing Sex Abuse by Sheikhs Out of the Shadows," *Religious News Service*, January 15, 2020, https://religionnews.com/2020/01/15/a-long-time-coming-these-muslims-are-bringing-sex-abuse-by-sheikhs-out-of-the-shadows/; "About the Hurma Project," *Hurma Project*, https://hurmaproject.com/about-us/.

24. Allison Jane Smith, "#ChurchToo: the Toxicity of Christian Complementarianism," *bitchmedia*, April 5, 2019, https://www.bitchmedia.org/article/church-too-one-year-later.

25. Adelle Banks, "Rachael Denhollander: Christian Colleges Key in Declaring Sex Abuse Is 'Evil,'" *Religious News Service*, January 31, 2020, https://religionnews.com/2020/01/31/rachael-denhollander-christian-colleges-key-in-declaring-sex-abuse-is-evil/.

26. Diana Garland, "The Prevalence of Clergy Sexual Misconduct with Adults: A Research Study, Executive Summary," *Baylor University*, https://www.baylor.edu/social_work/index.php?id=936023.

27. For example, Anne Ream began the Voices and Faces Project to support writing by survivors of sexual violence. Voices and Faces Project, "About," https://voicesandfaces.org/about/.

28. Hillary Jerome Scarsella and Stephanie Krehbiel, "Sexual Violence: Christian Theological Legacies and Responsibilities," *Religion Compass* 13, no. 9: e12337, https://doi.org/10.1111/rec3.12337.

29. James S. Evinger, "Clergy Sexual Abuse Bibliography," 35th revision, January 20, 2020, *Faith-Trust Institute*, https://faithtrustinstitute.org/resources/bibliographies/clergy-sexual-abuse.

30. Elizabeth Dias, "Southern Baptist Convention Removes Church with Registered Sex Offender Pastor," *New York Times*, February 18, 2020, https://www.nytimes.com/2020/02/18/us/southern-baptist-church-expelled.html?nl=todaysheadlines&emc=edit_th_200219&campaign_id=2&instance_id=15983&segment_id=21400&user_id=8246feed8242ad1dfc0eec441cb24799&regi_id=664167560219.

BIBLIOGRAPHY

Banks, Adelle. "Rachael Denhollander: Christian Colleges Key in Declaring Sex Abuse Is 'Evil.'" *Religious News Service*, January 31, 2020.

Benchimol, Guila, and Marie Huber. "A Silence That Speaks: The Missing Discourse on Safety, Respect, and Equity." *Jewish Philanthropy*, January 28, 2020.

Brownmiller, Susan. *Against Our Will*. New York: Simon & Schuster, 1975.

Bussert, Joy M. K. *Battered Women: From a Theology of Suffering to an Ethic of Empowerment*. Division for Mission in North America—Lutheran Church in America, 1986.

Cooper-White, Pamela. *Cry of Tamar: Violence against Women and the Church's Response*. Minneapolis, MN: Fortress Press, 1995, 2012.

Davis, Jim. "Church Allowed Abuse by Priest for Years," *The Boston Globe*, January 6, 2002, https://www.bostonglobe.com/news/special-reports/2002/01/06/church-allowed-abuse-priest-for-years/cSHfGkTIrAT25qKGvBuDNM/story.html.

Dias, Elizabeth. "Southern Baptist Convention Removes Church with Registered Sex Offender Pastor." *New York Times*, February 18, 2020.

Evinger, James S. "Clergy Sexual Abuse Bibliography." 35th revision. January 20, 2020. FaithTrust Institute. https://faithtrustinstitute.org/resources/bibliographies/clergy-sexual-abuse.

Fortune, Marie M. *Is Nothing Sacred? When Sex Invades the Pastoral Relationship*. San Francisco: Harper & Row, 1989.

———. *Keeping the Faith*. New York: HarperCollins, 1987.

———. *Sexual Violence: The Sin Revisited*. Cleveland: Pilgrim Press, 2005.

———. *Sexual Violence: The Unmentionable Sin*. Cleveland, OH: Pilgrim Press, 1983.

Garland, Diana. "The Prevalence of Clergy Sexual Misconduct with Adults: A Research Study, Executive Summary." Baylor University.

Goodman, Trudy. "Us Too." *Lion's Roar.* October 2, 2019.

Griffin, Susan. "Rape: The All-American Crime." *Ramparts Magazine.* September 1971.

Hibbins, Paxton. *Henry Ward Beecher.* New York: George H. Doran Co., 1927.

History.com editors. "Women's Christian Temperance Union." History.com. Updated August 21, 2019. Woman's Christian Temperance Union - HISTORY.

Khan, Aysha. "'A Long Time Coming': The Muslims Are Bringing Sex Abuse by Sheikhs Out of the Shadows." *Religious News Service.* January 15, 2020.

Langone, Alix. "#MeToo and Time's Up Founders Explain the Difference between the 2 Movements—And How They're Alike." *Time.* Updated March 22, 2018.

Medea, Andra, and Kathleen Thompson. *Against Rape.* Toronto: McGraw-Hill Ryerson Ltd., 1977.

Me Too. "Get to Know Us: History and Inception." me too. Movement | Get To Know Us (metoo mvmt.org). Accessed February 23, 2021.

Sacco, Lisa N. Violence against Women Act: Overview, Legislation, and Federal Funding. Congressional Research Service 7-5700, R42499, May 26, 2015, https://www.utsystem.edu/sites/default/files/offices/police/files/annual-promotional-exams/vawa.pdf.

Scarsella, Hillary Jerome, and Stephanie Krehbiel. "Sexual Violence: Christian Theological Legacies and Responsibilities." https://onlinelibrary.wiley.com/doi/pdf/10.1111/rec3.12337.

Smith, Allison Jane. "#ChurchToo: The Toxicity of Christian Complementarianism." *bitchmedia.* April 5, 2019.

West, Traci. *Wounds of the Spirit: Black Women, Violence, and Resistance Ethics.* New York: New York University Press, 1999.

CHAPTER 17

Femicide in Global Perspective

··

A Feminist Critique

Rev. Dr. Helen T. Boursier, PhD, College of St. Scholastica

ABSTRACT

Feminist voices have documented and advocated about femicide for almost 50 years, but it remains much less known than its common precursors: sexual harassment, domestic violence, and rape. Femicide is a chameleon of evil, blending in with culturally accepted norms like misogyny, dowry deaths, and honor killings as the rationale that males give for killing females because they are females. This essay explains the startling reality of femicide in global context, gives a tighter focus on Central America, includes a case study of Guatemala, and introduces state complicity to feminicide.

Before feminists invented the term *sexual harassment* or called out domestic violence and rape as human rights violations against females, these injustices were ignored, dismissed, and/or accepted as normative by society. Feminism defined, challenged, and reshaped public perspective through education and advocacy. Similarly, feminists have been forcing attention to the grim reality of femicide for almost fifty years, but it remains much less known than its common precursors: sexual harassment, domestic violence, and rape. Femicide is a gender-specific term, adapted from the gender-neutral homicide, to force attention to the grim reality of males killing females because they are female, including women, teens, girls, and babies. This interreligious and cross-cultural gender-specific brutality kills an estimated 66,000 females around the world each year.[1] If ever there was a global interreligious topic that warrants what Elisabeth Schüssler Fiorenza calls "a feminist systemic analysis of oppression and struggle for change,"[2] it is femicide. Femicide is "sexist terrorism" and the most extreme form of gender-related violence against females, which creates a ripple effect of suffering.[3] Compared to homicides, femicides frequently have more indirect casualties, including children, witnesses, and bystanders.[4] Families are destroyed, and children are left without their primary caregiver. Femicide tentacles also cross the boundaries from one nation-state to another when females flee their homelands to seek asylum elsewhere.

DEFINING TERMS: FEMICIDE AND FEMINICIDE

Femicide means the brutal murder of women and girls because of their gender, and feminicide connects the same violent acts of femicide to encompass state culpability.[5] Although femicide slowly has been increasing its voice on a global scale, there is no universally accepted term or definition for the killing. In its Global Burden of Armed Violence 2015 (GBAV) report, the Geneva Convention uses the broad term *female homicide* to encompass the murder of females. Some countries, like Guatemala, Costa Rico, and Mexico, have specific legislation designed to help combat femicide with its definition limited to intimate partner femicide.[6] Other countries treat femicide as an aggravated homicide without specifying the gender-specific hate behind the crime. For example, femicides are lumped together as regular homicides in US legal language, and there rarely is a specific connection made of the violent act being specifically a hate crime against females by males because they are female.[7]

Diana Russell, an early leader in femicide research and advocacy, defines femicide as "the murder of females by males because they are female," which highlights the gender-based primacy of males (men, teens, and boys) perpetuating this hate crime committed against females (women, teens, girls, and babies). She calls the "significant minority" of murders of females by females "female-on-female," and she categorizes these based upon whether the female acted as an agent of patriarchy, of male perpetrators, or as her own agent. Russell's sub-categories include intimate-partner femicides, familial femicides, femicides by known perpetrators, or stranger femicides.[8] Russell also includes "botched abortions," forced marriages of extremely young females to much older men, experimental birth control methods that cause death, and "the deliberate preference given to boy children in many cultures that results in countless female deaths from neglect, illness, and starvation in numerous impoverished nations such as China and India."[9] Other forms of femicide include honor killing, female feticide, female infanticide, bride burning, dowry murders, and multicidal femicide, which are "committed by serial murderers and mass murderers and systematic femicide is committed during armed conflict when females are systematically slaughtered."[10] Covert femicide encompasses the indirect or less visible forms of femicide that cause females to die because of patristic laws, practices, and actions of individuals and/or social institutions, like border policies that limit or deny access for females fleeing femicide in their homelands to seek asylum elsewhere. Femicide legislation in Guatemala specifies economic infringement on a female's right to earn a living to provide for herself and her family.[11]

Given the various studies and topologies for femicide, estimates vary considerably for the number of females who are killed from intimate femicide, ranging from 40 to 70 percent of all femicide.[12] Femicide also occurs within wider-scale genocide, like the

Rwanda genocide (approximately April 6–July 16, 1994) when females were gang raped before they were murdered.[13] When the numbers climb unchecked for individual cases of femicide, the collective responsibility becomes *feminicide*.

FEMINICIDE

Feminicide broadens accountability from individual perpetrators to include people and institutions that were and are in a position of authority and power that could and should provide protection for females who live within its jurisdiction. Explained in greater detail in chapter eighteen, *feminicide* is an accusatory term, which points to the non-response of the state, whether from ineptitude or disinterest, for failure to protect females. It encompasses political, judicial, and social factors.[14] States outside the boundaries of where femicides occur also have culpability connection to feminicide through global systems that intersect between nations. For example, when any nation develops border policies to limit or deny access to asylum seekers fleeing probable femicide, it becomes directly culpable to feminicide.[15] Interestingly, the terms *femicide* and *feminicide* often are used interchangeably in Latin America, which consistently has among the highest femicides in the world. It almost seems as if, by removing the distinguishing aspect of feminicide and government complicity, these states somehow seek to lessen their guilt regarding failure to protect females from femicides that occur within their boundaries. With more than 400 unsolved cases of brutal murders of females, Ciudad Juárez, Mexico, has the notoriety of bringing feminicide to the forefront in Central America.[16] (The next chapter explains state culpability to feminicide through the use and abuse of border controls for exclusion from asylum.)

GLOBAL CONTEXT

Gaps exist in femicide research due to lack of documentation, particularly in developing countries. However, when studies are conducted, the numbers can be staggering. The Geneva Declaration reported its findings in GBAV, the largest ever worldwide study to document femicides. The 2011 database on global femicide excludes conflict-related deaths. Otherwise, this inclusive data indicates that "an average annual total of about 44,000 femicides were reported in the 104 countries and territories under review between 2004 and 2009."[17] To determine the realistic total number of femicides globally, researchers applied femicide rates to the countries with no femicide data to calculate that there is an estimated 66,000 females killed around the world each year. The per capita rate is one femicide for every 100,000 persons of the total population.[18] The updated GBAV 2014 analyzed data between 2007 and 2012 to net an average of 60,000 femicides per year.[19] The rate decreased in some countries, but it increased in others.

The global baseline rate for femicide is 6.0 per 100,000 population. El Salvador has the highest per capita femicides (14.1 per 100,000), and Honduras is second with 10.9 per 100,000. Both countries also rank the highest for the "overall homicide rates, with 73 persons killed per 100,000 population in Honduras and 59 in El Salvador, indicating particularly high mortality rates due to intentional violence."[20] Lethal violence of females in El Salvador is higher than "the overall rate of male and female homicides in some of the 40 countries with the highest rates worldwide, such as Ecuador, Nicaragua, and Tanzania."[21] A study conducted in South Africa, based on court testimony and newspaper accounts, discovered that "a woman is killed by her intimate partner in South Africa every six hours. This is the highest rate (8.8 per 100,000 female population 14 years and more) that has ever been reported in research anywhere in the world."[22] A study in Jamaica notes that it was not until after 1998 that homicide data was classified by gender, so the high generic homicide rate overshadowed the previously unknown femicide rate. Once the male/female data was specified, femicide was identified in Jamaica as being "a very big problem, with 13 females for every 100,000 females murdered every year."[23] Specifying the gender distinction adds clarity to where females are most at risk for femicide.

Femicide might seem like an isolated anomaly in the United States, where it has a lower statistic than other places around the globe, but it does occur there. The term *femicide* is rarely used in the media and/or to technically define the instances of violent death of females by males because they are female. In fact, research suggests "that a crime committed against a minority group (African-Americans, Asian-Americans, Latinos, Jews, or gay men) was more likely to be considered a hate crime than crimes against women."[24] The United States has its statistics and grim testimonies of femicide. For example, in an otherwise peaceful Amish community located in rural Pennsylvania, Charles Carl Roberts IV committed femicide when the 32-year-old white male American entered an Amish schoolroom in Lancaster County to conduct a revenge killing on females. Upon arrival, he separated the children by gender and allowed the boys to leave. Then, he systematically conducted femicide as he "lined the girls against a blackboard, bound their feet with wire ties and plastic handcuffs, and then shot them execution style. Five little girls were killed: Lena Miller, 7; Mary Liz Miller, 8; Naomi Ebersol, 7; Anna Mae Stoltzfus, 12; and Marian Fisher, 13."[25] The details provide gruesome sensationalized headline news, but, once the story fades from public view and the shock wears off for all but the surviving families, the concept of femicide tends to diminish from reality in the United States, but it does occur. North Carolina has high rates of lethal violence against women,[26] and American Indian and Alaskan Native females experience a grossly disproportionate amount of gender-related sexual violence, a common precursor to femicide, than any other ethnic group in the United States.[27]

MALE RATIONALE FOR KILLING FEMALES

The rationale males use to justify killing females differs by culture and context. For example, Israa Ghareeb, a 21-year-old Palestinian woman in the West Bank, was brutally murdered by her brother in September 2019 because her father and brothers believed she had dishonored Islam and her family when she posted a video on social media of herself with her fiancé the day *before* she was to be engaged. Israa was physically assaulted in the Ghareeb family home and later admitted to the Arab Society Hospital in Bethlehem, where her brother brutally and fatally stabbed her multiple times in the hospital bed. An audio recording quickly went viral on social media of a young woman screaming while being tortured. Although the voice was not independently confirmed as being Israa's, #WeAreAllIsraa immediately became a popular hashtag with more than 50,000 tweets posting it on Arabic Twitter.[28]

So-called honor killings also are used by males in Jordan to justify their actions, where a female could be killed for "financial or inheritance claims, being a victim of rape or incest, becoming pregnant out of wedlock, engaging in an 'illegitimate' or extra-marital affair, marrying a man against her family's wishes, being seen talking to a man who is not a family member, running away from home, being caught in a brothel or mere rumors about or suspicion of any of the above."[29] The conservative estimate is that 15 to 20 females in Jordan are beaten or stabbed to death by family members each year in the name of honor. The guestimate for annual honor killings in Syria is 200, 400 in Yemen, 52 in Egypt, 27 in Palestine, and 122 in Iraq, with another 124 female suicides that could have a link to femicide through honor killings.[30] In Turkey, females must act in ways that adhere to current socially accepted standards. Otherwise, they "deserve" whatever injustice their male oversight "superior" deems appropriate. Physical violence against females is considered acceptable when females do not comply with the existing "social and political realm within which laws are enacted, interpreted, and applied."[31] Femicide becomes the next step in this societal norm that subjugates females because they are female.

Killing a bride because her family did not meet the dowry demands is a form of femicide in India that crosses all socioeconomic lines. Instead of the family of the bride doing the killing because they feel dishonored, the bride's new family, her in-laws, do the killing when they believe that the bridal dowry price was insufficient. Dowry disputes contribute to an estimated 25,000 brides who are "killed or maimed worldwide every year." It brings suspicion when a bride dies unexpectedly, including from suicide within seven years of being married. Research indicates that the most popular ways to inflict femicide or suicide for dowry disputes, in descending order, "are burning (bride burning), poisoning, hanging, strangulation, and head injury."[32] Regardless of the justification or method, it is femicide when a male kills a female because she is female.

While political rhetoric and social media cast the blame for femicide against a specific religion and / or nation / region of the world, the root problem is the ever-pervasive patristic idea that gives males their misogynistic justification to exert power or authority over females simply because of the gender differential. Femicide occurs worldwide, including in countries whose citizens have primary religious affiliations to Christianity, Islam, Buddhism, and Hinduism. Overall, "Femicide remains firmly anchored in the continuum of gender-based violence, intimate partner violence, and domestic violence."[33] The higher the tolerance level is for any form of violence against females by the population at large, including by females and males, the higher the femicide rate is in that country.

When domestic violence and rape are culturally normative, femicide can become the harsh consummation amid the social and government acceptance of violence against females by males. For example, a study in the Dominican Republic confirmed that every single time a femicide victim "was killed by her partner, the femicide was preceded by harassment, persecution, and threats."[34] People close to femicide victims knew about domestic violence warnings, but these were never documented through the legal system. The odds of femicide increase when intimate partner violence also includes stalking, particularly when a relationship has ended and the female has physically separated to a new housing location.[35] For example, the mother of three children reported that her former husband came to her mother's home, where she had sought safe haven, and dragged her by the hair back to his residence. He told her that, if she ever left him again, he would kill her. She told me she had suffered domestic violence from him "too many times to count." The next day, she left her older children with her mother and fled for America with her youngest child to seek asylum.[36] Mothers fleeing from probable femicide in the Northern Triangle often report "That evil man will not find me in the United States. Here I will be safe." A mother who fled with her six-year-old son from Honduras said, "I woke up one morning and left. The problem that I had there was too great. It forced me to leave. I had no time to plan. I left in emergency."[37] She and her son were forcibly separated at the border, during the Trump administration's family separation atrocity, when they crossed into the United States on June 6, 2018, to request asylum (see cover artwork/center image and figure 18.1, p. 249).[38]

ZEROING IN ON THE NORTHERN TRIANGLE: GUATEMALA, EL SALVADOR, AND HONDURAS

Since 2014, I have spoken with several thousand females fleeing violence in Guatemala, El Salvador, and Honduras. Each one personally knows a female who was killed because she was female, including mothers, sisters, aunts, cousins, daughters, neighbors, and friends. These women, teens, and girls are not exaggerating their fears. They have been living in a nightmare. They know that males do not make idle threats. Examples of previously fulfilled promises of violent death are self-evident. They consistently include domestic violence and rape in their credible fear claims for asylum in the United States.[39] Global femicide documentation validates their fearful reality. From 2010 to 2013, "El Salvador has had the highest rate of femicide in the world, with 2,250 femicides, Guatemala had the third and Honduras the seventh highest rate of femicides."[40] In Guatemala and El Salvador, "the rate of homicides against women is growing at a faster pace than those against men."[41] Overall, seven out of the ten highest rates for femicide in 2012 are countries in Latin America.[42] An Economic Commission for Latin America (CEPAL) 2014 report on femicide in Latin American countries indicates that 88 women in Colombia, 83 in Peru, 71 in the Dominican Republic, 46 in El Salvador, 25 in Uruguay, 20 in Paraguay, 17 in Guatemala, and 16 in Chile were victims of femicide (see the testimony of a mother fleeing gender-based violence in El Salvador; figure 17.1).[43]

Femicide in Brazil takes the top standing in South America, where an average of four women were murdered each day during 2019 becauses of their gender, with another 67 attempted femicides.[44] Despite how bad these statistics are, sexual violence

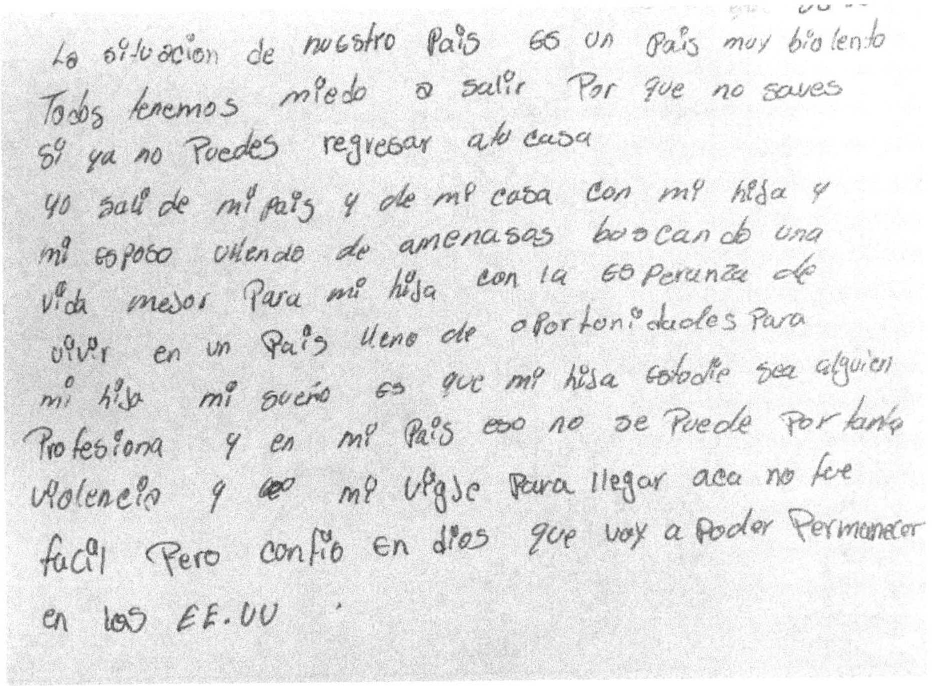

La situacion de nuestro Pais es un Pais muy biolento
Todos tenemos miedo a salir Por que no saves
Si ya no Puedes regresar a tu casa
Yo sali de mi pais y de mi casa con mi hija y
mi esposo uilendo de amenasas booscando una
vida mejor Para mi hija con la esperanza de
vivir en un Pais lleno de oPortunidades Para
mi hija mi sueño es que mi hija estodie sea alguien
Profesiona y en mi Pais eso no se Puede Por tanta
Violencia y el mi viaje Para llegar aca no fue
facil Pero confio en dios que voy a Poder Permanecer
en los EE.UU .

FIGURE 17.1. A mother detained at the GEO for-profit Immigrant Family Residential Center located in Karnes City, Texas, explains she wants to live in El Salvador, but that there is so much violence. She knows the journey will not be easy, but she trusts in God that they will be allowed to live in the United States.

is not accurately reflected because too much violence against females is not reported. For example, *Diario Libre* reported that in El Salvador the "constant threat saturates the environment and slows the complaint because "sexual abuse is so widespread since childhood that, in many cases, rape is experienced as part of the process of moving into adulthood and those who can, leave the country in search of security before dreaming of finding justice in one more system accustomed and characterized by impunity" in their homeland.[45] There is no "safe" age for females in high-risk nations like El Salvador, where young girls are kidnapped and put to "evil use," where being raped is so normal it is almost considered a rite of passage to adulthood (see figure 17.2).[46]

The key contributing factors for the culture of violence against females in Guatemala, El Salvador, and Honduras include drugs, guns, gangs, economic instability, police and government corruption, and the pervasive machismo culturally predisposed perspective, which is accepted and supported by males *and* females. The families fleeing violence in their homelands often mention that they want a "better life," a technical term that means *bare life*. They are not seeking the yellow brick road to happily ever after; rather they simply want life for themselves and their children. When remaining in their homeland becomes an inevitable death sentence, they desperately flee for their lives (see figure 17.3).

Gender oppression needs to be transformed within the cultural context, but receiving nations can and must name this as a viable reason to seek safe asylum elsewhere.

FIGURE 17.2. Mono print portrait acrylic paint on Greystone paper of a mother and daughter at a shelter in Nuevo Laredo, Mexico who are fleeing femicide from El Salvador to seek asylum in the United States.

© *Helen T. Boursier*

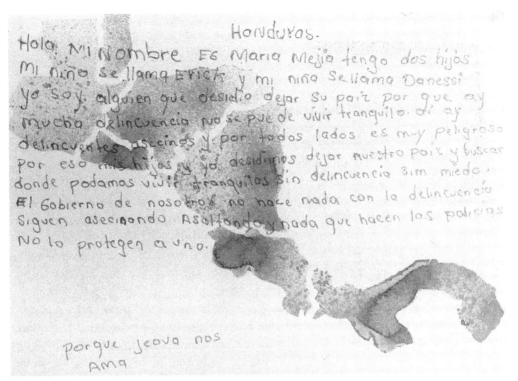

FIGURE 17.3. A mother detained at the for-profit immigrant family detention center located in Karnes City, Texas shares her reasons for fleeing Honduras: violence, fear, beaten, and "so much delinquency" that pervades her homeland. She is requesting asylum in the United States because it is a safe place where she can live without fear.

CASE STUDY: GUATEMALA

There is the most documentation on Guatemala about femicide, perhaps because its Decree 22–2008 is among the earliest and most complete femicide legislation in Central America.[47] This landmark legislation defines femicide as the "violent murder of a woman motivated by her gender" and specifies "25 to 50-year prison term without possibility of reducing the term." Article 7 stipulates that violence against a woman includes "physical and sexual violence, any type of harm or suffering inflicted on a woman's body, as well as prohibiting a woman from using methods for family planning or the prevention of sexually transmitted diseases" and mandates 5 to 12 years behind bars. It also specifies psychological abuse, "including intimidating actions towards a woman or her family members or attempting to control her or damage her self-esteem" and warrants a 5- to 8-year prison term. Article 8 on economic violence defines "any action that endangers a woman's right to work or possess and dispose of her property as she chooses, or using other forms of violence to obtain woman's earnings or assets" and mandates a 5- to 8-year prison term. The detailed law also stipulates the state's responsibility to provide free legal counsel for female survivors of violence, to develop and oversee specialized training and investigative services, and to create a plan to eradicate violence against females. This legislation makes phenomenal advancements for females in Guatemala, but it ultimately has done virtually nothing to stave off the increasing lethal violence against females. Impunity runs rampant.[48]

FROM NOMINAL PUNISHMENT TO 100% IMPUNITY

Denounce is the common term used by families who are searching for justice for their murdered loved ones. The majority of these denouncers are females—mothers, sisters, daughters, aunts, and grandmothers—who demand justice for femicide victims. The process to find justice for victims of domestic or lethal violence against females is fraught with gender bias sinkholes. The roadblocks include government and police corruption and complicity, gender and victim blaming and shaming, and zero political will to ensure safety and justice for females because they are female.[49] Discrimination begins at the police station, where victims of sexual violence in particular must endure "psychological violence due to the use of bad techniques to interview by the police, or in the form of repeated physical abuse including rape by the officer who takes the report."[50] These denouncers "face indifference, discrimination, lies, cover-ups and complicity, and outright hostility within the justice system. They often are treated like criminals for insisting on solving crimes involving their loved ones and 're-victimized' by mistreatment at the hands of the legal system itself."[51] It also consistently is reported that Guatemala, like other Central American countries where femicide runs unchecked, has "a dysfunctional judicial system with insensitive prosecutors and judges."[52] Females are too familiar with law enforcement incompetence and gender bias in their local communities. For example, a mother who had been a nurse in Guatemala filed a police report when gang members robbed her car. She explained:

> They began to make phone calls and death threats because I reported them to the police. They (gang members) came to my house and told me that because I had denounced them, that it would cost me my life. They gave me 72 hours to leave the country or they would murder me and my daughter. One month before, my aunt was murdered by strangulation, and they said the same thing would happen to me. With much fear and trembling, I quickly left. For this reason, I am appealing to the USA that they can grant me asylum.[53]

Police incompetence and gang retaliation are common realities that deter females from filing claims in their home country for nonlethal gender injustice, such as domestic violence and rape. They know that doing so would not be helpful. Instead, it likely would generate gang retribution and/or more gender injustice against them by police and government officials and also from their husband or partner. Females who fled gender violence in Guatemala to seek asylum in the United States regularly report that their spouse/partner mocked them, taunting them that going to the police to report a crime or death threat would be useless.[54] Consequently, the common precursors to femicide, domestic violence and rape, are grossly underreported. Femicides also are underreported. When reported, they are not investigated, or barely investigated such that very few perpetrators are ever tried or convicted, which nets the 97 to 98 percent impunity as femicide cases in Guatemala remain unsolved.[55]

For the miniscule who are convicted, the sentences often are set so low that the guilty perpetrator of femicide pays a nominal fine in lieu of incarceration. State complicity to feminicide is evident in the accusation that "judges purposely sentence male aggressors to the five-year minimum so they will not have to serve any time in jail."[56] For example, in Guatemala, the fine ranges "from 5–100 Quetzales per day (or approximately USD $0.60–$13 per day)."[57] The abysmally low conviction rate in Guatemala is similar in other Latin American countries.[58] When there are virtually no consequences for femicide, there is nothing to slow down or stop the atrocity.[59] A policewoman who fled Honduras with her family after repeated human rights violations against her family because of her vocation explained that she did not file a complaint with the police because, "even though I do not want to accept it, and it embarrasses me, some of the police officers from the upper ranks have ruined that honorable institution because there are so many who are involved with the gangs."[60] She said that she knew that their lives would have been at risk if she had filed a report with the police. When the local state fails to protect its citizens, the best hope is for them to run for their lives and seek safety elsewhere (see figure 17.4). If migrants survive the dangerous and daunting journey, they must transgress the gauntlet of (unjust) policies and practices designed for exclusion from asylum.

FIGURE 17.4. View of the US border wall from Nogales, Mexico looking north toward Nogales, Arizona.
© *Helen T. Boursier*

NOTES

1. Geneva Declaration, "When the Victim Is a Woman," in *Global Burden of Armed Violence* 2015, http://www.genevadeclaration.org/fileadmin/docs/GBAV2/GBAV2011_CH4_rev.pdf, 117.

2. Elisabeth Schüssler Fiorenza, *Jesus: Miriam's Child, Sophia's Prophet: Critical Issues in Feminist Christology* (New York: Continuum, 2004), 29.

3. Jane Caputi and Diana E. H. Russell, "Femicide: Sexist Terrorism against Women," in *The Politics of Woman Killing*, ed. Jill Radford and Diana E. H. Russell (New York: Twayne Publishers, 1992), 13–26.

4. "When the Victim Is a Woman," 113.

5. See, e.g., Helen T. Boursier, *The Ethics of Hospitality: An Interfaith Response to U.S. Immigration Policies* (Lanham, MD: Lexington Books, 2019); and *Desperately Seeking Asylum: Testimonies of Trauma, Courage, and Love* (Lanham, MD: Rowman & Littlefield, 2019).

6. See, e.g., Geneva Declaration, "Lethal Violence against Women and Girls," in *Global Burden*, 87–129.

7. Brianne Berry, "Ni Una Menos: Argentina Takes the Lead against Sexism and Gender Violence in Latin America," *Council on Hemispheric Affairs*, June 23, 2015, http://www.coha.org/ni-una-menos-argentina-takes-the-lead-against-sexism-and-gender-violence-in-latin-america/.

8. Diana E. H. Russell, "Femicide: Politicizing the Killing of Females," 26, and Monique Widyono, "Conceptualizing Femicide," 7, in *Strengthening Understanding of Femicide: Using Research to Galvanize Action and Accountability*, https://path.azureedge.net/media/documents/GVR_femicide_rpt.pdf; see also, Radford and Russell, eds., *Femicide: The Politics of Woman Killing*. For current qualitative studies and data collection initiatives on femicide in Latin America, see, e.g., "When the Victim Is a Woman," 116.

9. Russell, "Femicide: Politicizing the Killing of Females," 29.

10. Janice Joseph, "Victims of Femicide in Latin America: Legal and Criminal Justice Responses," *TEMIDA*, 29, no. 1 (2017): 5, http://www.doiserbia.nb.rs/img/doi/1450-6637/2017/1450-66371701003J.pdf. For honor killings, see, e.g., "Lethal Violence against Women and Girls," 87–129.

11. Kelsey Alford-Jones, ed., "Guatemala's Femicide Law: Progress against Impunity?," Guatemala Human Rights Commission USA, May 2009, http://www.ghrc-usa.org/Publications/Femicide_Law_ProgressAgainstImpunity.pdf.

12. L. L. Dahlberg and E. G. Krug, "Violence: A Global Public Health Problem," in *World Report on Violence and Health*, ed. E. G. Kurg et al. (World Health Organization, Geneva, 2002): 321, cited in Shanaaz Mathews, Naeemah Abrahams, Lorna J. Martin, Lisa Vetten, Lize van der Merwe, and Rachel Jewkes, "Every Six Hours a Woman Is Killed by Her Intimate Partner: A National Study of Female Homicide in South Africa," *MRC Policy Brief* (2004): 5, https://www.files.ethz.ch/isn/104994/sixhours.pdf.

13. Fulata Lusungu Moyo, "Gang-Raped and Dis-Membered: Contextual Biblical Study of Judges 19:1–30 to Re-Member the Rwandan Genocide," in *Sexual Violence and Sacred Texts*, ed. Amy Kalmanofsky (Cambridge, MA: Feminist Studies in Religion Books, 2017), 125–39; and Nancy Sai, "Rwanda," Women under Siege, Women's Media Center, February 8, 2012, http://www.womensmediacenter.com/women-under-siege/conflicts/rwanda.

14. See, e.g., Boursier, *Ethics of Hospitality*, and *Desperately Seeking Asylum*; Nancy Pineda-Madrid, *Suffering + Salvation in Ciudad Juárez* (Minneapolis, MN: Fortress Press, 2011), and "Feminicide and the Reinvention of Religious Practices," in *Women, Wisdom, and Witness: Engaging Contexts in Conversation*, ed. Rosemary P. Carbine and Kathleen J. Dolphin (Collegeville, MN: Liturgical Press, 2007), 61; and Widyono "Conceptualizing Femicide," 10–11.

15. Examples in the next chapter focus on US immigration policies and practices, but a parallel argument could be made for any nation that uses border policies and practices that prevent international access to females fleeing probable femicide.

16. See, e.g., Pineda-Madrid, *Suffering + Salvation*.

17. "When the Victim Is a Woman," 113–44. For details on population data and regional classifications, see the online methodological index at www.genevadeclaration.org.

18. "When the Victim Is a Woman," 117.

19. "Lethal Violence against Women and Girls," 90.

20. "Lethal Violence against Women and Girls," 94.

21. "Lethal Violence against Women and Girls," 94.

22. Mathews et al., "Every Six Hours," 4.

23. Glendene Lemard, "Femicide in Jamaica," in *Strengthening Understanding*, 45.

24. Jocelyn Jacoby, "Sexual Violence Is a Hate Crime," *Ending Violence against Women* (blog), May 9, 2017, *National Organization for Women*, https://now.org/blog/sexual-violence-is-a-hate-crime/, citing Donald A. Saucier, Tamara L. Brown, Raquel C. Mitchell, and Audrey J. Cawman, "Effects of Victims' Characteristics on Attitudes Toward Hate Crimes," *Journal of Interpersonal Violence* 21, no. 7 (2006): 890–909.

25. Jacoby, "Sexual Violence Is a Hate Crime." See also, e.g., Raymond McCaffrey, Paul Duggan, and Debbi Wilgoren, "Five Killed at Pennsylvania Amish School," *Washington Post*, October 3, 2006, http://www.washingtonpost.com/wp dyn/content/article/2006/10/03/AR2006100300229.html.

26. See, e.g., Kathryn E. Moracco, Carol W. Runyan, and John D. Butts, "Femicide in North Carolina, 1991–1993: A Statewide Study of Patterns and Precursors," *Homicide Studies* 2 (1998): 422–46, https://doi.org/10.1177/1088767998002004005. For intimate femicide, see, e.g., Margaret A. Zahn, C. Block, and J. Campbell, "Intimate Partner Homicide," *National Institute of Justice Journal* 250 (November 2003): 1–64.

27. Elena Mieszczanski, "Indigenous Women Can't Get Justice: You Should Care," *Ending Violence against Women* (blog), April 11, 2019, https://now.org/blog/indigenous-women-cant-get-justice-you-should-care/.

28. Emina Osmandzikovic and Hazen Balousha, "Murder of Israa Ghareeb Renews Debate over Honor Killings in Middle East," *Arab News*, September 2, 2019, https://www.arabnews.com/node/1548306/middle-east. See also, e.g., Adam Eliyahu Berkowitz, "Tlaib Blames Israel for Muslim Honor Killings," *Israel365 News*, September 2, 2019 (israel365news.com).

29. Rana Husseini, "Honor-Related Crimes in Jordan: Reasons Women Are Killed in Jordan," in *Strengthening Understanding*, 85.

30. Osmandzikovic and Balousha, "Slain in the Name of Honor."

31. Meltem Ahiska, "Violence against Women in Turkey: Vulnerability, Sexuality, and Eros," in *Vulnerability in Resistance*, ed. Judith Butler, Zeynep Gambetti, and Leticia Sabsay (Duke University Press, 2016), 212. See also, e.g., Ayse Gül Altinay and Yesim Arat, *Violence against Women in Turkey: A Nationwide Survey* (Punto Istanbul: Punto Publishing Solutions, 2009), 35, http://research.sabanciuniv.edu/11418/1/Violence_Against_Women_in_Turkey.pdf.

32. Virenda Kumar, "Dowry Deaths (Bride Burnings) in India," in *Strengthening Understanding*, 89–90.

33. "Lethal Violence against Women and Girls," 109.

34. María Jesús (Susi) Pola Z., "Feminicide in the Dominican Republic," in *Strengthening Understanding*, 53.

35. See, e.g., Judith M. McFarlane, Jacquelyn C. Campbell, Susan Wilt, Carolyn J. Sachs, Yvonne Ulrich, and Xiao Xu, "Stalking and Intimate Partner Femicide," *Homicide Studies* 3, no. 4 (1999): 300–16.

36. Interview with the author July 13, 2019; shared by permission.

37. This mother shares her family separation experience in Boursier, *Desperately Seeking Asylum*, 85–87.

38. Maya Rhodan, "Here are the Facts about President Trump's Family Separation Policy," *Time*, June 18, 2018, https://time.com/5314769/family-separation-policy-donald-trump/.

39. See, e.g., Boursier, *Ethics of Hospitality*, and *Desperately Seeking Asylum*.

40. Joseph, "Victims of Femicide in Latin America," 7; see also, e.g., Karen Musalo and Blaine Bookey, "Crimes without Punishment: An Update on Violence against Women and Impunity in Guatemala," *Hastings Race and Poverty Law Journal* 10 (Summer 2013): 269. https://cgrs.uchastings.edu/sites/default/files/Musalo_Bookey_CrimesWithoutPunishment_2013.pdf.

41. Ana Carcedoa, "Femicide in Central America 2000–2006," in *Strengthening Understanding*, 43.

42. "Lethal Violence against Women and Girls," 92.

43. For more examples of testimonies from asylum seekers, see Helen T. Boursier, *Art As Witness: A Practical Theology of Arts-Based Research* (Lanham, MD: Lexington Books, 2021), and *Refugee Art: Testimonies of Immigrant Families Seeking Asylum* (blog), https://refugeeartblog.com/.

44. Erica Sanchez and Sophie Maes, "Four Women are Killed Every Day in Brazil as Femicide Persists," *Global Citizen*, February 5, 2019, https://www.globalcitizen.org/en/content/femicide-brazil-2019.

45. *Diario Libre*, "Violación de mujeres, otro sello de las pandillas (1 de 2)" [Violation of women, other stamp of the gangs (1 of 2)], November 8, 2014, https://www.diariolibre.com/noticias/violacin-de-mujeres-otro-sello-de-las-pandillas-1-de-2-AHDL870761.

46. See, e.g., Boursier, *Desperately Seeking Asylum* and *Ethics of Hospitality*.

47. Alford-Jones, "Guatemala's Femicide Law."

48. See, e.g., Center for Gender and Refugee Studies, "Central America: Femicides and Gender-Based Violence," University of California Hastings College of the Law, accessed December 10, 2019, https://cgrs.uchastings.edu/our-work/central-america-femicides-and-gender-based-violence; and Joseph, "Victims of Femicide in Latin America."

49. See, e.g., Katharine Ruhl, "Guatemala's Femicides and the Ongoing Struggle for Women's Human Rights: Update to CFR's 2005 Report *Getting Away with Murder*," Center for Gender and Refugee Studies, 14, https://cgrs.uchastings.edu/sites/default/files/Guatemalas_femicides_ongoing_struggle_Ruhl_2006_0.pdf.

50. My translation from the Spanish. Lisa Davis and Bradley Parker, "Informe sobre Violaciones de Derechos Humanos de las Mujeres en Guatemala," New York, Human Rights Commission of the United Nations, March 13–30, 2012. https://www2.ohchr.org/english/bodies/hrc/docs/ngos/RVWHR_Guatemala_HRC104_sp.pdf, 7.

51. Nobel Women's Initiative, "From Survivors to Defenders: Women Confronting Violence in Mexico, Honduras, and Guatemala," http://nobelwomensinitiative.org/wp-content/uploads/2012/06/Report_AmericasDelgation-2012.pdf?ref=196, 21.

52. Joseph, "Victims of Femicide in Latin America."

53. Interview with the author; shared by permission in Boursier, *Ethics of Hospitality*, 125.

54. See, e.g., Boursier, *Desperately Seeking Asylum*, 91–108.

55. Alford-Jones, "Guatemala's Femicide Law." See, e.g., "Central America: Femicides and Gender-Based Violence," and Joseph, "Victims of Femicide in Latin America."

56. Musalo and Bookey, "Crimes without Punishment," 287.

57. Musalo and Bookey, "Crimes without Punishment," 287.

58. See, e.g., Ruhl, "Guatemala's Femicides," 14.

59. See, e.g., Joseph, "Victims of Femicide in Latin America."

60. Testimony (#22), November 6, 2019.

BIBLIOGRAPHY

Ahiska, Meltem. "Violence against Women in Turkey: Vulnerability, Sexuality, and Eros." In *Vulnerability in Resistance*. Edited by Judith Butler, Zeynep Gambetti, and Leticia Sabsay, 211–35. Durham, NC, and London: Duke University Press, 2016.

Alford-Jones, Kelsey, ed. "Guatemala's Femicide Law: Progress against Impunity?" Guatemala Human Rights Commission USA, May 2009. http://www.ghrc-usa.org/Publications/Femicide_Law_ProgressAgainstImpunity.pdf.

Altinay, Ayse Gül, and Yesim Arat. *Violence against Women in Turkey: A Nationwide Survey*. Punto Istanbul: Punto Publishing Solutions, 2009. http://research.sabanciuniv.edu/11418/1/Violence_Against_Women_in_Turkey.pdf.

Bala, Nila, and Arthur Rizer. "Trump's Family Separation Policy Never Really Ended; This Is Why." NBC News. July 1, 2019. https://www.nbcnews.com/think/opinion/trump-s-family-separation-policy-never-really-ended-why-ncna1025376.

Berkowitz, Adam Eliyahu. "Tlaib Blames Israel for Muslim Honor Killings." *Israel365 News*, September 2, 2019. https://israel365news.com/136456/tlaib-blames-israel-for-muslim-honor-killings/.

Berry, Brianne. "Ni Una Menos: Argentina Takes the Lead against Sexism and Gender Violence in Latin America." Council on Hemispheric Affairs. June 23, 2015. http://www.coha.org/ni-una -menos-argentina-takes-the-lead-against-sexism-and-gender-violence-in-latin-america/.

Boursier, Helen T. *Art As Witness: A Practical Theology of Arts-Based Research*. Lanham, MD: Lexington Books, 2021.

———. *Desperately Seeking Asylum: Testimonies of Trauma, Courage, and Love*. Lanham, MD: Rowman & Littlefield, 2019.

———. *The Ethics of Hospitality: An Interfaith Response to U.S. Immigration Policies*. Lanham, MD: Lexington Books, 2019.

———. *Refugee Art: Testimonies of Immigrant Families Seeking Asylum* (blog). https://refugeeart blog.com/.

Butler, Judith. *Precarious Life: The Powers of Mourning and Violence*. London and New York: Verso, 2004, 2006.

Caputi, Jane, and Diana E. H. Russell. "Femicide: Sexist Terrorism against Women." In *The Politics of Woman Killing*. Edited by Jill Radford and Diana E. H. Russell. New York: Twayne Publishers, 1992.

Dahlberg, L. L., and E. G. Krug. "Violence: A Global Public Health Problem." In *World Report on Violence and Health*. Edited by E. G. Kurg et al., 3–21. World Health Organization, Geneva, 2002.

Davis, Lisa, and Bradley Parker. "Informe sobre Violaciones de Derechos Humanos de las Mujeres en Guatemala." New York, Human Rights Commission of the United Nations, March 13–30, 2012, 7. https://www2.ohchr.org/english/bodies/hrc/docs/ngos/RVWHR_Guate mala_HRC104_sp.pdf.

Diario Libre. "Violación de mujeres, otro sello de las pandillas (1 de 2)" [Violation of Women, Other Stamp of the Gangs (1 of 2)] November 8, 2014. https://www.diariolibre.com/noticias/viola-cin-de-mujeres-otro-sello-de-las-pandillas-1-de-2-AHDL870761.

Geneva Declaration. "When the Victim Is a Woman." In *Global Burden of Armed Violence* 2015, 113–44. http://www.genevadeclaration.org/fileadmin/docs/GBAV2/GBAV2011_CH4_rev.pdf.

Jacoby, Jocelyn. "Sexual Violence Is a Hate Crime." *Ending Violence against Women* (blog). May 9, 2017. https://now.org/blog/sexual-violence-is-a-hate-crime/.

Joseph, Janice. "Victims of Femicide in Latin America: Legal and Criminal Justice Responses." *TEMIDA* 29, no. 1 (2017): 3–21. http://www.doiserbia.nb.rs/img/doi/1450-6637/2017/1450 -66371701003J.pdf.

Lusungu Moyo, Fulata. "Gang-Raped and Dis-Membered: Contextual Biblical Study of Judges 19:1–30 to Re-Member the Rwandan Genocide." In *Sexual Violence and Sacred Texts*. Edited by Amy Kalmanofsky, 125–39. Cambridge, MA: Feminist Studies in Religion Books, 2017.

Mathews, Shanaaz, Naeemah Abrahams, Lorna J. Martin, Lisa Vetten, Lize van der Merwe, and Rachel Jewkes. "Every Six Hours a Woman Is Killed by Her Intimate Partner: A National Study of Female Homicide in South Africa." *MRC Policy Brief*, 2004. https://www.files.ethz.ch/ isn/104994/sixhours.pdf.

McCaffrey, Raymond, Paul Duggan, and Debbi Wilgoren. "Five Killed at Pennsylvania Amish School." *Washington Post*. October 3, 2006. http://www.washingtonpost.com/wp-dyn/con tent/article/2006/10/03/AR2006100300229.html.

McFarlane, Judith M., Jacquelyn C. Campbell, Susan Wilt, Carolyn J. Sachs, Yvonne Ulrich, and Xiao Xu. "Stalking and Intimate Partner Femicide." *Homicide Studies* 3, no. 4 (1999): 300–16.

Mieszczanski, Elena. "Indigenous Women Can't Get Justice: You Should Care." *Ending Violence against Women* (blog). April 11, 2019. https://now.org/blog/indigenous-women-cant-get-jus tice-you-should-care/.

Moracco, Kathryn E., Carol W. Runyan, and John D. Butts. "Femicide in North Carolina, 1991–1993: A Statewide Study of Patterns and Precursors." *Homicide Studies* 2 (1998): 422–46. https:// doi.org/10.1177/1088767998002004005.

Musalo, Karen, and Blaine Bookey. "Crimes without Punishment: An Update on Violence against Women and Impunity in Guatemala." *Hastings Race and Poverty Law Journal* 10 (Summer 2013): 265–92. https://cgrs.uchastings.edu/sites/default/files/Musalo_Bookey_CrimesWithoutPun ishment_2013.pdf.

Navarez, Allana. "Latin America's War on Gender Violence." *International Policy Digest*. June 12, 2015. http://www.internationalpolicydigest.org/2015/06/12/latin-america-s-war-on-gender-violence/.

Nobel Women's Initiative 2012. "From Survivors to Defenders: Women Confronting Violence in Mexico, Honduras, and Guatemala." http://nobelwomensinitiative.org/wp-content/uploads/2012/06/Report_AmericasDelgation-2012.pdf?ref=196.

Osmandzikovic, Emina, and Hazen Balousha. "Murder of Israa Ghareeb Renews Debate over Honor Killings in Middle East." *Arab News*, September 2, 1019. https://www.arabnews.com/node/1548306/middle-east.

Program for Appropriate Technology in Health (PATH), InterCambios, Medical Research Council of South Africa (MRC), and World Health Organization (WHO). *Strengthening Understanding of Femicide: Using Research to Galvanize Action and Accountability*, 2009. http://acrath.org.au/wp-content/uploads/2011/02/Strengthening_Understanding_of_Femicide_Apr2008.pdf#page=14.

Pineda-Madrid, Nancy. "Feminicide and the Reinvention of Religious Practices." In *Women, Wisdom, and Witness: Engaging Contexts in Conversation*. Edited by Rosemary P. Carbine and Kathleen J. Dolphin. Collegeville, MN: Liturgical Press, 2007.

———. *Suffering + Salvation in Ciudad Juárez*. Fortress Press, 2011.

Radford, Jill, and Diana E. H. Russell, eds. *Femicide: The Politics of Woman Killing*. New York: Twayne Publishers, 1992.

Rhodan, Maya. "Here Are the Facts about President Trump's Family Separation Policy." *Time*, June 18, 2018.

Ruhl, Katharine. "Guatemala's Femicides and the Ongoing Struggle for Women's Human Rights: Update to CFR's 2005 Report *Getting Away with Murder*." University of California, Center for Gender and Refugee Studies. Hastings College of Law, September 2006. https://cgrs.uchastings.edu/sites/default/files/Guatemalas_femicides_ongoing_struggle_Ruhl_2006_0.pdf.

Sai, Nancy. "Rwanda." Women under Siege. Women's Media Center, February 8, 2012. http://www.womensmediacenter.com/women-under-siege/conflicts/rwanda.

Sanchez, Erica, and Sophie Maes. "Four Women Are Killed Every Day in Brazil as Femicide Persists." *Global Citizen*, February 5, 2019. https://globalcitizen.org/en/content/femicide-brazil-2019/.

Schüssler Fiorenza, Elisabeth. *Jesus: Miriam's Child, Sophia's Prophet: Critical Issues in Feminist Christology*. New York: Continuum, 2004.

University of California Hastings College of the Law. Center for Gender & Refugee Studies. "Central America: Femicides and Gender-Based Violence." n.d. https://cgrs.uchastings.edu/our-work/central-america-femicides-and-gender-based-violence.

Zahn, Margaret A., C. Block, and J. Campbell. "Intimate Partner Homicide." *National Institute of Justice Journal* 250 (November 2003): 1–64.

CHAPTER 18

Call to Accountability

· ·

Women's Studies in Religion Critiques
State Culpability to Feminicide
through Border Controls and
Exclusion from Asylum

Rev. Dr. Helen T. Boursier, PhD, College of St. Scholastica

ABSTRACT

The evil tentacles of femicide cross international boundaries to bordering nations that become culpable to the bigger systemic violation of feminicide through unjust policies and practices that force females seeking asylum from probable femicide to remain in harm's way. Feminism examines US immigration policies as a case study and critiques state culpability to feminicide through unjust border controls and exclusion from asylum. Feminism calls for education, advocacy, and public witness through civic actions to challenge and change this lethal violence against females by males because they are female.

Not every female has the option to flee before it is too late, such as the case of the 21-year-old Palestinian woman who was brutally murdered by her brother (see chapter seventeen). When females do have the ability to cross an international border to escape probable femicide to seek safety elsewhere, and other nations then do not provide a reasonable path to asylum, the receiving nation becomes drawn into the international web of feminicide. Feminism renounces femicide and feminicide, and demands state responsibility to protect females living within its boundaries, whether or not those females are legal residents, transients, or refugees seeking asylum *from* femicide *for* life.

CASE STUDY: INTERNATIONAL CULPABILITY TO FEMINICIDE AT THE US-MEXICO BORDER

Politics is very much a factor for gender injustice, and it is particularly so for femicide, feminicide, and exclusion from asylum at the US-Mexico border. Under the United Nations High Commissioner on Refugees (UNHCR) and the Convention and the 1967 Protocol, of which the United States is a signatory nation, people have an internationally recognized right to flee for their lives and seek asylum elsewhere when their home country cannot or will not protect them.[1] The United States also has existing laws that are meant to guarantee that asylum seekers have access to safety.[2] The initial point of access through the tedious due process for asylum is for migrants to show that they have "credible" or reasonable fear for their lives. Many mothers who fled for their lives with their children to seek safety and protection in the United States were forcibly separated from their children upon arrival to the United States. See figure 18.1, a watercolor portrait of a Honduran mother reuniting with her 6-year-old son on July 12, 2018, following six weeks of forced family separation after they presented themselves to Customs Border Patrol at the US-Mexico border to request asylum. She was fleeing a death threat and probable femicide in her homeland.[3]

Family separation quietly continued long after the public outcry against this official policy gave the impression that it would no longer be used against families seeking asylum.[4] A mother of four who journeyed from El Salvador through Mexico to the United States with her 18-year-old daughter and two-year-old son explained that she was surprised when her daughter was admitted to the United States, while she and her son were forced to remain in Mexico for the court process. Then, she discovered that her daughter was being deported back to Honduras alone, while the mother and son wait for their court appointments while staying in a church-supported migrant shelter in Nuevo Laredo.[5] Another mother reported that, when she entered the United States, immigration "prevented me from going to where my husband and my daughter are." Immigration gave her two options: return to Honduras or to go to Mexico and to challenge the case there. She lamented, "For me to be so close to my little girl and my husband, but then to not be allowed to reunite with them, and knowing that where they sent me and my son is very dangerous. . . . My heart breaks every time I think of everything [my daughter] told me. Please help us."[6]

A mother who crossed an international bridge at a legal point of entry to request asylum shared her family's experience of US injustice against asylum seekers: "The court asks, 'Are you an American citizen? Do you have permission to come to the United States?' Questions that we obviously aren't going to answer the way they want. After those questions, they say that, because of what we answered, they have the proof they need to deport us and remove us from the United States."[7] US Customs Border Patrol officers escort asylum seekers *back* across the bridge and leave them to fend for

FIGURE 18.1. Watercolor portrait of a Honduran mother reuniting with her 6-year-old son on July 12, 2018, following six weeks of forced family separation after they presented themselves to Customs Border Patrol at the U.S.-Mexico border to request asylum

© Helen T. Boursier

FIGURE 18.2. Customs Border Patrol agents escorts migrants back across the bridge from Laredo, Texas, to Nuevo Laredo, Mexico.
© Helen T. Boursier

themselves (see figure 18.2). The cartels post "watchers" on the Mexico side of the border whose job is to watch for returning migrants to kidnap. During my pastoral care visits to church-supported migrant shelters in Nuevo Laredo, Mexico, one of the most dangerous cities along Mexico's northern border, the mothers regularly share their horror stories of being kidnapped by the cartels, who contact family members in the United States and demand that they pay exorbitant ransom fees to release their loved ones.

The harsh border policies, enacted by the Trump administration January 24, 2019, with its so-called Migrant Protection Protocols (MPP),[8] forced vulnerable asylum seekers to "remain in Mexico" while they await news of their asylum case. Instead of respecting their international right to seek asylum, which includes the nonrefoulement priority that no one should be returned to their country if their lives would be at great risk,[9] these vulnerable victims of violence in their homelands were forced to huddle along the southern side of the US-Mexico border in horrendous conditions where femicide is extremely high,[10] like a Honduran mother and 12-year-old daughter fleeing for their lives and forced to remain in Nuevo Laredo, Mexico. This mother and daughter were kidnapped by the cartels at the bus station upon their arrival to the border, and now they remain locked inside a small house that serves as a shelter for migrants, with 90–120 other asylum seekers while they await "due process" to enter the United States (see figure 18.3).

It is common knowledge that the Mexico side of our southern border is *not* a safe place. The United States warns its own citizens of the violence along the Mexico side of the southwest border, but forces asylum seekers to remain in this same dangerous region for weeks and months before they are admitted to the United States (if at all).[11] A mother whose family was forced to remain in Nuevo Laredo, Mexico, while awaiting their asylum case in the United States, explained they fled her homeland because "it was save our lives and leave or wait to be killed." She added, "This is a nightmare because here it is the same, if not worse than in Honduras. . . . we are in even more danger here in Nuevo Laredo."[12] She specified that staying locked inside the church-sponsored migrant shelter equates to being in jail: the family cannot leave because of the danger outside with the cartels watching on every corner. One of the migrant shelters in Nuevo Laredo has an enclosed interior courtyard where the families sleep and hang their laundry on ropes strung back and forth; the only view of the outdoors is from looking up toward the sky (see figure 18.3). A second church-sponsored shelter has a small courtyard in front of the house, enclosed with an 8-foot-high locked iron gate to keep the families safely locked inside (see figure 18.4).

Femicides in Mexico have increased 40 percent since 2006. It is particularly prevalent in the Mexican state of Chihuahua, which borders the United States at New Mexico and nearly halfway along Texas to Big Bend National Park. Chihuahua has a femicide rate of 34.73 per 100,000, more than 15 times higher than the global rate.[13] Part of the high rate is attributed to femicides in Ciudad Juárez, but the entire border region is infamous for its extreme violence.[14] As many migrants report, "Nuevo Laredo is the most dangerous place in Mexico." The cartels are everywhere, competing to be the controlling force along the river that separates Mexico from the United States.

FIGURE 18.3. Refugee families seeking asylum sleep on stacked cots outdoors under a canopy in an interior courtyard at a church-sponsored shelter for migrants in Nuevo Laredo, Mexico.
© Helen T. Boursier

FIGURE 18.4. A locked gate offers some protection from the cartels for refugee families seeking asylum at a church-sponsored shelter for migrants in Nuevo Laredo, Mexico.
© Helen T. Boursier

'SAFE' THIRD COUNTRY

The US Departments of Justice and Homeland Security issued a joint Interim Final Rule (IFR) July 15, 2019, for asylum seekers who did not first seek asylum in at least one "third" country outside of their home of citizenship, which the rule states is "a lawful exercise of authority provided by Congress to restrict eligibility for asylum. The United States is a generous country but is being completely overwhelmed by the burdens associated with apprehending and processing hundreds of thousands of aliens along the southern border."[15] Four months later, the Trump administration began deporting asylum seekers to Guatemala as the forced "third country" for migrants from other countries to make their claim for asylum. Instead of being allowed to seek asylum in the United States, migrants were forcibly removed to Guatemala as an alternate "safe" nation to receive shelter.[16] Amid the COVID-19 global pandemic, "seventy-five percent of migrants deported to Guatemala on a single flight tested positive for coronavirus,"[17] adding further life-threatening risks to an already dangerous "safe" nation.

An asylum seeker who is fleeing death threats in Honduras with her 11-year-old son explained that she did not request assistance in Guatemala because "it is a joke that they classify Honduras, El Salvador, and Guatemala as 'Safe Third Countries.'" She added,

"Let an American try to live one day in one of these countries, and they will see that I am right." With the Migrant Protection Protocols already in place, this mother and her son were living in a church-sponsored migrant shelter in Nuevo Laredo while her court case was being determined in the United States. She specified that, if her home country is "unsafe and violent, that the United States government clearly does not care. It only cares that Mexico keeps us. If our country or Mexico is a risk to our lives, well, that is our problem."[18] Asylum seekers were forced to remain in this dangerous "suspended zone," where they were deprived of basic human rights, "neither living in the sense that a political animal lives, in community and bound by law, nor dead and, therefore, outside the constituting condition of the rule of law,"[19] like the thousands of asylum seekers the Trump administration forced to remain in Mexico during its Migrant Protection Protocols (see figure 18.5 of the migrant encampment in Matamoros, Mexico, with the bridge to Brownsville, Texas, in view above the trees).

Many of the females never make it to the United States to make their claim for asylum because of the suffering and violence they must endure during their overland journey through Mexico. Others are "caught" by Mexican authorities and forced to return to their homelands, not unlike how the United States "catches" migrants in the United States and deports them back from whence they came. Whether "caught" and forcibly returned from Mexico or from the United States, the state becomes culpable to feminicide when vulnerable females are deported back to their homeland or to another high-risk country in Central America.[20]

FIGURE 18.5. In May 2020, as many as 1,500 migrants seeking asylum in the United States slept in tents outdoors in Matamoros, Mexico, beside the Rio Bravo/Rio Grande River, within sight of the arches of the international bridge to Brownsville, Texas.

FLEEING DOMESTIC VIOLENCE

I suffered
>> much domestic violence
>> physical abuse
>> emotional abuse
> from my partner.
>> He did drugs.
> I suffered from depression
>> panic attacks
>> constant fear
> I took legal action.
> I got a restraining order.
>> He disobeyed.
>> He pursued me.
> In my home
>> to continue his violent abuse.

*

I called the police.
>> He was taken away.
>> Locked up.
> My lawyers told me
>> leave my country
>> for my safety and my son's.

*

We reached the United States.
>> It took two months.
> We asked at the border for help.
> We were informed:
>> "We are not allowing anyone to enter."
> We were heartbroken.
> All our suffering along the way
>> wasted.

*

My former partner is out of jail.
He is looking for me.
>> I am afraid.

Mother
November 5, 2019[21]

This mother fleeing likely femicide from a former partner who continues to pursue her after three years became trapped in the exclusion from asylum policies enacted by the Trump administration. She and her young son were forced to remain in a migrant shelter in Nuevo Laredo, Mexico, while her court case made its slow journey through US Immigration, with deportation the ultimate outcome given the Trump administration's policies and practices at the US-Mexico border. Deportation very likely could be a death sentence.[22] The probable femicide that females like this mother are fleeing, inevitably faces them upon return home when the United States plays its dangerous game of feminicide and denies credible fear for those who are desperately seeking asylum.[23] A mother whose credible fear for asylum was denied explained, "I think that they want me to have missing body parts or to have lost one of my children in order to show credible fear."[24] This mother is particularly concerned about the cartel "watchers" who photographed her children as they were preparing to go to their court appointment in the United States. She said, "Most of all they are watching my oldest one. She is 13 years old. We are so afraid."[25]

ETHICAL RESPONSE FOR INTERNATIONAL WELCOME

As an alternative to focusing on how much "burden" a nation is expected to bear in welcoming and assisting refugees seeking asylum, ethicist Joseph Carens cautions "the much more important issue is the moral wrong involved in the use of techniques of exclusion to keep the numbers within bounds."[26] In other words, the receiving nation needs to be looking at the harm, injustice, and moral horror that it perpetuates with exclusion from asylum as a government enacts injustice by tweaking, adapting, inventing, and/or flat disregarding national and international treaties, laws, and humanitarian standards for border controls policies and practices.[27] The nonrhetorical questions Judith Butler poses in regard to feminism in general, apply to culpability to feminicide through border policies for exclusion from asylum, covert femicide, as she asks:

> At what price, and at whose expense, does it gain a purchase on "security," and in what ways has a chain of violence formed in which the aggression the United States has wrought returns to it in different forms? Can we think of the history of violence there without exonerating those who engage it against the United States in the present? Can we provide a knowledgeable explanation of events that is not confused with a moral exoneration of violence?[28]

The challenge is to force individuals, institutions, and governments to acknowledge and enforce these human rights for *all* females, including females fleeing probable femicide to seek safe asylum elsewhere.[29] Justice includes calling the perpetrator to accountability.

CALL TO RESPONSE: EDUCATION FOR ACTION

Femicide is an extreme example of a social evil that Judith Herman would call "the *unspeakable*."[30] This trauma specialist's emphasis that "Remembering and telling the truth about terrible events are prerequisites both for the restoration of the social order and for the healing of the individual victims"[31] applies in the larger scale to nations, regions, and the world. Ignoring or disregarding information about femicide, particularly as it intersects with a nation's border policies and practices of exclusion from asylum, would be a form of "willful ignorance," deliberately choosing not to acknowledge the existence of this lethal violence against females.[32] Silencing femicide includes disregarding or ignoring the witness of potential victims, voices of victims' families demanding justice, impunity for perpetrators, and state complicity that permits systemic femicide to flourish. This silence must be broken. The unspeakable must be spoken.

There are practical ways to challenge and change the nightmare reality of femicide. Herman's important work on trauma theory from her research with rape victims applies to the larger scale of the systemic injustice connected to femicide and feminicide, particularly because:

> In order to escape accountability for his crimes, the perpetrator does everything in his power to promote forgetting. Secrecy and silence are the perpetrator's first line of defense. If secrecy fails, the perpetrator attacks the credibility of his victim. If he cannot silence her absolutely, he tries to make sure that no one listens. . . . After every atrocity one can expect to hear the same predictable apologies: it never happened; the victim lies; the victim exaggerates; the victim brought it upon herself; and in any case it is time to forget the past and move on. The more powerful the perpetrator, the greater is his prerogative to name and define reality, and the more completely his arguments prevail.[33]

It follows that presidential policy for exclusion from asylum exemplifies a powerful perpetrator that will stop at nothing to justify its injustice.

To break the pattern of misinformation and lies that contribute to femicide and feminicide, the reality must be brought into public view. Begin by talking within your circle of influence (i.e., friends, family, colleagues, and peers). It does not make popular dinner table conversation, but it is a conversation that needs to happen to raise awareness that brings people to a sense of outrage that moves them to responsible response through advocacy and action.[34]

DENOUNCE FEMICIDE AND FEMINICIDE THROUGH PUBLIC WITNESS AND CIVIC ACTION

One way to counteract legitimization is to break the silence by listening to the voices of family survivors and also to the "almost victims" who ran for their lives after receiving pointed death threats that could, and likely would, result in femicide if the females remained in their unsafe homeland.[35] Listen to their witness, hear their words, and then unite with them in denouncing these human rights violations.[36] Join with femicide and feminicide denouncers who educate, advocate, lobby, and march for justice. For example, the *Ni Una Menos* campaign started in Argentina March 26, 2015, to protest the femicide of a young woman found in a garbage bag on March 16. Then, an estimated 300,000 protestors marched through Buenos Aires on June 3, 2015, in the aftermath of another femicide, carrying signs with *"Ni Una Menos."*[37] The slogan is short for "Not even one woman less! We want us all alive!"[38] Protests like #NiUnaMenos and the symbolic pink femicide crosses in Mexico need to be included in education and advocacy events around the world, such as a local version of #WomensAgenda, #WomensMarch, and #LightsforLiberty.[39]

ADVOCATE THROUGH ELECTED US OFFICIALS

Elected officials need to be confronted with the reality that their hands are not clean. Silence is not an option. Engage in civic action to hold elected officials accountable to femicide and feminicide culpability at the US-Mexico border. Write, email, telephone, and/or visit elected officials and ask them to:

- Denounce violence against females of all ages and in all forms, including covert violence through border policies and practices that force females to remain in harm's way.
- Advocate to bring legislation in line with international standards on overt and covert violence against females and formulate specific legislation that criminalizes femicide.
- Establish specific guidelines and procedures for all steps of criminal investigation reports of violence against females.
- Institute a standard system for collecting data on violence against females.
- Implement femicide and feminicide training for Customs Border Patrol and Immigration and Customs Enforcement agents, judges, prosecutors, investigators, and other officials.
- Create zero tolerance for gender-based human rights violations with mandatory disciplinary action for officials who make groundless public statements; obstruct investigations; fail to take immediate action to prevent injury to women and girls at risk; and/or who harass, or intimidate family members, witnesses, or organizations who support them.[40]

Through civic actions like protests, marches, advocacy, and challenging elected officials, response to femicide offers solidarity and becomes what Nancy Pineda-Madrid terms "a praxis of salvation," which she defines as "the integral relation between human thought and action (or practice) on behalf of the future whole that God intends for all humanity and creation."[41] The collective "we" make femicide more visible as together we cry out against this evil and advocate toward a transformative difference. Actions today cannot negate the horrors of lives already lost, but collective advocacy and witness can become part of the bigger picture that demands the full humanity of every single person, such that future lives will not be cut short and that all females in all countries shall enjoy their full human rights to live without fear of femicide. This seemingly lofty goal embraces the hope and future that are embedded in virtually all world religions. The evil of this world is not the will or way of any god. As followers in faith, the response to participate with the divine through transformative action from evil for love, evil is thwarted through our collectively enacted spirituality of resistance.

NOTES

1. See, e.g., Helen T. Boursier, *The Ethics of Hospitality: An Interfaith Response to U.S. Immigration Policies* (Lanham, MD: Lexington Books, 2019), 62–65; and *Desperately Seeking Asylum: Testimonies of Trauma, Courage, and Love* (Lanham, MD: Rowman & Littlefield, 2019), 54–57.

2. See, e.g., Boursier, *Desperately Seeking Asylum*, 58–59.

3. This mother shares her family separation experience in Boursier, *Desperately Seeking Asylum*, 85–87.

4. Nila Bala and Arthur Rizer, "Trump's Family Separation Policy Never Really Ended; This Is Why," Think, NBC News, July 1, 2019, https://www.nbcnews.com/think/opinion/trump-s-family-separation-policy-never-really-ended-why-ncna1025376.

5. Excerpt from written testimony (#27) November 6, 2019, from an asylum seeker at a church-sponsored migrant shelter in Nuevo Laredo; collected by Sister Denise LaRock. Hereafter, the reference cites the testimony number and the date; all are shared by permission.

6. Testimony (#31) December 4, 2019.

7. Excerpt from written testimony (#42) December 4, 2019.

8. U.S. Department of Homeland Security, "Migrant Protection Protocols," January 24, 2019, https://www.dhs.gov/news/2019/01/24/migrant-protection-protocols.

9. See, e.g., Boursier, *Desperately Seeking Asylum*, 55.

10. See, e.g., Gustavo Solis, "Remain in Mexico: Not a Single Migrant Has Been Granted Asylum, Data Shows," *San Diego Union-Tribune*, July 30, 2019, https://www.sandiegouniontribune.com/news/immigration/story/2019-07-30/remain-in-mexico-trac-data-legal-representation; and Transactional Records Access Clearinghouse (TRAC) "Access to Attorneys Difficult for Those Required to Remain in Mexico," Syracuse University, July 29, 2019, https://trac.syr.edu/immigration/reports/568/.

11. Amanda Holpuch, "U.S. Sends Asylum Seekers to Mexico's Border Towns as It Warns Citizens of Violence in Region," *The Guardian*, October 10, 2019, https://www.theguardian.com/us-news/2019/oct/10/us-migrants-return-mexico-border-towns-violent-crimes?fbclid=IwAR1eDxnaJcMcTPqbeETGQHYekPEyZqbsqcCk4BeuPJ9FRA3ZqXa3pwBYLD4.

12. Testimony (#22) November 6, 2019.

13. Nobel Women's Initiative 2012, "From Survivors to Defenders: Women Confronting Violence in Mexico, Honduras, and Guatemala," http://nobelwomensinitiative.org/wp-content/uploads/2012/06/Report_AmericasDelgation-2012.pdf?ref=196, 8.

14. See, e.g., Anabel Hernandez, "Against the Current: Femicide in Mexico on the Rise and Growing More Brutal," *Deutsche Wells*, August 21, 2019, https://www.dw.com/en/against-the-current-femicide-in-mexico-on-the-rise-and-growing-more-brutal/a-50119043?maca=en-Facebook-sharing&fbclid=IwAR0cEGJojecsePijt3cHmz4A6T14z91OXIpBF6EMRAs17IQttYKvljQHpSY.

15. US Department of Homeland Security, "DHS and DOJ Issue Third-Country Asylum Rule," July 15, 2019, https://www.dhs.gov/news/2019/07/15/dhs-and-doj-issue-third-country-asylum-rule.

16. Geneva Sands, Priscilla Alvarez, and Michelle Mendoza, "Trump Administration Begins Deporting Asylum Seekers to Guatemala," CNN, November 21, 2019, https://www.cnn.com/2019/11/21/politics/guatemala-asylum-agreement/index.html.

17. Conor Finnegan, "Seventy-Five Percent of Migrants Deported to Guatemala on a Single Flight Tested Positive for Coronavirus," ABC News, April 15, 2020, https://abcnews.go.com/International/75-migrants-deported-guatemala-single-flight-tested-positive/story?id=70156471&cid=clicksource_4380645_10_heads_posts_card_hed&fbclid=IwAR3j-I-gaWnXl0e40iILYy5JTYJF7u6NduR_JCkau3GuPYXPmh36e7oEIhM.

18. Testimony (#43) December 4, 2019.

19. Butler's context is different, but her ideals apply to refugees forced to remain in Mexico. See Judith Butler, *Precarious Life: The Powers of Mourning and Violence* (London and New York: Verso, 2004, 2006), 67. See also, e.g., Giorgio Agamben, *Etat de'exception: Homo Sacer, II* (Stanford, CA: Stanford University Press, 1995).

20. See, e.g., Theodore Bunker, "Trump Admin to Deport Migrants to Guatemala," Newsmax, November 19, 2019, https://www.newsmax.com/newsfront/deport-migrants-guatemala/2019/11/19/id/942348/.

21. Helen T. Boursier, ed., "Fleeing Domestic Violence," *Refugee Art: Testimonies of Immigrant Families Seeking Asylum* (blog), May 4, 2020, https://refugeeartblog.com/?p=915. Participant voiced poem; excerpt from testimony (#23) November 6, 2019.

22. See, e.g., Sarah Stillman, "When Deportation Is a Death Sentence," *The New Yorker*, January 15, 2018, https://www.newyorker.com/magazine/2018/01/15/when-deportation-is-a-death-sentence.

23. Sibylla Brodzinsky and Ed Pilkington, "U.S. Government Deporting Central American Migrants to Their Deaths," *The Guardian*, October 12, 2015, https://www.theguardian.com/us-news/2015/oct/12/obama-immigration-deportations-central-america.

24. Testimony (#42) December 4, 2019.

25. Testimony (#42) December 4, 2019.

26. Joseph H. Carens, *The Ethics of Immigration* (Oxford: Oxford University Press, 2013), 209.

27. See, e.g., Boursier, *Desperately Seeking Asylum*, 77–90.

28. Butler, *Precarious Life*, 42.

29. See, e.g., United Nations Office of the High Commissioner on Human Rights, "The Equal Status and Human Rights of Women," *Vienna Declaration and Programme of Action*, June 25, 1993, para 38. https://www.ohchr.org/EN/ProfessionalInterest/Pages/Vienna.aspx; and Emilie M. Townes, "Washed in the Grace of God," in *Violence against Women and Children: A Christian Theological Sourcebook*, ed. Carol J. Adams and Marie Fortune (New York: Continuum, 1995), 61.

30. Judith Herman, *Trauma and Recovery: The Aftermath of Violence from Domestic Abuse to Political Terror* (New York: Perseus Books, 1992, 1997, 2015), 1.

31. Herman, *Trauma and Recovery*, 1.

32. For a parallel argument on disregarding vulnerability, see, e.g., Errin C. Gilson, *The Ethics of Vulnerability: A Feminist Analysis of Social Life and Practices* (London and New York: Routledge, 2014), 79. For an examination of the church's willful ignorance about immigration, exclusion from asylum, and the US-Mexico border, see Helen T. Boursier, *Willful Ignorance: Overcoming the Limitations of Love for Refugees Seeking Asylum* (Lanham, MD: Lexington Books, forthcoming).

33. Herman, *Trauma and Recovery*, 8.

34. See, e.g., Emilie M. Townes, "Living in the New Jerusalem: The Rhetoric and Movement of Liberation in the House of Evil," in *A Troubling in My Soul: Womanist Perspectives on Evil and Suffering*, ed. Emilie M. Townes (Maryknoll, NY: Orbis Books, 1993), 78.

35. See also, e.g., the glossary of organizations in the appendix section for specific organizations in Central America that work for human rights justice for females.

36. For an example of congressional testimony about human rights violations against children while detained in US custody, which also includes teens fleeing femicide in their homelands, see, e.g., Hope Frye, "Hope Frye's Testimony on Child Migrant Detention," Facing History and Ourselves, Resource Library, https://www.facinghistory.org/resource-library/hope-fryes-testimony-child-migrant-detention.

37. Brianne Berry, "Ni Una Menos." See also, e.g., "#NiUnaMenos 2015: Pregnant 14-Year-Old Girl Allegedly Murdered by Boyfriend Sparks Massive Domestic Violence March in Argentina," *Latin Post*, June 4, 2015, http://www.latinpost.com/articles/57610/20150604/pregnant-14-year-old-girl-allegedly-murdered-by-boyfriend-sparks-massive-domestic-violence-march-in-argentina.htm; and Paula Amor, Ixchel Cisneros, and Gabriela Jauregui, "#NiUnaMenos," *Quién*, January 2020, 38–45.

38. See, e.g., Elisabeth Jay Friedman and Constanza Tabbush, "#NiUnaMenos: Not One Woman Less, Not One More Death!" *NACLA Report on the Americas*, September 11, 2016.

39. See, e.g., Galo Cañas, "Sorority: Mexican Women Are Protecting Each Other," Editorial, *El Universal*, August 24, 2019, https://www.eluniversal.com.mx/english/sorority-mexican-women-are-protecting-each-other.

40. Adapted from Katharine Ruhl, "Guatemala's Femicides and the Ongoing Struggle for Women's Human Rights: Update to CFR's 2005 Report *Getting Away with Murder*," Center for

Gender and Refugee Studies, 25–27. https://cgrs.uchastings.edu/sites/default/files/Guatema
las_femicides_ongoing_struggle_Ruhl_2006_0.pdf. For more suggestions see, e.g., Nobel Wom-
en's Initiative 2012, "From Survivors to Defenders," 29.

41. Nancy Pineda-Madrid, "Feminicide and the Reinvention of Religious Practices," in *Women, Wisdom, and Witness: Engaging Contexts in Conversation*, ed. Rosemary P. Carbine and Kathleen J. Dolphin (Collegeville, MN: Liturgical Press, 2007), 73; see also Nancy Pineda-Madrid, *Suffering + Salvation in Ciudad Juárez* (Minneapolis, MN: Fortress Press, 2011).

BIBLIOGRAPHY

Agamben, Giorgio. *Homo Sacer: Sovereign Power and Bare Life*. Stanford, CA: Stanford University Press, 1995.

Amor, Paula, Ixchel Cisneros, and Gabriela Jauregui. "#NiUnaMenos." *Quién*, January 2020, 38–45.

Berry, Brianne. "Ni Una Menos: Argentina Takes the Lead against Sexism and Gender Violence in Latin America." Council on Hemispheric Affairs. June 23, 2015. http://www.coha.org/ni-una -menos-argentina-takes-the-lead-against-sexism-and-gender-violence-in-latin-america/.

Boursier, Helen T. *Desperately Seeking Asylum: Testimonies of Trauma, Courage, and Love*. Lanham, MD: Rowman & Littlefield, 2019.

———. *The Ethics of Hospitality: An Interfaith Response to U.S. Immigration Policies* Lanham, MD: Lexington Books, 2019.

———. *Refugee Art: Testimonies of Immigrant Families Seeking Asylum* (blog). https://refugeeart blog.com/.

———. *Willful Ignorance: Overcoming the Limitations of Love for Refugees Seeking Asylum*. Lanham, MD: Lexington Books, forthcoming.

Brodzinsky, Sibylla, and Ed Pilkington. "U.S. Government Deporting Central American Migrants to Their Deaths." *The Guardian*. October 12, 2015. https://www.theguardian.com/ us-news/2015/oct/12/obama-immigration-deportations-central-america.

Bunker, Theodore. "Trump Admin to Deport Migrants to Guatemala." Newsmax. November 19, 2019. https://www.newsmax.com/newsfront/deport-migrants-guatemala/2019/11/19/ id/942348/.

Butler, Judith. *Precarious Life: The Powers of Mourning and Violence*. London and New York: Verso, 2004, 2006.

Cañas, Galo. "Sorority: Mexican Women Are Protecting Each Other." Editorial. *El Universal*. August 24, 2019. https://www.eluniversal.com.mx/english/sorority-mexican-women-are-protecting -each-other.

Carens, Joseph H. *The Ethics of Immigration*. Oxford: Oxford University Press, 2013.

Diario Libre. "Violación de mujeres, otro sello de las pandillas (1 de 2)" [Violation of Women, Other Stamp of the Gangs (1 of 2)] November 8, 2014. https://www.diariolibre.com/noticias/ violacin-de-mujeres-otro-sello-de-las-pandillas-1-de-2-AHDL870761.

Finnegan, Conor. "Seventy-Five Percent of Migrants Deported to Guatemala on a Single Flight Tested Positive for Coronavirus." ABC News, April 15, 2020. https://abcnews.go.com/Interna tional/75-migrants-deported-guatemala-single-flight-tested-positive/story?id=70156471&cid= clicksource_4380645_10_heads_posts_card_hed&fbclid=IwAR3j-I-gaWnXl0e40iILYy5JTYJ F7u6NduR_JCkau3GuPYXPmh36e7oEIhM.

Friedman, Elisabeth Jay, and Constanza Tabbush. #NiUnaMenos: Not One Woman Less, Not One More Death! *NACLA Report on the Americas*, September 11, 2016.

Frye, Hope. "Hope Frye's Testimony on Child Migrant Detention." Facing History and Our-selves, Resource Library. https://www.facinghistory.org/resource-library/hope-fryes-testi mony-child-migrant-detention.

Gilson, Errin C. *The Ethics of Vulnerability: A Feminist Analysis of Social Life and Practices*. Routledge Studies in Ethics and Moral Theory. London & New York: Routledge Taylor & Francis Group, 2014.

Herman, Judith. *Trauma and Recovery: The Aftermath of Violence from Domestic Abuse to Political Terror.* New York: Perseus Books, 1992, 1997, 2015.

Hernandez, Anabel. "Against the Current: Femicide in Mexico on the Rise and Growing More Brutal." *Deutsche Wells*, August 21, 2019. https://www.dw.com/en/against-the-current-femicide-in-mexico-on-the-rise-and-growing-more-brutal/a-50119043?maca=en-Facebook-sharing&fbclid=IwAR0cEGJojecsePijt3cHmz4A6T14z91OXIpBF6EMRAs17IQttYKvljQHpSY.

Holpuch, Amanda. "U.S. Sends Asylum Seekers to Mexico's Border Towns as It Warns Citizens of Violence in Region." *The Guardian*, October 10, 2019. https://www.theguardian.com/us-news/2019/oct/10/us-migrants-return-mexico-border-towns-violent-crimes?fbclid=IwAR1eDxnaJcMcTPqbeETGQHYekPEyZqbsqcCk4BeuPJ9FRA3ZqXa3pwBYLD4.

Latin Post. "#NiUnaMenos 2015: Pregnant 14-Year-Old Girl Allegedly Murdered by Boyfriend Sparks Massive Domestic Violence March in Argentina." June 4, 2015. http://www.latinpost.com/articles/57610/20150604/pregnant-14-year-old-girl-allegedly-murdered-by-boyfriend-sparks-massive-domestic-violence-march-in-argentina.htm.

Nobel Women's Initiative 2012. "From Survivors to Defenders: Women Confronting Violence in Mexico, Honduras, and Guatemala." http://nobelwomensinitiative.org/wp-content/uploads/2012/06/Report_AmericasDelgation-2012.pdf?ref=196.

Pineda-Madrid, Nancy. "Feminicide and the Reinvention of Religious Practices." In *Women, Wisdom, and Witness: Engaging Contexts in Conversation.* Edited by Rosemary P. Carbine and Kathleen J. Dolphin. Collegeville, MN: Liturgical Press, 2007.

———. *Suffering + Salvation in Ciudad Juárez.* Minneapolis, MN: Fortress Press, 2011.

Ruhl, Katharine. "Guatemala's Femicides and the Ongoing Struggle for Women's Human Rights: Update to CFR's 2005 Report *Getting Away with Murder.*" University of California, Center for Gender and Refugee Studies. Hastings College of Law. September 2006. https://cgrs.uchastings.edu/sites/default/files/Guatemalas_femicides_ongoing_struggle_Ruhl_2006_0.pdf.

Sands, Geneva, Priscilla Alvarez, and Michelle Mendoza. "Trump Administration Begins Deporting Asylum Seekers to Guatemala." CNN, November 21, 2019. https://www.cnn.com/2019/11/21/politics/guatemala-asylum-agreement/index.html.

Solis, Gustavo. "Remain in Mexico: Not a Single Migrant Has Been Granted Asylum, Data Shows." *San Diego Union-Tribune*, July 30, 2019. https://www.sandiegouniontribune.com/news/immigration/story/2019-07-30/remain-in-mexico-trac-data-legal-representation.

Stillman, Sarah. "When Deportation Is a Death Sentence." *The New Yorker*, January 15, 2018. https://www.newyorker.com/magazine/2018/01/15/when-deportation-is-a-death-sentence.

Townes, Emilie M. "Living in the New Jerusalem: The Rhetoric and Movement of Liberation in the House of Evil." In *A Troubling in My Soul: Womanist Perspectives on Evil and Suffering.* Edited by Emilie M. Townes, 78–91. Maryknoll, NY: Orbis Books, 1993.

———. "Washed in the Grace of God." In *Violence against Women and Children: A Christian Theological Sourcebook.* Edited by Carol J. Adams and Marie Fortune. New York: Continuum, 1995.

Transactional Records Access Clearinghouse (TRAC). "Access to Attorneys Difficult for Those Required to Remain in Mexico." Syracuse University, July 29, 2019. https://trac.syr.edu/immigration/reports/568/.

United Nations Office of the High Commissioner on Human Rights. "The Equal Status and Human Rights of Women." *Vienna Declaration and Programme of Action*, June 25, 1993. https://www.ohchr.org/EN/ProfessionalInterest/Pages/Vienna.aspx.

US Department of Homeland Security. "DHS and DOJ Issue Third-Country Asylum Rule." July 15, 2019. https://www.dhs.gov/news/2019/07/15/dhs-and-doj-issue-third-country-asylum-rule.

———. "Migrant Protection Protocols." January 24, 2019. https://www.dhs.gov/news/2019/01/24/migrant-protection-protocols.

CHAPTER 19

Doctrine of Discovery

....

A Mohawk Feminist Response to Colonial Domination and Violations to Indigenous Lands and Women

Dr. Dawn Martin-Hill, PhD, McMaster University

ABSTRACT

This chapter offers an Indigenous feminist critique of gender injustice, white supremacy, patriarchy, and other aspects of inequality that impose disparate burdens on Indigenous / Native American women. It highlights examples of ongoing genocidal acts by the state of Canada. Exploring what conditions are required to *manufacture consent* to commit acts of ecocide and genocide in north America, such as sterilization, mass abduction of children, destruction of ecosystems, and murder? Dehumanization, justification, and normalization of ecocide and acts of genocide on Indigenous lands and bodies were set in motion centuries ago through the Doctrine of Discovery, shaping science to ensure Indigenous peoples were positioned as inferior, pagan, and without institutions. The 2019 Missing and Murdered Indigenous women in Canada's Inquiry reports, racialized violence is an "epidemic," yet no laws or government policies are in place to protect land and life. Solutions are found by restoring the traditional leadership roles of women and upholding the United Nations Declaration of Indigenous People.

Indigenous knowledge has a multiplicity of sources, including traditional, spiritual, and empirical; it engages a holistic paradigm that integrates assessing the emotional, spiritual, physical, and mental well-being of a people. The vast array of cultural diversity across Indigenous peoples is addressed through the recognition that Indigenous knowledge (IK) is inherent in the language landscape and culture from which it emerges. The concepts developed by pre-contact Haudenosaunee society demonstrate the immense universal consciousness that existed prior to the arrival of Europeans. The Haudenosaunee geopolitical territory perimeters/borders expand across what is now known as New York, Pennsylvania, and Ohio found within/in the United States of America and the provinces of Quebec and Ontario in Canada. The philosophy held by the founder of the Haudenosaunee Confederacy, the Peacemaker, promoted participatory democracy based upon peace and the rule of women as authority figures. The Haudenosaunee operate their society on an intellectually developed set of principles. Women are essential in order to preserve the heritage, land, and spiritual teachings, transmitting IK to the next generation. Moving forward through continuous colonization and criminalization of Indigenous culture, Indigenous lands, people, and especially women must navigate through another wave of trauma while attempting to preserve sacred ancient knowledge.

Sustaining ancient knowledge in an era of climate change mostly caused by industry, and effectively combatting the rise in racism under the Trump administration, is critical to our survival now, more than ever. For almost four decades now, mainstream media has begun to increasingly highlight the clashes between Indigenous peoples and various industries across the globe. Industries that continue to permanently devastate land and communities, such as the numerous oil companies operating worldwide, as well as mining, logging, and fishing. Mantras of "we are still here" and "land back" are responses from young Indigenous people to the colonizer's/state's assertion of ecocide, genocide, and environmental racism. Colonial attempts to control all things Indigenous, including the Haudenosaunee people, has resulted in not just a physical clash, but equally important, an intellectual one. For example, the removal and criminalization/outlawing of ancient Haudenosaunee knowledge systems, and furthermore, the relegating of intellectual legacies of IK as "myth." For example, colonial institutions, such as academia's systematic oppression of Haudenosaunee knowledge, is evidenced in over 70 scholarly publications about the "Iroquoians." There is ample documentation of Haudenosaunee contributing to the progress of Western knowledge; the eradication of Haudenosaunee political and social complexities, agricultural techniques, medical capabilities, and advanced philosophy were depreciated, only to be viewed as mere footnotes.[1]

The anthropological rendition of origin stories, and the *Kaianeraserakowa* (also spelled Kayanere'ko:wa; The Great Law of Peace), was a systematic undermining of the foundation of the Haudenosaunee people's constitution, a constitution that mandates the rights and relationships to the natural world and each other. Colonial Christian laws were, and are, in direct contradiction of the Great Law of Peace; Canadian and US foundations are built on the pope's Doctrine of Discovery, *terra nullius* (land is empty or territory is not annexed by any nation), which violates inherent Indigenous rights. Settlers then created a "white man's Indian" mythology to perpetuate racism leading to a north American narrative of dehumanization, dehistoricization, objectification, delegitimization, and demonization of Indigenous people. The Western tradition of attacking the legitimacy of Indigenous people's rights through a propaganda campaign that served to justify and normalize genocidal legitimacy of settler occupation. In Canada, the government officially acknowledged their agencies' policies impact on Indigenous peoples had genocidal consequences for Indigenous people.[2]

What started as a public apology by Canadian Prime Minister Harper and later, Prime Minister Trudeau launched the Truth and Reconciliation Commission. The (TRC) acknowledged "cultural ethnocide," referring to the horrific abduction of Indigenous children herded off to prisons run by churchs known as "residential schools." The 2015 TRC *Call to Action* provided 94 ways in which citizens, government, and industry should begin to engage in a process of reconciliation; sadly, as we fast-forward to 2020, most of these initiatives have only received lip service without much action under a prime minister who promised to resolve the injustices inflicted on Indigenous people. Canadian Prime Minister Justin Trudeau also funded a $50 million inquiry advocated by Indigenous women. The National Inquiry into Missing and Murdered Indigenous Women and Girls (MMIWNI) findings reinforced the claim there were, and still are, multiple acts of genocide being carried out against Indigenous women, girls, and 2SLGBTQQIA people by settlers. The inquiry states:

> Violence the National Inquiry heard about amounts to a race-based genocide of Indigenous Peoples, including First Nations, Inuit and Métis, which especially targets women, girls, and 2SLGBTQQIA people. This genocide has been empowered by colonial structures, evidenced notably by the Indian Act, the Sixties Scoop, residential schools and breaches of human and Indigenous rights, leading directly to the current increased rates of violence, death, and suicide in Indigenous populations.[3]

In Canada over 1,700 Indigenous women are reported as missing or murdered; it's an epidemic that is similar in the United States. According to historian Robert Berkhofer, Hollywood and academia fed the public a steady diet of dehumanizing the "Indian," similar to then US President Donald Trump's campaign of toxic disinformation on Muslims, African Americans, and Mexicans. Propaganda is sustained through symbiotic ideological institutions of media, academia, government, and the church.[4] The trajectory of violence against Indigenous people began with the Dum Diversas (1452), issued by Pope Nicholas V, that granted the King of Portugal "full and free permission to invade, search out, capture, and subjugate the Saracens and pagans and any other unbelievers and enemies of Christ wherever they may be, as well as their kingdoms, duchies, counties, principalities, and other property . . . and to reduce their persons into perpetual servitude."[5] In 1492, when Columbus sailed to the New World, understanding that he was authorized by the pope to take possession of any lands he discovered that were "*not under the dominion of any Christian rulers.*"[6] The Spanish Pope Alexander VI issued another Papal Bull on May 3, 1493, granting to Spain the right to conquer the lands that Columbus had already found, as well as any lands that Spain might "discover" in the future. Pope Alexander also stated his desire that the "discovered" people be subjugated and brought to the faith itself.[7] The debate in 1550 in Valladolid, Spain, between Las Casas and Sepulveda, argued their conceptions of Indigenous people as human or nonhuman; Las Casas won and laws protecting Indigenous people were passed by the Spanish King but were opposed and ignored by the colonists.[8]

How would a democracy, such as Canada, or a republic, such as the United States, tell its history of murder and mayhem of Indigenous people, all the while espousing freedoms and human rights? Both nations utilized their ideological institutions and created a brand marketed by Hollywood's 2,000 western movies. The brand builds on the pope's Doctrine of Discovery by adding a new spin, *manifest destiny*, and academia cements blaming the victims through Darwin's *survival of the fittest*, a colonial global human evolution mythology. The imperialist regimes collectively deleted India, Africa, Middle East, China, and American histories by repackaging their dogma as "pre-history" and "great mysteries." North America and the imperial mother country, Great Britain, were the epicenter of pillaging and appropriating the histories and cultures of all "others," now proudly displayed in their museums or, in my view, public house of horrors. The colonial racist propaganda generated in the West spread like a virus across the globe, justifying the imperialist dominion.

THE THREATENING POWER OF GENDER IN COLONIAL NARRATIVES

The earliest European literature about North America fed Europe a steady diet of "the white man's Indian," references dating back to as early as the 16th century, in Lewis Henry Morgan's ethnography of the Iroquois.[9] The great military might/force/presence of the Confederacy was prized, renowned, and sought after by imperial powers, first by the Dutch and then by the British and French. Facilitated by Morgan's ethnography, the imagination of European men was unleashed, and their ideological inclinations set the stage for the interpretative binary of communism or democracy. Intellectuals were referred to as the "fathers of enlightenment," such as Emile Durkheim and Benjamin Franklin, and they developed a narrative immersed in racism and sexism that is still felt by Haudenosaunee to this day. Emile Durkheim, drawing from Morgan's work, argued for the evolution of civilization in this way:

> In the same societies, female functions are not very clearly distinguished from the male. Rather, the two sexes lead almost the same existence. There are even now a very great number of savage people where the woman mingles in political life . . . in the Indian tribes of America, such as the Iroquois, the Natchez; in Hawaii she participates in myriad ways in men's lives, as she does in New Zealand and in Samoa.[10]

From the aforementioned literature, it seems the stage had been set to support the narratives of patriarchy by the *Fathers of Democracy* and *the Fathers of Enlightenment*, but what of their mothers?

SUFFRAGE MOVEMENT, EUROPEAN WOMEN'S IMAGINATION UNLEASHED

One of the first women to receive a doctorate for work in women's studies, Sally Roesch Wagner, examines how Iroquoian laws respected the rights of women and women's leadership. Wagner noted in her book *Sisters in Spirit* that the suffragists "believed women's liberation was possible because they knew liberated women, women who possessed rights beyond their wildest imagination: Haudenosaunee women."[11] Wagner argues the influence of the earliest American women's movement was inspired by the Iroquois women. The movement's early musings of the suffragettes highly regarded the autonomy of Haudenosaunee women, which was in direct opposition to colonial laws. Wagner states:

> At the 1888 International Council of Women, they listened as Alice Fletcher, a noted white ethnographer, spoke about the greater rights of American Indian women. Fletcher made clear that these Indian women were well aware that when they became United States citizens, they would lose their rights. "As an Indian woman I was free. I owned my home, my person, the work of my own hands, and my children should never forget me. I was better as an Indian woman than under white law." Fletcher also quoted an Indian man who reproached white men: "Your laws show how little your men care for their women. The wife is nothing of herself."[12]

Fletcher was not alone in chastising white men for their asserted domination over women. Wagner reiterates a more contemporary discussion with an Onondaga Clan Mother, Audrey Shennondoh:

> Then Audrey talked matter-of-factly about the responsibilities of Haudenosaunee women in their system of gender balance. Iroquois women continue to have the responsibility of nominating, counseling, and keeping in office the male chief who represents the clan in the grand council. In the Six Nations of the Iroquois confederacy, she explained, Haudenosaunee women have worked with the men to successfully guard their sovereign political status against persistent attempts to turn them into United States citizens. In Audrey's direct and simple telling, the social power of the Haudenosaunee women seemed almost unremarkable—"We have always had these responsibilities," she said. I caught my breath again, remembering that radical suffragists also knew such women who lived their vision.[13]

How does a nation based on freedom justify state-sponsored oppression and genocide? Edward Herman and Noam Chomsky's *Manufacturing Consent* examines how propaganda is subtly interwoven into academia and government and overtly present in media. The term "terrorist vs. freedom fighters" is one example of ways in which colonial institutions perpetuate bias. The discourse developed by colonial regimes positions all non-Caucasian peoples as inferior in the linear metric positioning of progress and development.[14] Over 2,000 Hollywood films were produced in the genre of "western" frontier settings.[15] These films served as propaganda to dehumanize, criminalize, and demonize Indigenous peoples, otherwise known as Native Americans. For example, the killing of an "Indian" was cheered on in theaters across our homelands, which is sadly no different from Hitler's propaganda against Jewish citizens. Posing a greater dilemma for settlers and fundamentally different from Nazi ideology, which proclaims Jewish people as immigrants to German homelands, Native Americans were not immigrants; conversely, the European settlers were the immigrants. This posed a fundamental problem of international law for colonial regimes. How were they able to lay claim to our lands across North America then? Colonial regimes used the pope's Doctrine of Discovery in support of the state claims, but this doctrine required they "get rid of the Indian problem." Unlike colonized people's enslavement in South Africa, where they are in need of Indigenous labor, North Americans' colonial regimes needed to *remove and erase* the Indian from the lands, and also from the consciousness of Americans and Canadians. The genocidal and racist tactics of the Indian Act became the rule of law in 1876, reducing Indigenous people to "wards" of the state and forcing patriarchy upon matriarchical cultures through tribal enrollment.[16] The legislated patriarchy was noted by ethnographer Alice Fletcher:

> A common mythology held that Christianity and civilization meant progress for women, but Stanton and Gage saw through it. . . . Wife battering was not tolerated by the Haudenosaunee, and rape was unheard of before the white man arrived on the continent. Among the clans, a family member could avenge a woman who was beaten by her husband, and it was believed that such a husband awaited eternal punishment in the afterlife. By contrast, American laws allowed a husband to physically punish both his wife and children as long as no lasting damage was done.[17]

Western intellectual tradition is considered epistemological violence by Indigenous scholars due to the institutional colonial hierarchies that systematically perpetuate racism and sexism through exclusion, erasure, and diminishment of Indigenous knowledge as "myths" and "unscientific."[18] Epistemic violence refers to the one racialized group positioning itself as being superior to the other. It is particularly common to justify doing so in the name of "science" as an all-encompassing "proof" that one group of people is supposedly superior over another, which creates "epistemic racism," and justifies racial superiority at the root source: the existence of the "superior" race simply is superior because of this so-called scientific explanation.[19] The intent of both the United States and Canada was to remove the "Indian problem," whether it was General Ulysses Grant's campaign of "extermination" or Superintendent of Indian Affairs Duncan Campbell Scott's ideology of "continue until there isn't a single Indian left," which was rampant throughout a variety of the tactics Scott enforced.[20] Scott, considered an "extreme assimilationist, was a Methodist preacher who ran the forced Indigenous residential school system in Canada during its heyday (1913 to 1932)."[21]

COLONIAL CLAIMS TO INDIGENOUS WOMEN'S BODIES

Canada had two eugenics committees established in 1928 in British Columbia and in 1934 in Alberta, long before Germany established any eugenics assessment structures. Thousands of Indigenous women were sterilized without their consent, and many believe this is still happening as a result of industrial contaminants being dumped in the environments of Indigenous communities. There is also evidence that the United States had similar sterilization programs.[22] In Canada, the *Missing and Murdered Indigenous Women* (MMIW) report concluded that "thousands of truths shared before the National Inquiry reinforced the existence of acts of genocide against Indigenous women, girls, and 2SLGBTQQIA people." In particular, the MWIW supplementary report highlights:

> The violence the National Inquiry heard about amounts to a race-based genocide of Indigenous Peoples, including First Nations, Inuit and Métis, which especially targets women, girls, and 2SLGBTQQIA people. This genocide has been empowered by colonial structures, evidenced notably by the Indian Act, the Sixties Scoop, residential schools and breaches of human and Indigenous rights, leading directly to the current increased rates of violence, death, and suicide in Indigenous populations . . . finds the term genocide best describes the Indigenous women's experiences. The Greek words *genos*, which means race or tribe, and *cide*, which derives from the Latin root *cidere*, to kill . . . atrocities perpetrated throughout history and identified three types of genocides: physical, biological and cultural. . . . physical genocide consisted of the physical destruction of a group, biological genocide was the destruction of the group's reproductive capacity, and cultural genocide yielded the destruction of structures and practices that allowed the group to keep living as a group.[23]

The legal team for the Commission on MMIWI detailing violence against Indigenous women specifies:

> In the Canadian Crimes Against Humanity and War Crimes Act, genocide is defined as: an act or omission committed with intent to destroy, in whole or in part, an identifiable group of persons, as such, that, at the time and in the place of its commission, constitutes genocide according to customary international law or conventional international law or by virtue of its being.[24]

Neither the United States nor Canada is prepared to address the grave injustices committed against Indigenous peoples, specifically the state-funded sterilization of Indigenous women without their consent. Forced and coerced sterilization have also been recognized by the United Nations as torture (Committee Against Torture, 2018), an act of genocide and a violation of human rights, medical ethics and reproductive rights.[25] It is a product of systemic discrimination (Amnesty International, 2018) and resulting from and informed by a context of colonialism and the expropriation of Indigenous lands and resources. Stote argues coerced sterilization must be considered in relation to the larger goals of Indian policy—to gain access to Indigenous lands by eradicating and eliminating the Indigenous population. Stote also frames sterilization in a manner that accurately understands it as an act of genocide, further exploring how Canada has undermined and avoided these accusations by controlling the narrative. Epistemic violence is deeply rooted in justifying horrendous actions toward Indigenous people, women in particular.[26] A further analysis of environmental considerations reveals vulnerability of Indigenous women to resource extraction and land exploitation.

The MMIWG Report finds the link between resource extraction projects and violence against Indigenous women is a "serious problem" that demands attention. The report recommends "federal, provincial and territorial governments to fund more inquiries into the relationship between resource extraction (e.g., oil companies' 'man camps') and violence against Indigenous women and girls."[27]

Prior to the MMIW Inquiry, the TRC report on residential school survivors and policy concluded that "cultural genocide" had taken place in the schools. These residential schools banned customs, languages, and spiritual practices to adhere to the notion of "save the child, kill the Indian," a social engineering campaign that was implemented by many churches and funded by the state government. Beginning in the 1830s all the way up until 1996 when the last school finally closed, there were 1,500 residential and industrial schools in Canada that stole over 150,000 children. The sexual abuse of children by priests and nuns was rampant; all the while physical abuse through severe punishment, such as whipping; starvation; and harsh adult labor were pervasive.[28] MacDonald's analysis of residential schools argues that recognition of genocidal policies, which not only encouraged but legalized the forced removal of children, is an important basis for meaningful discussions of how to engage Indigenous–settler relations in respectful and proactive ways.[29]

The United States is far more reluctant to address residential schools (commonly and deceptively known as boarding schools in the United States), but similar to the practice in Canada, the "lessons" taught at these schools did not involve standard academics but served as training for domestic servants. Young girls were taught sewing, cooking, and cleaning while boys were taught to operate farming equipment and operations. The social engineering of Indigenous children failed to completely exterminate their identity, Indigenous culture, and ways of being, but the layered impacts of intergenerational trauma are still felt today.

Racist assimilation policies were finally repealed in the 1980s.[30] Reserves were viewed as Indians' "dying grounds," leaving parents and grandparents childless, as they abducted children and forced them to assimilate further in cities. Infrastructure and sustainable resource development on reserves was not planned nor implemented. Reserves were further under attack as colonial regimes continued spreading propaganda that encouraged extinguishing Indigenous nations so that their lands and resources would be available for resource extraction. Today, the consequences are still felt on reserves across North America: employment and the lack of basic amenities, such as access to clean water and food security. A 2019 UN Water Report finds:

> Women and girls regularly experience discrimination and inequalities in the enjoyment of their human rights to safe drinking water and sanitation in many parts of the world. Ethnic and other minorities, including indigenous peoples, migrants and refugees, and people of certain ancestries . . . lower levels of access to water and sanitation services can be observed among ethnic minorities and Indigenous peoples.[31]

The natural world is declining at a faster rate than at any other time in human history according to a UN Report. The UN Intergovernmental Panel on Climate Change

2019 Special Report on Climate Change and Land further acknowledges that, as human population grows and depends on nature's resources to survive during a time of accelerating and unparalleled loss of biodiversity, it will pose a 'direct threat' to people "living in all regions of the world."[32] Indigenous knowledge provides an undeniable link between Indigenous bodies and Indigenous lands; understanding interconnectedness as the health of the land determines/defines/dictates the livelihood of humans' well-being. Lived experiences testify to the assault on life through sterilization, violence toward women, and MMIWG that mirror the colonial practice of raping/plundering/pillaging the land. Can we deny the lived experience of many Indigenous women as they face ongoing attempts to destroythem through social engineering, legislative policies, and violent force on a daily basis? Indigenous peoples are resilient, and in some cases have persevered and managed to remain sovereign and in control of their own bodies, culture, and lands in order to continue thriving.

Indigenous Knowledge

So what exactly are Indigenous knowledge and environmental management, and how do they connect? IK is best understood through Haudenosaunee creation stories that provide the ecocentric worldview that places intrinsic value on all living things. Haudenosaunee people's relationship with the natural environment is centered around the *responsibility* of being stewards of ecosystems whose legacy is a healthy planet for the coming generations. Women transmit teachings to their children and mobilize their communities to protect their environment. Indigenous knowledge is holistic in principle: health is viewed as all-encompassing by including the emotional, spiritual, and physical well-being of a people. Sustaining reciprocal relationships with the natural and spiritual worlds and families is foundational and vital to Indigenous societies, including the Haudenosaunee.

Preservation of Haudenosaunee knowledge is increasingly threatened by the loss of Indigenous languages, which affects its transmission through personal narratives, storytelling, song, and ceremony. For example, Haudenosaunee law acknowledges all of creation as interdependent and interconnected to human beings. As stated by the late Chief Deskahe, "The guiding philosophy Rotinonshonni or Haudenosaunee (People of the Longhouse), our perspective on the river and the relationships of respect and responsibility that should exist among all parts of creation are contained in the words of our Ohe'n:ton Karihwate'hkwe (Thanksgiving Address). . . . We believe that in order to gain a true understanding of any aspect of the natural world, respect must be shown for the entire web of relationships that exist and form our natural environment." The Haudenosaunee Ohe'n:ton Karihwate'hkwen "offers greetings and acknowledgement to the natural world," guiding humans to give thanks and maintain respect for the entire web of relationships that forms our environment; in other words, it asserts that all of creation has the right to existence and respect, not just humans.[33] In Haudenosaunee spiritual practice, reciprocal relationships are continuously renewed throughout the seasonal ceremonial cycles; it is this act of giving thanks through song and dance that kept these values maintained throughout, in spite of the colonial legislation of the "Indian Act" still in place today.

In 1910 a campaign to "outlaw" ceremonies, dancing, and gatherings had been amended by the Indian Act legislation in Canada and the United States. The criminalizing of Indigenous people's way of life resulted in imprisonment for "breaking the rule of law." Stifling economic growth meant that Indigenous people needed the white Indian agent's "pass" to leave the reserve for their livelihood, as selling produce off reserve was outlawed. For Indigenous women, the rule of law was even more oppressive.[34] In the Great Law, women have authority within their clans (social systems). The term *Clan Mother* is a spiritual socio-political title that values certain characteristics in women, peace and compassion being the primarily/highly esteemed attributes.

The Great Law of Peace endows women with the power of appointing their clan *Sachem*, otherwise known as the male leader. The Clan Mother is able to use her best judgment to determine which of the children in her longhouse has the attributes of a leader. For example, a Clan Mother is an expert in assessing kindness, peace, generosity, and other valued characteristics that a male leader should possess. She could (and still can) impeach her appointed Sachem if he displays unbecoming or immoral conduct. Clan Mothers are utilizing their knowledge to solve social issues in their communities, socioeconomic challenges/obstacles often tied to the trauma of family separation, and the abuse in residential schools inflicted on generations of families. The forced removal of children from their mothers is understood today as a form of torture. Healing families and communities is the highest priority in Indigenous communities. Suicide, incarceration, chronic poor health, and social distress and upheaval are double, triple, and even quadruple compared to that of non-Indigenous peoples in Canada or in the United States. Haudenosaunee matriarchs have developed healing strategies to improve the health and well-being of their communities. A case study of one such initiative was funded by the Canadian Institutes of Health Research (CIHR) and has proven to be extremely impactful as an intervention and prevention strategy/tool/technique for youth in two Haudenosaunee communities.[35]

CASE STUDY: DECOLONIZING THROUGH REMATRIATION AND OHERO:KON RITES OF PASSAGE

Louise McDonald, a Mohawk Clan Mother, has been applying traditional Haudenosaunee teachings to restore, reclaim, and rematriate stolen generations. She states:

> As women leaders were pushed aside while white men of importance would only speak to the "Chief," over time women were relegated to the kitchen. Part of my work through rites of passage is to re-train and re-educate our young men and women regarding the true roles and responsibilities embedded in our Great Law. We must "rematriate" our Clans and Nations to re-establish the Matriarchal law which was eroded over residential schools, loss of language and identity.[36]

Throughout the colonial era, Haudenosaunee women's voices were silenced through multiple agencies. Haudenosaunee culture adopted English; thus, Western worldviews of women and their authority were eroded. The role of gender within colonialism developed as a critical issue in the pursuit of decolonization.

Kim Anderson demonstrates the significant role that colonial subjugation played in the loss of status and power experienced by Indigenous women, which in turn crippled or fragmented societal and family structures. That older Indigenous women were most revered for their authority and responsibilities was highlighted, while colonial subjugation was completely contradictory to this aspect of IK. She notes, "It may seem incredible that this territory we now know as Canada once hosted societies that afforded significant political power to those currently most marginalized: older women."[37] Anderson's central thesis is that women have always played a central role as spiritual and political leaders, as well as stewards of the law and environment. Through the rites of passage, Haudenosaunee women are able to impart the importance of protecting land and water while healing historical trauma in order to strengthen their societies. Many Haudenosaunee refused the adoption of Christianity and the patriarchal tradition of women as chattel, though, sadly, in some communities, the view of women as possessions, legally owned by their fathers and then their husbands, had been adopted by Christian Haudenosaunee and remained until the last century.

The imposition of the Indian Act cemented the oppression of Haudenosaunee women. To demonstrate the brilliance of Haudenosaunee female leaders, Louise McDonald re-introduced the cultural practice of the "rites of passage," which restore knowledge, values, beliefs, and healthy functional and beneficial family dynamics. Together, we secured a Canadian Institutes of Health Research grant through the Institute of Aboriginal Health; it was the first ever health research grant funding for an Indigenous way of knowing research project. The Tehtsitewa:kenrotka:we (meaning "Together we pull it from the earth again") Ohero:kon Rites of Passage core premise is revealing multiple layers of being, parallel to harvest time when corn is revealed after husking. Ohero:kon, "under the husk," is an educational, instructional, and ritualized ceremonial process drawn from the Haudenosaunee Skyworld creation story known as the "Earth-grasper." Two Haudenosaunee communities, Akwesasne and Six Nations, provided youth between the ages of 10 and 18 weekly cultural teachings from the winter season into spring. The weekly teachings ultimately prepare the youth for the culmination practice of fasting. Ceremonial land-based activities are a process of restoring a youth's connecting to traditional ways, lands, roles, and responsibilities. Over four years, youth are mentored throughout adolescence, becoming healthy young adults integral within Haudenosaunee society. The objective of this project is to implement Onkwe:honweh neha (Haudenosaunee ways of knowing) as a prevention and healing journey for youth. They resurrect the ancient process of matrilineal lineage of clanships that teach and guide nieces and nephews into adulthood. Restoring the traditional roles of uncle and auntie mentorship has had a significant impact in healing families who were often torn apart through residential schools or child welfare's removal of children from the home.

Over 16 years, Ohero:kon has been developed and implemented; during this time it has received just under 1,000 youth participants from five communities. Six Nations was the first community to work with and attempt to apply the model of Akwasasne's rites of passage program. It is a process of personal and collective transformation through shared learning, self-discovery, ritual seclusion, expansion of community relationships, and spiritual growth through fasting. A significant outcome overall is the building and nurturing of leadership skills, interpersonal relationships, and the restoration of the rightful position women hold. Such an understanding of respect for women's leadership and responsibilities can be difficult to impart to youth still living under the colonial state, mainstream media of power and influence. By training, teaching, guiding, and supporting the development of young males, Ohero:kon aimed to counteract these ideological institutions' mythology and assimilative practices that still penetrate Indigenous communities. The mentorship of uncles and aunties nurturing nieces and nephews with land-based skills is an asset to communities. Ohero:kon is not only a ceremonial ritualization of youth into adulthood but also a celebration of life passages, such as first menses, sexual relations, and childbearing. Transformative teachings use both Western and Haudenosaunee knowledge to empower young men and women to cherish and govern their bodies through self-care and self-advocacy.

The young men learn their traditional roles and values, emphasized in communication skills, self-discipline, and respect for their families and partners. "Two-spirit" (LGBTQ) youth are provided space to learn traditional concepts of gender. The "coming of age" is a journey in self-awareness and strengthening mind, body, and spirit, upholding the principles of reciprocity by encouraging Ohero:kon graduates to return as teachers or mentors for new niece and nephew initiates. The key developmental markers for youth initiates are finding their voice, understanding their responsibility to carry forward their culture, understanding the importance of protecting the land and water, and continuing the healing from within their families to reduce their community's collective historical trauma. The program requires a huge commitment from youth and some sacrifice, as it spans across several months in order to understand seasonal cycles and land-based teachings. Activities include harvesting, creating art, sewing cultural regalia, basket making, fishing, hunting, and gardening; creating sustainable activities serves to empower and increase self-esteem, self-worth, and positive self-identity within a world that has historically demonized and degraded Indigenous peoples. Reclaiming the role of matriarchs and nurturing a new generation to respect women's authority and leadership in decision making is a long-term prevention strategy that will be impactful in reducing social ills, such as domestic violence.

Youth who have fasted at the end of their training share their visions, dreams, or concerns with leadership, aunties, uncles, and peers. A great majority of the youth have shared their grave concerns regarding the future of Mother Earth and their surrounding environment. What weighs on them heavily is related to climate change, cultural continuity, family, and their purpose on earth. During hosted roundtables, youth often discussed practical goals of accessing clean water and maintaining food security through harvesting the bounty of the land. They have also discussed ways to develop the skills and tools to deconstruct settler narratives, improve education through land-based learning, increase food and water security, and learn within their own language and cultural milieu. Many graduates of Ohero:kon have begun to represent themselves and their stories by making films, speaking publicly, producing art, and supporting a "Rematriation Magazine." The resurgence and revitalization of this initiative has become a movement of all genders to recognize the inherent strength and leadership of matriarchal governance. A recognition of Indigenous ways of knowing is a guide in uncertain times, holding the wisdoms needed to address ecological distress, social distress, food and water security, and cultural resilience. Central to rebuilding nations are families, mothers, grandmothers, aunties, and daughters working with grandfathers, grandsons, fathers, uncles, and brothers to restore balance internally and externally.

CONCLUSION

Mother Earth and the cosmos *are* the sacred spaces for worship. Indigenous identities, cultures, and spirituality are formed and embodied within these powerful natural forces, shaping relationships and understanding of interconnectedness. Protecting the land is as natural as protecting your family for Indigenous people, from the Amazon to the Arctic, which have and continue to resist destruction. Haudenosaunee people *know* without a doubt that the continuation of life is reciprocally dependent upon continuing the well-being of the land. Inherent to Indigenous knowledge is *knowing* all living creation has a divine right to exist. The Great Law of Peace of the Haudenosaunee outlines responsibilities, not rights; that is the fundamental principle that a Western paradigm so desperately lacks. We are witnessing the extinction of 80% of all biodiversity today because of the West's exploitative ideologies that focus on human rights, which are demonstrably humanity's abuse of power over nature. The early colonial encounters that gave rise to survival of the fittest, manifest destiny, and *terra nullus* have created a mythology deeply woven into the Western psyche, which has laid to waste so much of the earth and polluted the waters, air, cosmos, and land.

Life cannot be sustained in a vacuum of capitalist consumption. However, science has begun to catch up with Indigenous knowledge in understanding the natural world. It realizes that humans have destroyed the earth beyond sustainability. The natural world is declining at a faster rate than at any time in human history, according to the UN Report, highlighting that humans depend on nature's resources to survive. This threat to people living in all regions of the world is reaching a cataclysmic point of no return. The Intergovernmental Panel on Climate Change and Land (IPCC), a special report on climate change, desertification, land degradation, sustainable land management, food security, and greenhouse gas fluxes in terrestrial ecosystems, highlights that environments that are not controlled by Indigenous peoples suffer the greatest impacts, particularly women and children. It also points out that, globally, lands and waters managed and controlled by Indigenous peoples are in the best condition.[38]

The greatest resistance to continued destruction to the environment is consistently mounted by Indigenous women. They serve as *land and water protectors* who are applying traditional teachings to peaceful, direct and indirect, actions. Their fruitful education and advocacy are evidenced in memes, such as the T-shirts sold by pow-wow venders, which reinforce the younger generation's resilience and pride. Slogans like *we are still here* and *strong resilient Indigenous woman* challenge racist ideologies such as (my personal favorite), pulled directly from the US Declaration of Independence, July 4, 1776, the meme *merciless Indian Savage*. The Declaration states "He has excited domestic insurrections amongst us, and has endeavored to bring on the inhabitants of our frontiers, the merciless Indian

Savage."[39] There also are now numerous Indigenous tiktoks to "Savage Daughter," a song by Sarah Hester, whose words describe "my mother's savage daughter" in various scenarios that challenge the suffering and oppression of Indigenous females. Instead of being forced to change to accommodate their white oppressor, the tiktok uses the songs while showing Indigenous mothers dressing their daughters in their full regalia.[40]

The resiliency of the Haudenosaunee women is rooted in their spiritual foundation, surviving centuries of genocide, war, displacement, ecocide, assimilation, and detrimental social engineering, only to emerge as global leaders in climate change, education, women's rights, law, justice, infrastructure development, healing techniques, medicine, sciences, and so much more. The Great Law of Peace, the traditional governing council, still follows the line of the mothers and inherited clans. The duties of matriarchs are maintained through oral culture, while "Indian Statues Cards" were issued by the government through paternal lineage. Haudenosaunee women continue to emerge in the 21st century as they did in the 17th and 18th centuries, proving to be moral and spiritual guideposts for a new generation wanting to reclaim, restore, and rebuild their Nations. Women continue to resist government identities by reasserting their rightful lineage through the matriarchal system. It is the women's duty to protect their lands under the Great Law of Peace. Let's be clear; oppression is still very much intact in legislation evidenced by inequitable access to basic human rights, such as infrastructure that provides clean and potable water. The United Nations identified that Indigenous people experience water inequality in Canada. Nearly 100 Indigenous communities are under boil-water advisories and/or have no access to/contact with water. Women experience the greatest burden of water insecurity because they are less mobile and are most often the primary caregivers of dependent children, youth, and the elderly. Sterilization and child apprehension are still extremely problematic today.[41] Only three years ago, Minister of Indigenous Affairs and Northern Development Carolyn Bennett herself said child apprehension was so prevalent that there are "more children in care now than at the height of Residential schools."[42] Genocide, as it is understood in the MMIW report, explains that Indigenous women are targets for racialized murder. The report also further outlines the connection between resource extraction and violence against Indigenous women. Delegitimizing Indigenous ways of knowing, oral cultures, and Haudenosaunee governance structures in particular is an ongoing assault on feminine ecocentric laws embedded within the Great Law of Peace.

The legitimacy of a sovereign nation was diminished by undermining women and actualized by state policies embedded into the Indian Act of both Canada and the United States, which are still currently in place. Epistemic violence was, and continues to be, a tool of Western institutions that consistently dispossess the legitimacy of Indigenous governance in an attempt to force colonial exploitation of the land and water. Countless Indigenous peoples confront, resist, and protest capitalistic mind frames that view our mother, the earth, as a mere resource to exploit and commodify. It is women who lead the resistance, in America, from the Amazon, Standing Rock, Oka to the Wet'suwe'en, Apache, and Cree, and, globally, from the Maori and Australian Aboriginal to the Sami in Finland, all standing for the land and water at a great personal risk. Indigenous women have always threatened colonial patriarchies, from early colonial encounters with Ben Franklin to President Donald Trump. Indigenous women lead the battle cries against oil and mining, from the Amazon to Standing Rock, and it is no coincidence that Indigenous women suffer the greatest murder, assault, and rape. Old Doctrine of Discovery narratives have come full circle with the new awareness of who the real terrorists are, white Christian men and their mysoginistic racist rhetoric and white Christian females who also are complicit in playing out poetically on the American stage for the world to witness. Canada's kinder *genteel* assaults are carried out quietly on Indigenous lands and women with the same goal and devastating result as their reviled bombastic neighbors.

All the while Haudenosaunee women continue to reclaim and restore through rites of passage, learning our language, writing books, making films, organizing resistance to destructive development, singing, welcoming new babies, installing new Clan Mothers and Chiefs, reciting the Great Law, carrying out ceremonies, giving thanks to the thunder, wind, sap running from the maples, seeds, harvests, waters, moon, sun, stars, and sky beings, and dancing for the creator as we have done for thousands and thousands of years. *We paint our faces, wear our regalia, get our doctorates, and be fierce: We are still here.*

NOTES

1. See, e.g., Kevin White, "Rousing a Curiosity: Hewitt's Iroquois Cosmologies," *Wicazo Sa Review* 28, no. 2 (2013): 87–111; and Theresa McCarthy, *Divided Unity: Haudenosaunee Reclamation at Grand River* (Tucson: University of Arizona Press, 2016).

2. See National Inquiry into Missing and Murdered Indigenous Women and Girls (MMIWG), *Reclaiming Power and Place: Final Report*, vol. 1a, 2019, https://www.mmiwg-ffada.ca/wp-content/uploads/2019/06/Final_Report_Vol_1a-1.pdf; and vol. 1b, 2019, https://www.mmiwg-ffada.ca/wp-content/uploads/2019/06/Final_Report_Vol_1b.pdf; see also MMIWG, *Reclaiming Power and Place: Executive Summary of the Final Report*, 2019, https://www.mmiwg-ffada.ca/wp-content/uploads/2019/06/Executive_Summary.pdf; and MMIWG, *A Legal Analysis of Genocide: A Supplementary Report of the National Inquiry into Missing and Murdered Indigenous Women and Girls*, 2019, https://www.mmiwg-ffada.ca/wp-content/uploads/2019/06/Supplementary-Report_Genocide.pdf.

3. MMIWG, *Reclaiming Power and Place*, Sec. 1a, 5.

4. See, e.g., Robert Berkhofer, *The White Man's Indian: Images of the American Indian, from Columbus to the Present* (Ann Arbor: University of Michigan, 1979).

5. Canadian Catholic Council of Bishops (CCCB). "The 'Doctrine of Discovery' and Terra Nullius: A Catholic Response," March 19, 2016, https://www.cccb.ca/indigenous-peoples/resources/doctrine-of-discovery-and-terra-nullius/, 10.

6. CCCB, "Doctrine of Discovery," 10.

7. CCCB, "Doctrine of Discovery," 11.

8. See, e.g., Steve Newcomb, *Pagans in the Promised Land: Religion, Law, and the American Indian* (Golden, CO: Fulcrum Publishing, 2008).

9. See, e.g., Berkhofer, *White Man's Indian*.

10. Emile Durkheim, *The Division of Labor in Society*, trans. George Simpson (New York: Macmillan, 1933), 58.

11. See Sally Roesch Wagner, *Sisters in Spirit: Haudenosaunee (Iroquois) Influence on Early American Feminists* (Summertown, TN: Native Voices, 2001).

12. Wagner, *Sisters in Spirit*.

13. Audrey Shennondoh, cited by Wagner in *Sisters in Spirit*.

14. See Edward S. Herman and Noam Chomsky, *Manufacturing Consent: The Political Economy of the Mass Media* (New York: Pantheon, 1988).

15. See, e.g., Berkhofer, *White Man's Indian*.

16. See, e.g., John L. Steckley and Bryan D. Cummins, *Full Circle: Canada's First Nations*, 2nd ed. (North York, ON: Pearson Education Canada, 2007).

17. Wagner, *Sisters in Spirit*, 50.

18. See Dawn Martin-Hill, *Traditional Medicine in Contemporary Contexts: Protecting and Respecting Indigenous Knowledge and Medicine* (Ottawa, ON: National Aboriginal Health Organization, 2003), http://epub.sub.unihamburg.de/epub/volltexte/2013/15417/pdf/research_tradition.pdf; *The Lubicon Lake Nation: Indigenous Knowledge and Power* (Toronto, ON: University of Toronto Press, 2007); and "Traditional Medicine and Restoration of Wellness Strategies," *International Journal of Indigenous Health* 5, no. 1 (2009): 26–42.

19. See C. L. Reading and F. Wien, *Health Inequalities and the Social Determinants of Aboriginal Peoples' Health* (Prince George, BC: National Collaborating Center for Aboriginal Health).

20. See Truth and Reconciliation Commission of Canada (TRC). *Honoring the Truth, Reconciling for the Future: Summary of the Final Report of the Truth and Reconciliation Commission of Canada* (Winnipeg, MB: Truth and Reconciliation Commission of Canada, 2015), http://www.trc.ca/assets/pdf/Honouring_the_Truth_Reconciling_for_the_Future_July_23_2015.pdf.

21. Facing History and Ourselves, "'Until There Is Not a Single Indian in Canada," *Stolen Lives: The Indigenous Peoples of Canada and the Indian Residential Schools*, https://www.facinghistory.org/stolen-lives-indigenous-peoples-canada-and-indian-residential-schools/historical-background/until-there-not-single-indian-canada, accessed April 21, 2020.

22. Karen Stote, *An Act of Genocide: Colonialism and the Sterilization of Aboriginal Women* (Black Point, Nova Scotia: Fernwood Publishing, 2015).

23. MMIWG, *Reclaiming Power and Place*, Sec. 2, 3.

24. MMIWG, *Reclaiming Power and Place*, Sec. 2, 2.

25. See Roger Collier, "Reports of Coerced Sterilization of Indigenous Women in Canada Mirrors Shameful Past," *Canadian Medical Association Journal* 189, no. 33 (2017), E1080–E1081. doi:10.1503/cmaj.1095471; Karen Stote, *An Act of Genocide: Colonialism and the Sterilization of Aboriginal Women* (Black Point, Nova Scotia: Fernwood Publishing, 2015).

26. See Stote, *Act of Genocide*.

27. MMIWG Report, 2019, 584.

28. TRC, *Honoring the Truth*, 2015.

29. David MacDonald, *The Sleeping Giant Awakens: Genocide, Indian Residential Schools, and the Challenge of Conciliation* (Toronto, Canada: University of Toronto Press, 2019).

30. Patricia Olive Dickason and William Newbigging, *Indigenous Peoples within Canada: A Concise History*, 4th ed. (Oxford: Oxford University Press, 2018).

31. United Nations, *World Water Development Report 2019: Leaving No One Behind*, March 2019, https://www.unwater.org/publications/world-water-development-report-2019/.

32. See, e.g., United Nations Intergovernmental Panel on Climate Change (IPCC) Climate Change and Land Special Report, 2019, https://www.ipcc.ch/srccl/.

33. Mario Blaser, Harvey A. Feit, and Glenn McRae, eds. *In the Way of Development: Indigenous Peoples, Life Projects, and Globalization* (Ottawa, ON: ZedBooks, 2004).

34. Gail Guthrie Valaskakis, Eric Guiond, and Madeleine Dion Stout, eds. *Restoring the Balance: First Nations Women, Community, and Culture* (Manitoba: University of Manitoba Press, 2009).

35. See Canadian Institutes of Health Research, https://cihr-irsc.gc.ca/e/193.html, 2020.

36. Louise McDonald, Clan Meeting, Six Nations, 2015.

37. Kim Anderson, *A Recognition of Being: Reconstructing Native Womanhood* (Toronto, Canada: Second Story Press, 2000), 70–78.

38. P. R. Shukla, et al., eds., "Climate Change and Land: Summary for Policymakers," Intergovernmental Panel on Climate Change (IPCC), 2019, https://www.ipcc.ch/site/assets/uploads/sites/4/2020/02/SPM_Updated-Jan20.pdf; and https://www.ipcc.ch/site/assets/uploads/2019/08/4.-SPM_Approved_Microsite_FINAL.pdf.

39. USA Declaration of Independence, July 4, 1776.

40. Sarah Hester, *Savage Daughter*, May 2020, Apple Music.

41. See Valaskakis et al., *Restoring the Balance*.

42. Jillian Taylor, "'The Ultimate Goal Is to Reduce the Number of Children in Care': Indigenous Affairs Minister," *CBC News*, March 27, 2017, https://www.cbc.ca/news/canada/

manitoba/manitoba-carolyn-bennett-child-welfare-1.4042484. See also Sima Sahar Zerehi, "Car-olyln Bennett Says Pan-Aboriginal Approach to MMIW Inquiry Won't Work for Inuit," *CBC News*, January 16, 2016, https://www.cbc.ca/news/canada/north/carolyn-bennett-says-pan-aboriginal-approach-to-mmiw-inquiry-won-t-work-for-inuit-1.3426222.

BIBLIOGRAPHY

Anderson, Kim. *A Recognition of Being: Reconstructing Native Womanhood.* Toronto, Canada: Second Story Press, 2000.

Berkhofer, Robert. *The White Man's Indian: Images of the American Indian, from Columbus to the Present.* Ann Arbor: University of Michigan, 1979.

Blaser, Mario, Harvey A. Feit, and Glenn McRae, eds. *In the Way of Development: Indigenous Peoples, Life Projects, and Globalization.* Ottawa, ON: ZedBooks, 2004.

Canadian Catholic Council of Bishops (CCCB). "The 'Doctrine of Discovery' and Terra Nullius: A Catholic Response." March 19, 2016. "Doctrine of Discovery" and Terra Nullius–Canadian Conference of Catholic Bishops (cccb.ca).

Collier, Roger. "Reports of Coerced Sterilization of Indigenous Women in Canada Mirrors Shameful Past." *Canadian Medical Association Journal* 189, no. 33 (2017), E1080–E1081. doi:10.1503/cmaj.1095471.

Dickason, Patricia Olive, and William Newbigging. *Indigenous Peoples within Canada: A Concise History.* 4th ed. Oxford: Oxford University Press, 2018.

Durkheim, Emile. *The Division of Labor in Society.* Translated by George Simpson. New York: Macmillan, 1933.

Hester, Sarah. *Savage Daughter*, May 2020, Apple Music.

Herman, Edward S., and Noam Chomsky. *Manufacturing Consent: The Political Economy of the Mass Media.* New York: Pantheon, 1988.

MacDonald, David. *The Sleeping Giant Awakens: Genocide, Indian Residential Schools, and the Challenge of Conciliation.* Toronto, Canada: University of Toronto Press, 2019.

Martin-Hill, Dawn. *The Lubicon Lake Nation: Indigenous Knowledge and Power.* Toronto, Canada: University of Toronto Press, 2007.

———. *Traditional Medicine in Contemporary Contexts: Protecting and Respecting Indigenous Knowledge and Medicine.* National Aboriginal Health Organization, 2003. http://epub.sub.unihamburg.de/epub/volltexte/2013/15417/pdf/research_tradition.pdf.

———. "Traditional Medicine and Restoration of Wellness Strategies." *International Journal of Indigenous Health* 5, no. 1 (2009): 26–42.

McCarthy, Theresa. *In Divided Unity: Haudenosaunee Reclamation at Grand River.* Tucson: University of Arizona Press, 2016.

National Inquiry into Missing and Murdered Indigenous Women and Girls (MMIWG). *A Legal Analysis of Genocide: A Supplementary Report of the National Inquiry into Missing and Murdered Indigenous Women and Girls,* 2019. https://www.mmiwg-ffada.ca/wp-content/uploads/2019/06/Supplementary-Report_Genocide.pdf.

———. *Reclaiming Power and Place: Executive Summary of the Final Report,* 2019. https://www.mmiwg-ffada.ca/wp-content/uploads/2019/06/Executive_Summary.pdf.

———. *Reclaiming Power and Place: Final Report,* vol. 1a, 2019. https://www.mmiwg-ffada.ca/wp-content/uploads/2019/06/Final_Report_Vol_1a-1.pdf.

Newcomb, Steve. *Pagans in the Promised Land: Religion, Law, and the American Indian.* Golden, CO: Fulcrum Publishing, 2008.

Reading, C. L., and F. Wien. *Health Inequalities and the Social Determinants of Aboriginal Peoples' Health.* Prince George, BC: National Collaborating Center for Aboriginal Health, 2009.

Shukla, P. R., J. Skea, E. Calvo Buendia, V. Masson-Delmotte, H. O. Pörtner, D. C. Roberts, P. Zhai, R. Slade, S. Connors, R. van Diemen, M. Ferrat, E. Haughey, S. Luz, S. Neogi, M. Pathak, J. Petzold, J. Portugal Pereira, P. Vyas, E. Huntley, K. Kissick, M. Belkacemi, and J. Malley, eds. "Climate Change and Land: Summary for Policymakers." Intergovernmental Panel on

Climate Change (IPCC) 2019. https://www.ipcc.ch/site/assets/uploads/sites/4/2020/02/SPM_Updated-Jan20.pdf; and https://www.ipcc.ch/site/assets/uploads/2019/08/4.-SPM_Approved_Microsite_FINAL.pdf.

Steckley, John L., and Bryan D. Cummins. *Full Circle: Canada's First Nations*. 2nd ed. North York, ON: Pearson Education Canada, 2007.

Stote, Karen. *An Act of Genocide: Colonialism and the Sterilization of Aboriginal Women*. Black Point, Nova Scotia: Fernwood Publishing, 2015.

Taylor, Jillian. "'The Ultimate Goal Is to Reduce the Number of Children in Care': Indigenous Affairs Minister." *CBC News*, March 27, 2017. https://www.cbc.ca/news/canada/manitoba/manitoba-carolyn-bennett-child-welfare-1.4042484.

Truth and Reconciliation Commission of Canada. *Honoring the Truth, Reconciling for the Future: Summary of the Final Report of the Truth and Reconciliation Commission of Canada*. Truth and Reconciliation Commission of Canada, 2015. http://www.trc.ca/assets/pdf/Honouring_the_Truth_Reconciling_for_the_Future_July_23_2015.pdf.

United Nations Intergovernmental Panel on Climate Change (IPCC) Climate Change and Land Special Report, 2019. Special Report on Climate Change and Land—IPCC site

United Nations. *World Water Development Report 2019: Leaving No One Behind*. March 2019. https://www.unwater.org/publications/world-water-development-report-2019/.

Valaskakis, Gail Guthrie, Eric Guiond, and Madeleine Dion Stout, eds. *Restoring the Balance: First Nations Women, Community, and Culture*. Winnipeg, Canada: University of Manitoba Press, 2009.

Wagner, Sally Roesch. *Sisters in Spirit: Haudenosaunee (Iroquois) Influence on Early American Feminists*. Summertown, TN: Native Voices, 2001.

White, Kevin. "Rousing a Curiosity: Hewitt's Iroquois Cosmologies." *Wicazo Sa Review* 28, no. 2 (2013): 87–111.

Zerehi, Sima Sahar. "Carolyn Bennett Says Pan-Aboriginal Approach to MMIW Inquiry Won't Work for Inuit." *CBC News*, January 16, 2016. https://www.cbc.ca/news/canada/north/carolyn-bennett-says-pan-aboriginal-approach-to-mmiw-inquiry-won-t-work-for-inuit-1.3426222.

CHAPTER 20

Women's Religio-Political Witness for Love and Justice

Prof. Rosemary P. Carbine, PhD, Whittier College

ABSTRACT

This essay offers critical and constructive theological reflection on the theological claims and political praxis of emerging US social justice movements that exemplify a praxis of worldmaking, of imagining and incarnating the world otherwise than rising gender and sexual violence, xenophobic hate crimes, and white nationalist movements. More specifically, this essay redefines and expands the public sphere of religion and politics in multiracial, multicultural, and multifaith ways by engaging feminist and womanist theory and theology to elaborate on love as a theo-political ethic of justice based on the Revolutionary Love Project and its trifold notion of love as seeing no strangers, tending personal and socio-political wounds, and birthing a new future. Pointing out unexpected key parallels with Mary Magdalene and with the Nuns on the Bus, this essay explores women's religio-political witness as one theological model for women's ways of doing public/political theology today, that is, of generating alternative possible futures of love and justice that foster the flourishing of all.

INTRODUCTION

Scholars have engaged with aesthetic, archeological, biblical/scriptural, contemplative, ecclesiological, historical, liturgical, missiological, mystical, pastoral, and practical studies of Mary Magdalene as a prism through which to critically question and reconsider women's limited and restricted roles in the church as well as to advocate for more egalitarian, inclusive, and fully participatory understandings of church leadership in particular and of the church in general to reflect the diverse people of God. In conversation with but going beyond these studies, this essay[1] explores theological and ecclesiological issues by resourcing the Magdalene's praxis of prophetic public witness and ministry for fresh insights into women's religio-political roles, or women's ways of doing public theology today, exemplified by the interfaith, intercultural Revolutionary Love Project.

First, I will offer critical and constructive theological reflections on Mary by tethering together feminist New Testament studies, including *The Gospel of Mary*, with Eastern Catholic liturgical traditions, in order to illuminate Mary's prophetic witness as a praxis of worldmaking, that is, imagining and incarnating the world otherwise than imperial and other kinds of violence.[2] The Magdalene's witness functions as one potent theological symbol for women's audacious ways of doing public and political theology today, that is, of generating alternative possible futures of love and justice. Second, I will describe the theological and political praxis of the Revolutionary Love Project (RLP), an emerging US social justice movement, as embodying this praxis of worldmaking other than contemporary gender and sexual violence, xenophobic hate crimes, and white nationalist movements that predominate in our day. Pointing out unexpected provocative parallels between Mary Magdalene and the RLP, I will engage feminist and womanist theology throughout this essay to elaborate on love as a theo-political ethic of justice based on the RLP's trifold notion of love as seeing no strangers, as tending personal and socio-political wounds, and as birthing a new future.

MARY MAGDALENE

Feminist scholarship within the ever-growing field of Magdalene studies,[3] or what I call Magdalenology, recovers Mary's praxis of theological and prophetic witness *via negativa*. As Sandra Schneiders remarks, the Magdalene's personal identity and religious roles are "historically confused, theologically contorted, and ecclesiastically manipulated and prostituted."[4] Thus, a feminist hermeneutics of suspicion critically names who and what Mary Magdalene is not, to dispel false misrepresentations and to clarify her personal and religious identity, roles, and relations.

Feminist biblical and theological studies disentangle Mary Magdalene from other notable women in the gospels—the unnamed woman with the alabaster jar at Simon the leper's dinner party in Bethany who anoints Jesus' head (Mk. 14:3–9; Mt. 26:6–13), the unnamed repentant sinner at Simon the Pharisee's dinner party who wept on and washes Jesus' feet with her tears and oil and then dries them with her hair and whom Jesus forgives due to her great love (Lk. 7:36–50), and Mary of Bethany at the festive dinner after Lazarus' resurrection who anoints Jesus' feet with oil and dries them with her hair (Jn. 12:1–8)—all of which seemingly symbolize Jesus' burial—or the unnamed adulterous woman saved by Jesus from stoning (Jn. 8:1–11).

In his renowned Easter homily 33 in the late sixth century, Pope Gregory the Great assembled and blended these women into a theological mosaic to signify—that is, to interpret, ingrain, reify, and ossify—Mary Magdalene in the Western Christian theological imaginary as the previously spirit-possessed and now radically reformed yet ever-repentant sexual sinner. Albeit for pastoral purposes in politically tumultuous times, Gregory's homily equates Mary's seven demons with the totality of vices, and he describes Mary's repentance from bold speech in ways that negate her prophetic witness: "She had spoken proudly with her mouth, but in kissing the Lord's feet, she fixed it [her mouth] to the footsteps of her Redeemer."[5]

Aside from the Dominican Order of Preachers, which heralds the Magdalene as an exemplary charismatic model, the predominant portrait of Mary Magdalene in Western Christian tradition as the perpetual penitent woman is frequently reiterated in religious and popular literature, legend, and the arts. But it obscures and effaces Mary's visionary and prophetic witness, which must be recovered and restored *via positiva* through a feminist hermeneutics of remembrance.

Black Catholic womanist theologian Diana Hayes leverages the notion of subversive memory—which "contradicts the assumed reality and presents a paradoxical perspective"[6]—to retell a predominantly white history of US Christianity so that it reclaims and integrates the rich diversity of US black Catholic history, culture, and religious experience, too long marginalized, dismissed, or whitewashed in an often Protestantized field of American religion and in the at times limited hermeneutical circle of Catholic theology. Inspired by Alice Walker's definition, Hayes's womanist theology challenges predominant race, gender, class, sexual, and religious stereotypes of black women, often ostracized as "outsiders-within"[7] various communities, including Christianity. As Hayes argues:

> Black Catholic women can bring to the forefront of womanist dialogue images of Black women that contradict the dominant perspective—women such as Hagar, abused and misused by both her master and her mistress, yet taught by God how to survive in the wilderness as African-American women had to do for centuries in this land. . . . And let us not forget the two Marys: the mother of God, who had the courage and audacity to say yes to God that shattered all of human history, proclaiming in her magnificent song her awareness of her cooperation with God in an act that would change us all, and Mary Magdalene, the apostle to the apostles, as she was honored in the early church, the first to see the risen Lord rather than the fallen and lowly woman whom Jesus had to save from stoning as she has been incorrectly described for far too long.[8]

Drawing on Hayes's approach to subversive memory, a feminist hermeneutics of remembrance actively retells the subaltern multidimensional stories, vision, and praxis of Mary Magdalene, that is, re-members Mary Magdalene in Christian history and tradition by examining particularly salient scenes in biblical and extracanonical gospels, which as I will show resonate and reverberate with some scholarly, liturgical, and popular contexts as well as powerful contemporary US faith-based social movements.

Mary Magdalene cannot be reduced to the archetypical repentant sexual sinner, and cannot be used as an imitative model of silent, submissive, servile women disciples. Perhaps the sixth-century papal theological signification of the Magdalene aimed to theologically sideline and suppress the institutional church-condemned but then still popular extracanonical Gnostic *Gospel of Mary*. This gospel reveals, in Karen King's analysis, early intra-church conflicts over women's leadership, especially gendered rivalry for early church leadership. Written in Greek in the second century CE, it circulated in the third century CE and persisted in Egyptian Coptic in the fifth century CE.[9]

The *Gospel of Mary* depicts Mary Magdalene in a Christological role. Immediately after the Savior commissions the disciples to preach the good news and then departs, she greets, assuages/consoles, and instructs the other disciples (at Peter's request!) by explaining secret teachings that she received from Jesus, which grants her equal or perhaps superior spiritual and salvific knowledge (GM 4:8–10; 5:1–9; 6–7:2). Peter contends with Mary for legitimate community leadership; that is, he (along with Andrew) questions both her teachings and her relationship with Jesus. He challenged and even outright denied her personal experience of Jesus' resurrection and her prophetic commission by the risen Jesus to publicly preach and teach the gospel—to see, hear, and be empowered to share this witness (GM 6:1–2, 10:1–10).

This extracanonical gospel tradition of the Magdalene and Petrine rivalry correlates with biblical gospel traditions that portray Peter's prominence among groups of men disciples (variously described as the twelve, the seventy, etc.) involved in Jesus' public ministry, in identifying Jesus as the Messiah (Mt. 16:13–19), and in the leadership of the Jerusalem church. Yet, as Sandra Schneiders elaborates, the biblical gospel accounts about Peter's leadership also feature Jesus correcting Peter's leadership style of hierarchical exclusionary power over others. He often chastises Peter for his false primacy, superiority, and insularity and instead models for Peter how to enact servant leadership (i.e., not to judge or exclude others but to welcome all, to wash each other's feet, etc.).[10] Moreover, in John, Peter's leadership is downplayed; he takes second place to the beloved disciple at the last supper (Jn. 13:24–25), in the race to the empty tomb (Jn. 19:35), and in recognizing the post-resurrection Jesus (Jn. 20:3–8). Thus, this Magdalene-Petrine rivalry echoes these other scriptural precedents, which record, as Elaine Pagels observes, rivalries between competing Christian groups, such as Petrine and Johannine Christians; Johannine and Thomas Christians; and now Magdalene Christians, who revere these particular apostles as figurative leaders.[11]

Mentioned thirteen times in the New Testament, Mary leads almost every gospel list of prominent women disciples who followed Jesus' itinerant ministry, except for Jn. 19:25, which lists his mother first among the women who stood at the cross. As Amy-Jill Levine argues, Mary epitomized or typified multiple options for first-century Jewish women: she enjoyed economic savvy and autonomy, freedom of time and travel, and the ability to appear and speak in public in a time when women's public witness was denigrated and debased.[12] Identified with the seaside fishing town of Magdala, or Migdal, on the western side of the Sea of Galilee and not by patriarchal relations, which likely signals her independent status and her break with home and family to join the Jesus movement, Mary was healed, was liberated from spirit/demon possession through Jesus' ministry of exorcism. Subsequently, she, with other Galilean and Judean women disciples (e.g., Joanna, Susanna, Martha and Mary of Bethany, "and many others"), financially patronized, supported, or in other ways backed, as well as participated in, the Jesus movement and its teaching, preaching, healing, and table fellowship ministries out of their own resources (Lk. 8:1–3, 10:38–42).

In both Roman and Eastern Catholic Churches, Mary is portrayed as a model prominent disciple, prophet, visionary, and leader, and is renowned as the Apostle to (or of) the Apostles as a result of her primary witness to and preaching about the resurrection (Mk. 15:40–16:11, Mt. 27:55–28:10, and Jn. 19:25–20:18). Mary Rose D'Angelo and

Barbara Reid note Luke's limits on women's roles in the resurrection story; the women do not encounter the risen Jesus and are not commissioned by him to announce the resurrection to the disciples (Lk. 24:1–12, 22–24).[13] Nonetheless, the gospels agree that Mary accompanied Jesus throughout the Paschal events; that is, she witnessed his crucifixion, death, and burial; waited and watched at his tomb with other myrrh-bearing women (who vary in each gospel's telling) to anoint Jesus' body; discovered and encountered the open empty tomb in the pre-dawn hours; primarily eyewitnessed[14] and was commissioned to prophetically proclaim Jesus' resurrection and future ministry in Galilee, not only once but in an ongoing way (to "all the rest" e.g., Lk. 24:9, 22–24); and attended Passover and later Pentecost gatherings with other disciples and thus was empowered and vivified by the Spirit to preach the gospel.[15]

As Barbara Reid observes, prophetic witness, especially but not only by women, is typically rejected.[16] Jesus was kicked out of the Nazareth synagogue, driven out of town, and threatened with death for prophetic preaching (Lk. 4:16–30). Also, in Luke's telling, Mary and the women are terrified at the empty tomb but are encouraged by the angels to remember Jesus' preaching and ministry; the angels announce the resurrection to the women, and the women in turn preach the resurrection to the disciples. Mary gives the good news to the disciples, but, in Luke's (and also Mark's) telling, her continued prophetic witness, which makes significant theological and Christological claims, is doubted and dismissed by them as an idle tale (Mk. 16:11; Lk. 24:10–11). Moreover, Mary is rejected as a suitable apostolic replacement for Judas among the 120 persons in Acts 1:12–26, although she fulfilled the requisite criteria of personal confession of and experiential encounter with the risen Jesus as well as prophetic witness to the gospel. In both the extracanonical *Gospel of Mary* and in Luke, the good news is delivered by Mary but incites controversy; it is contested and must be patriarchally confirmed by Peter, who is amazed upon seeing the empty tomb and only later receives an appearance of the risen Jesus (Lk. 24:34).

In John's telling,[17] Mary's persistent prophetic witness is still not believed. Peter and the beloved disciple competitively race to the empty tomb to confirm the resurrection (only the beloved disciple is reported to see and believe in Jn. 20:8, but they do not see the risen Jesus). Yet, then the narrative shifts. Mary stays and mourns at the tomb alone after Peter and the beloved disciple abruptly left, almost as quickly as they fled the scene of Jesus' arrest and execution. She encounters two angels in the empty tomb and then a supposed gardener, both of whom she audaciously asks for the body of Jesus (to presumably anoint and re-bury), and then sees and greets the risen Jesus himself (who offers her an alternative future plan!). She recognizes the risen Jesus through her tears when he calls her name. In this brief moment of tearful recognition and joyful reunion, Jesus gives Mary, in my view, a twofold commission: first, not to hold on or cling to him since he can no longer be localized or circumscribed as the risen Jesus of Nazareth but is now radically universally present as the cosmic Christ, and, second, to boldly go and tell, to proclaim the good news to the disciples and to the world. Part of Mary's ministry involves globalizing the good news ("I have seen the Lord") to the whole people of God, which strengthens the other disciples for their future encounter with the risen Jesus and for their new post-Easter ministries among and with all nations. Mary functions as a prophetic leader in the early Christian community, because, as womanist theologians claim, God has made a way out of no way for her, God has encouraged her toward a new way of seeing, a new way of envisioning, empowering, and enacting a new life with new future possibilities.

The twenty-three Eastern Catholic Churches in communion with Rome uphold this powerful portrait of Mary's prophetic witness. As a Catholic feminist theologian, I inhabit and struggle to survive, negotiate, and thrive at the intersections of creative tension, of critical engagement with yet creative appropriation of both Roman and Eastern Catholic traditions in the United States. I am a cradle (born and raised) member of the Byzantine Catholic Church in America (specifically Carpatho-Rusyn or Ruthenian) but was socialized throughout my education in a bi-ritual way in both Roman and Byzantine Catholic Churches. The Byzantine Catholic Church in the United States consists of an archeparchy led by an archbishop (in Pittsburgh, Pennsylvania), three other eparchies led by bishops (Passaic, New Jersey; Parma, Ohio; and Phoenix, Arizona), and SS. Cyril and Methodius Seminary (in Pittsburgh, Pennsylvania). Because of this background, I am equally liturgically and theologically accustomed to statues and icons, holy water and incense, instrumental or *a cappella* music, notions of salvation as justification/sanctification and transfiguration, and so on. However, I am also equally liturgically and theologically alienated in both traditions by egalitarian ideals that get implemented as exclusive theologies and practices.

Byzantine Catholics revere Mary's praxis of resurrection witness and gospel proclamation during the Holy Saturday vigil service, called Resurrection Matins.[18] Also known as Paschal Matins, this service (without epistle, gospel reading, sermon, or Eucharist) consists primarily of the celebrant, cantor/choir, and people initially participating in a procession that recalls the myrrh-bearing women's journey to and wait at the tomb, followed by singing *a cappella* the canon or liturgical poem of St. John Damascene (d. 749), as well as chanting some Psalms (specifically the praises from Ps. 148–150), all of which is interspersed with litanies and hymns. Excerpts from Damascene's canon in the Resurrection Matins emphasize the theologically significant role of the Magdalene's prophetic witness.

> The women with Mary before the dawn found the stone rolled away from the tomb, and they heard the angel say: "Why do you seek among the dead, as a mortal, the One who abides in everlasting light? Behold the linens of burial. Go in haste and proclaim to the world that, having conquered Death, the Lord is risen; for he is the Son of God, the Savior of all."—Hymn after Ode 3[19]
> Christ is risen from the dead! Pious women ran in tears to you, O Christ, bringing myrrh to you as dead; but instead, they adored you in joy as the living God and announced your mystical Passover to your disciples.—Stanza in Ode 7[20]

Whether received from the angel or the risen Jesus, Mary fulfills this prophetic commission by saying to the other disciples: "I have seen the Lord." In the Resurrection Matins, Byzantine Catholics are cast in that same Magdalene role and continue her commission by repeatedly singing Christ is Risen throughout the service.

The Resurrection Matins also include praises based on the Psalms, and hymns called the Paschal *stichera*. During the *stichera*, the people akin to the Magdalene venerate the cross, gospel book, and icon of the resurrection and then announce the good news in multiple languages per church tradition and per Pentecost.

> Celebrant: Christ is risen! Response: Indeed he is risen!
> Christós voskrése! Voístinnu voskrése! (Slavonic)
> Christós anésti! Alithós anésti! (Greek)
> Al Maseeh Qam! Haqqan Qam! (Arabic)
> Kristus vstal zmr'tvych! Skutočne vstal! (Slovak)
> Krisztus feltámadt! Valóban feltámadt! (Hungarian)
> Hristus a Înviat! Adeverat a Înviat! (Romanian)
> Cristo ha resucitado! En verdad, está resucitado! (Spanish)

Some *stichera* specifically recall the Magdalene commission and the people's role in continuing it.

> O women, be the heralds of good news and tell what you saw; tell of the vision, and say to Zion: "Accept the good news of joy from us, the news that Christ has risen." Exult and celebrate and rejoice, O Jerusalem, seeing Christ the King, coming forth from the tomb like a bridegroom.
> Pasch so delightful, Pasch of the Lord, is the Pasch—most honored Pasch now dawned on us. It is the Pasch! Therefore, let us joyfully embrace one another. O Passover, save us from sorrow; for today, Christ has shown forth from the tomb as from a bridal chamber and filled the women with joy by saying: Announce the good news to the Apostles.[21]

Francine Cardman examined Mary Magdalene in different Western and Eastern Christian historical, cultural, and liturgical contexts as a lightning rod for understanding those particular times' and places' contextual and pastoral needs.[22] At the advent of the twenty-first century, Diane Apostolos-Cappadona suggested that interest in the Magdalene resurged in the aftermath of the 9/11 terror attacks in the United States, when loved ones lacked a body to mourn and bury, and instead faced an empty tomb but yet hoped to be gifted like the Magdalene with the affirmation of new life.[23] In our own time, aside from the Magdalene's popularity in cultural, pious, and ecclesial imaginaries, disrupting and dismantling the Magdalene tradition's negative effective history *via negativa* continues in the liturgy; the arts, including film; and anti-sexual violence movements in order to restore *via positiva* the Magdalene's image and consequently enhance women's status. Pope Paul VI in 1969 changed the liturgical lectionary readings about Mary Magdalene from the unnamed penitent woman in Luke to Mary's witness of the resurrection in John. Fifty years later, resurgent interest in Mary Magdalene occurs in our own day and demonstrates the intersection of a newly released film with the #MeToo movement.

In 2019, Focus Films released the film *Mary Magdalene*, which rehabilitates Mary's image as the misrepresented penitent sex worker that has predominated in Christian theology, devotion, legend, art, literature, drama, and film. In the film, Mary is portrayed as the apostle to/of the apostles, is involved in what the *Guardian*'s review calls "a platonic apostle-mance" with Jesus,[24] and is cast as a primary witness to the important events and major purpose of his ministry, death, and resurrection. In a revisionist twist, the film's screenwriters stylize Mary as an unmarried midwife who is considered mad because she rejects marriage and prays alongside men in the synagogue; her father and brothers punitively subject Mary to a failed midnight seaside exorcism ritual to rid her of her so-called demon of resistance to patriarchal familial and religious norms and practices. She encounters Jesus after barely surviving this violent ritual, is baptized by him, and then leaves her family to follow him. In another feminist twist, the film was distributed by the Weinstein Co., bankrupted and sold as a result of Harvey Weinstein's three decades of sexual harassment, assault, and abuse of allegedly hundreds of aspiring actresses, journalists, and models that re-ignited the #MeToo movement, in addition to civil and class-action lawsuits as well as criminal investigations and charges against Weinstein. As previously mentioned, Mary's prophetic witness to the resurrection and to the ongoing post-Easter Jesus movement's ministries is recorded in the biblical and extracanonical gospels as disbelieved, dismissed as nonsense (Mk. 16:11, Lk. 24:11, GM 10:1–10). Likewise, the #MeToo movement that was created by civil rights and anti-sexual violence activist Tarana Burke in 2006 for young women of color in marginalized communities resurged in 2017 with an albeit whitewashed Hollywood celebrity focus which sidelined women of color, including queer and trans folxs. #MeToo lifts up women's and all survivors' testimonies for the purpose of empowerment and healing through empathy and transformative justice, because survivors of all genders are still discounted and disregarded.[25]

Exactly one year after Weinstein's disgraced downfall due to countless survivors' testimonies, Dr. Christine Blasey Ford of Palo Alto University and Stanford University demonstrated personal and political courage to publicly testify before the US Senate Judiciary Committee about her accusations of sexual assault against then US Supreme Court nominee Brett Kavanaugh. In solidarity with Amanda de Cadenet, Glennon Doyle, Tracee Ellis Ross, and America Ferrera, Tarana Burke @MeTooMVMT issued a love letter to Dr. Ford, expressing gratitude and support for her political courage. Despite Ford's compelling testimony of traumatic events from the early 1980s, Justice Kavanaugh was narrowly confirmed to the US Supreme Court. He sits on the high court alongside another fellow Catholic, Justice Clarence Thomas. Nearly three decades ago in 1991, Professor Anita Hill of Brandeis University, then a University of Oklahoma law professor, testified during the US Senate Judiciary Committee hearing for Justice Thomas about her allegations of sexual harassment against him. The Kavanaugh hearings recalled the Thomas hearings, with a Senate committee that feigned an understanding of and sensitivity to sexual violence but instead interrogated or outright grilled survivors about their credibility, their allegations (in graphic detail!), and their lack of reporting. Both hearings, as Professor Hill observed, chose a politically expedient end rather than a fully transparent process with an independent third-party investigation.[26]

When women prophetically announce good news or denounce bad news, they are disbelieved; nevertheless, they persist. Moreover, when women stand in solidarity for racial, gender, sexual, and social justice and for broad civil and human rights, they are interrupted, rebuked, silenced, criminalized, and politically disenfranchised as nonpersons, with chants like "lock her up" and more recently "send her back"; nevertheless, they persist. On February 7, 2017, Senator Elizabeth Warren incorporated into her speech on the US Senate floor a 1986 letter and statement from Coretta Scott King in order to oppose Attorney General nominee Senator Jeff Sessions. Senate Majority Leader Mitch McConnell interrupted her speech, citing a Senate rule about inappropriate speech that impugns another Senator. In her exchange with McConnell, Warren protested the exclusion of Coretta Scott King's words, witness, and testimony from the Senate's deliberative debate. "She was warned. She was given an explanation. Nevertheless, she persisted," said McConnell. After Warren was silenced and barred from participating during the rest of the Sessions debate on the Senate floor, Warren finished her speech, including the letter and statement, outside the Senate on Facebook. Warren's savvy strategy created an alternative more inclusive and just counterspace for political discussion and debate to continue, as well as galvanized further racial and gender solidarity not only about women's political participation and leadership but moreso about civil and human rights. Paraphrasing her mother Coretta Scott King who linked women with saving the soul of the nation, Bernice King thanked Warren on Twitter for being the soul of the Senate during the Sessions hearing. Warren critically and creatively—innovatively—turned a rebuke into an intersectional feminist rallying cry: nevertheless, she persisted.

Where do we see the Magdalene tradition of prophetic public witness carried on, continued, persisting in dynamic ways today? According to Sandra Schneiders and Mary Ann Hinsdale, Mary Magdalene's ecclesial leadership and ministry is not limited to her but creates a biblical and historical tradition for those who continue to embody that Magdalene tradition of preaching the good news for the purpose of the well-being and flourishing of the whole body of Christ, for the whole people of God.[27] The rest of this essay builds on these theological insights about Mary Magdalene's prophetic witness *via positiva*, and paves new paths for women doing political/public theology today, especially by tending to those social movements that offer an alternative possible future beyond our presently oppressive status quo.

PUBLIC THEOLOGY

Public theology religiously vivifies our political dialogue, deliberative debate, and decision making about pressing issues that impact US common life and that enhance human dignity and rights, justice, and the common good. In the US Catholic context, women's religio-political witness operates in the highly contested site of who and what counts as the authoritative agents and practices of public Catholicism.

Catholic public theology is often equated with institutional church leaders' or spokespersons' statements about the so-called non-negotiable beginning and end of life issues for Catholic voters (e.g., abortion, embryonic stem cell research, euthanasia, human cloning, and same-sex marriage), emphasized since the 2004 US presidential election and amplified since 2012 in the US Conference of Catholic Bishops–sponsored Fortnight for Freedom, recently renamed Religious Freedom Week. In this context, women are disregarded as public theologians for Christological reasons. Women are barred from imitating and resignifying Christ in episcopal leadership positions, and thus are excluded from public ministry, from doing public theology.

By contrast, Vatican II's Constitution on the Church in the Modern World associates the Church's faith-based public engagement with realizing the already-present but always ever-coming eschatological reign of God, that is, the good society of love, justice, and peace. This constitution identifies the Church's public role as a critical advocate for a broad social justice agenda that seeks to subvert injustice and inequality along gender, race, class, socio-political, religious, and inter/national lines. To enact this agenda, this constitution calls for emulating the prophetic life-ministry of Jesus. Living out a political kind of discipleship based on Jesus' prophetic lifework for the kingdom of God serves as a theological touchstone for women to reclaim their baptismal and religio-political rights to faith-based activism for justice in the US public sphere.[28]

US Catholic sisters' social and eco-justice ministries have stood at the forefront of such prophetic praxis. Prophetic praxis often entails nonviolent, grassroots, collective action that confronts the prevalent socio-political order and also attempts to educate about and partly actualize an alternative possibility to it by forging solidarity with marginalized groups, thereby edging us toward a more inclusive, transformative, and just quality of life.

In my prior scholarship, I have highlighted the sisters' political praxis, especially NETWORK's Nuns on the Bus road trips, as a refreshing resource for a constructive feminist public theology.[29] The Nuns on the Bus tours from 2012 to 2018 illustrate the prophetic political praxis of US Catholic women, firmly founded on Catholic theological commitments to solidarity, the option for the poor, and the common good. The nuns' activism prophetically witnesses to an alternative political reality; the tours re/imagine and re/create a more interdependent, interconnected sense of community, thereby generating or bringing to birth possibilities for renewed common life amid a deeply divided US body politic.[30]

Birthing a new world resists *both* Catholic magisterial anthropologies, which essentialize and politicize women's bio-physical abilities to give birth, *and* traditionalist political ideologies, which domesticize and thereby disqualify women as citizens in the public sphere and instead portray their interests as aligned solely with the nonpolitical or private sphere, that is, with the reproduction of future citizens. Rather than concede to patriarchal theologies and politics, birthing metaphors can be reclaimed for their religio-political salience. Birthing metaphors need not be trapped in and need not entrap women in a reductive view of reproductivity. For example, biblical texts describe all creation groaning (in travail, in childbirth) for fulfillment, that is, for a just and peaceful society (Rom. 8:18–23). Together with creation and the cosmos, all are called to play a part in actively creating, generating, or birthing a new society. From this feminist and Magdalene-inspired perspective, creativity broadens, deepens, and democratizes the agents and the doing of public theology. Women are enabled to reclaim their right to do public theology through religio-political prophetic praxis of creating communities of justice and peace.

In scriptural prophetic traditions, God re-members; that is, God sees, hears, and acts for the well-being and eventual liberation of the oppressed. According to Dianne Bergant, the needs of the people determine through whom God works, often in unconventional means and methods.[31] Prophets are perennially needed to edge our seemingly intransigent racist, global capitalist, heterosexist, and patriarchal religious and political institutions toward right, loving, and just relations with multiply minoritized, marginalized, and disenfranchised peoples.

The encounter between Jesus and the Samaritan woman (Jn. 4:7–42), cited by NETWORK's Executive Director Sr. Simone Campbell, models women's innovative and prophetic intercultural and interreligious religio-political engagement that moves toward such right and just relations.[32] As a multiply disadvantaged foreign women with a complex sexual history hailing from a minoritized religious community and cultural background, the unnamed Samaritan woman transgresses these socio-cultural, religious, gender, and sexual borders and addresses Jesus' basic needs by drawing him some water from Jacob's well. Alone in public at the well, their conversation progresses, as Mary Catherine Hilkert describes, from reflections about personal identity and differing religious practices to theological debate about the presence of God.[33] She announces this good news of God's presence in Jesus to her Samaritan neighbors, who also see and believe through her witness. Like Mary Magdalene, the Samaritan woman is energized by this encounter to prophetically testify to what she has seen and heard and is empowered to act upon it to change others' lives.

Women's public or religio-political engagement taps a shared human capacity for creativity, and women's approaches to public theology stress a prophetic and solidarity-based praxis, which opens up a new vista for our theo-political imagination and activism, especially in interreligious, intercultural ways. Doing public theology interreligiously takes place in contemporary social movements like the Revolutionary Love Project.

REVOLUTIONARY LOVE PROJECT

Mary Magdalene's prophetic witness gives fresh insights into a feminist public theology of love and justice, with implications for the role and purpose of religion in US public and political life. The Magdalene's witness in pre-dawn places, between death and new life, accentuates that we live in liminal times, in the times between an oppressive present and an alternative more just future, in the spaces between seemingly perennially polarized groups. These interstitial times and spaces offer opportunities for new perspectives and movements to arise and build solidarity, especially but not only articulated and lead by marginalized peoples.[34]

In my view, The Revolutionary Love Project exemplifies women's faith-based public engagement for prophetic worldmaking, that is, the fusion of religion and politics to denounce and criticize an unjust US public life, on the one hand, and to announce and actualize—imagine and partly incarnate, or envision and enflesh—an alternative more just liberative world, on the other hand. Witnessing to a more just common life takes place in single leaders and social movements that induce through their praxis the birthpangs of the reign of God (Rom. 8:18–23).

Valarie Kaur stands out among contemporary religious leaders in the US public square involved in prophetic work.[35] Kaur is a Sikh activist, award-winning documentary filmmaker, and civil rights lawyer who partnered with communities of color (Sikh, Muslim, Black, Latinx, LGBTQ+, and indigenous peoples) since the 9/11 terrorist attacks and since the November 2016 US presidential election to oppose the rise in Islamophobic and white nationalist hate crimes. Emerging from this solidarity work, Kaur launched the Revolutionary Love Project (RLP) in 2016, housed at the University of Southern California Office of Religious Life.[36] RLP sponsored a multi-city nationwide Together Tour before the 2016 US presidential election that emphasized love as a public ethic that opposes racism, nationalism, and hate directed at Sikh, Muslim, and Asian American communities. After the election, Kaur collaborated with many movement leaders to host a Watch Night Service at the historic Metropolitan AME Church in Washington, DC, on New Year's Eve in which millions nationwide participated, as well as coordinated a fast, multifaith prayer gathering, and march on Inauguration Day. In 2017, RLP sponsored 100 film screenings, workshops, and keynotes for college students, as well as lobbied Congressional leaders to oppose multiple versions of the US Muslim travel ban (which recalled the US Supreme Court Korematsu decision that justified Japanese American incarceration in World War II) along with other discriminatory immigration and refugee policies, such as racial profiling and surveillance, special registries, detention and family separation, deportation, and border walls. After the mass shootings of Sikhs in the gurdwara in Oak Creek, African American Christians in Mother Emanuel AME Church in Charleston, Jews at the Tree of Life Synagogue in Pittsburgh, and Muslims at Christchurch, New Zealand mosques, RLP stood on the frontlines, echoing the Magdalene's witness, in my view: "Through our tears, we must act swiftly."

RLP's activities through 2020 spanned, for example, a book, book clubs and accompanying reading guides about racial justice and solidarity; media (e.g., podcasts, virtual meditations, film, and TV, including an Emmy-award winning episode on Sikhs in America for CNN's United Shades of America); an annual conference for more than 300 grassroots leaders and a Sikh women leaders retreat; and, grassroots nonviolent direct action campaigns, such as keynotes, anti-racism workshops, sermons in multifaith communities, get out the vote rallies, and letters of love and solidarity to immigrants, especially but not only women and children, seeking asylum at the US border. RLP co-sponsored a solidarity rally with the Poor People's Campaign on June 23, 2018, 200 dialogues about practicing revolutionary love as well as 2,000 #VoteTogether gatherings during the US Congressional midterm elections in Fall 2018. Also, Kaur organized with thirty-two diverse women leaders the third annual Women's March on January 19, 2019. All these activities oppose intersectional injustices of racism, poverty, militarism, sexism, and ecological devastation that manifest in the rollback of voting rights, women's rights, immigrant rights, health care, and climate change policies. Most importantly, these activities embody love as a public ethic that births a new future.

Kaur delivered a highly acclaimed TEDTalk during the TEDWomen gathering in New Orleans, Louisiana, in November 2017 which elaborated a feminist love ethic. Titled "Three Lessons of Revolutionary Love in a Time of Rage," this one million-plus-viewed talk[37] also informed Kaur's address to the 2018 Parliament of the World's Religions. In this PWR address, she reiterated this ethic's three main practices of love of others, opponents, and ourselves to over 8,000 attendees, whom she described as "midwives . . . tasked with birthing a new future for all of us . . . [who] labor for justice with and through love together . . . [who] can begin to deliver the world we dream," a world that is multiracial, multicultural, multifaith, and rooted in revolutionary love seeking justice.[38] Since its inception, RLP has joined with about 550 organizations annually on Valentine's Day to reach 14 million+ people, both personally and virtually, to reclaim love as a public ethic. RLP partnered with more than fifty organizations for the V-Day activities in February 2019, including NETWORK, CLUE, and other interfaith and faith-based groups, to articulate its three practices in a Declaration of Revolutionary Love.[39]

Both of Kaur's talks examine this three-pronged feminist love ethic and its public practices, which she described at the PWR as "a human birthright, a kind of labor that all of us are capable of," to advance and enhance a more just world for all. Kaur states in her TEDTalk, "Revolutionary love is the choice to enter into labor for others who do not look like us, for our opponents who hurt us, and for ourselves. . . . Love must be practiced in all three directions to be revolutionary."

First, love for others entails a practice, Kaur states, of seeing no stranger. Listening to others' stories in humility and in wonder enables us to see no stranger, to challenge the stereotypes that distort our vision of "black as criminal, of brown as illegal, of queer and trans as immoral, of indigenous peoples as savage, and of women and girls as property," and ultimately to stand in solidarity with others, to labor with others through vigils, marches, and other forms of political participation and engagement. In my view, seeing no stranger, which Kaur claims is "a part of me I do not yet know," evokes a new theological anthropology, or religious understanding of the human person, not as a ruggedly independent individual but as inherently interrelated in and with all communities of origin and of solidarity, including the Earth community. As the Declaration of Revolutionary Love proclaims, "we vow to see one another as brothers, sisters, and siblings. Our humanity binds us together, and we vow to fight for a world where all of us can flourish."

Second, love for opponents necessitates a practice, Kaur argues, of tending the wound. Tending the wound in others, even enemies, entails moral and pragmatic practices; it reveals oppressive systems and structures that normalize and radicalize harm as well as erode the capability to love. As stated in the Declaration of Revolutionary Love, "We vow to fight not with violence and vitriol, but by challenging the cultures and institutions that promote hate." Beyond resisting and replacing bad political actors and policies, birthing a new just world begins by tending personal and socio-political wounds, by challenging and remaking those intersectional systems and structures of injustice that collide and collude in all of us and in our world to de-create, to undo all of our belonging and flourishing.

Third, love for ourselves is characterized by Kaur as the practice of breathe and push. Love for others and oppressors requires self-love, as Kaur says to "love our own flesh" and "make our own flourishing matter." Self-love takes place in community in order to fully embrace ourselves and push through these hostile times together. Self-love in community is emphasized in the Declaration of Revolutionary Love: "We will protect our capacity for joy. We will rise and dance. We will honor our ancestors whose bodies, breath, and blood call us to a life of courage." Also, practicing self-love inspired Kaur to release in Spring 2019 a meditation app with four tracks, titled Breathe and Push, that stress connections between self-care (breathing together) and community care (pushing together for change).

Kaur notes that the "labor for justice . . . [will be] so much harder, so much longer, and so much more painful, not for the next few years, but for decades to come." Like the Magdalene, Kaur offers encouragement to persevere and persist in these bleak times. Merging similar ideas from both her talks, which Kaur initially developed for her Watch Night address, Kaur states:

> What if this darkness in the world is not the darkness of the tomb, but what if it is the darkness of the womb? What if our future, our America is not dead but is a country, a nation still waiting to be born? What if a new world is waiting to be born? . . . What if the story of America is one long labor? . . . What if this is our nation's, our time of great transition? The midwife tells us to breathe and then to push. Because if we don't push we will die. If we don't breathe we will die. If we don't push now, our nation will die. Tonight we will breathe, tomorrow we will labor. Revolutionary Loves requires that we breathe and push through the fire.[40]

Although Kaur outlined this feminist love ethic by drawing on Sikh theology and the writings of Black feminist bell hooks and others, RLP unexpectedly parallels what I have outlined here as the Magdalene tradition as a basis for women's ways of doing public theology.

Mary watched and waited at Jesus' tomb to anoint his buried body, to tend his bodily wounds inflicted by imperial indignities and injustices of Roman crucifixion. Black Catholic womanist theologian M. Shawn Copeland articulates a political Christology in which the body of the crucified Jesus refracts the wounds inflicted on marginalized peoples by contemporary empires.[41] Opposition and otherness based on dominant and subordinate relations along race, gender, class, religious, sexual, and many other marks of our differences in turn justify assault, conquest, occupation, detention, torture, incarceration, sexual shame and abuse, even execution. Prophetic social movements identify and tend these wounds in order to effect social change and justice.

Moreover, Mary experienced multiple turnings or conversions to new ways of seeing—from the grief and loss of the empty tomb to seeing through her tears with new eyes no stranger and no gardener, but the risen Jesus, and ultimately to seeing beyond Jesus, to take what she has seen and heard and to prophetically proclaim the good news, repeatedly, to all. Seeing no stranger creates new visions of life-giving communities that as Copeland states "re-order us, re-member us, restore us, and make us one" not only in the body of Christ, but also in the US body politic.[42]

Finally, self-love and communal solidarity occur together, as illustrated by Kaur's questions in her PWR address: "How are you breathing today? . . . Who are you breathing with . . . with the ones you love . . . with the earth, sea, and sky . . . with some of the ancestors at your back? . . . Can you breathe in order to remember all that is beautiful and good and worth fighting for?" In deeply distressing times, Mary regrouped with the women disciples in the Jesus movement. They waited, grieved, organized, and mobilized their ongoing witness together, that is, their self-love empowered them to envision, preach about, and realize new life in post-Easter ministries.

CONCLUSION

In sum, the Magdalene tradition continues in women's prophetic witness and praxis in contemporary US faith-based social movements like the Nuns on the Bus and the Revolutionary Love Project that begin to birth a new world that supports and safeguards civil and human rights for all people of all genders, races/ethnicities, classes, orientations, abilities, and religions. A concluding reflective exercise inspired by the RLP will aid us in doing the community building, the worldmaking, of a feminist public theology, that is, to imagine and incarnate, to envision and enflesh, a more just world for the flourishing of all. Kaur guides us in this exercise:

> Close your eyes. Can you feel it? What does it feel like in your body to live in that future? How would your life be different? How would it change the lives of the people you love? If we can inhabit this vision in our minds and bodies, then we can birth it.[43]

Building on its trifold public ethic of love which links personal and sociopolitical change, RLP leads the way in such worldmaking by planning a People's Inauguration in 2021. Starting on January 21, 2021, and continuing into the following week, the People's Inauguration will encourage all people to individually and collectively take oaths to recommit to one another, to core moral values, and to themselves, in order to envision and enact a US public life that is inclusive, anti-racist, equitable, and sustainable for the common good of all of "we, the people."

NOTES

1. This essay is based on an invited talk titled "Nevertheless, She Persisted: Women's Religio-Political Witness for Love and Justice," which I delivered for the annual Magdala Lecture at Boston College, July 19, 2019. I am so honored to stand among the women witnesses in the communion of saints who delivered the prior Magdala lectures and constructed different portraits of the Magdalene.

2. Rosemary P. Carbine, "Critical Constructive Theology as a Praxis of Worldmaking," *Critical Theology: Engaging Church, Culture, and Society* 1, no. 1 (Fall 2018): 8–12.

3. Mary Ann Hinsdale, "St. Mary of Magdala: Ecclesiological Provocations," *CTSA Proceedings* 66 (2011): 67–90, esp. 73–74 n.19 and 76 n.26.

4. Sandra M. Schneiders, "Encountering the Risen Jesus: Mary Magdalene as Prototype," Magdala Lecture, July 19, 2013, https://www.bc.edu/content/dam/bc1/schools/stm/continuing%20education/encore/pdf/mary-magdala-2013.pdf.

5. Homily 33 in *Forty Gospel Homilies by Gregory the Great*, trans. Dom Hurst (Piscataway, NJ: Gorgias Press, 2009), 268–79, at 270.

6. Diana L. Hayes, *Standing in the Shoes My Mother Made: A Womanist Theology* (Minneapolis, MN: Fortress Press, 2010), 17.

7. Hayes, *Standing in the Shoes My Mother Made*, 15–16.

8. Hayes, *Standing in the Shoes My Mother Made*, 13–14.

9. Karen L. King, *The Gospel of Mary of Magdala: Jesus and the First Woman Apostle* (Santa Rosa, CA: Polebridge, 2003).

10. Schneiders, "Encountering the Risen Jesus."

11. Elaine Pagels, *Beyond Belief: The Secret Gospel of Thomas* (New York: Vintage, 2004), 48–73.

12. Amy-Jill Levine, "Telling Stories about Women," Magdala Lecture, July 22, 2016, https://www.bc.edu/content/bc-web/schools/stm/sites/encore/main/2016/stories-women.html.

13. Mary Rose D'Angelo, "Reconstructing 'Real' Women in Gospel Literature: The Case of Mary Magdalene," and "(Re)Presentations of Women in the Gospel of Matthew and Luke-Acts," in *Women and Christian Origins*, ed. Ross Shepard Kraemer and Mary Rose D'Angelo (New York: Oxford University Press, 1999), 105–28, 180–91. Also, Barbara Reid, "Mary Magdalene and the Women Disciples in the Gospel of Luke," Magdala Lecture, July 21, 2017, https://www.bc.edu/content/dam/bc1/schools/stm/continuing%20education/encore/pdf/Mary%20Magdala%20Day%202017%2C%20Transcript%20of%20Barbara%20Reid%20Lecture.pdf.

14. For scholarly studies of the first witnesses of the resurrection of Jesus, see Hinsdale, "St. Mary of Magdala," 74–75 n.22.

15. Jane Schaberg, *The Resurrection of Mary Magdalene: Legends, Apocrypha, and the Christian Testament* (New York: Continuum, 2002).

16. Reid, "Mary Magdalene and the Women Disciples in the Gospel of Luke."

17. Sandra M. Schneiders, *Written That You May Believe: Encountering Jesus in the Fourth Gospel* (New York: Crossroad, 1999), and "Encountering the Risen Jesus."

18. *Matins of the Resurrection* (Pittsburgh, PA: Metropolitan Cantor Institute, 2011).

19. Recording available at https://mci.archpitt.org/recordings/ResurrectionMatins/07Hypakoje.mp3.

20. Recording available at https://mci.archpitt.org/recordings/ResurrectionMatins/13ResurrectionCanonOde7.mp3.

21. Recording available at https://mci.archpitt.org/recordings/ResurrectionMatins/18ThePaschalStichera.mp3.

22. Francine Cardman, "Mary Magdalene: Pieces of A Natural History," Magdala Lecture, July 20, 2018, https://www.bc.edu/content/dam/bc1/schools/stm/continuing%20education/encore/pdf/Mary%20Magdala%20Day%202018%2C%20Transcript%20of%20Francine%20Cardman%20Lecture.pdf.

23. In the documentary film *Dan Burstein's Secrets of Mary Magdalene*, directed by Rob Fruchtman (New York: Hidden Treasures Productions, 2006).

24. Peter Bradshaw, "Mary Magdalene Review—Toothless Attempt to Overturn Sunday School Myths," *The Guardian*, February 27, 2018, https://www.theguardian.com/film/2018/feb/27/mary-magdalene-review-rooney-mara-sunday-school-myths.

25. Rosanna Maule, "'Not Just a Movement for Famous White Cisgendered Women': #Me Too and Intersectionality," *Gender and Women's Studies* 2, no. 3 (2020): 4. I thank my student Sumitra Bernardo for this reference.

26. Anita Hill, "How to Get the Kavanaugh Hearings Right," *New York Times*, September 19, 2018, https://www.nytimes.com/2018/09/18/opinion/anita-hill-brett-kavanaugh-clarence-thomas.html.

27. Schneiders, "Encountering the Risen Jesus," and Hinsdale, "St. Mary of Magdala."

28. Rosemary P. Carbine, "'Artisans of a New Humanity': Revisioning the Public Church in a Feminist Perspective," in *Frontiers in Catholic Feminist Theology: Shoulder to Shoulder*, ed. Susan Abraham and Elena Procario-Foley (Minneapolis, MN: Fortress Press, 2009), 173–92.

29. Rosemary P. Carbine, "Creating Communities of Justice and Peace: Sacramentality and U.S. Public Catholicism," *Journal for the Academic Study of Religion* 29, no. 2 (2016); and "Birthing a New World: Women, Sacramentality, and the U.S. Public Church," *The Ecumenist: A Journal of Theology, Culture, and Society* 50, no. 2 (Spring 2013): 5–12.

30. Simone Campbell, *A Nun on the Bus: How All of Us Can Create Hope, Change, and Community* (New York: HarperCollins, 2014).

31. Dianne Bergant, "Women in the Old Testament: Then and Now," Magdala Lecture, July 22, 2010, https://www.bc.edu/content/dam/bc1/schools/stm/continuing%20education/encore/pdf/mary-magdala-2010.pdf.

32. Simone Campbell, "Politics, Faith, and Prophetic Witness," Annual Evelyn Underhill Lecture in Christian Spirituality, Boston College, July 12, 2014, https://www.bc.edu/bc-web/schools/stm/sites/encore/main/2014/politics-faith.html.

33. M. Catherine Hilkert, "On the Strength of Her Testimony," Magdala Lecture, July 22, 2015, https://www.bc.edu/content/bc-web/schools/stm/sites/encore/main/2015/strength-testimony.html.

34. Rosemary P. Carbine, "Public Theology: A Feminist Anthropological View of Political Subjectivity and Praxis," in *Questioning the Human: Toward a Theological Anthropology for the 21st Century*, ed. Lieven Bove, Yves de Maeseneer, and Ellen van Stichel (New York: Fordham University Press, 2014), 148–63.

35. Valarie Kaur, *See No Stranger: A Memoir and Manifesto of Revolutionary Love* (London: One-World, 2020).

36. See Revolutionary Love Project, 2020, https://revolutionaryloveproject.com/.

37. Valarie Kaur, "Three Lessons of Revolutionary Love in a Time of Rage," TEDWomen '17, November 2017, https://revolutionaryloveproject.com/ted/.

38. Valarie Kaur, "Parliament of the World's Religions," February 19, 2019, https://www.youtube.com/watch?v=jnCf3NL-0dI.

39. For the full text of the Declaration of Revolutionary Love, see https://reclaimlove.us/.

40. Valarie Kaur, "Video: Valarie Kaur Delivers Rousing Speech in Church," SikhNet, January 20, 2017, https://www.sikhnet.com/news/video-valarie-kaur-delivers-rousing-speech-church.

41. M. Shawn Copeland, *Enfleshing Freedom: Body, Race, and Being* (Minneapolis, MN: Fortress Press, 2009).

42. Copeland, *Enfleshing Freedom*, 82–83 and 128.

43. Valarie Kaur, "Rainbow Wave! What's Next after the Midterms," November 7, 2018, https://valariekaur.com/2018/11/rainbow-wave-whats-next-midterms/.

BIBLIOGRAPHY

Bergant, Dianne. "Women in the Old Testament: Then and Now." Magdala Lecture. July 22, 2010. https://www.bc.edu/content/dam/bc1/schools/stm/continuing%20education/encore/pdf/mary-magdala-2010.pdf.

Bradshaw, Peter. "Mary Magdalene Review—Toothless Attempt to Overturn Sunday School Myths." *The Guardian*. February 27, 2018. https://www.theguardian.com/film/2018/feb/27/mary-magdalene-review-rooney-mara-sunday-school-myths.

Campbell, Simone. *A Nun on the Bus: How All of Us Can Create Hope, Change, and Community*. New York: HarperCollins, 2014.

———."Politics, Faith, and Prophetic Witness." Annual Evelyn Underhill Lecture in Christian Spirituality, Boston College. July 12, 2014. https://www.bc.edu/bc-web/schools/stm/sites/encore/main/2014/politics-faith.html.

Carbine, Rosemary P. "'Artisans of a New Humanity': Revisioning the Public Church in a Feminist Perspective." In *Frontiers in Catholic Feminist Theology: Shoulder to Shoulder*, edited by Susan Abraham and Elena Procario-Foley, 173–92. Minneapolis, MN: Fortress Press, 2009.

———. "Creating Communities of Justice and Peace: Sacramentality and U.S. Public Catholicism." *Journal for the Academic Study of Religion* 29, no. 2 (2016): 182–202.

———. "Critical Constructive Theology as a Praxis of Worldmaking." *Critical Theology: Engaging Church, Culture, and Society* 1, no. 1 (Fall 2018): 8–12.

———. "Public Theology: A Feminist Anthropological View of Political Subjectivity and Praxis." In *Questioning the Human: Toward a Theological Anthropology for the 21st Century*, edited by Lieven Bove, Yves de Maeseneer, and Ellen van Stichel, 148–63. New York: Fordham University Press, 2014.

Cardman, Francine. "MaryMagdalene: Pieces of a Natural History." Magdala Lecture. July 20, 2018. https://www.bc.edu/content/dam/bc1/schools/stm/continuing%20education/encore/pdf/Mary%20Magdala%20Day%202018%2C%20Transcript%20of%20Francine%20Cardman%20Lecture.pdf.

Copeland, M. Shawn. *Enfleshing Freedom: Body, Race, and Being*. Minneapolis, MN: Fortress Press, 2009.

Fruchtman, Rob, dir. *Dan Burstein's Secrets of Mary Magdalene*. New York: Hidden Treasures Productions, 2006.

Hayes, Diana L. *Standing in the Shoes My Mother Made: A Womanist Theology*. Minneapolis, MN: Fortress Press, 2010.

Hilkert, M. Catherine. "On the Strength of Her Testimony." Magdala Lecture. July 22, 2015. https://www.bc.edu/content/bc-web/schools/stm/sites/encore/main/2015/strength-testimony.html.

Hill, Anita. "How to Get the Kavanaugh Hearings Right." *New York Times*. September 19, 2018. https://www.nytimes.com/2018/09/18/opinion/anita-hill-brett-kavanaugh-clarence-thomas.html.

Hinsdale, Mary Ann. "St. Mary of Magdala: Ecclesiological Provocations." *CTSA Proceedings* 66 (2011): 67–90.

Hurst, Dom, trans. *Forty Gospel Homilies by Gregory the Great*. Piscataway, NJ: Gorgias Press, 2009.

Kaur, Valarie. "Parliament of the World's Religions." YouTube. February 19, 2019. https://www.youtube.com/watch?v=jnCf3NL-0dI.

———. "Rainbow Wave! What's Next after the Midterms." November 7, 2018. https://valariekaur.com/2018/11/rainbow-wave-whats-next-midterms/.

———. *See No Stranger: A Memoir and Manifesto of Revolutionary Love*. OneWorld, 2020.

———. "Three Lessons of Revolutionary Love in a Time of Rage." *TEDWomen '17*. November 2017. https://revolutionaryloveproject.com/ted/.

———. Video: Valarie Kaur Delivers Rousing Speech in Church." *SikhNet*. January 20, 2017. https://www.sikhnet.com/news/video-valarie-kaur-delivers-rousing-speech-church.

King, Karen L. *The Gospel of Mary of Magdala: Jesus and the First Woman Apostle*. Santa Rosa, CA: Polebridge, 2003.

Kraemer, Ross Shepard, and Mary Rose D'Angelo, ed. *Women and Christian Origins*. New York: Oxford University Press, 1999.

Levine, Amy-Jill. "Telling Stories about Women." Magdala Lecture. July 22, 2016. https://www.bc.edu/content/bc-web/schools/stm/sites/encore/main/2016/stories-women.html.

Maule, Rosanna. "'Not Just a Movement for Famous White Cisgendered Women': #Me Too and Intersectionality." *Gender and Women's Studies* 2, no. 3 (2020): 4.

Pagels, Elaine. *Beyond Belief: The Secret Gospel of Thomas*. New York: Vintage, 2004.

Reid, Barbara. "Mary Magdalene and the Women Disciples in the Gospel of Luke." Magdala Lecture. July 21, 2017. https://www.bc.edu/content/dam/bc1/schools/stm/continuing%20education/encore/pdf/Mary%20Magdala%20Day%202017%2C%20Transcript%20of%20Barbara%20Reid%20Lecture.pdf.

Schaberg, Jane. *The Resurrection of Mary Magdalene: Legends, Apocrypha, and the Christian Testament*. New York: Continuum, 2002.

Schneiders, Sandra M. "Encountering the Risen Jesus: Mary Magdalene as Prototype." Magdala Lecture. July 19, 2013. https://www.bc.edu/content/dam/bc1/schools/stm/continuing%20education/encore/pdf/mary-magdala-2013.pdf.

———. *Written That You May Believe: Encountering Jesus in the Fourth Gospel*. New York: Crossroad, 1999.

SECTION FIVE

FUTURE MOVEMENT—
THE BECOM*ING* OF
WOMEN'S STUDIES
IN RELIGION

....

CHAPTER 21

Feminism, Religion, and the Digital World

Gina Messina, PhD, Ursuline College

ABSTRACT

This chapter explores the ways religious feminists have adopted the model of online feminism to create a space for voice, build community, and carry out activist efforts. While highlighting the benefits of the digital world, the limitations of access, inclusion, intersectionality, and corporate influence are also considered. Finally, this chapter questions what an intentional and inclusive digital space would look like and the need to address our own blind spots to avoid reproducing the injustice feminist movements seek to disrupt.

On December 16, 2012, Jyoti Singh, who became known around the world as "Delhi Braveheart," was tortured and gang raped by six men on a bus in South Delhi. Her male friend who accompanied her was also beaten unconscious, and their stripped bodies were thrown from the vehicle onto a national highway after the assault. Following five surgeries and thirteen days in critical condition, Singh succumbed to her injuries and died.

Sexual violence was so prevalent in Delhi that it had become known as "Rape City." Inadequate laws, sparse sexual assault prosecutions, and lack of protection left women in a constant state of fear. Responding to the brutality of the crime, citizens took to the streets to protest the government's ongoing failure to address sexual violence and prevalent attitudes that perpetuated the rape culture. As women, men, and children organized across the city, they picked up their cell phones and began tweeting their outrage, sharing photos, and tagging every social media share with the hashtag #DelhiBraveheart.

The result was staggering. Within minutes, news of the protests traveled around the globe. Soon, crowds were gathering in solidarity in cities all over the world; there was an international cry for justice for "Delhi Braveheart" and a demand for stricter laws in Delhi and beyond.

Eve Ensler, author and organizer of the global campaign to end sexual violence, One Billion Rising, traveled to India during the demonstrations. She commented:

> After having worked every day of my life for the last 15 years on sexual violence, I have never seen anything like that, where sexual violence broke through the consciousness and was on the front page, nine articles in every paper every day, in the centre of every discourse, in the centre of the college students' discussions, in the centre of any restaurant you went in. And I think what's happened in India, India is really leading the way for the world. It's really broken through. They are actually fast-tracking laws. They are looking at sexual education. They are looking at the bases of patriarchy and masculinity and how all that leads to sexual violence.[1]

Six men were prosecuted and new laws were passed that have been viewed as a model for other governments to follow. #DelhiBraveheart has become a foundational example of the possibilities that exist when social media is woven into movements against injustice.

SOCIAL JUSTICE AND ONLINE FEMINISM

Historically, information for public consumption, such as op-eds, editorials, broadcast news, and other sources of commentary, have been dominated by white male voices. The perspectives of those who have been disenfranchised rarely entered socio-political conversations, allowing power structures to remain firmly intact. However, the development of websites, blogs, and social media forums presented a new way of sharing ideas and broadening conversations. Suddenly, voices that had been limited to living rooms and coffee shops had access to an international audience.

Circa 2008, platforms such as YouTube, Twitter, and Facebook became well entrenched within our societal fabric, and feminist blogs like *Feministing* and *Jezebel* were widely embraced for their seemingly democratizing value and ability to broaden dialogue around feminist issues. With this cultural shift, online feminism was birthed. A pillar of what has been defined as the "fourth wave,"[2] online feminism has been critical in demonstrating the possibilities that exist by harnessing the energy of social media. It offers an opportunity to uplift voices that have traditionally been silenced, allows for the sharing of personal experience, transforms the way we engage social justice issues, and enables organizing movements that have a global reach.

The model of online feminism and access to social media have given way to the mobilization of activism efforts that have shifted power. Public outcry coupled with broader support have enabled many who have been silenced to collectively exert pressure on policymakers, the media, and others in powerful positions to address issues that have been perpetuated by unjust social structures. As #DelhiBraveHeart used a Twitter hashtag to demand justice for Singh and the implementation of effective laws against sexual violence, #BlackLivesMatter, #SayHerName, #MeToo, #TimesUp, and the Women's March became global movements through digital activism.

Nonetheless, online feminism is not without flaws. Comparable to the first, second, and third waves of feminism, this era grounded in technology has blind spots. Although women's voices have been given a platform allowing them to be front and center with a much wider reach, they have been primarily white voices focused on issues that are concerns of white women. Likewise, as Monica Coleman has pointed out, the Majority World[3] does not have the same access to technology that is readily available in the Minority World.[4]

Further investigation demonstrates that racial segregation is an issue within digital platforms, at least among Americans. According to Kate Ott, "many of us make the mistake of assuming that the 'open' nature of social media automatically means we are reaching a larger, more diverse audience. However, research related to social networking shows that they are much more homogeneous than most of us would like to admit."[5] The Public Religion Research Institute (PRRI) published a report that found that social networks for Americans have a tendency to mirror one's ethnic or racial background, although this varies depending on ethnicity and race. According to PRRI,

> Among white Americans, 91% of people comprising their social networks are also white, while five percent are identified as some other race. Among Black Americans, 83% of people in their social networks are composed of people who are also black, while eight percent are white and six percent are some other race. Among Hispanic Americans, approximately two-thirds (64%) of the people who comprise their core social networks are also Hispanic, while nearly 1-in-5 (19%) are white and nine percent are some other race.[6]

As we consider the purpose of activist efforts carried out through social media, the objective is to reach a larger and more diverse audience. However, if our own social media networks are segregated, as Ott notes, it would seem that we are "talking to ourselves." Additionally, these statistics lead to bigger questions about who we choose to engage with, who we exclude, and why? It appears that our social networks within the United States represent the ongoing struggle with bigotry that is embedded within our history.

In addition to the many intersectional issues that need to be addressed within the digital world, dependence on corporations, lack of funding, and difficulty sustaining efforts also require a close examination. As Alison Winch explains:

> Online activism faces acute problems, given that digital culture is primarily owned and monitored by corporations. Although younger women have been very visible in online media campaigning, they have been hindered by problems of resources and funding. Much feminist activism and debate must inevitably take place within—and often with the support of—corporations, most notably Google and Facebook. And branded spaces benefit from the unpaid labour of users, who participate in the creation of content, and also offer up lucrative data.

All this produces ethical dilemmas about how to sustain a website and maintain feminist connections while being dependent on big business and advertisers: *Feministing* is reliant on advertising, as are *Jezebel* and many bloggers.[7]

With exponential profits being earned by social media platforms from the unpaid labor of those who are embracing the social media effect, it is necessary to be realistic about the deficiencies of digital spaces. Ott argues that feminist activists need to be "critical about hacking platforms to generate diversity and social goods rather than have their free labor exploited and networks silently shaped by corporate goods."[8]

Admittedly, my earlier writings demonstrated such blind spots. Wowed by the possibilities, anxious to join the conversation, and influenced by lived experience and privilege, like so many white feminists, I jumped without considering whose voices are still being excluded and whose power is being bolstered. The benefits of technology interwoven with social justice must be examined using an intersectional lens, and it is critical to acknowledge that, although social media has offered a platform for some, due to overlapping forms of oppression, many are excluded.

What has become known as "hashtag feminism"[9] is an example of a response to some of these issues. Mikki Kendall's creation of #SolidarityIsForWhiteWomen confronted the exclusion of women of color from current feminist dialogue and sparked the development of other hashtag campaigns, including #BlackPowerIsForBlackMen and #NotYourNarrative, which challenges the Western media's portrayal of Muslim women.

While 140 characters are limiting and do not allow for a full exploration of issues, these hashtags have launched a critical dialogue about feminism, intersectionality, and digital feminist practices that are necessary to address identity politics, power structures, and the ways liberative movements create new forms of oppression. They have called us to do our own internal work while remaining conscious that feminism is committed to addressing gender inequities. It recognizes the intersectional nature of oppression and, thus, demands that we uproot all oppressions wherever they exist; because we cannot uproot one if we do not uproot all. Online feminism is uniquely positioned to make strides toward these efforts when blind spots are addressed.

FEMINISM, RELIGION, AND THE DIGITAL WORLD

While some have considered the imbrication of feminism and religion misguided, in fact they are deeply intertwined. Religion offers us a system of values and beliefs that honor the humanity of all persons and yet has been warped by those in power positions. Infused with patriarchy, religion is the foundation of our socio-political culture and overarching structures that perpetuate the marginalization of those historically disenfranchised. Thus, the application of a feminist lens grounded in intersectionality is necessary.

The practice of feminist studies has demonstrated the ways that religion has functioned to relegate the disenfranchised to the underside of dualism. Religious teachings and interpretations have been dictated by those in power, primarily white men. Women, marginalized, and colonized populations have been excluded from leadership and ritual practices, and their voices are absent from sacred texts. Thus, the lived experiences and perspectives of most of the population are largely missing within the fabric of religious traditions.

Many women experience what Mary Bednarowski calls religious ambivalence, having a dual identity of both insider and outsider within their traditions. Religious beliefs shape world views, and yet exclusionary practices deny women's full humanity. Such tension can result in ingenuity and creativity as women seek self-understanding.[10] As a result, multi-level revolutions have ensued. I use the word *revolution* to define activism grounded in compassion that works toward positive social change and disrupts injustice without reproducing it. They occur on both micro and macro levels and can begin in the home or take place as global organized efforts. Within religion, women are dismantling oppressive systems with a multiplicity of strategies, one being the digital world.[11]

Following the model of online feminism, new practices have developed in an effort to expand borders and create new frontiers. Online spaces, particularly blogs and social media platforms (websites, Facebook, Instagram, Twitter, etc.), have been generated that allow the conversation to evolve beyond scholars and religious leaders. They encompass religious feminist values in that they break silence, raise consciousness, cultivate a hermeneutic of suspicion, and build diverse community.[12]

Most religious feminist sites are led by women. Conversations are directed and shaped by female voices that use lived experience as a source of religious interpretation. Community engagement is a distinctive feature of the online movement. Unlike print materials, blogs encourage connection without hierarchy between writers and readers, resulting in constructive dialogue and the fostering of positive relationships. "With this sense of solidarity and support from online friends, creativity flourishes as bloggers are emboldened to tread into difficult new territory."[13] Caroline Kline poignantly describes this:

> Over the years, my online connections have become real-life, life-changing relationships, and at times when I might have felt utterly alone in my questions or pain, I have had the blog and blogging friends to turn to for support and advice. I'll never forget the day I didn't know whether I should move forward with holding my infant son in our Sunday service for his baby blessing, given my bishop's disapproval and strong advice that I not. (Traditionally, Mormon baby blessings consist of the father and other male friends and relatives holding and encircling the baby to pronounce a blessing.) Feeling discouraged, I turned to my blog friends for advice, and within an hour, I had twenty messages telling me to move forward, to think of what I would wish I had done when I look back on my life, and to push past my fear and hold my child. With their support, I gathered up my courage and did so. This is one very important thing the blog has given me and others—beloved friends who are there to make us strong when we are weak and discouraged.[14]

Because blogs and other social media forums are not sponsored by churches, mosques, synagogues, and temples, they have no control over their content. Kline explains, "the material has not been 'correlated,' that is, filtered through the centralized bureaucratic structure that approves all materials. . . . [Thus] writers are free to speculate theologically or discuss unconventional practices or rituals they have privately created."[15] Likewise, such projects allow for "[participation] in the incarnation, the embodiment of a divine new reality that begins with us and is shared and worked out in participation with others in a particular tangible place."[16] Their very format challenges power structures while naming them as sinful.

RELIGIOUS FEMINIST BLOGGING PROJECTS

Mormon feminist blogs have been a cornerstone of feminist religious movements within the digital world. *Feminist Mormon Housewives*[17] and *The Exponent*[18] are examples of women-led sites that have cultivated dialogue around feminist issues in the Mormon Church that embody thousands of voices from around the world. Both have grown over time and now include podcasts. They also offered a foundation for the launching of the "Ordain Women" campaign in 2013, which publicly called for the ordination of women and the need to address gender inequity in the Mormon Church. With the use of social media, "Ordain Women" created a website that displays profiles, a purposeful mirroring of the "I am Mormon" Campaign by the Church of Latter Day Saints (LDS), of mostly Mormon individuals, as well as some non-LDS members, who support the movement.[19]

Jewish feminist blogs have also been an early leader in religious feminist blogging projects. *The Sisterhood*[20] and *JewFem*[21] are popular sites that further dialogue around gender issues within Judaism, although *Lilith* may be the most well known. Like *The Exponent II*, *Lilith Magazine* was founded in 1976 with the mission of being "the feminist change-agent in and for the Jewish community, amplifying Jewish women's voices, creating a woman-positive Judaism, spurring gender consciousness in the Jewish world and empowering Jewish women and girls to envision and enact change in their own lives and their communities."[22] With evolving technologies, *Lilith* embraced the opportunity to further its reach, create a larger community, and encourage diverse voices to join the conversation by launching its blog. According to Rachel Barenblat, "Where can an Orthodox Rebbetzin, a radical Jewish Renewal poet and the world's only certified *soferet* (female Torah scribe) meet—across continents and ideological divide—to discuss Torah and politics, family and gender roles? This is my corner of the Jewish women's blogosphere, and it's not your mama's Sisterhood."[23] Jewish feminist blogs have offered an online sisterhood that have become a critical space in her life and for many Jewish feminists who seek community and dialogue about life and religious practice for women.

Altmuslimah (AltM)[24] and *Muslimah Media Watch*[25] are blogs that have created a platform for Muslim feminist voices to explore patriarchal issues within Islam and engage in dialogue with community. "Hashtag feminism" has also been embraced as a means of responding to Muslim women's issues; Rabia Chaudry created the #FireAbuEesa Twitter campaign in response to Imam and teacher for making derogatory statements on Facebook about International Women's Day, feminists, and rape. In response, Hind Makki acknowledged men who support women and feminism with #MuslimMaleAllies.[26]

Inspired by the success of religious feminist blogs and recognizing the need for a platform where feminist voices across traditions could come together, *Feminism and Religion* (FAR)[27] was founded in 2011. With the help of *The Exponent* founder, Kline, FAR has worked to expand boundaries, building diverse relationships that are not limited by geography, and encourage ongoing inter-religious dialogue that names and disrupts unjust systems. To date, *Feminism and Religion* shares a multitude of voices and is read in 181 countries.

Following this trend, the non-profit organization Feminist Studies in Religion, Inc. (FSR), which publishes the *Journal of Feminist Studies in Religion*, added a digital component to its work in 2013. Its companion website, www.fsrinc.org, hosts an online version of the journal and the *Feminist Studies in Religion Forum* where both academia and grassroots movements are brought together to further dialogue and create space to generate new feminist scholarship in religion.

It is important to note that, although a primary starting point, digital feminist activism is not limited to blogs. As stated, podcasts have launched as a way to offer commentary on feminist issues in religion that are widely accessible. Likewise, Facebook, Instagram, Twitter, Vimeo, and YouTube continue to be significant sites of resistance where information is shared and accessed, allowing communities to grow. Yet the success of these blogs reveals the need for such platforms that provide a space to speak truths, explore feminist questions, and find a supportive community. It also demonstrates that, while blogs do not solve accessibility issues, they can create access to information and opportunity to engage in dialogue and community that might not be available otherwise. Nonetheless, questions of inclusion and intersectionality within digital feminist religious movements are not that different from secular feminism and are critical to address.

INCLUSION AND INTENTIONAL SPACE

Although blogging projects allow for the sharing of experience, democratic participation, and dialogue across boundaries, such feminist practice occurs only if we act with intention. Engagement across differences is challenging, regardless of the format. We define feminism in different ways, and adding religion to the conversation creates another level of complexity. According to Xochitl Alvizo, "[I] have witnessed the tensions and conflicts, silencing and belittling, and complete disconnect that can take place among feminists when we encounter one another on blogs."[28] Relating to our conversation partners across our diversity of ideas in a constructive way requires significant effort, inclusiveness, and a willingness to remain engaged in the work; however, that does not always happen.

Sometimes, there is such a disconnect among religious feminists that a real dialogue never begins and potential conversation partners are excluded. As Jennifer Zobair explains, although feminist studies in religion as a field have made strides with the use of technology, Muslim women are often doubly othered—treated as outsiders in both Muslim and feminist communities. "There are notable points of departure for feminist studies in Islam. . . . The extent of Muslim women's exclusion from both religious and feminist spheres is profound."[29]

The marginalization due to geopolitical forces endured by Muslim women is not one many feminists can relate to. Because Islam has been deemed as inherently violent toward women and is practiced in nations where imperialism dominates, the guise of defending women's human rights has been used to justify military efforts while fueling fear of Islam. As a result, rather than including Muslim feminist voices, Western feminists have created a larger divide with viral campaigns to "save" Muslim women. For instance, the activist group FEMEN holds demonstrations where participants are topless with paint across their chests and flowers in their hair. Islamic treatment of women and girls is a primary target of their protests, which are displayed across social media. Such acts ignore the shared critique across patriarchal traditions, singling out a religious community that has been socially and politically marginalized. They also attack the values and beliefs of Muslim women and reinforce dualistic ideas that feminist efforts seek to disrupt. The result, as Zobair explains, is "a double silencing at the hands of Muslim patriarchy and 'white savior' feminism,"[30] which has found its voice in the digital world.

While Muslim feminists are engaging social media as a revolutionary act, they often do so without the support of other religious and secular feminists. The field of feminist studies in religion has been dominated by Christianity, and, whether or not deliberate, non-Christian traditions have generally been excluded.[31] In particular, Muslim feminists have been ostracized while experiencing attacks and insults and being branded as victims who can be saved only by the oppressor.

Religious feminists across traditions must prioritize meaningful collaboration beyond boundaries that honor the lived experiences of all persons while embracing the goals of intersectionality. Opportunities to connect with feminists, regardless of physical, political, and dogmatic divides, offer enormous potential for inclusive revolutionary action that acknowledges the value of a multiplicity of voices. Too often, we allow ourselves to be trapped within silos that deny the justice we seek. Our blind spots keep us shackled to the very systems we work to disrupt.

CONCLUSION

The use of social networks has changed the way activist efforts are carried out, and campaigns like #DelhiBraveHeart, #BlackLivesMatter, and #MeToo have demonstrated the possibilities that exist when we harness the power of online spaces. Feminist religious activism within the digital world is making progress, and social media offers an effective method that should continue to be embraced. In fact, with the evolution of technology, online activism is almost necessary to achieve forward movement in our continued efforts. However, we must be aware of the limitations that exist through such platforms while acknowledging the destructive nature of our own biases.

Feminism is defined in different ways. Alvizo demonstrates the complexities around our interpretations asking, "what 'feminism' are we talking about? Do we mean feminism as agency? power? resistance? The definitions can be so disparate that feminists may not recognize themselves in the feminism of another."[32] These are critical questions.

Indeed, as Alvizo argues, we should understand that feminism exists in a plurality and it is more accurate to refer to it as "feminisms." Nonetheless, our feminisms must be intersectional and recognized as calling us to uproot oppression wherever it exists; this includes religion and requires each of us to deeply consider the ways our own actions perpetuate such systems.

Online spaces must be *intentional* spaces. Revolutions are not made by mediums, and social media is not feminist; it is the visionary act of creating space that is grounded in feminist principles and challenges oppressive norms that is revolutionary. Inclusive and collaboratively cultivated spaces are essential if feminist religious activism is to create equitable change that interrupts the reproduction of injustice experienced within the patriarchies of our own traditions. "The more people with whom we can share the microphone and the more varied feminist voices that are present, the greater the potential for creative exchanges, liberative critique, and the disruption of kyriarchal[33] modes of relating."[34] Meaningful engagement within an intentional space requires that we be vigilant in allowing feminist principles to guide our actions, prioritize the goals of intersectionality, and welcome all voices to the virtual table.

NOTES

1. "One Billion Rising: Playwright Eve Ensler Organizes Global Day of Dance against Sexual Abuse," *Democracynow.org*, February 16, 2013, https://www.democracynow.org/2013/2/14/one_billion_rising_playwright_eve_ensler#transcript.

2. Ruxandra Looft, "#GirlGaze: Photography, Fourth Wave Feminism, and Social Media Advocacy," *Continuum: Journal of Media and Cultural Studies* 31, no. 6 (2017): 892–902. Also, see Constance Grady, "The Waves of Feminism and Why People Keep Fighting over Them," *Vox*, July 20, 2018, https://www.vox.com/2018/3/20/16955588/feminism-waves-explained-first-second-third-fourth.

3. I use the language "Majority World" to refer to the 80 percent of the world that lives on $10 a day or less and "Minority World" to refer to the West as a reminder that those of us who live in the West are a very small part of the global population. It also diverges from language that is hierarchical, offensive, and geographically incorrect.

4. Monica Coleman, "Religious Feminists and the Digital Divide," Roundtable: Feminism, Religion, and the Internet, *The Journal of Feminist Studies in Religion* 31, no. 2 (Fall 2015): 144–48.

5. Kate Ott, "Hacking the System," Roundtable: Feminism, Religion, and the Internet, *The Journal of Feminist Studies in Religion* 31, no. 2 (Fall 2015): 140.

6. Public Religion Research Institute, "Race, Religion, and Political Affiliations of American's Social Networks," August 3, 2016, https://www.prri.org/research/poll-race-religion-politics-americans-social-networks/.

7. Alison Winch, "Feminism, Generation, and Intersectionality," *Soundings* 58 (Winter 2014): 13.

8. Ott, "Hacking the System," 144.

9. Hashtag feminism is the practice of feminist activism through the use of Twitter hashtags to call attention to a specific issue with the goal of creating widespread awareness, encouraging dialogue, and shifting cultural norms.

10. Mary Bednarowski, *The Religious Imagination of the American Woman* (Bloomington, IN: Indiana University Press, 1999).

11. Xochitl Alvizo and Gina Messina, eds., *Women Religion Revolution* (Cambridge, MA: FSR Books, 2017).

12. Monica Coleman, "Blogging as Religious Feminist Activism," in *Feminism and Religion in the 21st Century*, ed. Gina Messina and Rosemary Radford Ruether (New York: Routledge, 2013), 20–33.

13. Caroline Kline, "Mormon Feminist Blogs and Heavenly Mother: Spaces for Ambivalence and Innovation in Practice and Theology," in *Feminism and Religion in the 21st Century*, ed. Gina Messina and Rosemary Radford Ruether (New York: Routledge, 2013), 36.

14. Caroline Kline, "Mormon Feminism: Embracing Our Past, Envisioning Our Future," in *Women Religion Revolution*, ed. Xochitl Alvizo and Gina Messina (Cambridge, MA: FSR Books, 2017), 56.

15. Kline, "Mormon Feminist Blogs and Heavenly Mother," 35.

16. Alvizo and Messina, *Women Religion Revolution*, 4.

17. Feminist Mormon Housewives (www.feministmormonhousewives.org) is the largest Mormon feminist blog.

18. *The Exponent* (www.the-exponent.com) was founded by Caroline Kline with the goal of continuing the efforts of *The Women's Exponent*, which was published from 1872–1914 in Salt Lake City, Utah, and is hosted on the *The Exponent II* website, a quarterly publication founded by Claudia Bushman and Laurel Thatcher Ulrich in 1974, which continues today in both print and digital formats and now offers "The Religious Feminist Podcast."

19. The Ordain Women movement has had success in its efforts; sadly, its founder, Kate Kelly, was excommunicated from the LDS Church for her work committed to gender equity and the ordination of women. See Laurie Goodstein, "Mormons Expel Founder of Group Seeking Priesthood for Women," *New York Times*, June 23, 2014.

20. See http://blogs.forward.com/sisterhood-blog/.

21. See http://www.jewfem.com.

22. "Mission," *Lilith Magazine*, https://www.lilith.org/about/mission/.

23. Rachel Barenblat. "Jewish Feminist Blogs—An Unlike Online Sisterhood," *Lilith Magazine*, Fall 2005.

24. See www.altuslimah.com.

25. See *Patheos*, www.patheos.com/blogs/mmw.

26. Jennifer Zobair, "The Depth and Weight of Feminist Studies in Islam: A Response to 'The Evolution of Feminist Studies in Religion.'" Roundtable: Feminism, Religion, and the Internet, *The Journal of Feminist Studies in Religion* 31, no. 2 (Fall 2015): 149–54.

27. *Feminism and Religion* (www.feminismandreligion.com) was co-founded by Gina Messina, Xochitl Alvizo, Caroline Kline, and Cynthia Garrity-Bond.

28. Xochitl Alvizo, "Participating for Transformation in Online Space," Roundtable: Feminism, Religion, and the Internet, *The Journal of Feminist Studies in Religion* 31, no. 2 (Fall 2015): 164.

29. Jennifer Zobair, "The Depth and Weight of Feminist Studies in Islam, 149–50.

30. Zobair, "The Depth and Weight of Feminist Studies in Islam," 151.

31. See Aysha A. Hidayatullah, *Feminist Edges of the Qur'an* (New York: Oxford University Press, 2014).

32. Xochitl Alvizo, "Being Undone by the Other," in *Feminism and Religion in the 21st Century*, ed. Gina Messina and Rosemary Radford Ruether (New York: Routledge, 2013), 48.

33. The term *kyriarchy* was coined by Elisabeth Schüssler Fiorenza as a way to re-conceptualize patriarchy and is derived from the Greed *kyrios*, meaning lord, master, father, and husband and the verb *archein*, meaning to dominate or rule. According to Fiorenza, "kyriarchy is best theorized as a complex pyramidal system of intersecting multiplicative social structures of superordination and subordination, of ruling and oppression." See Elisabeth Schüssler Fiorenza, *Democratizing Biblical Studies: Toward an Emancipatory Educational Space* (Louisville, KY: John Knox Press, 2009), 112.

34. Alvizo, "Participating for Transformation in Online Space," 166.

BIBLIOGRAPHY

Alvizo, Xochitl. "Being Undone by the Other." In *Feminism and Religion in the 21st Century*, edited by Gina Messina and Rosemary Radford Ruether, 47–56. New York: Routledge, 2013.
———. "Participating for Transformation in Online Space." Roundtable: Feminism, Religion, and the Internet. *The Journal of Feminist Studies in Religion* 31, no. 2 (Fall 2015): 163–67.

Alvizo, Xochitl, and Gina Messina, eds. *Women Religion Revolution*. Cambridge, MA: FSR Books, 2017.

Barenblat, Rachel. "Jewish Feminist Blogs—An Unlike Online Sisterhood." *Lilith Magazine*. Fall 2005.

Bednarowski, Mary. "Religious Feminists and the Digital Divide." Roundtable: Feminism, Religion, and the Internet. *The Journal of Feminist Studies in Religion* 31, no. 2 (Fall 2015): 144–48.

———. *The Religious Imagination of the American Woman*. Bloomington, IN: Indiana University Press, 1999.

DemocracyNow.org. "One Billion Rising: Playwright Eve Ensler Organizes Global Day of Dance against Sexual Abuse." February 16, 2013. https://www.democracynow.org/2013/2/14/one_billion_rising_playwright_eve_ensler#transcript.

Grady, Constance. "The Waves of Feminism and Why People Keep Fighting over Them." *Vox*. July 20, 2018. https://www.vox.com/2018/3/20/16955588/feminism-waves-explained-first-second-third-fourth.

Hidayatullah, Aysha A. *Feminist Edges of the Qur'an*. New York: Oxford University Press, 2014.

Kline, Caroline. "Mormon Feminism: Embracing Our Past, Envisioning Our Future." In *Women Religion Revolution*, edited by Xochitl Alvizo and Gina Messina, 53–58. Cambridge, MA: FSR Books, 2017.

———. "Mormon Feminist Blogs and Heavenly Mother: Spaces for Ambivalence and Innovation in Practice and Theology." In *Feminism and Religion in the 21st Century*, edited by Gina Messina and Rosemary Radford Ruether, 34–46. New York: Routledge, 2013.

Lilith Magazine. "Mission." Accessed March 5, 2020. https://www.lilith.org/about/mission/.

Looft, Ruxandra. "#GirlGaze: Photography, Fourth Wave Feminism, and Social Media Advocacy." *Continuum: Journal of Media and Cultural Studies* 31, no. 6 (2017): 892–902.

Messina, Gina, and Rosemary Radford Ruether, eds. *Feminism and Religion in the 21st Century*. New York: Routledge, 2013.

Ott, Kate. "Hacking the System." Roundtable: Feminism, Religion, and the Internet. *The Journal of Feminist Studies in Religion* 31, no. 2 (Fall 2015): 140–44.

Public Religion Research Institute. "Race, Religion, and Political Affiliations of Americans' Core Social Networks." August 3, 2016. https://www.prri.org/research/poll-race-religion-politics-americans-social-networks/.

Schüssler Fiorenza, Elisabeth. *Democratizing Biblical Studies: Toward an Emancipatory Educational Space*. Louisville, KY: John Knox Press, 2009.

Winch, Alison. "Feminism, Generation, and Intersectionality." *Soundings* 58 (Winter 2014): 8–20.

Zobair, Jennifer. "The Depth and Weight of Feminist Studies in Islam: A Response to 'The Evolution of Feminist Studies in Religion.'" Roundtable: Feminism, Religion, and the Internet. *The Journal of Feminist Studies in Religion* 31, no. 2 (Fall 2015): 149–54.

CHAPTER 22

Documenting, Changing, and Reimagining Women's Mosque Spaces Online

Dr. Krista Melanie Riley, Vanier College,
Montreal, Quebec, Canada

ABSTRACT

The issue of mosque spaces in North America (and elsewhere), particularly with regard to gender, has received increasing attention in recent years, both within and outside of Muslim communities. This chapter will focus on discussions about gendered mosque spaces taking place online. Taking as case studies three North American Muslim feminist bloggers, this chapter examines how online and offline spaces interact and how some Muslim women move in and out of these spaces in order to shift the gendered dynamics in their contexts. This chapter will conclude with a reflection on what these examples can tell us about gender and power in online and offline spaces and about the possibilities and limitations revealed as these conversations move between physical and online worlds.

In February 2010, blogger Ify Okoye published a post titled "The Penalty Box" on the popular group blog Muslim Matters.[1] The post began with a description of a recent experience where she and a friend had stopped at a mosque to pray on their way to a restaurant. Ify[2] wrote that the mosque's women's section was so small and uncomfortable that her friend joked that it "would be more rightly utilized as a penalty box for the men who come late to the *salah* [ritual prayer], as a rebuke and punishment." The two women decided instead to pray at the back of the men's section and later found themselves having to explain their decision to a man who reprimanded them for not praying in the designated women's section.

Ify's narration of this incident then led her to talk, in the same blog post, about a number of other experiences in mosques in which she found the spaces accorded to women to be systemically inadequate and inferior to the men's spaces. She also talked about the injustice of giving women "inferior seat choices," usually at the back, at conferences and seminars where women had paid the same amount as men to attend. By and large, Ify provided little commentary and seemed to want to let these stories speak for themselves. Aside from an indirect reference to one *hadith*, Ify did not reference any primary texts of scripture or *hadith* in this article. She did make reference to a religious course she had taken on Islamic jurisprudence surrounding the ritual prayer, also somewhat indirectly, mentioning only that the course addressed the topic of "the right of women to see the imam." Most of the post, however, was focused on stories of her own personal encounters with inequality with regard to the cleanliness, safety, comfort, aesthetics, and accessibility of women's spaces as opposed to men's. In the virtual space of the Muslim Matters blog, accessible to readers across a wide span of geographic locations, Ify drew on narratives of localized experiences to make an argument not only about the unjust nature of those particular physical contexts but also about broader trends related to gendered spaces within mosques and Muslim community events.

While Ify was far from the first person to write about this issue—and, in fact, this was a topic she had already addressed several times earlier on her own blog[3]—the Muslim Matters text was particularly widely read and has had lasting resonance that most of her other posts have not had. The post continued to be referenced in other online articles even years after its publication,[4] serving as a kind of rallying cry that has continued to resonate among Muslim women (and people of all genders) long since it was first published and reflecting a significant public intervention in debates within many Muslim communities.

The "Penalty Box" post and the responses to it offer a glimpse into some key questions around gender and space in North American Muslim communities and is an example of how those questions are discussed and debated online. How do online spaces such as blogs serve as forums for collective translocal public discussions about gender dynamics in local physical spaces? How are these discussions affected by the fact that most of their participants do not share, and have never shared, the same physical space with one another? What role might online spaces play in providing alternate sources of community for those who do not feel welcome in local organized religious spaces? What is gained and lost through these collective processes of imagining new kinds of spaces?

Mia Lövheim writes about young women's blogs as ethical spaces; in this understanding, blogs serve both as *platforms*, where particular content and perspectives are shared and as *spaces* of encounter, where ethical deliberations take place at least in part through the interactions among bloggers and audiences.[5] Lövheim writes that blogs "become not only a space for private self-expression and reflection but also for collective negotiations of social norms and meanings."[6] A similar phenomenon reflected in the strategies that the bloggers cited in this chapter employ through their writing on Islamic norms and ethics and their public sharing of ideas and experiences helps build a blogging environment in which ethical issues are collectively debated. The heavy presence of personal narratives in the comment sections of many of the blog posts suggests that many readers feel themselves personally interpellated and respond accordingly with their own testimonials, co-creating these spaces of personal sharing and ethical deliberation on the blogs. This chapter will illustrate some of the different ways that "collective negotiations" take place on these blogs, both in cases of (often productive) tension and in cases that reflect a more collaborative orientation.

The issue of mosque spaces in North America (and elsewhere), particularly with regard to gender, has received increasing attention in recent years, both within and outside of Muslim communities. Among other issues, these discussions address the increased presence of barriers between men's and women's sections in many mosques, along with problems with the condition of women's spaces, physically inaccessible spaces, and a lack of leadership opportunities for women; of course, the situation can vary quite dramatically from one mosque to another. It is also important to clarify that not all Muslim women are opposed to separate spaces for women and men within mosques; some in fact prefer the privacy of a space that allows them to connect with other women or to nurse their children without having to worry about covering themselves as they would when in the presence of men.[7] Separate women's spaces in Muslim centers can even sometimes share goals and characteristics with separate women- and non-binary-centered safe spaces advocated by other feminist groups.[8] Still, the result is often that men effectively have privileged access not only to the main prayer area but also to the leadership roles within it.[9] Arguments against gender segregation tend to take up this question of access, especially as it affects women's abilities to take part in religious activities, whether this means being able to see and hear religious lectures or being able to follow the movements of the imam leading the communal prayer.[10] In many cases, the recommendation is to have a separate space available for women who prefer not to be in the same space as the men, while ensuring that women who want to pray in the main prayer area have access to it.[11] It should also be noted that these discussions are very often based on a binary understanding of gender and that the challenges of gender-segregated spaces are further complicated when more than two genders are taken into account.

This chapter will focus on discussions about gendered mosque spaces taking place online. Taking as case studies three North American Muslim feminist bloggers, this chapter examines how online and offline spaces interact and how some Muslim women move in and out of these spaces in order to shift the gendered dynamics in their contexts. The narratives from the blogs explored in this chapter bring physical spaces into online discussions and use online discussions to (try to) influence physical spaces. These posts also often have the effect of creating spaces online for those who would not be able to connect offline, whether because of physical or geographic barriers or because they have disengaged from local communities where they do not feel welcome or comfortable.

COMPETING AUTHORITIES

Let us return to Ify's discussion of the "Penalty Box."[12] Looking at the comment section of the original blog post, many of the responses were positive and thank Ify for bringing attention to the topic. These came largely from women who share Ify's frustrations and experiences, but some male commenters also offered their support.[13] Others, both women and men, took issue with Ify's comments. This blog post and the extensive discussion it provoked reflect a space where a wide range of ideas were shared and heatedly challenged. Fiercely debated too were questions about who was properly qualified to develop and share some of the ideas circulating on the post and in its comment section.

For example, some of the negative responses to Ify's blog post specifically posited that she should be basing her claims solely on scholarly opinions or on religious texts, implicitly rejecting the arguments Ify made based on her own observations and experiences. In response to some of these comments, Ify did ground her decision to pray in the men's section in more "traditional" Islamic sources, noting not only that she and her friend prayed at the back of the room, with space between them and the men, but also that the earliest period of Islamic history had no physical barrier between the women's and men's prayer sections. Even this, however, did not settle the matter. Instead, it seemed to invite alternative interpretations of such sources or references to other sources also seen as having authority.

In other cases, participants in the discussion suggested that Ify does not have the authority in the first place to use or interpret the sources she cited. One commenter interjected, "Salaam, can we get a scholar in here please!!"[14] and another noted that they "haven't seen anyone quote what an *actual scholar* has to say on this issue."[15] Ify did note in one comment that "The people of knowledge that [she respects] have also validated other seating arrangements" than those requiring women to sit at the back during religious classes, but she also emphasized that, in her view, these calls for scholarly or scriptural permission were missing the point. In a reply to the commenter's demand for the opinion of an "actual scholar," Ify wrote,

> I don't need a fatwa or opinion of a scholar . . . to tell me that I don't feel included or valued or even able to participate effectively in discussions or questions and answer sessions that take place "somewhere over there on the brothers' side." I don't need a fatwa to tell me that it is not only possible but Islamically acceptable to treat women better and afford them better accommodation. These things are common sense. In Islam, we respect the people of knowledge and defer to them to guide us and our actions as they are the inheritors of the prophets, yet Allah has also given us laypeople an intellect with the capacity for critical thinking.[16]

Ify's response here did not dispute the status or authority of the "actual scholars" to whom the commenter refers, but she did take issue with the suggestion that their authority would be the only one that mattered or that it should forcibly supersede the "common sense" and "critical thinking" that she also claimed as God-given sources of Islamic knowledge. Ify made the case that the story she told, as well as her innate sense of what is right and appropriate, served as an entirely legitimate basis for religious interpretation. She concluded her response to one of the commenters by telling him to visit women's prayer spaces himself, essentially so that he could better know what he's talking about. In other words, Ify also challenged the sources *he* used to arrive at his opinions, and in this case she suggested that a lack of firsthand experience also reflected an inadequate understanding of her point. The stories she told in her original post that provoked this discussion reflected a weight and value given to personal experience (in this case, at mosques and conferences) as a way of knowing definitively that something is wrong with the situation. Although Ify may have used textual sources to corroborate that knowledge, she rejected the suggestion that her argument should be *dependent* on such sources. The "Penalty Box" post thus became a space of ethical deliberation not only about the state of mosques and women's prayer spaces but also about the basis upon which one can make arguments about Islam and Muslim communities.

WHAT IS A PICTURE WORTH?

At the end of her "Penalty Box" post, Ify wrote that she was considering creating a photoblog with images of women's prayer spaces in the mosques that she visited. Sure enough, a week after that post was published, Ify created a photo blog project called "Oursides," whose purpose was to post pictures of mosques, and especially of women's prayer spaces. The Oursides photo blog included several sets of pictures from mosques mainly in Ify's local area of Maryland and Virginia, along with images submitted by readers of mosques from other parts of the United States as well as from Morocco and Dubai.[17]

The visual images involved in a photo blogging project of this kind served a powerful rhetorical purpose to support the written arguments made by Ify and others about inequalities between women's and men's mosque spaces. The public visual documentation of so many spaces together acted as evidence that this phenomenon was widespread and systemic. In a later post on her own blog, responding to questions about whether mosques really have a problem when people (men) have never heard women complain, Ify reiterated that, because women have no access to the "community discussions" happening only among men in the men's section, they have no way of making their complaints heard.[18] In my interview with her, Ify also noted another, perhaps even more basic, function of the photo blog. Because men generally do not have access to women's prayer spaces (particularly in mosques that are entirely segregated by a barrier or a curtain or the men's and women's sections being on different floors), most men who pray in segregated spaces do not know what the women's section in their own mosque looks like. She explained that, in response to the "Penalty Box" post, "I think a lot of the men were like, oh I don't think it's that bad. I'm like, how the hell would you know? You've never been in the women's section." She also told me about an experience in her local mosque where the exit from the women's section would sometimes be chained shut from the inside, posing a fire hazard as well as an annoyance. When she raised this with the all-male mosque council, she was told that they had stopped chaining the door "years ago," even though she had just been there and seen it chained the previous weekend. Although she was frustrated that this man did not know, she also noted that he had no real way of knowing, "because he never goes in on the women's side. . . . he goes in through the men's side, which is perfect and nice."

Posting these photos online serves not only to document a systemic problem but also to allow men virtual access to these spaces, access that they do not have to the physical spaces, even if they regularly pray in the same building, so that they can see for themselves the disparities the women encounter in many mosques. Masserat Amir-Ebra-himi describes a similar role of blogging within her work on Iranian women's blogs. By talking openly about their everyday experiences as women, she argues, these bloggers expose men to private experiences that they may not have known about otherwise.[19] While the role of exposing a larger public to private experiences is one that blogging may play in any context, it is perhaps an especially significant one within the framework of communities that have a certain level (or ideal, however contested) of gender segregation and where there are many women's spaces or experiences to which men simply do not have access. Publicly exposing and naming mosques online, especially when accompa-nied by visual evidence, may also serve to hold mosques accountable to a wider Muslim audience than their local communities. A board member of one of the mosques Ify wrote about even left a comment on her post about that mosque, responding to some of her concerns and explaining some of the mosque's plans to better accommodate women.[20]

Ultimately, the Oursides project was relatively short-lived and eventually merged with Ify's own blog in July 2011. The Oursides link is still available, but any mosque photo posts after that date were published on Ify's personal blog.[21] A similar idea was taken up a year later by Chicago-based activist Hind Makki on a Tumblr page called "Side Entrance," described as featuring "Photos from mosques around the world, show-casing women's sacred spaces, in relation to men's spaces. We show the beautiful, the adequate and the pathetic."[22] Side Entrance does not explicitly acknowledge the earlier work by Ify, and it is unclear whether Hind Makki was aware of Ify's previous efforts in this area when she started the site. A post that Makki wrote on the blog *AltMuslim* explains that she started Side Entrance out of exasperation after having heard too many bad mosque stories and having had too many bad experiences herself.[23]

Regardless of whether Side Entrance was deliberately intended to mimic Oursides, it is a very similar project, where readers are invited to submit photos from the mosques that they visit, illustrating both the good and the bad. The site also includes links to relevant articles and occasional testimonials unaccompanied by photographs. Still rela-tively active, Side Entrance has received more submissions representing a much wider geographic area than Oursides and has also received more attention within the blogo-sphere,[24] as well as in some more mainstream media outlets.[25] When I asked Ify about her thoughts on Side Entrance, she laughed at how an issue that was once difficult to raise and seen as a fringe topic that only a few people were touching is now something that "everyone and their brother" is talking about. Her overall reaction to Side Entrance, however, was one of support and appreciation, noting that "the more voices we can con-tribute to the work, the better, like it doesn't matter, as long as we get there."

Ify's use of the photoblog (and Hind Makki's use of a similar medium with Side Entrance) represents one way that the online environment is not only shaped by offline realities but also has the potential to shape these offline spaces. One of Ify's original intentions in starting the blog, after all, was to convey to the people (men) in power what women's spaces in mosques were often like so that those making decisions about mosque spaces would be forced to confront the implications of those decisions for female community members. At the very least, the men she described as ignorant of the state of women's spaces would be left without the excuse that they had no way of knowing.

Publicly exposing and naming mosques online, especially when accompanied by visual evidence, may also serve to hold mosques accountable to a wider Muslim audience than their local communities. A board member of one of the mosques Ify wrote about even left a comment on her post about that mosque, responding to some of her concerns and explaining some of the mosque's plans to better accommodate women.[26]

By inviting participants to submit photographs and by posting pictures of the spaces she visited, Ify worked to build new understandings and experiences of shared space among her readers. The online environment became a means through which participants could invite one another into visual representations of their physical spaces, regardless of gender, which is not always possible in the actual physical space. They could then also share conversations about that space, whether or not it was one they inhabit physically together. In this way, Ify's photo posts challenged the relegation of women's spaces to only a matter of private concern for women and instead attempted to transform the larger conversations about mosques in ways that frame women's spaces as being of public importance.

GLOBAL MESSAGES TO LOCAL MOSQUES

At other points, the public identification of problems with specific mosques comes with more direct incitement to take action. In August 2012, during Ramadan, blogger Nahida Sultana Nisa posted an article on her blog, *the fatal feminist*, about the renovation plans for her local (and "favourite") mosque.[27] The post described mixed feelings upon initially hearing about the renovation plans; Nahida liked her quiet, humble mosque as it was but also hoped for a larger women's area. She then told readers about the announcement that she had heard at the mosque the previous evening: that the new mosque would provide space for up to 393 men and 160 women. The post also included an image of the proposed layout for the redesigned mosque. Nahida expressed her frustration with the renovation plans and made a very heartfelt plea to readers of the blog to contact the mosque themselves and voice their concerns.

In this case, her blog became a space to share her experience and commiserate with others and to appeal for members of her online community to take action to help change the plans for her local mosque. Several people left notes confirming that they had emailed the mosque as she had asked. Although they were geographically far away, they were able to participate in the project in Nahida's local area, and their actions demonstrated a sense of collective investment in the transformation of mosque spaces, even when this particular space may not be one they would ever visit.

Nahida later wrote a follow-up post to update readers on the status of the mosque renovations, explaining that the mosque had recently said that, in response to complaints, they were planning to "'fix something' about the discrepancy in the space allotted to women compared to men," although she also said she "[doesn't] really trust the committee" or have any details on what the proposed changes are. Nonetheless, she expressed gratitude (in the form of "A THOUSAND HUGS!") to readers who offered support, and especially to those who sent complaints to the mosque.[28]

While the commenters' support for Nahida could be read as simply reflecting their respect for her as a writer or their sense of affection or friendship toward her (both of which are likely true for many of the commenters), several of the comments suggest that something else is at play as well. In most of the comments left in response to the first post about the proposed mosque renovation, readers described their own similar experiences of frustration in mosques that they had frequented. The first commenter wrote that "Nothing breaks my heart more than having to go and pray in a women's prayer room, it truly hurts me," and proceeds to tell a story about an experience of her own.[29] Another commenter noted that she was "facing exactly this with a mosque in [her] area."[30] There is a sense that the commenters' responses were directly linked to their own experiences and many of them seemed to be acting, at least in part, in response to *their* experiences and not only to Nahida's. In this interaction, the shared virtual space of the blog carried a particularly strong connection to the physical spaces that these online participants occupied, such that their sense of shared experience—and the action that they took as a result—took precedence over any suggestion that they were not "really" sharing the same physical space.

In the last post she published about the mosque renovation, Nahida again affirmed her "love" for the readers who took the time to contact the mosque administration.[31] After a discussion about how the tone of women's protests could be policed and ignored—with polite protests being quietly dismissed, while more vocal or aggressive activists can be reprimanded for not being sufficiently polite—Nahida gave the latest update:

> *To speak of barriers*, the construction project is not yet complete, and the letters were not addressed. It is *especially* easy to ignore polite requests when they are not embodied in people who are demanding a response with their presence, and must instead write letters. However, because of a couple of women who walked out of the prayer area due to how *degrading* the separation of this space is the mosque board announced that the new building will not have a barrier. I don't believe them.
>
> Other than the fact that the word of a Muslim man is just about as reliable as Pluto's planetary status, men . . . will, being the sparkling politicians they are, say whatever sounds like great PR at the moment. No victory cries until the project is complete.[32]

Nahida's gratitude for her readers' support was tempered here with an acknowledgment of the limitations of online activism in relation to physical prayer spaces. As she noted, the fact that some of those protesting were not physically present meant that those making decisions may not have felt accountable in the same way to make changes. At the same time, given Nahida's lack of faith in the mosque board's promised changes, even when in response to the actions of women who were physically present, it remains uncertain whether the requests sent by email were actually any less effective than the actions of the women who were physically present in the space. We might then conclude that all of these forms of solidarity and activism find their value, at least as far as Nahida is concerned or until evidence of concrete changes is available, primarily as symbolic gestures of protest against an unequal situation. Still, the role of the readers' participation in contacting the mosque in reinforcing community online suggests that their value is not only symbolic and not wholly contingent on whether the mosque administration makes the requested changes.

CO-CREATING NEW SPACES

In February 2012, Kirstin S. Dane published a blog post on her blog, *wood turtle*, about a mosque that seemed to have everything. The imam was animated and funny. The men's and women's sections were side by side, allowing families to sit together in the middle, with segregated sections at the back for those who preferred it. The post described the mosque's soup kitchen, community garden, babysitting services, counseling services, and library. It was accessible to people with disabilities and was constructed in an environmentally sustainable way. The mosque's board included "an equal number of men and women"; it hosted lectures on "Living with HIV" as well as drug abuse and racism; and it offered "registered chaplaincy courses for *anyone* interested in becoming an imam"—both men and women. It was a space where Kirstin and her family felt at home and "an example of what is possible when women and equity allies are given a platform to actualise their opinions and affirm their rights in Islam."[33]

The catch? Halfway through the post, Kirstin referred to her daughter Eryn as a teenager, signaling—especially to regular readers, who knew that Eryn was only a toddler at the time Kirstin wrote the post—that she was not describing a real mosque but rather projecting herself into the future, illustrating her vision of what an ideal mosque would look like.

The post received several comments from readers who were captivated by the space described in the post and disappointed to learn that this mosque did not actually exist. The first comment began, "In my mind I was thinking, I want to move where you live and go to this mosque too! It's like a fantasy land! Then I came to the part where Eryn was a teenager . . . nooooo it IS a fantasy land!"[34] More than one commenter talked about being brought to tears by the post, reflecting its high level of emotional resonance and perhaps also the collective frustration felt by many readers with the actual state of their local mosques. One reader noted the importance of providing sign language interpretation in order for this imagined mosque to be considered truly accessible, adding her voice to further expand its possibilities.

Kirstin's act of describing this mosque served as a rhetorical invitation to her readers to enter into a shared sacred space with her. In this context, it is important to consider not only what was lacking—a real physical mosque that fits Kirstin's description—but also what was made possible by the online environment: in this case, a collective imagining of space by those who do not (and likely will never, in most cases) occupy the same physical spaces, and thus a kind of sharing of sacred space and religious community that can only happen virtually. Moreover, Kirstin's description of this ideal space allowed her to bypass some of the constraints imposed by what was lacking in the physical spaces available to her; the virtual world was not alone in not entirely fulfilling her needs and desires. Kirstin's imagined mosque can be seen not only as reflecting distance and absence from where she would like to be but also as a way of accessing a space, and bringing readers to it, that was otherwise (at least for now) inaccessible to her.

Given that a "lack of community" is one of the criticisms made against some mosques, one might ask if the internet provides some kind of replacement, or substitution. Predictably, the answer is more complicated than a simple yes or no. On the one hand, when I posed this question to Kirstin in an interview, she was clear that, for her, the online environment functions differently from a mosque: it can create and sustain interpersonal connections, but it does not replace the mosque. In response to one comment on her blog, Kirstin wrote that "[online worlds] shore you up when you need to vent, discuss and even offer support and sympathy—but when it comes down to the needs of a physical structure (for such important things as life events: aqeeqas [rituals conducted after the birth of a baby], janaazas [funerals], weddings, etc), the virtual world sadly falls short."[35] Many of these "life events" are also subject to legal requirements that people be physically present in order for the ritual to be valid, which further highlights the ways that the online context cannot completely replace the physical one.

On the other hand, while it is clear that online communities are not replacing mosques in the sense of fulfilling all of the roles that mosques may be expected fulfill, in many cases, the mosques are not fulfilling all their desired functions either. In the absence of mosques that respond sufficiently to the needs of community members, it is the internet, and not the inadequate mosques, that seems to be the next best thing for many of the bloggers and their readers. In other words, even if the blog space does not replace a mosque, it is nonetheless being used by some Muslims instead of a mosque to foster community and connection. Moreover, there are some ways the blog space allows for communities that couldn't come together in a physical mosque because of the geographic distance between them; there are elements that are both lost and gained through this creation of online communities.

CONCLUSION

It could be easy, especially in today's Islamophobic context, for some of the struggles discussed here to be construed as examples of Islam as inherently oppressive and Muslim women as its victims. It feels important to highlight that the examples described here—which represent so many others—are of Muslim women who are fighting for a way *into* mosques and religious communities, not out of them. And whether it is through documenting the spaces that exist, calling on online communities to help influence spaces under construction, or imagining entirely new possibilities, Muslim women are continuing to find ways to challenge the physical spaces in which they find themselves and to harness creative ideas for building new communities. Through leaving comments or contributing photographs, Muslim feminist bloggers and their readers join in the co-construction of online ethical spaces by adding their own stories and expanding a field that becomes one of collective deliberation and interpretation. Although fluid and unpredictable, the communities formed through these collective processes are far from incidental. The practice of blogging for these blogs and their writers thus becomes a way not only of using personal narratives to inform religious interpretations but also of using these processes to form networks and communities, which in turn push their feminist interpretive work forward.

NOTES

1. Ify Okoye, "The Penalty Box: Muslim Women's Prayer Spaces," *Muslim Matters* (blog), February 8, 2010, http://muslimmatters.org/2010/02/08/the-penalty-box/.

2. Although academic convention would usually favor referring to writers with their last names, I have instead used first names for the bloggers discussed in this chapter, to remain consistent with the usual practices within the online spaces they inhabit.

3. See, for example, Ify Okoye, "The Masajid around Seattle," *Ify Okoye* (blog), August 24, 2007, http://ifyokoye.com/2007/08/24/the-masajid-around-seattle/; Ify Okoye, "Second Class Believers: An Unfortunate Sign at the Masjid," *Ify Okoye* (blog), October 13, 2007, http://ifyo koye.com/2007/10/13/very-unfortunate-sign-in-the-masjid/; and Ify Okoye, "Modern Muslim Chivalry," *Ify Okoye* (blog), December 22, 2008, http://ifyokoye.com/2008/12/22/modern-mus lim-chivarly/.

4. See, for example, Shireen Ahmed, "Privilege and Prayer Spaces: An Interview with Hind Makki of Side Entrance," *Muslimah Media Watch* (blog), August 29, 2013, http://www.patheos .com/blogs/mmw/2013/08/privilege-and-prayer-spaces-an-interview-with-hind-makki-of -side-entrance/; and Kirstin S. Dane, "niqab is not the problem," *wood turtle* (blog), April 15, 2011, http://woodturtle.wordpress.com/2011/04/15/niqab-is-not-the-problem/.

5. Mia Lövheim, "Young Women's Blogs as Ethical Spaces," *Information, Communication & Society* 14, no. 3 (2011): 338–54, https://doi.org/10.1080/1369118X.2010.542822.

6. Lövheim, "Young Women's Blogs," 350.

7. Juliane Hammer, *American Muslim Women, Religious Authority, and Activism: More than a Prayer* (Austin: University of Texas Press, 2012), 128.

8. Jasmin Zine, *Canadian Islamic Schools: Unravelling the Politics of Faith, Gender, Knowledge, and Identity* (Toronto: University of Toronto Press, 2008), 201.

9. Zine, *Canadian Islamic Schools*, 197.

10. Hammer, *American Muslim Women*, 128.

11. Sarah Sayeed, Aisha al-Adawiya, and Ihsan Bagby, "Women and the American Mosque," *The American Mosque 2011*, March 2013, http://www.hartfordinstitute.org/The-Ameri-can-Mosque-Report-3.pdf, 13.

12. Okoye, "The Penalty Box."

13. Of course, any impressions one can gain about a commenter's gender are based on their username or on any additional information they provide, but cannot be externally verified.

14. From a comment left by a commenter identified as Usman on Okoye, "The Penalty Box."

15. From a comment left by a commenter identified as Abd-Allah on Okoye, "The Penalty Box," emphasis in original. It is also worth noting that several commenters had, in fact, already cited Yaser Birjas, a graduate of the Islamic University of Madinah and teacher of AlMaghrib's Fiqh of Salah course (presumably the same one that Ify refers to in the post, although she does not name him herself). They cite him as having argued for the right of women to see the imam during congregational prayer. Emphasis in original is in bold type.

16. From a comment left by Ify Okoye on Okoye, "The Penalty Box."

17. "Muslim Women's Prayer Spaces," https://oursides.wordpress.com/.

18. Ify Okoye, "Pray in Accordance to the Sunnah: Women Protest against Marginalization," *Ify Okoye* (blog), June 8, 2010, http://ifyokoye.com/2010/06/08/pray-in-accordance-to-the-sun nah-women-protest-against-marginalization/.

19. Masserat Amir-Ebrahimi, "Transgression in Narration: The Lives of Iranian Women in Cyberspace," *Journal of Middle East Women's Studies* 4, no. 3 (2008), 89–115.

20. Ify Okoye, "Prince George's Muslim Association (PGMA) in Lanham, Maryland," *Ify Okoye* (blog), February 9, 2011, https://oursides.wordpress.com/2011/02/09/prince-georges-mus lim-association-in-lanham-maryland/.

21. Ify Okoye, "Pray-In Updates & Merging Oursides Blog," *Ify Okoye* (blog), July 11, 2011, http://ifyokoye.com/2011/07/11/pray-in-updates-merging-oursides-blog/.

22. "Side Entrance," http://sideentrance.tumblr.com/.

23. Hind Makki, "Where's My Space to Pray in This Mosque?" *AltMuslim* (blog), July 27, 2012, http://www.patheos.com/blogs/altmuslim/2012/07/wheres-my-space-to-pray-in-this-mosque/.

24. Ahmed, "Privilege and Prayer Spaces."

25. See, for example, Monique Parsons, "Muslim Women Challenge American Mosques: 'Now Is The Time,'" NPR, January 15, 2014, http://www.npr.org/2014/01/15/262408057/muslim-women-challenge-american-mosques-now-is-the-time; and Yasmine Hafiz, "Women's Prayer Spaces Featured in 'Side Entrance' Blog: A Call for Improved Conditions in Mosques," *Huffington Post*, July 20, 2013, http://www.huffingtonpost.com/2013/07/20/women-prayer-spaces-mosques_n_3624084.html.

26. Okoye, "Prince George's Muslim Association."

27. Nahida Sultana Nisa, "A Favor?," *the fatal feminist* (blog), August 13, 2012, http://thefatalfeminist.com/2012/08/13/a-favor/.

28. Nahida Sultana Nisa, "On the Mosque Reconstruction: An Update," *the fatal feminist* (blog), December 20, 2012, http://thefatalfeminist.com/2012/12/20/on-the-mosque-reconstruction-an-update/.

29. From a comment left by a commenter identified as Redd on Nisa, "A Favor?"

30. From a comment left by a commenter identified as qatheworld on Nisa, "A Favor?"

31. Nahida Sultana Nisa, "Barrier Update, and Men You Should Follow," *the fatal feminist* (blog), August 31, 2014, http://thefatalfeminist.com/2014/08/31/barrier-update-and-men-you-should-follow/.

32. Nisa, "Barrier Update," emphasis in original.

33. Kirstin S. Dane, "Dreaming of Eryn's Sermon," *wood turtle* (blog), February 2, 2012, https://woodturtle.wordpress.com/2012/02/02/eryns-sermon/.

34. From a comment left by a commenter identified as qatheworld on Dane, "Dreaming."

35. Kirstin S. Dane, "Unmosqued: Finding Community," *wood turtle* (blog), February 27, 2013, https://woodturtle.wordpress.com/2013/02/27/unmosqued-part-four/.

BIBLIOGRAPHY

Ahmed, Shireen. "Privilege and Prayer Spaces: An Interview with Hind Makki of Side Entrance." *Muslimah Media Watch* (blog). August 29, 2013. http://www.patheos.com/blogs/mmw/2013/08/privilege-and-prayer-spaces-an-interview-with-hind-makki-of-side-entrance/.

Amir-Ebrahimi, Masserat. "Transgression in Narration: The Lives of Iranian Women in Cyberspace." *Journal of Middle East Women's Studies* 4, no. 3 (2008), 89–115.

Dane, Kirstin S. "Dreaming of Eryn's Sermon." *wood turtle* (blog). February 2, 2012. https://woodturtle.wordpress.com/2012/02/02/eryns-sermon/.

———. "Niqab Is Not the Problem." *wood turtle* (blog). April 15, 2011. http://woodturtle.wordpress.com/2011/04/15/niqab-is-not-the-problem/.

———. "Unmosqued: Finding Community." *wood turtle* (blog). February 27, 2013. https://woodturtle.wordpress.com/2013/02/27/unmosqued-part-four/.

Hafiz, Yasmine. "Women's Prayer Spaces Featured in 'Side Entrance' Blog: A Call for Improved Conditions in Mosques." *Huffington Post*. July 20, 2013. http://www.huffingtonpost.com/2013/07/20/women-prayer-spaces-mosques_n_3624084.html.

Hammer, Juliane. *American Muslim Women, Religious Authority, and Activism: More than a Prayer.* Austin: University of Texas Press, 2012.

Lövheim, Mia. "Young Women's Blogs as Ethical Spaces." *Information, Communication & Society* 14, no. 3 (2011): 338–54. https://doi.org/10.1080/1369118X.2010.542822.

Makki, Hind. "Where's My Space to Pray in This Mosque?" *AltMuslim* (blog). July 27, 2012. http://www.patheos.com/blogs/altmuslim/2012/07/wheres-my-space-to-pray-in-this-mosque/.

Nisa, Nahida Sultana. "Barrier Update, and Men You Should Follow." *the fatal feminist* (blog). August 31, 2014. http://thefatalfeminist.com/2014/08/31/barrier-update-and-men-you-should-follow/.

———. "On the Mosque Reconstruction: An Update." *the fatal feminist* (blog). December 20, 2012. http://thefatalfeminist.com/2012/12/20/on-the-mosque-reconstruction-an-update/.

———. "A Favor?" *the fatal feminist* (blog). August 13, 2012. http://thefatalfeminist.com/2012/08/13/a-favor/.

Okoye, Ify. "The Masajid around Seattle." *Ify Okoye* (blog). August 24, 2007. http://ifyokoye.com/2007/08/24/the-masajid-around-seattle/.

———."Modern Muslim Chivalry." *Ify Okoye* (blog). December 22, 2008. http://ifyokoye.com/2008/12/22/modern-muslim-chivarly/.

———. "The Penalty Box: Muslim Women's Prayer Spaces." *Muslim Matters* (blog). February 8, 2010. http://muslimmatters.org/2010/02/08/the-penalty-box/.

———. "Pray in Accordance to the Sunnah: Women Protest against Marginalization." *Ify Okoye* (blog). June 8, 2010. http://ifyokoye.com/2010/06/08/pray-in-accordance-to-the-sunnah-women-protest-against-marginalization/.

———. "Pray-In Updates & Merging Oursides Blog." *Ify Okoye* (blog). July 11, 2011. http://ifyokoye.com/2011/07/11/pray-in-updates-merging-oursides-blog/.

———. "Prince George's Muslim Association (PGMA) in Lanham, Maryland." *Ify Okoye* (blog). February 9, 2011. https://oursides.wordpress.com/2011/02/09/prince-georges-muslim-association-in-lanham-maryland/.

———. "Second Class Believers: An Unfortunate Sign at the Masjid." *Ify Okoye* (blog). October 13, 2007. http://ifyokoye.com/2007/10/13/very-unfortunate-sign-in-the-masjid/.

Parsons, Monique. "Muslim Women Challenge American Mosques: 'Now Is the Time.'" NPR. January 15, 2014. http://www.npr.org/2014/01/15/262408057/muslim-women-challenge-american-mosques-now-is-the-time.

Sayeed, Sarah, Aisha al-Adawiya, and Ihsan Bagby. "Women and the American Mosque." *The American Mosque 2011*. March 2013. http://www.hartfordinstitute.org/The-American-Mosque-Report-3.pdf.

Zine, Jasmin. *Canadian Islamic Schools: Unravelling the Politics of Faith, Gender, Knowledge, and Identity*. Toronto: University of Toronto Press, 2008.

CHAPTER 23

Minoritized Sexual Identities and the Theo-Politics of Democracy

Ludger Viefhues-Bailey, PhD, LeMoyne College

ABSTRACT

There has been a shift in the field of women's studies to include minoritized sexual identities. Recent scholarship has demonstrated how religious practices or texts enable non-normative and queer sexualities. Yet many contemporary religious actors are also invested in maintaining the importance of an essential difference dividing the sexes. This chapter investigates from the perspective of political philosophy the political context enabling both the insistence on and dissolution of clearly bounded sexual identities. To this end, I will turn to Chantal Mouffe's vision of passionate politics and her distinction between a democratic and liberal logic of democracy. The former requires that legitimate political acts represent the will of *the people*. This logic mobilizes the passion of sex and forces us to construct women as biological and cultural reproducers of the nation. The liberal logic appeals to a framework of universal human rights transcending and subverting the need for clear-cut sexual identities. The seesawing entrenchment and weakening of the boundaries of the sexual are embedded in the modern democratic project.

MINORITIZED OR MAJORITIZED SEXUALITIES ARE MADE NOT GIVEN

From the beginning, two intertwining questions moved the field of women's studies forward: what constitutes gendered and sexual identities and how does their making produce (and not merely channel) political power? In the words of Sojourner Truth or Simone De Beauvoir, Mary Daly, Audrey Lourdes or bell hooks, we find an awareness that sexual and political identities are intertwined. This awareness is particularly strong in the contributions of Black or Latinx feminist or womanist writers as well as of those who embody a subaltern, postcolonial, or anti-colonial positionality. To De Beauvoir's insight that sexual identities are made and not given by birth, these works add that this making is embedded in other intersecting networks of power, such as racialization or imperial domination. Hence, answering the question of who counts as a sexual majority or minority requires more than simply counting bodies that have particular folds of flesh in their reproductive anatomy. Rather, answering it requires accounting for the mechanisms of power that aim to determine whose bodies should count and how. In other words, sexual majorities or minorities are not there, but they are made for the purposes of creating power differentials. This raises the question motivating this article: What arrangements of political power enable the production of heterosexuality as a normative system for what counts as a natural way to sort sexual bodies into *women* and *men*? Instead of treating minoritized sexualities as problem or curiosity, I want to treat in turn the heterosexual difference as something we need to account for. By italicizing in the following the allegedly natural identity markers of *women* or *men*, I want to startle the reader into realizing that I am talking about markers that are constructed to produce and distribute particular modes of political power.

This approach reflects the guiding insight of queer theories, that is, works that both continue and critique the project of women's studies. Philosophers, like Judith Butler, use it to destabilize the conceptual core of feminism. *Woman* is not given as a natural kind (akin to elms or birches) ready for feminist use but results from complex performances. Likewise, the sociologists Zimmerman and West argue that, in modern Western societies, performances of gender served to first establish and then naturalize a social system of heterosexual differentiation. They call these performances "doing gender." "Doing gender means creating differences between girls and boys and women and men, differences that are not natural, essential, or biological." Heterosexual differentiation results from social practices. Spinning new and liberating modes of being sexual into being requires journeying beyond the political framework that makes into *women* or *men* human beings with bodies of varying capacities for reproduction and pleasure.[1]

If the differentiation between "girls and boys and women and men" is performative, then the heterosexual difference is not simply a reflection of biological nature. Our various sexual anatomies are in the service of "doing gender." Thus, the following question arises: Why and how are sexual majorities and minorities made? What is the social or political urgency to which *defending* the heterosexual difference responds? And yet also the opposite is true: if any mode of sexual identification reflects modes of power, then we can likewise ask, what is the social or political urgency to which *critiquing* the heterosexual difference and attending sexual minoritized bodies responds.

This is the task of the current chapter. And, indeed, the answer will be the same for both questions. What I will describe as the competing logics operating in democratic governance enable both the maintenance and critiquing of heterosexual differentiation or the making and unmaking of sexual majoritization. Hence, it makes sense that we find religious and political activists on both sides of debates about how natural the heterosexual difference is, and thus on who or who does not count as a sexual minority. Given the space constraints of this paper, I will focus, however, only on Christian activism defending this difference, particularly those supporting illiberal democracies in Europe and the United States. I have written a more ethnographical account on Christian activism resisting same-sex marriage, and I am thus aware that political motivations are not the same as religious ones. However, here, I want to reflect from the perspective of political philosophy on the opportunities that the system of democracy affords to the shaping of religious activism on issues of sexual majoritization and minoritization.[2]

Theopolitical movements supporting illiberal democracy are not a novelty. They have developed and gained steady ground over the last three decades on both sides of the Atlantic. Anti-LGBT movements are violently active in US and European politics, from Hungary or Poland, to Germany and France. And their activist roots reach deep. In the US case, let me only point to Phyllis Stewart Schlafly's successful political and religious mobilizations against the Equal Rights Amendment in the 1970s. In Europe, the networks of religious and political organizations agitating against what they call "gender ideology" and defending "gender complementarity" were formed also in the 1970s. Tracing them, we find moreover, active connections between the United States and European conservative religiopolitical movements. Thus, it would a mistake to see this kind of theopolitical activism in fervent support of the heterosexual difference as a historical fluke that has nothing to teach us about the relationship between politics and sexualities. Indeed, what these movements can teach us is that they respond to a systematic problem in democratic governance. In this sense, they are not anti-democratic but rather defenders of a particular vision of democracy. But what is this vision? What kind of democracy do these activists defend and why does the heterosexual difference play such a prominent role for them? Why does their defense of democracy require defending the majoritizing of the heterosexual difference at the expense of trans, queer, or intersex bodies?

Turning to the political philosopher Chantal Mouffe's concept of passionate politics allows us to answer these questions from the perspective of a sexually aware political theology: sexual passions are part of "the political" that must be incited and domesticated through politics. Christian heteropatriarchy can meet this systemic demand. Given the constraints of this chapter, I will point to the US context only to provide examples for this project. The goal is to think with the populists about democracy in order to then understand how the political order enables or disables sexual majoritization and minoritization.

First, I will establish the need for attending to sexuality in the pursuit of political and theological analyses of illiberal populist movements. In political science, demand-side explanations of these movements focus on the failure of elites to capture their population's socio-economic grievances. These works overlook the heteropatriarchal theology that these movements mobilize. Thus, I will expand, secondly, on Chantal Mouffe's framework to discuss the passionate construction of the *we/they* divide as constitutive for the theopolitical production of the people. Third, I will turn to the politics of contraception in the United States, to further analyze the passion missing in Mouffe's ontology of the political: sex. Extending Mouffe demonstrates that by domesticating sex through heteropatriarchy, illiberal populism answers to a systemic demand all democracies share: the (re)production of the people as citizens.

This analysis allows us to understand why Christian and political activists focus on the heterosexual difference. At a time when neoliberal globalization made the replacement of labor less pressing for capital and when national sovereignty weakened, un-reproductive sexual passions could be folded into the maintenance of the state. Queer political sexualities and the weakening of the heterosexual difference became possible. Yet, even if employers and global capitalists do not require the reproduction of "the people," the democratic state needs it and with it the heterosexual difference. Sexual passions are part of the political, and Christian heteropatriarchy stands ready to incite and domesticate them.

ATTENDING TO SEXUAL PASSIONS

To begin, let me quickly clarify some central concepts, like "populism" or "illiberal democracy." Chantal Mouffe is suspicious of the term and fearing that it is used to delegitimize political movements that challenge the neoliberal consensus.[3] And yet turning to Mouffe allows us to get a more precise handle on the phenomenon of populism: she points out that the current historical project of democracy as it arose in the North Atlantic cultural nexus exists as tension. This is the tension between a liberal logic of universal human rights and individual freedoms, on the one hand, and the democratic logic based on equality and popular sovereignty, on the other. The conflictual intertwining of both logics that makes liberal democracy work: the liberal logic challenges the exclusionary tendencies inherent in the need to produce the sovereign people; the democratic logic assures that the rights and freedoms of citizens are the product of the sovereign will of the people.

In a Mouffean picture, the democratic logic of democracy is by definition illiberal because it is invested in the production of a particular people as sovereign. The competing logics must be instantiated in institutions of governance and of political life. When the pressures of global capital or of supra-national political integration instantiate an order of rights and freedoms that is universal but not legitimized by the people concerned, the balance of the liberal and democratic logic of democracy is out of whack. We should, therefore, expect movements to emerge that marshal the logic of democratic sovereignty, which is by definition an "illiberal" logic.

Mouffe allows us to offer, what I want to call a systemic demand-side explanation for the emergence of populist movements in support of the democratic logic of democracy. In an institutional environment characterized by supra-national political and global economic integration, policy decisions (including those purportedly in the service of universal human rights) lack democratic legitimacy. This institutional demand-side explanation can link with empirical comparative studies by political scientist Daphne Halikiopoulou and others that demonstrate that economic grievances per se are insufficient to account for the rise of illiberal populist movements. Instead, what predicts such movements are unmet economic demands together with a crisis of legitimacy of democratic institutions.[4]

For this chapter, I want to focus on what Matthew Golder calls "exclusionary" populists, that is, movements that seek to exclude certain groups from "the people" and thus limit their access to citizenship. Central for Golder is the construction of a homogeneous vision of "the people," as the main concern for populism. This construction can be inclusionary or exclusionary: Inclusionary populism tries to extend material and political benefits to "historically disadvantaged and excluded groups. In contrast, exclusionary populism seeks to exclude certain groups from 'the people' and thus limit their access to these same benefits and rights." In short, I am concerned here with the marriage of right-wing religious and political movements as examples of an exclusionary populist movement (Golder) in support of the democratic logic of democracy (Mouffe).[5]

What remains however unaccounted for, is the marked presence of hetero-patriarchal discourses in the populist movements in support of the democratic logic of democracy. Why are concerns over gender, transgender rights, reproductive freedoms, and marriage rights at stake in these movements? Why is the doctrinal innovation of gender complementarity a battle cry uniting conservative Catholics and white Evangelicals in Europe and the United States?

MOUFFE'S PASSIONATE POLITICS

Focusing on the problem of national reproduction allows us to see that the passionate politics on display in current populist movements are not a novelty. Rather, they express a latent feature of Western secular democracies reflecting a systemic demand inherent in the Western ideal of popular sovereignty: This is the urgency of how needing to create what the sociologist John Lie calls "peoplehood," the deep sense of belonging to a nation or particular ethnic group commanding or allowing political attachment. Democracies can only function as such if they produce their people.[6]

Mouffe's reworking of Schmitt gives an account of the production of peoplehood that lays bare the libidinal element in the political. For her, the people as a cohesive moral unity are produced by mobilizing the passions of antagonism. We know who *we* are by defining who is our enemy. The friend/enemy distinction establishes *us* as a people, in contrast to other people or others who are not a people. The *we* that any polity must produce as a moral center establishes itself in defiance of its other, the *them*. And because this very center is ontologically empty, the process of antagonistic identity formation has to repeat itself and is always incomplete.[7]

If antagonism shapes the outside of a people, these passions must be modulated for the working of a democracy within a state. The political processes within a particular democracy should be marked by the conflicts that are not a matter of the (moral) death or life of the people. Thus, the task of politics is to domesticate the antagonistic passions that the state must mobilize to establish its defining borders into the constrained struggle of political agonism inside those borders. This domestication requires that *we* stop seeing *them* as moral evil to be eradicated. Instead, the other becomes a partner in a political struggle. The goal of this struggle must be to vanquish the political opponent but not by extinguishing them. To function, the democratic state must incite passions and control them. In the following, I will argue that a similar modulation of passions is necessary if it comes to the passion missing in Mouffe's account: sex.

QUEERING MOUFFE'S PASSIONATE POLITICS

Mouffe does not attend to an important other libidinal register in the service of (re)producing the people: sexual passions. This is surprising, given the extensive literature on sexuality and the nation, ranging from Nira Yuval-Davis's groundbreaking work to Anne Stoler's *Carnal Knowledge and Imperial Power*, or Pascal Blanchard's *Sexe, race et colonies*.[8]

Inciting Sexual Passions and the Making of Heterosexuality at the Border

Yuval-Davis following Cynthia Enloe argues that in nationalist war rhetoric, men are supposed to fight for "womenandchildren" (*sic*). Women are not only like children (helpless and in need of male protection), but also women-and-children together represent the reproductive future of the nation. Hence, attacking another nation at its core will always imply attacking their reproductive future by attacking their women. Militarized rape then is the clearest form of war. By fusing the emotions men are supposed to associate with the nation (honor, collective power) with those associated with reproduction (eros), the border of the nation becomes violently eroticized.[9]

The current contestations over immigration in the United States supply ample evidence for this eroticization of the nation's border. President Donald Trump's rhetoric is full of images of violent "Mexican" rapists who enter the nation unchecked. In this rhetoric, the threat to the nation is encoded as (unlawful) penetration.[10] The nation's borders, in contrast, appear as passive and vulnerable spaces. A physical cordon preventing penetration is necessary. At the border, the bodies that represent the reproductive future of a nation are indeed encoded as "womenandchildren." Bodies that represent the reproductive threat of sexual violence are encoded as *men*. The threat emanating from foreign "womenandchildren" is their reproductive power. Border sex requires the imagination and incitement of a particular heterosexual distinction, along the familiar heterosexist lines of female passivity and male aggression. Given this need, it is clear that trans and queer bodies make this type of border sex impossible. By drawing attention to the complexities of biological reproduction and sexual performance, they disrupt the performative nature to a sexual order that naturalizes the heterosexual distinction between violent *men* and passive *women* who are vessels of reproduction.

Controlling Sexual Passions and Making of Women's Bodies

Areletta Norval has shown that identity formation, including that of group identity, does not require antagonism. The self is not only constructed through aversion but also through the desires of attraction and fusion. Sexual passions produce flows of power by mobilizing all of these in messy ways. Making the *us* that constitutes the popular sovereign is not only a matter of defining borders but also one of mobilizing and controlling sex. For the internal maintenance of a functioning democracy, the sexual passions aroused in antagonistic border sex must be modulated so that those produced as *women* can be seen as both vessels of national reproduction and as citizens. Christian activists defending the heterosexual distinction stand ready to serve this need.[11]

All democratic states face the problem of how to reproduce the people as sovereigns correctly, as it were, and thus must produce and control *women's* bodies. Yuval-Davis notes that in democratic states *women* exist in two spheres: On the one hand, they exist as human citizens whose reproductive capacities do not matter. In this sense their bodies conform to the liberal logic of democracy. We share civic rights because we are human, not because we are set aside as *women* or as *men*. On the other hand, those whose bodies are capable of reproduction, that is, of bearing children, are singled out as *women*. As such they are subjected to a myriad of laws and regulations policing their reproductive bodies. Their bodies conform to the democratic logic of democracy. As *women* their bodies are in the service of the people.

As citizens, *women* are supposedly equal in their right to participate in the economic and political life of the nation and shape it. In this sense their bodies are private since a citizen's reproductive anatomy does not matter for these pursuits. At the same time, the nation's reproductive needs require *women's* bodies to be controlled by the urgency to reproduce the sovereign people correctly. In this sense, the reproductive anatomy of citizens matters. The reproductive capacities of *women* are what a state needs. Their bodies are public property. As my word choice indicates, the distinction between *women* and *men* is salient for the democratic logic of democracy. Here, it matters that we can separate out the kind of bodies that are capable of reproducing the nation. We have to know whose bodies to control. Hence, the democratic logic of democracy requires the heterosexual difference by defining some bodies as *women*, that is, as those capable of bearing children. According to the liberal logic of democracy, citizens are unsexed; according to the democratic logic of democracy, citizens in the service of reproduction are *women*. Hence, defenders of that logic focus intently on the question of who is and who is not *women*. Their bodies must be sexualized to incite sexual passions and controlled to ensure the right reproduction of the nation. The ability to define and control who is and who is not *women* is central for the democratic logic of democracy. Again, trans or queer bodies threaten this ability.

Increasing access to political and economic equality does not negate the urgency for some citizens to serve the people as *women*. Rather, increasing economic participation will only provoke the need to invest in a discourse that naturalizes motherhood. The French philosopher Elizabeth Badinter argues that, as fewer humans with reproductive abilities require marriage and motherhood for their economic survival, motherhood, and with it becoming a *woman*, will be optional. At this point, Badinter claims, discourses flourish that celebrate how "natural" motherhood is for those tasked to be "women." She singles out for critique feminist and philosophical movements in Europe that naturalize motherhood. However, her point can shed light as well on conservative Christian discourses in the United States.[12]

The economic situation of many *women* in the United States (and presumably Europe) is less rosy as Badinter describes. *Women* in the United States experience the pressure to lean into their private citizen bodies, by pursuing economic success. Without their work a family cannot hold onto the vestiges of middle-class life. Yet privatizing their bodies by following the liberal logic of democracy does not liberate them from being public property. The contrary is the case. This privatization increases the need to incentivize reproduction by making it allegedly natural for *women* (as Badinter argues) and by policing their bodies.

The complexities of White Evangelical theologies of gender serve to maintain this double life of *women*. As I have traced in previous work, they are not discouraged to be citizens and even become competitive and leaders in the world of business and, to a degree, in that of politics. At the same time, as *women*, they have to be submissive to their husbands in the home and fulfill what is imagined to be their natural destiny: becoming mothers.[13]

In particular, the Evangelical and Catholic discourse of gender-complementarity aims to present a sexual order where equality and submissions co-exist. In a surprising theological alliance, both white Evangelicals and Catholics agree that the goal of marriage is biological reproduction. And since *women* and *men* are unequally situated on this account, the theopolitics of gender-complementarity allows that both are treated differently, if it comes to issues of reproduction. By making the reproduction into a central goal, demand, and desire for married life, these types of Christianities provide anthropological and theological incentives for *women* to take on the unequal burdens of reproductive labor, as if it was natural for them to do so.

Theo-political incentives are particularly necessary in the United States given that the privatization of the costs of reproduction makes it economically irrational for *women* to bear children. Anne Crittenden notes that motherhood is the biggest risk factor predicting poverty in old age for any American *woman*. A team of economists around Ilyana Kuziemko found that the more American *women* are burdened unequally with reproductive labor, the more they tend to favor patriarchal family models. It seems that for these American *women* the economics of child raising make understandable the claim that they are naturally suited to be mothers.[14]

In an increasingly neoliberal economy, white American Christian theologies of gender and sexuality respond to a political opportunity structure arising out of the need to reproduce the sovereign people. *Women* are market actors like anyone else but since they must take on an unfair burden to satisfy the nation's need for reproduction, these theologies present them with supernatural incentives. At the same time, the systemic urgency that the democratic logic of democracy produces presents White American Christianity with an opportunity to imbricate itself into the body politic.

We can trace this mutual embedding of White Christian theologies of gender and sex in the politics of national reproduction in the increasing use of police power to control *women's* bodies, through various abortion and fetal personhood laws. The racial and classed nature of the application of these laws results in making reproduction even more dangerous and costly for minoritized *women*.

By making the bodies of poor and racially minoritized *women* into reproductive problems requiring state control, the legal framing of opposing a fetus with their delinquent mother contributes further to the privatization of reproductive labor. In this framing, the mother's private problematic life choices endanger the child. At the same time, the bodies of minoritized *women* are persecuted, policed, and further marked as unruly, threatening the imaginary natural reproductive order of the nation. This control allows to maintain the idea that *women* are simply equals as citizens, while also controlling the reproduction of those whose bodies do not matter to the state.

Hand in hand, with this encroachment of religiously sanctioned state power, goes an equally religiously sanctioned retraction of state power: the creation of spaces that are exempt from public mandates to provide *women* with medical care enabling reproductive choice. Through religious liberty legislation and jurisprudence, Congress and the US Supreme Court have created a "huge religious zone where the employment laws do not apply, and individuals lose their constitutional and statutory rights." This is a zone of "private" spaces that protects the sincerely held religious beliefs of religious institutions and closely held private companies.[15]

The religious or moral beliefs in question concern in particular the gendered nature of reproduction. Here, the alliance between white Evangelicals and US Catholics managed to restrict access to birth control and abortion, while increasing the costs of having children for minoritized *women*. Hence, the Christian discourse of heterosexual gender complementarity appears as a tool well suited for the reproductive needs of a democratic nation following the democratic logic of democracy. In this way of conceiving the heterosexual difference, Christian activists can have it both ways: They can claim on the one hand that the sexes are equal and thus acknowledge the liberal logic of democracy; and they can assert, on the other hand, that this equality does not lead to universally equal treatment before the law thus serving the democratic logic of democracy. Conceiving the heterosexual difference in terms of gender complementary supports the creation of the two bodies of *women* for the sake of national reproduction.

CONCLUSION

Needless to say, the nation could reproduce itself through migration. Yet this prospect threatens the antagonistic demarcation of the nation. *We* cease to be distinguishable from *them*. The nation's future as this particular (white) American nation is at stake. This is the core of the hard-right fear of replacement, that is, the idea that the dominant White population is being replaced by culturally alien migrants. Proponents of this theory, like the Republican Congressman Steven Arnold King, connect this fear of replacement to the providing of contraception through the mandates of Obamacare. Such a provision would drive down the American birth rate below that necessary to keep the white population at a stable level. To ward off this feared replacement of American families by aliens, the nation has to intervene where the reproductive choice happens, namely, in the allegedly private sphere of the family. Here, lies the urgency for an allegedly private mechanism of controlling and incentivizing *women* to reproduce. The need to define the nation's borders, leads to the urgency to marshal internally the powers of *women's* bodies to reproduce the nation—and to control them.

At a time when neoliberal globalization made the replacement of labor less pressing for capital and national sovereignty weakened, non-reproductive sexual passions could be folded into the maintenance of the state in some cases. Yet, even if employers and global capital do not require national reproduction, the democratic state needs it. Sexual passions are part of the political, and Christian heteropatriarchy stands ready to incite and domesticate them.

NOTES

1. Candace West and Don H. Zimmerman, "Doing Gender," *Gender and Society* 1, no. 2 (1987), 137; Judith Butler, *Gender Trouble: Feminism and the Subversion of Identity, Thinking Gender,* (New York: Routledge, 1990).

2. See, e.g., Ludger Viefhues-Bailey, *Between a Man and a Woman? Why Conservatives Oppose Same-Sex Marriage* (New York: Columbia University Press, 2010).

3. Chantal Mouffe, "The Populist Challenge," 2016, 2019, www.opendemocracy.net/democra ciaabierta/chantal-mouffe/populist-challenge.

4. Daphne Halikiopoulou and Sophia Vasilopoulou, "Breaching the Social Contract: Crises of Democratic Representation and Patterns of Extreme Right Party Support," *Government and Opposition,* January (2016).

5. Matt Golder, "Far Right Parties in Europe," *Annual Review of Political Science* 19 (2016), 479.

6. Daphne Halikiopoulou, Steven E. Mock, and Sophia Vasilopoulou, "The Civic Zeitgeist: Nationalism and Liberal Values in the European Radical Right," *Nations and Nationalism* 19, no. 1 (2013); John Lie, *Modern Peoplehood* (Cambridge, MA: Harvard University Press, 2004).

7. Chantal Mouffe, *Agonistics: Thinking the World Politically* (New York: Verso Books, 2013).

8. Ann Laura Stoler, *Carnal Knowledge and Imperial Power : Race and the Intimate in Colonial Rule* (Berkeley: University of California Press, 2002); Pascal Blanchard, ed., *Sexe, Race et Colonies* (Paris: La Découverte, 2019); Nira Yuval-Davis, *Gender & Nation, Politics and Culture* (Thousand Oaks, CA: Sage Publications, 1997).

9. Cynthia H. Enloe, "Women and Children: Making Feminist Sense of the Persian Gulf Crisis," *The Village Voice* 19, no 2 (1990): 51–52.

10. Amy N. Heuman and Alberto González, "Trump's Essentialist Border Rhetoric: Racial Identities and Dangerous Liminalities," *Journal of Intercultural Communication* 47, no. 4 (2018).

11. Aletta Norval, "Trajectories of Future Research in Discourse Theory," in *Discourse Theory and Political Analysis: Identities, Hegemonies and Social Change,* ed. David J. Howarth et al. (Manchester: Manchester University Press, 2000), 223.

12. Elisabeth Badinter, *The Conflict: How Modern Motherhood Undermines the Status of Women* (New York: HarperCollins, 2013), iii.

13. Viefhues-Bailey, *Between a Man and a Woman?*

14. Ann Crittenden, *The Price of Motherhood: Why the Most Important Job in the World Is Still the Least Valued* (New York: Metropolitan Books, 2001), 27; Ilyana Kuziemko et al., "The Mommy Effect: Do Women Anticipate in the Employment Effects of Motherhood?" Working Paper No. 24740, National Bureau of Economic Research, Cambridge, MA (2018).

15. Leslie C. Griffith, "A Word of Warning from a Woman: Arbitrary, Categorical, and Hidden Religious Exemptions Threaten LGBT Rights," *Alabama Civil Rights & Civil Liberties Law Review* 7 (2015), 98.

BIBLIOGRAPHY

Badinter, Elisabeth. *The Conflict: How Modern Motherhood Undermines the Status of Women.* New York: HarperCollins, 2013.

Blanchard, Pascal, ed. *Sexe, Race et Colonies.* Paris: La Découverte, 2019.

Butler, Judith. *Gender Trouble: Feminism and the Subversion of Identity.* New York: Routledge, 1990.

Crittenden, Ann. *The Price of Motherhood: Why the Most Important Job in the World Is Still the Least Valued.* New York: Metropolitan Books, 2001.

Enloe, Cynthia H. "Women and Children: Making Feminist Sense of the Persian Gulf Crisis." *The Village Voice* 19, no 2 (1990): 51–52.

Golder, Matt. "Far Right Parties in Europe." *Annual Review of Political Science* 19 (2016): 477–97.

Griffith, Leslie C. "A Word of Warning from a Woman: Arbitrary, Categorical, and Hidden Religious Exemptions Threaten LGBT Rights." *Alabama Civil Rights & Civil Liberties Law Review* 7 (2015): 97–128.

Halikiopoulou, Daphne, Steven E. Mock, and Sophia Vasilopoulou. "The Civic Zeitgeist: Nationalism and Liberal Values in the European Radical Right." *Nations and Nationalism* 19, no. 1 (2013): 107–27.

Halikiopoulou, Daphne, and Sophia Vasilopoulou. "Breaching the Social Contract: Crises of Democratic Representation and Patterns of Extreme Right Party Support." *Government and Opposition*, January (2016): 1–25.

Heuman, Amy N., and Alberto González. "Trump's Essentialist Border Rhetoric: Racial Identities and Dangerous Liminalities." *Journal of Intercultural Communication* 47, no. 4 (2018): 326–42.

Kuziemko, Ilyana, Jessica Pan, Jenny Shen, and Ebonya Washington. "The Mommy Effect: Do Women Anticipate the Employment Effects of Motherhood?" Paper No. 24740 June 2018, National Bureau of Economic Research. Cambridge, MA.

Lie, John. *Modern Peoplehood*. Cambridge, MA: Harvard University Press, 2004.

Mouffe, Chantal. *Agonistics: Thinking the World Politically*. New York: Verso Books, 2013.

———. "The Populist Challenge." 2016, 2019. www.opendemocracy.net/democraciaabierta/chantal-mouffe/populist-challenge.

Norval, Aletta. "Trajectories of Future Research in Discourse Theory." In *Discourse Theory and Political Analysis: Identities, Hegemonies and Social Change*, edited by David J. Howarth, David R. Howarth, Aletta Norval, and Yannis Stavrakakis, 219–36. Manchester: Manchester University Press, 2000.

Stoler, Ann Laura. *Carnal Knowledge and Imperial Power: Race and the Intimate in Colonial Rule*. Berkeley: University of California Press, 2002.

Viefhues-Bailey, Ludger. *Between a Man and a Woman? Why Conservatives Oppose Same-Sex Marriage*. New York: Columbia University Press, 2010.

Yuval-Davis, Nira. *Gender & Nation, Politics and Culture*. Thousand Oaks, CA: Sage Publications, 1997.

Zimmerman, Candace West, and Don H. "Doing Gender." *Gender and Society* 1, no. 2 (1987): 125–51.

CHAPTER 24

Spiritual Homelessness and Homemaking

··

A Nomadic Spirituality for Survivors of Childhood Violence

Denise Starkey, PhD, College of St. Scholastica

ABSTRACT

Being lost, displaced, and homeless is the cost of survival for many survivors of childhood and interpersonal violence. Survivors often have an all-consuming desire to belong. Yet, when they look to their religious communities, the idealized talk of home is inadequate for the needs of healing and flourishing. I name this experience spiritual homelessness: the displacement and exile that results when survivors cannot find belonging in their faith traditions and search elsewhere. This searching is often judged as misguided, but I argue that this is a holy and healing quest that opens possibilities for a new future. Authentic presence to one's experience may require moving toward the ambiguous, the unmapped, and the undetermined. In this chapter, I explore feminist metaphors and practices of home-making and propose a blueprint for a nomadic spirituality of home.

INTRODUCTION

Being displaced and homeless is the cost of survival for many survivors of childhood and interpersonal violence. When (and if) physical and psychic safety are achieved, the journey toward healing evolves, and many survivors discover an all-consuming desire to belong. They often look to religious communities to find a sense of belonging and home. Some survivors may go to great lengths to adapt to a certain religiosity, while others come to recognize that the explanations of suffering or salvation that fail to distinguish between the sinner and the sinned-against do not help with their healing or coming to belonging. They refuse to accept that suffering is the result of their sin or that their suffering is redemptive.

As theologian Wendy Farley observes, "for the sources of suffering to come from the church and be justified by its Scripture and traditions is a kind of toxic, crushing pain that is hard to endure."[1] If God is all-knowing and all-powerful, as many religions teach, survivors may also see God as responsible and feel abandoned. The idealized, other-worldly talk of home and belonging is inadequate for the needs of healing and flourishing *in the present*. They often feel doubly bereft when a spiritual refuge cannot be found. "When the church withholds divine love, where can we go to learn our true name?"[2] The path toward healing meanders; it is neither linear nor predictable. So survivors look elsewhere. They search.

I name this experience "spiritual homelessness," by which I mean the displacement and exile that results when survivors of childhood violence, looking for hope and *looking for home*, feel they must lose God and their religious communities in order to heal. Authentic presence to one's experience, a requirement for healing, may require moving toward an ambiguous and unmapped state of exile. Edward Said, in his eloquent "Reflections on Exile," describes exile as "the unhealable rift between a human being and a native place, between the self and its true home: its essential sadness can never be surmounted."[3] This displacement, an involuntary or coerced movement necessitated by survival, is compounded when the rift includes one's religious beliefs.

In recent decades, feminist scholars of religion have unearthed treasure troves of narratives, practices, and languages that mediate understandings of the divine as present and near in the experience of suffering. These understandings challenge traditional teachings rooted in male experience that emphasize only distance between the divine and humanity. My belief is that drawing upon these rich resources means that the work of home-making for survivors is not one of *creatio ex nihilo*—creation from nothing. Instead, feminist revisions of the practices of home-making may offer a blueprint for a nomadic spirituality of home that opens a different possibility for belonging and healing.

SURVIVING CHILD ABUSE

Although much research, activism, and prevention work has happened in the last few decades, the understanding of the long-term consequences of child abuse remains incomplete. Plenty is known about its scope and shape: child abuse crosses all socioeconomic and international borders.[4] According to the World Health Organization "child abuse or maltreatment constitutes all forms of physical and/or emotional ill-treatment, sexual abuse, neglect or negligent treatment or commercial or other exploitation, resulting in actual or potential harm to the child's health, survival, development or dignity in the context of a relationship of responsibility, trust or power."[5] Yet the often lifelong effects of abuse remain misunderstood and stand in sharp contrast to the romanticized view of childhood in many developed countries.

In *Too Scared to Cry: Psychic Trauma in Childhood*, Lenore Terr observes, "[i]f one could live a thousand years, one might completely work through . . . childhood trauma by playing out the terrifying scenario until it no longer terrified. The lifetime allotted to the ordinary person does not appear to be enough."[6] The aftermath of complex trauma is often an experience of living death, repressed memory, frozen desire, and engraved betrayal. The present is held hostage to an over-present past. Cathy Caruth notes that the crisis at the core of trauma is a pressing question, "Is trauma the encounter with death or the ongoing experience of having survived it? An oscillation between a crisis of death and the correlative crisis of life: between the story of the unbearable nature of an event and the story of the unbearable nature of its survival."[7] The central dialectic of trauma is the will to deny the trauma and the will to proclaim the truth about the trauma. One of the pernicious consequences of surviving is the way the trauma spirals back again and again.

In her classic work on posttraumatic stress disorder, Judith Herman describes the difficult "act of knowing" wrought by trauma for those who do survive.

> The traumatic event challenges an ordinary person to become a theologian, a philosopher, and a jurist. The survivor is called upon to articulate the values and beliefs that she once held and that the trauma destroyed. She stands mute before the emptiness of evil, feeling the insufficiency of any known system of explanation. . . . In order to develop a full understanding of the trauma story, the survivor must examine the moral questions of guilt and responsibility and reconstruct a system of belief that makes sense of her undeserved suffering. Finally, the survivor cannot reconstruct a sense of meaning by the exercise of thought alone. The remedy for injustice also requires action. The survivor must decide what is to be done. As the survivor attempts to resolve these questions, she often comes into conflict with important people in her life. *There is a rupture in her sense of belonging within a shared system of belief.* Thus, she faces a double task: not only must she rebuild her own "shattered assumptions" about meaning, order and justice in the world but she must also find a way to resolve her differences with those whose beliefs she can no longer share. [emphasis added][8]

The violence many children experience is committed by those charged with caring for them. When the abuse is justified by religious demands to honor parents and the dominant language used to name God is parental, survivors too often find themselves struggling for survival on their own. In order to heal, a moment or movement of dissent—in other words, the great sin of disobedience—is required to displace the "assumed" knowledge spoken in patriarchal religious answers.[9] Thus, movement toward healing may also necessitate rejecting God because it would be masochistic to pursue a relationship with a divine perpetrator.[10] Spiritual homelessness can feel like standing on a deserted island in the center of a large city. The cacophony of discordant narratives requires survivors to become explorers and archaeologists digging for different metaphors and practices. This is arduous work.

HOME SWEET HOME?

Spiritual homelessness resides in the wasteland between idealized notions of home as place and home as emotional and spiritual belonging. Home is often understood as a geographic and material point in space and time that we come from and return to and that is invested with psychological and religious meanings. The *Oxford English Dictionary* defines *home* as "a dwelling place; a person's house or abode; the fixed residence of a family; . . . A refuge, a sanctuary; a place or region to which one naturally belongs or where one feels at ease." Davidson and Gitlitz observe, "Home is frequently the locus of a person's sense of identity. It is the territory of the clan, of the family burial plot, of childhood memories, of the events that gave shape to a person's life."[11] In his influential work, geographer Edward Relph defines home as "a central point of existence and individual identity from which you look out on the rest of the world; the place where "practical and religious feelings about place are interwoven."[12] Relph defines place as the experience of rootedness, authenticity, and insidedness, and the absence of these is placelessness.[13]

Many people seem to have a positive, even romantic, view of material home, the place they come from, or the idealized place they think constitutes home. For others home is known by its absence. "Having a home may be an unlived, phantom condition, or only a distant memory, a half-lived, or now-lost experience."[14] Nothing, it seems, alleviates the universal yearning for home, even if one has never had one. Frederick Buechner uses the idea of "homesickness" to name this universal longing.[15]

Spiritual and religious narratives that ground understandings of what home and belonging should be often fail to account for those who have been displaced. Zen priest Zenju Eathlyn Manuel notes, "The words 'I am home' don't resonate" for those who have been a "target of hatred and violence . . . those who are dehumanized are never home."[16] Although Buddhist "teachings on find[ing] home are profound . . . they often leave out the experiences of those who are dehumanized in their own homeland."[17] This includes the millions of refugees risking life and limb fleeing to refuge and safety by cramming into inadequate vessels heading into open waters. It includes members of the LGBQTIA community who find themselves shoved to the margins by families and religions. And it also includes the invisible millions of children and women who experience intimate hatred and violence in places that are anything other than sanctuaries.

Nowhere does the normalization of violence have deeper roots than in traditional understandings of home. The poet Adrienne Rich first observed that home is the most dangerous place on earth for women.[18] In *Sexual Harassment of Working Women*, philosopher Catherine MacKinnon argued that the "intimate violation of women by men is sufficiently pervasive in American society as to be nearly invisible."[19] Joshua Price also challenges the "apotheosis of home"—a divinized ideal of home as "a place of safety and refuge." The lived reality of home for many women and children is a space that maintains and obscures violence.[20]

Feminist scholars, beginning with Simone de Beauvoir, have understood meanings of home as the source for women's oppression and the socialization of girls into patriarchal norms. Women have long been deemed the creators of this domestic private space in which men find home, comfort, and nourishment. Home as traditionally constructed has not been a place where women find their own subjectivity and nourishment. Beauvoir observed that the "comforts and supports of house and home historically come at women's expense. . . . Few tasks are more like the torture of Sisyphus than housework, with its endless repetition. The clean becomes soiled, the soiled is made clean, over and over, day after day."[21] In Beauvoir's withering view, this structure restricts women to immanence while making men's access to transcendence, and, therefore subjectivity, possible.

In Talmudic literature, "home is a woman." The first exile people experience is the ejection from the home of a woman's body. In a reflection on his own longing for home, Holocaust survivor Elie Wiesel, who promotes this Jewish understanding of women as the homemakers, also posits the idea that the opposite of home is not prison, but exile. "The opposite of home," Elie Wiesel observes, "is not the prison—which may, eventually, become home—but exile. More than prison, exile suggests uncertainty, anguish, solitude, suspicion, hunger, thirst and a constant feeling of guilt." Longing itself means to "be in exile and yearn for redemption which, in the Jewish tradition, is interpreted as returning home."[22] If woman is the source of home for men, what is the source of home for women?

For survivors from dysfunctional or violent homes the loss of home is complex. The pain of homesickness is intensified by the loss or deprivation of belonging. If survival required running away, choosing exile in order to survive, then the focus on home as arrival, homecoming, welcoming, to a fixed, known space or community of relationships eclipses experiences of violence. Religious celebrations of Mother's and Father's Day and other rites of family often promote idealized notions of home in ways that reinforce this homelessness.

Peled and Muzicant's study of the meaning of home for teenage Israeli girls who ran away found that their understanding of home resides in a liminal space between home as an idealized place of comfort and home as a prison.[23] "The girls spoke of the meanings of the absence of home both when they are at home and when they are running away."[24] They described an "intolerable gap between home as it could and should be, and their own home."[25] As Rachel, an interviewee explained,

> I'm not looking for a house, you know, a villa and stuff like that. I want to have a warm home, neither big nor small, a warm and loving home, I'll know, I'll know how to raise my children and whatever they ask for I'll try to give them. Because I know what it's like, 'cause there are things that I wanted and never got to this day, and today I'll do it by myself.[26]

This begs the question: Can a place that tries to annihilate you ever be considered home? Is return, homecoming, ever a possibility? And if not, where does that leave one? How does one, as Rachel and many dream of, learn to create something never known? The abyss that threatens to swallow those who experience trauma into dissociation, addictions, "placelessness"—the stuckness of trauma—is the absence of immanence, relationship, and presence. Many survivors mime normalcy to find belonging in a place not their own, to be at home or at least some approximation of it (and often experience further violence).

It is not surprising then that persons who experience the absence of home physically and psychologically would also experience that in their spiritual lives. Spiritual homelessness is more than an exile from home, place, and belonging. It is also an exile from God when the metaphors and images for God do not offer a foundation for finding one's self at home with God. Just as one's material home may not be a safe place, spiritual homelessness means God is also not a safe place.

METAPHORS AND PRACTICES OF HOME-MAKING

Perhaps a helpful way out of this morass of exile and homelessness is a rethinking of the metaphors and practices of home. In *The Journey Is Home*, pioneering theologian Nelle Morton argued that images are "'infinitely more powerful than concepts,' because they function with our emotions, even outside our awareness, and, especially beyond our willful control."[27] Philosopher Erazim Kohák describes the search for home and belonging as a quest for metaphors: "Metaphors . . . shape the context of our experience as a meaningful whole, deciding in the process not only what is primary and what is derivative, but also who we ought to be and how we ought to act."[28] The insightful revisioning of home-making by feminist philosophers and theologians offers metaphors and practices of home freed from their oppressive, gendered origins that provide blueprints for those looking to create an authentic home that is more than a mere replication of what was lost.

In her essay "House and Home: Feminist Variations on a Theme," philosopher Iris Marion Young agrees with Beauvoir's prescient critique[29] about home-making, yet presses for richer understandings of home-making because she is not ready to "toss the idea of home out of the larder of feminist values" since "the idea of home also carries critical liberating potential because it expresses uniquely human values."[30] Young argues for a political and philosophical revisioning of home that provides a foundation for the practice of home-making that transcends a "commodity-based identity" dominant in consumerist societies "at the expense of those projected and excluded as Other."[31] Young suggests four core normative values for this practice.[32] First, society as home should be a place of safety, not a place of exclusion, oppression, or violence. Second, home must be a place for individuation. A person without a home is quite literally deprived of individual existence. Home is an extension of the person's body. Young recognizes the material limits of this idea and diverges from problematic understandings of the private sphere that women were relegated to. Third, home should be a place where privacy is respected, a place where "the autonomy and control a person has to allow or not allow access to her person, information, and things meaningfully associated with her presence" is protected.[33] Fourth, home must be a site of collective history and meaning for the individual with all that signifies—and that includes the safeguarding of meaningful things, rituals, and stories. She reflects on the significance of this practice of home-making for people who have been displaced due to conflicts and economic and natural disasters, where home becomes the "primary place of the expression of cultural identity and continuity with their native lands."[34]

Theologian Seforosa Carroll also understands this mobile sense of home as she reimagines home-making from her context as a Pacific Islander who migrated to Australia. Carroll identifies three key assumptions for the practice of home-making. First, home should not be understood as fixed, impermeable, or permanent; instead, it is relational and involves movement. The practice of making home is created when "people offer each other material, emotional, and spiritual support."[35] For survivors who may not have this implied community, the work of healing self can contain practices of meaning-making through the recognition of one's "placeness" and belonging within the web of creation.

Carroll's second practice sees home as dwelling, a form of "embodied being" made possible by mutuality. Homes represent "where [people] are . . . and embodies something of who they are." Society as home is created "by contributions, not claims" and demolishes dualistic notions of private and public, us versus them. Drawing from the insights of Rabbi Jonathan Sacks, "What matters is that together we build something none of us could make alone."[36] Finally, Carroll says that home is made through practices that "enable and nurture the creation of a habitus for meaningful inhabitation" where all creatures are nourished.[37] This home-making is predicated on the kind of hospitality that is mutual, where others are invited to make themselves *at home* by being themselves rather than performing a version of who they think they must be in order to belong.[38] The alternative metaphors and practices of home-making sketched here suggest resonant ways to remodel, or even flip, conventional idealizations of home.

A NOMADIC SPIRITUALITY OF HOME

Philosopher Rosi Braidotti coined the term "nomadic subjects" to name, from a feminist, post-colonial, and anti-racist perspective, the ways that migration impacts bodies, identities, and belongings. Nomad and nomadic are compelling terms for offering a language of identity beyond that of victim and survivor. In *Agency, Culture, and Human Personhood*, Jeanne Hoeft argues "'victim' has . . . become an identity category lacking in ambiguity. . . . [W]hile it was once used to stress the harm done . . . it is now used to pathologize women."[39] The same argument can be made about the term survivor if it foregrounds trauma as the central component of one's identity.

Nomads are recognizable by a number of qualities: nomads are or become comfortable with change and transitions; they do not cling to permanence and stability; they find themselves at home "in transit." As Lisa Isherwood observes, "Christianity has often imaged itself as a pilgrim and resurrection community and so it should not be too difficult for such a community to understand its role as that of 'nomadic subjects' dislocating the grip of patriarchy."[40] Nomad also highlights agency, the capacity to search, to discern, to make home what it needs to be, including a practice of resistance that prevents further violence and trauma. Likewise, nomadic is a rich way to understand and symbolize the lifelong work of survival; it celebrates nomads for their resilience and resistance and names in positive ways the search survivor-nomads embark upon when they reject spiritual teachings and norms that do not liberate or heal. A nomadic spirituality recognizes the beauty found in fluid and impermanent practices of home-making.

EMBODIMENT, IMPERMANENCE, AND DWELLING

Embodiment, impermanence, and dwelling are key trailheads in a nomadic spirituality. Feminist scholar Sandra Schneiders defines spirituality as "the experience of conscious involvement in the project of life-integration through self-transcendence toward the ultimate value one perceives."[41] Spirituality is both an outward and inward dimension of human existence that engages reality (outward) and "one's most vital and enduring self (inward)." Bringing together the outward and inward is achieved by "the existential task of discovering one's truest self in the context of reality apprehended as a cosmic totality."[42] Self-transcendence—rising above—is a critical component of spirituality, especially in the development of regard for others outside the myopia of suffering. The need for immanence—indwelling, remaining within, sheltering—is also important to locate a dimension of spirituality in the idea of *being-at-home with* the self.

Interfaith theologian Beverly Lanzetta offers an expansive spirituality that describes the emergence of an embodied understanding of spirituality as one where we:

> are not enlightened by virtue of giving over our identities for an undisclosed future. . . . Through accepting responsibility for our embodiment, and for the ordinary events that give life meaning, we glimpse the habitation of the sacred within our midst. And somehow, in the throes of everything else, comes *a spiritual belonging that feels at home everywhere but resides nowhere.* It lays down before us an invisible blanket of meaning that imposes nothing but informs everything [emphasis added].[43]

The poet and playwright Ntozake Shange eloquently captures this homing work in her declaration "i found god in myself / and i loved her, / i loved her fiercely."[44]

Manuel describes this as the practice of *cultivating* home. Begin, she writes, by attending to the trauma and the experience of being "dispirited." Recognize that many have experienced "disregard" due to violence, oppression, and displacement. "Begin with this body, this life" and understand that "true home" is not a status symbol or an acquisition. "True home is impermanent. It cannot be possessed. Only a home that comes into being, arises, and ceases to be is a true home."[45] The process of living wholeheartedly in the present results in the creation of sanctuary, which she understands as an ever-evolving home where, when seen through the eyes of impermanence, means that "all of life is home."[46]

Lucinda Stark-Huffaker locates home-making in the metaphor and practice of dwelling. The metaphor of dwelling also offers an embodied practice.[47] Stark-Huffaker situates dwelling in feminist understandings of women as "embodied selves" that must "be embraced as where we fit, our situated perspective, our place in the whole."[48] Since "dwelling" is both a noun and a verb, both a "place and a practice," it offers an apt model for "emerging selfhood." To see the self as a dwelling harkens to the biblical understanding of *temenos*, a sacred place where transformation as well as shelter and comfort are found.[49]

> Dwelling as a practice carries connotations of attending to the present place and moment, commitment to the quality of our relational connections, and an

assessment of our human finitude. Because dwelling counterbalances striving, it affirms self-acceptance and encourages satisfaction and contentment. . . . Dwelling as a place and as a practice come together in self-acceptance, without which our fears of inadequacy and possible rejection make us unable to offer hospitality, receiving others as the image of God.[50]

Stark-Huffaker celebrates Nelle Morton's paradoxical recognition that the journey as home is "not so much a journey ahead, or a journey into space, but a journey into presence."[51]

In both Jewish and Christian theology, the idea that God dwells with us is powerful. The presence of God was carried across the desert after liberation from slavery in Egypt and was seated in the temple. *Shekinah,* the indwelling presence of God, is said to have gone into the Babylonian exile with the Jewish people in 587 BCE when the temple was destroyed.

In *The Female Face of God in Auschwitz,* a remarkable study of memoirs by Jewish women survivors, Melissa Raphael captures the integral ways that women experienced the dwelling of Shekhinah, the female face of God.[52] Unlike male Jewish theology that emphasized God's hiddenness, "women's bodily presence alone" turned an abandoned farmhouse in a storm from "an empty shell into a temporary home." The ways in which women "practically and imaginally cover[ed] and protect[ed] the body by the practices and functions of 'home'. . . also covered and protected the divine spark. They made a sanctuary for the spark of the divine presence that saved it from being extinguished."[53]

Women's home-making work in the camps, Raphael notes, "can be read . . . as anticipating and carrying forward the long work of *tikkun*—the end of exile, where exile is understood as separation from the holy." One practice through which "home could still be carried on the body" was through the "beggar bundle, known in the women's camp as a *pinkly.* The pinkly consisted of a scrap of rag, a sock, stocking or old cap tied into a bag in which women kept their bread, margarine, or perhaps, if very fortunate, an object such as an almost toothless comb."[54] These pinkly served as talismans of women's humanity and belonging, something that the Nazis could not take. They point to an understanding of home as both a welcoming shelter and a sanctuary. A further remarkable aspect of the Shekhinah's presence in the camps was the women's practice of God, not as an intervening powerful God that rescued them from the terror and horror, but rather as "a God of loving attention and consolation. . . . God is the one who sustains the sufferers in their struggle to maintain, as long as possible, a life of dignity and self-respect." This presence enabled women like Etty Hillesum to care for others as well as for "a defenceless God whose survival depends on the work of human beings to defend the world from destruction."[55]

CONCLUSION

A nomadic spirituality of home relies on a plethora of maps, metaphors, and meanings. I see resonances of the nomadic in Said's naming of the paradoxical gift of exiles: "seeing 'the entire world as a foreign land' makes possible originality of vision. Most people are principally aware of one culture, one setting, one home: exiles are aware of at least two, and this plurality of vision gives rise to an awareness of multiple dimensions. . . . Exile is nomadic, decentered, contrapuntal: but no sooner does one get accustomed to it than its unsettling force erupts anew."[56]

The spiral of trauma often "erupts anew," but adapting metaphors and practices that speak truthfully of experience relocates the focus from a longing for something one never had or will have in the conventional sense, to seeing the beauty all around and within making possible a spirituality that heals and expands. This is not a romantic view. Nor should it be an appropriated metaphor that diminishes the material reality of exile for refugees from conflict, violence, and poverty. A nomadic spirituality of home tells the truth. It embraces liminality (in-betweenness) and impermanence. It requires an embodied making of home in the present moment. A nomadic spirituality is a spherical process that locates home in the journey itself, rather than in the arrival at a proscribed destination.

NOTES

1. Wendy Farley, *Gathering Those Driven Away: A Theology of Incarnation* (Louisville, KY: Westminster John Knox Press, 2011), 5.

2. Farley, *Gathering Those Driven Away*, 137.

3. Edward Said, *Reflections on Exile: And Other Literary and Cultural Essays* (London: Granta, 2012), 137.

4. US Department of Health and Human Services, Administration for Children and Families, Administration on Children, Youth and Families, Children's Bureau (2020). *Child Maltreatment 2018*, https://www.acf.hhs.gov/cb/research-data-technology/statistics-research/child-maltreatment. The *Child Maltreatment Report* reports that of "the 3,534,000 million (rounded) children who were the subject of an investigation or alternative response in fiscal year 2018, 678,000 (rounded) children were determined to be victims of maltreatment, up from 674,000 (rounded) victims in 2017. In total, 60.8 percent of victims were neglected, 10.7 percent were physically abused and 7.0 percent were sexually abused. More than 15 percent were victims of two or more maltreatment types." The number of child fatalities due to child abuse and neglect increased in fiscal year 2018. The number and rate of victims have fluctuated during the past five years. A national estimate of 1,770 children died from abuse and neglect in fiscal year 2018 compared to an estimated 1,710 children who died in fiscal year 2017.

5. "Child Maltreatment," World Health Organization, https://www.who.int/news-room/fact-sheets/detail/child-maltreatment. As of 2017, 1 in 4 adults were abused as children worldwide. "Child maltreatment is the abuse and neglect of people under 18 years of age. It includes all forms of physical and/or emotional ill-treatment, sexual abuse, neglect or negligent treatment or commercial or other exploitation, resulting in actual or potential harm to the child's health, survival, development or dignity in the context of a relationship of responsibility, trust or power. Four types of child maltreatment are generally recognized: physical abuse, sexual abuse, psychological (or emotional or mental) abuse, and neglect."

6. Lenore Terr, *Too Scared to Cry: Psychic Trauma in Childhood* (New York: Basic Books, 1992), 186, 200.

7. Cathy Caruth, *Unclaimed Experience: Trauma, Narrative, and History* (Baltimore, MD: Johns Hopkins University Press, 2016), 7. Also see Laura S. Brown's insightful conversation of the normalcy of violence against women and children in "Not Outside the Range: One Feminist Perspective on Psychic Trauma," in *Trauma: Explorations in Memory*, ed. Cathy Caruth (Baltimore, MD: Johns Hopkins University Press, 1995), 100–12.

8. Judith Lewis Herman, *Trauma and Recovery: The Aftermath of Violence: From Domestic Abuse to Political Terror* (New York: Basic Books, 2015), 178.

9. Addressing questions of knowing in the context of childhood trauma can be a double-edged sword. For some, survival requires repressing memories in order to pursue some level of functioning and may also result in multiple forms of paralysis. As Alice Miller observes, "I have come to the conclusion that individuals abused in childhood can attempt to obey the Fourth Commandment [honor your father and mother] only by recourse to a massive repression and detachment of their true emotions," in *The Body Never Lies: The Lingering Effects of Hurtful Parenting* (New York: W.W. Norton, 2006), 14–15.

10. I agree with Rita Nakishima Brock's description of atonement theologies that argue for the necessity of the crucifixion as "cosmic child abuse." See *Journeys by Heart: A Christology of Erotic Power* (New York: Crossroad, 1988).

11. Linda Kay Davidson and David M Gitlitz, *Pilgrimage: From the Ganges to Graceland: An Encyclopedia* (Santa Barbara, CA: ABC-CLIO, 2002), 248.

12. Edward Relph, *Place and Placelessness* (London: Pion Limited, 1975). Quoted in Joshua M. Price, "The Apotheosis of Home and the Maintenance of Spaces of Violence," *Hypatia* 17, no. 4 (Fall 2002): 40.

13. Relph, *Place and Placelessness*. Quoted in Caroline Leigh Speed, *Sustainable Dwelling: A Phenomenography of House, Home and Place* (Berlin: Verlag, 2002).

14. Michael Allen Fox, *Home: A Very Short Introduction* (Oxford: Oxford University Press, 2017), 11.

15. Frederick Buechner, *The Longing for Home: Reflections at Midlife* (San Francisco: HarperOne, 2009), 19.

16. Zenju Earthlyn Manuel, *Sanctuary: A Meditation on Home, Homelessness, and Belonging* (Somerville, MA: Wisdom Publications, 2018), 4.

17. Manuel, *Sanctuary*, 3.

18. Adrienne Cecile Rich, *A Wild Patience Has Taken Me This Far: Poems 1978–1981* (New York: W.W. Norton, 1993), 26.

19. Catharine A. MacKinnon, *Sexual Harassment of Working Women: A Case of Sex Discrimination* (New Haven, CT: Yale University Press, 1979), 1.

20. Joshua Price, "The Apotheosis of Home," 40–70.

21. Simone de Beauvoir, *The Second Sex*, trans. H. M. Parshley (New York: Random House, 1952), 451.

22. Elie Wiesel, "Longing for Home," in *The Longing for Home*, ed. Leroy S. Rouner (Notre Dame: University of Notre Dame Press, 1996), 17–29.

23. Einat Peled and Amit Muzicant, "The Meaning of Home for Runaway Girls," *Journal of Community Psychology* 36, no. 4 (2008): 439.

24. Peled and Muzicant, "The Meaning of Home for Runaway Girls," 442.

25. Peled and Muzicant, "The Meaning of Home for Runaway Girls," 443.

26. Peled and Muzicant, "The Meaning of Home for Runaway Girls," 445.

27. Nelle Morton, *The Journey Is Home* (Boston, MA: Beacon, 1985), 120.

28. Erazim Kohák, "Of Dwelling and Wayfaring: A Quest for Metaphors," in *The Longing for Home*, ed. Leroy S. Rouner, vol. 17 (Notre Dame: University of Notre Dame Press, 1996), 31.

29. The term "third shift" is a metaphor that builds on sociologist Arlie Russell Hochschild's use of "second shift" to describe the domestic, family, and community work that women come home to when they finish their time at the office or factory. See Arlie Hochschild and Anne Machung, *The Second Shift: Working Parents and the Revolution at Home* (Viking, 1989).

30. Iris Marion Young, *On Female Body Experience: "Throwing Like a Girl" and Other Essays* (New York: Oxford University Press, 2009), 123–24. Young also draws from Luce Irigaray's critique of Heidegger's gendered notions of home. Men have a home "at the expense" of women's homelessness. "As homeless themselves, women are deprived of the chance to be subjects for themselves," 128. Luce Irigaray and Carolyn Burke, *An Ethics of Sexual Difference* (Ithaca, NY: Cornell University Press, 2014).

31. Young, *On Female Body Experience*, 148.

32. Young, *On Female Body Experience*, 150–54.

33. Young, *On Female Body Experience*, 152.

34. Young, *On Female Body Experience*, 144.

35. Seforosa Carroll, "Homemaking: Reclaiming the Ideal of Home as a Framework for Hosting Cultural and Religious Diversity," in *Colonial Contexts and Postcolonial Theologies: Storyweaving in the Asia-Pacific* (New York: Palgrave Macmillan, 2016), 225.

36. Carroll, "Homemaking," 226.

37. Carroll, "Homemaking," 226.

38. Carroll agrees with Robert Ginsberg's description of persons as "inherently home-makers . . . how we function as persons is linked to how we make ourselves at home. . . . Our residence is where we live, but our home is how we live." Robert Ginsberg, "Meditations on Homelessness and Being at Home: In the Form of a Dialogue," in *The Ethics of Homelessness: Philosophical Perspectives*, ed. J. M. Abbarno (Amsterdam: Rodopi B.V, 1999), 31.

39. Jeanne M. Hoeft, *Agency, Culture, and Human Personhood: Pastoral Theology and Intimate Partner Violence* (Eugene, OR: Pickwick Publications, 2009), 162–63.

40. Lisa Isherwood, *The Good News of the Body: Sexual Theology and Feminism* (New York: New York University Press, 2000), 34.

41. Sandra M. Schneiders, "The Study of Christian Theology: Contours and Dynamics of a Discipline," in *Minding the Spirit: The Study of Christian Spirituality*, ed. Elizabeth A. Dreyer (Baltimore, MD: Johns Hopkins University Press, 2005), 6–7.

42. Peter Van Ness, *Spirituality, Diversion, and Decadence: The Contemporary Predicament* (Albany: State University of New York Press, 1992), 273–74.

43. Beverly Lanzetta, *Emerging Heart: Global Spirituality and the Sacred* (Minneapolis, MN: Fortress Press, 2007), 65–66.

44. Ntozake Shange, *For Colored Girls Who Have Considered Suicide/When the Rainbow Is Enuf* (New York: Bantam, 1982), 84–85.

45. Manuel, *Sanctuary*, 74.

46. Manuel, *Sanctuary*, 75.

47. Lucinda A. Stark-Huffaker, *Creative Dwelling: Empathy and Clarity in God and Self* (Atlanta, GA: Scholars Press, 1998), 124.

48. Stark-Huffaker, *Creative Dwelling*, 126.

49. Stark-Huffaker, *Creative Dwelling*, 129.

50. Stark-Huffaker, *Creative Dwelling*, 129.

51. Morton, *The Journey Is Home*, 131.

52. Melissa Raphael, *The Female Face of God in Auschwitz: A Jewish Feminist Theology of the Holocaust* (London: Routledge, 2006), 143.

53. Raphael, *Female Face of God in Auschwitz*, 79.

54. Raphael, *Female Face of God in Auschwitz*, 143.

55. Raphael, *Female Face of God in Auschwitz*, 117.

56. Said, *Reflections on Exile*, 148–49.

BIBLIOGRAPHY

Beauvoir, Simone de. *The Second Sex*. Translated by H. M. Parshley. New York: Random House, 1952.

Braidotti, Rosi. *Nomadic Subjects: Embodiment and Sexual Difference in Contemporary Feminist Theory*. New York: Columbia University Press, 2011.

Buechner, Frederick. *The Longing for Home: Reflections at Midlife*. San Francisco: HarperOne, 2009.

Carroll, Seforosa. "Homemaking: Reclaiming the Ideal of Home as a Framework for Hosting Cultural and Religious Diversity." In *Colonial Contexts and Postcolonial Theologies: Storyweaving in the Asia-Pacific*, edited by M. Brett and J. Havea, 219–29. London: Palgrave Macmillan, 2016.

Caruth, Cathy. *Unclaimed Experience: Trauma, Narrative, and History*. Baltimore, MD: Johns Hopkins University Press, 2016.

"Child Maltreatment." World Health Organization. Accessed March 1, 2020. https://www.who.int/news-room/fact-sheets/detail/child-maltreatment.

Davidson, Linda Kay, and David M Gitlitz. *Pilgrimage: From the Ganges to Graceland: An Encyclopedia*. Santa Barbara, CA: ABC-CLIO, 2002.

Farley, Wendy. *Gathering Those Driven Away: A Theology of Incarnation*. Louisville, KY: Westminster John Knox Press, 2011.

Fox, Michael Allen. *Home: A Very Short Introduction*. Oxford: Oxford University Press, 2017.

Herman, Judith Lewis. *Trauma and Recovery: The Aftermath of Violence from Domestic Abuse to Political Terror*. New York: Basic Books, 2015.

Hoeft, Jeanne M. *Agency, Culture, and Human Personhood: Pastoral Theology and Intimate Partner Violence*. Eugene, OR: Pickwick Publications, 2009.

Holland, Nancy J., and Patricia J. Huntington, eds. *Feminist Interpretations of Martin Heidegger*. University Park: Pennsylvania State University Press, 2001.

Irigaray, Luce, and Carolyn Burke. *An Ethics of Sexual Difference*. Ithaca, NY: Cornell University Press, 2014.

Isherwood, Lisa. *The Good News of the Body: Sexual Theology and Feminism*. New York: New York University Press, 2000.

Kohák, Erazim. "Of Dwelling and Wayfaring: A Quest for Metaphors." In *The Longing for Home*, edited by Leroy S. Rouner, vol. 17, 30–46. Notre Dame, IN: University of Notre Dame Press, 1996.

Lanzetta, Beverly. *Emerging Heart: Global Spirituality and the Sacred*. Minneapolis, MN: Fortress Press, 2007.

Manuel, Zenju Earthlyn. *Sanctuary: A Meditation on Home, Homelessness, and Belonging*. Somerville, MA: Wisdom Publications, 2018.

Miller, Alice. *The Body Never Lies: The Lingering Effects of Hurtful Parenting*. New York: W.W. Norton, 2006.

Morton, Nelle. *The Journey Is Home*. Boston, MA: Beacon, 1985.

Peled, Einat, and Amit Muzicant. "The Meaning of Home for Runaway Girls." *Journal of Community Psychology* 36, no. 4 (2008): 434–51.

Price, Joshua M. "The Apotheosis of Home and the Maintenance of Spaces of Violence." *Hypatia* 17, no. 4 (Fall 2002): 40–70.

Raphael, Melissa. *The Female Face of God in Auschwitz: A Jewish Feminist Theology of the Holocaust*. London: Routledge, 2006.

Relph, Edward. *Place and Placelessness*. Los Angeles, CA: Sage, 2016.

Rich, Adrienne Cecile. *A Wild Patience Has Taken Me This Far: Poems 1978–1981*. New York: W.W. Norton, 1993.

Rouner, Leroy S. *The Longing for Home*. Notre Dame, IN: University of Notre Dame Press, 1996.

Said, Edward. *Reflections on Exile: And Other Literary and Cultural Essays*. London: Granta, 2012.

Schneiders, Sandra M. "The Study of Christian Theology: Contours and Dynamics of a Discipline." In *Minding the Spirit: The Study of Christian Spirituality*, edited by Elizabeth A. Dreyer, 5–24. Baltimore, MD: Johns Hopkins University Press, 2005.

Shange, Ntozake. *For Colored Girls Who Have Considered Suicide/When the Rainbow Is Enuf*. New York: Bantam, 1982.

Stark-Huffaker, Lucinda A. *Creative Dwelling: Empathy and Clarity in God and Self*. Atlanta, GA: Scholars Press, 1998.

Terr, Lenore. *Too Scared to Cry: Psychic Trauma in Childhood*. New York: Basic Books, 1992.

Wiesel, Elie. "Longing for Home." In *The Longing for Home*, edited by Leroy S. Rouner, vol. 17, 17–29. Notre Dame, IN: University of Notre Dame Press, 1996.

Young, Iris Marion. *On Female Body Experience: "Throwing Like a Girl" and Other Essays*. New York: Oxford University Press, 2009.

CHAPTER 25

Hope Now

··

Rev. Dr. Cynthia L. Rigby,
Austin Presbyterian Theological Seminary

ABSTRACT

What might it look like for feminist theologians and scholars of religion to have hope? First, I name some ways our hopes have *not* been realized. For example, feminist work in religion still seems to be neglected by non-feminist peers, which makes it difficult to have the kinds of constructive conversations necessary to move toward transformation. Next, I point out that it is tempting but problematic to work under the illusion that things will get better as long as we are patient. I argue that we need to let go of this assumption, using the example of Jimmy Carter to argue that hope may often manifest more as impatience than patience. Third, hope is always funded by remembering the "why" of our work and our being and the "who" we do it for. Finally, I close with reflection on Nelle Morton's advice that we remember the journey itself is home, which reminds us that our hope isn't contingent on measurable outcome but characterizes our day-to-day reality as we share life with one another and work for a more equitable, peaceable world.

HOPE NOW: NAMING DISAPPOINTMENTS

I have been honored with the assignment of offering a kind of charge, here at the end of this volume, that we writers and readers might be inspired by its rich content to "go forth" and continue doing feminist work in theology and religion. As we have been asked before, so we will no doubt be asked again (and again): Is such work really necessary? Look how far women have come!

I have to confess that I was once among those who were hoping we wouldn't have need, by this point in time, to label distinctively *feminist* theologies and *feminist* approaches to religion. This isn't because I thought they were peripheral, faddish, or only useful as temporary stopgaps—in fact, quite the opposite was true of my thinking. From

··

the time I began drinking from the well of feminist insights, it seemed to me so obvi-ous that feminist wisdom was nourishing and healing for everyone (not only women) that I imagined it would eventually be embraced by all religious thinkers. I hoped and expected that, by now, feminist scholars of religion would not be seen only as limning the boundaries of religious traditions but as making contributions at the heart of them.

When I read Valerie Saiving and Judith Plaskow on sin, for example, it expanded my understanding of how those who are self-deprecating, as well as prideful, can find healing.[1] When I read Elisabeth Schüssler Fiorenza, I gained ways to read between the lines of Scripture that have helped countless people with whom I've shared—including those who might never think to identify themselves as feminist—continue to identify with the biblical narrative.[2] When I read Rosemary Redford Ruether's opening midrash on "the *kenosis*[3] of the Father" (divine self-emptying) in *Sexism and God Talk*, I learned how to creatively convey a theological insight she shares (at least in some significant ways) with Karl Barth: that God's character eschews abusive earthly fatherliness.[4] When I read Elizabeth Johnson's *She Who Is*, it seemed so obvious to me that honoring the mystery of God and condemning idolatry—a value in so many religious traditions—is facilitated by using expansive imagery for God.[5] When I read *Sisters in the Wilderness*, Delores S. Williams convinced me that it is not simply that all women are oppressed in relation to all men, who are the oppressors. Rather, many of us in different ways must work both to resist subjugation and to repent of subjugating others.[6] When I read Delores S. Williams, Rita Nakashima Brock, Rebecca Parker, and others, I began thinking very differently about atonement theory, noticing that stu-dents in my seminary classes and church education classes were eager to think about the cross differently (even when they didn't agree on how, they were grateful feminist and womanist insights opened up the conversation).[7] And when I read Sharon Welch and Ada María Isasi-Díaz,[8] I gained a clearer understanding of what Gustavo Gutié-rrez means when he challenges us to attend to how God is moving in the communities of the world (*koinonia*) and to join in.

But the integration of feminist theological ideas into the field of theology hasn't happened in the way I expected it would. Just a few days ago, for example, I opened—with very positive expectations—a new book on theology and imagination. I was dis-couraged to see that the author, in one short section, talks of "Christian theologians . . . facing . . . the feminist challenge" as though Christians would not raise such a challenge among themselves. He makes the case that "the appropriate language" for God is "mas-culine" and only masculine.[9] A scholar has the right to make whatever theological case is true to their convictions, of course, but what troubles me is that this author makes judgments without giving feminist thinkers a fair hearing, or even a hearing at all. In a subsection titled "the Kenotic Masculinity of God," for example, he assesses that "femi-nist theologians seem generally to have missed the irony of biblical patriarchy" without even mentioning the foundational work feminist thinkers have done on kenosis.[10] As earlier mentioned, Ruether's now-classic feminist theological text opens precisely by attending to the dark irony that, *despite* the divine kenosis emphasized in Scripture, God has been portrayed through the ages as a male patriarch in ways that have led to the subjugation of women. And Elizabeth A. Johnson (also not cited in his discussion), says, in *She Who Is*, "The crucified Jesus embodies the exact opposite of the patriarchal ideal of the powerful man. . . . The cross . . . stands as a poignant symbol of the 'kenosis of patriarchy,' the self-emptying of male dominating power in favor of the new humanity of compassionate service and empowerment."[11] Johnson sees the irony, I'm sure.

The real question is, How could the author of this new book not even mention Johnson's and Ruether's work on kenosis, patriarchy, and God-language in the course of explaining the problem he has with feminist misunderstandings of kenosis, patriarchy, and God-language? What's it going to take for feminist theologians and feminist scholars of religion to be engaged as insiders? And perhaps more to the point, how disappointing to have missed the opportunity to enter into a rich and meaningful dialogue on God-language, founded in an obvious shared interest in considering the implications of the divine kenosis.

The realization that even the most widely read and acclaimed works in feminist studies are not taken as seriously as we might assume, and have not made as much of a difference as we thought they would, by now, can be quite discouraging. Given this, how shall we hope as we move out from our writing and reading of this book into our continued work and lives?

HOPE NOW: DON'T BE PATIENT

I realize now that I started my teaching career, twenty-five years ago, with the assumption that—slowly, slowly but surely, surely—women would gain ground in theological and ecclesiological circles and we wouldn't have to spend as much time making the case and making a space for women's perspectives, gifts, and leading. My confidence that there would be a steady improvement was likely founded in the way I had been taught American history, on the one hand, and Christian faith, on the other. If it were indeed true that the United States is a land where we ultimately care about "freedom and justice for all," it made sense to me to believe opportunities for women and other marginalized groups would continue opening up as time went along. And if I "rested in the Lord and waited patiently," I would, as Psalm 37:4 promises, be given "my heart's desires" (which, truly, were simply to use the gifts for teaching theology and preaching that God had given me).

I remember when I first had the horrible realization that things could go *backward* for women. Four months after my ordination in the year 2000 as Minister of Word and Sacrament in the Presbyterian Church (USA), Jimmy Carter left the Southern Baptist Convention because they renounced the ordination of their own female ministers, citing a return to a more literalistic interpretation of Scripture. Carter described this decision as "exclusionary" and "onerous,"[12] saying he, a third-generation Baptist, was sad to leave.

My dad was a Baptist minister. I, too, had left the conservative Baptist church because of its literalistic interpretation of certain passages of Scripture which, I believed, were inconsistent with the message of the Bible as a whole. I also left so I could follow my calling to be a theologian and a minister, which the Baptists would not allow me to do. But there had been progress in the Baptist church even as I had been transforming into a bona fide theologian, ordained minister, Reformed and feminist scholar. I and my dad, both, were hopeful that the church of my youth was coming along. "Just hang on, honey, things will get better," he'd say, whenever I complained about how long it was taking for women's gifts to be celebrated and used. I remember when I called him about Carter's exodus. "Things aren't getting better, Dad," I remember saying, with sadness, hopelessness, and probably a little fear in my voice. "We are going *backward*. Things are not going to change *automatically*. We have to be more aggressive, and we can't let up or things will snap back."

And Jimmy Carter didn't let up. He kept on teaching Sunday School in his Baptist home church, emphasizing every chance he had that he did so only because his church did have women deacons and would have no problem having a female pastor. Meanwhile, he kept working on the issue of women and religion. Nine years after leaving the Southern Baptist Convention, he wrote and published a public letter, titled "Losing My Religion for Equality." In it, he indicted not only Southern Baptists for their destructive teachings about women, but leaders of many global religions:

> The truth is that male religious leaders have had—and still have—an option to interpret holy teachings either to exalt or subjugate women. They have, for their own selfish ends, overwhelmingly chosen the latter. Their continuing choice provides the foundation or justification for much of the pervasive persecution and abuse of women throughout the world. This is in clear violation not just of the Universal Declaration of Human Rights but also the teachings of Jesus Christ, the Apostle Paul, Moses and the prophets, Muhammad, and founders of other great religions—all of whom have called for proper and equitable treatment of all the children of God. It is time we had the courage to challenge these views.[13]

As we move from writing and reading to whatever next project we are moved to undertake, Carter's example challenges me to ask, What are we being too patient about? Are we ready to take a strong stand against momentum that moves us "backward" in relation to equality and justice, even if it costs us something in relation to our most beloved communities?

HOPE NOW: REMEMBER WHY AND FOR WHOM

The main character of *The Handmaid's Tale* (Margaret Atwood's novel and now a TV series on Hulu)[14] has learned the hard way that things don't inevitably improve if one is patient and cooperative, hardworking, or clever. Things can definitely go "backward," in fact. The key to maintaining any modicum of hope is to recognize the power one has and be ready to use it whenever one has the opportunity, for one might not get a second chance to act. For June, it is essential to her being ready to act in the moment to remember why she is resisting her subjugation: she is determined to get her daughter out of the oppressive place called Gilead so Hannah can be free to be her own person.

In April 2014, I was driving across Austin with NPR on the radio, our eight-year-old daughter, Jessica, in the back seat. All of a sudden she exclaimed, with alarm, "What do they mean, 216 girls have been kidnapped from a school in Nigeria? How did *that* happen?" Every single day, for weeks following, Jessica asked me, with a confident tone, whether we had gotten the girls out yet and what the plan was for doing so. She seemed to believe our own family should get more actively involved in a rescue operation and began suggesting (Princess Leia-inspired) plans of her own. Finally, I told Jessica she didn't need to ask me every day, promising I would tell her whenever I heard a news update. Over time, she finally stopped asking. Five years later, I heard that Boko Haram had released about a hundred girls. True to my word, I told Jessica (who was by then 13), the good news. I wasn't sure she would even remember the story. "What about the others?," she immediately asked, without missing a beat. "Are they going to get them back, too?" Even as I stuttered out some answer, a verse from the prophet Isaiah came to mind: "Because God is great in strength, mighty in power, *not one is missing.*"[15] Jessica wasn't going to let God—or us—off the hook until every one of those girls was found.

It helps us keep on in the work to remember that we do what we do so that every girl, woman, child, boy, man, person, and creature will have a place and a life. And we are interpreters and shapers of religion—a powerful force in relation to these values.

If you will indulge me one more time in relation to the example of Jimmy Carter, I will tell you this: He never forgets the why of his—and our—work. He never lets up on analyzing and educating about how religion can be used to justify the harming of women and girls. Fourteen years after leaving the Southern Baptist Church, but still teaching the Sunday school class he loved, he published *A Call to Action: Women, Religion, Violence, and Power.* In it he writes:

> Although economic disparity is a great and growing problem, I have become convinced that the most serious and unaddressed worldwide challenge is the deprivation and abuse of women and girls, largely caused by a false interpretation of carefully selected religious texts and a growing tolerance of violence and warfare, unfortunately following the example set during my lifetime by the United States. In addition to the unconscionable human suffering, almost embarrassing to acknowledge, there is a devastating effect on economic prosperity caused by the loss of contributions of at least half the human beings on earth. This is not just a women's issue. It is not confined to the poorest countries. It affects us all.[16]

In November 2014, Carter addressed the American Academy of Religion on both climate change and gender equality, commending us, as scholars of religion, to remember the importance of our work to the well-being of all. I left feeling hopeful but also appropriately burdened, rededicating myself to participate in the mending of the world.

To hope now, as we remember why we do what we do and who we do it for, necessarily entails experiencing a great deal of anguish. This is because recognizing suffering is painful, and imagining a world without violence, by contrast, may only exacerbate our present pain. But we must resist setting our expectations low or underestimating our own capacities in order to avoid discomfort. Those girls in Nigeria—and our girls and boys riding in the back seats of our cars, sneakily listening to the news—are depending on it.

HOPE NOW: ATTEND TO TODAY

While feminist hope is fed by keeping the big "why" and "for whom" of our work in view, that alone is not enough to sustain it. As embodied, finite creatures with our own needs and fears, we also need to attend to *today*, to be present to ourselves and to each one. If we focus only on the goal of getting *all* the girls back, without celebrating the hundred that *have* come back *so far*, we will miss out on the gift of being in communion with those hundred.

In the introduction to her book *How to Do Nothing*, Jenny Odell suggests that attending to maintenance (of our bodies, schedules, homes, imaginations, artistic propensities, etc.) is at least as important to the well-being of the world as being productive. In our consumeristic, capitalistic global economy, she argues, we need to reclaim the value of being "useless," for it is only then that we will be able to re-discover our creativity and transform the world. But, of course, if our goal for doing nothing is to refuel so we can produce more transformation, we've missed the point. Doing nothing must be done for its own sake, or it is doing something, O'Dell implies.[17]

We feminist, religious types are very good at these kinds of reflections, but not as good, perhaps, at taking them to heart. Yet attending to maintenance, to presence, to today is critical to living a hopeful, beautiful life.

Feminist theologian Nelle Morton similarly suggests that it is important not to allow our joy to be contingent on worldly conceptions of success, which (as we have noted) can be elusive. It is not that we should ever give up on having "no one missing" but that we should allow ourselves the pleasure of working with this vision in mind, day by day, hand in hand with others, in communities of resistance and solidarity.[18] I suggest we receive Morton's insight as our final charge and perhaps, even, benediction. As feminist students, theologians, and scholars of religion, may we not only hope so hard that we are impatient, keeping the why and for whom of what we are doing pushing us forward until everyone is safe and whole. May we also be present to the moment, learning when to do something, but also when to do *nothing*, so we will continue to be open to possibilities for the *new*. May we be nourished by the journey itself, able freely to share with one another and with the whole world.

NOTES

1. Valerie Saiving, "The Human Situation: A Feminine View," in *Womenspirit Rising*, ed. Carol Christ and Judith Plaskow (San Francisco: Harper & Row, 1979), 25–42; Judith Plaskow, *Sex, Sin, and Grace* (Lanham, MD: University Press of America, 1980).

2. Elisabeth Schüssler Fiorenza, *In Memory of Her: A Feminist Theological Reconstruction of Christian Origins* (New York: Crossroad, 1992).

3. *Kenosis* means "self-emptying" in Greek and is celebrated in Philippians 2:6–8.

4. Rosemary Radford Ruether, *Sexism and God-Talk* (Boston, MA: Beacon Press, 1983). For an interview with Rosemary Radford Ruether, Mary Daly, and Sidney Cornelia Callahan by William F. Buckley Jr. recorded on June 24, 1968, see, "The Rib Uncaged: Women and the Church," *Firing Line with William F. Buckley Jr.*, WOR-TV, New York (YouTube) July 4, 2019, https://www.youtube.com/watch?v=TxdBLDmBT6k&feature=youtube.

5. Elizabeth A. Johnson, *She Who Is: The Mystery of God in Feminist Theological Discourse* (New York: Crossroad, 1993).

6. Delores S. Williams, *Sisters in the Wilderness: The Challenge of Womanist God-Talk* (Maryknoll, NY: Orbis, 1993).

7. See Williams, *Sisters in the Wilderness*; Rita Nakashima Brock and Rebecca Parker, *Proverbs of Ashes* (Boston: Beacon, 2002); and Margit Trelstad, ed., *Cross Examinations* (Minneapolis, MN: Fortress, 2006).

8. Sharon D. Welch, *Communities of Resistance and Solidarity* (Eugene: Wipf & Stock, 2017); Ada María Isasi-Díaz, *En la Lucha/In the Struggle: A Hispanic Woman's Liberation Theology* (Minneapolis, MN: Fortress, 1993).

9. Garrett Green, *Imagining Theology: Encounters with God in Scripture, Interpretation, and Aesthetics* (Grand Rapids, MI: Baker Academic, 2020), 141.

10. Green, *Imagining Theology*, 140.

11. Johnson, *She Who Is*, 161.

12. Somini Sengupta, "Carter Sadly Turns Back on National Baptist Body," *New York Times*, October 21, 2000, https://www.nytimes.com/2000/10/21/us/carter-sadly-turns-back-on-national-baptist-body.html.

13. Jimmy Carter, "Losing My Religion for Equality," *The Age*, July 15, 2009, https://www.theage.com.au/politics/federal/losing-my-religion-for-equality-20090714-dk0v.html.

14. Margaret Atwood, *The Handmaid's Tale* (New York: Doubleday, 2019).

15. NRSV Isaiah 40:8 (my emphasis).

16. Jimmy Carter, *A Call to Action: Women, Religion, Violence, and Power* (New York: Simon & Schuster, 2014), 2.

17. Jenny Odell, introduction to *How to Do Nothing: Resisting the Attention Economy* (New York: Melville House, 2019).

18. Nelle Morton, *The Journey Is Home* (Boston, MA: Beacon Press, 1985), xxviii.

BIBLIOGRAPHY

Atwood, Margaret. *The Handmaid's Tale*. New York: Doubleday, 2019.

Carter, Jimmy. *A Call to Action: Women, Religion, Violence, and Power*. New York: Simon & Schuster, 2014.

———. "Losing My Religion for Equality." *The Age*. July 15, 2009. https://www.theage.com.au/politics/federal/losing-my-religion-for-equality-20090714-dk0v.html.

Green, Garrett. *Imagining Theology: Encounters with God in Scripture, Interpretation, and Aesthetics* (Grand Rapids: Baker Academic, 2020), 141.

Isasi-Díaz, Ada María. *En la Lucha/In the Struggle: A Hispanic Woman's Liberation Theology*. Minneapolis, MN: Fortress, 1993.

Johnson, Elizabeth A. *She Who Is: The Mystery of God in Feminist Theological Discourse*. New York: Crossroad, 1993.

Morton, Nelle. *The Journey Is Home*. Boston, MA: Beacon Press, 1985.

Nakashima Brock, Rita, and Rebecca Parker. *Proverbs of Ashes*. Boston: Beacon, 2002.

Odell, Jenny. Introduction to *How to Do Nothing: Resisting the Attention Economy*. New York: Melville House, 2019.

Plaskow, Judith. *Sex, Sin, and Grace*. Lanham, MD: University Press of America, 1980.

Ruether, Rosemary Radford. *Sexism and God-Talk*. Boston: Beacon Press, 1983.

Ruether, Rosemary Radford, Mary Daly, and Sidney Cornelia Callahan. Interview by William F. Buckley Jr. "The Rib Uncaged: Women and the Church." *Firing Line with William F. Buckley Jr.* WOR-TV, New York, June 24, 1968. Updated on YouTube July 4, 2019. https://www.youtube.com/watch?v=TxdBLDmBT6k&feature=youtube.

Saiving, Valerie. "The Human Situation: A Feminine View." In *Womenspirit Rising*, edited by Carol Christ and Judith Plaskow, 25–42. San Francisco: Harper & Row, 1979.

Schüssler Fiorenza, Elisabeth. *In Memory of Her: A Feminist Theological Reconstruction of Christian Origins*. New York: Crossroad, 1992.

Sengupta, Somini, "Carter Sadly Turns Back on National Baptist Body." *New York Times*. October 21, 2000. https://www.nytimes.com/2000/10/21/us/carter-sadly-turns-back-on-national-baptist-body.html.

Trelstad, Margit, ed. *Cross Examinations*. Minneapolis, MN: Fortress, 2006.

Welch, Sharon D. *Communities of Resistance and Solidarity*. Eugene, OR: Wipf & Stock, 2017.

Williams, Delores S. *Sisters in the Wilderness: The Challenge of Womanist God-Talk*. Maryknoll, NY: Orbis, 1993.

CHAPTER 26

Resources for Clarification, Education, and Action

....

GLOSSARY OF HASHTAGS

#2SLGBTQQIA: Two spirited, lesbian, gay, bisexual, transsexual, transgender, queer, questioning, intersex, asexual. This expansive acronym refers to the many orientations and gender expressions under the "queer" umbrella.

#BlackLivesMatter: Three radical Black organizers, Alicia Garza, Patrisse Cullors, and Opal Tometi, created this movement in response to the acquittal of Trayvon Martin's murderer. Its purpose is to demand an end to police brutality against all Black people.

#ChurchToo: A movement that started on social media to bring to light the sexual harassment, abuse, and assault that happens within churches/faith communities. It is a collective story of individuals who have been harmed. It is also the story of the failure of religious communities and institutions.

#DelhiBraveheart: On December 16, 2012, Jyoti Singh, who became known around the world as "Delhi Braveheart," was tortured and gang raped by six men on a bus in South Delhi. People shared the hashtag #DelhiBraveheart in tweets, texts, and social media to protest the sexual violence that was so prevalent in Delhi that it had become known as "Rape City." #DelhiBraveheart has become a foundational example of the possibilities that exist when social media is woven into movements against injustice.

#FireAbuEesa: Rabia Chaudry created a Twitter campaign using this hashtag in response to an imam and teacher for making derogatory statements on Facebook about International Women's Day, feminists, and rape. In response, Hind Makki acknowledged men who support women and feminism with #MuslimMaleAllies.

#LightsforLiberty: Billed as "a Vigil to End Human Detention Camps," people gathered at Lights for Liberty rallies across the United States, July 12, 2019, to protest the Trump administration's detention of immigrants. Leaders from pro-immigrant agencies, such as RAICES Texas, Immigrant Families Together, and Border Angels, organized five main events, which were held in El Paso, Texas; Homestead, Florida; San Diego, California; New York City; and Washington, DC. It became a worldwide vigil, with at least one event in every state in the United States and also five continents. Overall, there were more than 700 events that protested border camps.

#MeToo: The Me Too movement originated in 2006 when American social activist and community organizer, Tarana Burke, began using it to fight against sexual assault and harassment against women.

#MuslimMaleAllies: Hind Makki acknowledged men who support women and feminism with this hashtag.

#NiUnaMenos: Originated in Argentina to signify "not one less woman" alive; not one more woman killed. The protest theme quickly moved into Latin American countries, where femicide and gender violence are out of control. Reports indicate there were some "138 separate protests in Argentina, 25 in Chile, seven in Bolivia, five in Mexico, two in Uruguay, two in Honduras, and others in the capital cities of Paraguay, Ecuador, Costa Rica, El Salvador, Guatemala, and beyond."[1]

#NotYourNarrative: Challenges the Western media's portrayal of Muslim women.

#SayHerName: It began when protestors outside of city hall chanted "Say her name!" after Sandra Bland died in police custody July 2015. The hashtag is used to create a social media presence with racial justice campaigns like #BlackLivesMatter to bring attention to the reality that Black females, not just Black males, are the victims of racism and police brutality.

#SayTheirNames: An expansion from #SayHerName, this social justice hashtag is an outcry against police brutality and anti-Black violence in the United States.

#SolidarityIsForWhiteWomen: Mikki Kendall created this to confront the exclusion of women of color from current feminist dialogue, sparking the development of other hashtag campaigns, including #BlackPowerIsForBlackMen and #NotYour Narrative.

#TimesUp: The Time's Up movement was formed in 2018 in response to sexual harassment.

#WeAreAllIsraa: Israa Ghareeb was a 21-year-old Palestinian woman in the West Bank who was brutally murdered by her brother because she posted a video on Instagram of herself and her fiance the day *before* she was to be engaged. Her father believed she had dishonored Islam and the family. She was physically assaulted in the Ghareeb family home. Due to severe spinal injuries, she had to be admitted to the Arab Society Hospital. The hashtag originated soon after an audio recording went viral on social media which, although never authenticated as her voice, was attributed to Israa screaming as her brother stabbed her while she was in a hospital bed while recovering from the severe injuries inflicted upon her earlier.

GLOSSARY OF PEOPLE

Margot Adler (1946–2014): A journalist, book author, and leader in contemporary Paganism. The granddaughter of the world-renowned psychotherapist Alfred Adler, Adler was raised in a secular Jewish family. A baby boomer, she discovered Paganism in the early 1970s. She worked as a journalist for National Public Radio (NPR) from 1979 through the rest of her career. She worked on *All Things Considered,*

Morning Edition, and *Weekend Edition* and was a familiar radio voice for decades. She combined her professional journalism expertise with her ties to the Pagan community to write the highly successful book *Drawing Down the Moon* (1979). The book has been relied on by practitioners and scholars alike since its publication. Adler published a revised, updated edition in 1986 and then further expanded editions in 1997 and 2006. Adler died in 2014 after contracting rapidly progressing endometrial cancer. A practicing Manhattan Pagan, Adler was close with Judy Harrow, another New York priestess, throughout their adult lives.

Susan B. Anthony (1820–1906): She organized the American Equal Rights Association; co-founded *Revolution,* a radical feminist newspaper; and (illegally) voted in the 1872 presidential election in Rochester, New York, her hometown.

María Pilar Aquino: A Catholic Latina theologian and prolific writer whose work focuses on liberation theology, social ethics, and feminist theologies. She wrote *Our Cry for Life: Feminist Theology from Latin America* (2002) and edited *A Reader in Latina Feminist Theology: Religion and Justice* (2002) with Daisy L. Machado and Jeanette Rodríquez.

Buddha: Means "Enlightened One." As a historical figure, Buddha is associated with Gautama Buddha, Siddhartha Buddha, or Shakyamuni Buddha. He lived in current Nepal in 5th to 4th BCE.

Grace Lee Boggs (1915–2015): Born to Chinese immigrants in 1915, Boggs grew up in Providence, Rhode Island. Despite her PhD from Bryn Mawr in 1940, Boggs could not find a job in the academy. Boggs relocated to Chicago, where she became involved in African American civil rights activism through her work with West Indian Marxist C.L.R. James. She married African American activist James Boggs, and the couple moved to Detroit in 1953. For many decades, they had played a key role in various social movements, including civil rights, Black Power, labor issues, women's rights, antiwar campaigns, environmental concerns, and Asian American rights.

Zsuzsanna "Z" Budapest: The founder of the largest branch of Dianic Wicca. Budapest's branch is sometimes labeled "Z Budapest Dianic Wicca" in order to differentiate it from a smaller lineage—McFarland Dianic Wicca, which shows ideological/thealogical similarities but a separate founding history. Budapest wrote the *Feminist Book of Lights and Shadows,* which was later republished as *The Holy Book of Women's Mysteries.* Claiming to have been taught Witchcraft by her Hungarian grandmother, Budapest developed a tradition that was clearly a radical feminist spin on existing Witchcraft traditions. Budapest has lived in California since 1970, first in Los Angeles and later in Northern California. Budapest accrued a large spiritual feminist following in the 1970s and beyond. In recent years, Budapest has received criticism for excluding transgender women from her tradition's practice and for the broader ideology known as trans-excluding radical feminism.

Katharine C. Bushnell (1856–1946): She was an early feminist who worked as a medical doctor in the United States and China. She studied the Bible in the original Greek and Hebrew to examine the biblical status of women.

Katie Geneva Cannon (1950–2018): A Presbyterian minister, theological scholar, pioneer, and a progenitor of womanist theology and ethics who was the Annie Scales Rogers Professor of Christian Social Ethics at Union Presbyterian Seminary and also taught at many other esteemed academic institutions. In 1974, Cannon became the first African American woman to be ordained in the Presbyterian Church (U.S.A.). In 1985, Cannon was the first person to present an essay on womanist theology at the American Academy of Religion, and in 1983 she became the first African American to earn the doctor of philosophy degree from Union Theological Seminary in New York. She is the author of several groundbreaking texts and essays, including her first full-length book, *Black Womanist Ethics*, published in 1988, considered a seminal text that launched the field of womanist ethics. Her other books include *Katie's Cannon: Womanism and the Soul of the Black Community* (1995) and *Teaching Preaching: Isaac R. Clark and Black Sacred Rhetoric* (2002). She edited other works including *The Oxford Handbook of African American Theology* (2011).

Carol P. Christ: An eco-feminist who argues for the interrelatedness of human beings and nature, integrating justice for ecology and for women. She graduated with a PhD from Yale University. Her 1974 dissertation was titled "Elie Wiesel's Stories: Still the Dialogue." While studying theology at Yale, Christ became disenchanted with sexism in traditional Abrahamic religion and in academe. She authored several books. A leader in women's Goddess Spirituality, she was one of the first to use the term "thealogy." She founded the Ariadne Institute, which offers Goddess pilgrimages to Crete. She also founded the Women's Caucus within the American Academy of Religion and Society of Biblical Literature. She has been a key player in interreligious feminist theology / thealogy for decades and has collaborated frequently with Judith Plaskow in particular.

Kimberlé Williams Crenshaw: A legal scholar who coined the term "intersectionality."

Philip Vera Cruz (1904–1994): Cruz came to the United States in the early 20th century and spent thirty years working on farms and in canneries and restaurants in Minnesota and Washington. After moving to California in 1950, he was involved in the Filipino labor movement and helped the Agricultural Workers Organizing Committee organize a series of effective strikes and boycotts. He was the vice president of the United Farm Workers under Chicano César Chávez until 1977. In his later years, he trained a new generation of activists.

Mary Daly (1928–2010): The first woman philosopher–theologian in the Anglo-American world of philosophy of religion, who authored *Beyond God the Father*. She challenged Thomas Aquinas [Thomist] arguments and ideals about there being a single Creator God who is all knowing, in control of everything, present everywhere, and eternal or everlasting. She ultimately renounced Christianity and became the first feminist to call herself post-Christian.

Françoise d'Eaubonne (1920–2005): French feminist who originated the term *ecofeminism*, when, in *Le Féminisme ou la Mort* (1974), she called upon women to lead an ecological revolution to save the planet.

Rachel Dehollander: An outspoken evangelical survivor who is challenging Christian colleges to train administrators to respond appropriately to victims and survivors and to take leadership in changing the cultural norms that support sexual violence.

Nancy DeMoss Wolgemuth: Created the "True Woman Manifesto" (https://www.reviveourhearts.com/true-woman/manifesto/) for the "Revive Our Hearts" theme of the first True Woman Conference. It is self-proclaimed as a Christ-centered antidote to feminist theology (https://www.reviveourhearts.com/true-woman/about/).

Sarah Forten (c. 1811–c. 1898): An abolitionist and early womanist, the words of this Black poet were printed on the covers of most of the Anti-Slavery Convention of American Women in 1837.

Miranda Fricker: Credited with bringing the phenomenon of epistemic injustice to the attention of analytic philosophers.

Diana Garland (1950–2015): Baylor University professor who directed the first national, random survey in 2008 to try to measure the extent of sexual abuse by clergy.

Israa Ghareeb (c. 1998–2019): A 21-year-old Palestinian woman in the West Bank who was brutally murdered by her brother in September 2019 because her father and brothers believed she had dishonored Islam and her family when she posted a video on social media of herself with her fiancé the day *before* she was to be engaged.

Jacquelyn Grant: An African Methodist Episcopalian minister, theological scholar, administrator, and a pioneering founder of womanist theology and ethics, who is currently the Fuller E. Callaway Distinguished Professor of Systematic Theology at the Interdenominational Theological Center. Grant founded the Center for Black Women in Church and Society at the Interdenominational Theological Center in 1981, where she continues to serve as director and professor. Grant is the first African American woman to ever earn a PhD in systematic theology, which she did from Union Theological Seminary in New York. Grant is the author of several ground-breaking literary works including *White Women's Christ and Black Women's Jesus: Feminist Christology and Womanist Response* (1989). In 1995 Grant also co-edited two volumes, *Perspectives on Womanist Theology and Recovery of Black Presence* with Randall Bailey.

Riffat Hassan: Is among the earliest Muslim feminists based in the West and influenced by the liberal thinker Fazlur Rahman and his holistic reading of the Qur'ān in order to seek the spirit behind its literalism. For example, Riffat Hassan interrogates Qur'ānic male interpretation that blames Eve for the fall of humanity.

Ada María Isasi-Díaz (1943–2012): A Cuban American theologian who developed the term "mujerista theology," which prioritizes specifically Latina concerns. She also was founder and co-director of the Hispanic Institute of Theology at Drew University until she retired in 2009.

Brett Kavanaugh: His US Supreme Court Justice September 2019 confirmation hearing was interrupted when his former classmate, Dr. Christine Blasey Ford, accused him of sexual assault while they were in high school in 1982. Situated amid the #MeToo movement, the accusation drew national attention.

Kate Kelly: A human rights attorney, she was excommunicated from the Mormon Church (formally, the Church Jesus Christ of Latter-day Saints) for her work committed to gender equity and the ordination of women.

Yuri Kochiyama (1921–2014): Born to Japanese immigrants in California in 1921, Kochiyama was incarcerated at the internment camp at Jerome, Arkansas, during World War II. After having moved to New York City with her husband, Bill, in the late 1950s, Kochiyama became seriously involved in the civil rights movement, connecting the emerging Asian American movement on the East Coast to the ongoing

African American civil rights movement. During the 1980s, she and Bill testified in the Commission on Wartime Relocation and Internment Civilians.

Christine Hoff Kraemer: She is a Pagan theologian who offers an extensive discussion of sexist language, concluding that inclusive language is political in nature.

Cheris Kramarae with Paula Treichler: Coined the phrase "feminism is the radical notion that wo/men are people."

Machik Labdron: The Tibetan founder of Chöd who lived from 1055 to 1149.

Fatima Mernissi: An influential Moroccan sociologist and feminist, Mernissi traced the subordination of women to fabricated hadith, rather than to the Qur'ān, and shed light on the many important roles that Muslim women have played historically while also conducting ethnographic work on contemporary Moroccan women's issues.

Gelongma Palmo: Founder of the Nyungne practice.

Judith Plaskow: Her scholarship is the first systematic feminist Jewish theology that focuses on recovering women's history and redefining women's relationship with the sacred.

Kwok Pui-lan: A Hong Kong-born postcolonial feminist theologian based in the United States who critically analyzes empire and colonialism, elaborating on crucial theological concepts such as hybridity, diasporic imagination, and transnationalism. She has written or edited more than 20 books in English and Chinese.

Diana E. H. Russell (1928–2020): An early leader in femicide research and advocacy, she defines femicide as "the murder of females by males because they are female." Born and raised in Cape Town, South Africa, before moving to the United States to attend Harvard University, she is one of the first feminist writers and activists to focus attention on femicide. Russell wrote numerous books and articles on sexual violence against females, including marital rape, femicide, incest, misogynist murders of females, and pornography.

Elisabeth Schüssler Fiorenza: German-born (1938) Harvard scholar provided models, methods, and metaphorical language for examining biblical texts through a feminist hermeneutical lens. Her many groundbreaking books include *In Memory of Her: A Feminist Theological Reconstruction of Christian Origins* (1983), *But She Said: Feminist Practices of Biblical Interpretation* (1992), *The Power of Naming: A Concilium Reader in Feminist Liberation Theology* (1996), and *Congress of Woman: Religion, Gender, and Kyriarchal Power* (2016).

Sa'diyya Shaikh: South African Muslim academic whose research on Sufi metaphysics and theology examines how gender justice can take place through re-visioning the legal and ethical formulations of women's place in society. She has also coined the term, a "tafsir of praxis" through which to shed light on Muslim women's embodied, experiential, and everyday understandings of Qur'ānic teachings, and has contributed to the theorization of Islamic feminism.

Miranda Shaw: A Buddhist feminist scholar who provided a gynocentric interpretation of Vajrayāna Buddhism that emphasized women's power.

Elizabeth Cady Stanton (1815–1902): In her publication of the *Woman's Bible* in 1895, she disputes the scriptural suggestion that sin and death were introduced into the world by a woman. She was an American suffragist, social activist, abolitionist, and leading figure of the early women's rights movement. Her Declaration of *Sentiments*, presented at the Seneca Falls Convention held in 1848 in Seneca Falls, New York, is often credited with initiating the first organized women's rights and women's suffrage movements in the United States.

Starhawk (Miriam Simos): Perhaps the most recognized leader in contemporary Paganism, Starhawk is the author of *The Spiral Dance* (1979) and a founding member of the Reclaiming Witchcraft tradition. Starhawk studied with several Pagan leaders before developing a new tradition. As a young adult living in the San Francisco Bay Area, Starhawk envisioned a socially progressive, politically active version of the Wiccan religion. With the assistance of other Witches, she helped make the dream a reality, establishing Reclaiming Witchcraft. Beginning as the Reclaiming Collective, the group has blossomed into a full-blown international organization, with member communities in Australia, South America, Europe, and North America. In addition to being a founding leader of the Reclaiming Witchcraft tradition, Starhawk speaks openly about her Jewish heritage and has been an influential spokesperson for the "Jewitch" tradition.

Gloria Steinem: An American feminist, journalist, social political activist, and a spokeswoman for the American feminist movement in the late 1960s and early 1970s. She famously said that "a feminist is anyone who recognizes the equality and full humanity of women and men."

Emilie M. Townes: An American Baptist minister, theological scholar, and womanist pioneer and leader who is the first African American to serve as dean of Vanderbilt Divinity School, where she also serves as the E. Rhodes and Leona B. Carpenter Professor of Womanist Ethics and Society. Townes also served as the first African American woman elected to the office of president at the American Academy of Religion in 2008. Townes' broad areas of expertise include Christian ethics, cultural theory and studies, postmodernism and social postmodernism, as she critiques American culture and empire from a womanist spirituality. Townes also engages deeply in African American health from a womanist perspective and coined the term "womanist ethic of care" as a theological approach to health care. A prolific author, Townes has penned several seminal works in womanist and theo-ethical thought, including *Womanist Ethics and the Cultural Production of Evil* (2006); *Breaking the Fine Rain of Death: African American Health Care and A Womanist Ethic of Care* (1998); *In a Blaze of Glory: Womanist Spirituality as Social Witness* (1995) and *Womanist Justice, Womanist Hope* (1993). She also co-edited *Womanist Theological Ethics: A Reader* (2011) with Katie Geneva Cannon and Angela D. Simms, and *Religion, Health, and Healing in African American Life* (2008) with Stephanie Y. Mitchem.

Paula Treichler with Cheris Kramarae: Coined the phrase "Feminism is the radical notion that wo/men are people."

Amina Wadud: Her landmark work, *Qur'an and Woman: Rereading the Text from a Woman's Perspective*, established hermeneutical principles that take context into account in interpreting the Qur'ān and show that the scripture upholds the equality of the sexes. Her tireless efforts toward establishing gender justice for Muslim women are expressed in her many lectures, teaching, and foundational role in organizations such as Musawah, a global movement for equality and justice in relation to family law. Her most recent work, *Inside the Gender Jihad: Women's Reform in Islam*, speaks from her embodied experiences as an African American Muslim woman, scholar, and activist to critique patriarchal structures.

Sally Roesch Wagner: One of the first women to receive a doctorate for work in women's studies in the United States (UC Santa Cruz, 1978). Dr. Wagner is also a founder of one of the country's first women's studies programs at California State University, Sacramento (1970).

Alice Walker: American author and poet who first used the word "womanist" in her 1979 short story, *Coming Apart*, and again in her 1983 book *In Search of Our Mothers' Gardens: Womanist Prose*. In her writings, Walker defines a "womanist" as a "Black feminist or feminist of color." Walker cites the phrase "acting womanish," which Black mothers said to a child who willfully acted serious, courageous, and grown-up rather than "girlish," as generally expected by society.

Renita J. Weems: An ordained elder and minister in the African Methodist Episcopalian Church, biblical scholar, womanist pioneer, writer and public intellectual, who currently serves as co-senior pastor of Ray of Hope Community Church in Nashville, Tennessee. Weems received her Ph.D. from Princeton Theological Seminary in 1989 and was the first African American woman to earn a doctorate in Old Testament studies, also from Princeton. Weems has taught at Vanderbilt Divinity School, Spelman College, and has served as academic dean at American Baptist College in Nashville. Weems has also authored of several books on women's spirituality and wholeness including *Just A Sister Away* (1987 & 2005); *I Asked for Intimacy* (1993); *Showing Mary: How Women Can Share Prayers, Wisdom, and the Blessings of God* (2003); and *What Matters Most: Ten Passionate Lessons from the Song of Solomon* (2004).

Delores S. Williams: An African American Presbyterian theological scholar and a founding scholar of womanist theology who was the Paul Tillich Professor of Theology and Culture at Union Theological Seminary. Williams authored the seminal text *Sisters in the Wilderness: The Challenge of Womanist God-Talk* in 1993, which helped concretize the field of womanist theology. In "Black Women's Faith, Black Women's Flourishing (Christian Century, 2019), theologian Eboni Marshall Turman notes how Williams, in *Sisters in the Wilderness*, "condemned the patriarchal assumptions of black liberation theology, particularly its emphasis on the significance of Jesus' suffering and death for the black community . . . [and] . . . white atonement theories . . . [as] Jesus' suffering does not save black women. To venerate the blood of the cross is to glorify surrogacy." Williams uses the biblical figure Hagar (Gen. 16, 21), who she identifies as an African slave woman, to challenge the sin of surrogacy by connecting Hagar's experiences of racial, gender, and sexual oppression and her ability to resist her oppressors, name God, and survive in the wilderness with many contemporary Black women. Williams' work has provided robust definitional and epistemological grounding to consider how womanist theology may be applied theoretically and practically through the lived experiences and social location of Black women.

Mary Wollstonecraft (1759–1797): In *A Vindication of the Rights of Women*, first published in 1792, Wollstonecraft proposed that the oppression of middle-class women was primarily because of their limited education. She argued that men do not have intellectual superiority over women; rather women were undereducated because of the norms of the time.

Morning Glory Zell (1948–2014) (aka Morning Glory Zell-Ravenheart): Born Diana Moore, Morning Zell was partnered with Oberon Zell (Oberon Zell-Ravenheart) for three decades, from their meeting in 1974 until her passing in 2014. The two had been prominent advocates for polyamory in addition to being influential Pagan leaders. Morning Glory publicly identified as bisexual. Her essay "A Bouquet of Lovers," first published in the Church of All Worlds newsletter *The Green Egg*, included the section "Rules of the Road" (by which title the essay is sometimes referred) and was a short primer on ethics in, and strategies for, healthy, successful consensual non-monogamy. Morning Glory died in May 2014 after a long battle with cancer. With long interests in performance and theater, Morning Glory requested to "attend her own wake," and a Celebration of Life was held at their residence "RavenHaven" in Northern California. Morning Glory passed away just over three weeks later.

GLOSSARY OF TERMS AND PHRASES

Akhāṛā: Literally, "wrestling ring." A religious or monastic society or organization that provides facilities of shelter and food, along with religious and martial arts training to its members.

Anthropocene: Invented by the chemist Paul Crutzen to describe our "human-dominated, geological epoch." Crutzen noted the following "geologic-scale changes" caused by human beings: "Human activity has transformed between a third and a half of the land surface of the planet. Most of the world's major rivers have been dammed or diverted. Fertilizer plants produce more nitrogen than is fixed naturally by all terrestrial ecosystems. Fisheries remove more than a third of the primary production of the oceans' coastal waters. Humans use more than half of the world's readily accessible fresh water runoff." Most significantly, Crutzen said, people have altered the composition of the atmosphere. Owing to a combination of fossil fuel combustion and deforestation, the concentration of carbon dioxide in the air has risen by 40 percent over the last two centuries, while the concentration of methane, an even more potent greenhouse gas, has more than doubled. Paul Crutzen, "Geology of Mankind," *Nature* 415 (2002).

Avalokitesvara (Sanskrit): The Bodhisattva of Compassion. As Buddhism integrated into indigenous traditions, deities such as Avalokitesvara (literally, the Lord who gazes down toward the world) and Tara, a female deity in her own right, were developed in different Buddhist cultures as either gods or goddesses who embody the compassion of the Buddha.

Bhikshuni (Sanskrit)/Bhikkuni (Pāli): Fully ordained female monastic in the Buddhist tradition.

Bhogī: A person who enjoys life; used in a pejorative sense in modern colloquial Hindi to describe a lustful person who has no control over his or her bodily desires and material nature.

Bodhisattva (Sanskrit): A being dedicated to returning to saṃsāra to help all sentient beings reach enlightenment.

Brahmacārinī: A female celibate student who follows a strict vegetarian diet and engages in a collection of ritual practices to enhance her purity. *Brahmacārinīs* typically wear white clothing to signify their vows of celibacy and lifestyle dedicated to purity. The celibate women living at Trikal Bhavanta's temple, however, do not limit themselves to white clothing. They wear what they want, but they maintain a strict diet and follow a daily schedule of ritual study and practice.

Bride burning: The most common way to kill or maim a bride in India due to a dowry dispute.

Chöd (Tibetan): A Tantric practice associated with Machik Labdron (1055–1149) that is distinctive due to its rhythmic incorporation of bells and drums.

Counter-memory: A concept initially developed by philosopher Michael Foucault which is utilized as rhetorical tool in womanist theological and theo-ethical thought. As a womanist ethical reflection, it narrows the focus and begins with the particular before moving toward the universal. Its purpose is to examine the past for "microhistories" to discern flawed interpretations and perspectives about the past that contain false assumptions and/or missing information that collectively generate a distorted assessment of the factual "truth" about a person, place, event, or circumstance.

Dharma (Sanskrit): A term used in Buddhist, Hindu, and other South Asian religious cultures. In the context of chapter 12, *dharma* is used to mean the teachings of the Buddha. Derived from the Sanskrit verbal root (*dhṛ*) meaning "to hold," "to support," and "to obtain," dharma *describes* that which "holds" the world/cosmos/ universe together; it is a term with a wide semantic range and thus references concepts such as "religion," "ethics," "customs," "traditions," "way of life," "order," "prescribed duty," and "universal common good."

Dharmakṣetra: Literally, "the field of religion." The female Shankaracharya of India, named Trikal Bhavanta Saraswati, invokes the concept to describe Hindu religious institutions in India.

Difference feminism: A variation that emphasizes "sexual difference, identifies women's reproductive function as the primary site of female oppression; the biological family structure is, then, the ground of patriarchal constructions of women as a subordinate class. This use of class for female reproduction is essentially a refinement of a Marxist conception of class oppression which is, then, equated with a biological function of women."[2]

Double consciousness: The term W.E.B. DuBois uses in speaking of Black people's duality of identity.

Double workload: María Pilar Aquino's term to describe the double oppression of Latina women who suffer as workers and also as women, who have the primary responsibility for domestic tasks in the home.

Durga: A name for the fierce, warrior goddess Durga in Hinduism. As the Goddess's name is based on the Sanskrit term for "fort," Durga is known as the "invincible" and "unassailable" feminine power of the universe. She defeats many demons who threaten to destroy order in the universe. Durga is beseeched by the gods and emerges from the primeval power of the goddess Parvati in order to battle the demons and restore cosmic order in the universe. In the Hindu traditions, Durga represents one of the three forms (or powers) of the Great Goddess Shakti and is extolled in the 6th-century text the *Devī-Māhātmya*, which is part of the *Markandeya Purāṅa*.

Ecocide: Human-induced extinction of massive numbers of species, including humanity itself.

Ecofeminism: Includes the connections between ecological and feminist concerns: discerning multiple associations between the feminist and ecological movements and between the historical and contemporary oppression and domination of women and the natural world. It is deemed to have originated with French feminist Françoise d'Eaubonne in Le Féminisme ou la Mort (1974) when she called upon women to lead an ecological revolution to save the planet.

Elohim: One of the names for God in the Hebrew Bible.

Exegesis: It is a systematic plan for coming to understand a biblical text. The origin of the word is from the Greek term *exegeisthai*, meaning "to explain" or "to interpret." It has been used to refer to explanations of Scripture since the early 17th century. This term is often used interchangeably with the word "hermeneutics," which refers to the interpretation of the Bible for preaching, as well as to the interpretation of sacred texts in the world's religions.

Femicide: It is a gender-specific variation from homicide that means to kill females because they are female. This interreligious and cross-cultural gender-specific brutality kills an estimated 66,000 females around the world each year.

Feminicide: This term broadens accountability from individual perpetrators who kill females because they are female to include people and institutions that could and should, but do not, provide protection for females who live within its jurisdiction. It is a accusatory term, which points to the non-response of the state, whether from ineptitude or disinterest, for failure to protect females. It encompasses political, judicial, and social factors.

Feminism lite: Chimamanda Nogozi Adichie uses this term to describe "conditional female equality," which she rejects outright. Judging women more harshly than men is an example: a man is applauded for being assertive and a real "go-getter," while feminist lite defines similar actions by a woman as being too "aggressive." Power and strength are applauded in men, but feminism lite views these traits as negative abnormalities in females.

Feminist consciousness: To be conscious of the reality that women are oppressed individually and as a people group.

Feminist preaching: It is a preaching practice designed to overcome gender oppression and injustice. It is a practice that is influenced by the women's liberation movement in the late 1960s. Feminist preaching is concerned with the advocacy for women, while challenging male preaching authority, sexist biblical interpretation, and use of inclusive language and that of illustration that justify gender-based violence. It also attends to the vocational element of preaching, including ordination of women and roles of women in ministry for Christian churches.

G*d: Elisabeth Schüssler Fiorenza uses this term to "degender" the male-gendered Greek term for the traditional spelling of God.

Gelongma (Tibetan): Fully ordained female monastic in Buddhist tradition.

Geshema (Tibetan): A female recipient of the highest academic philosophical degree in the traditional Tibetan Buddhist learning system.

Guru: A religious teacher or preceptor who is considered to be enlightened. Meaning, from the perspective of authoritative Hindu religious texts and popular Hindu imagination, the guru is thought to have realized the highest state of unitive consciousness with the divine. The guru's direct experience of the divine is said to be the source of his or her religious wisdom / knowledge.

Homiletician: A professional academic who studies the art and science of preaching.

Homiletics: The art of preaching or writing sermons, which also includes the study of preaching styles, techniques, and interpretation processes.

Homily: It is a concise liturgical sermon. The word came from the Latin word *homilia* as a translation of the Greek meaning for conversation, discourse, or address. It is often referred to as a short lesson preceding the Eucharist in Roman Catholic and Episcopal contexts. Homily and sermon are often interchangeable.

Honor killings: Justification by males for killing a female because the female has "dishonored" the family. Reasons include financial or inheritance claims, being a victim of rape or incest, becoming pregnant out of wedlock, unacceptable engagement to an unacceptable male, marrying a man against her family's wishes, or any "suspicious" activity.

Inclusive language: It is language that intentionally aims to recognize and include the wide diversity and many differences of people present in and beyond worship. Inclusive language became a movement that emerged out of the women's liberation movement in the late 1960s and the early 1970s. It draws attention to power embedded in language for the sake of decentering that power in all forms of oppressions, such as classism, racism, sexism, ageism, and ableism. Preachers committed to inclusive language make use of language for God that is beyond a male God.

Intersectionality: Legal scholar Kimberlé Crenshaw coined this term that encompasses the interconnected aspect through diverse social categories, such as race, gender, class, sexuality, and imperialism.

Kyriarchy: Coined by Elisabeth Schüssler Fiorenza as a way to re-conceptualize patriarchy and is derived from the Greed *kyrios*, meaning lord, master, father, or husband (senior male in the household who holds authority above all others), and the verb *archein*, meaning to dominate or rule. She uses kyriarchy instead of patriarchy to express the various levels or categories of domination in the overall system of domination.

Lama (Tibetan): A Buddhist teacher.

Liberal feminism: Actively participates in the various waves or expressions of feminism. "'Liberal' describes one of feminism's earliest forms. Liberal feminism is identified by its political agenda to eradicate the social and legal inequalities suffered by women."[3]

Majority World: Refers to the 80 percent of the world that lives on $10 a day or less.

Mahāyāna Buddhism: A form of Buddhism found in East and Inner Asia that is distinct through its use of Sanskrit language canon.

Mani (Tibetan): A short way of referring to the popular six-syllable mantra "Om mani padme hung."

Mani Lhakhang (Tibetan): A temple associated with practice dedicated to Avalokitesvara, the Bodhisattva of Compassion.

Mantra (Sanskrit): A short saying that can be repeated to inspire meditation and focus; used as a sacred hymn, prayer, or invocation to connect with deities and/or calm the mind.

Masculinist: Similar to "male chauvinist," it designates anti-feminist positions.

Minority World: Refers to the West as a reminder that those of us who live in the West are a very small part of the global population. It also diverges from language that is hierarchical, offensive, and geographically incorrect.

Model minority stereotype: A model minority stereotype emphasizes Asian Americans' cooperation and assimilation with mainstream American society. Asian immigrants are praised for their hard-working, economic success; emphasis on education; and respect for American values and culture. However, many Asian American scholars criticize this stereotype for hiding the high level of poverty and low level of education, especially among intercity Asians and Southeast Asian refugees. Moreover, Korean Americans are the largest uninsured ethnic group. The stereotype also dismisses structural racism to the individual problem as though anyone would achieve the American dream if they had worked hard like Asian immigrants. Thus, the stereotype creates the political tension between Asians and other racial minorities. A model minority stereotype is also called a "middleman stereotype," as Asians are placed between whites and other racial minorities. The middleman stereotype, however, rightfully points out that a large percentage of economically independent Asian Americans are the owners of small businesses; Asian Americans rarely hold leadership positions beyond middle management positions in the government or professional organizations. A model minority stereotype is a hindrance to the development of Asian American communities and solidarity between Asian American communities and other racial minorities.

Mujeres de Negro: Several civic organizations in Chihuahua City, Mexico, gathered in November 20, 2001, when approximately 300 women dressed in black and wearing pink hats interrupted the parade in Chihuahua City to protest the discovery of eight women's corpses in Ciudad Juárez.

Mujerista/mujerist **theology**: Ada María Isasi-Díaz developed what she defined as *mujerista* theology, which prioritizes a preferential option for Latina women and their struggle for freedom. Since her conception of this term, many US Latina theologians prefer instead to be known as "Latina feminists" to support their efforts at self-identity in the public square and to establish conversation with the rich tradition of Latina/Chicana feminism.

Nepantla: A Nahuatl word for an in-between, liminal state, that uncertain terrain one crosses when moving from one place to another.

Northern Triangle: The region in Central America that includes Guatemala, El Salvador, and Honduras.

Nyungne (Tibetan): A visualization, prayer, and fasting practice associated with Avalokitesvara, attributed to Gelongma Palmo (dates unknown).

Postcolonial feminist theology: Postcolonial feminist theology decolonizes a masculinist theological tradition, constructed on the long heritage of European colonialism defined by white, middle-class, Eurocentric norms. It seeks to reconceptualize the relation between theology and empire through the multiple lenses of gender, race, class, sexuality, colonialism, and religion. Developed in the 1990s, postcolonial feminist theology challenges Western feminist studies that essentialize women in the postcolonial world experiences as homogeneous, failing to recognize the connection of imperial and racist domination in their own scholarship.

Poststructuralist feminism: Recognizes patriarchy as "an ideological structure permeating every aspect of life. Poststructuralists, especially those informed by French psycholinguistics, tend to assume a conception of language as the ground of all meaning and value."[4]

Priesthood of all believers: It is a doctrine, a chief principle of the churches of the 16th-century Reformation, both Lutheran and Reformed, and the Protestant Free churches that arose from the Reformation churches. The doctrine asserts that all humans have access to God through Christ, the true high priest, and thus do not need a priestly mediator. This introduced a democratic element in the functioning of the church that meant all Christians were equal. The ordained clergy thus were representatives of the entire congregation, preaching and administering the sacraments.

Pulpit: It is a raised stand for preachers in a Christian church. The origin of the word is the Latin *pulpitum* (platform or staging). The traditional pulpit is raised well above the surrounding floor for audibility and visibility. Though sometimes highly decorated, it is not for purely decorative purposes but can have a useful acoustic effect in projecting the preacher's voice to the congregation below.

Radical feminism: Patriarchy is considered an "all-pervasive and a-historical system. 'Radical' refers to the belief that patriarchy is deeply rooted, inherently hierarchical and aggressive, existing independently of social changes. A key condition of the radical is: that the shifts from one economic or political structure to another would not make any difference to women's subjugation."[5]

Rasquache is a bricolage, kitsch aesthetics claimed by Latinx artists.

Repulsions of Asian Exclusion Acts: (1) The Magnusson Act of 1943 repealed the 1882 Chinese Exclusion Act by making Chinese immigrants eligible for citizenship and establishing a quota for Chinese immigrants. (2) The 1945 War Brides Acts temporarily lifted the ban on Asian women married to American soldiers and Asian children adopted by American servicemen. (3) The McCarran-Walter Act of 1952 abolished the 1917 Asia Barred Zone concept, replacing it with quotas of 100 persons annually for countries within the Asia-Pacific Triangle and allowing Asian immigrants to be naturalized. (4) The 1965 Immigration and Nationality Act abolished discrimination in immigration and naturalization based on race and national origins.

Sādhu: A generic term for a holy person in India; its usage in northern Indic contexts describes ascetics who leave behind family and social duties in order to devote themselves to the divine.

Samsara (Sanskrit): The cycle of death and rebirth.

Sangha (Sanskrit): The Buddhist monastic community.

Sannyāsī: A term for the world renouncer in Hinduism; it characterizes a radical and unconventional life of severing ties with family and society in order to realize the divine.

Sarveshwar Mahadev Vaikunth Dham Mukti Dwar Akhara Pari: "The Army of Angels." The monastic society that the female Shankaracharya of India named Trikal Bhavanta Saraswati formed for female *sādhus* in 2014. It serves as a shelter for abused and homeless women and children, as well as a monastic center of learning where women across the age, caste, and class spectrum can study Vedic and other literature and receive martial arts training in self-defense.

Shakti (śakti): While the term translates as "power," it references the Goddess (Shakti), women, and the dynamic and creative, divine feminine power of world. In Hinduism, women are said to have more *śakti* than men because they are thought to share in the Goddess's femaleness.

Shankaracharya: A religious title and office that pertains to the highest levels of the traditional Hindu power structure within institutionalized forms of the Hindu religion in India. Historically, this leadership role, and by implication, lineage tradition, has been reserved for Brahmin men. The institution of the Shankaracharya leadership is traced to the 9th-century religious reformer Adi Shankaracharya. Besides writing numerous book and commentaries on the theology of non-dualism, he is said to have organized four or five monasteries in the four corners of India.

Shari'a: A catch-all term to mean Islamic law, but Islamic jurisprudence should properly be called *fiqh*. *Shari'a* denotes the divine and moral principles behind the system of Islamic law and is not monolithic.

Shekhinah: God's presence, or the Shekhinah dwells among the exiled community of Israel.

Shiva: A great god in the Hindu pantheon.

Socialist feminism: Seeks to "change the concrete circumstances of women's lives; that is, their social and material situations. The 'socialist' feminist assumes that the solidarity and interdependence of men as grounded on a material and economic base enables men to dominate women."[6]

Strīdharma: A term that translates as "the *dharma* of women." In the orthodox Brahmanical Sanskritic tradition of Hinduism, *strīdharma* characterizes the duty of women to marry and procreate, to worship their husbands as their lord, and to cultivate self-effacement, obedience, loyalty, and respect for their husbands and families. From the perspective of Brahmanical Hindu orthodoxy, a wife and mother of sons has the highest status. She represents the ideal woman.

Strī kī śakti: Literally, "the power of women." The female Shankaracharya of India named Trikal Bhavanta Saraswati draws on the concept in connection with her religious teachings and practices to advance the idea of autonomy and equality as "powers" intrinsic to the female sex.

Sūtra (Sanskrit): A text in the Mahāyāna Buddhist canon.

Tantric Buddhism: Also known as Vajrayāna Buddhism; a form of Buddhism that embraces all experiences as potential paths to enlightenment.

Testimony: It is a truth telling by a witness to the power of the gospel. It is a display of one's faith not simply as a matter of individual stories but as stories that are responsible to and for the Christian community and the world. Preaching as testimony has been developed in order to rediscover centuries old women preaching tradition that is largely hidden in the dominant history of Christianity.

The*logy: Elisabeth Schüssler Fiorenza swaps the letter "o" for the asterisk symbol to "degender" what is otherwise a male-gendered rendering for the traditional spelling of God.

Thealogy: Naomi Goldenberg first used this term in her book *Changing of the Gods* (1979); countering and correcting the patriarchal theology of the Abrahamic religions is "thealogy," the discourse of the feminine divine (thea) in contrast to the male God (theo), providing a framework for giving voice to representations of the divine in a female form.

Theravāda Buddhism: A form of Buddhism found in South and Southeast Asia that is distinct due to its use of the Pāli language canon.

Therīgāthā **(Pāli)**: Collected songs of the earliest female monastics in Buddhism.

Trinity: It is a Christian doctrine that holds that God is one God with three divine beings. The etymology of the word came from the Latin word, *trinus* meaning "threefold." God as the Father, the Son (Jesus Christ), and the Holy Spirit are "one God in three Divine persons." The three persons are distinct, yet are one substance, essence, or nature.

Triveni Sangam: Literally, the confluence of three rivers. A sacred pilgrimage place located in Prayagraj, Uttar Pradesh, where the Ganga, Jamuna, and hidden Saraswati rivers converge. According to Hindu sacred texts, upon the creation of the world, the gods and the demons fought one another in order to retrieve the elixir of immortality, which was produced from the cosmic churning of the world and put in a vessel known as the *kalāśa* (waterpot). The deity who was carrying the *kalāśa* spilled the mixture, which fell to the earth. One of the spots where the elixir is said to have fallen is Prayagraj. In the Hindu lunar calendar, there are a number of holy days and festivals, during which Hindu pilgrims and others take a ritual bath to cleanse themselves of their karmic "sins." It is thought that ritual bathing in the Triveni Sangam, a practice which is prescribed by Hindu texts, can liberate the devotee from the eternal cycle of rebirth.

US laws that exclude Asians from immigration, citizenship, and ownership of property: 1882 Chinese Exclusion Act; 1917 Asian Indian (South Asian) Exclusion Act/Asia Barred Zone Act; 1924 Japanese (and Korean) Exclusion Act; and the 1934 Filipino Exclusion Act.

Vajrayāna Buddhism: Also known as Tantric Buddhism; a form of Buddhism that embraces all experiences as potential paths to enlightenment.

Vinaya: Monastic law for Buddhist monastics.

White gaze: This attends to the ways in which Black people's bodies are interrogatively surveilled by white persons, resulting in distorted stereotypical perceptions. White gaze is grounded historically and globally in white supremacy ideology that creates a systemic flux of ongoing racialized micro-aggressions, structural oppression and cultural violence travailed by Black people in varied spaces and places.

Wo/man: Elisabeth Schüssler Fiorenza uses this term to signify everyone who is excluded from democracy or democratic processes, outsiders who have secondary status than the dominant/prominent.

Womanist theology: Womanist theologians analyze the impacts of class, gender, and race in a context of Black life and religious worldviews to formulate strategies for the elimination of oppression in the lives of Black Americans and the rest of humanity by centering the experience and perspective of Black women. Similar to womanism in general, womanist theology also examines how Black women are marginalized and portrayed in inadequate or biased ways in literature and other forms of expression while simultaneously working for the liberation of all people of all genders. American author and poet Alice Walker first used the word "womanist" in her 1979 short story *Coming Apart* and again in her 1983 book *In Search of Our Mothers' Gardens: Womanist Prose*. Among the progenitors of womanist theology, Black women theological scholars include Katie Geneva Cannon, *Black Womanist Ethics*; Jacquelyn Grant *White Women's Christ, Black Women's Jesus*; and Renita Weems *Just a Sister Away*. Delores Williams authored the seminal text *Sisters in the Wildnerness: The Challenge of Womanist God-Talk* in 1993. These scholars move in a long trajectory of other Black women religious thinkers who may be referred to as *proto-Womanists*, a term developed by womanist systematic theologian JoAnne Marie Terrell.

WomanistCare: WomanistCare is a term co-created by pastoral theologian Marsha Foster Boyd and other womanist caregivers convened by Linda Hollies in 1991, who also was an editor for the first book on WomanistCare in 1991.

Womanist ethic of care: Social ethicist Emilie Townes coined this term as a theological approach to health and health care.

WomanistHealthCare: This term was coined by doctoral student Anjeanette Allen as a reprisal and response to health care's dismissal and cultural erasure of Black women's pain. It is a womanist practical theology of health and health care that is an expansion of the term "WomanistCare," which was co-created by pastoral theologian Marsha Foster Boyd and other Womanist caregivers convened by Linda Hollies in 1991, and it also builds on social ethicist Emilie Townes's focus on a "Womanist Ethic of Care." WomanistHealthCare seeks to advocate for the creation of safe spaces, rituals, and practices embodied by love, beneficence, and justice for Black women, specifically in health care settings. A WomanistHealthCare approach is a critical pedagogy that yields understanding on the nuances between space, place, and power by situating Black women's bodies and the spaces they inhabit for care as sites for radical resistance and redemptive healing. WomanistHealthCare makes operable, for Black women and the Black community at large, the Hippocratic Oath and upholds the principle of nonmaleficence, which asserts an obligation to not inflict harm or evil on others, which, in medical ethics, is associated with the maxim *Primum non nocere*, "Above all do no harm."

Women's consciousness: To be aware or conscious of women as a distinct group of people.

YHWH (without vowels): One of the names for God in the Hebrew Bible.

Yogī: A spiritual aspirant who is said to have restrained his or her bodily senses, material desires and cravings, and lower material nature. Similarly, a spiritual aspirant who has "yoked" herself or himself to a practice of discipline in order to attain the highest state of unitive consciousness.

Zanan: One of the most notable Muslima women's magazines, it was founded in Iran in 1992 under the Khatami regime by Shahla Sherkat and closed down under the Ahmadinejad regime in 2008. The magazine created a forum for translation into

Persian of key feminist works, discussions of topics ranging from the nature of women's rights and the scope of freedom of the press to new interpretations of Islamic texts and legal issues.

GLOSSARY OF LOCATIONS, ORGANIZATIONS, EVENTS, MOVEMENTS

Asociación de Mujeres para Estudios Feministas Guatemala **(AMEF)** [Association of Women for Feminist Studies]: Founded on June 23, 2010, in Guatemala City in the context of a post-conflict patriarchal society, as an association committed politically, ideologically, and ethically to defending women's rights: the right to a life with dignity, to be heard, to holistic health, to the recognition of cultural knowledge, to social and political participation, justice, and ethnic diversity (http://amefguatemala.blogspot.com/).

La Asociación Maya Uk'ux B'e Guatemala [Mayan Association Uk'ux B'e]: A Mayan organization with the capacity to promote the reconstitution of the Mayan People (Mayab' Tinamit). From the perspective of Mayan cosmology and culture, the association seeks to contribute to the inter-generational formation of Mayan leadership and the re-vindication and exercise of Mayan historic rights through education, health, teaching and research (http://ukuxbe.org/Index.html).

Asociadas por lo Justo (JASS) Mesoamerica—Guatemala: Strengthens and leverages the collective power of women to promote justice, safety, and accountability in a context of impunity and violence (http://www.justassociates.org/meso/index.htm).

Asociadas por lo Justo (JASS) Mesoamerica—Honduras: Strengthens and leverages the collective power of women to promote justice, safety, and accountability in a context of impunity and violence (http://www.justassociates.org/meso/index.htm).

Aztlán: Located in northwestern Mexico and the Southwest United States; was understood as the historic and mythic homeland of the Mexica people who migrated to central Mexico to found Tenochtitlan. For many Chicano artists in the 1960s, restoring the memory and claim to this ancient border homeland was significant.

Beijing Platform for Action [Geneva Declaration, p. 87]: 1979 United Nations Convention on the Elimination of All Forms of Discrimination against Women (CEDAW).

Benefit Corporations: Certified Benefit Corporations, or B Corps, are businesses that achieve at least a minimum score on the B Impact Assessment, which measures a company's social and environmental impact. Benefit corporations are legally structured to put social mission first and also have third-party certification of the ways in which they meet their goals of treating employees justly (for example, paying a living wage, and not just a minimum wage), meeting social needs directly through their goods and services, and exercising environmental responsibility.

Center for Women's Rights (CDM)—Honduras: A social and feminist institution, *el Centro de Derechos de Mujeres* (CDM) is dedicated to protecting and promoting women's human rights in Honduras through legal aid, legal education, advocacy, and community organizing (http://www.derechosdelamujer.org/).

Center for Women's Studies—Honduras: *Centro de Estudios de la Mujer-Honduras* (CEM-H) is a legally constituted NGO since 1987, nationally and internationally recognized as one of the most important feminist organizations in Honduras, specialized in incidence and investigations on the situation of women in Honduras (http://www.cemh.org.hn/).

Committee of Relatives of the Disappeared in Honduras (COFADEH): The *Comité de Familiares de Detenidos Desparecidos en Honduras* (COFADEH) is an NGO with national and international activities whose fundamental aim it is to fight against all different forms of impunity as well as to revive the memory of the victims (http://www.cofadeh.org/).

Feministas en Resistencia (FER) Honduras [Feminists in Resistance]: An alliance of diverse women and organizations from across Honduras who came together in response to the 2009 coup in Honduras to promote a return of democratic order and to protect democratic and women's rights gains over the last 20 years (http://feministascontraelgolpehn.blogspot.com/).

Japanese Internment Camps: Following imperial Japan's attacks on Pearl Harbor, the US government issued Executive Order 9066. Within weeks of EO 9066 being signed, a series of exclusion and incarceration of all persons of Japanese ancestry happened throughout Canada and the United States. Both countries forcibly removed and confined almost their entire Japanese populations. In the United States alone, the government incarcerated 120,000 Japanese Americans, including over 1,100 transferred from Hawai'i and 6,000 born in the camps located across the country—two thirds of them US citizens and comprising less than 1 percent of the total US population.

The Katie Geneva Cannon Center for Womanist Leadership: As described in its mission statement, the Center for Womanist Leadership is "committed to convening Black women around common issues for wisdom sharing, networking, problem solving, and mobilization, and to giving Black women thinkers, activists and artists opportunities to expand existing efforts and connect them for sustainable collaboration." The mission statement reflects the visionary insight of the late Dr. Katie Geneva Cannon who was the Annie Scales Rogers Professor of Christian Social Ethics at Union Presbyterian Seminary. In 1974, Cannon became the first African American woman to be ordained in the Presbyterian Church (U.S.A.). Union Presbyterian Seminary developed the Center for Womanist Leadership "to inspire, equip, connect and support Black women divinely motivated to serve as change makers in their community." In 2019, the seminary named the center in memory of the Dr. Katie Geneva Cannon. In July 2019, Rev. Melanie C. Jones joined the Katie Geneva Cannon Center for Womanist Leadership as its newest director and next visionary leader (https://www.upsem.edu/cwl/).

National Network of Women Human Rights Defenders in Honduras, Women for Life Forum: *Foro de Mujeres por la Vida* (http://forodemujeresporlavidazonanorte.blogspot.com/).

National Network of Women Human Rights Defenders in Mexico Tlachinollan Human Rights Center: *Centro de Derechos Humanos de la Montaña Tlachinollan* is based in Tlapa de Comonfort and has worked for over 15 years in one of the poorest regions in Mexico, the Montaña and Costa Chica regions of the state of Guerrero, where poverty, discrimination, and abandonment of the indigenous communities are common, and these communities are deprived of the right to justice and dignity (http://www.tlachinollan.org/).

National Organization for Women (NOW): Founded in 1966 as a grassroots arm of the women's movement, its current five national campaigns include (1) End the Criminalization of Trauma; (2) Ratify the Equal Rights Amendment; (3) Mobilize for Reproductive Justice; (4) Advance Voting Rights; and (5) Protect Immigrant Rights (https://now.org/).

Network: An advocacy for justice organization inspired by Catholic sisters. Its "Nuns on the Bus" has driven thousands of miles across the United States to speak prophetically for justice and to advocate for adequate federal policies for budget, housing, income, immigration, taxes, voting and democracy, and women and families (https://networklobby.org/2020vision/).

Nobel Women's Initiative: Uses the prestige of the Nobel Peace Prize and six courageous women peace laureates—Mairead Maguire, Rigoberta Menchú Tum, Jody Williams, Shirin Ebadi, Tawakkol Karman, and Leymah Gbowee—to magnify the power and visibility of women working in countries around the world for peace, justice, and equality. The six women bring together their extraordinary experiences and work to spotlight, amplify, and promote the work of grassroots women's organizations and movements around the world. The Nobel Women's Initiative was established in 2006 (https://nobelwomensinitiative.org/).

Ordain Women Movement: This campaign was launched in 2013 to publicly call for the ordination of women in the need to address gender inequity in the Mormon Church.

Pacific Asian North Asian American Women in Theology and Ministry (PANAAWTM): PANAAWTM began as a small group of women, predominantly from Asia, who were enrolled in graduate theological institutions or working in ministry in the United States. With the assistance of Professor Letty Russell of Yale University Divinity School, these women convened in the fall of 1984 to explore common interests and the possibility of forming a network. Out of this gathering, thirteen Asian women formed the group, Asian Women Theologians, Northeast US Group. Within a year, a small number of Asian American women were added to the group from the West Coast, affiliated with the Pacific and Asian Center for Theology and Strategy. A significant development in the group over the years has been the increasing participation of Asian American women who bring perspectives and issues that often differ dramatically from those of their Asian sisters. Asian American issues have included racism, identity, and sexism within the Asian American community, as well as tokenism and marginalization within US society at large and homophobia. In the early 1990s, Asian Canadian women began to join and become active in the network. In response to these changes, the group's name became Pacific, Asian, and North American Asian Women in Theology and Ministry. Since then, PANAAWTM has published three anthologies, mentored Asian and Asian American doctoral students and emerging scholars, and produced critical scholarships on feminist theology and biblical studies.

Seneca Falls Convention 1848: Although it is considered by many to be the beginning point of the women's rights movement in America, abolitionist women, Black and white together, gathered at the Anti-Slavery Convention in New York City, May 9–12, 1837—11 years earlier. The Seneca Falls Convention passed a resolution that called for the right to vote for women and became the starting point for the suffrage movement. It was 72 years later before women finally received the right to vote.

Sinergia No'j Guatemala: Founded in 2006 with the objective of strengthening the leadership of social movements, in particular those of indigenous peoples, women and youth in Guatemala (http://www.sinergianoj.org/index.php).

True Woman Movement: A worldwide grassroots movement, organized by Nancy DeMoss Wolgemuth and birthed on October 11, 2008, as a Christ-centered antidote to counter feminist ideals, which this group sees as counter what it means to be a "true woman" from a biblical perspective (https://www.reviveourhearts.com/). It includes the "True Woman Manifesto," which affirms the biblical justification for patriarchy (https://www.reviveourhearts.com/true-woman/manifesto/).

La Unidad de Protección a Defensoras y Defensores de Derechos Humanos, Guatemala (UDEFEGUA): Unit for the Protection of Human Rights Defenders in Guatemala was founded in 2004 with the objective of promoting the security of human rights defenders in Guatemala and to contribute to the protection of the political space in which they work (http://www.udefegua.org/).

Women's Alliance for Theology, Ethics, and Ritual (WATER): Founded in 1983 by Mary E. Hunt and Diann L. Neu, WATER nourishes a growing network of theologians, religious studies scholars, religious professionals, and activists. The organization engages theological training and scholarship to engender social change as it works for "empowerment, justice, peace, and systemic change (https://www.waterwomensalliance.org).

Union Nacional de Guatemaltecas (UNAMG) [National Union of Guatemalan Women]: Founded in 1980 on International Women's Day, UNAMG is an autonomous feminist organization that promotes equal rights, social justice, and respect for ethnic and cultural diversity (http://unamg.org/v1/).

NOTES

1. See, e.g., Elisabeth Jay Friedman, and Constanza Tabbush, #NiUnaMenos: Not One Woman Less, Not One More Death! *NACLA Report on the Americas*, September 11, 2016.

2. Pamela Sue Anderson, *Re-visioning Gender in Philosophy of Religion: Reason, Love and Epistemic Locatedness* (Surrey, UK: Ashgate Publishing Ltd., 2012), 9.

3. Anderson, *Re-visioning Gender*, 9.

4. Anderson, *Re-visioning Gender*, 9.

5. Anderson, *Re-visioning Gender*, 9.

6. Anderson, *Re-visioning Gender*, 9.

Index

capitalism: Kimmerer on exploitative, 76–77; Tanner on, 77, 91nn8–9

Cardman, Francine, 287

Carpenter, Dennis, 130

Carroll, Seforosa, 345

Carter, Jimmy, 355–56, 357

Caruth, Cathy, 341

Catholic Church: Daly on patriarchy in, 25; De Boer on, 170; faith leaders sex abuse in, 226; on Mary Magdalene prophetic witness, 286; Nuns on the Bus road trips, 290; Religious Freedom Week and, 289; women position in, 39

Catholicism: Berger, T., on gender and liturgy in, 26–27; Daly rejection of, 26

celibacy vow, at *Akhāṛā Pari* monastery, 176–77

¡Cesen Deportación! (Stop Deportation!), by Garcia, R., 51

Changing of the God (Goldenberg), 29

Charter for the Protection of Children and Young People, 226

Chicano movement, 51

child abuse, 348n4; trauma and, 341, 345–46, 348, 349n9; WHO on, 340, 348n5

childhood violence survivors: embodiment, impermanence and dwelling, 346–47; home definition, 342–44; home-making metaphors, 5, 344–45, 350n38; home nomadic spirituality, 345, 347–48; spiritual homelessness of, 5, 339, 340, 341

Chinese Exclusion Act (1882), 159

Chinese Women's Jeleab organization, of APA women, 161

Chinese YWCA of APA women, 161

Cho, Grace, 158

Chöd, 144, 148

Choi, Jin Young, 158–59

Chomsky, Noam, 267

Christ, Carol P., 124, 129, 133

Christian Church: APA women in, 156; women preaching leadership in, 205–14

Christian feminism, 14

Christian feminist theology: Daly and, 25–26; McFague and Ruether on, 26; Schüssler Fiorenza on, 26; *Woman's Bible* and, 14, 25

Christianity: APA and, 156, 164; Daly rejection of, 26; ecofeminism and, 66–67; Ruether on, 136; Tanner on capitalism and, 91nn8–9

Christianity and the New Spirit of Capitalism (Tanner), 77

The Church and the Second Sex (Daly), 15

#ChurchToo movement, 221–22

Circle Sanctuary, of Fox, 130, 133

Citizenship Act of 1955 amendment, in India, 171, 179n9

Clifford, James, 48

Clifton, Chas, 125, 133

climate justice, ecofeminism and, 71

Coleman, Isobel, 197

Coleman, Monica, 303

colonialism: Black slave women and, 109–10, 116n5; Native American women bodies claims in, 268–71; patriarchy narratives and, 266

The Color Purple (Walker), 17–18

Las Comadres, in US-Mexico border, 51–52

community economies: ethical decision making in, 78; Gibson-Graham on, 75, 77–78; Kimmerer on, 75–77; Sanchez on, 76; Schor on, 75, 77; Tanner on, 77, 91nn8–9

Cook County Commission on Social Innovation: Anaya of, 87; economic sustainability and, 87–90; Garcia, J., of, 87, 89; Lane of, 87–88; Malone on objectives of, 88, 88–90

Copeland, Shawn, 114, 294

counterpatriarchal framework, of Buddhism, 31

Covenant of the Goddess: Harlow and, 140n39; Pendderwen and Kelly, A., of, 129; Ruether on, 129–30

COVID-19 pandemic: Asians attack during, 159, 165; asylum seekers and, 252

Coyle, T. Thorn, 135

"The Creation of a Feminist Theology" (Trible), 15

credibility: Day on, 98–99; harms of excess, 99–101; IPCD, 96–98, 103; IPCE, 97–100, 104n22; male perpetrators sympathy and, 94–95; Medina on excess, 95; in sexual assault testimonies, 94–95

Crenshaw, Kimberlé, 206

Crimes Against Humanity and War Crimes Act, Canada, 269

Crittenden, Anne, 334

Crosby, Fanny J., 108, 116

Cruz, Philip Vera, 163

cultural violence, of Black women, 109

Daly, Mary, 15, 63, 327; on Catholic Church patriarchy, 25; Christian feminist theology of, 25–26; as Pagan and Goddess Spirituality leader, 133; radical feminism of, 133, 135

dance, women religion studies on, 40

Dane, Kirstin S., 321–22

Davis, Addie, 207

Dawson, Barbara, 111

Day, Keri, 98–99

The Death of Nature (Merchant), 63

on, 97–98, 104n12; harms of, 99–101; Jones on, 97–98; Medina on, 98, 101; Taylor, C., on recognition respect, 100–101; white supremacy and, 99–100, 104n22

IFR. *See* Interim Final Rule

IJSO. *See* Institute for Judaism and Sexual Orientation

IK. *See* indigenous knowledge

Ikaria Design Company, 80–83, 91n21

illiberal democracy, 329, 330

illiberal populist movement, 330

immigration. *See* Asian American history; asylum seekers; US-Mexico border

Immigration and Nationality Act (1965), 161, 163

inclusion, intentional space and, 307–8

inclusive language, 21, 27, 32n2; Kim on, 211–12; Reform Movement and, 25

India: Citizenship Act of 1955 amendment, 171, 179n9; sexual violence demonstrations in Delhi, 301–2; Srinivas on Hindu nationalist government in, 171

Indian Act (1876), 271; genocidal and racial tactics of, 268; Haudenosaunee women oppression and, 273

indigenous knowledge (IK), 263; Haudenosaunee creation stories and, 271; Haudenosaunee oppression of, 264, 273

indigenous Native American women, 277; Canada and US violence toward, 265–66; colonial claims to bodies of, 268–71; colonial narratives of gender, 266; Durkheim and Franklin on, 266; Fletcher on greater rights of, 267, 268; Haudenosaunee Confederacy and, 264, 265, 267, 271–75; IK and, 263–64, 271–72; involuntary sterilization of, 268–69; Mohawk feminist response to violations against, 5, 263–76; rematriation case study, 272–75; resiliency of, 276; suffrage movement and, 266–68; TRC *Call to Action*, 265, 270; United Nations Declaration of Indigenous People and, 263, 269. *See also* Iroquois Indians; Laguna Pueblo/Sioux people

inequality: Mataji response to Hinduism sexual, 169–79; in mosque spaces for women, 313–14

In Memory of Her (Schüssler Fiorenza), 15

Institute for Judaism and Sexual Orientation (IJSO), 188

Institute of Medicine (IOM), *Unequal Treatment* report by, 112–13

intentional space, inclusion and, 307–8

Intergovernmental Panel on Climate Change and Land (IPCC), 270–71, 275

Interim Final Rule (IFR), for asylum seekers, 252

international initiatives, ecofeminism and, 64

interpretation: Biblical on women preaching, 212–13; patriarchy and Qur'ān, 194; of Qur'ān, 28, 193, 197–98

intersectionality: Crenshaw on, 206; ecofeminism and, 64

interstitial integrity, of APA women, 155, 163–65

intimate partner violence, 235–36

Invisible Visits (Sacks), 113

IOM. *See* Institute of Medicine

IPCC. *See* Intergovernmental Panel on Climate Change and Land

IPCD. *See* identity-prejudicial credibility deficit

IPCE. *See* identity-prejudicial credibility excess

Iroquois Indians: Morgan ethnography of, 266; suffrage movement inspired by, 267; Wagner on women respect by, 266–67

Isasi-Díaz, Ada María, 17, 354; on ethnography, 47–48; on ethnomethodology, 55n7; on Mujerista theology, 28

Islam: misconceptualizations of, 192; SIS and, 200, 201; women in, 192–93

Islamic Family Law Act (1984), 200

Islamic feminist theology, 28–29, 197–98

Islamophobia, Kaur on, 291–92

Japanese WWII internment camp, 159, 161, *162*, 166n29

Jesus and the Disinherited (Thurman), 102

Jewish feminism: activism and, 183–84; feminist thought and depatriarchalization, 186–88; Halakhah and, 186; Holub and, 186; lesbian, 187; prayer groups growth, 184–85; Reconstructionist Movement and, 188; Twilight People Opening Prayer, 188; WCGLBTJ and, 187–88; Weisberg on, 184–85; women in movement, 183; women rabbi ordination, 183, 184, 189n4

Jewish feminist thought: of Adler, R., 24, 33n22, 187; depatriarchalization and, 186–88; of Falk, 24, 25, 33n23, 187; gender-inclusive language in Jewish prayer book, 25; of Heschel, 24; key figures of, 33n17; liturgy changes, 25; of Plaskow, 24, 186; on sexuality, 187; of Umansky, 24

Jewish law. *See* Halakhah

Jewish mysticism, Scholem on, 35n45

Jewish prayer book, 25, 183

Jewish texts: androcentrism in, 23–24, 183, 184–85; gender-inclusive language in prayer book, 25

marital rape, 224–25

Mary Magdalene, 289, 294; Cardman on, 287; Hayes on, 283; King, K., and, 283–84; Peter rivalry with, 284; Pope Gregory on, 12–13, 282–83; Pope Paul VI on, 287; prophetic witness of, 285–86, 288, 291

Mary Magdalene (film), 287–88

masculine language of God, 22, 23

Mataji. *See* Saraswati, Trikal Bhavanta "Mataji"

Matthews, Pack, 81, 91n21

McConnell, Mitch, 289

McDonald, Louise, 272–75

McFague, Sallie, 26, 32n4

Medea, Andra, 223

Medical Apartheid (Washington), 110

medical racism: Black women gynecological mutilation and sterilization, 110–11; on Black women pain disbelief, 110–12; King, M., on, 113; pregnancy-related deaths and, 113; of Sims, 110–11; social media platforms on, 112; Tuskegee syphilis study, 110; *Unequal Treatment* IOM report, 112–13

Medina, José, 95, 98, 101, 102

Merchant, Carolyn, 63

Mesa-Bains, Amalia, 52

methodology, of women religion studies, 4–5, 38

#MeToo movement, 1, 5, 100, 308; background of, 222–23; Burke as founder of, 93, 222–23, 288; #ChurchToo movement and, 227; faith leaders sexual abuse, 221–22, 225–27; Garland and, 227; GBV religious context, 222, 224–25; Kavanaugh and, 93–94; Nassar and, 94; religion and, 221–28; on sexual violence, 221–28; Weinstein and, 93–94

migrant shelters, at US-Mexico border, 2–3, 250–51, *251*, *252*, 253, *253*, 258n5

Milano, Alyssa, 222–23

Miles, Marie, 63

military brides, in Asian American history, 161–62

minoritized sexual identities, 336; De Beauvoir on, 327–28; illiberal democracy, 329; Mouffe passionate politics, 329, 331–35; political power and, 327–28; queer theory, 328

misogyny, in textual traditions, 39

Missing and Murdered Indigenous Women and Girls (MMIWG), Canada National Inquiry into, 265–66

Missing and Murdered Indigenous Women (MMIW) report, 269

missionary movement, in Greco-Roman cities, 15–16

mixed-gender membership, of Reclaiming Witchcraft, 129

MMIW. *See Missing and Murdered Indigenous Women*

MMIWG. *See* Missing and Murdered Indigenous Women and Girls

model minority stereotype, 158, 163

Models of God (McFague), 26

Moffett, Samuel, 155

Mohanty, Chandra Talpade, 192

Mohawk feminists. *See* indigenous Native American women

Mohawk rematriation case study, 272–75

monastery society. *See akhāḍā*

monastic institutions: freedom beyond, in Buddhist communities, 148–50; freedom within, in Buddhist communities, 147–48

Morgan, Henry, 266

Morton, Nelle, 344, 353, 358

mosque spaces for women online: collective negotiations in, 315; competing authorities, 315–16; Dane on co-creating new spaces, 321–22; global message to local mosques, 319–21; inequality in, 313–14; Lövheim on blogs for, 314–15; Nisa on, 319–21; Okoye on, 313–14; Oursides photo blog, of Okoye, 317–19; Side Entrance photo blog, of Makki, 318

Mother Earth, 29, 274, 275

motherhood, 333–34

Mouffe, Chantal: on illiberal populist movement, 330; passionate politics, 329, 331–35

Mujerista theology, Isasi-Diaz on, 28

music, women religion studies on, 40

Muslim Matters blog, 314

Muslim theology, 191; Qur'ānic feminist hermeneutics, 197–99; text, law and women history in, 193–97; women activism, 199–201, 307–8; women in Islam, 192–93

Muslim women: activism of, 199–201, 307–8; Coleman, I., on, 197; *hijāb* head covering of, 195–96; SIS organization, 200; veiling and seclusion of, 194, 201n5

an-Na'im, Abdullahi, 200

Nassar, Lawrence, 94

The Natural History of the Human Species, 111

nature: feminine connection with, 63; feminist theology on humanity connection with, 32

Negro Project, in eugenics movement, 111

neopaganism, 27, 29, 133

nepantla, 50, 53–54

Neto, Charles Redden Butler, 135

New Age and Neopagan Religions (Pike), 133

Nisa, Nahida Sultana, 319–21

non-maleficence principle, WomanistHealthCare and, 107, 115

Northern Triangle, femicide in, 236–39, 237, 238

Norval, Areletta, 332

"Notes Toward Finding the Right Question" (Ozick), 24

#NotYourNarrative, 304

Nuns on the Bus, 281, 290

Nyungne Amla, of Nyungne prayer practice, 149

Nyungne prayer practice: male lamas as leaders of, 150; Mani Mother or Nyungne Amla of, 149; Palmo and, 148

Odell, Jenny, 358

Okoye, Ify, 313–16

On Being a Jewish Feminist (Heschel), 24

One Billion Rising, of Ensler, 302

online feminism: Coleman, M., on, 303; Kline on, 305–6; of Muslim feminists, 307–8; Ott and Winch on, 303–4; social justice and, 302–4. See also blogs; digital world

oppression, 3; of APA women, 157; ecofeminism and, 67; IK of Haudenosaunee, 264, 273; US Asian, 159–63, 162, 166n29

Ordain Women movement, of Kelly, K., 310n19

ordination of women, 1, 214n1, 355–56; Buddhism, 146–47; as Jewish rabbi, 183, 184, 189n4; preaching leadership and, 210; sangha and, 144

Orthodox Bhramanical worldview, 173, 174

Osman, Fathi, 200

Ott, Kate, 303–4

Oursides photo blog, of Okoye, 317–19

Ozick, Cynthia, 24, 186

Pacific Asian North Asian American Women in Theology and Ministry (PANAAWTM), 155, 156, 157, 159

Padma'tsho, 147

Pagan and Goddess Spirituality leaders: Adler, M., 133; Buckland, 126, 133; Budapest, 124, 126, 129, 130, 133, 135, 136; of Christ, Daly, Fox, Valiente, 133; Farrar, J., as, 126, 130, 133; Feminist Witchcraft/Goddess Religion, 134; Traditional/Eclectic Wicca and Paganism, 134; Zell, 126, 133

Paganism: Berger, H., on gender ratio of, 128; Clifton study of, 125; Farrar, J., and Farrar, S., on, 130; feminism influence on, 124; Fox as leader of, 130; leaders of, 126; Reece on, 138; Wicca and, 124

Pagels, Elaine, 284

Palmo, Gelongma, 148

Pandey, Jyoti Singh, 177

passionate politics, of Mouffe, 329, 331–35; queering of, 332–35; sexual passions incitement and border heterosexuality, 332; women bodies and sexual passions control, 332–33

Pass Me Not, O Gentle Savior (Crosby), 108, 116

patriarchy: colonial narratives on, 266; gender injustice and, 3; kenosis, 354–55; Qur'ān interpretation and, 194

Paul VI (pope), 287

Paxson, Diana, 126

"Penalty Box" (Okoye), 313, 314, 315–16, 323n15

Pendderwen, Gwydion, 129

people, planet and profit balances, in B Corporations, 78

People's Inauguration, in 2021, 295

Perceptions and Realities, of SIS, 200

Peter, Mary Magdalene rivalry with, 284

Pew Research Center, on Black women religion, 116n2

Picturing Paradise project, in Lima, Peru, 46, 54; activist research of, 49; of displaced women, 47; ethnography of, 47–48; visual arts fabric pictures, 47, 47, 48, 49

Pike, Sarah M., 133

Plaskow, Judith, 354; on Halakhah, 186; Jewish feminist thought of, 24, 186

Plenitude (Schor), 77

Plumwood, Val, 63

Politics of Piety (Mahmood), 198

populism, 330

populist movements: Golder on exclusionary, 330–31; illiberal, 330

postcolonial feminist theology, 146, 207

posttraumatic stress disorder, Herman, J., on, 341

praxis-based learning: ethnography and, 40; hermeneutical circle in, 41–42, 42; theological reflection in, 41

prayer: Jewish book of, 25, 183; Jewish feminism groups growth, 184–85; quorum in Judaism, 38–39, 184. See also Nyungne prayer practice

preaching leadership of women, in Christian Church: Biblical interpretation, 212–13; changes in, 207–8; Florence on testimony of, 208; Gross, N., on, 210; Hall on, 205–6; Hartford Institute of Religion Research on, 209–10; of Hutchinson, 207; Kim on, 207; language of, 211–12; male and female differences, 213–14; ordination and, 210; physicality of preaching, 209–11; preaching as testimony, 208–9; Theresa of Avila and, 210; women movement four waves, 206–7

pregnancy-related deaths, medical racism and, 113

Priestess, Mother, Sacred Sister (Sered), 126

priesthood of all believers, 210

prophetic witness, by women, 289, 295; of Mary Magdalene, 285–86, 288, 291

Prothero, Stephen, 135–36

PRRI. *See* Public Religion Research Institute

psychic wounding, of Black women, 109

Public Religion Research Institute (PRRI), on social media, 303

public theology, 282–83, 289–94

queer theory, 78, 328

Quiet Odyssey (Lee, M.), 155–56

Qur'ān: Ahmed on, 193; al-Hibri on, 197; Barlas on, 197–98; feminist hermeneutics, 197–99; on gender equality, 193; Hassan on, 197; interpretation of, 28, 193, 197–98; patriarchal interpretation of, 194; Rahman holistic reading of, 28; Shaikh interpretation of, 28; Stowasser on, 194; on veiling and seclusion, 194, 201n5; Wadud interpretation of, 28, 197–98

"Racial Bias in Pain Assessment and Treatment Recommendations, and False Beliefs About Biological Differences between Blacks and Whites" medical report, 112

radical feminism, 123, 126; of Daly, 133, 135; religion criticism by, 29; Ruether on, 136; Wicca and, 132, 137

Rahman, Fazlur, 28

Rainbow of Pride. *See* Keshet Ga'avah

rape: Baldwin on, 99; Buddhism and 170, 173, 177; colonial oppression and, 110, 157; culturally normative, 235; credible fear for asylum and, 236; "Delhi Braveheart," 301; femicide and, 231, 237; gender-based violence as, 222, 224; honor killings and 235; indigenous women and, 268, 277; marital, 224–25; militarized, 232; as rite of passage, 237; police complicity and, 240; preaching and (Hilkert), 211; "Rape" (Griffin), 223; Rwanda and 232–33; trauma theory and (Herman), 256; scripture and, 224; Weinstein and, 93–94; white man complicity to, 268

"Rape" (Griffin), 223

Raphael, Melissa, 347

rasquache, 51

Reclaiming Witchcraft, 124; Berger, H., Leach, and Shaffer on, 128; mixed-gender membership of, 129; Starhawk founding of, 126, 128, 132

Reconstructionist Movement, Jewish feminism and, 188

Reece, Gwendolyn, 138

"Reflections on Exile" (Said), 340

Reformed Congregation of the Goddess, 135

Reform Movement, 25

Reid, Barbara, 212–13, 285

religions: ecofeminism meets, 61–73; history of, 38; Pew Research Center on Black women and, 116n2; sex abuse crisis of, 170; shifts within, 71; taxonomy of, 65

religio-political approach to love and justice, 5; introduction to, 281–83; Mary Magdalene and, 12–13, 282–89, 291, 294; public theology and, 282–83, 289–94; RLP, 291–94; US social justice movement, 281

religious feminist blogging projects, 306–7

Religious Freedom Week, 289

religious language and symbols, 22

religious traditions, 4, 5

research questions, for women religion studies, 42–43

resistance, US Asian, 159–63, *162*, 166n29

restorative interventions: of Latina women through art and activism, 45–55; in Lima, Peru, 45; at US-Mexico border, 45, 50–51

Resurrection Matins, 286–87

Revolutionary Love Project (RLP), 12, 281, 282, 291–93

Rhimes, Shonda, 223

righteous behavior. *See dharma*

The Right Question is Theological (Plaskow), 24

Rig Veda, 30

rites of passage, of Haudenosaunee, 265, 269, 273, 274

rituals, 24, 40

River, Falcon, 135

River, Jade, 135

Rizzuto, Ana-Maria, 13

RLP. *See* Revolutionary Love Project

Roberts, Charles Carl, IV, 234

Rohr, Richard, 18

Roman Catholic Church. *See* Catholic Church

Ruether, Rosemary Radford, 15, 124, *131*, 132, 133, 354; Christ and, 129; Christian feminist theology of, 26; on Christianity, 136; on Covenant of the Goddess, 129–30; on ecofeminism, 61, 62; on feminist theology and women full humanity, 16; on feminist Wicca, 129, 136; Gardner reference by, 128, 129; on Wicca, 128–30, 136

Rush, Bonita, 112
Russell, Diana, 232
Russo-Japanese War (1904-1905), 156
Ryan, Tamra, *84*, 84–87

Sacks, Tina, 113
sādhu: equality fight of, 178; female inferior to male, 169; male gurus dependence by, 172–73; Mataji as, 172; moral character of, 173; societal perception of female, 173; stereotypes of women, 171
Said, Edward, 340
Saiving, Valerie, 15
Sakyadhita, Buddhist women organization, 146
Sales, Ruby, 12
Salomonsen, Jone, 136–37
Salving, Valerie, 354
Sanchez, Carol Lee, 76
Sanders, Maxine, 126
Sanger, Margaret, 111
sangha, women ordination and, 144
Sannyāsī, 171–73
Saraswati, Trikal Bhavanta "Mataji": *akhāḍā* monastery society founded by, 169, 176; *Akhāṛā Pari* monastery of, 176–78; female *sādhus* societal perception, 173; female society formation by, 176–77; good woman revisioning by, 177–79; on guru devotion, 174–75; on Hinduism sex abuse crisis, 171, 174, 176–77; Hinduism sexual inequality and violence response by, 169–79; personal sexual abuse story, 171–73; as Shankaracharya female leader, 170–71, 176–78; *tan, man, and dhan* ideology, 173–76
Sarsour, Linda, 12
Scarsella, Hilary, 227
Schlafly, Phyllis Stewart, 329
Schneider, Nicole, 148
Scholem, Gershom, 35n45
Schorr, Juliet, 75, 77
Schreiner, Olive, 4
Schrempf, Mona, 148
Schüssler Fiorenza, Elisabeth, 15–16, 310n33, 354; Christian feminist theology of, 26; on femicide, 231
Scott, Duncan Campbell, 268
seclusion, of Muslim women, 194
Second Vatican Council (1962-1965): feminist theology and, 15; on social justice, 290
sefirot, Zohar on, 33n13
self-trust, Jones on distortions in, 97–98
separatist Wicca, 132, 135, 138; Budapest as founder of, 130, 133; Starhawk on, 124, 129
Sered, Susan Starr, 126–27

sex abuse crisis, of religions, 170, 179n1, 180n11; faith leaders sexual abuse, 221–22, 225–27; Mataji on Hinduism, 171, 174, 176–77
sex-based harm, 93
Sexism and God-Talk (Ruether), 15, 354
sexist language, Kraemer on liturgy, 27
sexual assault testimonies: credibility distortions and, 94–95; Kavanaugh effect and, 93–94; Nassar and, 94; Weinstein and, 93–94, 206, 222, 288; women indictments in, 94–95
sexual harassment, women's movement and, 206, 214n6
Sexual Harassment of Working Women (MacKinnon), 342
sexual inequality, Mataji response to Hinduism, 169–79
sexuality, Jewish feminist thought on, 187
sexual passions: border heterosexuality and incitement of, 332; women bodies and control of, 332–33
sexual violence, 1, 5; in Delhi, India, 301–2; feminist ethics on, 93–103; Hinduism response to, 169–79; #MeToo movement and, 221–28
Shaffer, Leigh S., 133; on Gardnerian Wicca, 137; on Reclaiming Witchcraft, 128; on Wicca, 127
Shaikh, Sa'diyya, 28, 191, 201
Shakti, 176
Shalom, 12
Shange, Ntozake, 18
Shankaracharya, Mataji as female leader, 170–71, 176–78
shared community concept, of WomanistHealthCare, 115
Shari'a, 195
Shaw, Miranda, 31
Shekhinah, 33n11; feminine name of, 23, 33n16, 347; Judaism on, 23, 25; in Zohar, 23–24, 33nn14–15
Shennondoh, Audrey, 267
Sheppard, Phillis Isabella, 115
She Who Is (Johnson), 354
Shiva, 176
Shiva, Vandana, 63
Side Entrance photo blog, of Makki, 318
Sikhs, public theology and, 292
Sikkim, 144
Simos, Miriam. *See* Starhawk
Sims, James Marion, 110–11
sin: gendering of, 15; Salving and Plaskow on, 354
Singh, Jyoti, 301, 302–3

transgender students, Reconstructionist Movement and, 188

transmigration, of Asian Americans, 160

transpacific studies: Kwok Pui-lan on dialogical imagination of, 159; Lee, M., on, 158; on US transpacific domination, 157. *See also* Asian transpacific feminist theology

trauma, child abuse and, 341, 345–46, 348, 349n9

TRC. *See* Truth and Reconciliation Commission

Triumph of the Moon (Hutton), 133

Triveni Sangam, 171, 173

Trump, Donald, 264, 265, 276; family separation policy, 236; Guatemala asylum seekers and, 252–54; US-Mexico border and, 161, 236, 250, 332

Truth, Sojourner, 327

Truth and Reconciliation Commission (TRC) *Call to Action*, 265, 270

Tuskegee syphilis study, 110

Twilight People Opening Prayer, 188

2SLGBTQQIA people, Haudenosaunee rites of passage and, 265, 269, 274

Umansky, Ellen, 24

Unequal Treatment report, by IOM, 112–13

UNHCR. *See* United Nations High Commissioner on Refugees

United Nations Declaration of Indigenous People, 263

United Nations High Commissioner on Refugees (UNHCR), on asylum seekers, 248

United Nations Sustainable Development Goals, 87, 92n34

United States (US), 164; Asian oppression, resistance and activism in, 159–63, *162*, 166n28; femicide civic action through elected officials, 257; femicide compared to hate crime in, 234; social justice movements, 281; transpacific domination by, 157

universal human rights, 5, 195, 327, 330

US-Mexico border: AMBOS and, 52–53, 57n31, 57n34; anti-immigration sentiment and, 50; Anzaldúa on art activists in, 50–51; Aushana on art activists in, 51; BAW/TAF on, 51, 53, 56n20; case study, 248–51; Chicano movement in, 51; civic action with elected officials, 257; *Las Comadres* in, 51–52; controls case study, 248–51; family separation at, 236, 248–49, *249*, 268n3; femicide at, 2, 248–51; Garcia, R., silkscreen art, 51; Mesa-Bains on, 52; migrant shelters at, 2–3, 250–51, *251*, *252*, 253, *253*, 258n5;

restorative interventions at, 45, 50–51; *Space In Between* sewing project, 53–54; Trump and, 161, 236, 250, 332; violence at, 250–51

Vajrayāna Buddhism, 144, 145, 148

Valiente, Doreen, 125, 126, 133

Vatican II. *See* Second Vatican Council

VAWA. *See* Violence Against Women Act

veiling, of Muslim women, 194, 201n5

violence: Black women cultural, 109; epistemic, 268, 269–70; Mataji response to Hinduism, 169–79; at US-Mexico border, 250–51. *See also* rape, sexual violence

Violence Against Women Act (VAWA) (1994), 224

Viswanath, Sunita, 12

Voices from the Pagan Census (Berger, H., Leach, and Shaffer), 133

Wadud, Amina, 28, 191, 197–98, 200

Wagner, Sally Roesch, 266

Walker, Alice, 17–18, 27, 283

Warren, Elizabeth, 289

Washington, Harriet, 110

WCGLBTJ. *See* World Congress of Gay, Lesbian, Bisexual, and Transgender Jews

Weinstein, Harvey, 93–94, 206, 222, 288

Weisberg, Dvora E. (rabbi), 184

Welch, Sharon D., 354

West, Candace, 328

Whitaker, Damaris, 12

white exceptionalism, WomanistHealthCare and, 115

white gaze, Yancy on, 109

white supremacy, IPCE and, 99–100, 104n22

WHO. *See* World Health Organization

Wicca, 123; -as-women's-religion myth, 137–38; Berger, H., Leach, and Shaffer on, 127; in *Encyclopedia of Women and Religion in North America*, 130, *131*, 132; as feminist, 125–26; Gardnerian, 125; gender ratio in, 124; in *Goddesses and the Divine Feminine*, 128–30; god representation in, 140n34; holy envy role in, 135–37; mass media growth impact, 125; representations of, 132–35; Ruether on, 128–30, 136; television shows and films on, 125; witchcraft and, 125; women religion defined, 126–28

Wiesel, Elie, 343

Willard, Frances, 222

williams, angel Kyodo, 12

Williams, Delores S., 13, 27–28, 354

Wilson, Liz, 146

Winch, Alison, 303–4

Winnicott, Donald, 13

About the Contributors

Anjeanette M. Allen is a PhD student and emerging scholar of religion at Chicago Theological Seminary whose research interests include practical theology, womanist pastoral theology, and bioethics. She is an ordained Baptist minister and oral historian and currently serves as a hospice chaplain. She has previous careers in the nonprofit sector, public policy arena, and social justice activism on local, state, and national levels.

Rebecca Berru Davis is assistant professor in the theology department at St. Catherine University, St. Paul, Minnesota. Her degree is in art and religion from the Graduate Theological Union. Rebecca's research focuses on the intersection of art, faith, and justice as a way to understand spiritual expressions of those living on the margins, particularly Latin American and US Latina women's creativity evidenced in home, church, and community.

Helen T. Boursier is a public theologian, educator, author, activist, ordained minister, and artist. She has been a volunteer chaplain with refugee families seeking asylum since 2014, and she teaches theology and religious studies at the College of St. Scholastica. Her books include *Desperately Seeking Asylum: Testimonies of Trauma, Courage, and Love* (2019), *The Ethics of Hospitality: An Interfaith Response to U.S. Immigration Policies* (2019), and *Art As Witness: A Practical Theology of Arts-Based Research* (2021), and *Willful Ignorance: Overcoming the Limitations of Love for Refugees Seeking Asylum* (forthcoming).

Rosemary P. Carbine is associate professor of religious studies at Whittier College. She specializes in Anglo and Asian American feminist, African American womanist, and Latina/mujerista theologies, theological anthropology, ecological and public/political theologies, and teaching and learning in theology and religion. In addition to nearly twenty articles in journals and edited volumes, she has co-edited and contributed articles to three books, *The Gift of Theology* (2015), *Theological Perspectives for Life, Liberty, and the Pursuit of Happiness* (2013), and *Women, Wisdom, and Witness* (2012). She is currently working on a book that offers a constructive feminist public theology in conversation with US faith-based social justice movements.

Antoinette E. DeNapoli is an associate professor of religion at Texas Christian University. Trained as a historian and ethnographer of religion, her research and teaching examine gender, religion, and authority in contemporary India. She wrote *Real Sadhus Sing to God: Gender, Asceticism, and Vernacular Religion in Rajasthan* (2014) and is currently writing her next monograph, *Female Agency: The Struggle for Gender Equality and Social Transformation in Contemporary Hindu Society.*

Heather Eaton is full professor of conflict studies at Saint Paul University in Ottawa, Canada. Her current research includes ecological, gender/feminist, and religious dimensions of peace and conflict studies and theories of conflict, social justice, non-violence, and animal rights. She publishes frequently, including *Immanent Religiosities, New Materialisms, and Planetary Thinking* with Karen Bray and Whitney Bauman (2021); *Advancing Nonviolence and Social Transformation* with Lauren Levesque (2016); *The Intellectual Journey of Thomas Berry* (2014); *Ecological Awareness: Exploring Religion, Ethics and Aesthetics* with Sigurd Bergmann (2011); *Introducing Ecofeminist Theologies* (2005); and *Ecofeminism and Globalization* with Lois Lorentzen (2003).

Marie M. Fortune is an author, teacher, ethicist, theologian, and pastor who was ordained in the United Church of Christ in 1976. In 1977, she founded the FaithTrust Institute, which has become an international training resource for addressing sexual and domestic violence/gender-based violence in faith communities. Her books include *Sexual Violence: The Sin Revisited, Keeping the Faith, Is Nothing Sacred?,* and *Love Does No Harm.*

Rabia Terri Harris, founder of the Muslim Peace Fellowship and first president of the Association of Muslim Chaplains, is co-founder of the Community of Living Traditions, a multi-religious, multifaith, multicultural, intergenerational intentional community of practice that cultivates the spiritual commitments of its members while striving to learn and teach models for authentic multifaith engagement, anti-racist praxis, and faith-rooted approaches to building peace, seeking justice, and serving and preserving the land.

Amy Holmes-Tagchungdarpa is an associate professor of religious studies at Occidental College. Her research focuses on Buddhist communities in Tibet, Sikkim, Bhutan, Nepal, and China, and she is the author of *The Social Life of Tibetan Biography: Textuality, Community and Authority in the Lineage of Tokden Shakya Shri* (2014).

Candace Jordan is a PhD candidate at Princeton University. Her research interests include African American religious traditions, the civic and political uses of resentment and anger, and the politics of testimony. Having been educated most formatively at Quaker institutions, Candace carries forth a spirit of service and simplicity into her political, professional, and personal commitments.

Zayn Kassam is the John Knox McLean Professor of Religious Studies at Pomona College in Claremont, California. She has authored an introductory volume on Islam and edited two volumes, one titled *Women and Islam* and the other titled *Women and Asian Religions.* Kassam is co-editor of the *Journal of Feminist Studies in Religion.*

Natalie Kertes Weaver is professor of religious studies and theology and pastoral ministry and co-director of the Master of Arts Program in Theology and Pastoral Studies at Ursuline College in Pepper Pike, Ohio. She has published several books, including *The Theology of Suffering and Dying: An Introduction for Caregivers* (2013). She currently is developing books on sex and the body and music and theology.

HyeRan Kim-Cragg holds the Timothy Eaton Memorial Church Professorship in Preaching and serves as graduate studies director at Emmanuel College in the University of Toronto, Canada. She has written eleven books and numerous articles in journals and edited volumes. Her recent books are *Postcolonial Preaching: Making a Ripple Effect* (2021) and *Interdependence: A Postcolonial Feminist Practical Theology* (2018). Her most recent article is found in the journal *Liturgy* (2019), "Probing the Pulpit: Postcolonial Feminist Approaches."

Yudit Kornberg Greenberg is the George D. and Harriet W. Cornell Endowed Chair of Religion and director of the Jewish Studies Program at Rollins College, Florida. She is the author and editor of books and articles in contemporary Jewish thought, comparative religion, women and religion, and cross-cultural views of love and the body, including the *Encyclopedia of Love in World Religions* and *The Body in Religion: Cross-Cultural Perspectives*.

Jacqueline J. Lewis is the senior minister of Middle Collegiate Church in New York City. She is a nationally acclaimed activist, author, public theologian, and organizer of an antiracist multicultural movement of love and justice. She has been featured in the *Washington Post, Wall Street Journal*, and *New York Times* and on PBS, NBC, CBS, and MSNBC. Her books include *The Power of Stories: A Guide for Leading Multi-Racial and Multi-Cultural Congregations* (2008), *Ten Essential Strategies for Becoming a Multiracial Congregation* (2018), the children's book, *You Are So Wonderful* (2020), and *Fierce Love: A Bold Path to a Better Life and a Better World* (2021).

Dawn Martin-Hill, Mohawk and a cultural anthropologist, is a Canada and US Fulbright scholar. Her primary research, spanning two decades, prioritizes working with ecological knowledge, healing, women and youth, and Indigenous ways of knowing and being. She also researches rites of passage for youth as suicide prevention and access to clean water, particularly with and for Indigenous communities.

Gina Messina is associate professor and department chair of philosophy and religious studies at Ursuline College. She is co-founder of FeminismAndReligion.com and has authored or edited five books, including *Faithfully Feminist*. Messina presented at the United Nations; has appeared on MSNBC, PBS, NPR, and the TEDx stage; and has been featured in the *Washington Post, HuffPost*, Associated Press, and *Boston Globe*. Her research is grounded in an intersectional lens and is committed to equity and social justice.

Michelle Mueller earned her PhD from the Graduate Theological Union. She is a member of the teaching faculty of Santa Clara University's Religious Studies Department.

She has published in *Theology & Sexuality*, *Nova Religio*, and *The Pomegranate*. Her first book, *New Religions and the Mediation of Non-Monogamy: Polyamory, Polygamy, and Reality Television*, is an expansion of her dissertation project and highlights the role of alternative religious populations in America's pop culture representations of non-monogamy.

K. Christine Pae is associate professor of religion/ethics and chair of the Department of Religion at Denison University. Her research interests include the ethics of peace and war, feminist spiritual activism, transnational feminist ethics, US overseas militarism, and Asia/Asian American religious ethics.

Cynthia L. Rigby is the W. C. Brown Professor of Theology at Austin Presbyterian Theological Seminary, where she has been teaching for 25 years. She is the author of *Holding Faith: A Practical Introduction to Christian Theology* (2018) and a general co-editor of the *Connections* lectionary commentary series. She is an ordained minister in the Presbyterian Church USA.

Krista Melanie Riley obtained her PhD in Communication Studies from Concordia University, where her research focused on Muslim feminist bloggers. She is the former editor-in-chief of *Muslimah Media Watch*, an international blog looking at media and popular culture representations of Muslim women, and currently works as a researcher and pedagogical counselor at Vanier College in Montreal.

Denise Starkey is professor of theology and religious studies at the College of St. Scholastica. Her teaching and academic research focus on feminist liberation theologies, feminist spirituality, and religion and psychology. She is the author of *The Shame That Lingers: A Survivor-Centered Critique of Catholic Sin-Talk*. Her current research focuses on spiritual homelessness, practices of pilgrimage, and multiple religious belonging in order to construct a nomadic spirituality of home for survivors of violence.

Ludger Viefhues-Bailey is distinguished professor of philosophy, gender, and culture at LeMoyne College in Syracuse, New York. His work analyzes the intersection of sexuality, politics, and religion. His most recent book is *Between a Man and a Woman? Why Conservatives Oppose Same-Sex Marriage* (2010).

Sharon D. Welch is affiliate faculty member at Meadville Lombard Theological School (Unitarian Universalist), after having served as provost and professor of religion and society for ten years. She has held positions at the University of Missouri and Harvard Divinity School. Welch is the author of six books, her most recent being *After the Protests Are Heard: Enacting Civic Engagement and Social Transformation* (2019).